THE IMPACT OF THE CIVIL WAR

A SERIES PLANNED BY
THE CIVIL WAR CENTENNIAL COMMISSION

AGRICULTURE AND THE CIVIL WAR
by Paul W. Gates

BONNET BRIGADES
by Mary Elizabeth Massey

HEARD 'ROUND THE WORLD
edited by Harold M. Hyman

A MORE PERFECT UNION
by Harold M. Hyman

In Preparation:

THE UNWRITTEN WAR
by Daniel Aaron (Literature)

ON PHILANTHROPY AND WELFARE
by Robert N. Bremner

ON SCIENCE
by Robert V. Bruce

ON GOVERNMENT AND ECONOMY
by Daniel Elazar

ON BUSINESS ORGANIZATION AND LEADERSHIP
by William Greenleaf

ON LABOR
by Herbert Gutman

ON ENTERTAINMENT
by Richard B. Harwell

ON NEGRO LIFE
by Leon Litwack

ON MEDICINE
by W. F. Norwood

THE NORTH TO POSTERITY
by James I. Robertson

A More Perfect Union

THE
IMPACT
OF
THE
CIVIL
WAR

[THE CIVIL WAR CENTENNIAL COMMISSION SERIES]

Planned by Allan Nevins

Edited by Harold M. Hyman

A
MORE PERFECT
UNION

The Impact of
the Civil War and Reconstruction
on the Constitution

by Harold M. Hyman

New York: Alfred · A · Knopf
1 9 7 3

Library of Congress Cataloging in Publication Data:
Hyman, Harold Melvin, date.
A more perfect Union.
(The Impact of the Civil War)
Bibliography: p.
1. United States—Constitutional history.
2. United States—Politics and government—Civil War.
3. United States—Politics and government—1865–1877.
I. Title. II. Series.
JK231.H9   320.9′73′07   72–2256
ISBN 0–394–46707–8

THIS IS A BORZOI BOOK
PUBLISHED BY ALFRED A. KNOPF, INC.

Manufactured in the United States of America
FIRST EDITION

To the memory of
ALLAN NEVINS

America! America!
God mend thine every flaw,
Confirm thy soul
In self-control,
Thy liberty in law!

Contents

Contents

Footnote Abbreviations

AAPSS	American Academy of Political and Social Sciences
ABA	American Bar Association
AHA	American Historical Association
AHR	*American Historical Review*
AJLH	*American Journal of Legal History*
ALHS	American Legal History Society
ALReg	*American Law Register*
ALRev	*American Law Review*
AM	*Atlantic Monthly*
AMA	American Medical Association
ANJ	*Army and Navy Journal*
APS	American Philosophical Society
APSR	*American Political Science Review*
AR	*Annual Reports*
Att. Gen. Ops.	*Attorney General, [U.S.] Opinions*
BHM	*Bulletin of the History of Medicine*
BHR	*Business History Review*
BMJ	Bureau of Military Justice
CalifLR	*California Law Review*
CentLJ	*Central Law Journal*
CG	*Congressional Globe*
CLR	*Columbia Law Review*
CM	*Continental Monthly*
CR	*Congressional Record*
CU	Columbia University
CUNY	City University of New York
CWH	*Civil War History*
Fed. Cas.	Federal Case
GU	Georgetown University
HL	Huntington Library
HLR	*Harvard Law Review*
HR	House Report
HSP	Historical Society of Pennsylvania

Footnote Abbreviations

HU	Harvard University
IndMH	*Indiana Magazine of History*
ISHS	Illinois State Historical Society
JAH	*Journal of American History*
JEH	*Journal of Economic History*
JHI	*Journal of the History of Ideas*
JHM	*Journal of the History of Medicine*
JHU	Johns Hopkins University
JNH	*Journal of Negro History*
JPE	*Journal of Political Economy*
JPL	*Journal of Public Law*
JPoli	*Journal of Politics*
JSH	*Journal of Southern History*
JSS	*Journal of Social Science*
LC	Library of Congress
LH	*Legal Historian*
LNLF	Lincoln National Life Foundation
LQ	*Lincoln Quarterly*
LSU	Louisiana State University
MA	*Military Affairs*
MH	*Magazine of History*
MHS	Massachusetts Historical Society
MHSP	*Massachusetts Historical Society Proceedings*
MichLR	*Michigan Law Review*
MinnLR	*Minnesota Law Review*
MLJ	*Mississippi Law Journal*
MLR	*Mississippi Law Review*
MLRep	*Monthly Law Reporter*
MoHS	Missouri Historical Society
MVHR	*Mississippi Valley Historical Review*
M&P	U.S. President, *A Compilation of the Messages and Papers of the Presidents*, comp. James D. Richardson (Washington, 1896–99)
NA	National Archives
NAR	*North American Review*
NCHR	*North Carolina Historical Review*
NDL	*Notre Dame Lawyer*
NE	*New Englander*
NEA	National Education Association
NEQ	*New England Quarterly*
NMHR	*New Mexico Historical Review*
NTA	National Teachers Association
NU	Northwestern University
NYBA	New York Bar Association
NYHSQ	*New-York Historical Society Quarterly*

Footnote Abbreviations

NYPL	New York Public Library
NYU	New York University
OAH	Organization of American Historians
OR	U.S., Army, *The War of the Rebellion: A Compilation of the Official Records of the Union and Confederate Armies* (Washington, 1880–1901)
PAH	*Perspectives in American History*
PMHB	*Pennsylvania Magazine of History and Biography*
PSQ	*Political Science Quarterly*
PU	Princeton University
RLR	*Rutgers Law Review*
RP	*Review of Politics*
RS	U.S., *Revised Statutes*
RU	Rice University
RUS	*Rice University Studies*
SAL	U.S., *Statutes at Large*
SAQ	*South Atlantic Quarterly*
SCR	*Supreme Court Review*
SDLR	*South Dakota Law Review*
SHA	Southern Historical Association
SHSW	State Historical Society Wisconsin
SIU	Southern Illinois University
SLR	*Southern Law Review*
SSQ	*Social Science Quarterly*
StLR	*Stanford Law Review*
SUI	State University of Iowa
TCU	Texas Christian University
TLR	*Tulane Law Review*
TSA	Texas State Archives
UA	University of Alabama
UC	University of Chicago
UChiLR	*University of Chicago Law Review*
UCLA	University of California at Los Angeles
UI	University of Illinois
UMd	University of Maryland
UMich	University of Michigan
UMinn	University of Minnesota
UP	University of Pennsylvania
UPLR	*University of Pennsylvania Law Review*
UR	University of Rochester
USC	University of Southern California
UT	University of Tennessee
UWash	University of Washington
UWis	University of Wisconsin
VaLR	*Virginia Law Review*

Footnote Abbreviations

WD	War Department
WLR	*Washington Law Review*
WMQ	*William & Mary Quarterly*
WVLQ	*West Virginia Law Quarterly*
YLJ	*Yale Law Journal*
YU	Yale University

Introduction

A Narrative of the Apprehension and Application of Principles

---

In 1870, replying to a request from the *Edinburgh Review* that he prepare an article on the changes in the American Constitution resulting from the Civil War and its aftermath, the young political commentator Henry Adams begged off. He asserted that the concept of War-caused constitutional change was defective. "The essential and fatal changes in our Constitution were not the result of the war, but of deeper social causes" too difficult and complex to cover properly in a book, much less an article—"each [deeper social cause] need[s] a volume to discuss."

Perhaps, as Adams suggested, his "disordered liver," not the scope or difficulty of the commission, was the real reason for his refusal.[1] Whatever it was, I wish earnestly that he had undertaken it so that his analysis could serve as a research asset. For, ninety years later, when Allan Nevins honored me with an invitation to prepare for the "Impact Series" the volume on the Constitution, I accepted.

That was ten years ago. I believed then that I was familiar with the relevant manuscript and printed sources of the pertinent legislation and resulting litigation, which was the stuff of constitutional history as I defined it at that time. My assumption was that, by re-examining those sources, I would produce an appropriate reconsideration of the constitutional impact of the War and Reconstruction.

But instead of being involved in relatively straightforward research, I soon found myself immersed in an enormous, varied

---

1. Ernest Samuels, *The Young Henry Adams* (Cambridge, 1948), 183.

literature, and I felt justified in excluding many themes and in compressing others. I entered research arenas strange to me because, in order to understand impacts, I felt that I had to know as well as I could contemporary understanding of the constitutional anvil on which the War and Reconstruction struck, as well as the ways in which the Constitution shaped the War and Reconstruction. I wondered how Lincoln's generation apprehended the thrust in their lives of the War and Reconstruction; what it meant to them, what they wished it to mean, and what they intended if possible to prevent it from meaning.

A painful, slow realization emerged that priorities and perceptions of the 1860's and 1870's involved public policy alternatives that often, for long periods, and for many persons, had little or nothing to do with the traditional concerns of Civil War and Reconstruction constitutional history—the Union, the South's states, the Negro. These alternatives included urban responses to cholera epidemics, political corruption, inadequate public services, and abused animals; states' concerns about mine safety, public health (the Slaughterhouse case wants attention in this context), defective professional standards among lawyers, pharmacists, physicians, and teachers, and rapacious entrepreneurs; and national decisions (and nondecisions) regarding appropriate institutional forms for aiding agriculturalists, antipornography crusaders, and freedmen, for associating with new technology such as the telegraph, and for obliterating slavery's persisting remnants in the South and polygamy and peonage in the West.

All these matters involved constitutional impacts of the Civil War and Reconstruction. Each required me to deal with sources, men, and measures which until this time I had more or less ignored. I learned that instead of being relatively tight and straightforward, the impact theme applied to the Constitution involved so many subjects, institutions, and individuals that, as Adams argued in 1870, complete coverage is impossible in one book.

Further complicating the evolution of this volume was the fact that, like Adams in 1870, inquirers have attended almost exclusively to only half the impact question, considering primarily the effects of the Civil War and Reconstruction on the Constitution. The other, largely ignored dimension of this question, perhaps more significant, asks: What were the Constitution's effects on the War and Reconstruction, on the nature of responses to felt wants by nation, state, and local governments, by individuals, by private associations, and by official institutions? If, as I now believe, ascertainable policy alternatives of the 1860's and 1870's were sharply limited as to number, kind, and duration by influential individuals' constitutional perceptions, then insight into those perceptions is in order. For the quarrels of a century ago not only shaped the Constitution, the Constitution shaped the quarrels.[2]

This addition to the fundamental research concept made more troublesome the fact that Civil War and Reconstruction constitutional impacts still manifest themselves, and will continue to do so. In the 1970's as in the 1870's, they inform American society's direction, velocity, and quality. Achievements and failures of the 1860's and 1870's help still to set the contours and purposes of political parties, to establish the uses and limits of public power, to modify relationships of nation to states to cities to individuals, to regulate the methods and standards of corporations, and to affect the coexistence patterns of races.

Such complex dynamism makes the constitutional historian's task particularly difficult. As Francis N. Thorpe noted in 1902, it is an extraordinarily elastic field, or at least it can and should be elastic. Thorpe applied to America's constitutional history an outer crust of definition derived from England's past— "a history of the origin and growth of a civil system embodied in a constitution, whether written or unwritten." But because

---

2. Arthur Bestor, "The American Civil War as a Constitutional Crisis," *AHR*, LXIX (1964), 327–52; Alfred H. Kelly, "Comment on H. M. Hyman's Paper," in *New Frontiers of the American Reconstruction*, ed. Hyman (Urbana, 1966), 40–58. Just as I finished writing this book, Charles Fairman's *Reconstruction and Reunion, 1864–88* ([VI, 1, *The Oliver Wendell Holmes Devise History of the Supreme Court of the United States*] New York, 1971) came into print. Fairman coped with complex matters that I had struggled painfully even to perceive. As example, his Preface, p. xvii: "Some readers may expect that a book about the Supreme Court will be entirely a composition in lofty strains. But . . . in this period the Court's work . . . included a mass of commonplace litigation on matters of private right, differing from what came before the State courts in nothing save that the parties must be citizens of different States." I add to this insight that, in 1865 *ff.*, many men saw jurisprudence and jurisdiction as opportunities not merely to advance private rights, but also concepts of public good. See further in Fairman, *Reconstruction*, chs. 1–5, 11, and *passim*. I acknowledge here our parallel concerns and, sometimes, judgments, reached independently, and derive comfort from the distinguished company.

Introduction

America's "civil system" was federal, not unitary, because unique forms of judicial review obtained here, and because mid-nine-teenth-century American politics had little parallel in Britain, Thorpe transformed latter parts of his definition into a descriptive guide to research materials. Constitutional historians here must look into the laws, high-bench decisions, customs, and constitutions of national, state, and local units of government; into the records of private associations such as political parties obviously affecting official policy (less obviously until recently, other private associations aiming at narrow or broad reforms also created constitutional history); into the works of legal commentators, philosophers, and statesmen. Then, perhaps to lessen the appre-hensions felt by would-be constitutionalists among his readers at the mountain of sources he was cataloguing, Thorpe retreated. "The entire testimony bears back to principles of government, few in number and comprehensive in character," he wrote. "A constitutional history is a narrative of the apprehension and application of these principles by the American people."[3]

Unfortunately, for decades thereafter constitutionalism lost Thorpe's anchor. On campuses the specialization became a branch of political science or public law more than of history, and took on a case-decisional stress that Thorpe would not have wel-comed, or perhaps even recognized. Seeking in 1929 to reclaim the field for history, James G. Randall insisted that "Constitu-tional history is no subject for the legalist. It is no subject for one whose interest in the forms of law blinds him to the essential forces that work through law."[4]

Still far from complete, constitutional history's reclamation continues in the broadly inclusive spirit Thorpe and Randall de-scribed. Helping in 1960 to set goals for Americans, Clinton Rossiter described constitutionalism in this context:

> . . . the essence of the democratic process has been respect for the rules; the guaranty of this respect in the public arena has been the spirit and practices of constitutionalism. Constitutionalism is the generic label for all those arrange-ments and techniques—separation of powers, checks and

---

3. Francis N. Thorpe, "What Is a Constitutional History of the United States?" AAPSS *Annals*, XIX (1902), 259.

4. James G. Randall, "The Interrelation of Social and Constitutional History," *AHR*, XXXV (1929), 2.

Introduction

balances, due process, bill of rights, the rule of law—that force our governors to think, talk, bargain, and explain before they act, and that institutionalize the procedures through which public policy is made, administered, and enforced.[5]

Agreeing with Hermann E. Von Holst and Allan Nevins that constitutional history is never "window-dressing,"[6] I try to apply in this book these inclusive and reciprocal definitions of constitutional history to the question of Civil War and Reconstruction impacts. The broad horizon made it necessary to hold reasonably tightly to relatively immediate rather than longer-term effects which are still manifesting themselves. Further, in light of the impact theme, a decision seemed justifiable to keep roughly to a chronological pace so that the interworking of one line of results with others could receive analysis and, I hope, a degree of clarification, in closely contemporary terms.

In disagreement with Professor Howard Mumford Jones, I perceive the existence of a "governing philosophic concept" in this period. This bedrock position was best expressed by William R. Brock: "The [Civil] war had . . . started to preserve the Union, but for the majority in the North it had become a war to create a more perfect Union." That purpose is the theme of this book. Now with far greater reason than Professor Arthur E. Sutherland, I repeat his disclaimer: "A confident statement of the immediate and the ultimate effects on American life of the [Civil] War years 1861–1865 [and their aftermath] would require much more wisdom than I can muster."[7]

Rice University   Harold M. Hyman
September 1972

---

5. Quoted in *AHR*, LXXVI (1971), 960. See also P. L. Murphy, "Time to Reclaim: The Current Challenge of American Constitutional History," *AHR*, LXIX (1963), 64–79.

6. Allan Nevins, "The Constitution, Slavery, and the Territories," in *The Gaspar G. Bacon Lectures on the Constitution of the United States, 1940–1950* (Boston, 1953), 97.

7. Howard Mumford Jones, *The Age of Energy: Varieties of American Experience, 1865–1915* (New York, 1971), ix; William R. Brock, *An American Crisis: Congress and Reconstruction, 1865–1867* (New York, 1963), 2; Arthur E. Sutherland, *Apology for Uncomfortable Change, 1865–1965* (New York, 1965), 19.

A More Perfect Union

Chapter I

Quarrels That the Constitution Shaped

Americans should have come to the secession winter well armed from experience and well equipped with institutions to deal with the strains involved. Forty years of sectional and party battles had made the secessionist position familiar. Repetitive contentions had resulted in the manufacture southward of heavy political weapons out of the constitutional theory of secession, but Americans had apparently mastered the art of bypassing them.

Great debates about the nature of the Union prepared Americans to argue over secession, but, as events were to prove, not to experience it. The enduring lesson from 1820, 1833, 1850, and 1854 was that secession was a gambit in sophisticated political confrontations that the federal system made possible; a weapon that was not supposed to go off. Until 1860 political palliatives salved the major sectional irritants. Parties continued to operate; democracy and federalism worked well enough. Successes in skirting secession hazards so heightened popular confidence in the nation's constitutional ways and political means that avoidances of confrontations became confused with solutions. Mid-nineteenth-century Americans judged from these successes that nothing in constitutional theory or political action was beyond the capacity of ordinary citizens to master. The rule of law, informed by open but restrained political democracy and arranged in a unique federal structure, would allow Americans to overpass the sad fates which history had recorded for less favored nations. In short, before the 1860–61 secession winter, confidence was widespread that American constitutional and political arrangements were adequate to cope with crises.

A common, pervasive, and tenacious belief was that this blessed competence derived from the Constitution, which had institutionalized commendable practices of political democracy, perpetuated the happy arrangements of federalism, and protected the rich rewards of unfettered capitalism. To be sure, awareness obtained that the United States deviated from an illusory, ideal democracy. But with all its closed enclaves, including slavery for most Negroes and hangover political limitations for many whites, in 1860, as earlier, America was visibly the world's most open society and democratic polity. Commonplace practices provided citizens with the best practical training men knew then in the operation of popular government and of a federal system. Ordinary Americans argued and decided as a right matters that elsewhere were monopolies for elites to enjoy, theoretical questions for scholars to chew on, or burning aspirations for conspirators to realize.

The continuing popular commitment to keeping the public law the public's law, and for mixing constitutional idiom into political argumentation, made attitudes toward and interpretations of the Constitution something higher than gamesmanship and more serious than partisanship.[1] Uncaring how patricians or professors fussed at the tenacious habit of mixing law and politics, Americans kept on debating the nature of the Union, and refused to place law outside of politics.[2] To debate made sense because, despite the alleged clarity of the Constitution, the Union's nature was demonstrably unclear, and because laymen understood that the stakes of power were inseparable from one

---

1. J. C. Hurd, *The Theory of Our National Existence as Shown by the Action of the Government of the United States Since 1861* (Boston, 1881), 95; G. Dietze, *America's Political Dilemma: From Limited to Unlimited Democracy* (Baltimore, 1968), 16.

2. Note the post-Appomattox argument of former Harvard University law professor Theophilus Parsons, that the mixture of constitutionalism and politics made politicians more intransigent, with the Civil War as consequence; Parsons, *The Political, Personal and Property Rights of a Citizen of the United States, How to Exercise and Preserve Them* (Hartford, 1874), 38.

interpretation or another of the Constitution. Political hustings as well as judges' sanctums were proper and obvious arenas in which to solve public difficulties.

Americans continued to play politics in the ways they knew how.[3] History's record during the first half of the nineteenth century encouraged popular confidence in political action. The great debates on national banking, tariff, and internal improvements policies, and on Missouri's admission and South Carolina's nullification adventure, provided a generation with unprecedented expertness in the theory of the Constitution and in the practice of politics. Questions about fugitive slave renditions, the Texas annexation, Congress's power to regulate slavery in the mushroomed federal territories, the troubles in Kansas, and the effects of the Dred Scott decision continued the tuition. In these and in other encounters, secession was a theme of varying prominence and undoubted presence.

In effect, the popular nature and extent of these debates democratized constitutional concepts and made them part of political dialogue. Wherever Americans gathered, discussion resulted of political issues cast in constitutional terms. Everyone claimed competence in public law and understood that secession was an omnipresent element in political discourse. Even when debate centered on a seemingly disparate theme—on the power of Congress to impose a tariff or to prohibit slave property from entering national territories, as examples—understanding obtained that behind it the secession threat lurked for southern spokesmen to employ.

This interweaving of secession constitutional theory with recurrent political issues made more significant the fact that debates on the one educated Americans about the other. As a result, the political-constitutional dialogue penetrated far beyond national, state, and local legislative halls.[4]

The propensity of laymen to intrude into areas of complex legal-constitutional interpretation drew blasts from some bright

---

3. R. M. Venable, "Partition of Powers between the Federal and State Governments," ABA *Reports*, VIII (1885), 258–9. See also B. J. Bledstein, "The Intellectual, the Professional, and the Problem of Democracy in America" (AHA paper, 1968 [with thanks to the author for a copy]); M. Bloomfield, "Law vs. Politics: The Self-Image of the American Bar (1830–1860)," *AJLH*, XII (1968), 306–23.

4. Allan Nevins, "The Constitution, Slavery, and the Territories," in *The Gaspar G. Bacon Lectures on the Constitution of the United States, 1940–1950* (Boston, 1953), 97.

lights of the bar, who assumed that the profession's technical training should automatically have brought with it political leadership.[5] The doubtful proposition that only lawyers understood the Constitution in prewar years made little or no impression on the general population. However widespread the popular reverence for the rule of law, however puzzling the mysterious science lawyers served, mid-nineteenth-century Americans were not inclined to leave to private lawyers any more than to public men the conception, execution, and interpretation of public law. The conviction was general that no aristocracy existed with respect to the Constitution. Like politics, with which it was inextricably joined, the Constitution was everybody's business. Superiority of lawyers in technical education was no passport to political power, albeit lawyers were beginning to crowd into political command posts.

Bending to popular currents which they could not dam, some prominent men of the law tried to educate the public in public law.[6] Most attorneys found distasteful the unending intrusion of common folk into constitutional questions, and, worse, the insistence of unlettered politicians to create from debates, election campaigns, and political manipulations policies in the form of laws. It was clear to would-be patricians of the robe that democracy was having a greater impression upon the law than the proper, reverse path.[7]

---

5. In January 1861, Professor Emory Washburn told Harvard law students that "In a busy, restless community like ours, somebody has to do the thinking, whose whole time and energies are not engrossed by the drudgery and details of physical labor or the eager pursuit of the means of comfort. . . . Notions, the wildest and most extravagant, are constantly struggling to gain a lodgment in the public mind, and so long as they are dealt with only by men who have but a single line of thought, and [who] have never been trained to scrutinize questions as having two sides . . . they often assume for the time being, a weight of importance which sinks into insignificance the moment such a test is applied. For the past thirty years, the public mind seems to have been constantly growing more and more ready to take up these opinions upon every thing, however grave. . . . The issues to which that period has given rise, have indeed been legion; so susceptible has the public sense been to any thing new and startling." Washburn, *Lecture Before the Members of the Harvard Law School, January 11, 1861* (Boston, 1861), 17–18.

6. Nathaniel Towle, *A History and Analysis of the Constitution of the United States* (Boston, 1860), iv.

7. Lemuel Shaw, "Influence of the Form of Government and Political Institutions upon the Law and Its Professors," *American Jurist and Law*

Quarrels That the Constitution Shaped

Especially obnoxious to profession-proud lawyers was the spectacle, as they saw it, of "pulpit politicians" sermonizing over the Constitution. "Unconstitutional divines" were far too inclined to comment on constitutional law, grumbled prestigious, acerbic Joel Parker of the Harvard Law School; the vulgarization of the Constitution had gone too far. Yet even Parker acknowledged that popular opinion was neither fooled nor foolish about the relevance of constitutional approaches to national problems.[8] The United States was not only a political democracy. It was also a federal system in which the functional arenas of the states and of the central governments were ill-defined and in flux. Contention was in order on such matters as the fugitive slave law and Congress's power to regulate slavery in national territories because the outcome of constitutional theorizing would become political policy.

As unparalleled in the mid-nineteenth century as its political democracy, American federalism was distinguished from all others by the extent of the country, by the mass of territorial expansion and amount of state-making after 1800, and by the basic policy determination and performance responsibilities that state governments and their local divisions retained jealously and tenaciously. Despite Cassandra-cries to the contrary, in 1860 a central leviathan was not in process of overshadowing states,

---

Register, VII (1832), 56–70; William Barry, "American Political Science," *Old and New*, III (1871), 309; Anton-Hermann Chroust, "The American Legal Profession: Its Agony and Ecstasy," *NDL*, XLVI (1971), 487–525.

8. In 1862 Parker suggested that "the innumerable speeches, in Congress and out of Congress, within the last few years, may serve to show with what diligence, if not with what success, constitutional law has been recently studied. If the speechmakers have not put the authors of the [Federalist] Papers to shame, by their recondite researches into the mysteries and rules of constitutional construction, they have at least shown that there may be expositions of the provisions of the Constitution, of which Hamilton, Madison, and Jay never had any conception." Parker, *Constitutional Law; With Reference to the Present Condition of the United States* (Cambridge, Mass., 1862), 9–10. See also Parker's *Constitutional Law and Unconstitutional Divinity: Letters to Rev. Henry M. Dexter and to Rev. Leonard Bacon, D.D.* (Cambridge, 1863); and David Christy, *Pulpit Politics: Or Ecclesiastical Legislation on Slavery in Its Disturbing Influences on the American Nation* (Cincinnati, 1863), on ministers and the law; Perry Miller, *The Life of the Mind in America: From the Revolution to the Civil War* (New York, 1965), 99–265; and see n. 3, above.

counties, or townships.[9] Instead a complex dual federalism or dual sovereignty existed in which, according to a recent statement by Daniel Elazar, "the federal and state governments pursued virtually independent courses of action during a period when government activity was, in any case, minimal."

By the 1850's national authority entered infrequently into functional arenas common abroad, and except for fugitive slave returns was irrelevant with most respect to individuals' civil rights and political practices. The political parties had long since adapted themselves to state-centered convictions about the proper spheres of government functional activity. States and their city, county, and township subdivisions, employing delegated powers of their states, did almost all the work of government that was done. Political history became the story of sporadic efforts to shape this tightening mold so that, on behalf of intrastate constituencies, congressmen could charter, or oppose chartering of, "national" banks or subsidize improved roadways westward.[10] Certain national issues, including the bank, the tariff, internal improvements, and extension of slavery, refused to recede and kept vital the continuing argument over the nature of the Union.

In a federal system that was a political democracy and an economic capitalism, men went for arguments to the written Constitution that undergirded the whole. "The configurative role that constitutional issues played is the point of crucial importance," Arthur Bestor argued recently in an admirable analysis. "It was constitutional theorizing, carried on from the very birth of the Republic, which made secession the ultimate recourse to any group that considered its vital interests threatened."[11]

Slaveowners, their human property shielded in states' laws,

---

9. In 1858, Chief Justice of the United States Roger B. Taney offered as realistic this definition of existing federal-state relationships: "The powers of the general government, and of the state[s], although both exist and are exercised within the same territorial limits, are yet separate and distinct sovereignties, acting separately and independently of each other, within their respective spheres." Ableman v. Booth, 21 Howard 506 @ 516 (1859).

10. Daniel Elazar, "Federal-State Collaboration in 19th Century United States," *PSQ*, LXXIX (1964), 248, and *passim.*; M. A. DeWolfe Howe, "Federalism and Civil Rights," *MHSP*, LXXVII (1965), 15–27.

11. Arthur Bestor, "The American Civil War as a Constitutional Crisis," *AHR*, LXIX (1964), 329. See too his "State Sovereignty and Slavery: A Reinterpretation of Proslavery Constitutional Doctrine, 1846–1860," *ISHS Journal*, LIV (1961), 1–64; Walter Hartwell, *American Theories of Federalism* (University, Ala., 1964), 127–63; Robert R. Russel, "Constitutional

felt threatened enough to shape state-rights constitutionalism into sophisticated restraints on almost all national government functions. The master constitutionalist John C. Calhoun allowed exceptions only when a domestic national function served the further to protect slave property, as in recapture clauses of fugitive slave laws. Calhoun's concerns over misdirections being taken by enfranchised majorities in nonslaveholding states were shared implicitly by many of the "best men" there. Fears persisted that the renunciation of England's common law, during and since the American Revolution, led to democracy's excesses. Therefore, the patrician proposition ran that steps were in order to seek greater social stability by increasing statutory and constitutional restraints upon popular actions.

By 1860, Calhoun's constitutional views were entrenched in the southern states and diffused widely if more thinly through the rest of the nation, especially in Democratic party councils. The general effect of such state-centered thinking helped to hold at minimum levels the vitality as well as the functions and size of the national government. Federal bureaucracy had become "a cave-dwelling affair," where national officials contented themselves with the "modest performance of minor duties," Bray Hammond concluded.[12]

Even the rush of communications and production technologies in the 1850's failed to stiffen the weak springs of national government; states released entrepreneurial energies rather than constrained them. Men who pressured states and nation to aid particular railroad, turnpike, or canal speculations wanted, and won, support without regulation, subvention without supervision. Only Indians and Negro slaves endured positive restraints so far as congressional legislation was concerned.[13]

The upshot was that though states' authorities were busy

Doctrines with Regard to Slavery in Territories," *JSH*, XXXII (1966), 466–86; Roy F. Nichols, "Federalism *versus* Democracy: The Significance of the Civil War in the History of United States Federalism," in *Federalism as a Democratic Process* . . . (New Brunswick, 1942).

12. B. Hammond, *Banks and Politics in America from the Revolution to the Civil War* (Princeton, 1957), 719–29; and see D. J. Boorstin, *The Americans: The National Experience* (New York, 1965), 391–430; C. Degler, "The Nineteenth Century," in *Theory and Practice in American Politics*, ed. W. H. Nelson (Chicago, 1964), 29–42, esp. 32.

13. David Potter, *The South and the Concurrent Majority* (Baton Rouge, 1972), *passim*; C. Goodrich, *Government Promotion of American Canals and Railroads, 1800–1890* (New York, 1960), chs. 1–5; J. W. Hurst,

with multitudinous local concerns, they were rarely venturesome in terms of innovative functions. As decades dragged on to 1860, national officials, immobilized by deepening sectional contentions, virtually abstained from significant activity. Presidency, Congress, and Supreme Court were dominated by state-oriented, dual-sovereignty representatives. The constitutional notion that tight limits existed on what government could do was a runaway favorite. The chief advocates and beneficiaries of this view, the southern Democracy along with many supporters in northern states, were adrift from moorings that seventy years earlier had given spirit to their party and vitality to the Constitution.

American political parties had rooted in differences in constitutional interpretation about the allowable limits of national functions, as stated in the familiar confrontation between Alexander Hamilton and Thomas Jefferson when both were members of Washington's cabinet. Hamilton asserted that the Constitution made necessary and proper the assumption by Congress of relatively numerous, significant, and large-scale economic and commercial activities. He was concerned especially to avoid weaknesses so painfully exhibited by the Continental and Confederation Congresses. They were bound to recur unless, under the 1787 Constitution, national authority proved itself adequate to impress foreign powers and to win Americans of uncertain allegiance. Therefore Hamilton aspired to raise, through tariffs and excises, revenues adequate for better armed forces and foreign policies, and to tie the self-interest of Americans to the destinies of the new nation.[14]

With respect to United States commercial policy Jefferson's goals were not essentially in conflict with those of his cabinet colleague. But the Virginian was more concerned than the New

---

Law and the Conditions of Freedom in the Nineteenth Century United States (Madison, Wis., 1956), *passim;* Elazar, "Federal-State Collaboration," 248 and n.; W. D. Farnham, " 'The Weakened Spring of Government': A Study in 19th Century American History," *AHR,* LXVIII (1963), 662–80; O. and M. Handlin, *The Dimensions of Liberty* (New York, 1966), 76; H. N. Scheiber, *Ohio Canal Era: A Case Study of Government and the Economy, 1820–1861* (Athens, O., 1969), *passim.*

14. C. L. Rossiter, *Alexander Hamilton and the Constitution* (New York, 1964), *passim.*

Yorker with holding domestic and foreign policy in line with the revolutionary heritage. Therefore, Jefferson more strictly construed the permissible limits of national action under the Constitution.

Then France's revolution and consequent foreign wars raised issues here of neutrality, maritime depredations, and recruitment in America for belligerents' forces, transcending the commercial issues on which Hamilton and Jefferson first split.

Fears that dissent would destroy the infant republic inspired Federalists in Congress to enact the famous Alien and Sedition laws. So doing, they tied economic alternatives to First Amendment negatives; state rights to national wrongs. A result was the creation of extraconstitutional political parties, loosely organized in two broad coalitions on echelons paralleling those of the federal system, but without hierarchical discipline.[15] While local party echelons retained primary interest in neighborhood bread-and-butter matters, state and especially national political spokesmen took on sharply divergent party positions centering on the Alien Act, and to a lesser extent, the Sedition law.[16] Federalists accepted as proved the nation's need to adopt economic as well as internal security functions, and they derided opponents' attempts to raise the First Amendment as a bar against congressional action. Their opponents, coalescing into Democratic-Republican organizations, adapted stricter-construction positions that Jefferson had worked out earlier against Federalist commercial policies. They preached the gospel of functional limits, equated localism with liberty, and asserted that federalism flourished best when central activity was less. In the Kentucky and Virginia Resolutions, Jefferson and his coadjutors erected the Bill of Rights into a bill of wrongs that Congress must not commit.[17] As result, by the

---

15. M. D. Peterson, "Thomas Jefferson and Commercial Policy, 1789–1793," *WMQ*, 3rd ser., XXII (1965), 608–10; *The Making of the American Party System, 1789–1809*, ed. N. E. Cunningham, Jr. (Englewood Cliffs, N.J., 1965); Morton Borden, *Parties and Politics in the Early Republic, 1789–1815* (New York, 1967); R. Hofstadter, *The Idea of a Party System: The Rise of Legitimate Opposition in the United States, 1780–1840* (Berkeley, 1969), offer recent brief surveys.

16. M. Smelser, "George Washington and the Alien and Sedition Acts," *AHR*, LIX (1954), 322–34; S. G. Kurtz, *The Presidency of John Adams: The Collapse of Federalism, 1795–1800* (Philadelphia, 1957).

17. L. W. Levy, *Legacy of Suppression: Freedom of Speech and Press in Early American History* (Cambridge, 1960), 266.

turn of the century American constitutional and political institutions and idioms united.[18] The Federalist party committed itself to a latitudinarian view of what the Constitution allowed Congress to do, at least while Federalists were running the Congress, although neither Jefferson nor Hamilton nor their parties fit too neatly or at all times into the postures required by their rhetoric.[19]

Federalists crossed the line to Jeffersonian means, especially to state-right constitutional positions, when opposition developed to national policies including the Louisiana Purchase, the embargo, and especially the war against Britain. Despairing of regaining direction of affairs through the ballot, Federalists assembled in the 1814 Hartford Convention and parroted Jeffersonian rhetoric about constitutional limitations, in order to protect not individual liberty but sectional power.[20]

With Louisiana's acquisition and embargo enforcement, the degree became apparent of the Jeffersonian crossover concerning national governmental functions. Such backings and fillings convinced some onlookers that political positions were mere conveniences. "States' rights and State sovereignty are expressions coined for party purposes, often by minorities, who happen to be dissatisfied with the measures of the General Government, and as they are . . . used, they produce only state delusion. In this business each large minority has had its turn," Harvard law professor Nathan Dane wrote disgustedly in 1829.[21]

---

18. C. P. Patterson, *The Constitutional Principles of Thomas Jefferson* (Austin, 1953). It should be noted that except for intermittent instances during the 1850's when men of conscience employed state-rights arguments to block slave-catching by national authorities, the years of the Federalist hegemony were the first and almost the last time when individuals' civil rights and state rights legitimately were paired. See also L. Hartz, *The Liberal Tradition in America: An Interpretation of the American Political Thought Since the Revolution* (New York, 1955).

19. See J. M. Smith, *Freedom's Fetters: The Alien and Sedition Acts and American Civil Liberties* (Ithaca, 1956); L. W. Levy, *Jefferson and Civil Liberties: The Darker Side* (Cambridge, Mass., 1963); J. Knudson, "The Jeffersonian Assault on the Federalist Judiciary, 1802–1805; Political Forces and Press Reaction," *AJLH*, XIV (1970), 55–75.

20. D. H. Fisher, *The Revolution of American Conservatism: The Federalist Party in the Era of Jeffersonian Democracy* (New York, 1966); T. J. Farnham, "The Federal-State Issue and the Louisiana Purchase," *Louisiana History*, VI (1965), 5–25; Allen Guttmann, *The Conservative Tradition in America* (New York, 1967); James M. Banner, *To the Hartford Convention: The Federalists and the Origins of Party Politics in Massachusetts, 1789–1815* (New York, 1970), *passim*.

21. Nathan Dane, *General Abridgement and Digest of American Law* (Boston, 1829), IX, App., 32–3.

During the 1830's and later, statesmen of the Old South found in Calhoun's formulations and distortions of state-centered Jeffersonianism a mighty fortress behind which to shelter slavery. Of the years 1840–60 a Republican party spokesman later recalled that "The [congressional] sessions produced little in the way of legislation beyond the tax and appropriation bills. . . . The Presidents of these half-forgotten years were as diligent . . . to explain why the Federal government could do nothing, as the Congresses were to do nothing. . . . Constitutional inhibitions were pleaded in excuse for all omissions."[22]

The contrast is striking between Democratic espousal of somnolence for the national government in almost all matters, and the thrusting national energy which the party's southern leadership demanded in recapturing runaway slaves. In 1850 as part of the "compromise" legislation, a new, stringent fugitive slave law went on the statute books. Almost as if to exaggerate contrasts between state-right professions and actions, the 1850 recapture law provided for creation of a substantial corps of federal court commissioners to enforce the augmented body of national criminal law the fugitive question created. In efforts to recapture alleged slave runaways, the commissioners enjoyed authority to interfere with persons and property within states— obviously, only within northern states.

Derivative strains proved to be too much for many Democratic party members.[23] As 1860 neared, signs grew clearer of an intraparty struggle between a faction of southern predominance strongly favored by incumbent President James Buchanan and a northern group under the leadership of Illinois Senator Stephen A. Douglas. The knife edge between them was the increasing northern antipathy to enforcement of the fugitive slave law and to the prospect of slave property blocking free white laborers'

---

22. [Anonymous], "Address of the Union Republican Congressional Committee," *The Republic*, III (1874), 51–3. It is less important whether this description is precisely accurate than that it represents what informed people believed in the 1870's to have been true about prewar conditions, and about the Civil War's impact on their generation. On the Calhounite rise, see Bestor, "State Sovereignty and Slavery," 117–80.

23. *Ibid.*, and see S. W. Campbell, *The Slave Catchers: Enforcement of the Fugitive Slave Law, 1850–1860* (Chapel Hill, 1970), ch. 6; L. Gara, "The Fugitive Slave Law: A Double Paradox," *CWH*, X (1964), 229–40; J. Yanuck, "The Fugitive Slave Law and the Constitution" (Ph.D. diss., CU, 1953); C. Warren, "Federal and State Court Interference," *HLR*, XLIII (1930), 346–78; C. A. Linquist, "The Origin and Development of the United States Commissioner System," *AJLH*, XIV (1970), 7–9.

entry into the nation's western territories. On these matters the state-rights men made it clear that their concern was with the exercise of power, not theoretical rights, with action, not philosophy. Southern pressure grew rapidly to favor positive congressional policies by which to protect slave property in territories and to reclaim runaways who had reached northern states. This pressure kept slavery a national political issue in a manner that the minority of abolitionists were incapable of achieving.

A very few southerners deplored the fact that by pressing for enactment and enforcement of the 1850 fugitive slave law, they were tacitly admitting Congress's adequacy under certain circumstances to act within states, at least through the national courts. But these protesters went unheeded. In political terms the South demanded the full measure of what the Constitution permitted, in paradoxical contradiction to the coexisting state-rights interpretation of what the Constitution forbade.[24]

By the 1850's the First Amendment concerns that had played so prominent a role in Jefferson's rise were no longer of interest in politics, except as fugitive slave recaptures unsettled matters. Almost no white Americans endured restraints from local or state governments save in criminal activities. On the national level, except for fugitive slave recapture questions, criminal law was thin indeed. Even the defeatist Federalists of 1814 did not move Congress to limit by a sedition act the untrammeled expression of opinion, or excite the President to seek in federal courts treason indictments against malcontents. All evidence sustains the Handlins' judgment that "By the middle of the nineteenth century Americans commonly thought of their rights as a solid barrier that could readily be defined in handbooks and that colored everything from the most general constitutional provisions to the details of business negotiations."[25]

This belief in the existence of rights deriving from the machineless functioning of the rule of law—the Constitution—received contradiction primarily from the political difficulties slavery created. Imposition during the mid-1830's of a gag rule in

24. W. E. Dodd, *Statesmen of the Old South, or From Radicalism to Conservative Revolt* (New York, 1911); R. F. Nichols, *The Democratic Machine, 1850–1854* (New York, 1923), 223–6.
25. Oscar and Mary Handlin, *Dimensions*, 59.

the Congress against introduction of antislavery petitions inspired John Quincy Adams to condemn the censorship involved as a violation of petitioners' rights guaranteed by the First Amendment. Similarly, the decision in executive departments of the national government by indirection to bar abolitionist tracts from the mails, and the destruction in the South by local postmasters of antislavery materials, received scattered condemnation in the North as violations of the Bill of Rights.[26]

Such reactions made some abolitionists look less critically on the Constitution. Perhaps it was less a hellish covenant if its commerce clause could interdict the interstate slave trade, if its Fourth Amendment's comity provision could counter slave states' laws with appropriate free states' analogies, or if its Fifth Amendment's due-process clause could block Congress from depriving persons of property or liberty without due process, as occurred in fugitive slave renditions. If constitutional law had developed a rhetoric protecting slave property, could not policy be altered by politics?[27]

Gradually, enough northerners became sensitive to such notions to count in terms of political weight. During the 1840's and 1850's "conscience" Whigs and Democrats found insupportable the dilemma the Constitution imposed on them with respect to congressional policies on runaway slave returns and western slavery extension. With the rise northward of concern over these matters, liberal constitutional exposition in major party politics, defined in the 1790's as the protection through law and politics of individuals against government excesses, again became possible. Joined by latter-day champions of multi-barreled internal improvements programs (who could feel as much as anyone else the moral rasps of slavery's expansion), dissenters from the southern Democracy's dogma organized in the mid-1850's as Republicans.

---

26. I. Brant, *The Bill of Rights: Its Origin and Meaning* (Indianapolis, 1965), 318–19; A. H. Kelly and W. A. Harbison, *The American Constitution: Its Origins and Development* (3rd edn., New York, 1963), 354–8.

27. *Ibid.*, 358–62; see too Frederick Douglass, *The Constitution of the United States: Is It Pro-Slavery or Anti-Slavery?* (Halifax [1860]), 8–16; E. H. Madden, *Civil Disobedience and Moral Law in Nineteenth-Century American Philosophy* (Seattle, 1968); R. D. Marcus, "Wendell Phillips and American Institutions," *JAH*, LVI (1969), 41–58; C. A. Miller, "Constitutional Law and the Rhetoric of Race," *PAH*, V (1971), 147–62; T. Lowi, "Politics and Public Policy" (OAH paper, 1971), considered the process of reciprocation between the two.

A single common assumption bound together Republicans of whatever motivation and of various opinions on the degree of or desirability of opposition to the fugitive slave law—that Congress enjoyed not only adequate constitutional power to exclude slave property from expansion farther into western territories, but also the responsibility to translate ability into political policy.[28]

28. L. Gara, "Slavery and the Slave Power: A Crucial Definition," *CWH* (1969), 5–18; E. Foner, *Free Soil, Free Labor, Free Men: The Ideology of the Republican Party Before the Civil War* (New York, 1970), *passim.*

Chapter II

Westward the Course

I f slavery—Negroes—had not become involved with the western territories, probably too few whites would have become antagonistic enough over the new Wests to cause political upsets. The territorial question was always politically potent because white Americans believed that the western lands offered safety-valve security and opportunity insurance. Men who probably never intended personally to be pioneers in western lands and who were not Negrophiles became intensely interested in holding slavery to its existing locations within states, in order that the West remain free; i.e., lily-white.

Common men comprehended that an American territory was far more than land. Instead it was a state in the process of becoming; a vital, viable element in the federal system. This dynamic connection between subordinate territory and co-ordinate state was a revolutionary, original, and constructive American contribution to the art of government and the practice of federalism. Since the birth of the nation the commitment had obtained that the immense acreages which wars and purchases brought under national jurisdiction were destined for separate and equal statehood. Americans had learned from recent history the lesson that subordination for colonies—territories in the American scheme—bred unrest. Instead, in the Northwest Ordinance and related legislation, a workable formula emerged for the incubation of new states. When an adequate population was resident in a federal territory, one or more states equal in every way to older eastern states might emerge from the territorial condition.

The question of the Negro slave's presence or absence in the territories marred the symmetry of the ingenious constitutional state-making machine that meshed so well with federalism, capitalism, and democracy.[1] Because the assumption was general North and South that slavery required growth in order to live, and that natural limits to its profitable expansion were illusory, the conclusion was logical that static boundaries for the institution would make it wither away (in a generation? a century? a millennium?) even in the eastern states of its origin.[2]

An increasing conviction developed northward in favor of a national containment policy. States still to emerge out of the territorial chrysalis would therefore be clean of the taint of slavery. By emigrating abroad, somewhere, Negroes would let whites bypass the problem of biracial coexistence on legal bases other than master-slave, about which even abolitionists were uneasy and divided. And meanwhile white men would inherit the western earth. The world's most democratic society would no longer expand beachheads for slavery as in Texas, meriting the scorn of censorious world Christendom, when everywhere else contraction was the pattern.[3]

In constitutional terms the only positive action required to achieve a slaveless West was for Congress to bar slave property from territorial lands. The Northwest Ordinance, containing such a bar, had easily passed the Confederation Congress and been re-enacted in the first Congress under the 1787 Constitution. Thereafter matters went less smoothly.

By 1815 the southern consensus was no longer (if ever it had been) that slavery had best die. Instead many slaveowners

---

1. The status of slavery in the District of Columbia was unquestionably under Congress's jurisdiction. Political leaders shied off from the question as long as they could, and most of their constituents were content to allow the bypassing. A. H. Kelly and W. A. Harbison, *The American Constitution: Its Origins and Development* (3rd edn., New York, 1963), 363; Eric Foner, *Free Soil, Free Labor, Free Men: The Ideology of the Republican Party Before the Civil War* (New York, 1970), 283.
2. Cf. C. W. Ramsdell, "The Natural Limits of Slavery Expansion," *MVHR*, XVI (1929), 151–71, and E. D. Genovese, *The Political Economy of Slavery: Studies in the Economy and Society of the Slave South* (New York, 1965), ch. 10.
3. See R. McColley, *Slavery and Jeffersonian Virginia* (Urbana, 1964), *passim*; S. Lynd, "The Abolitionist Critique of the United States Constitution," in *The Antislavery Vanguard: New Essays on the Abolitionists*, ed. M. Duberman (Princeton, 1965), 209–39.

wished to enlarge regions open to their peculiar property. Since slavery was a function of a state's property code, the need was obvious for appropriate parts of the national territories to become slaveowning states. The national Congress became the political cockpit of sectional interests centered on slavery. These interests focused on state-rights constitutional doctrines, especially the Fifth and Tenth Amendments, because the result desired was the buttressing of allegedly inviolable states' slave property laws by restraining Congress from excluding slaves from national territories. The upshot was a protracted debate on the question of the admission as a state of a portion of the lands acquired in the Louisiana Purchase.[4] A solution of sorts came forth in the "Missouri Compromise" legislation of 1820.

But the issue remained alive. The annexation of Texas twenty-five years later, and the conquest soon after of vast Mexican lands reaching the Pacific's shore, upset sectional equilibriums. By mid-century California's swelling population demanded admission as a state. David Wilmot, a Pennsylvania congressman and Democrat of uncertain antislavery convictions, introduced in the form of a resolution in Congress a "proviso" that slavery not exist in lands won from Mexico. Congress did not enact Wilmot's proviso. But its reintroduction in succeeding sessions of Congress reflected considerable and spreading northern opinion that a containment policy was in order with respect to the expansion of slavery, grown so monstrous of late; ten years later this minority opinion became northern majority policy.

In 1850, Congress created another "compromise" including prohibition of the slave trade in the District of Columbia, enactment of a more stringent fugitive slave law, and California's admission as a free state. By buck-passing to local residents of Utah and New Mexico territories the decision at the time they became states to have slavery or not—a political stratagem dignified as "popular sovereignty" or less elegantly as "squatter sovereignty"—aging Lewis Cass of Michigan and young Stephen Douglas of Illinois believed that they had gotten around the slavery-territory hazard.[5]

---

4. P. H. Detweiler, "Congressional Debate on Slavery and the Declaration of Independence, 1819–1821," *AHR*, LXIII (1958), 598–616.

5. Eric Foner, "The Wilmot Proviso Revisited," *JAH*, LVI (1969), 262–79. But even the most wishful thinking about popular sovereignty failed to result in the complete exclusion of Congress from decision. The

The 1820 legislation had provided for the allocation of slave property in lands acquired by the Louisiana Purchase; the 1850 statutes, extending to the Pacific, apparently were final solutions for the nation's significant territories. Within a man's life span Congress had shaded the racial complexion of areas larger than western Europe. In the process it had coped with the most sensitive public issues that the nervous American society had produced. Only distaste in some northern communities for the new fugitive recapture law rippled political waters.

Then the fabric that had appeared to be complete ripped apart again. The occasion was Senator Douglas's ultimately successful drive to push through Congress what became the 1854 Kansas-Nebraska law. Douglas convinced himself that the Constitution did not allow Congress to bar slave property from the nation's territories. His Kansas-Nebraska Act repealed the slave-prohibition provision of the 1820 law embracing the flatlands. A white or piebald future was up for grabs again in the trans-Mississippi West, now so close to settled areas just across the mighty river.

Douglas never understood why a storm came. He buttressed his constitutional conviction with assertions that nature forbade bondsmen in the West, a doubtful proposition when slave labor served in varied industrial and agricultural situations and conditions of climate and terrain. Further, the argument that American Negro slavery endured simply as a profit-making arrangement, and was on its way out, rings hollowly.

Whatever Douglas's motives, he helped sharply to lessen Congress' capacity to continue its hard-won function as sectional compromiser. After 1854 the Congress could no longer balance constitutional contentions, politicians' goals, and sectional interests in ways acceptable North or South.[6]

One result of the Kansas contention was the creation of the Republican party. Its first (1856) platform insisted that the Congress had the power and duty positively to exclude slave prop-

---

territorial governor or Congress might disallow a decision in a territory to have or not to have slavery. R. R. Russel, "What Was the Compromise of 1850?" *JSH*, XXII (1956), 296 *ff*. The 1850 statute is in *SAL*, IX, 462–5.

6. Kelly and Harbison, *American Constitution*, 375; H. D. Woodman, "The Profitability of Slavery: A Hardy Perennial," *JSH*, XXIX (1963), 303–25; *The Crisis of the Union, 1860–1861*, ed. G. G. Knowles (Baton Rouge, 1965), 51–5; Roy F. Nichols, "The Kansas-Nebraska Act: A Century of Historiography," *MVHR*, XLII (1956), 187–212; R. S. Starobin, *Industrial Slavery in the Old South* (New York, 1970), *passim*.

erty from territories and that the Fifth Amendment's due process clause required such action. At the same time, southern Democrats were discovering in the same Amendment a requirement for Congress actively to protect slaves in regions under national jurisdiction.

It is less remarkable that the Fifth Amendment's meaning, like beauty, should depend upon the beholder, than that opposite conclusions should rise from America's political parties. Earlier, the American way of politics had blended issues rather than sharpened them. But by the mid-1850's certain subjects defied softening. The public's concern was with its future. Decisions in Washington about territories and race would set matters in the West for as long as men could foresee. Therefore in Kansas partisans committed excesses along the Ossawatomie in order to influence policy along the Potomac. In Washington, as men sought support for their positions, attention shifted to portions of the Constitution little studied or understood, such as the Fifth Amendment. Auguries were that traditional political processes would settle matters, and that if a formula failed initially to please, second go-rounds were possible at another election.

Not so, decided the Supreme Court of the United States in 1857. Congress had no power to bar slavery from the national territories, ruled Roger B. Taney, Chief Justice of the United States, in the famous Dred Scott decision. Despite half a century of precedents favoring congressional regulation of internal territorial affairs, the Court judged that only territorial residents could arrange property matters, else their vested rights as American citizens suffered. Among these rights, the Fifth Amendment's guarantee against property deprivation by Congress without adequate procedures of law was pre-eminent. The 1820 Missouri Compromise statute hardly provided the process due a slave-owning citizen, since he could not take his slave into a national territory north of an arbitrary line. Therefore, the 1820 Missouri legislation had substantially violated property rights. Notwithstanding Douglas's 1854 repeal of the slavery prohibitions in the 1820 statute, in 1857 Taney again voided the earlier enactment.

A heavy weight of legal and historical gloss has accumulated around the opinions set down in this case by the Chief Justice and his discordant associates. One recent analysis deserves restatement here:

> The Dred Scott Case was on the whole a sorry episode in Supreme Court history. Both majority and minority opin-

ions betrayed a clear attempt to interfere in a political controversy to extend aid and comfort to one side or the other in the slavery controversy. Taney's reasoning was questionable on several points. His argument that Congress had no general police power in the territories ignored historical realities, while his attempt to draw a substantive limitation upon congressional power from the due process clause of the Fifth Amendment and his assertion that a state could not define even state citizenship [in instances of northern states that permitted Negroes status as citizens] within the meaning of the Constitution were at least open to dispute.[7]

As a bid to settle political issues, the Dred Scott venture was a ghastly failure. Instead of pacifying, it created worse turbulence. It forced politicians and the public into more intense and agonizing reappraisals of Constitution and parties, centering on the question of Congress's allowable role concerning slavery in national territories.

Although Democrats employed the Chief Justice's views on the Fifth Amendment, southern sentiment moved to a constitutionally more radical position of demanding positive congressional protection for slave property in territories. Concerted Democratic cuts frayed the Republicans' position that, Dred Scott notwithstanding, under the Constitution Congress could exclude slaves from the territorial West. Denying the validity of the Scott decision and continuing to insist that Congress keep the West slaveless incurred considerable political risk for Republicans. But in addition to the moral taint involved in surrender, abandoning that position made electoral defeat even more likely. If the Republican organization shattered, then Americans who opposed the expansion of slaveholding lost their only political home. It was not nightmare fear of partisan rhetoric to worry that perpetuation for slavery in the home of the free was the consequence of the disruption of the Republican organization, should it occur.

Probably almost all Republicans had the interests of whites,

---

7. Kelly and Harbison, *American Constitution*, 390–1; and see also Foner, *Free Soil*, 292–3; E. S. Corwin, "The Dred Scott Decision in the Light of Contemporary Legal Doctrines," *AHR*, XVII (1911), 52–69; W. Mendelson, "Dred Scott's Case—Reconsidered," *MinnLR*, XXXVIII (1953), 16–28; V. C. Hopkins, S.J., *Dred Scott's Case* (New York, 1951); Allan Nevins, "The Constitution, Slavery, and the Territories," *passim*; C. B. Swisher, "Dred Scott One Hundred Years After," *JPoli*, XIX (1957), 167–83.

not Negroes, in mind when advancing the need for Congress to insulate territories from slavery. Democratic opponents condemned as "radical" this concern for a slaveless future. Yet the Republican constitutional position was not radical. Again to employ Bestor's analysis, "The fact that the controversy of 1846–1860 turned on the extension of slavery to the territories (and, to a lesser extent, on the fugitive-slave law) showed that antislavery leaders, far from flouting the Constitution, were showing it a punctilious respect. Had they been disposed, as their opponents alleged, to ride roughshod over constitutional limitations, they would hardly have been bothered with the question of the territories or the question of fugitive slaves."[8]

Insight into Republicans' commitment to constitutionalism emerges from examination of Lincoln's relentless pressure on Douglas during their 1858 senatorial contest to reconcile popular sovereignty with the Scott decision, and from Douglas's desperate counterthrusts about Republicans' alleged disrespect for judicial decisions.[9] Further insight derives from Ohio Republican Senator Benjamin F. Wade's response to Mississippi's Senator Albert G. Brown's March 1860 demand that Congress not merely admit slavery everywhere the national flag flew, but protect it actively; a position that many southern Democrats were moving toward that year. During the ensuing debate, adverting to northern interferences with the operations of the 1850 fugitive slave law, Senator Robert Toombs of Georgia asserted that sectional tensions were on the rise only because of aggressions by a Republican-abolitionist coalition.

Wade privately revealed his intended rebuttal strategy: "I shall plant myself upon 'State Rights' and shall invoke the [Virginia and Kentucky] Resolutions of [17]98–9 as containing the proper remedy for cases like the present . . . to [oppose] the execution of the 'Fugitive Slave Law' as they [were the proper remedy to oppose] . . . the old 'Alien and Sedition' Law." Doing so, and having Republicans shield themselves in the state rights

---

8. A. Bestor, "State Sovereignty and Slavery: A Reinterpretation of Proslavery Constitutional Doctrine, 1846–1860." ISHS *Journal*, LIV (1961), 127; M. L. Wilson, "The Repressible Conflict: Seward's Concept of Progress and the Free-Soil Movement," *JSH*, XXXVII (1971), 533–56.

9. H. V. Jaffa, "Expediency and Morality in the Lincoln-Douglas Debates," *Anchor Review* (1957), 180–204; Mark M. Krug, "Lyman Trumbull and the Real Issues in the Lincoln-Douglas Debates," ISHS *Journal*, LVII (1964), 380–96.

mantle long monopolized by Democrats, delighted the tough campaigner from Ohio. "Compelling them to take their own physic" was poetic justice, he gloated.[10]

Wade's purgative took the form of a biting review of injuries which northern states and citizens experienced by operation of the 1850 fugitive recapture statute. Its enforcement commissioners were an extraordinary corps of venal federal police, who exercised within states semijudicial powers destructive to individuals' rights, he argued. Abruptly removed from one state to another, alleged fugitives rarely had an opportunity to win habeas corpus hearings before ordinary judicial tribunals. Little wonder that a swiftly increasing number of northerners considered that law to be unconstitutional, and, becoming Republicans, wished through politics to amend its harsh features.

Though opposed to the fugitive slave law and to further territorial expansion of slavery, Republicans did not deny or resist the constitutional requirement that runaways from servitude be returned to masters. What galled were the methods to which the 1850 law resorted, violative of white men's rights. Therefore Ohio and other states, Wade hoped, would protect their white citizens against oppression from national slave-catching police through passage and enforcement of personal liberty legislation.

In a sudden shift to the nationalist strain prominent in Republican constitutional doctrine, Wade insisted that, Dred Scott notwithstanding, Congress could drop a free-labor curtain west of which slaves might not go.[11] The Supreme Court, not Congress,

---

10. Benjamin Wade to Benjamin Stanton, May 30, 1859, owned by Stanton T. Allison. See also Hans L. Trefousse, *Benjamin Franklin Wade: Radical Republican from Ohio* (New York, 1963), 116 and *passim*.

11. *CG,* 36 Cong., 1 sess., App. 150–3. Years later the constitutional commentator John Norton Pomeroy wrote: "The Republican party was organized avowedly in support of the national theory of constitutional interpretation. . . . The national theory was the very *raison d'être* of the Republican party; and this fact was recognized by its early opponents as well as by its early leaders. The distinctive doctrine concerning slavery, which it advocated,—that slavery should be restricted to the States where it already existed, and should not be permitted to spread into the Territories belonging to the United States,—was but a legitimate consequence of . . . constitutional interpretation in conformity with the national theory. The leaders of the Republican party perceived this truth, and accepted it to its fullest extent and with all its results. In Congress and elsewhere they advocated the restriction of slavery as a direct and necessary consequence of the broad conception of the United States as a nation, and

had overstepped proper functional boundaries, the Ohioan told senators; the Dred Scott judgment was not above criticism although "the decisions of courts of late are magnified into much importance." Not even the Supreme Court could read into the Constitution the strange new southern Democratic doctrine that required subservience by all Americans to judicial decisions favoring slavery extension. "Our safety . . . consists in keeping close to the Constitution," Wade concluded.[12]

Such comments made sense to increasing numbers of northerners because of their sensitivity to a rough national presence in the form of fugitive-slave-law-enforcement officers. In 1854, a Wisconsin crowd had rescued a runaway Negro from recapture and sent him to Canada. Two of the rescuers found themselves under arrest, charged with violations of national law. A Wisconsin judge, by a habeas corpus writ, brought the lawbreakers before him, discharged them, and declared the 1850 fugitive slave law unconstitutional.

Wisconsinites cheered the state judge. He had thrust the "state" habeas corpus writ into the procedural gap Congress left in the fugitive slave law when it omitted jury trials for alleged runaways and prohibited testimony by them. On reflection (and reflection was needed, because diminutions of the conditions of freedom were so rare for whites), these were basic, minimal recourses for free Americans. So ignored, the Fifth Amendment's due-process clause lost substantive meaning as a realistic protection against Congress.

A participant in the Wisconsin litigation, Timothy O. Howe, subsequently United States Senator, recalled how Sherman Booth,

---

of the [C]onstitution as the organic law of a nation." Pomeroy, "The Supreme Court and State Repudiation—The Virginia and Louisiana Cases," *ALRev*, XVII (1883), 687–8; and see Eric Foner, *Free Soil*, chs. 1–3.

12. Certainly Wade was then no racial egalitarian. The westward movement of free white labor and capital was what he wished to build up. Free northern Negroes, unhappily "despised by all," and with whom white coexistence was undesirable and improbable on terms decent for the blacks, with government assistance should find tropical homes. "I hope, after that is done, to hear no more about negro equality or anything of that kind," Wade said. *CG*, 36 Cong., 1 sess., App. 150. On another occasion Wade wrote privately of his disgust with "old lawyers of Cincinnati" who refused to oppose enforcement of the fugitive slave law. "The Almighty has designed them for understrappers and bootblacks, niggers in soul and spirit. He forgot only to kink their hair and black their faces. . . ." Wade to Benjamin Stanton, May 30, 1859, owned by Stanton T. Allison.

one of the men freed, was rearrested for having helped to rescue another runaway Negro. This time the complainants avoided state authorities and went to the Federal District Court in Wisconsin. Tried, convicted, and imprisoned in the federal court, Booth found that the state's supreme court had issued another habeas corpus writ on his behalf. Again the state's judges ordered the nation's prisoner freed.[13]

Howe remembered that even enthusiasts for state interpositions against the federal recapture law realized that Wisconsin's action made the federal system unworkable. Nevertheless, merchants, publishers, judges, lawyers, and bankers felt that exigencies justified "incorporating the principles [of state defiance of unpopular national law] into the creed of Wisconsin Republicanism. . . . Here was open conflict between the . . . tribunals of the respective governments [state and national]."[14]

The open conflict deepened. Federal Marshal Ableman obtained a writ of error to the United States Supreme Court in order to overcome the habeas corpus obstruction Wisconsin's highest court had built. Despite the refusal of the Wisconsin court officially to notice the subsequent Washington proceedings, what followed was a confrontation of national and state judiciaries. In 1859, deciding Ableman v. Booth, the United States Supreme Court upheld the legitimacy of Congress's 1850 fugitive slave law. In his well-balanced opinion, Taney underscored the need in a federal system for national laws and courts to operate without harassment by state courts' writs.[15] In Wisconsin, Booth and others involved, learning of Taney's decision, again appealed to

---

13. In Howe's words, one of the Wisconsin supreme court judges "asserted the ultimate of the State sovereignty theory. He argued that the [federal] law having been pronounced unconstitutional by the Supreme Court of the State, it was therefore void within the State, regardless of what might be thought or resolved by the Federal Courts. Even this proposition as it seemed to offer the surest protection against an odious act, was hailed with great satisfaction by the great majority of those who opposed that [federal] law." Howe to J. M. Bundy, Sept. 26, 1870, in Bundy, *Are We a Nation?: The Question as It Stood Before the War* (New York, 1870), 5–8. For texts of states' personal liberty laws, see E. McPherson, *The Political History of the United States of America during the Great Rebellion* (2nd edn., Washington, 1865), 44–7; and see also S. W. Campbell, *The Slave Catchers: Enforcement of the Fugitive Slave Laws, 1850–1860* (Chapel Hill, 1970), ch. 6 and *passim*.

14. T. O. Howe, in Bundy, *Are We a Nation?* 7.

15. Ableman v. Booth, 62 US, 506 (1859).

the state high court for another habeas corpus proceeding. "Had that effort succeeded," Howe reminisced, "it is not easy to see how Wisconsin could have escaped an open rupture with the National Government; so that Mr. Lincoln . . . would have found instead of one, two hostile forces in the field, having not the least sympathy with each other, yet both denying the National authority."[16]

Perhaps other northern states in addition to Wisconsin would have engaged in outright defiance of the federal courts. Wade was trying to have Ohio's supreme court emulate Wisconsin's. Momentarily unsuccessful, in 1859 he wrote of his regret "that we have not a [state] supreme bench on whom we can rely in this emergency . . . [to] follow in the footsteps of Wisconsin." Wade estimated that state courts' libertarian defiances of federal courts' claims could be immensely valuable political capital, adequate to attach to the Republican side perhaps a third of Ohio's Democrats. For what decent man could tolerate constitutional interpretations of the Scott and Ableman sorts? The former denied Congress power to keep the nation's territories free of slaves; the latter sustained the nation's power and duty to thrust deep into northern states in pursuit of runaway slaves. So interpreted, the Constitution was out of balance.[17]

The onset of the Civil War averted a possibility of other confrontations over slave-return jurisdiction between national and Wisconsin or Ohio courts. By the end of 1862 Congress had repealed the vexatious recapture statute, which, combined with ratification in 1865 of the Thirteenth Amendment abolishing slavery, reversed the Dred Scott decision and imparted a wholesome flavor to the Ableman case.

Republicans discerned a useful bridge across the federal system in the expansion of national judicial power over states' courts which Taney's Ableman opinion envisaged. During the Civil War, several states' courts impeded national policies. Congress substantially enlarged the national courts' jurisdiction over certain actions by states' courts, thereby creating new, direct links between the nation and individuals.[18]

16. T. O. Howe, in Bundy, *Are We a Nation?* 7–8.
17. Benjamin Wade to Benjamin Stanton, May 30, 1859, owned by Stanton T. Allison.
18. See for background J. C. Hurd, *A Treatise on the Right of Personal Liberty, and on the Writ of Habeas Corpus* (Albany, 1858), 120–32; D. H. Oaks, "Habeas Corpus in the States—1775–1860," *UChiLR*, XXXII (1965), 288; Charles Warren, "Federal and State Court Interference,"

But in 1860 popular attention centered on the territorial issue and the Dred Scott decision more than on the fugitive recapture question and the Ableman case. By mid-year Republicans meeting in convention placed into the party platform a statement of constitutional conviction, in correct anticipation that it would attract broad northern electoral support: "That the new dogma that the Constitution, of its own force, carries slavery into any or all of the territories . . . is a dangerous political heresy, at variance with the explicit provisions of that instrument itself, with contemporaneous exposition, and with legislative and judicial precedent; is revolutionary in its tendency, and subversive of the peace and harmony of the country."

The Republican platform builders made obeisance to the "inviolate . . . right of each state to order and control its own domestic institutions according to its own judgment exclusively," and denounced violent, John Brown–style invasions of a state by residents of other states. According to the Republicans' platform, the Fifth Amendment was a prop to liberty of persons everywhere in the land including the territories; not merely a protection of slave property. If elected in adequate numbers, Republicans promised "by legislation, whenever such legislation is necessary, to maintain this provision of the Constitution [the Fifth Amendment] against all attempts to violate it; and we deny the authority of Congress, of a territorial legislature or of any individuals, to give legal existence to slavery in any territory of the United States." Lincoln's nomination on this platform—and in all public utterances and private communications he hewed tightly to it—signified a consensus that despite Dred Scott, Congress enjoyed not only the right but the duty to prevent the entrance into territories of human property.[19]

Democratic disunity contrasted sharply with the Republican agreement on fundamentals. Splitting at their convention, Demo-

---

358–9, 363; W. M. Wiecek, "The Reconstruction of Federal Judicial Power, 1863–1875" (M.A. essay, UWis, 1966), 3 (encapsulated under the same title in *AJLH*, XIII [1969], 333–59).

19. D. E. Fehrenbacher, "The Republican Decision at Chicago," in *Politics and the Crisis of 1860*, ed. N. A. Graebner (Urbana, 1961), 32–60. The platform text is in K. H. Porter and D. B. Johnson, *National Party Platforms, 1840–1960* (2nd edn., Urbana, 1961), 32.

crats failed to put their party's sectional pieces together again in time for the fall balloting. Douglas had worked out a tortuous formula in hope of bypassing the Dred Scott decision, so unpalatable in the North, without openly violating it, a course unacceptable in the South. The Douglas solution was, if possible, to get Congress off the hook of decision-making about slavery in a federal territory. Douglas wanted to shift responsibility westward. In 1858 and 1860 he argued that territorial lawmakers—creatures of Congress—somehow could do what the Dred Scott decision said Congress must not do; that territorial legislatures could exclude slaves simply by failure to enact ordinances making criminal the theft or other abuse of human property. Slaveowners would be unlikely to bring their chattels to areas where to interfere with slavery was not a crime.[20]

Douglas men were in a far more radical constitutional position than the Republicans. In the Republican argument of 1860, unaltered since 1857, Congress could not evade its responsibility to govern, to seek a solution to the territorial dilemma through ordinary legislation, perhaps looking toward a constitutional amendment, or to try in another suit to test again the issue of the Scott case.[21]

Considering the immediate advantages which the Democratic party would have gathered from closing ranks behind Douglas, it is remarkable that it did not. Had Democrats fallen into step quickly enough, they would have taken the rapidly approaching elections and fixed into constitutional law, as perpetually as possible, the state-centered, slave-focused position their southern pacemakers demanded. But dissident Democrats,

---

20. A. Kelly and W. Harbison, *American Constitution*, 392–3; D. Wells, *Stephen Douglas: The Last Years, 1857–1861* (Austin, 1971).

21. *The Collected Works of Abraham Lincoln*, ed. R. P. Basler *et al.* (New Brunswick, 1953), II, 401. In 1858, Lincoln held that "The Republican party . . . holds that . . . slavery is an unqualified evil. . . . Regarding it as an evil, they will not molest it in the states where it exists; they will not overlook the constitutional guards which our forefathers have placed around; they will do nothing which can give proper offence to those who hold slaves by legal sanction; but they will use every constitutional method to prevent the evil from becoming larger." *Ibid.*, III, 92. (Henceforth, this collection is cited as Lincoln, *Works*.) T. J. Pressly, "Bullets and Ballots: Lincoln and the 'Right of Revolution,'" *AHR*, LXVII (1962), 647–62, especially n. 21, offers a guide to Lincoln's references to his constitutional position.

chiefly southerners, found both the Douglas and the Republican positions unacceptable.

If Douglas's strategy had reunited the Democracy, the cost to democracy would have been very high; to Negroes, incalculable. Since the clear logic of politics was unable to hold in check the emotional reverberations of slavery, it is difficult to see why the uncertain logic of economics would have kept slaves from western lands. Obeying dictates of a united Democracy speaking with a southern drawl, Congress could only have opened territories to bondsmen. Of course a possibility existed that Douglas as President could have worked an exclusion of slaves from the West without direct congressional action. But events since 1819, and especially since 1848, had made clear that southerners were unlikely to let any direct or indirect rein on their peculiar institution slide by unnoticed. Certainly in the opinion of Douglas's contemporaries the odds were that anyone who wished to keep Democratic factions in step accepted a cadence counted by southern drillmasters in the party.[22]

Instead of uniting, southern Democrats withdrew from their party's convention. Organized as a separate party for the election, with support from the Buchanan Administration, the southerners offered as presidential aspirant John C. Breckinridge of Kentucky. They presented as platform their unyielding constitutional variant derived from Calhoun's theory and Taney's Dred Scott reference to the Fifth Amendment's property protection possibilities. The southern Democrats insisted that Congress could not exclude from national territories property that was legitimate under national statutes or any states' laws. Then, undermining Douglas's evasive strategy, the breakaway spokesmen claimed that Congress must not only admit slave property to territories but protect it there, whatever the convictions and votes on the matter of local residents or of citizens generally. In sum, the only power that the nation could exercise in this subject so central to popular concern was to support the western advance of slavery. Posterity—future politics—could not alter this commitment, according to the southern Democrats. Heretofore, the primary restraints on Congress had existed in the Bill of Rights, with

---

22. I employ in this analysis the lucid position of Bestor, "American Civil War as a Constitutional Crisis," 347–9. An alternative view is in Robert W. Johannsen, "Douglas at Charleston," in *Politics and the Crisis of 1860*, ed. Graebner, 61–90.

purpose to guard certain individual liberties. In 1860 a bill of southern white-rights-only came to the fore, sustaining slavery and promising to upend the federal system.

Obviously, the southern Democrats of 1860 shared with Republicans the assumption that Congress enjoyed power to act in the territories and should do so, but only in a certain way. Southern spokesmen agreed with the sweeping pronouncement that Senator Toombs had made four years earlier, that "Congress has no power to limit, restrain, or in any manner to impair slavery: but on the contrary, it is bound to protect and maintain it in the States where it exists, and wherever its flag floats, and its jurisdiction is paramount."[23] By this reasoning the slave laws of the southern states somehow acquired instantaneous existence and validity within a national territory the moment the American flag went up. Stated in future tense, which was the argument's core in 1860, the southerners looked forward to an ever-expanding nation in which slavery had to follow the flag, and in which southern states' slave codes must penetrate even free-soil northern states in instances of runaways.

In this Orwellian Union the slave states were more sovereign than others. Even if Congress wished them to, free states' law codes could not gain export to national territories. However, the slave provisions of southern states must have entry into territories whatever the degree of popular desire to the contrary. Simultaneously and without evidencing a sense of the paradoxes involved, southern spokesmen insisted that in the recapture of runaway slaves Congress must exert within northern states enormous police powers and punitive functions.

This phantasmagoric conception of the Union was presented as an election appeal. Linked with slavery, the argument for state sovereignty had become the hallmark of the South as a very self-conscious minority.[24]

These minima of 1860 not forthcoming, and Lincoln's election seeming to retard their achievement for at least four years, southern leaders prepared to take their states into secession. In constitutional terms secession was not the goal of the state sovereignty argument. Instead men employing that argument had sought, within the Union, positive policies agreeable to the main-

---

23. In Alexander H. Stephens, *A Constitutional View of the Late War Between the States* (Philadelphia, 1868–70), I, 625.
24. Arthur Bestor, "State Sovereignty and Slavery," 180.

tenance and increase of their slave institution.[25] But the Union—
at least the "old" Union—had become exposed as constitutionally
defective and so its disruption was in order.

In the fall of 1860 awareness was so general of the South's
determination to reshape the Constitution's machinery as to inspire creation of still another political alternative, the Constitutional Union party, with John Bell of Tennessee as presidential
candidate. Its strength was in the border states. Men from that
region were supposed somehow to possess a peculiar aptitude for
arranging sectional compromises through politics in the pattern
set in 1820 and 1850. With secession of southern states under
way or imminent following Lincoln's election, border-state leaders
tried again to create a constitutional principle out of their conviction that a sectional political compromise was in order. The would-
be compromisers of 1860 intended to cement terms into the
Constitution beyond the power of popular majorities to alter by
ballot; to exclude from democratic consideration subjects about
which millions of Americans had indicated by votes just cast that
action was necessary.

Action was forthcoming. November's balloting brought
promise that by the succeeding March, Republicans would have
formal control of national policies. Movement began to separate
states of the deep South from the federal Union. By Christmas
1860 American constitutional history appeared to have come to a
dismal close. A relative of the historian George Bancroft, whose
work centered on the formation of the 1787 Constitution, wondered what would become of the scholar-politician. "His occupation will certainly be gone. Nobody will want to read in history of
the formation of a government by our forefathers which we have
let fall to pieces."[26]

However, the onset of secession raised, not lowered, history's
curtain on the American Constitution. Events brought men to
estimate carefully their government and society, so that one

---

25. A. Bestor, "American Civil War as a Constitutional Crisis," 350.
No more than Professor Bestor can I accept the conclusion that the slavery-
territory question in politically or constitutionally significant terms was
ever merely rhetorical. See James G. Randall, *Lincoln the President* (New
York, 1945), I, 125; Russel, "Constitutional Doctrines," 486.

26. William D. Bliss to "Sandy," Dec. 18, 1860, Bancroft-Bliss Papers,
LC.

commentator of 1861 was moved to the judgment that "The apparatus for studying our Constitution has improved more rapidly since the integrity of the Union was threatened than at any preceding period."[27] But in 1860–61 the question was whether it was not already too late for action or reflection to avert disaster.

---

27. In an unsigned review of George S. Williams, *The Constitution of the United States for Use of Schools and Academies* (Cambridge, 1861), in *NAR*, XCIV (1862), 271; and see Joel Parker, *Constitutional Law*, 9–10.

Chapter III

The Shock of Weakness[*]

Soon after Lincoln's election, the lame-duck President James Buchanan complained to a visitor at the White House: "I think it is very hard [that] they can not let me finish my term of office in peace, at my time of life."[1] There was to be no peace, in the sense of stability, for which Buchanan yearned, and at the end of 1860 the close of his tenure stretched distantly ahead. The Constitution's curious rhythm required that he hold his office a third of a year after the election had chosen a successor whose policies differed markedly from his own. During this interregnum Buchanan had little power. But he might have influenced events in a constructive manner.

Tragically, Buchanan's limitations denied the nation the only possible effective national leadership. On Capitol Hill the Congress was caught up in contention. The Supreme Court was discredited in the North because of the Dred Scott decision and had nothing more to say to the South. If sectional reconciliation was to come forth its source had to be the White House. Lesser performance meant failure on the part of every institution the nation possessed to cope with the worst crisis the nation had ever faced. Resort to some extraordinary expedient—plebiscite, peace

---

* This chapter has appeared in essentially similar form in *Freedom and Reform: Essays in Honor of Henry Steele Commager,* ed. Harold M. Hyman and Leonard W. Levy (New York, 1967), 149–66.

1. Ms. memorandum by John C. Ropes, Feb. 8, 1870, of conversation in Sept. 1869 with Edwin M. Stanton, H. Woodman Papers, MHS.

congress, or constitutional convention—was an implicit acceptance of incapacity on the part of Constitution, President, Congress, Court, and parties.

Attention focused on the White House because then as now America was a President-centered political society. All other elected officials, including United States senators and representatives, were essentially states' men. The public was not deceived by the anachronistic Electoral College into misreading the character of the presidential office. It had come to be the only wholly national possession. Despite weak Democratic Presidents and the Whigs' weak-executive theory, the heritage of Washington, Jefferson, and Jackson provided Buchanan with a reservoir of potential effectiveness, even, men hoped, to the point of dealing constructively with the determined southern spokesmen.

It was also apparent that enormous obstacles stood in the way of such an accomplishment. Buchanan had proved unable to hold his Democrats together. Unless he swiftly altered his constitutional views he could not hope to win Republican support, for in the election just past Buchanan had backed dissident Breckinridge Democrats who were sparking the secession process in a half-dozen states. In the North the public had sustained either Douglas Democrats or upstart Republicans, implicitly repudiating the President. Fretful at such treatment from the North, Buchanan felt betrayed by his erstwhile friends in the South.

Buchanan pleaded ignorance of nationalist constitutional development, to which he was unsympathetic. A confidant advised him "to show the Country a grand example of the teachings of the Jackson school in which we were educated," to which Buchanan replied that he did not know his predecessor's position during the 1832 nullification crisis. "I was out of the country as Minister to Russia during the Nullification times and I really don't know the arguments on the question," Buchanan asserted.[2]

To his credit, the President brought into his cabinet men of antisecession attitude to replace defectors of southern persuasion. In stormy meetings, the new cabinet officers tried to bring the old

---

2. *Ibid.* Differing interpretations on Buchanan are in P. S. Klein, *President James Buchanan: A Biography* (University Park, Md., 1962), *passim,* and in B. P. Thomas and H. M. Hyman, *Stanton: The Life and Times of Lincoln's Secretary of War* (New York, 1962), chs. 5–6; R. A. Mohl, "Presidential Views of National Power," *Mid-America,* LII (1970), 171–89.

man to a more respectable Unionist posture.[3] They lessened the flaccidity that had characterized Buchanan's manner and public utterances under earlier prosouthern tutors. But the influence of the incoming advisors is easily overestimated; they perceived no new modes of national action against states' secessions. Consider this testament by Joseph Holt, the new Secretary of War, who in mid-January 1861 wrote to a Louisiana friend:

> The thought of employing force to oblige a state to remain in the Union has never been entertained by the President or any member of his cabinet—He has held, as I do, that it is his duty to protect the public property in his charge as well as he can—But this principle is virtually an abstraction since with two or three exceptions the arm[orie]s and forts of the Un[ited] States have been seized throughout the South. . . . No effort to regain them will be made. . . . The Union is passing away like a band of fog before the wind—But the fate of the South will be that of Sampson— She will pull down the temple, but she will perish amid the ruins.[4]

Early in December 1860 Buchanan addressed the lame-duck session of the 36th Congress on the sorry state of the Union. He revealed that his basic constitutional position was unchanged from what it had been before the elections. His classic dual-federalism view envisaged functional orbits for the national government to travel, which, because of the Tenth Amendment, never intersected with those of the states. Secession was unconstitutional. But no branch of the national government could do anything to impede the process. Coercion was out of reason, the President insisted in what the scholar John W. Burgess later described as "one of the most unfortunate state papers of our history."[5]

Buchanan's speech deserved Burgess's description. To Buchanan the possible destruction of the Union from efforts by the nation to stem states' secessions by force was worse than the certain destruction of the Union by acquiescence in illegal seces-

---

3. James Buchanan to Harriet Lane, Nov. 4, 1860, Buchanan-Johnson Papers, LC.

4. Joseph Holt to James O. Harrison, Jan. 14, 1861, Harrison Papers, LC.

5. John W. Burgess, *The Civil War and the Constitution, 1859–1865* (New York, 1901), I, 80.

sion. Even if the Constitution allowed the central government to wage war upon a state or states in order to thwart secession, Buchanan opposed recourse to this desperate expedient. "War [by the nation against a state] would not only present the most effectual means of destroying it [the Union] but would banish all hope of its peaceable reconstruction," he stated. Only mutual good will between the sections would serve.

But this improvement could occur only when the South's terms were met. If in 1857 the Dred Scott decision had been accepted as a finality in constitutional law, as Buchanan believed it should have been, then southern views on the issues "settled" by that case might have rested where they were. Unfortunately "a very large proportion of the people of the [northern] United States still contest the correctness of that decision, and never will cease from agitation and admit its binding force," the President said crossly, careless of his own earlier concern over the need for a consensus. Northern recusancy explained why the South raised demands from the 1857 level to the 1860 Breckinridge heights. Now the rest of the nation must give evidence that secession was unnecessary as well as unlawful.

In the face of the Republican and Douglas Democratic ballots so recently counted, which meant a northern mandate to Congress to cope with the westward march of slavery, the President brought forth a proposal to reverse the verdict of that election. He wanted an "explanatory" amendment to the Constitution to confirm the legitimacy of slave property in slaveowning states (in 1860 it was under attack in none); congressional protection for slave property in national territories until state constitutions with or without slavery replaced the territorial condition (the Kansas troubles had occurred because men were convinced that a slaveowning territory must become a slaveowning state); and a reaffirmation of the 1850 fugitive slave law, coupled with a clause voiding obstructive personal-liberty laws of northern states.[6]

In the North the President's message unleashed a wave of criticism. Sickened by what they considered to be the craven course of action—or inaction—in Washington, Americans wondered what was wrong with governing institutions. Until this time, despite implicit agreement that slavery had extended far enough, little effective co-operation had existed between Republi-

6. *M&P*, VI, 626–37.

can "professionals," intellectuals, reformers, and literary pace-
setters. By today's inapplicable standards, these men and women
exhibited curious mixtures of antislavery and Negrophobe attitudes, of opposition to secession and elitist antipathies to democracy's excesses, of pacifism and militant patriotism. But in mid-
nineteenth-century terms these people became the consciences of
American society, in the same sense that the Republican party
was the only on-hand vehicle with which to oppose in politics the
western advance of slavery.[7] Buchanan's view of the federal
system and his overblowing of the Tenth Amendment pushed
men of disparate purposes into more effective political concert
than had been thought possible. If the Republican party backtracked from its central principle and accepted a "compromise"
similar to those of 1820 and 1850, free society was impossible.[8]

To be sure, definitions varied widely of the nature of free
government and desirable social purposes. Aristocrats and equalitarians, theorists and activists, shared a growing conviction that
the Constitution was at a crossroads. A wrong turn on the part of
the Republican party in the direction of acquiescence to
Buchanan's constitutional invocations would mean disaster for all
purposes.

Now men must stand up to the South; perhaps a stiff spine
might save American society, if it was worth saving. To para-
phrase the title of a sermon by Reverend Henry W. Bellows, a
prominent Unitarian minister, the advantage to be gained by
testing American principles without further delay could overcome
the South's long-time customary lead and purify a society grown
flabby from preoccupation with things.[9]

---

7. See George M. Frederickson, *The Inner Civil War: Northern In-
tellectuals and the Crisis of the Union* (New York, 1965), ch. 4; G. S.
Henry, Jr., "Radical Republican Policy Toward the Negro During Recon-
struction, 1862–1872" (Ph.D. diss., YU, 1963), chs. 1–2; W. G. Cochrane,
"Freedom Without Equality: A Study of Northern Opinion and the Negro
Issue, 1861–1870" (Ph.D. diss., UMinn, 1957), 2–44.

8. As an example of sensitivity to the speech and its effects, and of
the need for Republicans to hold firm to their central constitutional view,
see J. E. Cabot, *Letter to the Governor of Massachusetts on the Occasion
of His Late Proclamation of August 20, 1861* (Boston, 1866), 198–203;
P. Paludan, "The American Civil War Considered as a Crisis in Law and
Order," *AHR*, LXXVII (1972), 1013–34.

9. Henry W. Bellows, *The Advantage of Testing Our Principles, Com-
pensatory of the Evils of Serious Times. A Discourse on Sunday Morning,
February 17, 1861, Before the Second Unitarian Society of Philadelphia*
(Philadelphia, 1861); and see D. D. Braden, "The Concept of Equality in
American Political Thought" (Ph.D. diss., USC, 1944), chs. 8–10.

Concern, occasioned by Buchanan's December 1860 message, that this sort of servile nature had taken over the White House, the Supreme Court, and Congress, with consequent total national corruption, led to a conclusion that constitutional confrontation was a superior alternative to continued cowardice.

The diffusion of belligerent sentiments[10] among normally cautious and conservative men like James Russell Lowell has impressed twentieth-century commentators. One historian concluded recently that "It was obvious by 1860 that . . . intellectuals were ready to welcome a great national catastrophe . . . [or] a 'chastising calamity,' [and] . . . hurried the country along toward civil war."[11]

Certainly by 1860 many "intellectuals" welcomed anything that might bring forth a decent resolution of the country's difficulties and cleanse its allegedly corrupted political apparatuses. Decency required that secession and the Juggernautish western advance of slavery stop. If force was necessary to realize these ends then these men were at the point of welcoming the abstract notion of war in the belief that, possessed of superior virtue, the North's cause must win.

But they did not advocate that Americans plunge into a civil war—certainly not into *the* Civil War—as a solution to the slave extension problem, for which in their view the Constitution already offered remedy, or in order to burn evils out of the American system. In 1860 Americans lived in an age of innocence with respect to the nature of mass war. A people of plenty, they flourished in the world's least military society. Certainly intellectuals of reformist bent did not look forward to a war as a desirable step in social change or in preventing further change.

When war came the intellectuals' concern remained what it had grown to by the time of the secession winter. They wanted to employ the Constitution and the national government in favor of stability, or in search of whatever improvements in American society they advocated, especially to keep the territories free from slavery. Obviously the Democracy had no appeal for this new breed of liberal; affiliation was possible only with Republicans.

---

10. J. R. Lowell to Charles Nordhoff, Dec. 31, 1860, in *Letters of James Russell Lowell*, ed. C. E. Norton (New York, 1894), I, 308.

11. Frederickson, *Inner Civil War*, 48–9; and see R. Albrecht, "The Response of the Transcendentalists to the Civil War," *NEQ*, XXXVIII (1965), 21–34; Martin Duberman, *James Russell Lowell* (Boston, 1966), ch. 10.

Once convinced that politics was the only way to win goals, even abolitionists, who had in some instances been fiercely antipolitical, antidemocratic, anti-institutional, and anti-Union, moved into Republican ranks. They shared with Republican "pros" the assumption that the Constitution was a source of power as well as limitations. The reformers' problem was to bend the party to their purposes. Meanwhile they kept close attention on Congress and the White House.[12]

In December 1860, holdover Republicans in Washington conducted a rear-guard operation so that the Lincoln Administration might have a capital to come to.[13] Party frontrunners revealed how unpalatable they found Buchanan's suggestion for constitutional amendment. Speaking on December 17, Senator Wade stressed the inability of political democracy to survive if, as Buchanan had proposed, losers of elections employed subsequent constitutional amendments to reverse popular verdicts. Republicans would not compromise away responsibilities that the recent balloting had imposed on them. But Wade insisted that southerners had no justification to take their states out of the Union, because once in office Republicans intended to obey the popular voice.

Wade was a member of a special Senate committee that was seeking a viable formula for sectional conciliation. Prospects were dismal for the success of the committee's efforts. There was a long distance between Wade's constitutional views and that of some of his colleagues.

One of Wade's committee mates, Toombs of Georgia, proposed to the group that it draft for the Senate's approval an irrepealable, unamendable amendment to the Constitution. The amendment would embrace perpetually the essentials of what, in the elections just past, the southern Democrats had demanded but failed to win as the price of unity.

---

12. R. D. Marcus, "Wendell Phillips and American Institutions," *JAH*, LVI (1969), 47–58; J. McPherson, *The Struggle for Equality: Abolitionists and the Negro in the Civil War and Reconstruction* (Princeton, 1964), chs. 3–5. J. Rosenberg, "Toward a New Civil War Revisionism," *American Scholar*, XXXVIII (1969), 250–72, offers opposite views without offering contrary evidence.

13. Charles Sumner to Governor John A. Andrew, Jan. 28, 1861, Andrew Papers, MHS.

The concept of an unamendable amendment—a fatally constrictive "Chinese shoe," the scholar Von Holst later called it— was novel. That it should have received serious consideration during the weeks following Lincoln's election is the measure of how low secession had brought the constitutional ethics of many Americans, and of how frightened the country was.[14]

Toombs insisted that the unalterable amendment should read that citizens were to have the right to move into all present and future national territories "with whatever property they may possess, including slaves," and enjoy protection for their goods, human and otherwise. Toombs further proposed, as a perpetual, irrevocable alteration in the federal system, to change interstate comity relationships so that slave and criminal codes of southern states would apply in free-soil states, but not the reverse. In Toombs's words:

> Persons committing crimes against slave property in one State, and fleeing to another, shall be delivered up in the same manner as persons committing crimes against other property, and that the laws of the States from which such persons flee shall be the test of criminality; that fugitive slaves shall be surrendered under the provisions of the Fugitive Slave Act of 1850, without being entitled either to a writ of Habeas Corpus, or trial by jury, or other similar obstructions of legislation in the state to which they may flee; and that Congress shall pass efficient laws for the punishment of all persons in any of the States who shall in any manner aid and abet invasion or insurrection in any other State, or commit any other act against the law of Nations, tending to disturb the tranquility of the people of government of any other State.[15]

Kentucky's Senator John J. Crittenden, resorting again to traditional border-state practices of balancing interests, proposed to escalate the pattern of crisis legislation made familiar in 1820 and 1850 onto Toombs's irreversible constitutional level. He proposed a "compromise of 1860" that essentially followed the Buchanan-Toombs lead. Crittenden's notion of acceptable com-

---

14. *CG*, 36 Cong., 2 sess., 99–104, for Wade, and see Charles Francis Adams, *The Constitutional Ethics of Secession* (Boston and New York, 1903); Hermann E. Von Holst, *The Constitutional and Political History of the United States* (Chicago, 1876–92), VII, 377.

15. Burgess, *Civil War and the Constitution*, I, 96–7.

promise was also to attach an unamendable amendment to the Constitution. He revived the old 36'30" line as a viable partition line for existing and future territories. North of that line no slavery could ever exist. But the enormous expanse south of it was always to be open to slavery and Congress must protect slave property. To be sure, Crittenden prescribed that future states carved from territories south of 36'30" might come into the Union with or without slavery as residents chose. However, if history was a guide, it stood to reason that enfranchised inhabitants of a slaveholding territory would choose to enter as a slave state.

In 1860 no one who rated a hearing in terms of political realities suggested that Congress could reach into states to end slavery. Even so, Crittenden specified that it could never do so. He would disarm Congress perpetually of a power it did possess; to abolish slavery in the District of Columbia or in other national enclaves inside slaveholding states. Slaveowners who were unable to recover runaways because of popular antipathy in northern states to enforcement of the fugitive slave law, would receive compensation from the national government. It would then extract a like amount from the county in which the fugitive found succor. In all events and for all time, Congress must rigorously enforce the fugitive slave ordinance, which in a sense also became unrepealable. Last, Crittenden wanted his amendment to declare null and void the personal liberty laws of northern states.[16]

In 1860 most white Americans felt unable to live in a situation in which slavery's western enlargement was not merely permitted but guaranteed, and placed forever beyond limitation by future political action. A favorable view of Crittenden's positions requires faith that politics could have dropped the slavery-extension question if the Kentuckian's specifications went on the books. A favorable estimate comes easiest from retrospective knowledge that the Civil War was waiting in the wings, and must come onstage in absence of a settlement agreeable to the South.

---

16. Crittenden hoped that northern states would repeal their personal-liberty laws in anticipation of the ratification of his amendment. *CG*, 36 Cong., 2 sess., 114; Bestor, "The American Civil War as a Constitutional Crisis," *AHR*, LXIX (1964), 341, 343; and for a differing analysis, Albert K. Kirwan, *John J. Crittenden: The Struggle for the Union* (Lexington, Ky., 1962), 366–421.

Consider the last point first. In December 1860 and January 1861, when Crittenden made his bid, few Americans anywhere seriously anticipated war, despite bellicose rhetoric. Men on the inside of the best information then available, who received warnings of the possibility of armed strife, found incredible the notion of a large-scale formal trial-at-arms between the sections.

But even in light of the war that was to come the Crittenden proposals were wretched levels on which to fix, as permanently as men knew how to do, the constitutional law of the United States. It is difficult to understand how a revision of the Constitution in Crittenden's terms could have opened in the foreseeable future opportunities to deal peaceably through politics with subjects that the Crittenden formula excluded forever from political consideration. Unless prejudgment exists that anything is preferable to confrontation, it strains credulity to rank Crittenden's proposal to enlarge areas open to slavery as a constitutionally or morally superior alternative to the Republican position of holding the line.

In the last days of 1860 confrontation was not the necessary consequence of rejection for the Crittenden package. Men were not desperately trying to fend off a war the onset of which they did not seriously anticipate.[17] The would-be compromisers were peacemakers, not war-avoiders; they were structuring as permanent a peace as they were able to do.

What confuses is that Crittenden employed a constitutional idiom for a political purpose. Because in the South's opinion slavery was too delicate to risk in politically democratic processes, Crittenden wished to provide it a permanent sanctuary in the Constitution and to sever the Constitution from politics; i.e., to cut from the Constitution the capacity to receive from politics continuing involvement with popular needs.

His way was to freeze the Constitution into a catatonic condition with respect to certain tender functional arenas of the national government and vital federal-state relationships. Perhaps actual secession would lever out of the North what threats of seceding had failed to force.

Secession's incredible reality shook many northerners so deeply that a few weeks after the election some were willing to

---

17. In addition to Buchanan's constitutional constrictions, disbelief in the chance of violence kept the President from allowing anything approaching adequate preparations. See Edwin M. Stanton to Ohio Senator Salmon P. Chase, Jan. 23, 1861, Chase Papers, HSP.

abandon their positions of November and to support Crittenden's way. Recent Constitutional Unionists swung away from their campaign slogan of "The Constitution and the Union" to approve a Constitution and Union reshaped to the South's demands. Douglas Democrats generally followed their leader's similar post-election shift, to favor perpetually exempting from the principle of popular sovereignty the vast lands south of the 36'30" partition line, apparently without worrying overmuch about the incongruities involved.[18]

In sharp contrast, Republicans held fast to their election position and to the constitutionalism that underlay it. Indeed, in early 1861, only a dozen years after the first submission of the Wilmot Proviso attracted a tiny minority of northerners, Republican professionals understood that the precarious coalition achieved in 1860 would shatter into futile fragments if members did not hold fast on the root issue of slavery containment. By the standards of 1860–61 the Republican position was adequate to fire hard-bitten political "pros" as well as reformer-intellectuals. Unlike Buchanan, Crittenden, Douglas, or Toombs, the Republicans assumed that practical alternatives, yet undiscerned, existed to ignominious capitulation. These alternatives could be reached through the ordinary processes of political democracy, not by closing them off or resorting to extraordinary expedients. The appealing Republican assumption was that the Constitution was adequate to cope with calamities, and that it deserved a better fate than to be welded forever to slavery.[19] A sense of injured nationalism and a conviction about the Constitution's adaptability were the essence of the new political liberalism and of the old constitutional attitude that by early 1861 was attracting all sorts and conditions of northerners into the Republican party.

. . .

18. Stephen A. Douglas to C. H. Lamphier, Dec. 25, 1860, George Fort Milton Papers, LC; Robert W. Johannsen, "The Douglas Democracy and the Crisis of Disunion," *CWH*, IX (1963), 231.

19. Reflecting on this matter of the Republicans' tenacious concern with the Constitution's adequacies and alternatives, Joshua Giddings recalled how "Mr. Crittenden appeared to think that the Union could only be preserved by so amending the Constitution as to change the essential character of the Government, making it a slave-sustaining federation, instead of adapting its energies to securing liberty." Giddings, *History of the Rebellion: Its Authors and Causes* (New York, 1864), 455; and see Burgess, *Civil War and the Constitution*, I, 99.

During the early weeks of 1861, the question rose whether some leaders of the party, especially the President-elect, could withstand the lure of the Crittenden sort of proposal. A variety of ad hoc compromise-seeking groups, including special committees of the House and Senate, a governors' conference, and a prestigious though fumbling peace congress at Washington were adding to the confusion.

During the interregnum Lincoln refused to commit himself or his administration to anything less or more than his party's 1860 platform and his previous statements specified.[20] Knowing that the information would be broadcast, Lincoln wrote to a member of the special House committee that was searching for a path to sectional reconciliation: "Entertain no proposition for a compromise in regard to the *extension* of slavery. The instant you do, they have us under again; all our labor is lost, and sooner or later must be done over. . . . Have none of it. The tug has to come, and better now than later."

For dissemination among states' governors then convened, Lincoln let it be known that as President: "I will be inflexible on the territorial question; . . . I think either the Missouri line extended, or Douglas' . . . Pop[ular] Sov[ereignty] would lose us everything we gained by the election; that filibustering [by southern whites in Latin America] for all South of us, and making slave states of it, would follow."

Lincoln was not immune to the need to placate southerners about his alleged bellicosity and to prove to northerners that Republicans were not aiming beyond duties that the Constitution imposed. Writing on February 1 to his Secretary of State-designate, William H. Seward, again with intention that the information leak to the public, Lincoln adverted to his imminent responsibility as President to enforce the 1850 fugitive slave law. Of this tender matter "and whatever springs of necessity from the fact that the institution [of slavery] is among us, I care but little, so what is done be comely, and not altogether outrageous," he stated. But he returned to what was basic that year: "I am for no

---

20. A caller at Willard's Hotel late in February 1861, after seeing the President-elect, described how "Everybody here seems to look to Lincoln and Lincoln says 'delighted to see you &c &c.,' but no one gets his tongue and everyone has his ear. . . . The peace Congress is a humbug." Wilder Dwight to Horace Gray, Feb. 27, 1861, Gray Papers, LC. A different judgment is in Robert A. Gunderson, *Old Gentlemen's Convention: The Washington Peace Conference of 1861* (Madison, Wis., 1961).

compromise which assists or permits the extension of the [slave] institution on soil owned by the nation."[21]

Lincoln's consistency on this critical position made him acceptable to almost all Republicans.[22] Evoked by the specter of expanding thralldom and made urgent by the shock of secession, this position had at its center the assumption that the national government under the Constitution had the power to hold the present line between free and slave regions, and a duty to do so arising out of the election results. The year 1860 was one of those points in history when a party's constitutional position was so involved with the nation's needs as to render irrelevant efforts to separate them.[23]

Yet secession pressure squeezed even Republican stalwarts. Under Seward's sponsorship, a proposal to amend the Constitution in the direction of a perpetual commitment to the sanctity of slave property in *states* where it then existed came from the special House committee on sectional conciliation.[24] In Congress an impressive number of Republicans supported this suggestion. It harmonized the Republicans' 1860 platform pledge against interference by the national government with the internal concerns of states, although the party had not offered this pledge in the form of a proposition for an ordinary amendment to the Constitution, much less a perpetual one. Nevertheless, the 1861 Seward amendment proposal offered hope of stabilizing one uneasy element in federal-state relationships. Perhaps approval for it would halt secession without requiring abandonment of the

---

21. The three quotations are respectively Dec. 11, 17, 1860, Feb. 1, 1861, in *The Collected Works of Abraham Lincoln,* ed. Roy P. Basler *et al.* (New Brunswick, N.J., 1953), IV, 150, 154, 183.

22. Lorraine A. Williams, "Northern Intellectual Attitudes toward Lincoln, 1860–1865," ISHS *Journal,* LVII (1964), 270–7.

23. A recent example of such an attempt is in Johannsen, "The Douglas Democracy and the Crisis of Disunion," 232, where the suggestion is made that "At the time, party position seemed [to Lincoln] more important than the nation's problems." Cf. C. D. Hart, "Why Lincoln Said 'No': Congressional Attitudes on Slavery Expansion, 1860–1861," SSQ (1968), 732–41.

24. By terms of the proposed addition, "no amendment shall be made to the Constitution which will authorize or give to Congress the power to abolish or interfere, within any state, with the domestic institutions thereof, including that of persons held to labor or service by the laws of said state." CG, 36 Cong., 2 sess., 1284–5, 1403. Note that the federal territories and the District of Columbia were not included in the terms of the proposal. See also Wilson, "The Repressible Conflict," 553–4.

primary Republican concern with keeping the territories free from slavery.

By March 1861 the proposed amendment had passed through Congress. It reached the White House in time for Lincoln to refer to it in his inaugural address. Such a restriction on Congress's power was already "implied constitutional law," Lincoln said. Therefore, he could not object "to its being made express, and irrevocable."[25]

The proposed amendment became a casualty of the war it was designed to avert. Less than two years after the amendment's proposal the idea of preserving slavery had become anachronistic, as, in vastly altered circumstances Lincoln issued his Emancipation Proclamation. By 1863, abolition pressure was increasing even in the loyal border states where slaveholding existed; by the close of 1865 a Thirteenth Amendment to the Constitution, embracing all states as well as territories, contradicted directly the 1861 proposal that would have become the Thirteenth Amendment if events had gone other ways. One measure of the Civil War's impact is to gauge differences between what might have been, and what came to be.[26]

The Civil War crushed not only the specific subject matter of the 1861 amendment proposal but also its novel and unsuitable method. After 1861 Americans did not attempt to add unamendable amendments to the 1787 Constitution.[27]

During the secession crisis, in addition to proposing unamendable amendments, conservatives suggested plebiscites, national referenda, and/or interstate conventions to reverse 1860's verdicts by ballots. Later, Edward Pollard, the effective chronicler of the Lost Cause, recalled how, during presecession arguments in Congress, Mississippi Senator Jefferson Davis revived one of Calhoun's "most beautiful and ingenious theories." Calhoun had "proposed that in cases of serious dispute between any State and the General Government, the matter should be referred to a convention of all the States for its final and conclu-

---

25. Lincoln, *Works,* IV, 270.

26. Herman V. Ames, "Proposed Amendments to the Constitution of the United States During the First Century of Its History," AHA *Annual Report* (1896), II, 23–49.

27. Burgess, *Civil War and the Constitution,* I, 99–100.

sive determination." Such a convention would rein in democracy's excesses through exercise of "august guardianship" by the states. Pollard professed to believe that such a convention of states would provide "that principle of adaptability to circumstances which is the first virtue of wise government."[28]

On January 3, 1861, Crittenden suggested that the Senate initiate a nationwide referendum to register popular opinion on his earlier propositions to amend the Constitution irrevocably. Douglas added his still-heavy weight on the side of the Kentuckian's plebiscite innovation, insisting that arguments from Republicans that the preceding November's balloting had already registered public opinion were unconvincing.

Seward retorted that it was frank blackmail for Democrats to exploit secession as a partisan opportunity to reverse the election's verdict. He condemned as unconstitutional any delegation of Congress's inescapable responsibilities to govern, by a ruse such as the one Crittenden wished the Senate to approve.[29]

Perhaps as a diversionary tactic designed to shield Republicans from any onus of insensitivity to conciliation, Seward himself put forward a notion of an over-all reconsideration of the Constitution by means of a national constitution convention. But, like Lincoln, Seward was holding Republican constitutional doctrine pretty much where it had been since the party assumed national prominence four years earlier. This position acknowledged that the Constitution required study and repair. It denied the southern and border-state tinkering that would have amputated functional arenas.[30]

All proposals failed for national constitutional conventions, plebiscites, or unamendable amendments. However, almost no one accounted the Constitution's passage, unaltered, through the secession winter as much of a triumph. The unopposed progress of secession and unimpeded creation of the Confederacy argued heavily that the 1787 Constitution was hopelessly defective as a frame for government.

---

28. Edward Pollard, *The Lost Cause Regained* (New York, 1868), 43; Roy Franklin Nichols, *Blueprints for Leviathan: American Style* (New York, 1963), 134–43.

29. Kirwan, *Crittenden*, 392–4; CG, 36 Cong., 2 sess., 211, 237, 264–7, App., 38–42.

30. CG, 36 Cong., 2 sess., 341–6; F. W. Seward, *An Autobiography, with a Memoir of His Life, and Selections from His Letters, by Frederick W. Seward* (New York, 1891), II, 494.

The Shock of Weakness

It is difficult to imagine a longer road for the Constitution to travel than the one stretching from Sumter to Appomattox. It is more difficult to explain the successful transit without appreciation of the narrow escape from capitulation during the secession winter, which the Republicans' constitutional position of refusing to admit the Constitution's defectiveness or inadequacy made possible.

Chapter IV

The Constitutional Commitment
to Capacity

On March 4, 1861, Lincoln's inauguration as President of the United States was a welcome sign that at least some portions of the creaking Constitution were in working order. Since his election four months earlier and the subsequent secessions of seven states, doubts had increased that it could operate at all.

Indeed, patriotic men had worried that the electoral machinery would stall or be jammed. As Inauguration Day drew closer fear had grown of disorders in northern cities and of invasion from the militant South, designed to block Lincoln's entrance into the Presidency. This final overload would shatter the apparently brittle constitutional structure, already strained by secession.

Any cause likely to prevent the inauguration was a national danger. If Lincoln was not installed on March 4 the government would be headless. No way existed to bypass the Constitution's rigid timetable, to keep Buchanan on as emergency place-holder, or to arrange for an interim substitute from among members of the House, Senate, or Supreme Court, as some concerned onlookers suggested.

The least consequence of instability in Washington must be to add stability to the self-proclaimed Confederate States of America at Montgomery. Beyond this men anticipated, with fear or with hope, the further Balkanization of the once-United States. Therefore, the fact that Lincoln's inauguration occurred at all evoked relief among northern patriots. That it went off without disturbance (few people knew of the extensive and largely unofficial security precautions that were in effect in Washington on Inauguration Day) was happy evidence that there was still life in the old Constitution.

And so at Harvard Law School three days later Professor Theophilus Parsons felt justified in sounding a hopeful note. Passion would ebb and the southern wanderers return, he predicted. The national government must exhibit "patient forbearance while that is possible." The Constitution required the exercise of gentleness, but it possessed also "exquisite adaptedness to any exigency; and therefore, of adequacy to any exigence which may call upon it . . . to bring into action its whole irresistible might."[1]

The view from Washington was remarkably different from Parsons's Cambridge vista. Settling in at the White House, the new President and leading Republican congressmen knew how complex and unstable the situation that they had inherited from Buchanan was. Out of patriotism and in default of adequate interparty and intragovernment channels, two cabinet officers in the Buchanan Administration, Buchanan's Secretary of War Joseph Holt and Attorney General Edwin M. Stanton, as well as the Army's senior general, Winfield Scott, had communicated clandestinely with Republicans destined for Lincoln's cabinet and for significant committees in the forthcoming Congress.[2]

Boiled down, this intelligence concluded that there was not much that the national government could do effectively to reverse secession, even if the Constitution allowed the use of force. Ridiculously small numbers of soldiers were at hand, for Buchanan had not dared risk upsetting the status quo by transferring eastward the small, tough frontier-based regular Army.

---

1. Theophilus Parsons, *The Constitution, Its Origin, Function, and Authority: Lecture at Harvard Law School, March 7, 1861* (Boston, 1861), 5, 28–30; C. P. Stone, "Washington in March and April 1861," *Magazine of American History*, XIV (1885), 7–8; J. Bayard to S. L. M. Barlow, Dec. 6, 1861, Barlow Papers, HL.

2. Joseph Holt's "Report on Fort Sumter," March 5, 1861, in Robert Anderson Papers, LC, was official, not clandestine. Hereafter I refer to it as "Holt Report." On the clandestine arrangements about the propriety of which contemporaries and historians have disagreed, see Benjamin P. Thomas and Harold M. Hyman, *Stanton: The Life and Times of Lincoln's Secretary of War* (New York, 1962), 93–118.

Much of the deep-water Navy was on foreign assignments. Another question was where to confront secessionists. The pattern of secession had physically isolated the deep South states behind a Europe-wide buffer of slaveowning but unseceding sisters. Any smell of coercion was likely to topple these border states into the secessionists' camp.

But if the United States government could, or would, not try to apply force against seceders, the same scruples did not rein in southern policy-makers. This disparity had tripped a time bomb at Fort Sumter and tossed it into the hands of the incoming Lincoln Administration. Odds were that the device would explode in a confrontation between secessionist officials and national authorities, or fizzle out with almost equally destructive effect for the United States government. If Washington disgraced itself again, through craven surrender of the fort, the Confederacy would likely win its experiment in rebellion.

Apparently the Constitution offered no guide to useful action. It spoke of precise, "normal" conditions—war, peace, invasion, and rebellion; it specified that the President "shall take care that the laws be faithfully executed."[3] Unfortunately, the framers had not provided for the combustible results of a faithful execution of the laws in 1861 at Charleston, South Carolina.

The seceded states had appropriated the civil and military properties of the federal government inside their boundaries. Under Buchanan no interference occurred as one by one southern post offices, mints, lighthouses, revenue facilities, shipyards, armories, and fortifications slipped into the hands of state officers or agents of the newborn Confederate central government.

Two exceptions marred the completeness of the secessionist takeover, and provided arenas where the United States and the seceded states still confronted one another. One of these locations was Fort Pickens, off Pensacola, Florida. A local arrangement between federal and state officers allowed ship-borne replenishment of the garrison's supplies. Thereby the situation at Pickens ceased to be critical.

Fort Sumter at Charleston was also an island position, but unlike Pickens, Sumter lay inside the harbor and city it had been built to protect. Revictualing vessels had to run past shore batteries of impressive weight. Further, South Carolina's and the

---

3. Art. II, sec. 3.

Confederacy's representatives at Charleston were less patient than their opposite numbers at Pensacola and allowed no equivalent to the Pickens "truce." Because Sumter's food stock had to run out, and the temper at Charleston was unbending, a built-in time limit existed.

Buchanan believed that he had no constitutional power to do more than to revictual the Sumter garrison, and Charleston's cannon prevented this. No war existed; no invader menaced from abroad; no states appealed to Washington for aid to suppress an insurrection. Therefore, the United States government had no right to use its troops, even to rescue besieged comrades.[4]

Yet, in ways the Constitution's framers intended, at least twenty-one times since 1789, Presidents of the United States had employed the nation's military force within states in order to enforce laws or judgments of federal courts and to suppress certain disturbances. Statutes of 1795, 1807, and 1833 allowed the interjection of national officials within states.[5] The pattern had evolved since 1795 that a President need not wait for an appeal for military assistance from a federal judge or other national officer, or from a state's governor, before calling into national service the regulars or the states' militias to enforce national policy or a state's peace.

Before 1860 general approval developed for a President to employ regulars as well as militiamen in intrastate disturbances, and sometimes to use regulars exclusively. The assumption was that professional soldiers would be neutral with respect to local issues and more restrained than the citizen-soldiers, who too often were uniformed partisans. A catalogue on pre-1860 employments of regulars, or of Congress's authorizations (sometimes retroactive) so to use them, includes the Burr conspiracy, the embargo, Nat Turner's revolt, the nullification controversy, the Dorr Rebellion, fugitive slave law violations, Mormon troubles in Utah, the Kansas "war," and John Brown's Harper's Ferry raid. The

---

4. Earlier, Buchanan had asked his last, contentious Congress for permission to call states' militias into federal service. So doing, he could muster a martial force that would deserve respect and simultaneously deny that manpower to secessionist authorities—if his orders were obeyed. Congress failed to afford him the requested permission. Nothing was done. "Holt Report."

5. *SAL*, I, 264, 271, 424; II, 443. See also Bennett M. Rich, *The Presidents and Civil Disorder* (Washington, 1941), chs. 1–4, 12–13; *Federalist Papers,* Nos. 28, 29.

weight of history and of constitutional interpretation was on the side of a President having all but complete discretion to decide when military intervention was needed in a state, and whether regulars or militiamen could better keep the peace and sustain the laws.

But because of the small number and scattered assignments of the regulars, Presidents relied on states' militiamen when minor crises occurred. When a state's militia might be unreliable in suppression of disorder, the militias of neighboring states formed a stand-by resource. Only during the War of 1812 and the abortive nullification controversy had governors refused to call out militias at presidential request. These exceptions aside, before 1861 the Constitution's internal peacekeeping provisions had worked.[6]

Taken together, the Constitution and the laws provided Buchanan with several alternatives, if his courage could mount to the employment of force. His new Unionist cabinet counselors reminded him that as recently as the late 1840's President Tyler had had to decide which of two contending state governments in Rhode Island, each demanding national military aid against the other, was the legitimate one.[7] By the time Buchanan referred seriously to statutes and precedents that allowed him to employ either regulars, militiamen, or mixed forces against secessionists, national officers were no longer resident in southern states except at Fort Sumter for military power to succor, and southern militias would not obey a summons into the "old" nation's service.

The immediate result of Buchanan's timidity was to encourage secessionists and to discourage men of national mind concerning the Constitution's provisions for suppressing local lawlessness.[8] Weakness in the White House convinced congress-

---

6. Robert W. Coakley, "Federal Use of Militia and the National Guard in Civil Disturbances," in *Bayonets in the Streets: The Use of Troops in Civil Disturbances,* ed. Robin Higham (Lawrence, Kan., 1969), 17–26.

7. In that instance Tyler had refused directly to intervene, thus sanctioning the incumbent state authorities; Luther v. Borden, 7 Howard, 1 (1849); Marlin S. Reichley, "The Federal Government and Civil Disturbances" (Ph.D. diss., GU, 1939), chs. 1–4.

8. A longer-run impact of the secession winter was a general loss of confidence among legislative leaders in the utility of the militia provisions of the Constitution and of derivative laws for the suppression of intrastate disorders. To be sure, statutes in 1861 and 1867 re-emphasized that Presidents might employ within states either states' militias or regulars, or both. But, Lincoln aside, except for Andrew Johnson's call in 1867 for

men that leadership properly belonged on Capitol Hill or in states. The effect of such judgments was to lessen further the prestige both of the presidential office and of the national government, just when neither had any to spare. It seems more accurate now to say that Buchanan's failure to accept responsibility was personal, not constitutional. But the important judgment is the contemporary one. Accurate or not, it became a factor in the ongoing story of secession.

No one can say whether invocation by Buchanan of ancient statutes, the assembling of federal marshals' posses, "federalized" states' militiamen, or even of regulars would have halted secession. The sounds of muster drums might have accelerated the process and tumbled the border states into association with their deep-southern sisters. On the other hand, calls to the nation's colors could have invoked the characteristic American reverence for law, at least enough to embarrass secessionist leaders. Centers of Unionism might have grown up, as they did after Sumter in western Virginia, eastern Tennessee, and Missouri, to give the lie to claims of a consensus in the South favorable to abandoning the Union.

Instead, out of its timid torpor during the secession months, the national government failed to nurture Unionism in the South. Antisecessionists had little reason to look to Washington. Instead of becoming centers of loyalist strength, many southern Unionists became exiles.

To govern at this unfortunate moment was to flounder among uncertainties. Lincoln learned quickly how fearfully state sovereignty constitutional thinking had diffused the energy of national government. Buchanan had so wasted the Presidency's symbolic capital that his successor had little choice except to continue the unstable equilibrium he had inherited. Initially, therefore, Lincoln's behavior did not appear sharply different from his predecessor's. He told his countrymen in his inaugural address that abandonment of the nation's properties located in southern states would cease, but no repossession would be at-

---

militiamen to repel Fenian raiders, Presidents after Buchanan did not again resort to militias or to more modern equivalents until in 1957 Dwight Eisenhower "federalized" the Arkansas National Guard to establish order in Little Rock. During the ninety years between the Johnson and Eisenhower employments, Presidents used regulars literally dozens of times. Coakley, "Federal Use of Militia," 25–8.

tempted of facilities already under control of Confederate authorities.

Such a restrained position could only displease men who wished matters to move to decision one way or another. Here and abroad observers were incredulous that any nation would allow itself to be dismembered. Meanwhile the temper of the slaveholding border states remained ambiguous and worrisome to the White House. Sumter's mounting peril required swiftest remedy. Inaction there confirmed the worst diagnoses of the nation's helplessness and of presidential ineptitude. Therefore, Lincoln continued efforts to get foodstuffs into Fort Sumter, and in other ways to seek less-than-bellicose resolutions of tensions. Rumors grew that he had decided on abandoning the fort, angering and depressing even some informed onlookers.[9]

This pessimistic analysis reflected a misreading of the President's ways and purposes. Lincoln carried into the White House his politician's habit of sniffing out the public's temper. To this end he listened to all sorts of men. Apparent vacillation on his part was a search for practical alternatives in view of on-hand resources, that would not transcend agreed notions of constitutional limitations on national government.

There is a tenacious tradition that Lincoln planned to yield Sumter while holding firm at Pickens. The evidence employed to sustain this depiction is thin and unconvincing, and lacks the substantiation of necessity besides. Because ships easily supplied it, Pickens never became subject to a time limit. Sumter did. Depending on the manner in which its garrison gave up the post, the United States could survive for a time or fall at once. If Sumter's flag had to come down it must do so in honorable manner, or all was lost. The yielding of the fort in advance of absolute necessity meant everything, because so much else had already fallen without resistance. Indefensible, Sumter was a last leaf that, falling prematurely, would signal an end to the youthful American experiment in democracy and federalism; a public admission that the United States government could not hold one fort, much less seven states.

Lincoln mused about abandoning Sumter. Several cabinet officers favored the gesture. But the evidence is strong that Lincoln neither agreed with these counsels nor promised to give up

9. Edwin M. Stanton to John A. Dix, March 16, 1861, in Martin Lichterman, "John Adams Dix, 1798–1879" (Ph.D. diss., CU, 1952), 413–14.

the fort.[10] Lincoln's constitutional views would not allow him to let the fort go without resistance. He had come to the White House committed to a nationalist interpretation of the Constitution and an organic theory of the nation. As he groped during the weeks after inauguration toward constructive ways to deal with the seceded states and the beleaguered fort, these principles could only convince him not to call it quits.

To describe Lincoln as a nationalist is not merely to contrast him with state-oriented secessionists, to say that he was patriotic, or to note that he found convincing inspiration in his constitutional convictions not to haul down the Sumter flag. Lincoln's nationalism was deep, impelling, and systematic. It was a faith, not a slogan. In his apotheosis of the republic the nation took on transcendent virtues.[11] Since the turn of the century, Marshall, Webster, and Story had given classic expression to nationalist doctrines. In the early weeks of 1861, Francis Lieber was advising law students at Columbia College that the Constitution's most important element "is its prominent and distinct nationality," and, at Harvard, law professor Washburn echoed the theme.[12] Like theirs, Lincoln's nationalist idiom was quiet rather than flamboyant. It tied together the nation, Constitution, and liberty in a trinity that he argued was inseparable. Together they made free government possible and worthwhile.

It was a common rhetorical flourish a century ago to equate free government with constitutional government. Lincoln's distinctive quality is in the intensity with which he clung to that equation. Secession placed on trial the object of his faith, not figuratively but actually. Lincoln came to the White House convinced that the failure of the United States to maintain national government and a free society would doom democracy globally; a

---

10. For critical evaluation of the evidence see, Grady McWhiney, "The Confederacy's First Shot," *CWH*, XIV (1968), 5–14; Richard N. Current, *The Lincoln Nobody Knows* (New York, 1958), 121–2; Kenneth P. Stampp, *And the War Came* (Baton Rouge, 1950), 205, 223, 241–6; James G. Randall and David Donald, *The Divided Union* (Boston, 1961), 171–5.

11. James A. Rawley, "The Nationalism of Abraham Lincoln," *CWH*, IX (1963), 283. Paul C. Nagel, *One Nation Indivisible: The Union in American Thought, 1776–1861* (New York, 1964), 136–7, and *passim*, offers background.

12. Francis Lieber, ms., "Lectures on the Constitution of the United States," 104, Lieber Papers, HL; Emory Washburn, *Lecture Before the Members of the Harvard Law School, January 11, 1861* (Boston, 1861), 19–20.

theme to which he was to return at Gettysburg. Secession proved how tender and experimental free government was even in America; abroad it was so rare as to make the American condition glorious. If secession killed democracy and federalism here, where could it live?

Lincoln never doubted that it deserved to live. Despite secession in America and analogous declines abroad in the vigor of democracy and of federalism, the American way could work, he believed, even in the face of mounting evidence against this proposition.[13]

Lincoln's office marked him off from others who shared similar views. He could shape events. Manipulation of men and measures were no novelty for the new President. Lincoln had been the man-to-see-in-Springfield when one wished something done or not done in Illinois. Events proved that he was able to transfer eastward the experience gained from midwestern politicking. He understood power, loved politics, and comprehended the need to exert the latter in order to employ the former.

The upshot was his quick comprehension during the 1860–61 winter, when confusion was the general condition, that secession was a rejection of normal politics. Even the provisions in the Constitution for pacific redress, including amendment, elections, assembly, and petition, though unique in the world, were inadequate to the South's escalating race-relations concerns. Far more swiftly than most of his contemporaries, Lincoln understood that secession was a *coup* in which the goal was the maintenance of slavery. The new President comprehended that the basic means of revolt was the ballot in the hands of southern whites who denied the verdicts of ballots cast by northern whites. In his judgment the secession revolution was an immoral as well as an unconstitutional distortion of democracy. Lincoln was not shocked that southerners sought to gain their ends through the exercise of force. But he saw no reason why force should not find employment on behalf of nobler, nationalist ends that he favored and that the Constitution embodied.[14]

---

13. Thomas D'Arcy McGee, *Notes on Federal Governments Past and Present* (Montreal, 1865), 40; Robert C. Brinkley, *Realism and Nationalism, 1852–1871* (New York and London, 1941), ch. 13; Carl J. Friedrich, *The Impact of American Constitutionalism Abroad* (Boston, 1967), 4, 49.

14. *The Collected Works of Abraham Lincoln,* ed. R. P. Basler *et al.* (New Brunswick, N.J., 1953), II, 366, hereafter cited as Lincoln, *Works;* T. J. Pressly, "Bullets and Ballots: Lincoln and the 'Right of Revolution,'" *AHR,* LXVII (1962), 647–62.

The Constitutional Commitment to Capacity

Lincoln also brought to the Presidency a nascent awareness that stable popular government required the broadest possible diffusion of equality and liberty. During the 1850's he was drawn to sections of the Constitution long ignored in political argumentation: the Bill of Rights and the guarantee of a republican form of government for each state. The Declaration of Independence fascinated him, and his excitement with its equalitarian preamble became a gauge by which Americans then and since measured themselves. These new stresses placed him into a new category of nationalist thinking. Through his concern with an enhanced level of liberty and progress, and his commitment to America's nationhood, Lincoln linked Jeffersonian aspirations with post–Civil War evolutionary approaches of Lieber and John W. Burgess.[15]

It is tempting but unrealistic to ignore chronology and anticipate the emancipator in the nationalist. Lincoln's hatred for slavery as an institution is well known. He welcomed the Republican party's commitment against its extension and he helped to formulate the proposition that in the territories Congress could and should rein slavery in. Lincoln judged even his beloved Constitution to be flawed, though not tainted incurably, because it sanctioned slavery. Excusing the framers for having included in the Constitution protections for state-defined slave property, Lincoln came to the White House convinced that the Constitution, slavery and all, was still "the charter of our liberties."[16]

In sum, the new President was not an abolitionist or a pioneering exponent of biracial equalitarianism. The governmental activism he had favored was of the traditional Whiggish cast that called for a weak executive, and a relatively energetic congressional program of support for certain internal improvements, including homestead legislation, plus the Republican gloss

---

15. Rawley, "Nationalism of Lincoln," 285; and see Charles Sumner's eulogy on Lincoln in Sumner, *Works*, IX, 380–93 (June 1, 1865); and the intriguing fragment in Lincoln, *Works*, IV, 168–9. W. Kendall and G. W. Carey, *The Basic Symbols of the American Political Tradition* (Baton Rouge, 1971), 88–95 and *passim*, attend almost uniquely to Lincoln's libertarian contribution. See also J. W. Cooke, "Freedom in the Thought of Abraham Lincoln," *Lincoln Herald* (1970), 10–16; C. A. Miller, "Constitutional Law and the Rhetoric of Race," *PAH*, VI (1971), 149.

16. Lincoln, *Works*, II, 501; G. E. Mulder, "Abraham Lincoln and the Doctrine of Necessity," *LQ*, LXVI (1964), 59; A. E. Strickland, "The Illinois Background of Lincoln's Attitude Toward Slavery and the Negro," ISHS *Journal*, LVI (1963), 474–94. Cf. S. Lynd, *Class Conflict, Slavery and the United States Constitution* (Indianapolis, 1967), 135–312.

of restricting slavery's further growth. He followed a line in politics that the careers of Hamilton, Webster, and above all Clay had blazed. In the law, in matters apart from ordinary bread-and-butter business, Lincoln paid homage to nationalist sermons that Marshall, Kent, and Story had preached. Beyond this, on March 4, 1861, when Lincoln took oath to uphold the Constitution and nation he revered, he was like both, a mass of incipiencies.

As the crisis increased at Sumter, the question with respect to any constitutional theory was not its accuracy but its relevancy. During the secession crisis the flounderings of the nation's highest officials revealed how inadequate nationalist doctrine was to meet strains without adequate physical power to backstop theory. If nationalist constitutionalism remained primarily a reaction to southern contentions on the nature of the Union, could it defuse secessionists' coercive power? Up to March 1861 nationalists had shown themselves to be too cautious and theoretical to cope with the daring adventurers who hoisted Calhoun's banner and under it sailed their states out of the Union. Far more was necessary than intoning "No" to the fact of secession. Unless Washington exhibited more courage, initiative, and stubbornness than appeared likely in the spring of 1861, the nationalist position exposed the Constitution of the United States to mockery as a paper tiger.

On April 12, 1861, the Sumter stalemate exploded. News of the bombardment outraged the North. Speeches, rallies, and parades contrasted vividly with the timid drift of preceding months. The common cry stressed a necessity to enforce the nation's rightful constitutional stand.[17]

But how, and out of what reservoir of resources? American law and constitutional theory even of the nationalist variety had paid almost no attention at all to any condition except formal war or localized disturbances. Yet Lincoln proved ready to function in a manner appropriate to the needs, resources, and temper of loyal men and states. His readiness was an impressive indication of the fully developed nature of his constitutional preparation and hand-at-the-helm insights.

It is a familiar story how, the day after Fort Sumter's garri-

---

17. Cf. Interior Secretary Caleb Smith to R. W. Thompson, April 14, 16, 1861, LNLF.

son surrendered honorably, Lincoln issued an executive proclamation to declare that an insurrection existed in seven states, too powerful for ordinary processes of law to suppress. Therefore, he employed a provision of the 1795 law that Buchanan had said was inapplicable, and called into national service for three months the militias of all the states, including those of the South (of course the governors of the seceded states rejected his call), to the number of seventy-five thousand men.[18]

On April 19, Lincoln announced the existence of a blockade to affect the seven seceded states, and subsequently added to the roster the later recruits to the Confederacy. Because the single railroad line that tied Washington to the loyal northern states ran through turbulently prosecessionist Baltimore, on April 27 Lincoln authorized the suspension in that neighborhood of the privilege of the writ of habeas corpus; his first resort to this expedient, later common.[19]

Other even less traditional outreachings of national executive authority followed. Unresting in his efforts to gain each day another day's worth of survival, on May 3 the President appealed for recruits for the regular Army, although the preceding Congress had not provided for enlargement of the military establish-

---

18. Even supporters of Lincoln's dramatic resort to this statute worried that it was simply inadequate, as indeed it proved to be. According to a Boston survey, the 1795 law "by which a feeble insurrection in a single state was sought to be suppressed" was hardly up to the strain involved in a civil war that involved all the Confederate states: "Direct Taxation and the Income Tax," *MLRep*, XXIV (1862), 257. On July 13, 1861, Congress modified the 1795 law so that a President could declare a state to be in insurrection whose citizens claimed to act by authority of that state: *SAL*, XII, 255.

19. As a matter of definition of what the habeas corpus writ is, this recent one deserves employment: "the Great Writ is simply a mode of procedure . . . its function has been to provide a prompt and efficacious remedy for whatever society deems to be intolerable restraints. Its root principle is that in a civilized society, government must always be accountable to the judiciary for a man's imprisonment; if the imprisonment can not be shown to conform with the fundamental requirements of law, the individual is entitled to his immediate release." Fay v. Noia, 372 US, 391, at 401 (1963). Of course this does not apply if the writ privilege is suspended. Note that the existence of martial law does not of itself or at all necessarily suspend the writ privilege or other civil processes unless the military commander specifies suspension. Sherrill Halbert, "The Suspension of the Writ of Habeas Corpus by President Lincoln," *AJLH*, II (1958), 95–116.

ment.[20] Lincoln disbursed public funds to private persons able and ready to use them effectively; so many commissioned officers were untrustworthy. A noteworthy example of this adventitious extralegal activity occurred when a delegation from western Virginia, wanting to split away from their seceding state and hoping to get federal weapons, gained an audience with Lincoln. The President listened to the appeal for arms, and replied "in his own inimitable manner, that 'he found that he must be very cautious in what he did, as he saw Alec Stephens [Vice President of the Confederacy] had declared his calling out of the 75,000 men to defend the Government, *wholly unconstitutional.*'"

Lincoln sent the delegation off to talk with counsellors who held the most expansive view of the inherent war powers of the national government and especially of the executive office. The President then let them convince him, and the arms went off to Wheeling—in time.[21]

This was action. There had been a widespread assumption in America and abroad that constitutional limitations bound up the national government in shackles that no emergency could loosen. A fear existed among well-wishers to the Union that American constitutional habits and governing institutions could not react appropriately or courageously to crisis. The charge was common—and it hurt—that, secession having proceeded unopposed from Washington, any injury would be borne without retaliation.

That collapse did not occur at once after Sumter was an obvious and impelling encouragement to continue politicking and to attend to the Constitution's configurations. A kind of victory for the Union came about because, however barely, it survived not only secession and the Sumter capitulation but the onset of war and even a succession of military reverses.

Government authorities found resources to place thousands of men in the field, to float a navy, and to try to cope with widespread home-front disloyalty, especially along the broad sweep of

---

20. For several reasons, Lincoln held off until April 15 from calling into special session the 37th Congress, which met on July 4.

21. *New York Times*, Aug. 29, 1865, on West Virginia. Other data in James G. Randall, *Constitutional Problems Under Lincoln* (rev. edn., Urbana, Ill., 1951), 49–50. Lincoln's defense for these extraordinary actions is in his message to Congress, July 1861, in *M&P*, VI, 20–31, and will be referred to later. On August 6, 1861, Congress sustained his immediate post-Sumter actions; *SAL*, XII, 326.

the border states. The rule of law might yet prevail; perhaps hope was justified instead of despair.[22]

Lincoln's spectacular and energetic moves confounded doomsayers and delighted relieved patriots. In Washington, former Iowa chief justice Charles Mason, a disgruntled prosecessionist since become chairman of the Democratic National committee, noted the overwhelmingly approving popular response to Lincoln's outreaching; and grumbled, that "vast numbers of my fellow countrymen . . . applaud it to the echo."[23] During the warm spring weeks of 1861, as the North bustled to improvise an army of three-month volunteers, it appeared that Lincoln's strokes of pen were inspired improvisations. They freed the nation for ninety days from Buchanan's style of restraints. This brief emergency period could be borne. Then, the Confederacy crushed and the rule of law sustained, matters would return to normal.

Lincoln had come unerringly to resources that the nation did not know it possessed. These ways and means proved to be capable of enduring far greater weights for periods unimaginably longer than ninety days. Moving first, forcefully, and appropriately, Lincoln gained precious advantages. It is the essence of the War's meaning for the Constitution that his career linked the Sumter surrender to the Appomattox capitulation, making the latter possible.

Beyond this, Lincoln took the initiative that they had held for forty years out of the hands of champions of constitutional inhibitions on national action. His rugged thrusts defined new arenas of constitutional and political contention centering on individuals' rights and national powers, and roughed in its primary characteristics. Henceforward constitutional-political arguments had to shift from secession's negatives to issues that Lincoln had raised. It no longer made much sense to ask—al-

---

22. See Theophilus Parsons, *An Oration Delivered on the 4th of July, 1861, Before the Municipal Authorities of the City of Boston* (Boston, 1861), 23; Rev. George F. Noyes, *Celebration of the National Anniversary by Doubleday's Brigade, at Camp Opposite Fredericksburg, Virginia, July 4, 1862* (Philadelphia, 1862), 9.

23. Entry, April 29, 1861, *Life and Letters of Charles Mason, Chief Justice of Iowa, 1804–1882*, ed. Charles Mason Remey (Washington, 1939), unpaginated copy in JHU Library; W. H. Toussaint, "Charles Mason's Influence on Iowa Jurisprudence," *Annals of Iowa* (1968), 372–87; *A Philadelphia Perspective: The Diary of Sidney George Fisher, Covering the Years 1834–1871*, ed. Nicholas B. Wainwright (Philadelphia, 1967), 396.

though the habit of asking persisted—whether the nation possessed an abstract right under the Constitution to oppose further secessions, to impose a blockade, and to try to crush rebellion on battle and home fronts. Instead the questions became how, when, and through what agencies of government it should do these things. The uses of power, not doubt as to its existence, became the issue in courtrooms and on the hustings. This was a basic shift from the disastrous year 1860, which closed with the epitaph from a Frenchman visiting in America: "I told you . . . that everything about the Constitution of the United States was wrong."[24]

Lincoln's hyperactivity during the early weeks of the War made it clear that at least something in it was right. Acting on the assumption that the nation possessed in its Constitution the "power and propriety" to protect itself in a civil war, Lincoln shaped the monumental constitutional questions that the Civil War provided opportunity for the nation to decide.[25] In effect his actions advanced a proposition that the Constitution deserved continuing attention and contention because it was a reservoir filled with might and means adequate to deal with the unhappy tasks that the War was opening. Therefore, it was worth efforts to sway policies, however untraditional, through traditional avenues of pressure such as politics, press, pulpits, and courts.

---

24. Dec. 14, 1860, in *A Casual View of America: The Home Letters of Salomon de Rothschild, 1859–1861*, ed. Sigmund Diamond (Stanford, 1961), 85.
25. See his phrase in *M&P*, VI, 25, and for effect, Fisher, *Diary*, 396. Fisher's continuing enthusiasm for Lincoln's policies can be seen in his reaction to the December State of the Union Message, Fisher, *Diary*, 410–11.

Chapter V

The Shock of Power

In comparison with ways that Europeans and Latin Americans then took for granted were necessary to wage wars, especially civil wars, and with the harsher standards of the mid-twentieth century, Civil War America remained an astonishingly free and open society. This openness helps to explain why unprecedentedly vigorous governmental actions occasioned such surprise. Freedom without restraint was habitual; freedom coexisting with power surprised a generation habituated to belief that such coexistence was impossible.

Almost totally civilian in habits and local in orientation, Americans were simply unready for the spectacle of "national" soldiers—even hastily uniformed neighbors—performing police functions. From the days after Sumter all through 1861, arrests of civilians by soldiers and suspensions of the revered though little understood privilege of habeas corpus were the most visible evidences of war. Indeed, for a year after the War began, little else occurred to hold popular attention. Secession and the Sumter crisis had whetted the public's appetite for high drama in the daily news. But the military actions did not sustain that tempo; the augmenting naval blockade was invisible offshore. As a result, interest focused on the internal-security improvisations of the Lincoln Administration.

Unrestrained journalism, unfettered communications, and unsubdued opposition politics attended to the "arbitrary arrests" of "political prisoners" and of "prisoners of state," and their incarcerations in "American Bastilles." There, military commissions pronounced ferocious penalties under the unknown and therefore doubly worrisome tenets of martial law. In this context, Lincoln's permissions to subordinates to "arrest and detain without the ordinary processes of law such individuals as they might deem dangerous to the public safety" proved to be the lever that pried constitutional argument away from secession and moved it on.[1]

Debate shifted to the habeas corpus suspensions, to the scope of "war powers" and of commander-in-chief functions, to the basic question whether what was going on was a war between nations or a civil war, to altering configurations of national-state relationships, to the applicability of the Bill of Rights to wartime ways, and to the role of the nation's and states' judiciaries in supplying answers to war-born uncertainties.

A hundred years ago, these matters were unstudied in law schools, ignored in universities, and unknown in West Point's curriculum. Among government officials, ignorance about them was all but complete. Legal literature on such themes was inadequate if not irrelevant.[2] After Sumter, persons who sought guidance on internal-security matters found themselves in an everyman's-land of assumptions, conjectures, and surmises. Precise questions did not exist, much less answers. It was all novel and startling.[3]

But in turning to its consideration, commentators continued to cast into precise constitutional idiom the uncertainties resulting from Lincoln's internal-security efforts. Lawyers and judges

---

1. *M&P*, VI, 24.

2. J. H. Hatcher, "Martial Law and Habeas Corpus," *WVLQ*, XLVI (1940), 188. In America, the privilege of the habeas corpus writ is suspended, not the writ, as in England. Henceforward, in this book the simpler phrase will often be employed, for brevity and clarity.

3. Late in 1861, Philadelphian Edward Ingersoll expressed this sense of the exacerbatingly unfamiliar: "Civil War and Revolution start strange topics of discussion. If any one, whether lawyer or layman . . . who had ever given a thought to the American Government, had been told so lately as . . . 1860, that at this day we would be discussing the question of the rightful power of the president of the United States to arrest and imprison its citizens at his discretion, what would such auditor have said? Would any earthly information have convinced him that such futurity was close at hand? Yet here we have it upon us . . . [and] we know that the exercise of this power is the new American fact . . . [It] seems vain any longer to say it was impossible, and turn from its consideration." Ingersoll, *Personal Liberty and Martial Law: A Review of Some Pamphlets of the Day* (Philadelphia, 1862), 1.

maintained the conventions of the adversary system in courtroom actions about arbitrary arrests; derivative political dialogue took the similar position that one point of view was wholly right, others completely wrong. The arbitrary-arrest issue ballooned into the major postsecession constitutional question because, evidence from secession notwithstanding, educated Americans were convinced that America lived always under a rule of law.[4] Northern men of law and letters went from this unshaken belief to outrage at the South for seceding, because the nation's disruption threatened not only the Union of states but the unity of law and the fabric of social order. Most northern commentators believed that their nation could—must—fight its war under the constitutional cloak that had weighed so lightly before Sumter. Any rents caused by secession in that revered fabric required attention and repair. But even parts long ignored such as the Bill of Rights must not become cast off.

Europeans thought all this childish; by the 1880's, even some American jurisprudents came to believe that "there is something exquisitely absurd in the supposition that a civil, any more than a public, war can be waged under the protection of the Bill of Rights."[5] But in white America of the 1860's, rights were "a solid barrier," not a phantom; a reality, not an aspiration; a possession, not a purpose.[6] Among northern writers a primary question was how to fight the South and suppress northern disloyalists more vigorously, so that, the war ending swiftly, patriots' rights, and everyone's responsibilities under law, would hold firmer.

A century ago the common denominator of American life was the village and small town. Before Sumter, lifetimes passed without encounter with national officials, especially uniformed ones. The national government was almost inert and without significance to the daily concerns of most Americans. Authority was adequately represented by the village constable, the city mayor,

---

4. O. and M. Handlin, *Dimensions of Liberty* (New York, 1966), 55; and see P. S. Paludan, "Law and Equal Rights: The Civil War Encounter— A Study of Legal Minds in the Civil War Era" (Ph.D. diss., UI, 1968), Intro., ch. 1. G. Garvey, *Constitutional Bricolage* (Princeton, 1971), attends to the configurative role of the legal adversary system.

5. John N. Pomeroy, *An Introduction to the Constitutional Law of the United States* (Boston, 1886), 379.

6. Handlins, *Dimensions*, 59; J. C. Hurd, *The Theory of Our National Existence, as Shown by the Action of the Government of the United States Since 1861* (Boston, 1881), ch. 5.

and the county sheriff. Except for Negroes almost everywhere, and Indians and Mexicans in some areas, public law did not restrain private citizens. Freedom was the condition of law. Questions of personal liberty, trial by jury, freedom of speech and press, and, since the Jacksonian reforms, of access to the ballot were rarely if ever matters of political or constitutional contention in courts or legislatures of nation or states. Property, not individuals, received the "parchment barriers" of protection by lawmakers and courts.[7]

Popular conviction had it that this way of almost-no-national-government that encouraged private interests was the source of Americans' good fortunes, low taxes, and high prospects. Lawyers and judges nourished the view of government as negation. The decline of the Whig party during the 1850's diminished prospects for functional vitality in the national government that Clay and Webster had envisaged. One commentator described American national government as totally "imbecile" and almost invisible; irrelevant to war because it had been futile in peace.[8]

These loose prewar ways were admirable by many measures. When the Civil War came, even onlookers who condoned the internal-security outreachings of the Lincoln Administration nevertheless regretted the decline in governmentlessness.[9] All had been quiet along the Potomac for so long in functional matters significant to common folk that any action from there shocked. People who condemned the arbitrary arrests extolled the prewar amorphous conditions of society that Carlyle had de-

---

7. P. Miller, *The Life of the Mind in America: From the Revolution to the Civil War* (New York, 1965), 227; Francis Lieber, *On Civil Liberty and Self-Government* (3rd edn., Philadelphia, 1875), esp. ch. 22; J. W. Hurst, *Law and the Conditions of Freedom in the Nineteenth Century United States* (Madison, Wis., 1956), *passim;* P. Paludan, "The American Civil War Considered as a Crisis in Law and Order," *AHR,* LXXVII (1972), 1013–34.

8. On "imbecile government," see Charles Fenton Mercer, *An Exposition of the Weakness and Inefficiency of the Government of the USA, by a Late American Statesman* (London, 1863), 35; and see Timothy Farrar, *Manual of the Constitution of the United States of America* (Boston, 1867), 473.

9. America "is as little administered as possible; an immense advantage, which might be weakened or disappear under the influence of existing events," worried Count Agénor de Gasparin, a dedicated friend to the Union's fortunes. Gasparin, *America Before Europe,* tr. Mary L. Booth (New York, 1862), 338.

scribed as "anarchy plus a street constable."[10] Neither critics nor supporters inquired seriously whether street constables or national troops were the only alternatives, or what constituted the permissible limits of dissent.

Instead, among critics especially, the "good old days" attitude resulted at once in hostile suspicion about the men and measures that authorities scratched together in early efforts to combat home-front disloyalty. Animadversions about arbitrary arrests employed the anticentralization idiom drawn from the essentially economic concerns of the ages of Jefferson and Jackson.

It is now clear that such sighing after a vanished happy time was more romantic than accurate. Prewar Americans had looked to governments on every level of the federal system for a variety of entrepreneurial aids and economic favors.[11] But the post-Sumter arbitrary arrests were different from these uncoercive prewar governmental interventions. After Sumter, men could no longer say "We hardly knew we had a national government except when the quadriennial contest for spoils of office came around."[12]

The rude, vigorous, and effective national presence in the dark days after Sumter pleased patriots who feared that the nation had become *di*visible because it was too *in*visible; that prewar federalism and the absence of direct national involvements with individuals had resulted in an inadequate reservoir of loyalty upon which the nation's officials could draw during and after the secession crisis.

Arbitrary arrests were unpalatable, however, even to many stanch patriots. They were the first intimations that the nation required obedience as well as devotion, wrote Charles Demond, a Williams College professor. Commencing at once after Sumter, and continuing at intervals throughout the war, martial-law im-

---

10. Quoted in Rev. Joseph P. Thompson, "The Test-Hour of Personal Liberty and Republican Government," *NE*, XXI (1862), 328.

11. Wallace D. Farnham, "The 'Weakened Spring of Government': A Study in Nineteenth-Century American History," *AHR*, LXVIII (1963), 662–80; Harry W. Broude, "The State in American Economic Development, 1820–1890," in *The State and Economic Growth*, ed. Hugh G. H. Aiken (New York, 1959), 4–25; Carter Goodrich, *Government Promotion of American Canals and Railroads, 1800–1890* (New York, 1960), *passim*.

12. Edwin Channing Larned, *The Great Conflict, What Has Been Gained, and What Remains to Be Done, Oration, 4th July, 1865, Aurora, Illinois* (Chicago, 1865), 5.

positions were the first assertions in the nation's happy history of the central government's "power to protect and punish us."[13]

Demond was a poor historian. So were all Americans, including Lincoln. Military arrests of civilians, loyalty-oath tests, inquisitorial legislative committees, and travel, trade, and election controls had been employed during the American Revolution and in intervening crises. But, save for sporadic attention paid to slavery, historians had ignored such unpleasant aspects of America's past.

By 1863 the fact that open politics continued unabated—indeed, invigorated—during the Civil War in northern states inspired new looks into American history. Evidence accumulated that Lincoln's internal-security "innovations" were not really new. But, coming late, substantiations from history failed to lessen shock at the apparent novelties.[14]

And so from Sumter on, the sudden thrusts of national officials, especially soldiers, continued to grate. The change was very intense from prewar amorphous conditions, Demond recalled, as after Sumter "the recruiting agent, the Provost Marshal, the [tax] assessor, the collector of taxes, all officers of the central government . . . entered into every town and village and dwelling, to gather up men and means." It fascinated Americans that Secretary of State Seward, whom, nominally at least, Lincoln had placed in charge of internal security out of distrust of War Secretary Simon Cameron, could send a telegraphic message to Maine or to California for soldiers to arrest named persons. Even patriots who cheered because known pro-Confederates were rendered harmless found this spectacle of soldiers imprisoning neighbors by orders from distant Washington or from strangers at a military headquarters distasteful. Impositions of loyalty-oath tests as conditions precedent to the exercise of suffrage, office, and travel occurred frequently in the border states and in the neighborhoods of Union Army field commands, and were a source of much irritation.[15]

---

13. Charles Demond, *Address Before the Society of the Alumni of Williams College, August 1, 1865* (Boston, 1865), 6–7.

14. Sidney Cromwell, *Political Opinions in 1776 and 1863; A Letter to a Victim of Arbitrary Arrests and "American Bastilles"* (New York, 1863); William A. Cook, *The Administration of Abraham Lincoln Sustained by the Sages and Heroes of the Revolution* (Washington, 1864); see also Harold M. Hyman, *To Try Men's Souls: Loyalty Tests in American History* (Berkeley and Los Angeles, 1959), ch. 7.

15. Demond, *Address*, 7; Samuel Harris, *Our Country's Claim: Oration . . . July 4th, 1861* (Bangor, Me., 1861), 8. See the exchange be-

The shock of the arbitrary arrests was the more intense because of the belief that America was an Eden whose people need never suffer repressive devices familiar abroad. Such belief, ignorance about precedent analogous situations, and an assumption that wars must restrict themselves to battlefields in the manner of eighteenth-century military prints were poor preparations for the characteristics the Civil War quickly developed.[16] Little wonder that the popular mind was ill-prepared for rigor on the part of the government when for so long flaccidity had been the habitual condition, reflected J. M. Sturtevant, an Illinois college president. The constitutional commentator John Codman Hurd estimated that Lincoln's way of vigor and courage, of bridging interstices in the federal system, and of employing every possible instrument of executive power, which replaced Buchanan's torpid timidity so abruptly, was "an astonishment and a puzzle to the people of the United States."[17]

As weeks passed after Sumter and the only news was of arbitrary arrests and the complaints of victims, "an unmanly depression" developed in the North, wrote one insightful observer,[18] replacing initial buoyancy. But this low mood rarely lasted long among men of patriotic bent. The internal-security procedures that occasioned uneasiness also improved morale, as their efficacy in subduing overt disloyalty became apparent.

One result of improvement was a shift in the interest of commentators from theories of government to realities of power. The Eden myth cracked a little. Sturtevant understood that the "delusive dreams of our national childhood" had to give way before different needs which the Civil War was revealing. Americans could live no longer "the unreflective life of the child," wrote Orestes Brownson. Of all nations, Brownson judged, the United States most needed knowledge of itself, but had less. The War was altering these loose patterns in favor of tougher, more real-

---

tween Illinois Senator Lyman Trumbull and Secretary of State Seward, Dec. 12, 1861, *CG*, 37 Cong., 2 sess., 67, 90–91, 2114.

16. See Henry James, Sr., *The Social Significance of Our Institutions, An Oration, Newport, R.I., July 4, 1861* (Boston, 1861), 26; Lorraine A. Williams, "Northern Intellectual Reaction to Military Rule During the Civil War," *Historian*, XXVII (1965), 335–9.

17. Hurd, *Theory of Our National Existence*, x; J. M. Sturtevant, "The Lessons of Our National Conflict," *NE*, XIX (1861), 894. See also Henry James, *Hawthorne* (London, 1879), 142–4.

18. Charles J. Stillé, *How a Free People Conduct a Long War* (New York, [1862]), 1.

istic estimations.[19] General Winfield Scott feared that the more muscular mood of 1861 would not last; that secession had withdrawn too much from the nation's spine to allow for long the more erect posture Lincoln initiated. Nevertheless, the hopeful sign was that collapse had not occurred at news of Sumter or antiwar riots on reports of Bull Run. The ongoing arbitrary arrests were resulting in swift releases of victims through loyalty oath subscriptions, and in rarer instances in lawyerlike confrontations, rather than in breakdowns of government.[20]

Because the Constitution was unexpectedly working for war as well as for peace, it was worth analyzing, concluded Robert L. Breck, a Kentuckian, whose divided state was an area of special interest to antidisloyalty operatives. Breck wrote of the predicament Americans faced who assumed that the existence of the Constitution guaranteed both nationhood and total liberty. The "past enjoyment of such innocence is one of the features of peril for the future," Breck worried. He noted that

> The American people are engaged in a great struggle in the process of which they begin to be, for the first time, thrown upon the serious discussion of the most fundamental and vital principles of enlightened and constitutional liberty. It is an evidence of their past happy exemptions from tempests such as those which have rocked other great nations, that these very elementary principles, these rudiments of liberty, are so little known and so feebly apprehended by them. They have lived so long in the almost unparalleled enjoyment of liberty, but have realized no occasion to study it, and have not analyzed or defined it. They have sailed upon a smooth sea, without the experience of a single storm to awaken serious apprehension for their safety, and have never examined the vessel which has borne them, to understand the great timbers and braces that hold it together.[21]

---

19. Sturtevant, "Lessons of Our National Conflict," 894; Orestes Brownson, *The American Republic: Its Constitution, Tendencies, and Destiny* (New York, 1865), 2; and see *A Philadelphia Perspective: The Diary of Sidney George Fisher, Covering the Years 1834–1871*, ed. Nicholas B. Wainwright (Philadelphia, 1967), 398.

20. Winfield Scott in Salmon Portland Chase, *Going Home to Vote: Speeches during his Visit to Ohio . . . October, 1863* (Washington, 1863), 34.

21. R. L. Breck, *The Habeas Corpus and Martial Law* (Cincinnati, 1862), 10.

. . .

The internal-security apparatus, whose bruising hyperactivity occasioned these reactions, is difficult to describe systematically. In technical terms it was a national, military, executive machinery that rested for constitutional sanction upon Lincoln's expansive view of presidential war powers. But the "system" was dominated by local and state civil officials and by private citizens and associations. Stated another way, when the war commenced the national government of the United States had almost no internal coercive resources. Its only "police" were the Treasury's and Post Office Department's fraud detectors and the special fugitive-slave commissioners. States' militiamen and regulars were urgently required for field service against Confederate armies.

Individuals took matters into their own hands. Sometimes in unofficial co-operation with marshals of federal courts or federal attorneys, often with only vague permission from a state's governor or a city's mayor, most often probably without any sanction, such persons and the associations they formed suppressed secession in border states and diminished prosouthern expressions in northern reaches. In sum, early Civil War internal-security policies were simply what people were already doing.

In the White House and Congress, men were keen enough to realize that this congeries was a powerful tool *if* the nation learned how to employ it, or a runaway weapon. Seward tried to win control of this elusive web. Careless of traditional separations of powers, he transformed federal judges, marshals, and attorneys into field agents, because they were already on hand in every judicial and congressional district and because they had reached their positions through links with states' political chieftains. Now, along with the Treasury's and the Post Office's field staffs, such partisan connections served the nation's needs.

Although differing details mark every locality from every other, a general pattern was for a federal marshal or attorney or postmaster or Treasury agent to bring his district's village constables, city police chiefs, county sheriffs, and state militia officers into rough co-operation; plus generals commanding field armies and purely private would-be counterspies. As a result, very swiftly after Sumter surveillance machineries existed in thousands of the small towns that then were the population centers of America. Citizens' posses, civilian police, militiamen, and any nearby national soldiers formed its muscle. With varying degrees of parallel activity and, sometimes, competition by Secretaries Blair, Cameron, Chase, Welles, and Attorney General Bates (the last almost completely outstripped by the pace of events), Seward tried to run everything by means of the telegraph. Odds were heavy against subordinating this unharmonious mélange to systematic direction. Always the imperative to keep it working took precedence over that of making it work perfectly.[22]

The first test of this hurriedly assembled machinery came in Maryland. If Maryland seceded, Washington was cut off from the loyal North and West, the Confederacy's bid for independence was assured, the United States was dead. Lincoln authorized in Maryland the war's first suspensions of habeas corpus. Spectacular military arrests took place, including some of Maryland's legislators and police heads.[23]

In the border slaveholding states from Maryland to Missouri, in uncertain southern counties of states fronting the Ohio River, and in northern states as well, similar expedients were applied. As they thrust southward, Union armies established internal security contrivances in salients of Dixie.

Allowing that some antidisloyalty action was in order, the major defect of this "system" was that it was never systematic. Too many uncontrollable private persons and local officials were more concerned with feeding potentially dangerous miscreants into the repressive machinery than with freeing them if they were innocent or harmless. Suppression and, far better, prevention of overt disloyalty were the goals; adequacy was the standard, not perfection; energy was its characteristic, not restraint.

The ramshackle devices Lincoln employed in 1861 probably prevented the border states from splitting off and the neutrality

---

22. In Harold M. Hyman, *Era of the Oath: Northern Loyalty Tests During the Civil War and Reconstruction* (Philadelphia, 1954), *passim;* and *To Try Men's Souls*, ch. 6, I have tried to deal with aspects of these questions, but no systematic inquiry is in print on the internal-security improvisations of the immediate post-Sumter period. James G. Randall, *Constitutional Problems Under Lincoln* (rev. edn., Urbana, 1951), ch. 7 is basic. Source-chronological files, Attorney General's Papers, RG 60, NA, offer details on the hectic scenes of the spring of 1861. Mr. John F. De-Porry diligently mined for me great masses of this collection, and I thank him especially for this service. I have based the above description primarily on his findings. See J. Syrett, "The Confiscation Acts: Efforts at Reconstruction During the Civil War" (Ph.D. diss., UWis, 1971), on cabinet clashes.

23. L. D. Asper, "The Long and Unhappy History of Loyalty Testing in Maryland," *AJLH* (1969), 103–5.

that Kentucky attempted. In succeeding years internal-security operatives under more effective national control made workable the administration's conscription, emancipation, trade-control, and Negro-enlistment policies. None of this is to extol mythic virtues in loyalty-security proceedings or to praise arbitrary arrests of civilians by soldiers. But the caution is well expressed by James G. Randall:

> That all of this procedure was arbitrary, that it involved the withholding of guarantees normally available, is of course evident. . . . It would be a mistake, however, to suppose that all the conditions of summary justice were present. The number of arrests made, though very large, has been commonly exaggerated. There was no "system" by which men [prisoners] were quickly advanced to the scaffold or to terms of imprisonment. There was no "revolutionary tribunal" such as that by which the guillotine was fed during the terror in France, nothing similar to the "Star Chamber" of the Tudor period in England.[24]

Although successful and relatively restrained, these security improvisations demand censure for their manifest imperfections. The frequent tinkering and continuing pressure needed even to keep the machinery going suggests the intrinsic weaknesses in its construction. Without question innocent persons suffered because of the competing and confused jurisdictions and the clumsy workings of the imperfect apparatus.

Many individuals who were subjected to arbitrary arrests wrote of their experiences without interference by authorities. Lincoln was a military dictator, partisan pamphleteers charged.[25] Such animadversions proved to be especially attractive to persons who believed democracy to be dangerous and who wanted its foremost practitioner in the world to die. An American pianist on tour abroad wrote in February 1862 that for almost a year he had read in European newspapers that in the northern states "the theaters are closed; that the public finances and private fortunes

---

24. Randall, *Constitutional Problems*, 152–3. One may add that Civil War loyalty-security techniques stand up very well in comparison with what took place in France in 1871, and with twentieth-century equivalents in Africa, Asia, Europe, and Latin America. See too Benjamin P. Thomas and Harold M. Hyman, *Stanton: The Life and Times of Lincoln's Secretary of War* (New York, 1962), 375–7.

25. Viz., An Eye Witness, *The Bastille in America, or, Democratic Absolutism* (London, 1861), 6–7.

are exhausted; that the North is a prey to famine; that the terrorism of Robespierre is revived by the American Republicans; that they kill each other in open day[light]."[26]

Some patriots expressed a certain pride in the existence of opposition to wartime internal-security policies. A *North American Review* editorialist wrote rather smugly that the loud criticism reflected credit on all Americans: "[I]ndeed it would be strange if in this, the land of freedom, above all others . . . now ruled by those accustomed from infancy to the exercise of the amplest liberty, any encroachment upon the rights of the citizen under the common law were not watched with extreme suspicion and jealousy. It would be a matter of discredit and disappointment were this not so."[27]

Lincoln was never a military dictator even by mid-nineteenth-century standards, much less by those of the mid-twentieth century. Keeping in mind the War's avalanching scope and the inherent prospects for excess which obtained, an astonishingly small degree of interference with free expression and opposition politics occurred. The tyranny accusation proved to be most appealing when for political purposes critics of the Lincoln Administration joined it with pitiable statements from victims of arbitrary arrests. Historians have attended more to victims' assertions of unmerited injuries than to justifications by officials, a sensitivity which reflects attitudes of our time, when the suggestion that *Staatsrecht* was ever an adequate reason for imposition of any security procedures is shrugged away because strong suspicion exists that, currently, such devices are overblown.

However deserving this judgment may be about today's restraints, extrapolation of similar judgments to 1861–65 presents substantial difficulties. The question of feasible alternatives to what came in after the Sumter bombardment has received little attention. Actual disloyalty existed in dangerous quantity and frightening concentration; some security measures were in order or else efforts were wasted to restore by arms the disrupting union of states. A society resentful of restraints was unlikely to accept unnecessary security fetters as passively as proved to be the case. False pleas of necessity could scarcely have convinced alert, self-appointed monitors of American institutions, morals, and ways.

---

26. Louis Moreau Gottschalk, *Notes of a Pianist,* ed. Clara Gottschalk (Philadelphia, 1881), 128–9.
27. "Military and Martial Law," *NAR,* CII (1866), 341.

The notion that officials could act secretly or mask excesses with fictions of mythical underground conspiracies was dubious at best. The antidisloyalty recourses of the Lincoln Administration were imperfect and galling; but they were neither irrelevant nor cynical.[28]

Opposition politics provided an obvious, ready-to-hand arena for dissent, and the internal-security growth was a free gift to Democrats. Historians have examined closely the disruption of the Democratic party in 1860. But little is known of its rapid reconstruction in all northern states after Sumter. This revival is the more remarkable in that large numbers among its presecession membership accepted "Union party" coalition with Republicans. Notwithstanding defections and the Republicans' tainting of the opposition with the brush of associative disloyalty, Democratic remnants swiftly became a respectable minority.

Antiwar Democrats applied familiar static constitutional doctrines about race and federal-state relationships, to the novel assertions from Washington about war powers. A peace-at-any-cost faction of the Democracy even espoused agreement to an independent Confederacy by a treaty, armistice, special election, referendum, or constitutional convention. These Democrats now looked hostilely on the national government. Beginning in 1861, they adopted an idiom of antipathy to martial ways and loyalty tests, of obeisance to the Bill of Rights, and, for a while at least, of respect for courts as defenders of individuals' liberties against internal-security policies. But, despite the Jeffersonian rhetoric involved, as before Sumter the wartime Democracy was engaged in a quest for static federalism racially ordered, for liberty as a factor of national inaction concerning slavery, for nationality as a reflection of local domination. Observing Democratic chieftains, Robert Trimble, an astute visiting Englishman, summarized their

---

28. James G. Randall, "Lincoln in the Role of Dictator," *SAQ*, XXXVIII (1929), 245–7; Charles Warren, "Attacks in Congress upon President Lincoln Because of His Requests for, and Exercise of, 'Arbitrary' and 'Despotic' Powers (1861–1863)," *New York Times*, May 12, 1918. Of course Warren, an assistant to the United States Attorney General when he assembled this data, was seeking to prove from history that Wilson's home-front security expedients were not excessive. See also Hyman, *To Try Men's Souls*, ch. 11; Robert D. Marcus, "Wendell Phillips and American Institutions," *JAH*, LVI (1969), 51–2.

strategy: "The most notable way of impeding [the Republicans'] effort is to knock them down with the 'Constitution' every time they rise to the surface and begin to swim out."

The Democratic party's spokesmen were anxious to disassociate from secession. Popular concern over the arbitrary arrests was a windfall for the War Democracy, which found an agreeable new image as opponents to security operations.[29] Yale professor Dutton's description appears sound, that the arrests created "a question . . . of more interest and importance than any which has arisen since the Constitution was adopted. . . . Many persons, even in the States which are still loyal, charge the President with usurpation. Many loyal citizens, though acquiescing . . . as a matter of necessity, still doubt its constitutionality."[30]

Negrophobia, accumulating war-weariness, and many other factors in addition to arbitrary arrests contributed to the Democracy's spectacular revival after Sumter. Support for Democrats was a natural way to express unhappiness with ways the War was taking. The Democrats' political revival provided a suitable, realistic, effective way for antiwar, antiadministration sentiment to express itself within permissible limits of dissent. In the absence of modern watchdog private organizations that center attention on civil-liberties infringements, the Democratic party partially performed that function.

Many Democrats who defended white men's civil liberties were also holdfasts on Negro slavery and accommodationists about an independent Confederacy.[31] Champions of the Bill of Rights against censorship or arbitrary arrests insisted also that

---

29. Robert Trimble, *A Review of the American Struggle in Its Military and Political Aspects* (London, 1864), 7, and see also S. S. Nicholas, *Conservative Essays, Legal and Political* (Louisville, 1867), I, 207; John Hubbell, "The Northern Democracy and the Crisis of Disunion, 1860–1861" (Ph.D. diss., UI, 1969), *passim;* Joel Silbey, "A Respectable Minority: The Democratic Party, 1860–1868" (AHA paper, 1968 [used with permission]).

30. Henry Dutton, "Writ of Habeas Corpus," *ALReg*, IX (1861 [pam. reprint, n.p., n.d.]), 1.

31. Consideration is very meager of the complex question of how men ascertained the permissible limits of dissent a century ago, or how nations at war allow or forbid "loyal oppositions." Allusion to this subject is in the remarks of Edward Everett to the Boston Union Club, Apr. 9, 1863, printed in the inside covers of Daniel Agnew, *Our National Constitution: Its Adaptation to a State of War or Insurrection* (Philadelphia, 1863). See also W. G. Carleton, "Civil War Dissidence in the North: The Perspective of a Century," *SAQ*, LXV (1966), 390–404.

the same restraints prohibited confiscations of rebels' property or emancipation of slaves.

For Republicans, the relatively latitudinarian constitutional base of their party adapted an "adequacy" approach to most conditions the War brought in. Julian boasted that "the Republican principle was as true in the midst of war as in seasons of peace."[32] Willing to employ the powers of government in the numerous ways that the War revealed were necessary, Republicans shifted liberalism to a posture of positives from its prewar stress on negatives; some "Radical" Republicans wished to make the War an opportunity to weld inseparably liberty *and* Union.

Of course antiwar Democrats condemned these Republican attitudes, aspirations, and policies. Unlike Democrats who, looking backward to better times, allegedly understood the Constitution better, Republicans "look exclusively to the future," charged one bitter Democrat. "Their policy is purely present and original. They are a band of reformers, with new schemes, new doctrines, and new purposes to promulgate and establish."[33]

Obviously this is oversimple. But Democrats did take a rigid stand and Republicans were relatively flexible. Each new day the nation endured, goals beyond Union or secession were realizable through politics' processes. The War opened up possibilities which had long been stopped up with constitutional inhibitions. After Sumter they appeared suddenly to be reachable if champions committed to politics enough money, time, energy, and organization, and if the Confederacy did not triumph.

Awareness of this openness brought into politics men who wished to direct change toward particular goals. Businessmen, educators, journalists, and ministers, especially of the radical Protestant-Transcendentalist varieties, became politicians as understanding grew that the causes of the War did not predetermine the results; that the stated War aim of the Union—reunion—did not exclude others that the War made achievable.[34]

Soon after Sumter political parties and adversary litigants

---

32. George W. Julian, *Political Recollections, 1840–1872* (Chicago, 1884), 223–4.

33. William C. DeWitt, *Sundry Speeches and Writings: Driftwood from the Current of a Busy Life* (Brooklyn, 1881), I, 74–5.

34. Robert Albrecht, "Theological Response of the Transcendentalists to the Civil War," *NEQ*, XXXVIII (1965), 21–34; George M. Frederickson, *The Inner Civil War: Northern Intellectuals and the Crisis of the Union* (New York, 1965), chs. 4–11; Marcus, "Phillips," 51–2.

took positions appropriate to the War's dynamic nature. Except in intensity, they continued much of the constitutional dialogue of prewar times. But prewar attention had centered on federal-state relationships and interstate property traffic. Even the slavery extension contention had partially resolved itself into the question whether the Congress might prevent state-defined legal property from entering a territory; secession argument had focused on the nature of federalism. The rhetoric of race had shied off constitutional law's thick walls.

After Sumter the intrusion of the arbitrary-arrest issue, the thrust of soldiers and other national agents into local scenes, shifted attention in courts and politics to questions of individuals' rights. Of course Republicans never intended to supply the Democracy with such a convenient and obvious means of party resurrection and rehabilitation as the arbitrary arrests proved to be. It was impossible to carry on the military arrests of civilians secretly. Indeed, since arrests aimed primarily to prevent trouble by overawing potential activists, many government officers arranged as much publicity as possible.[35]

Experts in politics, Lincoln's cabinet and congressional intimates were also trained in the law. They anticipated that the arrests would result in damage suits against officers involved for false imprisonment and unwarranted seizures. But in April 1861 no one expected that the first court test would feature the Chief Justice of the United States.[36]

---

35. B. P. Thomas and H. M. Hyman, *Stanton*, 157–8; General John A. Rawlins, *General Grant's Views in Harmony with Congress: Speech, Galena, Illinois, June 21, 1867* (Washington, 1867), 8.

36. On 1861 apprehensions of suits, see William Whiting's comments, Secretary of War "Policy Book," 9–11, RG 110, NA; Francis Lieber's ms. memorandum on habeas corpus, Lieber Papers No. 2422, HL.

Chapter VI

Taney and Treason

This confrontation did not occur by chance. Chief Justice Roger B. Taney seized the first opportunity to broadcast, as an exercise of his judicial office, his private views about the conduct of the Civil War.[1] Taney looked backward to days when white men knew few restraints, when soldiers were an irrelevance to existence, and when national authority was rarely visible. He was one of many men in 1861 and later who saw no alternatives between helpless acquiescence in the secession of the South and the inevitable rise of a military dictatorship in the North, if the government tried to restore the cleft Union of states by force.[2]

Only six weeks after Sumter, Taney worked out a vivid staging for delivering this sermon on the Constitution to the President and the nation. He employed as backdrop Baltimore, Maryland, his home city and state, which encapsulated many issues involved in the secession and War. The Chief Justice knew that only in Missouri were arbitrary arrests by soldiers of civilians more numerous and spectacular than in Maryland. However, the

---

1. C. B. Swisher, *Roger B. Taney* (New York, 1935), 550–54; C. G. Haines and F. Sherwood, *The Role of the Supreme Court in American Government and Politics, 1835–1864* (Berkeley and Los Angeles, 1957), 465; M. R. Cain, *Lincoln's Attorney General, Edward Bates of Missouri* (Columbia, Mo., 1965), 142–61, esp. 145.

2. See Taney to Franklin Pierce, June 12, 1861, in Swisher, *Taney*, 554. R. M. Spector, "Lincoln and Taney: A Study in Constitutional Polarization," *AJLH*, XV (1971), 199–214.

"show-me" state was far from the center of popular attention.[3] Following Sumter's surrender, Baltimore mobs, with overt aid from city police, attempted to block passage through the city of northern militiamen who were trying to hurry to Washington's defense. The danger was clear and present that secessionists might take Baltimore and all Maryland into partnership with the Confederacy; at least they would keep the city and state so turbulent that the vital link connecting Washington to the loyal hinterland was uncertain. Either condition might be a final weight to snap the Union's backbone.

Therefore, on April 27, as noted, Lincoln authorized along the Washington-Philadelphia corridor the War's first suspensions of habeas corpus. Acting on accurate information supplied by loyal Baltimoreans, on May 25 soldiers arrested John Merryman, a prominent suburbanite and known secessionist, and jailed him in Fort McHenry.

Lincoln had sent round a circular on May 17, cautioning officials to limit arrests of civilians by military officers to extreme instances.[4] Granting that many officers were not too careful about the meaning of "extreme," Merryman fit the condition.

An unplanned but widespread aspect of the first arrests, later made official policy, was that most jailers permitted prisoners who could afford the luxury to enjoy access to lawyers. Perhaps this commendable permissiveness reflected class conditions and the localistic focus of internal-security operations. The new officialdom must often have hesitated to deny arrested persons very much. No one knew how long the antidisloyalty work would go on; how long the Union would endure. At some uncertain date present prisoners would likely return to positions of local prominence. Perhaps, too, permissiveness with respect to counsel reflected respect for civil law's orderly processes. And, of course, no officials had any experience in the matters at hand. Confident assertions by prisoners concerning right to counsel must have been impressive.

In any event, the same day his client was jailed, Merryman's family lawyer hurried to Washington and petitioned "The Chief

---

3. Judge Samuel Treat in St. Louis acted and felt much as Taney did; yet In re McDonald, 16 Fed. Cas. No. 8751 (1861), 17–33, made far less impression on the nation than what Taney took on in Baltimore.
4. *Collected Works of Abraham Lincoln*, ed. R. Basler *et al.* (New Brunswick, N.J., 1953), IV, 372.

Justice of the United States and presiding Judge of the United States Circuit Court, Baltimore" for a writ of habeas corpus.

Here was the opportunity for which Taney had been waiting. He issued a writ at once, taking care first to strike the designation of himself as a circuit jurist from the petition. Consequently, the paper that went to General George Cadwalader, in charge at the fort, came from the nation's highest judicial officer. Yet, despite having removed his circuit title from the petition, Taney specified that the officers in charge of Merryman produce the prisoner in Baltimore, not Washington. That same day Taney traveled to the circuit courtroom in Baltimore.

Later Taney explained the title change and trip as devices to relieve Cadwalader from going to Washington. However, according to a lawyer who accompanied Taney on the hurried ride to Baltimore, and in the opinions of scholars, the jurist wanted also to escalate Merryman's imprisonment to the highest levels. He won that trick. A President of the United States had employed military force to arrest a citizen. Now Merryman was to slip from the military's grasp through an order from the Chief Justice of the United States. If Lincoln obeyed Taney's paper all was won; other jurists would follow the pattern. But if the President refused to give way then he must stand exposed in a tyrant's posture.[5] The upshot of Taney's shrewd arranging was that the law faced the sword in Baltimore in simple terms that laymen could appreciate.

The city still fumed from the suppression only a month earlier of the anti-Union rioters, although the Army now maintained surface calm. In April Taney's partner on the federal circuit bench, Judge William Giles, while serving alone as the district court justice, had futilely raised some of the issues involved in the Merryman petition. Coming only three weeks later, and recruiting into the drama the Chief Justice of the United States, the Merryman case, according to Carl Brent Swisher, at the very least provided "additional prestige . . . to arguments of the type which Judge Giles had advanced."[6]

---

5. A. S. Ridgeley to Salmon P. Chase, Dec. 28, 1866, Chase Papers, ser. I, box 98, #1472D, LC; A. H. Kelly and W. A. Harbison, *The American Constitution: Its Origins and Development* (3rd edn., New York, 1963), 439; Cain, *Bates*, 145.

6. Swisher, *Taney*, 550, and 448–550 on Giles. A similar incident involving Justice Wayne and General Scott is in A. A. Lawrence, *James Moore Wayne, Southern Unionist* (Chapel Hill, N.C., 1943), 186–7.

Sixty years earlier, when John Marshall decided to hear the petition of an obscure would-be justice of the peace, he had won the safe stage he sought from which to attack President Jefferson. In 1861, Taney could not help but gain a nationwide audience by confronting Lincoln, who tried to avoid the encounter. On May 27 a uniformed emissary from Cadwalader offered the jurist an accurate description of the conditions that had prompted Merryman's arrest. The general requested Taney to let matters rest briefly until the President provided the Army with instructions. Legal custom was that officials deserve from judges a presumption of rectitude.[7] Nothing impelled Taney to his next step.

He issued an attachment naming Cadwalader as offender. The court's marshal tried to serve the citation at Fort McHenry. Sentries blocked his way. Next day, before a crowd of two thousand people, including newspapermen, the marshal informed Taney officially that the jurist's order was frustrated. Violence was expected. Starting for the courtroom, Taney remarked that before nightfall he might be a prisoner in the fort.[8]

This emotional spirit affected everyone in the courtroom. After reading from a prepared text the details leading to the marshal's helplessness at Fort McHenry, Taney departed from the written opinion, and noted that his marshal could summon a posse comitatus to seize Cadwalader; Taney could fine and imprison him for willful usurpation of judicial authority. Unfortunately the Army officer commanded forces that overawed any posse. Under these circumstances the Chief Justice discharged the marshal from further attempts to serve the attachment, and asked the President to instruct the general to obey the orders of the court. Subsequently he filed his opinion respecting Merryman, with orders that the President receive a copy.[9]

---

7. Martin v. Mott, 12 Wheaton, 19 @ 33 (1827).

8. Swisher, *Taney*, pp. 551, 553. This apprehension on Taney's part has appeared to be the overexcited fear of a partisan. But in an unpublished memorandum, Francis Lieber noted that Lincoln contemplated Taney's arrest, and issued Ward Hill Lamon, marshal for the District of Columbia, permission to arrest him. The jurist may have heard rumors of the decision, leading to his perturbation. Lieber Papers No. 2422, HL. If it was ever intended or considered, Lincoln did not allow the arrest to occur.

9. Taney's oral comments are in Edward McPherson, *The Political History of the United States during the Great Rebellion* (2nd edn., Washington, 1865), 155. Ex parte Merryman, 17 Fed. Cas. No. 9,487 (1861), 144 at 147, contains only a résumé of the oral comment.

This famous opinion at once became a landmark in constitutional lore and partisan politics. It is rich in curious features. One recent commentator has remarked not only on its precipitate temper, but also on "the extreme legal propositions" the opinion advanced.[10]

Taney commenced in lawyerlike manner by establishing his jurisdiction. The 1789 Judiciary Act in its fourteenth section authorized national judges to issue in certain circumstances habeas corpus writs "for the purpose of an inquiry into the cause of [a petitioner's] commitment," he stated. Then he came to the question whether Lincoln's proclamation had suspended the writ privilege. The Chief Justice insisted that he had listened "with some surprise" to the general's claim of exercising a delegated power from the President, "for I had supposed it to be one of those points of constitutional law upon which there was no difference of opinion, and it was admitted on all hands, that the privilege of the writ could not be suspended, except by acts of Congress."[11]

As proof of this allegedly proven point, Taney noted that in Article I of the Constitution, dealing entirely with legislative matters, the framers had specified that: "The privilege of the writ of habeas corpus shall not be suspended, unless when, in cases of rebellion or invasion, the public safety may require it." Immediately following, as if regretting the need to allow suspension under any circumstances, the framers had listed matters with which even Congress might not deal. Suspension of the writ privilege except in dangerous conditions of rebellion or invasion "is first in the list of prohibited powers," Taney stated.

Who, then, could decide when adequate danger existed to warrant the exception and then to suspend the writ privilege? Language in the Constitution "too clear to be misunderstood by anyone" gave a complete monopoly to the Congress, Taney said. Executive suspension was usurpation of Congress's prerogatives. A judge was bound to protest against this dangerous imbalance.

But even if Congress suspended the habeas corpus writ privilege, civilians could not thereby become subject to military detention or to military trials. The Bill of Rights stood in the way,

---

10. John H. Hatcher, "Martial Law and Habeas Corpus," *WVLQ*, XLVI (1940), 189.

11. Ex parte Merryman, 147–8. On jurisdiction, see *SAL*, I, 81; Paul A. Freund *et al.*, *Constitutional Law* (3rd edn., Boston, 1967), I, 46–8.

said the Chief Justice. He had employed the Fifth Amendment in the 1857 Dred Scott decision as a protection for slave property. On Merryman's behalf, Taney insisted that the Fifth and Sixth Amendments forbade national officials from depriving any person of liberty without due process of law, and from prosecutions lacking in adequate speed and assistance by counsel.

By Taney's depiction the normal operation of courts must be Lincoln's chief concern; the only occasion he would allow of a President exercising military authority over American citizens was as a sort of glorified assistant for marshals' posses in support of the judiciary.[12] The apparatus of civil justice—courts, judges, attorneys, marshal—was in operation. If Merryman was guilty of something, then the Army officers should have brought notice of his offenses to civil officials who would have attended to him in the usual processes of courts. Therefore, Merryman was wrongly imprisoned because his arrest had occurred under executive, military authority.

Concluding this lecture to the President, Taney reminded him to exercise with restraint his commander-in-chief powers and to keep in check his uniformed subordinates. Failure in this basic responsibility threatened free government with collapse and allowed a military form to replace it.[13]

The Taney opinion and resulting polemical debate revealed that the Chief Justice and a very large number of his countrymen, including lawyers, possessed fanciful notions about the habeas corpus writ and its role in America as a defense of individuals' liberty. The Blackstonian tradition had set hard that habeas corpus was "the most celebrated writ in the English law" and that it was "great and efficacious . . . in all manner of illegal confinement."[14] James Kent had written thirty years before Sumter that England's "most wholesome" statute of 1679 on habeas

---

12. Ex parte Merryman, 149; Horace Binney, *The Privilege of the Writ of Habeas Corpus under the Constitution* (2nd edn., Philadelphia, 1862), 37–8.

13. Ex parte Merryman, 150–3.

14. William Blackstone, *Commentaries on the Laws of England* (Oxford, 1768), Book III, 129, 131. All references to the habeas corpus writ are to the form habeas corpus ad subjiciendum, as defined in John Bouvier, *A Law Dictionary, Adapted to the Constitution and Laws of the United States* (4th edn., Philadelphia, 1852), I, 575, and see also Fay v. Noia, 372 US, 391 (1963); and above, ch. 4, n. 19.

corpus had come implicitly into American law through the nation's and states' constitutions, and was "a common law right."[15]

In 1861 Taney was only the most prestigious legalist who assumed the English writ and its American offshoot to be the same effective pretrial remedy. But such judgments were cloudy. They failed to take into account "the enormous difference that federalism made in the way the writ actually operated," Professor Bestor insists.[16] Further, the presence of slavery had made habeas corpus protection irrelevant for millions of persons. Notwithstanding the 1787 Constitution's stipulation, repeated in essence in almost all states' constitutions, that the writ privilege must not be suspended except in grave emergencies, it had been permanently suspended in every slave state "for over seventy years . . . so far as colored persons are concerned, and practically suspended so far as white men [who] should assume to plead their cause," complained one antislavery veteran.[17]

Taney's statement that the habeas corpus writ had actually been a bulwark against oppression in America defied fact. Federal habeas corpus writs could serve only in instances involving congressional enactments, executive actions as in Merryman's case, or other national-level proceedings, but constitutional history to 1861 exhibited no significant marks of such service. States, not the nation, had almost always been the source of oppressive enactments. The nation's courts had never enjoyed authority to pluck from states' courts individuals who suffered from state policies by habeas corpus or other writs.[18] Thirty years before

---

15. Kent stated that the writ applied even where an explicit state constitutional provision or statute to that effect was wanting. James Kent, *Commentaries on American Law* (2nd edn., New York, 1832), II, 26–32. See too Helen A. Nutting, "The Most Wholesome Law—The Habeas Corpus Act of 1679," AHR, LXV (1963), 527–43; Dallin H. Oaks, "Habeas Corpus in the States—1776–1860," UChiLR XXXII (1965), 243–88.

16. Arthur Bestor, "The Two Habeas Corpus Acts of the Fifth of February, 1867, and Their Untoward Sequel, The McCardle Case" (OAH paper, 1966), 6–7 (used with permission); Rollin C. Hurd, *A Treatise on the Right of Personal Liberty, and on the Writ of Habeas Corpus* (Albany, 1858), esp. 120–32, 136–8; W. M. Wiecek, "The Reconstruction of Federal Judicial Power, 1863–1875" (M.A. thesis, UWis, 1966), 44–9 (used with permission).

17. Edward F. Bullard, *The Nation's Trial: The [Emancipation] Proclamation: Dormant Powers of the Government: The Constitution a Charter of Freedom and Not "A Covenant with Hell"* (New York, 1863), 60.

18. Wiecek, "Federal Judicial Power," 47. In 1789 a proposed amend-

Merryman, the Supreme Court of the United States had exhibited publicly its powerlessness to wrest a Georgia prisoner, whose offense was protecting Indians, from the state's clutches, despite a finding that the Reverend Samuel Worcester's jailing was a violation of the United States Constitution.[19]

In dramatic contrast to the weakness national courts exhibited in the Worcester case, in 1859 Taney asserted in the Ableman litigation the existence of great strength in the federal judiciary. But it was national strength directed against a state's habeas corpus writs which were being exercised for once to aid individual liberty. In Ableman Taney forthrightly denied to state courts any right to impede slave recaptures which the 1787 Constitution assigned to Congress.[20] In 1857, moreover, Taney's Dred Scott decision had denied Congress power to keep slavery from the national territories. The Worcester incident had made clear that the nation could not protect individuals who were caught up in a state's penal apparatus. In Merryman, Taney broadcast historical misinformation about the habeas corpus writ. He cast it in a role it did not deserve in America's court history on any level of the federal system, as the tried writ of liberty. In the context of the secession winter and the Sumter surrender, obedience by Lincoln to Taney's order would likely have diminished, not enhanced, liberty.

Naturally, antiwar and Democratic partisans at once employed Taney's Merryman opinion to flay the Republican Administration. Until the 1866 Milligan case replaced it, the Merryman statement

---

ment was lost in the U.S. Senate that would have applied against the states the essence of the First Amendment; *Annals of Congress*, 1 Cong., 1 sess., 433–6; *Senate Journal*, entry Aug. 25, 1789 (1820 reprint), 63–4; and see Charles Warren, "Federal and State Court Interference," *HLR*, XLIII (1930), 353; Joel Parker, "Habeas Corpus and Martial Law," *NAR*, XCIII (1861), 494–6; Joseph K. Angell, *A Treatise on the Limitations of Actions at Law and Suits in Equity and Admiralty* (Boston, 1869), 19; T. D. Morris, "Free Men All: The Personal Liberty Laws of the North, 1780–1861" (Ph.D. diss., UWash, 1969), *passim*.

19. Worcester v. Georgia, 6 Peters, 515, esp. 562, 597 (1832). The U.S. Supreme Court heard Worcester's plea on a writ of error, not a habeas corpus. Had the latter existed from federal to state jurisdictions, the Court's decision would have been directed to Worcester's jailer. In its absence the Court addressed its finding to the Georgia tribunal, which ignored it. Bestor, "The Two Habeas Corpus Acts," 14–15.

20. Ableman v. Booth, 21 Howard, 506 (1859); Oaks, "Habeas Corpus," 288.

was the single most important item of opposition literature. The Democratic theme was that the Chief Justice had proved the truth of conservative charges about the transformation of the prewar republic into a centralized military despotism.

Undoubtedly more to Taney's satisfaction, his Merryman stand won the accolade of emulation by other jurists in federal and state courts.[21] But he had not accepted Merryman's petition in order to initiate a great debate on the Constitution, to provide antiwar Democrats with proofs of Republican excesses, or to establish a citation for like-minded jurists to employ. Instead, Taney intended the decision to be the last word—a judgment—that would check what the War was loosing.[22]

Taney was misreading signs. None of the reaction to Merryman swerved the President from the muscular course he had chosen. The arbitrary arrests continued. In Congress and nationwide, impressive evidence of support for his ways accumulated.

Naturally, Republican stalwarts lined up behind Lincoln, and some of them were very able constitutional lawyers. Prominent nonpolitical legal commentators questioned sharply every point the Chief Justice had made in the Merryman opinion, comforting Lincoln with assurances that Congress's monopoly in suspending the writ privilege was by no means so clear as Taney had suggested. The division of informed judgment on this essential issue led only to the Scottish verdict, not proved.[23]

Critics of Taney's Merryman opinion were able to play the debater's game of employing his own words, drawn from earlier situations, against an opponent. A dozen years before Sumter, in a case rising out of Rhode Island's Dorr Rebellion, Taney had read this proposition into the Court's record:

> After the President has acted, and called out the militia, is a . . . Court of the United States authorized to inquire whether his decision is right? . . . Could the Court, while the parties were actually contending in arms for the posses-

---

21. Partisan reaction is in Gerald I. Jordan, "The Suspension of Habeas Corpus as a War-Time Political Control Technique" (Ph.D. diss., UCLA, 1941), ch. 9; judicial application is in Ex parte Benedict, 3 Fed. Cas. No. 1292 (1862), 159; In re Kemp, 16 Wis., 382 (1863).

22. Taney to Judge Samuel Treat, June 5, 1861, in Swisher, *Taney,* 554.

23. An able survey of the large literature on these points is in Sydney George Fisher, "The Suspension of Habeas Corpus During the War of the Rebellion," PSQ, III (1888), 454–88; and see Hatcher, "Martial Law," 187–95.

sion of the state [i.e., Rhode Island] government, call witnesses before it to inquire which party represented a majority of the people? If it could, then it would become the duty of the Court (provided it came to the conclusion that the President had decided incorrectly), to discharge those who were arrested or distrained by the troops in the service of the United States, or the government which the President was endeavoring to maintain. If the judicial power extends so far, the guarantee contained in the Constitution of the United States [against a state suffering domestic violence] is a guarantee of anarchy and not of order.[24]

It is difficult to reconcile Taney's 1861 point that Lincoln enjoyed no discretion to decide when emergency existed adequate to warrant habeas-corpus-writ-privilege suspension, with his contrary emphasis in the earlier Dorr Rebellion case. Supporters of the President's policies argued that Taney had been correct in 1849 but not in 1861; that assumption of jurisdiction by any civil court in an appeal from a military arrest was doubtful according to existing standards. Yale law Professor Henry Dutton typified a library-full of similar queries, in asking: "What has a general to do with a bench warrant, and who ever heard of such an officer rendering an account of his conduct to a judge?"

Dutton concluded that the Chief Justice had radically outreached proper judicial functions. Were judges to tell a President during a war what his soldiers could do? Common sense boggled at the proposition. Dutton resented a suggestion that the framers of the 1787 Constitution had failed to provide posterity with practical ways to cope with rebellion; i.e., that the Constitution was inadequate and defective. Taney's point was laughable that a judicial rein was needed on the President's writ-privilege suspension orders in order to preserve private rights. "For what purpose

---

24. Luther v. Borden, 7 Howard 1 @ 43 (1849). In that case Taney had quoted approvingly from an earlier precedent. Back in 1827 then Chief Justice Marshall had vigorously sustained a President's right under the Constitution and statutes to judge when conditions justified summoning states' militias into active service. Marshall had asserted that "whenever a statute gives discretionary power to any person, to be exercised by him upon his own opinion of certain facts, it is a sound rule of construction that the statute constitutes him the sole and exclusive judge of the existence of those facts." Martin v. Mott, 12 Wheaton 19, @ 29 (1827). Attorney General Bates, replying to Taney, hit hardest on this phrase by Marshall. See John P. Frank, "Edward Bates, Lincoln's Attorney General," *AJLH,* X (1966), 43 n.

is such a strict construction [as Taney required in the Merryman case] to be applied to the suspension of the writ of habeas corpus?" If Taney's construction held, then the Union and the Constitution collapsed; "If the Constitution is destroyed, of what use is the [writ] privilege?"

Dutton was unimpressed with Taney's argument that because civil courts were open in Baltimore there was no need for action by Army officers of the sort that had landed Merryman in Fort McHenry's dungeon. After all, unimpeded by these courts, the miscreant had helped to organize a company of men with admitted intention to join Confederate forces. In this war no sharp line separated battlefront from home front, Dutton concluded. "It is impossible to make any sound distinction between the capture of a rebel in Maryland by Gen. Cadwalader, and one in North Carolina by Gen. Butler."

Dutton's views paralleled those of many antislavery veterans[25] of libertarian battles as well as defenses which Lincoln offered to Congress on the occasion of its July 1861 assembly. Lincoln stated that the only impossible role had been inactivity: "A choice of means . . . became indispensable" the moment he assumed the Presidency. Adverting to the arrests of civilians by soldiers, which he knew interested the congressmen to a degree second only to the conduct of the War itself, Lincoln cautioned that "Of course some consideration was given to the questions of power and propriety before this matter was acted upon." In passages frequently quoted, Lincoln described the dilemma of democracy caught up in crisis; contended that the Constitution "is silent" as to whether suspension was a congressional or a presidential function. But the provision for suspension "was plainly made for a dangerous emergency." That being so, hesitation to act would have lost the certain substance out of excessively tender regard for the uncertain letter.

Then, in passages almost forgotten, Lincoln referred to the themes closest to him, of the popular character of the war, and of Americans' responsibility to preserve their peculiarly worthy government: "Our popular Government has often been called an experiment [he continued]. Two points in it our people have

---

25. Dutton, "Writ of Habeas Corpus," *ALReg*, IX (1861 [pam. reprint]), 3, 12–13; Bullard, *The Nation's Trial*, 61; and see Jacobus ten Broek, *The Antislavery Origins of the Fourteenth Amendment* (Berkeley and Los Angeles, 1951), 94–110.

already settled—the successful *establishing* and the successful *administering* of it. One still remains—its successful *maintenance* against a formidable internal attempt to overthrow it."

To contradict directly the Chief Justice's suggestion that no necessity—not even civil war and widespread disloyalty—was adequate to loosen the Constitution's alleged restraints, Lincoln argued that the defense of the government against instant and total destruction required recourse to "the war power." Short of this decision, the rebels would already have won no matter what courses battles took. Acquiescence after Sumter in a doctrine of constitutional helplessness would have nullified the popular verdicts given in the 1860 balloting. And he implied that the Chief Justice erred in trying to decide what was essentially a political question as a matter of constitutional law. "The people themselves, and not their servants, can safely reverse their own deliberate decisions," Lincoln concluded.[26]

In unhappy support of the President, his Attorney General, the Missouri conservative Edward Bates, took the position not that Lincoln had acted correctly but that the Chief Justice had behaved wrongly. Confused by the sweep of events, stirred by patriotism but unable to shake off misconceptions on habeas corpus, and awed by the Chief Justice, Bates resorted to legal fictions and created a fragile geometry of the Constitution. In it, the three branches of the nation's government were not only virginally separate but neatly balanced in the manner of numerous eighteenth-century disquisitions on government. None of these branches could inhibit another, as Taney had assumed to do by a writ. Bates admitted that the weight of precedent favored Congress, not the President, suspending the habeas-corpus-writ privilege. But Lincoln was serving as a sort of steward of Congress or as a civil magistrate, Bates continued. In the peculiar circumstances that had existed since Sumter, the President had acted rightly to keep the peace.[27]

It impressed onlookers that Congress, numbering excellent

---

26. *M&P*, VI, 25, 30–31.
27. Cain, *Bates*, 145, 149. Binney, *Privilege*, 37, wrote in response: "There probably has been, and still is, a strong professional [lawyer's] bias in favor of the power of Congress [to suspend the writ privilege], perhaps a judicial bias, if that be possible. It was not easy to avoid the bias under the influence of the English analogy. . . . But there is nothing on this point that is judicially authoritative." That Binney, an octogenarian legal expert, supported Lincoln, was a heavy weight in the President's favor among lawyers. See also, Frank, "Bates," 34–50.

constitutionalists in its ranks, failed to exhibit the same concern about its alleged prerogatives in habeas corpus matters that the Chief Justice had shown, and displayed far greater philosophical resiliency than Bates. Although habeas corpus questions continued to come up frequently for discussion, for two years more Congress permitted the President to go on doing what the Chief Justice had condemned, and then, in 1863, created arrangements to supplement (not replace) those which Lincoln had worked out. One line of thought, then and since, is that by their deliberate speed, lawmakers implicitly approved the President's concurrent right to suspend, in contradiction to Taney's monopoly assignment to Congress. An August 1861 joint resolution, ratifying what Lincoln had done concerning the military establishment since March, is a point in substantiation.[28] An alternative proposition, judging courts to be irrelevant as enforcers of internal security, was expressed by Professor Randall.[29] Similar sentiment obtaining in 1861, the easy, politically safe course was for legislators to allow Lincoln to bear the arbitrary arrest responsibility as long as possible. No one gained votes or glory from connection with the habeas-corpus-writ suspensions.[30]

Real dangers and hidden opportunities abounded in Taney's Merryman opinion. The dangers were not those the Chief Justice catalogued, however. The military despotism he predicted was an unlikely consequence of Lincoln's Presidency, although the policies Taney condemned continued on augmenting scales. Breakdowns did not occur in the tripartite equipoise of the national government or in the vitality of the states in the federal system. Dutton's midsummer judgment rings true that no President could suspend the habeas-corpus-writ privilege unless Congress and the mass of the citizenry supported the extraordinary expedient.[31]

---

28. *SAL*, XII, 326. On the March 3, 1863 habeas corpus law, see ch. 15.

29. James G. Randall, "The Indemnity Act of 1863: A Study in the Wartime Immunity of Governmental Officers," *MichLR*, XX (1922), 589–613.

30. See Dutton, "Writ," 11–12; James G. Randall, *Constitutional Problems Under Lincoln* (rev. edn., Urbana, Ill., 1951), 128–30; George C. Sellery, "Lincoln's Suspension of Habeas Corpus as Viewed by Congress," History Series, UWis *Bulletin*, I (1907), 213–26; and Donald G. Morgan, *Congress and the Constitution: A Study of Responsibility* (Cambridge, Mass., 1966), ch. 6.

31. Dutton, "Writ," 13.

From Maryland to Missouri disloyalty posed such clear threats as to align an impressive segment of public opinion in support of the President, in a society unaccustomed to much federal presence at all, especially of a coercive nature. However haphazard, imperfect, and unsystematic by modern standards, the security network that wove itself in 1861 was one of the two major evidences that democracy and federalism could respond appropriately to danger and disloyalty. Amassing Union armies formed the other one. If the Union was to survive its test hour its champions desperately needed such evidences.[32] Unopposed and unpunished, disloyal sentiment would have completed the Union's dissolution of spirit and structure.

Punishment for Merryman exclusively through judicial processes, as Taney prescribed, ran headlong into the solid fact that disloyalty was not a crime in 1861. Treason was the only offense under national law by which civil officials could seek to curtail Merryman's capacity to do further harm and to punish him for what he had already done; the one crime that the Constitution's framers had troubled to spell out and to enjoin Congress to punish.[33] Obedient to this stipulation, in 1790 members of the first Congress to meet under the newly ratified Constitution stipulated that convicted traitors had to suffer death.[34] In May 1861, when Army officers arrested Merryman, the 1790 statute constituted almost the whole body of appropriate national criminal law. Alternatives to the treason statute and to a prosecution under its elaborate prescriptions consisted of laws enacted between 1790 and 1860 to punish offenders under counterfeiting, bribery, patent, postal, slave-trading, and fugitive-slave regulations. Unless a treason indictment was issued against Merryman, federal statutes offered no way to punish him at all, much less quickly,

---

32. William B. Allison, *The Strength of Our Government, an Address at the Commencement of the State University of Iowa, June 22, 1887* (The University, 1887), 11, and *passim*.

33. Art. III, sec. 3. This definition is exclusive. In Kawakita v. U.S., 717 US @ 741 (1952), the Supreme Court agreed that "no matter the reach of the legislative power in defining other crimes, the constitutional requirements for treason remain the same. The crime of treason can be taken out of the Constitution by the processes of amendment; but there is no other way to modify it or alter it."

34. *SAL*, I, 112. In 1790 another statute punished misprision of treason; the crime of having knowledge of treason with failure to communicate the information to authorities. *Ibid.*, 656.

because an unbridged gap existed between the treason statute and other penal provisions too minor for employment in Merryman's instance.[35]

Later, federal district judge Peleg Sprague outlined the government's problem that derived from the absence of adequate criminal provisions. In 1861 the convicted murderer of a United States marshal could receive under national law a maximum sentence of one year in jail and a fine of three hundred dollars, even if conviction for such a murderer could occur in places of Baltimore's prosouthern temper. What price the unimpeded action of national courts and obedience of President and Army to Taney's claims, Sprague asked, if the courts' marshals were fair game for assassins? "Such was the condition of our [national] criminal jurisprudence for the protection of the life of the government, and to secure the enforcement of the laws, up to the time of the breaking out of the rebellion," Sprague continued. "How far it fell short . . . is now [1863] seen by the light of the conflagration which was permitted to be kindled."[36]

Obviously, Lincoln and his cabinet coadjutors read more clearly than the Chief Justice the fact that the nation's criminal laws, enforced by the ordinary processes of the federal courts, were too slow in effect to be relevant and too low-pitched to be adequate. The President did not grope clumsily among irrelevant minor federal criminal provisions.

If a treason prosecution had been appropriate to Lincoln's immediate concern of securing swiftly the safety of such places as Baltimore and with them the capacity of what was left of the Union to mount a war, the odds are that he would have resorted to it. But the unhappy fact was that the Constitution's arrangements and the conditions of 1861 made a recourse to its treason provision implausible.

First, there was so much treason. The national machinery

---

35. Randall, *Constitutional Problems*, 74–6; Joel Prentiss Bishop, *The Criminal Law* (Boston, 1868), II, 651–78; Bradley Chapin, *The American Law of Treason: Revolutionary and Early National Origins* (Seattle, 1964); J. W. Hurst, "Treason in the United States," *HLR*, LVIII (1944, 1945), 226–72, 395–444, 806–57. The best summary is Catherine M. Tarrant, "To 'Insure Domestic Tranquility': Congress and the Law of Seditious Conspiracy, 1859–1861," *AJLH*, XV (1971), 107–23.

36. Peleg Sprague, *What Is Treason? A Charge . . . to the Grand Jury for the District of Massachusetts, at the March Term, A.D. 1863* (Salem, 1863), 6.

was simply inadequate to cope; the Chief Justice was unrealistic to imply that individual trials could handle actual disloyalty.[37] Of course, recruitment theoretically could have augmented the number of federal judges and attorneys. But there is considerable doubt that congressmen would create quickly the small army of court officials needed to mount the treason trials the Chief Justice had specified. Many ardent Republicans were suspicious of federal judges because of southern dominance, and were hagridden by Victorian concerns over the North's allegedly empty purse; many antiwar Democrats could be depended upon to oppose any administration effort designed to enlarge national strength. Once mounted, treason prosecutions would very likely aggravate northern divisions of opinion rather than increase unity.[38] And the best reason against initiating treason trials was that the odds against winning convictions were so high.

The Constitution required that treason indictments and trials take place within the district where the alleged offense occurred. Obviously this was impossible with respect to the seceded states.[39] But as a practical matter it was highly dubious in Maryland if the government aspired to win litigation. The requirement of local venue meant that neighbors of the accused would form the jury panel. Merryman stood in little peril of suffering a guilty verdict in a treason trial conducted anywhere in Maryland. Even after Appomattox it proved impossible to carry through the treason trial of Jefferson Davis in Virginia. A great deal happened between John Merryman's and Jefferson Davis's

---

37. Not a cabinet department until 1870, in 1861 (and in 1865) the staff of the Attorney General's office, which in 1861 for the first time since 1789 was supposed to superintend inferior law officers, consisted of 8 men; there were 70 federal judges (78 in 1865); and 81 federal attorneys, solicitors, marshals, and other court officers (93 in 1865). Paul P. Van Riper and Keith A. Sutherland, "The Northern Civil Service: 1861–1865," *CWH*, XI (1965), 357; R. F. Fenno, *The President's Cabinet* (Cambridge, Mass., 1959), 17.

38. Bray Hammond, "The North's Empty Purse, 1861–1862," *AHR*, LXVII (1961), 1–18; and see Senator William Pitt Fessenden's comments, *CG*, 37 Cong., 2 sess., 2016; Frank, "Bates," 43 n.

39. A member of a Georgia militia company who during the secession weeks had helped to take over a federal fort there, and who was in Philadelphia immediately after the Sumter attack, was arrested and brought before a national district court in Philadelphia. The judge decided in a preliminary hearing that there was evidence enough to hold the accused for trial on a treason charge. But he released him on $10,000 bond until a trial could take place in Georgia. It never did. U.S. v. Griener, 26 Fed. Cas. No. 15,262 (1861).

imprisonments. But no modernization occurred of the treason clause of the Constitution or of derivative statutes.[40]

The Constitution specified also that a person accused of treason must have been waging war against the United States, and that two witnesses must testify to these overt acts. This meant that if treason trials were the only recourse, the government had to stand by while many Merrymans committed further acts detrimental to the already groggy Union. There was no way around the Constitution if the Lincoln Administration viewed it as an obstacle; "The [federal] criminal code touched no measure [when the War began] that had not ripened into an overt act of levying war, or actual interference with the administration of the law," Judge Sprague complained in 1863. "All the incipient and preparatory measures, leading to the overthrow of the government, were left without punishment or reprehension."[41]

History added its weight to the unemployability of the Constitution's treason clause. Half a century before Sumter, prosecutions arising out of Aaron Burr's western misadventures had placed in the record the tight definitions of what constituted overtly levying war against the nation, so troubling to federal attorneys in 1861.[42] "Abundant dicta" but few certain guidelines for prosecutions had emerged from the Burr precedent, observed Joel Prentiss Bishop, the leading criminal law scholar of the Civil War and Reconstruction period. He noted that when the War

---

40. U.S. v. Jefferson Davis, 7 Fed. Cas. No. 3621a (1868); Roy Franklin Nichols, "United States v. Jefferson Davis," *AHR,* XXXI (1926), 266–84.

41. Sprague, *What Is Treason?* 6; U.S. v. Greathouse, 26 Fed. Cas. No. 15,254 (1863) suggests the difficulties involved in coming to agreement about what levying war consists. Even under the act of July 17, 1862 (12 *SAL,* 589) that punished acts of disloyal nature which did not fit the Constitution's stipulations, judicial punishments were uncertain. Further, the question intruded whether rebels were enemies of the United States, thus bringing into play the offense of aiding them, leading to treasonous actions.

42. Ex parte Bollman, 4 Cranch 75 (1807); U.S. v. Burr, *ibid.,* App. 470 (1807). Offered a law partnership, ex-CSA General S. B. Buckner hesitated because he knew no law. His would-be associate, former Georgia Governor George A. Brown, replied (Dec. 15, 1865): "Neither did Vattel [know any law], nor Chief Justice Marshall, but Halleck and Chase [Marshall's successor after Taney as U.S. Chief Justice] are pregnant with it. A few sentences from the first named author should be read to Halleck occasionally to show him what a fool Vattel was, while Chase should hear occasionally the case of U.S. v. Burr, while he sits to condemn [Jefferson] Davis for Treason . . . that he might pronounce Marshall a goose." No. SB 127, HL.

started (or when it ended for that matter) no agreement existed whether, as in Merryman's instance, one man could levy war, and so doing, come under the Constitution's treason definition. The leading doctrines of criminal law in national and most states' courts required proof of intention to commit a crime as prerequisite for finding guilt. Mere "evil imagining" or conspiracy did not serve as a base for prosecution, Bishop concluded.[43]

In 1861 the treason and related criminal clauses of the 1787 Constitution did not serve the nation's needs as a deterrent against or a punishment for disloyalty or treason. As the sole weapon against disloyalty, the treason clause left authorities far too lightly armed for effective home-front combat. Lawyers in the government's service including the President, as well as observers in America and abroad, understood better than the Chief Justice that the Constitution's apparently pellucid treason clause actually was murky and shifting.[44]

Sensitivity to hazards implicit in Taney's Merryman opinion was clear and immediate at the White House, a fact that deserves encomiums. A view of the Constitution requiring (not suggesting) that conspiracies actually (not theoretically) devoted to the violent upset of the Union's remnants must (not could) remain unimpeded until they erupted, led only to disaster. Instead, the decision was quick and certain that the Constitution allowed the middle way that Lincoln chose to travel. The continuing great debate on the arbitrary arrests should not obscure the fact that the President never suffered repudiation on Capitol Hill, at the polls, or in the nation's highest courts.

---

43. Bishop, *Criminal Law*, II, 1201, and see ch. 63. See also Judge David Davis's charge to grand jurors, on treason, in Indianapolis *Star*, May 6, 1863.

44. Justice Jackson's comment is applicable: "The framers' efforts to compress into two sentences the law of one of the most intricate of crimes, gives a superficial appearance of clarity and simplicity which proves illusory when it is put to practical application." Cramer v. U.S., 35 US 1 @ 46 (1945). Even foreigners estimated matters more accurately than Taney. A retrospective judgment by a London law writer was that the law of treason in the United States did not approach "anything like the certainty of the law of treason in any other political system that has ever existed. . . . History has overwhelmed this simple text [the U.S. Constitution's treason clause] with such difficult and numberless glosses as to have given this extraordinary quality to the Constitution . . . that it is almost impossible to say of almost any act of war against the central government, either that it does or does not come within the definition of treason." R. E. F., "Trial of Jefferson Davis," [London] *Law Magazine and Law Review*, XXI (1866), 259–60.

Chapter VII

The Inadequate Constitution

Another danger rising from the Merryman epicenter of disturbance was the exposure of disagreement among the nation's highest officials about the Constitution they served. This exposure, coming so closely together with secession and the onset of war, impacted with avalanche effect. That generation had revered the Constitution but had paid it little attention as an instrument of power. The Civil War was to alter the innocent prewar attitude.[1]

Suits of the Merryman sort could set Constitution against nation, nation against states, courts against patriotism, law against allegiance. The prewar popular reverence for law and judges, however romantic, might reverse into contempt if other jurists emulated the Chief Justice's early effort to pit the Constitution against the Union, or if Taney managed other confrontations with President or Congress. Once idolized, but now perilously close to becoming defiled, the Constitution might become a casualty no matter who won a final military verdict.

Many laymen saw little wrong in an argument that the Constitution was silent while the War lasted, at least with respect to less-than-patriotic persons. A literature came quickly into being in 1861, and continued through the War, the message of which

---

1. Francis Lieber, *What Is Our Constitution—League, Pact or Government? Two Lectures on the Constitution of the United States . . . Law School of Columbia College . . . 1860 and 1861* (New York, 1861), 6 n.; Lorraine A. Williams, "Northern Intellectual Reaction to Military Rule During the Civil War," *The Historian*, XXVII (1965), 339.

was that victory was unobtainable unless the Constitution was acknowledged to be irrelevant. "Great crisis required great measures," editorialized the *Continental Monthly*; another commentator concluded that the time was past for arguments on the Constitution's construction.[2]

This outpouring disquieted persons such as George Ticknor Curtis who held that Jeffersonian negatives on governmental action must always apply. The Constitution's salvation lay less in winning the war than in maintaining unaltered all connections "between the political past and the political future."[3] Such judgments took on more extreme shadings among vigilantes who would willingly have set aside the Constitution for the duration, and far-right Democrats who wished it to apply as if nothing going on since Sumter was different from what obtained earlier. These extremists misunderstood Lincoln's basic point that the Constitution was adequate for all seasons; that new situations called up from the 1787 reservoir appropriate if novel means to cope with crisis.[4]

However it was interpreted, disagreement in high places about the Constitution hurt, because for more than seventy years Americans had believed that it was a perfect, finished work that since initiation had required only technical adjustments in the form of two amendments. Then, with accumulating pressure, the thrusts of secession, war's inception, and the Lincoln-Taney altercation, broke the customary crust of satisfaction with the Constitution as the core of the rule of law. No longer could reasonable men think of the Constitution as "a final rule of right, behind which there was nothing to which good citizens were called to look for guidance," wrote Edwin Lawrence Godkin. The Merryman hearing made necessary evaluations of the Constitution as a

---

2. *CM*, III (1863), 631–2; Sidney Cromwell, *Political Opinions in 1776 and 1863: A Letter to a Victim of Arbitrary Arrests and "American Bastilles"* (New York, 1863), 18.

3. G. T. Curtis, *Constitutional History of the United States from Their Declaration of Independence to the Close of Their Civil War*, ed. Joseph Culbertson Clayton (New York, 1896), II, 547–8.

4. As example, one antiwar, antiemancipationist commentator indignantly condemned the fact that "the Constitution, founded on the right of Revolution, is set at nought by those who claim to be its special champions, upon the ground that it is unfit for revolutionary times, or such periods of popular uprising as that to which it owes its birth." An Eye-Witness, *The Bastille in America, or, Democratic Absolutism* (London, 1861), 6–7.

defective power arrangement rather than as a source of perfect government. Thereafter the Constitution deserved respect, not adoration; employment, not adulation. In short, in 1861, "criticism has been let loose even upon the Constitution of the United States," Godkin concluded.[5]

The degree of malaise occasioned by realization that defects existed in the Constitution is roughly measurable by the inner civil war intellectuals suffered during the crisis of the Union. Men went off in several directions as they searched for ways to pin supports or condemnations of what was going on to the Constitution. What impresses is not that partisans came to prejudiced judgments[6]—it is the continuing concern for finding bases in the Constitution for harmonizing liberty and power; the persisting agreement that the Constitution mattered; the compelling insistence that what Robert Dale Owen described as the "War-Gulf" be as narrow as possible. Only by sensing the tenacious hold that the *idea* of the Constitution had on most Americans is the impact of the War's revelations about the Constitution's defectiveness measurable.[7]

---

5. E. L. Godkin, "The Constitution, and Its Defects," *NAR*, XCIX (1864), 120, 123. Forgetting his own insights, Godkin's "Some Things Overlooked at the Centennial," *The Nation* (Sept. 2, 1887), 226, dates initiation of criticism in the 1880's, as do Herman Belz, "The Constitution in the Gilded Age: The Beginnings of Constitutional Realism in American Scholarship," *AJLH*, XIII (1969), 110; H. E. Von Holst, *The Constitutional and Political History of the United States* (Chicago, 1876), I, 68; Woodrow Wilson, *Congressional Government: A Study in American Politics* (Boston, 1885), 4–6, 332. For a contrary view, dating criticism in 1861, see my introduction to a new edition of Sidney George Fisher's *Trial of the Constitution* (New York, 1972 [not in print, however, as I write this, and so I refer henceforward to the 1862 edition published in Philadelphia]). By 1866 it was visible in England that the American Constitution, "so long regarded as an institution of almost divine authority, is, in reality, full of defects." R. E. F., "Trial of Jefferson Davis," [London], *Law Magazine and Law Review*, XXI (1866), 259–60.

6. George M. Frederickson, *The Inner Civil War: Northern Intellectuals and the Crisis of the Union* (New York, 1965), 77–8; Williams, "Northern Intellectuals," 334–49.

7. R. D. Owen, "Looking Back Across the War-Gulf," *Old and New*, I (1870), 579–89. The son of one of the War's major commentators on the Constitution remembered vividly the unsettling feeling of uncertainty caused by the Merryman clash that in 1861 sent his father hurrying to histories and to reference books: "There were few things in American history more worthy of discussion than the power exercised by Lincoln. . . . It was absolute and arbitrary and, if unauthorized, its exercise was a tremendous violation of the Constitution. Whether it was justifiable

A More Perfect Union

The Constitution defective? Before 1861 this suggestion was almost unuttered except by abolitionist heretics. Even secessionist leaders justified their centrifugal courses from the allegedly unconstitutional excesses of northern democracy, and insisted that secession and the initiation of the Confederacy were returns to proper nation-state constitutional relationships. Popularly, the idea never flourished that the Constitution was irrelevant to the War. It violated Americans' "curious reverence [and] superstitious faith in the Constitution," in the derisive phrase of England's *Saturday Review*.[8]

Coming so soon after secession and Sumter, the Taney-Lincoln contention challenged that faith and forced into northern consciousness a sense of crossroads. "This war is a test of the Constitution," wrote the Philadelphia lawyer Sidney George Fisher. "We stand today beside one of those catapult plunges in human history," echoed a Boston minister, "[at a] test-hour for all that we have hitherto regarded as fixed and valuable in popular constitutional history, and especially the test-hour of a national government [built] upon the basis of republican freedom."[9]

In the sense that they broadcast imprecisions about constitutional relationships, the comments that issued in the wake of Merryman's hearing mitigated against successful passage of the test. Defenders and attackers took up every point that Taney raised or that Lincoln employed as counter. And every writer in this large and energetic crew "flushed and put upon the wing a whole covey of reviewers," remarked one of the most significant of the propresidential scribes.

Retrospectively, however, the ongoing arguments were bene-

---

and necessary is another matter. If it was unconstitutional and yet necessary in order to save the Union, it shows that the Constitution is defective in not allowing the government the proper means of protecting itself." Sydney George Fisher, "The Suspension of the Habeas Corpus During the War of the Rebellion," *PSQ*, III (1888), 457.

8. [London] *Saturday Review* (March 10, 1866), 283. Pessimistic at the prospects for a viable federal arrangement for his aspiring land because of events southward, a Canadian asked, "What verdict could be more crushing to any Constitution, than half a century after its establishment, the foremost men [of the United States], born and bred under its provisions, should be unable to agree as to whether it was the mere agent of the several States, or 'a government proper'?" Thomas D'Arcy McGee, *Notes on Federal Governments Past and Present* (Montreal, 1865), 40; Robert D. Marcus, "Wendell Phillips and American Institutions," *JAH*, LVI (1969), 50–1.

9. Fisher, *Trial of the Constitution*, 357; Rev. Joseph P. Thompson, "The Test-Hour of Popular Liberty and Republican Government," *NE*, XXI (1862), 222–3.

ficial. They kept the Constitution relevant to policy alternatives and encouraged resolutions within political and judicial processes rather than outside them, as had occurred with secession.[10] But such a judgment requires the insight that hindsight allows. In 1861 the revelations of imprecision in the Constitution, the disagreements of self-styled legal experts, and the debates by politicians led many individuals to despair rather than comfort. One of Lincoln's staunchest and ablest defenders in this controversy, the aged Horace Binney, admitted candidly in a public letter to Lieber: "We have talked and written much to each other on this Habeas Corpus question. It is a political rather than a legal question,—a mixed political and a legal question. . . . No one should be dogmatical, or very confident, in such a matter."[11] Despite this admirable precept, many persons were dogmatic and very confident on habeas corpus and related matters. Still, perception existed that, instead of being a final word, Taney's Merryman mandate was "a first impression" on the plastic pages of American constitutional law, as Binney contended.[12]

Binney's defenses of Lincoln's ways comforted men in the White House and the War Department. But it was no comfort that this distinguished lawyer and scholar admitted the imprecise condition of the Constitution on the all-important habeas corpus question. At least Binney's frank inconclusiveness hit closer to constitutional realities than Taney's negative certainty or Bates's responsive geometry.

---

10. Horace Binney, as paraphrased in Fisher's "Habeas Corpus," 465. *Ibid.*, 485–8, Fisher listed approximately 50 publications on the habeas corpus question. Much later, James G. Randall, *Constitutional Problems Under Lincoln* (rev. edn., Urbana, Ill., 1951), 531–63, presented a full bibliography. A recent reconsideration of the polemical literature is in Williams, "Northern Intellectual Reaction," *passim*. An obscure but perceptive Ohioan summarized the War's effects in the following manner: "To arrive at just conclusions we are thus compelled to look the great Constitutional questions in the face. In the absence of unanimity in the interpretation of these, the humblest citizen may examine these great questions and decide for himself the path of practical duty. If any apology were necessary for plain people attempting a discussion of Constitutional questions it may be found in the fact that hitherto our political leaders have proven themselves to be blind leaders of the blind." William P. Cutler, *The Duty of Citizens in Reconstruction: Address, Belpre, Ohio, July 4, 1865* (Marietta, O., 1865), 9.

11. Dec. 23, 1861, in Horace Binney, *The Privilege of the Writ of Habeas Corpus Under the Constitution* (2nd edn., Philadelphia, 1862), unnumbered prefatory page.

12. *Ibid.*, 37–8.

Continuing revelations of the imprecision of the Constitution concerning the prevention and conduct of civil war led some commentators to conclude that the American experiment was a flat failure. In 1861 some individuals gave way, momentarily at least, to black despair. Caught up in this depression, Senator Timothy O. Howe advised a young relative:

> Don't anchor yourself to any policy. Don't tie up to any platform. The very foundations of the Government are rocking. All the signs portend an eruption. God only knows what sort of a landscape will be exhibited when the convulsion is over. No mere policy or platform can outlive the storm. Clutch hold with both hands and with your teeth also that great eternal principle underlying all government both of God's and men—that authority is of men and government for their use and that all government is usurped and unconstitutional which does not seek their good. Keep your eye on these principles and you will come ashore somewhere but whether in time or in eternity, I'm sure I do not know.[13]

Reflecting such pessimism, an anti-Republican party literature grew up quickly that assumed the death in 1861, after Merryman, or in 1863 after emancipation, or any time Union arms suffered reverses, of the "old" Constitution. These morbid polemics outlined assertedly superior new frames for government, involving, usually, permanently gerrymandered restraints on democracy, perpetual protections for slavery, and increased restrictions on national power and functions. This theoretical inquiry largely ended when the Confederacy collapsed.

Unlike the theoreticians and polemicists of 1861–65, creators of the Confederacy's national constitution were involved in an intensively practical application of the defectiveness theme. Too often their administrative-fiscal improvements have been misinterpreted as substantive advances in the art and practice of federalism and democracy. Not so.[14] But during the War, Union-

---

13. T. O. Howe to nephew James, Dec. 30, 1861, typescript, Howe Papers, SHSW.

14. On utopian and antiutopian literature, see Burnett, *The American Theory of Government Considered with Reference to the Present Crisis* (New York, 1861) (see review of the 1863 edition in *Brownson's Quarterly Review*, IV [1863], 243–9); W. W. Handlin, *American Politics: A Moral*

ist politicos and jurisprudents felt constrained to rebut all charges that the 1787 Constitution was defective.

A heavy weight of European comment, to which American intellectuals were sensitive, ridiculed this concern over constitutions while agreeing that the Constitution was dead. In 1861 Parisians enjoyed the barbed story of a bookseller who received a request for a copy of his nation's new constitution. "We do not deal in periodical literature," he replied. A touring Illinois college president reported that "English people consider us . . . under the influence of a hallucination . . . on this point [of constitutionalism]."[15] Many European intellectuals felt that written constitutions deserved no respect because they were not keeping ships of state on straight courses. Soon after the Merryman clash, the English journalist William Howard Russell in New York City "had bought the 'Constitution' for three cents . . . and had read it carefully, but . . . could not find that it was self-expounding; it referred . . . to a Supreme Court, but what was to support the Supreme Court in a contest with armed power, either of government or people?" The American national government was "groping in the dark," Russell decided, without much illumination from the disappointingly murky Constitution. Americans' habit of looking back to 1787 for light in 1861 amused Sir James Fitzjames Stephen, who derided the folly of employing lawyers' adversary techniques as guidelines for peace, much less for war. But the Americans' "reverence for law" impressed Robert Trimble, espe-

---

and *Political Work, Treating of the Causes of the Civil War, the Nature of the Government, and the Necessity for Reform* (New Orleans, 1864); Lewis John Jennings, *Eighty Years of Republican Government in the United States* (New York, 1868); John Williams, *The Rise and Fall of "The Model Republic"* (London, 1863). Concerning the Confederate Constitution, see William R. Leslie, "The Confederate Constitutions," *Michigan Quarterly Review*, II (1963), 153; Eric L. McKitrick, "Party Politics and the Union and Confederate War Efforts," in *The American Party Systems: Stages of Political Development*, ed. William N. Chambers and Walter D. Burnham (New York, 1967), 117–51. I exploit these perceptive essays throughout this section. They deal with matters ignored in Charles R. Lee, Jr., *The Confederate Constitutions* (Chapel Hill, N.C., 1963). The insights of R. T. Takaki, *The Agitation to Reopen the African Slave Trade* (New York, 1971), 231–43, deserve close attention.

15. For the bookseller, Roger Foster, *Commentaries on the Constitution of the United States, Historical and Juridical* (Boston, 1895), I, 1–2; for the college president, J. M. Sturtevant, *English Institutions and the American Rebellion: Extracts from a Lecture Delivered at Chicago, April 28, 1864* (Manchester, Eng., 1864), 8–9.

cially as it impelled Lincoln's compatriots to accept Taney's Merryman opinion without violence.[16]

As here, the conviction spread abroad that the American Constitution was both a cause and a casualty of secession and war. The overtouted Constitution's innate rigidity made responsiveness to the swift pace of change improbable. Political democracy and federalism were conditions of American life too unstable to be contained by a past generation's formula, no matter how wise. History had outstripped 1787, until in 1861 the sections came to separation and war. A conclusion emerged among Victorian critics of democracy that a written constitution could lead only to moribund, static societies.[17]

Conservative convictions took inspiration from the American events of 1861. Since they allegedly proved that democracy and federalism were unsuitable bases for effective government in America, eminent Europeans concluded that America's experience proved democracy to be unsuitable for their countries as well.

Walter Bagehot, according to G. M. Young "the greatest Victorian," in mid-1861 confessed his surprise that Americans incomprehensibly desired to compress politics and law—two of man's most innately complex pursuits—into neat codes and rules. Little wonder that the product proved to be evanescent. Law and politics were transitory, not fixed. But, even if incorrect, Americans so revered their fundamental law—later Bagehot wrote that America was "the most law-loving of Countries"[18]—that the reasons for its failure deserved study.

Bagehot uncovered without difficulty what undermined the

---

16. W. H. Russell, *My Diary North and South*, ed. Fletcher Pratt (New York, 1965), 9; Sir James Stephen, *Liberty, Equality, Fraternity* (New York, 1873), 168–9; cf. Robert Trimble, *A Review of the American Struggle in Its Military and Political Aspects* (London, 1864), 24–5; and Carl J. Friedrich, *The Impact of American Constitutionalism Abroad* (Boston, 1967), *passim*.

17. Thornton P. Terhune, *The New Regime in the Nineteenth Century: A Research in the Analogy Between Western Europe and American Political Evolution, 1860–1870* (Toulouse, France, 1933), 19–20, 47; Gottfried Dietze, *America's Political Dilemma: From Limited to Unlimited Democracy* (Baltimore, 1968), 17.

18. *The Works of Walter Bagehot*, ed. Forrest Morgan (Hartford, 1891), IV, 40. (Henceforth this collection is cited as Bagehot, *Works*). See also H. C. Allen, "The Impact of the Civil War and Reconstruction on Life and Liberalism in Great Britain," in *Heard Round the World: The Impact of the American Civil War Abroad*, ed. Harold M. Hyman (New York, 1968), 3–97.

Constitution. Federalism was one of his two villains, and he likened it to a cancer. From the end of the American Revolution to the onset of the Civil War, the malignancy of localism had grown larger. But until 1861 it did not collapse the national structure in which it fed, Bagehot wrote. The built-in defect, semi-autonomous states, received continuing nourishment from the effects of "certain elaborate provisions [in the Constitution] which were believed [in 1787] to be the best attainable safeguards against analogous dangers and difficulties."[19]

According to Bagehot, semiautonomy in the states led to belief in their sovereignty. To be sure, in 1787 some genuflection was necessary in the direction of the states. But the framers should have adopted Hamilton's notion and made the states "mere municipalities" analogous to Liverpool under England's constitution. This done, secession would have become unlikely; effective conduct of war by secessionists impossible.

Bagehot admitted that he was close to heresy in criticizing American federalism; that peculiar "Union with a top to it." Nineteenth-century Europeans praised no invention in government more.[20] But what was going on in the un-United States proved that federalism was suitable only for placid seas. "At every critical period the sinister influence of the imperium in imperio will be felt," Bagehot decided.

Here Bagehot switched from federalism to expose the even more virulent malignancy that underlay it—political democracy. Through its provisions for periodic elections, especially of the President, held within states, the Constitution tied the federal structure unhealthily to political democracy. Every presidential election was a constitutional crisis. Even a "homogenous and simple" nation would hesitate ever to indulge in the internecine tugs that Americans suffered every four years. As a result, the United States was "the most separable of political communities."

He noted how slavery strained further the inherently defective federal system and democratic political structure. Slavery

---

19. Walter Bagehot, "The American Constitution at the Present Crisis," [London] *National Review*, XIII (1861), 465–93 (I employ the text in *Bagehot's Historical Essays*, ed. Norman St. John-Stevas [New York, 1966], 348–9); see also M. Churchman, "Walter Bagehot and the American Civil War," *Dublin Review*, CCXXXIX (1965–66), 377–92.

20. *Bagehot's Historical Essays*, 357. Of course Bagehot failed to realize that American federalism had grown up since 1607, not since 1776, despite the inability of England's Constitution to adapt to alternative arrangements.

existed under states' laws, but dominated national politics. When a possibility threatened that the national government under Republican party leadership might be inhospitable to slave property, the southern states began their centrifugal courses. These "magical consequences" of the 1860 balloting were the clear result of inadequately tough efforts by the framers of 1787 to subordinate masses to elite classes and states to nation, Bagehot judged.[21]

Devices which the framers had built into the Constitution to maintain the federal system were incapable of effective operation, save when it was not very important if they worked. In this connection Bagehot considered the Supreme Court to be merely "a pre-eminently judicial tribunal" unsuitable and unable to decide contention between states or between states and the national government. Thus, Bagehot concluded, in the 1860–61 secession winter the Court played no role in the most basic question of constitutional law. How could it? The defect that brought on secession was in the federal nature of the Union, not in law,[22] and overly democratic democracy worsened the effects of the Constitution's inherent flaw. The "lower orders" spoke loudly in all American elections, and, as all Englishmen knew, even interfered with the proper conduct of foreign relations. Because the "low vulgarity" of American politics so displeased "the cultivated mind of Europe," few in the Old Country would mourn the collapse of the New World's maverick society. And collapse it would. No permanent reunion was possible even if the Confederacy quit its war. The same destructive factors would operate that had led to Sumter.[23]

Buchanan's lame-duck incumbency was the final proof Bagehot required to condemn the Constitution's arrangements as defective and unimprovable. Such as it was, the nation's power had been in Buchanan's hands during the fateful months of November 1860 to March 1861. Any head of state owed his people the plain duty to oppose the overturn of their government. Buchanan's rejection of this duty in favor of legalistic rhetoric illustrated "a singular defect in the American Constitution, that

---

21. *Ibid.*, 362–3. The only virtue that Bagehot could discern in the Constitution was that once in office, unless impeached and convicted a President could not be removed. *Ibid.*, 377. See too Benjamin E. Lippincott, *Victorian Critics of Democracy* (Minneapolis, 1938), *passim*.

22. *Bagehot's Historical Essays*, 363–4.

23. *Ibid.*, 363, 365. Joseph M. Hernon, Jr., "The Use of the American Civil War in the Debate over Irish Home Rule," *AHR*, LXIX (1964), 1022–6.

[through elections] it gave power at the decisive moment to those least likely to use that power well."[24] The English critic derided the Constitution's prohibition against executive or judicial officers holding seats in Congress. This bar made impossible—indeed illegal—the amassing of executive and legislative expertness that distinguished Parliament. Worse by far, the Constitution's lack of clarity on the scope of the nation's powers, even in a time of civil war, was thrusting the untried Lincoln Administration into desperate improvisations. Bagehot recognized that the framers of the Constitution may well have avoided detailing how the nation should cope with rebellion for fear of admitting the possibility of internal strife. But now the bitter fruit of eighteenth-century caution had ripened. Almost every action that the wartime President and his subordinates were taking to counter the rebels exposed each official to peril in the form of damage suits or unpunished retribution. Little wonder that officers were either timid or despotic.[25]

The Constitution did not deserve "the deference and the admiration with which all Americans used to regard it," Bagehot believed, despite its "ingenious devices and superficial subleties." The wonder was not that calamity had come in 1860 but that it had not occurred sooner, he concluded.[26]

Thus, only a few weeks after Sumter, a prestigious European had from his Burkean perspective found America's Constitution innately and irreparably defective. Bagehot's almost offhand essay came to conclusions that were not surprising in the light of the author's nationality, class, and concerns about democracy's rise in Britain.[27] It is more surprising that almost at the same time

---

24. *Bagehot's Historical Essays*, 370–1.
25. *Ibid.*, 378–9. Bagehot asserted that in analogous situations Parliament would condone every "well-intentioned and beneficial irregularity [in defense of the realm] by an act of indemnity. But the American Congress can not do so" because express warrant for acts of indemnity is not in the Constitution. *Ibid.*, 379.
26. *Ibid.*, 379–80. See too Alistair Buchan, *The Spare Chancellor: The Life of Walter Bagehot* (London, 1959).
27. Note that Bagehot's 1861 essay on the American Constitution, not his 1867 effort on England's (in *Works*, IV), is the first of his analyses to compare cabinet and presidential forms of government, to the detriment of the latter. See William H. Riker, "Sidney George Fisher and the Separation of Powers During the Civil War," *JHI* (1945), 399, as an example of the common error on this point of date. In America, fortunately for the Union's survival, Bagehot had little influence until after Appomattox. See

Bagehot's essay appeared in print, an American should reach parallel conclusions.

Sidney George Fisher's prominent Philadelphia family provided him a superior education at Dickinson College and distinguished mentorship in the law. Fisher became a Whig in politics, then a Republican. Independently wealthy, he devoted his time to gentlemanly farming and to writing belles-lettres, until the Kansas-Nebraska legislation inspired him to add pamphleteering to his activities.

Fisher's pre–Civil War pamphlets reflect strongly nationalist constitutional views appropriate to a self-styled Websterian. He lashed out against the restraints on national action in the Kansas-Nebraska law and the Dred Scott decision. In other matters, however, William H. Riker, the most careful student of the Philadelphian's career, has judged that Fisher's prewar writings "display a curious hodge-podge of convictions," including Constitution-worship and belief in majority rule, Republican party affiliation, and racism so deep as to come close to support for Negro slavery. This "potpourri of ideas," curious by our standards but not by those of Fisher's time, would have left Fisher properly forgotten had the Civil War not lifted him to a higher plane of consistency and content.[28]

Lincoln inspired the initial escalation. Reading the President's July 4, 1861 message to Congress, Fisher marveled how "in this hour of its trial the country seems to have found . . . a great man." Deriving courage from Lincoln's posture in the Merryman litigation, Fisher began to question his own doubts, reminiscent of Bagehot's, concerning America's constitutional machineries.[29]

Prominent Philadelphians, including members of Fisher's select family and circle of acquaintances, were blatantly antiwar and dangerously pro-Confederate. Some fell victims to arbitrary

---

also John E. Acton, *Essays on Freedom and Power*, ed. G. Himmelfarb (Glencoe, Ill., 1949), ch. 7; John E. Acton, *Historical Essays and Studies*, ed. J. Figgis and R. V. Laurence (London, 1908), ch. 4.

28. Riker, "Sidney George Fisher," 402. I employ this admirable essay throughout the following treatment of Fisher. See also U. B. Phillips, "The Central Theme of Southern History," *AHR*, XXIV (1928), 31; Belz, "Constitution in the Gilded Age," 111–12.

29. *A Philadelphia Perspective: The Diary of Sidney George Fisher Covering the Years 1834–1871*, ed. Nicholas B. Wainwright (Philadelphia, 1967), 396.

arrests of the sort that Merryman endured. Fisher wasted no tears on them.[30] These arrests made him particularly sensitive to the savant's storm that blew up nationwide in the wake of Taney's Merryman opinion. Enlisting in Lincoln's favor his knowledge of the law, Fisher set out to prepare a modest pamphlet, expecting that the task would occupy a few dozen hours over several weeks. Fisher's intention was merely to confirm from the Constitution his assumption that Lincoln had acted correctly in arresting Merryman.

Instead, Fisher found himself caught up in a year of intensive labor. He produced a four-hundred-page book instead of a brief pamphlet, and even so he felt a need to apologize for the brevity of his study. "The flight of events is now so rapid, that he who wishes to influence opinion must now speak quickly, and cannot therefore bestow much time on careful and artistic execution," Fisher noted in the preface to his swollen literary product.[31]

Apology was unnecessary. Fisher's book, entitled *The Trial of the Constitution,* led from the habeas corpus controversy into a far-ranging survey of the capacity of the American Constitution to cope with crisis. *Trial* is an account of Fisher's discovery and exploration of a realistic constitutional world that was markedly different from the neat geometry favored in Taney's Merryman opinion and in Bates's reply to the Chief Justice; and to the failed verdict Bagehot offered. By contrast, Fisher's Constitution was dynamic, chaotic, and uncompleted.

Basic in Fisher's education was reverence for Bacon, Blackstone, Burke, Coke, Grotius, and Vattel among foreign legal commentators, and, of Americans, for *The Federalist,* Marshall, Kent, Story, and Webster. Only the Civil War's enormous impacts could have wrenched loose the hold of "the learned doctors of our law," Fisher confessed. The "new light" the War was shedding onto the "principles and meaning" of the Constitution revealed that before 1861 American government had been untested. Now, "when it is for the first time subjected to the test of a severe ordeal, its defects are becoming manifest."[32]

---

30. *Ibid.,* 405. Fisher's antiwar relatives and friends included Charles Ingersoll, author of *An Undelivered Speech on Executive Arrests* (Philadelphia, 1862); and J. Francis Fisher, who wrote *The Degradation of Our Representative System and Its Reform* (Philadelphia, 1863).

31. Fisher, *Trial* (1862 edn.), vii.

32. *Ibid.,* v–vi. See also Belz, "Constitution in the Gilded Age," 112.

Fisher described candidly the self-instruction into which his research had plunged him. He had begun work without thought that the Constitution might not supply final answers. To Fisher the real problem that the Taney-Lincoln-Bates dialogue revealed was not whether President or Congress enjoyed a mechanical priority to cope with disloyalty or whether the Chief Justice could legitimately call to heel other branches of government. What mattered was that the law was still unsettled; that in 1861 it was "necessary to write on the subject at all"; that "no man can tell what are the actual, undoubted powers of the Government" in such a vital arena as internal security or "the security afforded, by the Constitution, to personal liberty."[33]

What was wrong with the Constitution that seventy years after its adoption such dangerous imprecision should still exist? The villain was excess rigidity. Men are no match for the centuries, Fisher wrote in criticism of the slow, clumsy amendment system that the Constitution specified; "the efficacy of a safety-valve depends on the promptness with which it can be opened and the width of its throttle."[34] Change was a constant factor in American life. But the American experience indicated how difficult—almost impossible—it was to win constitutional changes. Frictions created by popular demands for alteration and the laggard responses had caused the periodic crises that spotted America's history. These crises had brought forth sectional treaties, misnamed compromises, that could not root because they did not tap the wellsprings of popular support.

Perhaps to his own surprise and with some evident distaste, Fisher found himself championing unrestrained congressional statutes based upon unlimited political democracy, to substitute for the rigid amendment process, as the only workable way to register the popular will quickly. Constitutional change must always be easy and responsive to the demands of the representatives of the passionate multitude.[35] Better that the Congress should react sensitively to the people's wants than that demagogues on the numerous state and local levels, too many to rein in, should mislead credulous provincials.

Every ill of 1861 stemmed from the Constitution's immobility and from the inability of the competing elements of the

---

33. Fisher, *Trial*, v–vii.
34. *Ibid.*, 26.
35. *Ibid.*, 20–36.

The Inadequate Constitution

government to work together. Lincoln's encounter with Taney had revealed the uncertain boundaries between executive and judicial authority, and the "weakness and uncertainty in a part of our system [the Presidency] where few expected to find it."[36] Congress should be neither weak nor uncertain. But Congress was dodging its responsibility to act, Fisher declared. It bore the sovereign's burden to rule exactly as Parliament carried that weight in England; Congress, like Parliament, was unrestrainable, the repository for the popular will as expressed in election returns. Acceptance of this doctrine incurred risks of runaway democracy that made conservatives shudder. But though Fisher shuddered, he saw no alternative to disaster save agreement that Congress by ordinary statute could do what the amending process could not possibly do.

Of course he recognized that he was suggesting abandonment of cherished traditions of federalism, of separation of powers, and, less revered, of judicial review. Fisher defended his departure by arguing that the War was revealing these peculiar features to be the cause of the Constitution's defective operation. If the unworkable amendment provision or Congress-President-Court competition made the incorporation of changes difficult or impossible, then disaster impended in the contest against the Confederacy and the seeds of future discord were sown. Congress must be able to cope with any subject; the only check was in voters' ballots, ready to praise or condemn. "These afford a better security than the weak protest of a [Supreme] Court which does not represent the people," Fisher wrote.[37]

Fisher's willingness to demean the states reflects the enormous initial impact of secession and civil war. State-rights advocacy had never been a southern or Democratic monopoly. Yet almost offhandedly, Fisher urged the scrapping of the federal system. He asserted that secession and civil war proved the intrinsic evil of semiautonomous states. Congress should assume the states' substantive functions, leaving merely administrative responsibilities to the lower echelons.

Fisher joined slavery and secession to federalism and separation of powers as causes of the Civil War. This conviction forced him to overcome temporarily his prewar Gobineau-derived

36. *Ibid.*, 202.
37. *Ibid.*, 199, for the quotation; and see 41, 54–7, 235–7.

113

Negrophobia and in 1861 to enter emancipationist ranks.[38] Congress must abolish slavery. Lincoln's September 1862 proclamation to that end, issued just before Fisher's book went to press, was well enough. But it was defective because it affected only rebel areas instead of being uniformly national, and it was reversible. Further, the President's proclamation violated Fisher's major precept of congressional initiative.

Fisher's bitter anger at southern leaders who engineered the unwarranted disruption of the Union is clear. They were the men who, earlier, had forced slave codes into northern states in the form of fugitive-slave-recapture laws. But the great sin was seceding. It could kill all the states, all law, all property, all social stability. Therefore, to salvage what was possible to save, centralization was worth trying.

In short, Fisher's Constitution remained the basis for the rule of law; in its defense patriots should proceed wherever necessity led. But the goal was to return to law and to familiar ways. As W. R. Brock has noted of Civil War and Reconstruction Republicans, "the idea of suspending the Constitution seemed to offer far more difficulties than remedies."[39]

Vigor, swiftness, and relevance were the needed improvements, Fisher judged, and few contemporaries denied the proposition. "We the people of 1862 are not to be commanded to our destruction, by even the best and wisest people of 1787 . . . whose spirits are perhaps now mourning over the destruction of their hopes," he wrote. Only "a madman" would suggest achieving the abolition of slavery through a constitutional amendment. Wartime was no time to convene a new constitutional convention of the sort that Seward had suggested in January 1861, to redraft the 1787 frame for government. Nothing was required "but to arm the existing Government by our support, with all the power that a [constitutional] Convention would have, that is to say, with all the power of the people."[40]

The present Congress was unlikely to heed Fisher's urging to transmute itself into a Parliamentlike body, and by his own argument amendment processes were all but useless. In England,

---

38. Cf. Fisher's *The Laws of Race as Connected with Slavery* (Philadelphia, 1860), and Riker, "Fisher," 402.

39. W. R. Brock, *An American Crisis: Congress and Reconstruction, 1865–1867* (New York, 1963), 6–8; Fisher, *Trial*, 199–200.

40. Fisher, *Trial*, 199–200, and see 314–15.

Cromwell had carried Parliament to primacy. Fisher's clear intimation was that Lincoln, a good, trustworthy man, should take on Cromwell's role and use the Union Army to reshape the Constitution: "If the Union and the Government cannot be saved out of the terrible shock of war constitutionally, then *a* Union and *a* Government must be saved unconstitutionally," he concluded.[41]

Fisher was America's first "student of the Constitution who wrote about it the way it actually worked rather than about the way it ought to work." He deserves not to be forgotten, as he was by the scholars and statesmen of his own time and as he has been by most historians since.[42] Fisher deserves to be remembered despite the fact that subsequent events proved that he and Bagehot were wrong. After they published their gloomy conclusions, American arms and institutions began to perform far better than had seemed to be possible during the first weeks and months after Sumter. Federalism, democracy, and other familiar ways which the Constitution prescribed or sanctioned were to prove themselves on a hundred battlefields and in a thousand freely contested wartime elections.

But these fortuitous turns were by no means inevitable when Bagehot and Fisher wrote their 1861 judgments. Both men were commendably sensitive to the initial effects of secession and civil

---

41. *Ibid.*, 199 for the quotation, and see 391. Yet in 1868, when Admiral David Dixon Porter, out of despair for democracy, looked forward to a military dictatorship under Grant, Fisher disliked Porter's tone. "It was that of a man who looked forward to such a result, not with regret as a dreary and dismal consequence of mob rule, but with satisfaction as a triumph for himself & his friends." *Diary*, 546.

42. Riker, "Fisher," 411. Fisher rated inclusion in *Dictionary of American Biography*, in a "brief and not altogether accurate sketch," (*Diary*, iii), but is unmentioned in Elizabeth Kelley Bauer, *Commentaries on the Constitution, 1790–1860* (New York, 1952), Frederickson, *Inner Civil War*, or Clyde E. Jacobs, *Law Writers and the Courts: The Influence of Thomas M. Cooley, Christopher G. Tiedman, and John F. Dillon upon American Constitutional Law* (Berkeley and Los Angeles, 1954). Edward S. Corwin, *The President: Office and Powers* (New York, 1940), 385, mentions Fisher in a footnote. The third edition (1948), elevates Fisher to the text and *Trial* is described as notable. Clinton Rossiter, *Constitutional Dictatorship* (Princeton, 1948), 224 n., calls *Trial* "great." See Riker, "Fisher," 409 n., the introduction to my edition of Fisher's *Trial;* Belz, "Constitution in the Gilded Age," 112; U. B. Phillips, "The Central Theme of Southern History," *AHR*, XXIV (1928), 31.

war. Their insights suggest how low the Constitution had fallen in 1861, and why many analysts judged that secession had killed it.

Orestes A. Brownson was a better-known though temporary representative of this school. The nation's weaknesses during the secession winter and the ensuing year confirmed his pre-existing antipopular commitments to state-rights doctrines derived from Calhoun, Roman Catholicism, and property law. Eager for ways to sustain social stability and to inhibit changes, Brownson worried that the vagaries of popular will expressed in elections would further sap the Union's apparently fragile strength.

But secession and rebellion worked on Brownson as they had on Sidney George Fisher, if more slowly. By 1864, Brownson had become so impressed by the nation's unanticipated survival resources as to recant his prewar constitutional views. He picked up a position John C. Hurd had advanced in 1858, in *The Law of Freedom and Bondage in the United States:* that sovereignty rested not in states, but in states united. Nevertheless the initial impact on Brownson of the nation's weakness of 1861 is to be kept in mind. In despair, like Fisher he began a systematic study of the Constitution (it was published in 1865), admitting himself "ambitious . . . to exert an influence on the future of my country."[43]

It is unlikely that most pessimistic commentators, expounding on the Constitution's inadequacies, expected actually to move men or to shape measures conformably with their formal schemes. But a few tried during the War to bind up the nation's wounds in constitutional fetters, with the purpose of ending the conflict and preventing social, racial, or other changes.

The idea implicit (though rarely explicit) in many writings of canceling, suspending, or terminating elections never caught on, whether propounded by neo-copperheads or patriots. Proceeding as though there was no war, ignoring the tradition abroad that suspended elections during crises, Americans in northern states balloted on every matter including war aims, race relations, and the price of victory or defeat. Every election was likely to be a contest over wartime ways and ends, although local candidates might aspire only to a sheriff's badge or a mayor's seat. The

43. Orestes A. Brownson, *The American Republic: Its Constitution, Tendencies, and Destiny* (New York, 1865), xv; Arthur M. Schlesinger, Jr., *A Pilgrim's Progress: Orestes Brownson* (Boston, 1966 edn.), 259–61.

parties functioned more vigorously after Sumter than before. Even soldiers voted whose states arranged absentee balloting or who made the trek home on election days. Except very rarely near battle areas, military interference with elections failed to oversway voters' wishes. For good or ill, the mechanical election rhythms that the nation's and states' constitutions required were obeyed.

During the early weeks of 1861 escape had been narrow from some form or another of unamendable amendment that would have excluded politics from certain arenas of American life, such as slavery. After Sumter, conservatives returned to unamendable amendments as the best means to achieve a reunion without victory. Especially as failures became evident first to keep the peace and then to win the War quickly, this appeal waxed. For example, during the early weeks of 1861 an American Society for Promoting National Unity came into being in New York City. Its membership sought ratification for the irreversible thirteenth amendment to which in March 1861 Lincoln had given his grudging assent.[44] Thereafter, Democratic spokesmen advanced the idea of the War's futility and the need for reviving the form and substance of this unamendable amendment.

Here was the single improvement the Constitution needed to repair defects in prewar federal-state relationships, Andrew Wilcox, a Baltimore lawyer and friend to Taney, wrote early in 1862. Douglas's principle of national nonintervention in intrastate matters, especially slavery, was the only acceptable position for Democratic candidates that year, Wilcox asserted, ignoring the contrary evidence. Alteration of the nation was in the cards; probably it was already too late to halt the process. Wilcox's solution was to remove slavery from contention forever by means of an unamendable amendment to the Constitution. Then white men could stop dying in the interests of Negroes or, rather, in the interests of allegedly unscrupulous Republicans who exploited patriots' concerns for nation and Negroes. Peace would then return to the divided land.[45]

Notwithstanding the progress of Lincoln's and Congress's

---

44. Harold M. Hyman, "Election of 1864," in *History of American Presidential Elections, 1789–1968*, ed. F. L. Israel and A. M. Schlesinger, Jr. (New York, 1971), II, 1155–6; McKitrick, "Party Politics and the Union and Confederate War Efforts," 117–51; American Society for Promoting National Unity, *Constitution and Appeal* (New York, 1961).

45. Andrew J. Wilcox, *A Remedy for the Defects of the Constitution* (Baltimore, 1862), 36–7.

emancipation policies, some Democratic spokesmen kept returning to the notion of protecting forever, by national amendment,
all slave property as defined by states' laws. The most prominent
to play the role of Lot's wife was Ohio Congressman Samuel Sullivan "Sunset" Cox. In May 1864 he spoke against Republican
wartime reconstruction policies, arguing that the only policy
necessary was to reverse history back to 1860. If the War ended at
that moment, major popular attitudes about race and federal relations would be unchanged North and South from what had
existed then, he asserted.

In a wistful what-should-have-been mood, Cox recalled that
in 1861 all efforts at compromise embraced some form of unamendable amendment. Those efforts had failed to remove permanently from political contention the irritant that had stymied
the Constitution; failed to provide "a final adjustment of the
character of all the territory, and a complete nonintervention by
Congress with the domestic relations of the Territories and of the
States." This principle, applied, "would have settled the difficulties."

But in 1861 the action of "intemperate and blood-desiring
men" defeated the proposed compromise amendment. There was
still time to turn back the clock. The Democracy in 1864 must be
"a party whose first and only preference is for the Union through
compromise, and who shall at least be allowed to try the experiment of reconciling the States by guaranties similar to those
proposed in 1861."[46]

Cox's recipe was too rich; the 1864 Democratic party platform ventured only to denounce the War as a failure and to call
for an armistice with the Confederacy. But Lincoln and Republicans took the victor's laurels. With this the impetus faded for
unamendable amendments; in late 1867 John Hay lumped the
perpetual amendment idea among other "morbid heresies left us
by a worn out generation."[47]

The impact of the Civil War was to ratify the Republican pre-

46. Samuel S. Cox, *The Nation's Hope in the Democracy—Historic
Lessons for Civil War* (Washington, 1864), 11. This is a pamphlet reprint
of his speech in the House of Representatives, May 4, 1864, in opposition
to the Wade-Davis bill and to Lincoln's Dec. 1863 proclamation on reconstruction. See too David Lindsey, *"Sunset" Cox: Irrepressible Democrat*
(Detroit, 1959); Forrest Wood, *Black Scare: The Racist Response to
Emancipation and Reconstruction* (Berkeley, 1968), 53–79.

47. John Hay to Charles Sumner, Dec. 19, 1867, Sumner Papers,
Houghton Library, HU.

Sumter constitutional position that, save for matters properly denied to the national government in the Bill of Rights, no subjects were exempt from political democracy. To look ahead to change remained for Republicans a viable position, because the Constitution survived the secession winter and the War without adding elements useless to try to reform through politics.

Balked by opposition to unamendable amendments, conservatives sought other byways around the Constitution that might end the War without a military decision and leave unaltered prewar racial and federal-state relationships. Attractive because superficially more democratic than the perpetual amendment proposal, nationwide plebiscites and constitutional conventions had significant proponents. Among the most prominent and politically high-placed was the New Yorker and Democratic national chairman August Belmont. Both sections were ripe for a negotiated settlement and reunification on the basis of a return to 1860, Belmont asserted at intervals from 1862 onward. A revamped Constitution likely to result from a special national plebiscite would freeze the slavery issue acceptably to the South.

In July 1862, Belmont wrote to Thurlow Weed that it was time for "one or two conservative men" with Lincoln's blessing to visit the Confederate capital discreetly and open peace negotiations. A sure way to attract support in Richmond was to include a commitment for the calling of a national constitutional convention "for the purpose of reconstructing the Federal compact, with such modification in the Constitution as our late sad experience had demonstrated to be necessary."

This effort failing, Belmont returned in late November to the central theme of a plebiscite to determine if the War should end, and how. Conservative candidates in congressional, state, and local elections won enough contests earlier that month to encourage Belmont. After communicating with Democratic party leaders, he employed Rothschild connections abroad to suggest that mediation was desirable by foreign powers to sell to the Lincoln Government the need for an armistice, to be followed by a "national" constitutional convention. The convention would "take away from the ultra men, North and South, the power of future mischief, and by a better defined limitation of Federal and State power prevent the recurrence of the calamities which have now befallen us . . . *any other solution* is impossible."

Presumably, Belmont's convention would fix permanently

the status of Negroes in American constitutional law at what obtained in 1860, even though by the time of the Belmont maneuver Lincoln had issued his Emancipation Proclamation. Belmont's appeal was to the most conservative instincts of the time with respect to racial relationships and to federal-state functional boundaries.[48]

This was true of almost all advocates of a national constitutional convention. As example, the Iowan Charles Mason, who had been chief justice of that state and in the war years was a Washington resident, was also a prominent right-wing Democratic party spokesman and extreme critic of the Lincoln Administration. In May 1863, Mason issued to intimates a call for a national convention. It was to be composed "only of those who desire the restoration of the Union and preservation of the Constitution as it had been and with such modifications as shall be deemed necessary and in strict accordance with its own provisions and purposes." Mason believed that the War had begun only because of "a mutual misunderstanding between the people of the antagonistic sections and by a departure from the spirit of the revered organic law." A return was necessary to "the old National compact," or else the Confederacy might—must—win.[49]

Belmont's and Mason's schemes received little encouragement within the parties. For Republican-Democratic Unionists, a call for a national convention would be a confession of weakness and an admission that the President and Congress were unequal to the tasks they faced. The only reason for a convention was to do things that Congress could not do, and by the close of 1862 belief in the adequacy of Congress and of the Constitution was an article of Unionist faith. Among antiwar Democrats, the encouraging results of the 1862 elections argued against risking further associative guilt with the seceders of 1860–61 who in some states had used conventions. The abortive efforts at conciliation had also taken conventionlike forms. "So we had a Peace Convention . . . sitting in Washington alongside of Congress, attempting to do its work but it could not prevent war," derided Sidney George Fisher.

---

48. August Belmont, *Letters, Speeches, and Addresses* (privately printed, 1890), 73–4, 79–83; Irving Katz, *August Belmont: A Political Biography* (New York, 1968), 109–10, 120.

49. May 24, 1863, *Life and Letters of Charles Mason, Chief Justice of Iowa, 1804–1882*, ed. Charles Mason Remey (Washington, 1939), unpaginated; W. I. Toussaint, "Charles Mason's Influence on Iowa Jurisprudence," *Annals of Iowa* (1968), 372–87.

Fear of runaway conventioners also made Fisher oppose appeals to support a national constitutional convention; i.e., the conservative purpose clashed with the conservative fear. Alluding to the untrustworthiness of men popularly elected through party apparatuses to a constitutional convention, he worried that once there, delegates "might play some fantastic tricks, which, if they did not make the angels weep, would more than ever divide sections and parties, inflame passions, and very probably produce the anarchy it was intended to prevent."[50]

Fisher's concern over runaway conventioners reflects one of the foulest blows secession struck at American constitutional institutions. An American contribution to the practice of popular government in which great pride was taken, constitutional conventions dated back to the Revolution. Secessionists employed them to pry states out of the Union and, in the North, antiwar spokesmen advocated the employment of conventions to arrange a military armistice on terms agreeable to the Confederacy. In Illinois, considered to be a center of copperhead disloyalty, constitutional conventioners of 1862 expressed "radical" notions about the limitlessness of the popular will extending even to state controls over entrepreneurial relationships.

Admittedly, conventions were the people's voice. But the Illinois claim that its convention voice was unlimitable even by judges, legislators, or governors shocked men already shaken by secession's swift passage through southern and border states' conventions. A view of unlimited conventions—i.e., of uncheckable popular democracy—frightened and offended people with other priorities. This view had been cropping up since state constitutional conventions in the 1820's. Its reappearance in Lincoln's state in 1862 especially outraged legal professionals, who, according to an Inns of Court commentator, "regard this constitutional restriction upon legislation as to corporate as well as individual property as something essential to really free government."[51]

---

50. Fisher, *Trial*, 387; Fisher, *Diary*, 445–6.
51. H. R. Droop, *Decisions in the United States as to the Constitutional Limits of Legislative Power* (London, 1869), 5. See also S. S. Nicholas, *Conservative Essays, Legal and Political* (Louisville, 1867), I, 10–13, III, 60–61; *Democracy, Liberty, and Property: The State Constitutional Conventions of the 1820's*, ed. Merrill D. Peterson (Indianapolis, 1966), *passim*, for analysis and documents on earlier views of conventions'

Shame at the nation's weakness during the secession winter had inspired Fisher to consider the Constitution's trial; shock at states' excesses during constitutional conventions, especially his own state's 1862 sessions, impelled John A. Jameson, an Illinois superior court judge and later a University of Chicago law professor, to begin the first systematic study of constitutional conventions. Jameson was especially aggrieved that the Illinois meeting "unwisely seized upon a time of national peril to endorse a disorganizing dogma."[52] He was ashamed that his state harbored copperhead conspiracies as well as the doctrine of the limitless constitutional convention. Jameson intimated that disloyal persons sowed this unholy seed; that Knights of the Golden Circle were the "certain influential members" at the 1862 Illinois constitutional convention who advanced "a claim of inherent powers amounting almost to absolute sovereignty."[53]

Like Fisher, Jameson was so shaken by the Civil War's impact that he began to open history's doors. Traditions, myths, or theories about conventions could not sustain his Burkean concerns about law and order. Toiling in research and writing about conventions until a year after Appomattox, the judge was to win the goal he sought. His 1866 treatise on constitutional conventions, reissued and enlarged for two decades thereafter, provided others of like mind with impressive precedents leading to the conclusion that constitutional conventions were restrainable after all. By early 1866 the United States Supreme Court accepted for the first time jurisdiction of a case involving a clause in a state's

---

powers; and Henry Hitchcock, *American State Constitutions: A Study of Their Growth* (New York, 1887), *passim*.

52. John A. Jameson, *The Constitutional Convention: Its History, Powers, and Modes of Proceeding* (New York, 1867), 2, 296. Internal evidence places the book's appearance in print in October 1866. In 1887, Jameson brought out a fourth edition of this work under a slightly altered title, Chicago, Callaghan publisher. Hereafter, citations to each will be Jameson, *Constitutional Conventions*, with the year of publication in parentheses.

53. Note that Jameson persisted in this belief twenty years later; *Constitutional Convention* (1887), iii. He cited as proof of excess the argument at the Illinois convention, "that though the Act of the General Assembly under which the Convention had met required it to submit the fruit of its labors to the people, for ratification or rejection, it might lawfully refuse to do so and put the Constitution it should frame in operation without any reference whatever to the people." Jameson did not see fit to note that this course was not followed. See also ch. 19, n. 5.

constitution; by 1871 a survey of "American Political Science" credited Jameson with curbing "political aspirants, party aggressions, and unscrupulous innovators." In the sense of inspiring an influential literature, the Civil War's impact must be accounted very large.[54]

Jameson's triumph, like the North's, lay in the future. Meanwhile, pessimists about the Constitution's chances for survival appeared to have the weight of events on their side.

---

54. W. Barry, "American Political Science," *Old and New*, III (1871), 303–4; Cummings v. Mo., 4 Wall., 277 (1867). See too James Speed to Francis Lieber, March 3, 1867, Lieber Papers, LI 3218, HL; Francis Newton Thorpe, "In Memoriam, John Alexander Jameson," AAPSS *Annals* (supplement, Jan. 1891). Indeed, revisers of post-Appomattox state constitutions had little literature to work with except Jameson's book, which, though largely ignored in general constitutional commentaries, was a common handbook at conventions. See Bernard Sage, *The Republic of Republics* (Philadelphia, 1878), App., 1–7; Charles S. Bradley, *The Methods of Changing the Constitutions of the States, Especially That of Rhode Island* (Boston, 1885), unnumbered prefatory page. Bradley was a former chief justice of the Rhode Island Supreme Court.

Chapter VIII

The Adequate Constitution

In 1861, only wild seers prophesied total defeat for the Confederacy. The United States government appeared to be strangling in negatives which Chief Justice Taney and others wove around the 1787 Constitution. Taken together with the amassing of northern armies and the absence of further secessions, Lincoln's tenacity gave the lie to critics here and abroad who had concluded that federalism and democracy could not cope with crisis. A global audience was impressed by these evidences of vigor and resilience. Americans were assembling armies large even by the Old World's standards and supplying them without strain; impressive feats in the light of Crimean War history. Manifestations of power were better understood than the weakness of the secession winter.[1]

By the War's first summer it was apparent that auguries of immediate disaster for the Union were wrong. Despite Cassandra-cries about the Constitution's defectiveness, democracy's rottenness, and federalism's fantasticality, America was thriving. Karl Marx and John Stuart Mill, among many others, sensed that the new, vital element in the world that America represented was not dead after all.[2]

---

1. Donaldson Jordan and Edwin J. Pratt, *Europe and the American Civil War* (Boston, 1931), 11–12; Goldwin Smith, *A Letter to a Whig Member of the Southern Independence Association* (Boston, 1864), 14; Auguste Laugel, *The United States During the Civil War*, ed. Allan Nevins (Bloomington, 1961), 186–8.

2. Gerald Runkle, "Karl Marx and the American Civil War," *Comparative Studies in Society and History*, VI (1964), 121; Mill to Henry

The Adequate Constitution

The unexpected thrust in seemingly moribund institutions exhilarated men who had nearly given up the Union's ghost. Popular faith revived in the Constitution's survival potential. Inquiring how this happy reversal had come to be, many Americans found the sources in the political democracy and federalism that Bagehot had condemned. By midsummer 1861 spokesmen for these views were in print with the happier judgment that existing constitutional and political institutions were relevant to the nation's needs.

Intimate reciprocation existed between the rapid restoration in public spirit and the stiffening spring of government. Growing vigorous from the rise in popular morale, government drifted less. Heartened officials sought to direct the flow of events, and citizens hoped to win goals which suddenly were within reach because government's thrust was muscular. Out of it all, politics revived, and the Constitution, pronounced dead, lived.

By the first wartime July 4, Harvard law professor Theophilus Parsons was restrainedly optimistic. He noted that the Union's survival was no longer a daily gamble; that political and constitutional institutions had not collapsed completely under the shame of secession and the strains of mobilizing military resources. Instead, men and matériel were assembling in masses unprecedented in the continent's history, and fear of punishments unknown before Sumter was forcing pro-Confederates underground or into overt quiescence.[3] Looking backward from the vantage point of a centennial observation, James Russell Lowell remembered his pleasure at the Constitution's capacity to be tough in 1861, so that "it really seemed as if we had invented a machine that would go of itself, and this begot a faith in our luck which even the Civil War itself but momentarily disturbed."[4]

What Lowell recalled in 1888 as "momentarily" stretched

Villard, Jan. 26, 1870 in JSS, V (1873), 138; Heard Round the World, ed. Harold M. Hyman (New York, 1969), passim; Carl J. Friedrich, The Impact of American Constitutionalism Abroad (Boston, 1967), 5.

3. Theophilus Parsons, An Oration Delivered on the 4th of July, 1861, Before the Municipal Authorities of the City of Boston (Boston, 1861), 23; Charles Demond, Address Before the Society of the Alumni of Williams College, August 1, 1865 (Boston, 1865), 6–7.

4. James Russell Lowell, The Independent in Politics: An Address Delivered Before the Reform Club of New York, April 13, 1888 (New York, 1888), 16–17; Martin Duberman, James Russell Lowell (Boston, 1966), 358–61.

out distressingly for men responsible in 1861 for the nation's survival. Nevertheless, the sense of Lowell's recollection is accurate. Recovery did occur remarkably quickly. Acceptance became general of a concept succinctly summarized by the informed Canadian, Thomas D'Arcy McGee. "One lesson has been . . . taught [by the Civil War's first months] to every just-minded observer," he wrote; "namely, that those who formerly held the Constitution of 1789 to be perfect, were not further from the truth, than those who have since [1860] spoken of it as a complete failure."[5]

By such reasoning, rejection of the Constitution was unjustified. Defeatists were out of touch with reality. The feeling spread that the 1787 Constitution was serviceable for war's wintry conditions as well as for the benign environment of long-continued peace; a sentiment best expressed by Jacksonian political veteran Elizur Wright:

> Do we condemn the great constitutional bridge which has carried the nation safe over three-quarters of a century, from beggary to the front rank of civilized nations? On the contrary, the less we count ourselves its bond-servants, the more we venerate it. It is a most excellent bridge—as far as it goes—and if it ever comes to harm it will be from those who seem determined that no part of any flood shall reach the sea except by going under its arches.[6]

Lincoln's role was essential in transforming April's defeatism into July's tougher stance. Antiwar spokesmen insisted that he managed the feat only through extra- and unconstitutional means. The President had descended since his Merryman defense to the plea of necessity, as old "as the reign of Tibereas [sic]; its

---

5. Thomas D'Arcy McGee, *Notes on Federal Governments Past and Present* (Montreal, 1865), 40.

6. Elizur Wright, *The Programme of Peace, by a Democrat of the Old School* (Boston, 1862), 3–4. Wright continued: "In our present circumstances, if we are to be indebted to our grandfathers for all the constitution we need, we must regard what they did as well as what they said. After their 19th of April [1775] they had the common sense to take their facts as they found them, and postpone their old theories. Since our 19th of April [1861] almost everybody has insisted that our peculiar facts must be governed by the theories of those who failed to foresee these facts." *Ibid.*, 5. See also my essay in *New Frontiers of the American Reconstruction*, ed. Harold M. Hyman (Urbana, Ill., 1966), 22–4, and Prof. Alfred Kelly's response, *ibid.*, 40–58.

limits should be looked for in Tacitus," Supreme Court Justice Catron wrote privately.[7]

Some historians have accepted the sense of Judge Catron's animadversion. But contemporaries close to Lincoln understood better than the jurist that the plea of necessity alone would have consigned the Constitution to a trash heap of obsolete state papers. Lincoln never believed that the Constitution was unworkable, and so never needed to descend to the argument of necessity to justify his actions. Instead he found substantiation in the Constitution for the wide-ranging policies that he unleashed and executed. Because the President managed this feat immediately after Sumter, lesser men were able to advance to the conclusion that the Constitution was adequate.[8]

Disaster was the likely consequence of a less confident or courageous tone or less relevant actions. Fortunately, as noted, Lincoln did not hesitate to preach the adequacy of the nation's Constitution, and to point out that existing ills were curable by means of ordinary elections or amendments.[9] He bought time by his readiness to act. His belief "that we may . . . act, [and that] we must study, and understand the points of danger," grew into a sectional conviction.[10] As a result, democratization continued of constitutional discourse on levels of intensity and significance higher than anything known in pre-Sumter years; politics remained confined within constitutionalism despite the swerve to-

---

7. John Catron to J. M. Carlisle, Feb. 26, 1863, in *LH*, I (1958), 52.

8. David M. Silver, *Lincoln's Supreme Court* (Urbana, Ill., 1956), 119: "Lincoln provided only one vindication of his policy; necessity justified the exercise of arbitrary power. . . ." Cf. the more acute insight by War Secretary Stanton: "The President felt it his duty to employ with energy the extraordinary powers which the Constitution confides to him in case of insurrection"; *M&P*, VI, 25.

9. See Nathaniel W. Stephenson, "Lincoln and the Progress of Nationality in the North," AHA, *AR* (1919) (Washington, 1923), I, 351–66; Gerhard E. Mulder, "Abraham Lincoln and the Doctrine of Necessity," *LQ*, LXVI (1964), 65; Morgan D. Dowd, "Lincoln, The Rule of Law and Crisis Government: A Study of His Constitutional Law Theories," *University of Detroit Law Journal*, XXIX (1962), 633–49; Willmoor Kendall and George W. Carey, *The Basic Symbols of the American Political Tradition* (Baton Rouge, 1971), *passim;* James A. Rawley, "The Nationalism of Abraham Lincoln," *CWH*, IX (1963), *passim.* Note also the intriguing "fragment on the Constitution and the Union," ca. Jan. 1861, in *Collected Works of Abraham Lincoln*, ed. Roy P. Basler *et al.* (New Brunswick, N.J., 1953), IV, 168–9 (cited hereafter as Lincoln, *Works*).

10. Lincoln, *Works*, IV, 169.

ward extreme alternatives discernible immediately after Sumter.

Obstacles in the way of rapid dissemination of optimistic constitutional ideas were substantial. No bureaucratic machineries existed to spread views. The public's access to issues was largely through uncontrollable private intermediaries, including lawyers, ministers, and journalists and other men of letters, through professional and popular periodicals, and through newspapers and organizational publications.

Of these, lawyers and judges formed the group most necessary to reach in order to counter Taney-ish stances. In Perry Miller's apt phrase lawyers were the "pontiffs of this society." Enjoying a swift rise in popular esteem, lawyers were increasing in number among states' legislators and congressmen. The recruitment into political life of lawmakers who were law-trained created problems as well as opportunities for the effective conduct of the War.

Lawyers were on the brink of conceiving a great leap forward in governmental efficiency. Repulsed at what they believed were Jacksonian corruptions and excesses of democracy, lawyers had theorized about governing by suprapolitical professionally appointed commissions staffed with expert administrators; devices that in rough form and always with political aspects were to be an early feature of the Civil War. But even commission advocates among lawyers feared simultaneously the politics-dominated processes and institutions that must establish these commissions. If seized by runaway passions or demagogic misdirections, the elitist commissions might threaten property and the rule of all law. Obsessed by fears of Jacksonian and socialistic assaults on property, jurisprudence was dedicated to holding federal-state relations and national and state governments' functions to familiar ways, and so law reformers marked time on the commission advance.

In 1860–61, lawyers and judges suffered a particular shock to their assumptions about the rationality of social processes because the Constitution failed to halt secession and to prevent war. As the War's pressures grew harsher, some lawyers broadcast notions of a revival of Hamiltonian-Marshall boundlessness, and insisted that even certain private and property rights had to give way to momentary exigencies. In legal circles the idea circulated that though the Constitution was adequate for conditions of war as well as peace, a war introduced temporary relationships not present when peace obtained. While a Taney preached constitutional constraints, other lawmen made acceptable the thesis of the Constitution's adequacy for war by stressing the differences separating war from peace and the continuums that allowed the Constitution to serve adequately in both.[11] Since critics of the War tied themselves to a Constitution that operated negatively in war or peace, it was important that prominent legal professionals should agree with Lincoln that an opposite judgment was correct.

For example, early in the War's first winter, Timothy Farrar, the respected former partner of Daniel Webster, published spirited tributes to the Constitution's adequacy for positive actions. Farrar asserted that in 1789 anti-Federalists had set too hard a tradition of state-centered antipathy to national functions. In order to gain ratification for the Constitution, its friends had felt impelled "to claim and exercise as little power as possible [for the central government], instead of being driven to assert its plenary adequacy to all the purposes of its creation." Thereafter until 1861, constitutional law enshrined restraints without testing the premises or conclusions of this attitude. As a result, "the adequacy of the Constitution to the exigencies of government and the preservation of the Union, has not hitherto been exhibited and proved in practice, nor fully asserted and insisted on by its friends, even in theory."

From its first day the Civil War had become the supreme practical test of the Constitution's adequacy.[12] Farrar insisted that the Constitution was not a checkrein against which officials must struggle. He presented a brief version of the Marshall-Webster-Story concept, which Lincoln shared, of the Union predating the states. The Declaration of Independence had made the United States a nation, Farrar insisted. To be sure, under the Continental Congresses and the Articles of Confederation, national authority had become "inefficient and almost extinct, by the constant and unauthorized aggressions of the local govern-

---

11. Perry Miller, *The Life of the Mind in America: From the Revolution to the Civil War* (New York, 1965), 230 and see 99–265, esp. 222; Alan Robert Jones, "The Constitutional Conservatism of Thomas McIntyre Cooley: A Study in the History of Ideas" (Ph.D. diss., UMich, 1960), ch. 4; Phillip S. Paludan, "Law and Equal Rights: The Civil War Encounter—A Study of Legal Minds in the Civil War Era" (Ph.D. diss., UI, 1968), ch. 6; Maxwell Bloomfield, "Law vs. Politics: The Self-Image of the American Bar (1830–1860)," *AJLH*, XII (1968), 319–21.

12. Timothy Farrar, "Adequacy of the Constitution," *NE*, XXI (1862), 51–2, 54.

ments." The 1787 Constitution was an effort on behalf of "renovation" of the national authority; 1861 echoed that noble theme.

Everything would collapse if popular opinion refused to sustain the War's costs, if officials proved to be incapable, if soldiers refused any longer to offer themselves. Alluding to the reciprocation noted earlier between governmental action and constitutional adequacy, Farrar asserted that "Our present business is to . . . see if the Constitution . . . is adequate to the exigency, in case the people and the administration fail not." The seventy-year-long "disposition to render the [national] Government inefficient" did not alter the intention of the framers to create an effective national administration.[13]

With respect to the burning habeas corpus issue, Farrar, like Horace Binney, stressed the ambiguities surrounding that writ and civil-military relationships generally. Undoubtedly the War's pressures would bring illumination. Meanwhile, President and Congress bore responsibility to flesh out the Constitution's spare frame.[14]

The guarantee clause (Article IV, section 4) was another proof to Farrar of his argument that the Constitution's lacunae were gates, not barriers. Since 1819, when the question of Missouri's admission as a slave state into the Union triggered the slavery extension debate, congressmen had argued sporadically whether the Constitution's guarantee of a republican form of government to every state was compatible with slavery. Southern congressmen had insisted then and during the intervening forty years that the guarantee provision conferred no power to act upon the national government, unless a state deprived its citizenry of republican government. These debates resulted in "no legislative aid" for understanding what the guarantee clause allowed the Congress to do. Nevertheless the clause "has significance not to be overlooked or disregarded," Farrar wrote in accurate prophecy.[15]

Summing up, Farrar asserted that the Civil War was revealing, in sudden, stark manner, undeveloped portions of the Constitution such as the guarantee clause and the habeas-corpus-

---

13. *Ibid.*, 55–64.
14. *Ibid.*, 59, 61, 64–6.
15. *Ibid.*, 70; and see Charles O. Lerche, Jr., "Congressional Interpretations of the Guarantee of a Republican Form of Government During Reconstruction," *JSH*, XV (1949), 192–3; Lieber to Sumner, Oct. 11, 1865, LI 3834, Lieber Papers, HL.

suspension provision. National officials were responding sensitively and swiftly to the disclosures and were exceeding no constitutional limitations, because "the provisions of the Constitution are the measure of the powers of Government."[16]

By the beginning of 1863, officials and lawmen had accepted the argument of the Constitution's adequacy. The War's dynamic character was becoming clearer, mused the prominent Pennsylvania judge Daniel Agnew. Now he understood that a great war was not a legal condition merely. His country had gone to war somnambulistically with respect to the relationships of war and the Constitution. "So long had we been resting in the arms of peace . . . and so trifling had been previous attempts at insurrection, that, as a people, we were unconscious of the sleeping powers of the Constitution," Agnew declared. Then reality raised the question whether the Constitution possessed "inherent vigor to meet the emergency." Americans surprised themselves by deciding that it did.

The surprise had been great because constitutional law had not dealt with war; scholars of the law had made "no correct exposition" of war because their "frame of mind . . . looks alone to a state of peace." Because legalists swiftly filled in these omissions, the Civil War became a cram course in unexplored aspects of the Constitution.[17] It was becoming clear that the Constitution's silence on waging war was necessary and proper. Neither the framers of 1787 nor congressmen since could foresee history's hazards. The choice of means had to lie with Congress and the

---

16. Farrar, "Adequacy," 73. Continuing preachments against constitutional adequacy by conservative antiwar spokesmen irritated Farrar. He wrote: "At a time like this, when by following the lead of southern politicians, into all their anti-federal and state-right doctrines, the country has been brought into its present condition, it would seem that patriotic statesmen and constitutional lawyers might find better employment than in exercising their critical skill and legal acumen, in endeavors to prove that the Constitution means nothing, but to blind its own prerogatives to utter inefficiency; that the nation has no power; and that the Government is destitute of any rights to defend and execute the supreme law." Farrar, "States Rights," *NE*, XXI (1862), 722–3, and see a review of Farrar's *Manual of the Constitution of the United States of America* (Boston, 1867), in H. T. Blake, "Judge Farrar on the Constitution," *NE*, XXVI (1867), 725–39.

17. Daniel Agnew, *Our National Constitution: Its Adaptation to a State of War or Insurrection* (Philadelphia, 1863), 11. Agnew was President-Judge (i.e., chief justice) of Pennsylvania's circuit court of appeals.

President, or appropriate reaction to unanticipatable events was impossible.

Agnew did criticize some of the ways in which Lincoln and other executive officers had used the vast powers the Constitution required them to exercise during war. Nevertheless, the jurist felt impelled to remind his audience that the source of the powers—not the judgment on the wisdom of their employment—was in the Constitution. It provided a wartime President with "express, unlimited, and unconditional authority to use the whole physical force of the nation . . . in quelling traitors, their aiders and abettors, and compelling them to submit to the laws." During wartime, constitutional limitations familiar from peace could not apply. The Constitution mocked itself in lunatic manner if effectiveness was stultified "by some peace-breathing clause."[18] Agnew agreed with and developed Lincoln's point to Congress in mid-1861 that raw necessity was not overriding the Constitution. The arbitrary arrests, the suspensions of habeas corpus, and the impositions of martial law flowed from the Constitution's recognitions of the employment of force in certain situations. No rule existed to gauge when the moment had arrived to exert force. Judges were not better fitted than the President or Congress to anticipate events or to know remedies. What was going on since the spring of 1861 was not the same as the localized Whiskey Rebellion or the South Carolina nullification.

Did it make sense to assert that formal laws of war allowed a commissioned Army officer to arrest suspicious civilians near a battlefield, but denied the President of the United States similar recourse behind northern lines when individuals' activity was inimical to the Union's safety? Agnew insisted that the proposition was absurd; the Civil War's actuality, as distinguished from theory, simply did not permit this neat dichotomy. Faith was necessary in the decency, judgment, and probity of the government's officers, or else any effective action was impossible and the

---

18. *Ibid.*, 16–17. See also William Whiting, *The War Powers of the President and the Legislative Powers of Congress, in Relation to Rebellion, Treason, and Slavery* (2nd edn., Boston, 1862), *passim*. Hereafter, I will cite all editions as Whiting's *War Powers*, with the year of publication in parentheses. In 1864, going on through the 43d edition in 1871, the major title altered to *War Powers Under the Constitution of the United States*. It is this last version which is the most valuable, for Whiting made it a cumulative depository for many documents otherwise difficult or impossible to obtain, spiced by his analyses and observations.

Constitution must crash into ruin. Agnew denied that "a peace view of the Constitution" must prevail or that the Constitution's peace and war clauses had to clash.[19] Instead the Civil War was jumbling peace and war zones in a manner confusing to a generation that had learned from simpler texts.

Alone, professional lawmen could not spread these ideas widely. To the Union's good fortune, an impressive proportion of the North's men of letters also understood the equation between the Constitution's adequacy and the Union's need for action that Lincoln had spelled out to the congressmen. War "was not a quadrille in a ball-room," wrote Walt Whitman. Emerson described the War as "the searcher of character, the test of men"; a "dynamometer," a "rack to try the tension of your muscle and bones"; a "new glass to see all our old things through, how they look." And he asked Lincoln's basic question: "Should we carry on the war by subscription, and politely?" No matter what individuals wished to reply to this question, the War was shaping its own answers. It was "a realist, shattering everything flimsy and shifty," and crashing down "party walls that have stood fifty or sixty years as if they were solid," Emerson continued. It simply would not lend itself to the remonstrances of "anxious statesmen" who wished to "keep it well in hand."[20] Intensely pleased that American men and institutions were meeting the test in manly fashion, Whitman applauded the fact that "our national democratic experiment, principle, and machinery could weather such a shock, and that the Constitution could weather it, like a ship in a storm, and come out of it as sound and whole as before, is by far the most signal proof yet of the stability of that experiment—Democracy—and of those principles and of that Constitution."[21]

Whitman's adoration of democracy was hardly typical. Like him, a sizable segment of the North's litterateurs welcomed a

---

19. Agnew, *Our National Constitution*, 20–6. All during the War and Reconstruction, insistence was heard that the view Taney had offered in Merryman of the Constitution as a single-speed mechanism unaffected by changes in context was the proper one. See Ex parte Milligan, 4 Wallace, 2 @ 120 (1866); and for criticism, see John H. Hatcher, "Martial Law and Habeas Corpus," *WVLQ*, XLVI (1940), 187–200.

20. *Walt Whitman's Civil War*, ed., Walter Lowenfels (New York, 1961), 293; "1861" in *Leaves of Grass*, numerous editions; *Journals of Ralph Waldo Emerson with Annotations*, ed. Edward Waldo and Waldo Emerson Forbes (Boston and New York, 1913), IX, 358, 411–12, 461–2.

21. *Whitman's Civil War*, 290, and see 283–4.

contest against the slave states as a test of the Constitution and of all American institutions and aspirations. Secession sickened them; the nation's acquiesence in secession was even worse. Many patriotic pamphleteers and orators were state-rights nationalists. They spoke of the Constitution's adequacy in order to return to constitutional normality—at least as they recalled pre-Sumter normality.[22]

These seeming cross-purposes and paradoxes led thoughtful Americans into numerous explorations of policy alternatives and constitutional potentialities. The prominent New York City Congregational minister Joseph P. Thompson, for example, writing a year after Sumter, held up the 1787 Constitution for respectful attention as history's best expression of restrained popular liberty. Liberty and the Constitution were flourishing in healthy symbiosis despite the general acquiescence "in unwonted [wartime] restrictions upon personal liberty, and, in certain emergencies, upon freedom of speech and of the press, as demanded by the public safety." A critic of unlimited democracy, Thompson's primary concern was that the Union win the War swiftly enough so that the people would not revolutionize existing institutions. Therefore, this conservative felt impelled to favor the most energetic conduct of the War and the assumption by government of extraordinary power and functions.

Suppose, he asked, the effort was too flaccid and the South won? Its slave expansion pressures into Latin America would keep the continent an armed camp. In order to face a victorious, permanently independent Confederacy, the diminished Union would have to maintain a huge standing army—the ultimate threat to liberty to mid-nineteenth-century Americans.[23]

Henry Ward Beecher was also apprehensive that wartime pressures might diminish even loyal states. In November 1861 he

---

22. Simeon Sterne, *Constitutional History and Political Development of the United States* (New York, 1882), iii–iv; and for different views, see George M. Frederickson, *The Inner Civil War: Northern Intellectuals and the Crisis of the Union* (New York, 1965), 65–78 and *passim*; Phillip Paludan, "John Norton Pomeroy, State Rights Nationalist," *AJLH*, XII (1968), 275–93.

23. Joseph P. Thompson, "The Test-Hour of Popular Liberty and Republican Government," *NE*, XXI (1862), 225, 231, 235, 243; and see Harold M. Hyman, "Reconstruction and Political-Constitutional Institutions: The Popular Expression," *New Frontiers of the American Reconstruction*, 14–21.

pleaded that "this conflict must be carried through our institutions and not over them. Revolution is not the cure for rebellion." But Beecher demanded also that patriots sustain the Lincoln Administration. He realized that its rude thrusts might force the government into unforeseen outlets, including abolition. Beecher detested any diminution of property rights. But nothing in the Constitution forbade the nation from saving itself. If the need rose, despite doubts and fears Beecher was willing to support the government's abolitionizing experiment as a step toward survival.[24] He was only a year in advance of Lincoln.

James Russell Lowell, perhaps the most influential commentator on the Constitution's adequacy, also disliked some doctrines that the War was letting loose. "Constitutional and unconstitutional propositions press upon us with such rapidity at the present day, that before we have time to dispose of one set of them, another claims our attention," he complained early in 1862.[25]

But Lowell did not believe that the Constitution forbade changes. Until secession ripped away prewar innocence, he had simply assumed that the ways of peace were permanent. Now he knew better. Armed with this more mature outlook, and blessed with a Constitution that was capable of coping with all threats and needs, Americans needed to be more wise than fearful, Lowell wrote. Because America's danger lay not in a threat of tyranny from Washington but in the nearer possibility of anarchy in ten thousand villages, Lowell professed to welcome centralization of functions in Washington rather than continuation of prewar state-centered patterns. Secession was the product of local autonomy southward; in the North, great cities writhed in control of corrupt rings and cliques. Everywhere, license, not liberty, resulted from localism defended by state-rights constitutionalism. Local and state authorities were too parochial in outlooks and too simple in forms to adjust to the "large interests" that the Civil War was exposing to view. Lincoln's "wisdom and vigor" justified optimism, Lowell asserted; "Every possible presage of success and perpetuity" existed in the fortuitous combination of a Constitution

---

24. Henry Ward Beecher, *Freedom and War: Discourses on Topics Suggested by the Times* (Boston, 1863), 156, 188–9.
25. James Russell Lowell, "Constitutional Law," *NAR*, XCIV (1862), 475–9. He was especially offended by Sumner's Senate resolutions that secession by a state lost its residents all constitutional protections and placed that state into a territorial condition under Congress's authority.

of powers in charge of a President who understood this muscular character.[26]

By the beginning of 1862 new champions of the adequate Constitution had come to approximately the position that Lincoln had reached the preceding April and had spelled out to Congress in July 1861—that extraordinary exertions were justifiable not as extraconstitutional spasms but as constitutional recourses. Employing this reasoning, men of widely disparate social goals and political purposes could applaud the military and internal-security efforts of the Lincoln Administration as necessary and proper. It had gone against the patriot grain to ascribe the existing crisis to the deficient handiwork of the 1787 framers. The way out that Lincoln showed suited deepset American habits admirably. Hamiltonian nationalism, Jacksonian traditions of the primacy of the democratic will, and elitist counterfears of mobocracy combined to champion the Constitution's adequacy for all purposes related to winning the War. Ideas of the Constitution's adequacy comforted patriotic lawyers, legislators, ministers, orators, and writers, who employed them in a Joseph's coat of variant but conformable imagery. By the close of 1861 the Constitution's adequacy received such frequent expression in Congress, states' legislatures, newspapers, classrooms, churches, and barracks as to warrant description as a consensus. This view permeated even the new military manuals that were in print by early 1863, as well as civilians' journals. Such diffusion helped to prevent alienation of soldier from civilian, a common pattern in wars abroad.

Consider the words of Durbin Ward, Ohio Democratic Congressman and, in early 1863, a combat officer in that state's federalized volunteer infantry. Ward was a conservative who would never have exalted the notion of a Constitution adequate for all purposes had not the War required temporary allegiance to this view. From his Tennessee bivouac Ward denounced antiwar Ohio Democrats who argued that harsh government policies relieved citizens of their allegiance. Aggrieved men retained access to the courts and to the ballot boxes, Ward retorted. In any event, allegiance was more than checkreins on government:

> If our rulers are restrained by the limits of constitutional power, they are also obligated by the grants of power which

---

26. James Russell Lowell, "Loyalty," *NAR*, XCIV (1862), 145–59.

the Constitution confers. That instrument is not merely a net-work of negatives. It clothes the Government in the panoply of national power; it affirms, as well as denies; it creates a government, and imposes on that government the duty of self-preservation; and for this purpose that government has a right to use all the legal means at its command.[27]

The popular consensus on the Constitution's adequacy made sensible—indeed, necessary—continued politicking in order to determine the paths which derivative policies should take. Political discourse retained the constitutional idiom of prewar times because an adequate Constitution served in war as in peace; politics followed as a matter of course. Confirmed in their political-constitutional habits, Americans overcame quickly the despair about their institutions of the secession winter, and exhibited again their reverence for their Constitution.

This stubborn insistence in the midst of a great war on quarreling over constitutionalism, this unwavering assumption that the results of those quarrels would be policy, deeply impressed European onlookers,[28] especially as the ninety-day militia muster that Lincoln sketched in his April 1861 proclamation developed into the longest, bloodiest, costliest conflict fought anywhere in the western world between 1815 and 1914.

Writing in 1873, Sir James Fitzjames Stephen argued that the American Civil War had developed into "the most pointed and instructive modern illustration" of the fact that "the manner in which war is conducted is worthy of much greater attention than it has received, as illustrating the character and limits of [a nation's] life." Who, Stephen asked, "looking at the matter dispassionately, can fail to perceive the vanity and folly of the attempt to decide the question between the North and the South by lawyers' metaphysics about the true nature of sovereignty or by conveyancing subtleties about the meaning of the Constitution and the principles by which the written documents ought to be interpreted? You might as well try to infer the fortunes of a battle from the shape of the firearms."[29]

---

27. *Life, Speeches and Orations of Durbin Ward of Ohio*, comp. Elizabeth Probasco Ward (Columbus, 1888), 55–6.

28. [London] *Saturday Review* (March 10, 1866), 283.

29. James Fitzjames Stephen, *Liberty, Equality, Fraternity* (New York, 1873), 170; and see H. R. Droop, *Decisions in the United States as to the Constitutional Limits of Legislative Power* (London, 1869), 5.

Yet that is precisely what Americans assumed was the way to do war's business. They went about the War and Reconstruction confident of their ability to draw from the Constitution approval or censure for all that went on, and of the worthwhileness of doing so. The retention of constitutional concerns even during such a war was never curious to Americans. *They* understood their Constitution, in the same sense, Edward Dicey noted, "as the knowledge of the books of the Veda is confined to the Brahmins."[30] Americans clung to Millsian libertarian notions which Sir James Stephen criticized sharply, and hesitated to accept the latter's insight that in modern societies compulsion, in the sense of direction by government toward approved goals, is "normal," and that war, especially a great war, increases the exercises of compulsion. Stephen insisted that because of their immersion in constitutional concerns, Americans failed to come to grips with bedrock matters:

> The compulsion of war is one of the principles which lie at the root of national existence. It determines whether nations are to be and what they are to be. It decided what men shall believe, how they shall live, in what mold their religion, law, morals, and the whole tone of their lives shall be cast. . . . It determines precisely, for one thing, how much and how little individual liberty is to exist at any specific time and place. From this great truth flow many consequences. . . . They may all be summed up in this one, that power precedes liberty—that liberty, from the very nature of things, is dependent upon power; and that it is only under the protection of a powerful, well-organized, and intelligent government that any liberty can exist at all.[31]

Even under the lash that the Civil War provided, such reasoning was too far outside familiar contexts for Americans to accept. "We are in the habit of saying and thinking that war is the abnormal and peace the normal condition of a nation," mused the Attorney General of the United States six weeks after Appomattox.[32] Six weeks after Sumter, when Merryman's appeal

---

30. Edward Dicey, *Six Months in the Federal States* (London, 1863), I, 117–18.
31. Stephen, *Liberty*, 170.
32. James Speed to Francis Lieber, May 26, 1865, Lieber Papers, HL.

elicited Taney's blast, the "habit" was so strong and prevalent, despite the surmounting of secession and the successful recruitment of an army and navy, as to make possible disaster for the Union out of variant interpretations of the Constitution before the augmenting armies fought a major battlefield clash.

The Constitution had worked well enough in March 1861 for Lincoln to be installed in the Presidency without violence. After Sumter, the Constitution, President, Congress, and states—the Union, in short—could work only as they associated with violence, and controlled it. The Army was the instrument of violence. Could constitutionalism, federalism, and democracy survive an army large enough to defeat the Confederacy?

Lincoln's views of 1861 triumphed over Taney's because most Americans shared the President's sense of intimacy with the Constitution to which Dicey referred, and derived optimism and confidence from the close relationship. They found his "adequacy" thesis relevant to their constitutional mystique and immediate needs. As Professor Randall has noted, it spoke to Americans' most pressing concerns "to admit that the Constitution is binding during war and yet to maintain that it sanctions extraordinary powers."[33]

Most of the political-constitutional battles of the Civil War and Reconstruction were fought out in the broad, ill-defined, middle arena which the argument of the adequate Constitution made possible. The military institutions were necessarily involved in many of these confrontations because, in the adequacy context, war powers are wedded to the Constitution. The President must obey the Constitution's injunction "to take care that the laws be faithfully executed"; he is also Commander-in-Chief of the armed forces. In Professor Corwin's phrase, Lincoln equated the war power "with the full actual power of the nation in waging war," and employed the war power concept to justify actions ranging from Merryman's imprisonment to emancipation. But Lincoln never admitted that a single presidential action exceeded what the Constitution allowed or obliterated any clause of the Constitution. By 1864 his view was general Republican doctrine, illustrated by the title of War Department Solicitor William Whiting's 1862

---

33. James G. Randall, *Constitutional Problems Under Lincoln* (rev. edn., Urbana, Ill., 1951), 31; and see Horace Helbronner, *Le Pouvoir judiciaire aux États-Unis* (Paris, 1872), 38–9.

support for Lincoln, *The War Powers of the President*. Two years later Whiting produced the tenth edition of his treatise, much enlarged, with the title, *War Powers Under the Constitution of the United States*.[34]

---

34. Edward S. Corwin, *Total War and the Constitution* (New York, 1947), 16–18, 35–7 (the quotation is from 37); Corwin, *The President: Office and Powers* (New York, 1940), 155–66. On Whiting, see n. 18, above.

Chapter IX

Mars and the Constitution

Whatever individuals believed about the Constitution's adequacy to undergird the Civil War, almost every American assumed that certain restraints governed their Army's conduct in any war. This was a remarkable attitude, in light of history's dismal verdict that the worst human behavior appears during civil wars, especially when race is involved. For four years the Civil War combined these inducements to excess. Yet the conduct of the Civil War was not discreditable.

Americans shared a consensus that ascending civilization had raised man too high for bestial wartime ways, common in the not-very-distant past, to reoccur. The censure of enlightened Christendom bound nations to wage war decently, to treat captives gently, and to abjure pillage, sack, and slaughter of civilians. Since Grotius's 1625 summary of the "law of war and peace," international laws, nations' domestic statutes, and armies' regulations had standardized these stipulations; the laws of nature and of nations governed the laws of war.[1] But in addition, Americans believed that their Constitution bound their armed forces in ways less blessed foreigners did not enjoy.

Within a year after Sumter, the Supreme Court reinforced this consensus. It allowed the Confederacy the position which the President and the armed forces accorded it, of a de facto belliger-

---

1. Hugo Grotius, *De Jure Belli ac Pacis Libri Tres,* trans. F. W. Kelsey *et al.* (Oxford, 1925) I, 38–44; Morris Greenspan, *The Modern Law of Land Warfare* (Berkeley and Los Angeles, 1959), ch. 1.

ent enemy, thereby sustaining Lincoln's blockading orders and the capture of neutral vessels which attempted to pierce the screen.[2] In diplomatic matters the United States government insisted that the Civil War was a purely domestic event. Though not a war between nations, the Civil War "was accompanied by the general incidents of an international war," the Supreme Court decided almost fifteen years after Appomattox; a policy which the Union's armed forces assumed at once after Sumter.[3]

Americans entered into the Civil War convinced that national law deriving from the Constitution applied to America's armies, making them automatically restrained and obedient to civilian overlords, especially to the President. America's unusually happy domestic history during the War of 1812 and the Mexican War, as well as its Constitution, justified the assumption that armies were susceptible to civilians' controls and that soldiers need not gall civilian populations. By 1860, ideas about war's restrained conduct had mixed with other tenacious constitutional views.[4]

When Attorney General Bates defended Lincoln's internal-security policies against Taney's attack from the bench, he argued that the three co-ordinate branches of national government were balanced in a neat geometry, and that none could inhibit another.[5] Bates's trizonal imagery appealed strongly to constitutional and political conservatives even among Republicans, who

---

2. Prize Cases, 2 Black, 635 (1863); Sir James Fitzjames Stephen, *Liberty, Equality, Fraternity* (New York, 1873), 170.

3. Dow v. Johnson, 100 US, 158, esp. 164 (1879); and see Coleman v. Tennessee, 97 US, 509 (1878). Although as early as the 1862 Prize Cases the Supreme Court reached the obvious conclusion that a war of huge mass was a more compelling factor in history than small conflicts, sometimes jurists forgot this. In an 1870 decision the Court decided that the Civil War "had the same properties as if it had been the insurrection of a county or smaller municipal territory against the State to which it belonged. The proportions and duration of the struggle did not affect its character." Hickman v. Jones *et al.*, 9 Wall., 197 @ 280 (1870). Of course "proportions and duration" affect the "character" of a war; indeed of the combatant society. James G. Randall, *Constitutional Problems Under Lincoln* (rev. edn., Urbana, Ill., 1951), ch. 3, deals fully with the Civil War's legal nature, and restatement is unnecessary.

4. Henry Wager Halleck, *Elements of Military Art and Science* (New York, 1846), 8–9; Louis Smith, *American Democracy and Military Power* (Chicago, 1951), 21–6; Carlton B. Smith, "The American Search for A 'Harmless' Army," *Essays in History*, X (1964–65), 29–43.

5. Randall, *Constitutional Problems*, 30–1.

asserted that Civil War America was divided constitutionally into strictly predictable and separate, though shifting, zones of law— civil, military, and martial—of almost planetary isolation from one another.[6]

Propositions of this sort received common expression soon after Sumter. Writing early in 1861 on "the laws of war," the important Democratic party theoretician and self-styled conservative essayist, Kentucky jurist S. S. Nicholas, set the theme: "There is not, there never can be, in this country, a law of war, different from the constitutional law of the land." And within two years after Appomattox, the United States Supreme Court reached a similar conclusion: "There is no law for the government of the citizens, the armies, or the navy of the United States, within American jurisdiction, which is not contained in or derived from the Constitution."[7]

Such confidence in the Constitution as the measure of military as well as of civilian behavior led to early and lasting confusion when collisions occurred between the supposedly discrete civilian and military worlds. In the first spring of the war, the editor of a major law journal could "readily perceive how, in the present posture of our National affairs, many questions arise . . . touching the precise relation which the military bear to the civil powers . . . in moments of extreme danger."[8]

Little useful clarification about this "precise relationship" occurred until mid-War, but the common belief was that it derived from the Constitution. Despite daily contrary evidence, this assumption rarely receded very far. In courtrooms as well as in politics, Americans continued substantiating from the Constitution what the Civil War required them to do, and of objecting even to military policies because they allegedly offended the 1787 formulation.

---

6. Joel Prentiss Bishop, *Commentaries on the Criminal Law* (4th edn., Boston, 1868), I, 23–4. Pleading for the government in the Prize Cases, R. H. Dana's figure of the war zone being defined by the shifting line of Union bayonets perfectly encapsulated these themes. See *Arguments and Addresses of Joseph Hodges Choate*, ed. F. C. Hicks (St. Paul, Minn., 1926), 57.

7. S. S. Nicholas, *Conservative Essays, Legal and Political* (Louisville, 1867), I, 207; Ex parte Milligan, 4 Wall., 2 (1866). A recent similar expression is in Arthur A. Ekirch, Jr., *The Civilian and the Military* (New York, 1956), ch. 7.

8. "Martial Law," *ALReg*, IX (1861), 498.

With respect to the armed forces' subordinate relationship to President and Congress, in 1861 imprecision appeared to many of Lincoln's contemporaries to be improbable, if not impossible. The Constitution's arrangements and derivative legislation apparently had created a "harmless army" that would remain obedient no matter how huge it grew. Belief prevailed that the Constitution enmeshed the Army in the check-and-balance complex so that civilian control emerged. Only Congress could declare war. The legislators controlled the military budget, supplied its basic regulations, approved (in the Senate) officers' commissions, and held similar checkreins over the states' militias in certain circumstances. The President was Commander-in-Chief of all armed forces. The Constitution's guarantee to each state of a republican form of government sanctioned the employment of national armed force under extraordinary conditions on behalf of a state or states.

All this appeared to be clear enough. But, unperceived by most of Lincoln's contemporaries, the Civil War continued an unofficial, gradual development in Army-Congress-President relationships that had been unfolding since 1789. That development linked the career Army closer to Congress than to the President. By 1861 some lawyers held the Whiggish view that in military matters Presidents served as Congress's steward; that under the Constitution Congress defined and the President merely administered the American Army.[9]

Career Army officers had reached a similar judgment long before Sumter. Presidents came and went, but like many congressmen, career Army personnel stayed on. The custom developed early for professional soldiers to look more to Congress

---

9. "In the United States, under the Constitution, the power of Congress over the army is absolute. The President commands the army when it is once created; but Congress alone has the power to diminish or increase its numbers and its strength at pleasure. The President possesses the ordinary powers and prerogatives of the commander-in-chief of an army; but he is limited and controlled in his actions by any general or special law which Congress may choose to enact in regard to him in his relation to the [armed] forces." *Ibid.*, 504, and see 498. The Constitution's deliberate mixture of presidential and congressional controls over the Army obviously had lowered a President's prerogatives below those enjoyed by a British king, with respect to American armed forces. *Federalist Papers*, Nos. 69, 74; Louis Smith, *American Democracy and Military Power: A Study of Civil Control of the Military Power in the United States* (Chicago, 1951), chs. 3, 11, 15.

than to the White House for decisions of real importance to the peacetime military about the size, organization, equipment, and funds of the Army and the military's intra-institutional laws.

The exceptional circumstances after Sumter and the exceptional personality in the White House obscured the habit of congressional priority in military affairs. "A vigorous executive, wielding formidable powers," Lincoln was able to raise his office as high as he did by combining Commander-in-Chief duties with the vague war power.[10] Events were to prove that his ascent was temporary. Alfred Conkling, a noted contemporary analyst of the Presidency, discerned that "the ample powers with which the President is armed as generalissimo in time of war . . . are altogether exceptional." The rise in presidential effectiveness associated with Lincoln's administration did not fundamentally alter ties that bound the military institution to Congress as well as to the White House. Conkling noted that "the war-making power was confided [in the Constitution] to Congress, and the President was declared commander-in-chief; and there the subject was, of necessity, left."[11]

After two years of trial and error, Lincoln and his able coadjutors in the Cabinet and in Congress created executive and legislative machineries and constitutional-legal treatises and compendia that fleshed out more adequately the Constitution's thin prescriptions about military subordination. But until these improved glosses and machinery took form, great confusion existed concerning the constitutional place of the Union Army.

The common assumption of 1861 was that civilian control existed immediately and automatically. In short, Americans believed that the Constitution, adequate for the United States Army, covered also the mass Union Armies. But soon after Sumter contentions over the Constitution's adequacy for unanticipated Civil War conditions became a prominent political divisor. Questions unanticipated in law schools or West Point, involving the natures and limits of military law and of martial law and the interactions of soldiers with civilians, advanced sharply in public

---

10. Adolphe de Chambrun, *The Executive Power in the United States: A Study of Constitutional Law*, tr. Madeleine Vinton Dahlgren (Lancaster, Pa., 1874), 256–7.

11. Alfred Conkling, *The Powers of the Executive Department of the Government of the United States, and the Political Institutions and Constitutional Laws of the United States* (Albany, 1866), 88.

attention. And as with secession and internal-security arrests, for a distressingly long while no one, even among the highest officials and most learned men, agreed on answers.

This unreadiness is visible in the mercenary instructional literature that issued soon after Sumter to feed the sudden public hunger for information about martial and military law. Almost all the authors and, by implication, readers accepted the idea that neat divisions existed between civil, martial, and military laws, and that these divisions delineated equally neat territorial and jurisdictional boundaries for warriors to obey. Such a lawyer's query of 1861 as: "Under what circumstances and by whose authority [may] the municipal law of the land . . . be rightfully superseded by what is known as the military or martial law?" presupposed precise, catechismal responses. Appearing in a leading law journal, this question confused martial and military law in a manner to suggest that lawyers' and generals' comprehensions concerning the military's place in constitutional life were no keener than the general public's.[12]

One reason for this confusion is that in 1861 no literature existed appropriate to American Civil War conditions about military law, much less about martial law. Before Sumter some American commentators were in print on these themes. But these rare writers so parroted major European theorists, especially Grotius and Vattel, that one disgusted reader of Henry W. Halleck's prewar treatise on international law remarked that Halleck "was pregnant" with Vattel.[13]

Pregnant, perhaps, but not fruitful enough to help Ameri-

---

12. "Martial Law," *ALReg*, 489: Note that generals and Supreme Court jurists also confused military and martial laws and such differing Army tribunals as courts-martial (for soldiers only and for offenses under the Articles of War) and military commissions (for soldiers and civilians) for offenses under military occupation regulations; Daniel Gardner, *A Treatise on the Law of the American Rebellion, and Our True Policy, Domestic and Foreign* (New York, 1862); James Russell Lowell, "Military and Martial Law," *NAR*, CII (1866), 334–56; G. N. Lieber, "What Is the Justification of Martial Law?" *NAR*, CLVI (1896), 549–63.

13. G. A. Brown to S. B. Buckner, Dec. 15, 1865, HL. And, as one British commentator remarked after surveying American legal attitudes of 1861, "But there's [always] Grotius." *Fraser's Magazine*, LXVI (1862), 259. Henry W. Halleck, *International Law: Or, Rules Regulating the Intercourse of States in Peace and War* (San Francisco, 1861), 775–841, noted the lack of appropriate provisions for Americans responsible for governing occupied regions, in the Constitution, statutes, or Articles of War.

cans cope quickly or easily with Civil War civil-military inter-actions and abrasions. Instead, in the words of William Whiting —who at the end of 1862, obedient to Lincoln's personal request, became the War Department's Solicitor—"the powers of war, the rights of war, and the courts of war, [in 1861 and 1862] seemed equally strange and alarming."[14]

It is less surprising that the ways of war should appear exotic to men steeped in the civil law, than that military careerists were equally ill-prepared to adjust to Civil War realities and responsibilities. But the fact was that American war men were no better prepared than lawmen to cope with what the Civil War brought in. By 1861, the United States Army had forgotten its own history. Regulars were unaware that the Revolutionary War had involved the Continental Army in civil-military interactions, especially with respect to internal security, analogous to Civil War situations. More recently, during the Mexican War, American Army officers had created temporary military governments to replace the vanquished Mexican authority. But this reservoir of experience failed to flow from Guadalupe Hidalgo to Sumter. Consequently, career military officers who by logic should have come to the Civil War equipped to employ military and martial laws were unready to do the job.

The Mexican War involved a "traditional" foreign foe, and the subsequent brief military occupation involved primarily simple police duties by the victorious American Army as it awaited completion of the armistice. By contrast, the Civil War pitted Americans against each other. Its battles raged on common land—common, that is, if the bluecoats won. And Union Army occupation of Confederate real estate involved Billy Yank in lengthy and complex economic, legal, social, and racial situations into which northern jurists and politicians injected sharply differing views. Despite these differences, by 1863 the partial applicability of the Mexican War experience was becoming apparent to some Civil War officials, who wondered why the relevance was not apparent earlier.[15]

The primary reason the Army lost its memory about Mexico

14. William Whiting, *War Powers Under the Constitution of the United States* (43rd edn., Boston, 1871), 159.

15. See "Status of the Rebel States Before and After Their Conquest," *MLRep* (Aug. 26, 1864), 537–57; Frank Freidel, "General Orders 100 and Military Government," *MVHR*, XXXII (1946), 541–2.

is that during the 1850's the careerists became almost totally divorced from the main currents of American life and thought. After the victorious homecoming, the volunteers quickly demobilized. Except as regulars competed in print for glory, the Army all but disappeared in frontier posts and Washington bureaus. Soldiers could not sustain compendious textbooks and periodicals in which to assemble a backlog of pertinent data and to circulate news of subsequent developments.[16]

For its part, the Army's top echelon failed to educate Capitol Hill overlords about civil-military relationships, martial law, and military government questions that the Mexican experience at least posed, so that when the Civil War and Reconstruction again thrust these matters forward the hazards of surprise and confusion were incurred.

A decade before Sumter, the bestarred galaxy let slip its best opportunity to transmit some lessons from Mexico. Senator Jefferson Davis, always concerned about military matters, introduced in 1850 a resolution which resulted in the assembly in Washington of a high-level Army board. One question the senators posed to these prestigious soldiers allowed consideration of the Army's experience administering martial law and military government: "What provisions are necessary to authorize officers of the Army to exercise civil functions in emergencies . . . and what restraints are expedient, to prevent such officers from usurping the powers of civil functionaries?"[17]

The official record suggests that the board's members tried seriously to answer the question; they offered this seemingly deliberate conclusion:

> . . . no necessity can arise, and no provision need be made by law, to authorize officers of the army to exercise civil functions within the United States in time of peace; nor in

---

16. In 1861, only one textbook on military and martial law was in print; John Paul Jones O'Brien, *A Treatise on American Military Laws: And the Practice of Courts Martial; with a Suggestion for Their Improvement* (Philadelphia, 1846). A poor piece of work, it served inadequately the armed horde that formed after Sumter. All efforts had failed during the 1850's to maintain from tax sources or private funds even one periodical devoted primarily to military science and law, at a time when Britain's *United Service Magazine* and France's *Le Spectateur militaire* and *Le Moniteur de l'armée* regularly circulated in those nations; Donald N. Bigelow, *William Conant Church* (New York, 1952), 103–4.

17. *Sen. Exec. Doc.* 5, 31 Cong., 2 sess.; CG, 31 Cong., 1 sess., 2072.

time of war can the necessity be so clearly anticipated as to be provided for by law. And the board is not aware that further provisions are necessary to prevent officers of the army from usurping the powers of civil functionaries. In regard to foreign territory which may be held in the military occupation of the United States in time of war, the board is of opinion that the laws of war invest the commander-in-chief with the powers necessary to enforce civil order.[18]

But a private account kept by a junior member, Colonel Ethan Allen Hitchcock, makes clear that the primary interest of the generals was another star for Winfield Scott, leaving almost no time for consideration of civil-military relations. The generals, "disposing of [this] one other point," adjourned.[19]

Later in the 1850's, displeased by what he deemed excessive curiosity on the part of Secretaries of War about the Army's inner workings, Scott moved the commanding general's headquarters out of Washington to New York City, not to return until the eve of secession. Meanwhile, to Scott's greater credit, he supported a suggestion from one of the nation's few experts (perhaps the only one) on the conduct of wars rather than of battles, the Columbia political theorist Francis Lieber, who wished to offer a course at West Point on the laws of war. But the Point's commandant resisted the notion on the grounds that the curriculum was already overcrowded, and the Army's future leaders remained as uneducated on this score as before.[20] As a result, in 1861 career officers were unprepared to cope with the mountainous problems that the Civil War let loose, or to instruct volunteer officers in

---

18. The board did look ahead a little, if perfunctorily. It requested Congress to provide a "permanent" statute to specify the powers of temporary civil administrators in territories newly acquired by conquest or purchase. Back in 1803 President Jefferson had obtained from Congress such a useful statute to apply in Louisiana. But the 1850 request for a guide to Army direction of civilian affairs in areas lacking civil government, where "the military authorities be required to assume the administration of the civil laws," received no response. *Sen. Exec. Doc.* 3, 31 Cong., 2 sess., 3.

19. Ethan Allen Hitchcock ms. diary, entries Nov. 8, Dec. 4, 1850, W. A. Croffut Papers, LC.

20. Frank Freidel, "General Orders 100," 542–3; Stephen Ambrose, *Duty, Honor, Country: A History of West Point* (Baltimore, 1966), chs. 8, 10; Benjamin P. Thomas and Harold M. Hyman, *Stanton: The Life and Times of Lincoln's Secretary of War* (New York, 1962), 146 and n.

their solution. Neither President nor Congress possessed machinery, beyond the Constitution's thin offerings, to control the blue-coated horde.

This unpreparedness extended even to military law, the branch or zone of law that was apparently the simplest and most precise, being "the legal system [prescribed by Congress] that regulates the [internal] government of the military establishment."[21] So long as only professional soldiers lived under military law, most people cared little about it or the fact that life under military law cut soldiers off from the Constitution's protections. Then Sumter brought the inflow of volunteers, militiamen, and, later, conscripts. Despite differences between the tiny prewar United States Army and the post-Sumter Union Army, the same military law served for internal discipline and government.[22]

Consider how literacy and its political consequences set off Mr. Lincoln's army from the regulars. Unlike them, Billy Yank corresponded with family, friends, legislators, ministers, and journalists, subscribed to newspapers and periodicals, and even voted. When suddenly concerned homefolks realized that their uniformed men were subject to unfamiliar military law, they received initial assurances in popular periodicals that military law was little different from civilians' codes.[23] But early in the war differing reports began to circulate. Journalists with troops and soldiers in letters home described the unpredictable ways of military discipline. Evidence mounted that officers' whims or a unit's habits more than Congress's regulations governed disciplinary relationships. Reports made clear that severe, near-barbaric

---

21. G. N. Lieber, "What Is the Justification . . . ?" 549.

22. "Our country came suddenly upon this new system of [military] law. We took the old laws, forms, and regulations provided for our little regular army, by which it has been governed through so long a time of peace, and applied them as well as we could to the great army of the present time." Lowell, "Military Law," 336.

23. Although it came late, the following statement is typical of a great many which defined military law as rational, regular, and understood: "Military law is a portion of the law of the land, by which the army is governed as a distinct organization. It has its own distinct laws and rules. . . . Military law exists by force of statute . . . exists both in peace and war . . . applies only to the army and those connected with it . . . only to the administration of criminal justice . . . exists normally as the necessary system by which a peculiar class of men are governed, by a method peculiar to that class, and suited to it as distinguished from the rest of society. . . . The rules of military law are fixed and definite." *Ibid.*, 336–7.

penalties were commonplace in some Army units, while in others milder consequences followed similar offenses. Blunders were publicized, and appeared comical, of new officers who stumbled in burlesque manner through courts-martial. But humor flagged when rugged sentences followed slipshod performances.

Prewar regulars, who had endured mutely the vagaries of military law as compared to precise congressional and War Department stipulations, mocked the fuss that rose up. Explaining in 1867 why these divergences existed, Army veteran and law-journal editor Oliver Wendell Holmes, Jr. noted that "Before the war, all knowledge on the subject of military law had to be derived from . . . bald and inaccurate treatises, from a dozen decided cases, and from a few official opinions scattered through the volumes of opinions by the Attorney General, and through the orders of the War Department." Two years after Appomattox, Holmes reported that "no branch of the law is so badly supplied with literature as that which relates to courts-martial."[24] This dearth of reliable literature on courts-martial diminished only after Joseph Holt began to reform the Judge Advocate General's office in 1863.

The basic "literature" of military law included Congress's several statutes for the government of the armed forces, plus executive orders and explanations, known collectively as the "Rules and Articles of War." After Sumter, commercial publishers supplied thousands of new Army and militia officers with copies and with editions of military-law manuals. Holmes was correct that these manuals were inaccurate and slipshod. He was not correct, however, in concluding that the erratic characteristics of Army discipline resulted only from the deficient characteristics of these manuals.

---

24. Oliver Wendell Holmes, Jr., *ALRev*, I (1867), 559–60. Only one even of the "bald and inaccurate treatises" was available before the War: O'Brien, *Treatise on American Military Laws*. Two others came in after Sumter: Capt. Stephen V. Benet, *A Treatise on the Military Law and the Practice of Courts Martial* (New York, 1862); and William De Hart, *Observations on Military Law, and the Constitution and Practice of Courts Martial, with a Summary of the Laws of Evidence as Applicable to Military Trials, Adapted to the Laws, Regulations, and Customs of the Army and Navy of the United States* (New York, 1862). The Confederate equivalent was Charles H. Lee, *The Judge Advocate's Vade Mecum; and the Practice Before Courts Martial, with an Epitome of the Laws of Evidence, as Applicable to Military Trials* (Richmond, 1863); Randall, *Constitutional Problems*, 140.

The prewar absence of enough administrative machinery and sustained civilian interest to compel obedience within the Army to President and Congress was a weightier factor. Some field officers, for example, never worked out the differences between courts-martial of soldiers and military commission trials of civilians, or perhaps never saw a need to. Two years after Sumter, General Henry W. Halleck, one of the small number of officers who was informed in the law of war, found it necessary to lecture field commander General William Rosecrans on the differences between military commissions and courts-martial. When high generals required instruction junior officers endured little control.[25]

Neither generals nor lieutenants received instruction or control from civilian judges. "I know nothing, literally, of the Law of Courts Martial," admitted Justice David Davis of the Supreme Court (he meant military commissions in this instance).[26] While the War lasted, Davis and his colleagues refused to accept jurisdiction of appeals coming to them from military tribunals; a stance that altered dramatically soon after Appomattox.[27]

It is remarkable that Americans did not find the inconsistencies and differences between their illusions about military law as a precise and certain code, and the realities that wartime experience revealed, deeply unsettling. No political pressure generated in the direction of establishment of a separate body of military law for the war-service-only multitude. Public interest never focused on the need wholly to reform or to restrain military

---

25. Henry W. Halleck to William Rosecrans, March 20, 1863, Stanton Papers, LC. Rosecrans was establishing military courts both for his soldiers and for civilians resident within his lines, and Halleck was aiding him in providing a dual system of Army-run courts. Here is Halleck's instruction: "Courts-martial, as you must be aware, are courts of special and limited jurisdiction, under the 'Rules and Articles of War,' both with regard to persons and offences. They cannot take jurisdiction of persons, or cognizance of offences, not specially authorized by those 'Rules and Articles.' But the laws of the United States, as well as the military usages of other countries, recognize courts of general military jurisdiction, over civilians as well as soldiers, under the common law of war. Such tribunals, are, with us, denominated 'Military Commissions.'"

26. David Davis to Joseph Holt, Oct. 11, 1862, Holt Papers, LC.

27. Even before Appomattox, Davis inveighed against military arrogance, as he saw it; see his charge to a federal grand jury, in Indianapolis Star, May 6, 1863. The wartime jurisdiction question is Ex parte Vallandigham, 1 Wall., 243 (1864); the post-Appomattox decision is Ex parte Milligan, 4 Wall., 2 (1866).

law. Judges did not concern themselves with establishing its constitutional limits. In short, military law did not create constitutional history.

This low-key response to disclosures about the defects of military law is the more remarkable when measured against the potent home-front connections the bluecoats enjoyed. Reciprocally, these influential connections formed part of the reason why the military-law imbroglio never became a constitutional issue. Complainants were satisfied when individual injustices were ameliorated. Politics provided volunteers and conscripts with effective individual avenues of complaint against rigors to supplement the inadequate intra-Army channels of appeal from court-martial decisions. Lincoln's sympathy for victims of alleged excessive discipline was well known. His sensitivity to the requests of congressmen, governors, or other influential persons on behalf of constituents caught in the Army's internal police linked politics to humanitarianism and blunted the sharp thrust of the rigorous, erratic ways of military law.

A second explanation for the public's placid temper about military law lies in the familiarity of Lincoln's generation with civil codes that also functioned uncertainly and harshly. By today's criteria the penal portions of states' criminal laws in the mid-nineteenth century were rugged and their application was uneven. Everywhere court reporting was a chancy affair.

Third, even commentators who were aware of the irregularities of military law agreed that no superior code existed. Indeed, many thought that America deserved congratulation because its sons adapted themselves quickly to the military's tough law. Surely a society was not irretrievably decayed whose youths accepted subservience to military discipline without undue visible strain. This acceptance was accounted another proof of constitutional government's great virtues.[28]

Fourth, the volunteer duration-only amateurs aped the professionals, and easily acquired the habit of glorifying and romanticizing the toughness of their training and discipline. Veteran soldiers and officers scorned the barracks-room-lawyer who demanded the full measure of justice allowable under the Articles of War. It was a part of the *code d'honneur* mutely to

---

28. Lowell, "Military Law," 335–6; George M. Frederickson, *The Inner Civil War: Northern Intellectuals and the Crisis of the Union* (New York, 1965), ch. 11; Bishop, *Criminal Law*, I, 47.

accept company punishments instead of courts-martial, in order to keep offenses unrecorded. This posture further confounded the theoretically consistent application of military law, and often closed off the slim avenues of appeals from military punishments that Army regulations allowed.[29]

Last, with few exceptions, military law primarily affected soldiers. A small number of civilian employees of field forces, such as stevedores, stewards, and teamsters, traditionally were also subject to military law and courts-martial. Employing delegated executive authority, Civil War Army commanders added balloonists, steamboat pilots, and telegraphers to the list. In mid-1862, Congress stipulated that corrupt civilian contractors should be "deemed and taken as a part of the land or naval forces," and be subject to military law; an 1863 statute extended further court-martial jurisdiction to other classes of contractors.[30] No compilation exists of how many courts-martial of civilians resulted from this expansion, but there were a fair number.

Yet no suits in civil courts took place alleging the unconstitutionality of these jurisdictional enlargements until after Appomattox. A federal district court decision in 1866 (unreported until 1878), reached the dubious conclusion that in 1862 and 1863 Congress had defined as contractors only persons already members of the armed forces, storekeepers and the like.[31]

Prospectively more significant was the provision in the 1863 statute that military personnel who defrauded the government or commited other crimes while in uniform, and who then became civilians, should remain subject to courts-martial whether or not civil courts were available for trials. Under the terms of this statute, post-Appomattox courts-martial tried and punished dishonest and larcenous soldiers-become-civilians for wartime crimes. Military law not only overshadowed these veterans but incorporated civilian crimes unknown in military law before Sumter, including embezzlement, murder, and rape. This 1863 statute remained in force until, in the mid-1950's, civil courts no

---

29. "The Education of Generals," *ANJ*, I (Sept. 5, 1863), 26.

30. *SAL*, XII, 594 (1862); *ibid.*, 696 (1863); *see* Holt's ms. opinion, Nov. 15, 1866, BMJ, WD, Letters Sent, XXIII, 331, NA.

31. Ex parte Henderson, 11 Fed. Cas. No. 6349 (1866), 1067; and see Hill v. U.S., 9 Ct. Cl. 178 (1873), which assumed the constitutionality of the maligned statutes. See too Robert Girard, "The Constitution and Courts-Martial of Civilians Accompanying the Armed Forces—A Preliminary Analysis," *StLR*, XIII (1961), 461–521.

longer sustained extension of military law to civilians who had been soldiers, or who were or had been connected to the armed services in certain contractual relationships.[32]

In the 1860's these novel military-law extensions excited little or no fears about military imperialism. Legal luminaries kept attention centered on martial law and military occupation concerns rather than military law. Despite all contrary evidence, military law continued to give off an illusion of rationality. It appeared to be relatively simple, and to hold easily to its proper "zone" and uniformed population. But none of these characteristics was strictly accurate.[33]

Far more complex questions came up from the wake of the Army's penetrations of the South. Moving there, Union troopers created the second "zone" of law—military occupation and government—into which the Civil War allegedly divided the land; placed in the "grasp of war" whatever came within the Union Army's "shifting line of bayonets."[34]

---

32. U.S. ex rel. Toth v. Quarles, 350 US 11 (1955) and Reid v. Covert, 354 US 1 (1957) probably ended this extension. Earlier decisions are surveyed in J. W. Bishop, Jr., "Court-Martial Jurisdiction over Military-Civilian Hybrids: Retired Regulars, Reservists, and Discharged Prisoners," *UPLR*, CXII, 317–77, esp. 325, n. 36; see too Garrard Glenn and A. Arthur Schiller, *The Army and the Law* (rev. edn., New York, 1943), ch. 4. In 1969 the "Pinkville Massacre" question revived these uncertainties.

33. See F. Whittaker, "The American Army," *Galaxy*, XXIV (1877), 388–98.

34. Hicks, *Choate*, 57; Samuel Shapiro, *Richard Henry Dana, Jr., 1815–1882* (East Lansing, Mich., 1961), 119–20.

Chapter X

A Chaos of Doctrines: Military Occupation and Martial Law

Feebly in 1861, then with accelerating vigor, territorial contraction became the central theme of Confederate history. Yankee military occupation areas and, later, military governments remained like glacial moraines in the wakes of Union combat men. This mobile zone or zones of military occupation and government, consisting of whatever areas of the Confederacy were rewon at a given time, formed the second division of law into which legal idiom, popular imagery, and military reality divided Civil War America.[1]

Occupied areas served Union field forces as communication, garrison, intelligence, and supply bases. Then, before 1861 ended, without concert or guidance, occupation concerns escalated to higher strategical and political-constitutional levels, because by then it was manifest that reunion would result from battlefield decisions and their aftermaths rather than from peace conventions or scholars' contentions. That is, combat victories

---

1. The sense of mobility is important. On it hinges the derivative question of the status of the occupied territory when military power existed. See the Prize Cases, 2 Black, 635 @ 667 (1863); and R. H. Dana to Sumner, Feb. 5, 1866, vol. 76, Sumner Papers, Houghton Library, HU, and n. 10, below.

followed by military occupations allowed northern civilian policy-makers to make policy in ever-augmenting Union Army toe holds.

Soon after Sumter, sensitive northerners in the Army, in high civilian offices involved with the Army, in Congress, and in the web of benevolent, charitable, patriotic, political, and religious organizations that knit the home front together became aware of opportunities that occupied areas represented to transform restorations into a reconstruction. Reconstructions thus began almost at once after Sumter, not the day after Appomattox, as Union Army military commanders developed policies that moved into the North's politics.[2]

The foregoing suggests orderliness in the evolution from military occupation as a tactical operation, to military government as a strategical concept, and then to Reconstruction policies as political-constitutional decisions. To be sure, evolution did occur. It took place adventitiously, however, without blueprints for the systematic instruction of generals or statesmen. Each step was a guideless tour filled with opportunities and pitfalls, but without commitment to a common goal except victory.[3]

As an illustration, consider that all the deficiencies in the literature and statutes on military law existed also with respect to military occupations and their consequence, martial law. Lacking even an agreed vocabulary, most commentators lumped military occupation questions under the catch-all rubric, martial law, as Henry W. Halleck noted.

Hazards to civilian direction of Reconstruction's political goals existed in this fuzzy categorization. All available manuals stressed the almost totally free rein that a martial conqueror enjoyed over the enemy civilians he ruled. Witness this permis-

---

2. William Whiting, *War Powers Under the Constitution of the United States* (43rd edn., Boston, 1871), 261–306, and, as a case history, George L. Hendricks, "Union Occupation of the Southern Seaboard, 1861–1865" (Ph.D. diss., CU, 1954).

3. See A. H. Carpenter, "Military Government of Southern Territory, 1861–1865," AHA, AR (1900), I, 467–98; William A. Russ, Jr., "Administrative Activities of the Union Army During and After the Civil War," *MLJ*, XVII (1945), 71–89; John G. Sproat, "Blueprint for Radical Reconstruction," *JSH*, XXIII (1957), 25–44; Laura Wood Roper, "Frederick Law Olmsted and the Port Royal Experiment," *JSH*, XXXI (1965), 272–84; Willie Lee Rose, *Rehearsal for Reconstruction: The Port Royal Experiment* (Indianapolis, 1964); James G. Randall, *Constitutional Problems Under Lincoln* (rev. edn., Urbana, Ill., 1951), ch. 10.

sive statement from the American military manual, by John O'Brien, that Union Army officers read far more than any other:

> Martial law, as Blackstone truly remarks, is in fact no law. It is an expedient, resorted to in times of danger, similar, in its effect, to the appointment of a dictator. The general, or other authority charged with the defence of a country, proclaims martial law. By so doing he places himself above all law. He abrogates or suspends, at his pleasure, the operation of the law of the land. He resorts to all measures, however repugnant to ordinary law, which he deems best calculated to secure the safety of the state in the imminent peril to which it is exposed. Martial law, being thus vague and uncertain, and measured only by the danger to be guarded against, exists only in the breast of him who proclaims and executes it. It is contained in no written code.[4]

This doctrine of unlimited and uncatalogued powers for military occupation commanders did not chafe until it became apparent that the Civil War was different from other conflicts. In "ordinary" wars, military occupations had involved foreign residents. Essentially without political purposes, earlier military occupations were brief holding operations waiting upon the return of the region to former sovereigns or its transfer to a new allegiance. John Marshall had set the theme into American constitutional law: "The usage of the world is, if a nation be not entirely subdued, to consider the holding of a conquered territory as a mere military occupation, until its fate shall be determined at the treaty of peace."[5]

But Civil War occupation questions involved other Americans, not foreigners. The destiny of the Union rested on bluecoats' postbattle decisions. Men who wished to direct those decisions, especially with respect to race relationships, asserted that restraints reined in occupation commanders after all; reined in

---

4. John Paul Jones O'Brien, *A Treatise on American Military Laws: And the Practice of Courts Martial; with Suggestions for Their Improvement* (Philadelphia, 1846), 26, and see Gerhard von Glahn, *The Occupation of Enemy Territory: A Commentary on the Law and Practice of Belligerent Occupation* (Minneapolis, 1957), 3–8; Henry W. Halleck, *International Law, or, Rules Regulating the Intercourse of States in Peace and War* (San Francisco, 1861), 775–841.

5. American Insurance Co. v. Canter, 1 Peters, 511 at 542 (1828); and see "Status of the Rebel States Before and After Their Conquest," *MLRep* (Aug. 26, 1864), 537–57.

those of differing views, at least. To be sure, the Constitution and statutes did not supply these checkreins, as was true in military law. They derived instead from the law of nations on the conduct of war. "Nothing is plainer in principle than that neither military law nor martial law is justified in running riot," wrote Joel Prentiss Bishop, and he criticized Blackstone along with the Duke of Wellington for agreeing that martial rule was the commander's whim.[6]

Bishop's pellucid principle was less plain than he imagined. With respect to civil-military relationships, the legal doctrine persisted of total permissiveness. But Union brass never exercised plenary powers regardless of theoretical plenitude. Instead, occupation commanders felt a need to discern the unspecified limits which political-constitutional imperatives placed on their freedom of action, and to work within them.

Those limits remained obscure for a long time. They derived from politics, not philosophy or international laws, and from the tenacious constitutional conservatism that characterized even "Radical" Republicans. Still, until the President, cabinet secretaries, and legislators specified permissible boundaries of action concerning such tender questions as the return by Union soldiers of rebels' runaway slaves, field officers shouldered the weights of decision, sometimes at great political risk. In short, the very openness which generals enjoyed in conquered zones bred confusion.

According to Freidel, "much of the original confusion came from the widespread belief that the army should apply [in the South] municipal law, the statutes of the United States, rather than international law for the suppression of the rebellion." This basic uncertainty led to many others. Again to quote Freidel:

> During the first two years of the war, confused and often conflicting policies among the many commands advancing into Confederate territory plagued the Union army. A considerable part of this confusion grew out of a lack of knowledge of the intricate technicalities of the international law of war regulating military government. How and when should martial law function? How should the army treat civilians and private property? What was the status of

---

6. Joel Prentiss Bishop, *Commentaries on the Criminal Law* (Boston, 1868), I, 46–7; and see *Miscellaneous Writings of the Late Hon. Joseph P. Bradley*, ed. Charles Bradley (Newark, 1901), 146–7.

property in slaves? What attitude should the government take toward loyal, neutral, and disloyal persons in occupied territory?[7]

Some of the confusion derived from the purposes of partisans—some of whom were in uniform—as well as from the uncertainties of generals. There was a common argument that American "municipal" law applied in rewon portions of the South. Residents there were rebels, not enemies under international law. As rebels, they were subject to the will of generals but also, as time passed, to the President's decrees on blockade and emancipation and to Congress's growing battery of laws on confiscation, conscription, conspiracy, and treason. Further, the brevity in the duration of a military occupation that international law recommended did not apply to rewon rebel areas under national control.

Among conservative Democrats, the treatment of the South as a rebel region was unpalatable. They favored applying to military occupation zones only "laws" governing international wars. This option provided southern whites with immunity from lengthy military overseership and congressional punitive laws concerning general property rights, which conquered rebels could not enjoy. If the conservative constitutional attitude held firm, the only upset likely to emerge from the Civil War was the suppression of secession.

Unfortunately for northern conservatives, pitfalls lined the seemingly clear pathway that this logic blazed. One unforeseen trap became visible before 1861 ended. Violators of Lincoln's blockade proclamations came up for trials in United States district courts. Judges agreed that the United States properly enjoyed the same belligerent rights as in an international conflict, including blockading "enemy" ports and taking as "prizes" ships that disobeyed the restraints, along with cargoes. Then it occurred to northern conservatives that the international war rubric was two-edged. It cut their way as a protection for southerners' property while hostilities lasted. But what of the South's status when the Confederacy gave up its experiment in rebellion? If at any time the United States enjoyed a belligerent status and won, would it not thereafter have conquerers' rights over the South, including

---

7. Frank Freidel, "General Orders 100 and Military Government," *MVHR*, XXXII (1946), 541-2; Randall, *Constitutional Problems*, 51-73; Bradley, *Miscellaneous Writings*, 147.

disposition of governmental institutions and of much private property?

This concern received succinct expression in 1862 by Judge Peleg Sprague, in a Prize Case opinion that became a lodestar for conservatives:

> An objection to the prize decisions of the District Courts has arisen from an apprehension of radical consequences. It has been supposed that, if the government have the rights of a belligerent, then, after the rebellion is suppressed, it will have the rights of conquest; that a State and its inhabitants may be permanently divested of all political privileges and treated as a foreign territory acquired by arms. This is an error,—a grave and dangerous error. The rights of war exist only while the war continues. . . . Conquest of a foreign country gives absolute and unlimited sovereign rights. But no nation ever makes such a conquest of its own territory.

The worried judge insisted that the national government acquired no new rights by suppressing rebellion. The Army's penetrations into the South merely restored prewar conditions. "No [military] success can extend the powers of any department beyond the limits prescribed by the original law," Sprague stated. Military government in the South could never "permanently" subject southern civilians to Army rule.[8]

Some conservatives took the position that the resurrection of civilian primacy was instantaneous upon Union occupation of a rebel region. As the constitutional commentator John C. Hurd described this position, it was akin to saying that the eleven Confederate states were truant schoolboys, who, forced back into class, lost nothing by their delinquencies.[9]

Most War Democrats and Republicans could accept these notions about instant reconstruction no better than conservatives

---

8. The Amy Warwick, 2 Sprague's Decisions, 147 (1862); and see *Reports of Cases Decided by Chief Justice Chase in the Circuit Court of the United States for the Fourth Circuit, 1865–1869,* ed. Bradley T. Johnson (New York, 1876 [new edn., ed. Ferne B. Hyman and H. M. Hyman, New York, 1972]), iii–xvii and *passim.*

9. John C. Hurd, *The Theory of Our National Existence as Shown by the Action of the Government of the United States Since 1861* (Boston, 1881), 262; S. S. Nicholas, *Conservative Essays, Legal and Political* (Louisville, 1867), I, 207–8.

could stomach Massachusetts Senator Charles Sumner's visions of the South as a conquered province. One popular middle recourse was the brainchild of novelist and federal attorney Richard Henry Dana, Jr. In 1863 Dana was delighted that in the Prize Cases the Supreme Court sustained the President's blockade imposition as an aspect of war powers, but later he warned Sumner, the leading exponent in Congress of the "state suicide" theory about the South, against making the Prize Cases decision a support for the senator's contention. All that the Court had said was that "enemy territory" subject to federal military control was a thin, mobile, "shifting line of bayonets."[10] Adverting to the Union capture of Norfolk, the federal attorney explained to the senator that as soon as Union troops were in "firm possession" of the city, "we were unable to condemn any property as enemy's, on the sole ground that the owner was domiciled there. When we got firm possession of all the rebel country, there was no 'enemy's territory' in the meaning of Prize Law." The Prize Cases decided only that since April 1861 there was a war on, that while it lasted "extraordinary power" came into play, and that this unusual condition ended very soon after guns ceased shooting in any battle area.[11]

Even the relatively restrained position in the Prize Cases was a great leap forward from Taney's Merryman stand two years earlier, which, obviously, he had failed to "sell" to his colleagues. Clinton Rossiter's view is justified that "The facts of history and the [constitutional] doctrine of the Prize Cases dovetail rather neatly." That dovetailing is best illustrated in Justice Grier's assertion that Confederates could not cloak themselves in the Constitu-

---

10. Samuel Shapiro, *Richard Henry Dana, Jr., 1815–1882* (East Lansing, Mich., 1961), 119–20. In the Prize Cases, 2 Black, 635 (1863), the Supreme Court unanimously agreed that after July 13, 1861, the eleven Confederate states were enemy territory in the meaning of international law, and in Ford v. Sturget, 6 Otto, 176 (1877), Chief Justice Waite stated that the Prize Cases settled that all residents of the South were liable to treatment as an enemy, without reference to individuals' sentiments. See also Quincy Wright, "The American Civil War," in *The International Law of Civil War,* ed. R. A. Falk (Baltimore, 1971), esp. 42–108.

11. According to Dana, the true status of the rebel states was "bodies politic under coercion of war." To Sumner, Feb. 5, 1866, vol. 76, Sumner Papers, Houghton Library HU. See too Justice Field in Williams v. Bruffy, 6 Otto, 187 (1877), and Choate's description of Dana in *Arguments and Addresses of Joseph Hodges Choate,* ed. F. C. Hicks (St. Paul, Minn., 1926), 77–8.

tion they were rebelling to destroy; rebels could not beg jurists "to affect a technical ignorance of the existence of a war . . . and thus cripple the arm of the Government and paralyze its power by subtle definitions and ingenious sophisms."[12]

Any way jurisprudents and partisans sliced it, the weight of northern judgment was that the 1787 Constitution spoke appropriately if implicitly to the Union's needs in military occupation matters. The area, people, and property behind rebel lines took on enemy characteristics for a time, duration unspecified, and generals set policy during this indefinite period. Awareness in the North of interaction between power and policy is plentifully visible in the close scrutiny paid to generals' behavior in the occupied South.[13]

Early in 1862 General Benjamin F. Butler established command of just-captured New Orleans. He had a limited number of troops with which to keep order in the explosive city, the South's largest. No rioting occurred, and the only civilian executed had cut down a national flag. Butler's "woman" order probably stopped behavior by females that was provoking confrontations between townsmen and bluecoats.[14] Even so, President Davis, who knew better, declared Butler an outlaw subject to hanging for violations of the laws of war. Historians have echoed Davis's theme that Butler was a prime example of the evil inherent in military rule over civilians. But within the context of contemporary standards and analogous events, Butler's policies were neither brutish nor inappropriate. Butler's conduct and constitutional ideas about occupation administration fit O'Brien's 1861 manual as well as the 1862 situation in New Orleans. Here is Butler's understanding of his own powers:

> Now, my theory of the law martial is this—that it is a well-defined part of the common law of this country . . . recognized in its proper place by the Constitution, and that proper place is the camp and garrison. Now the best definition of martial law that I have ever heard [of] was that by

---

12. Clinton Rossiter, *The Supreme Court and the Commander-in-Chief* (Ithaca, N.Y., 1951), 75–6; Grier in The Amy Warwick, 2 Black, 635 @ 670 (1863); Shapiro, *Dana*, 122.

13. Freidel, "General Orders 100," 543.

14. Cf. Carpenter, "Military Government," 496–8; Gerald M. Capers, Jr., "Confederates and Yankees in Occupied New Orleans, 1862–1865," *JSH*, XXX (1964), 405–26.

. . . [the] Duke of Wellington . . . : 'The will of the Com-
m[an]d[in]g. General exercised according to natural equity.'
. . . Thus civil government may well exist in subordination to martial law . . . when . . . efficient to the end
desired. When [not] . . . that [civil] government is . . .
to be cast aside.[15]

Freidel has concluded that the amorphousness which Butler
described created "a basic problem" because it allowed partisans
in uniform to exceed bounds.[16] But in addition to problems and
dangers arising from lack of reins on generals, this amorphousness also allowed opportunities for the creation of desirable
policies. Therefore, from the White House down, civilian politicians, the Army's nominal overlords—President, cabinet officers,
congressmen—received encouragement actually to monitor and
to direct generals' ways in occupation matters.

The Army's interactions with racial matters, however inconsistent, consistently were in every spotlight which Americans
knew how to turn on. Journalists, legislative investigating committees, presidential and intra-Army inquiries, evaluations by
private associations interested in the bodies and souls of blacks,
and, ultimately, decisions by ballot-casting citizens, thousands of
whom were in uniform, allowed little to pass by unobserved. The
result was that occupation-reconstruction policy built from existing needs rather than from pre-existing theories. By 1863 Army
experience had become an essential source of emancipation and
Reconstruction politics. Generals were as aware as politicians of
the Army's innately political role. From the War's early days,
most of the highest brass bent to civilian goals, notwithstanding
permissive constitutional doctrines that allowed generals free
rein.

Some generals professed to stand aloof from civilian politics.
George Brinton McClellan was unhappily aware that his soldiers
harbored runaway slaves in defiance of the 1850 fugitive rendi-
tion law. Many northerners including bluecoats did not love the
fugitive Negroes. But they hated disloyal slaveowners and did not
want the Army to return the refugee property.

Some of McClellan's most ardent backers admitted privately

---

15. See for opinion on Butler and his quotation, James G. Randall
and David Donald, *The Divided Union* (Boston, 1961), 515–16.

16. Freidel, "General Orders 100," 543, and see James Russell Lowell,
"Military and Martial Law," *NAR*, CII (1866), 336–7.

that the Union Army was involved in this hot political question merely by being in the South. "Every step taken [by the Army] in the rebel territory is complicating the necessity for some action to be taken by the Federal authority, as to the disposal of the slaves belonging to the rebels found in arms," wrote a field correspondent of S. L. M. Barlow's New York *World.* "I can see how the question will again and again force itself upon the [public] mind."[17]

Indeed it did. For occupation commands were places where national power, confronting rebel society, could shape it or allow its familiar configurations to remain largely unaltered. In 1861 military security needs and political ambitions inspired General John Charles Frémont, the Republican party's first presidential candidate, and General David Hunter to emancipate and arm slaves domiciled within their respective commands. Lincoln felt impelled to override both generals. His decision incurred large risks of snapping Army obedience to its civilian commander and of disrupting the internal harmony of his party. Confederate victory was the least consequence of either happening.

McClellan held views opposite to Hunter's or Frémont's. He wished the War to end without alteration from prewar race relationships and aimed to make himself President. McClellan decided military strategy and played political games involving the Army with as much enthusiasm as Butler or Frémont. But he and others such as W. T. Sherman tried to hide conservative purposes in the professional soldier's mantle of neutral innocence with respect to policy.[18]

McClellan did not fool himself or the influential civilians who were hoping to lever him into the White House. He knew

---

17. H. D. Bacon to S. L. M. Barlow, Dec. 4, 1861, Barlow Papers, HL.

18. George Brinton McClellan, *McClellan's Own Story* (New York, 1887), 149–66, 476–80, and *passim;* Warren W. Hassler, *McClellan: Shield of the Union* (Baton Rouge, 1957), *passim.* See also W. T. Sherman's pious 1865 statement to the American Peace Society: "What is this army of the United States of which you speak? It is the body of men chosen and paid by the national Government to enforce its laws and carry out its wishes. We take no part in your legislation," in Rev. A. P. Peabody, *Lessons from Our Late Rebellion: An Address at the Anniversary of the American Peace Society, May 19, 1867* (Boston, 1867), 27–8; and see John L. Peyton, *The American Crisis: Or, Pages from the Note-Book of a State Agent During the Civil War* (London, 1867), I, 294–5; Joseph Harsh, "General George Brinton McClellan and the Conservative Strategy in the Civil War" (Ph.D. diss., RU, 1970), *passim.*

that what his soldiers did about runaway Negroes was a political question of escalating importance. "Help me to dodge the nigger,—we want nothing to do with him," McClellan pleaded in 1861 with his would-be Warwick and Democratic makeweight, S. L. M. Barlow. The general wanted to win the war with the Union as it had been before Sumter. "To gain that we can not afford to mix up the negro question. It must be incidental and subsidiary," he insisted.[19]

What McClellan yearned to dodge the Army learned to embrace. Because the Union's armies were enmeshed in political decisions involving slaves and masters, dodging and embracing were both reasonable courses for generals and politicians to seek. In the opinion of nonabolitionist northerners in and out of the Army, it made increasingly less sense for Union troops to safeguard any property of disloyal southern whites, as international law required if the latter were foreign enemies, or to preserve for the South its basic labor resource by returning fugitive slaves to probably disloyal masters.

Some generals tried compromises between McClellan's static path on Army-Negro interaction and the Frémont-Hunter diversions. When fugitive slaves reached Butler's headquarters, he labeled them "contrabands of war," admitted them to his lines, and put them to work. An anonymous officer on McClellan's staff, a man of moderate antislavery but not abolitionist leanings, expressed his disgust with these deviant and contradictory patterns that were occurring on the highest field-command levels:

> . . . the people have . . . been brought to regard the Constitution . . . as an almost invincible barrier to [the nation's] acknowledged welfare, and all have set themselves to finding a method by which to overreach it. Some have said that, for once, it should be disregarded; others, that all slaves being *prima facie* freemen, the army should not stop to inquire as to the reality of their condition, but that they should be allowed to proceed as fugitives. . . . Much has been said of the "war power," and that, under the plea of the national safety, there should be worked out a national emancipation. And thus it would seem as though we

19. Nov. 8, 1861, Barlow Papers, HL; and on expressions of McClellan's concern with what other commanders were doing, *OR*, ser. I, vol. VIII, 552–3.

are all trying to elude the Constitution by constitutional evasions.[20]

Little profit exists in censuring or praising by quotation of theories the courses generals chose to take, or expressing shock at military impacts into civilians' lives and institutions. The only attitude that Union Army commanders in the South could *not* afford about belligerent New Orleans ladies or runaway slaves was to have no attitude. Democracy's test in the 1860's was what it has been since 1941—the creation and maintenance over long periods of time of an enormous military institution capable of harming the enemy but simultaneously restrained from injuring civilian values. In this sense, the Civil War's impact was not merely temporary or restricted to the South's occupied areas. It was nationwide and permanent.

While generals enforced military law within the North's Army and under martial law oversaw occupied regions in the South, Union soldiers sometimes imposed martial law on individuals in the North as well. When national armed forces temporarily replaced or supplemented civilian authorities as when arbitrary arrests occurred of civilians by soldiers, it was common to say that a condition of martial law existed. Technically, even the suspension of habeas corpus did not automatically bring in martial law. Suspension did create a third zone of law in Civil War America, that in terms of generals' freedom of action was dissimilar to those in occupation areas southward. In the South, martial rule automatically displaced all civil law, authorities, institutions, and procedures save as Union commanders wished them to function. Not so northward. Coexistence under martial-law conditions

---

20. An Officer in the Field, *The Coming Contraband: A Reason Against the Emancipation Proclamation Not Given by Mr. Justice Curtis* (New York, 1862 [reprinted in *Magazine of American History,* extra number 49, 1916]), 5–6. See also Benjamin R. Curtis, *Executive Power* (Boston, 1862), reprinted in George Ticknor Curtis, *Constitutional History of the United States from Their Declaration of Independence to the Close of Their Civil War,* ed. Joseph Culbertson Clayton (New York, 1896), II, 668–86. Note that a year passed after Sumter before Congress enacted an addition to the Articles of War prohibiting military or naval personnel from serving as slave catchers; *SAL,* XII, 354. Randall, *Constitutional Problems,* ch. 15, describes the "steps toward emancipation" that led in confused and overlapping manner toward an uncertain end.

of civilian and military courts, as in Merryman's instance, prevailed, not exclusive military substitutions.[21]

As with military-law and military-occupation questions,
Americans expected precision in the definition and performances
of martial law, and were puzzled that exactness never emerged.
"The public is sensitive to all questions of power," historian
George Bancroft warned Lincoln.[22] After Sumter, martial law
intrusions were the most visible power manifestations which the
majority of northerners encountered.

Puzzlement is understandable. Americans were heirs to a
tradition which was unsympathetic to martial-law exercises. But
unstudied antipathy against martial law required balancing with
a parallel jurisprudential tradition in Britain and here which
sustained martial-law employments. On this score, Professor
Randall's judgment deserves quotation: "a series of decisions may
be cited sustaining executives who have initiated martial law and
declaring that, where the action was *bona fide,* the courts would
make no inquiry into the causes thereof."[23]

As the Civil War progressed, it became understood that
unlike military law, martial law was not susceptible to neat
cataloguing. "Nothing in the Constitution or laws can define the
possible extent of any military danger," wrote War Department
Solicitor Whiting, to whom Lincoln paid close attention. "Hence it
is worse than idle to attempt to lay down rules of law defining the
territorial limits of military operations, or of martial law, or of
captures and arrests."[24]

It required enormous pressure to push Whiting, Lincoln, and
their peers in administration, politics, and the law into agreement
with Whiting's sweeping doctrine of the plenary character and
primacy of martial law. The presence of disloyalty and the inadequacy and irrelevance of civilian weapons against it, along with
military occupations, provided the pressure. Merryman's imprisonment during the War's first weeks typified the continuing

---

21. Randall, *Constitutional Problems,* 142, on the openness of the
courts in the Merryman situation, and Indiana Judge McDonald's comment: "Our Federal Court is sitting; but inter arma, silent leges." In
"Hoosier Justice: The Journal of David McDonald, 1864–1868," ed. D. O.
Dewey, *IndMH,* LXII (1966), 185.

22. Quoted in Lorraine A. Williams, "Northern Intellectual Reaction
to Military Rule During the Civil War," *Historian,* XXVII (1965), 339.

23. Randall, *Constitutional Problems,* 147.

24. Whiting, *War Powers* (1871), 169.

problem, and supplied dialogue for derivative political and constitutional confrontations. But the basic fact was that disloyalty was not a theory. Northern prosoutherners could lose the War for the North in spite of battlefield advances, as in the mass rioting in 1863 against conscription.[25]

Seen in this light of the inadequacy of on-hand ways to punish disloyalty, the Lincoln-Taney confrontation centered less on whether President or Congress properly could suspend the habeas corpus writ privilege than whether America's Constitution and laws offered relevant means to meet immediate problems. Taney insisted that only existing procedures centering in civil courts were appropriate for the nation's salvation. Lincoln denied the claim. The President's view prevailed with respect to Merryman, because his "war powers" umbrella included martial law as a primary strut.

The upshot was that increasing numbers of Lincoln's Republican colleagues in Congress and his countrymen generally came to comprehend that in 1861 there were not enough institutions or laws appropriate to cope with the danger which disloyalty posed. There was not enough government, in short, to allow Lincoln any recourse between doing nothing and employing martial law. The latter resort involved other dangers, however, including a ballooning of executive power, a mushrooming of military pretensions over nominal civilian superiors, and an apparent decline in the vitality and relevance of states' actions. Alternatives to martial law had to come into being, or else the Union was lost through overdoses of military remedies for civilian ills.

History records that there was swift understanding of the existence of as well as the need for alternatives. "There is nothing . . . that necessarily implies that due process of law must be judicial process," Thomas M. Cooley wrote later.[26] The applicability of these words to 1861 is evident from examination of the alternatives both to military commission trials under conditions of habeas corpus writ suspension or martial law, and to civil treason trials, that Lincoln and his cabinet and congressional coadjutors

---

25. Stanton's report, Feb. 1862 in *M&P*, VI, 102–3. On 1861 hiatus, see Halleck, *International Law*, 775–841.

26. Weimar v. Bunbury, 30 Mich. 203 (1874), in Alan Jones, "Thomas M. Cooley and the Interstate Commerce Commission: Continuity and Change in the Doctrine of Equal Rights," *PSQ*, LXXXI (1966), 607; cf. R. M. Spector, "Lincoln and Taney: A Study in Constitutional Polarization," *AJLH*, XV (1971), 199–214.

dredged up from ignored recesses of the Constitution and the laws.

President, Congress, and courts commenced searching for better ways to provide simultaneously for internal security and for the operations of the world's most open political democracy; for the coexistence of the nation's mass Army and the Constitution's Bill of Rights; for states' vitality and nation's needs. The results of the political pressures generated by military law, military occupations, martial law, and writ-privilege suspensions were remarkable adaptations to the War and Reconstruction. In the form of War-born institutions, procedures, and statutes, these adaptations eventually permitted the Union Army to amass the strength it required to crush Confederate forces, occupy the South, and hold disloyalty adequately in check in northern states, while maintaining and even improving Americans' political and civil liberties and the vigor of the check-and-balance and federal systems.

Chapter XI

Years of Precision—
Congress

The enlargement of liberty's dimensions during a civil war through creation of coercive or punitive statutes and bureaucratic apparatuses is an exceptional pattern in any nation's history. Civil War and Reconstruction Americans achieved this rare design. To be sure, the aim was less liberty than effective military and internal-security policies. Liberty enlarged because government's effectiveness increased and because there occurred also what the Handlins described as "the confining of force within rules of procedure." The Handlins noted that "the process of securing consent [to this confinement] was itself a mechanism for the accommodation of differences; and necessities accepted by free choice blurred the abstract distinction between compulsion and permissiveness."[1]

Antidisloyalty laws and bureaucratic-judicial procedures initiated by the 37th and 38th Congresses partially to sustain the legislators' devotion to the separation of powers created the first interlacings in this pattern. Eventually some of these innovations also made more certain civilian control over the armed forces, more restrained and rational the conduct of military law and military occupations, and more infrequent the resorts to martial law. Last, new bridges between nation and state came into being,

---

1. Oscar and Mary Handlin, *The Dimensions of Liberty* (New York, 1966), 47.

with effects enduring into our time. According to one insightful anonymous analyst of 1871, this "shifting of power [was] the first revolution effected by the late civil war and the legislation of reconstruction." This power shift "established more definite and better understood relations—whether better or worse is not here the question—between the general and state governments" and between citizens and all levels of government.[2]

What follows is an effort to trace wartime developments in Congress leading to this impact.

Congress entered the antidisloyalty arena during its historic midsummer 1861 session, and it rarely bowed out during the ensuing decade. Along with holdovers, the 37th Congress was composed of men elected with Lincoln. Secession flaccidity, the Bull Run reverse, and exposures of prosouthern sentiments among northern officials had shaken congressmen. Dispirited, they approved Crittenden's July 1861 resolution that the Union's sole war aim was reunion, not racial upset; a gratuitous hobbling in that context. But despite agreement on this commitment to inequality, many congressmen shared Lincoln's resilient patriotism and sensitive educability.

History taught other men nothing. Antiwar Democrats never understood the dynamic impact of a massive war on a plastic society. But even Republicans who came to the Civil War with relatively flexible constitutional attitudes, looked backwards for values to retain more than for Edens to discover. Further, though Republicans operated on the conviction that the Constitution could function even in war, they wished Whiggishly that Congress, not the President, should direct operations, as in prewar decades. Considering these constitutional assumptions, historical understandings, and institutional affections, it is not surprising that congressmen were unwilling to give center stage to executive or judicial officers more than was necessary.[3] Republican con-

---

2. "The Shifting of Power," AM, XXVII (1871), 665; Leonard P. Curry, *Blueprint for Modern America: Nonmilitary Legislation of the First Civil War Congress* (Nashville, 1968), *passim*.

3. A tenacious tradition continues that "Radical" Republican congressmen asserted legislative leadership as part of a determined effort to win legislative primacy. I believe that in 1861 virtually all congressmen assumed that Congress's leadership already existed. Cf. James MacGregor Burns, *The Deadlock of Democracy: Four-Party Politics in America* (rev. edn., Englewood Cliffs, N.J., 1963), 70–3; Sidney George Fisher, *The Trial of the Constitution* (Philadelphia, 1862), *passim*; Timothy Farrar, "Ade-

gressmen were thus caught up in tensions and loyalties transcending but never totally divorced from partisanship that centered on the legislature as the historical locus of leadership. Lincoln's party colleagues on Capitol Hill were sensitive to popular and political demands for national functional innovations ranging from aid to farmers to freedom for rebels' slaves. At the same time, these lawmakers revered property as states defined it; were state-rights nationalists, in Professor Paludan's phrase. Antipathy to "class" legislation, bureaucracies, and unbalanced budgets were typical congressional "sets." With remarkably few exceptions, congressmen of all parties and factions were loyal Congress-men. They resented deeply any judicial interferences with national aims of the sort Taney essayed in the 1861 Merryman hearing or extralegal plots by antiwar Democrats to take Congress over, and reacted sharply against executive surprises like Lincoln's 1864 pocket veto of the Wade-Davis bill.

Such attitudes required appropriate institutionalization before they could determine intergovernmental relationships, and in certain terms, Congress was better prepared than the President or the courts to accommodate the war's ways. Congressional instruments, especially its committees, proved adequate without much tinkering to produce the initial, lurching investigations and legislation "for the emergency."[4]

With respect to disloyalty, congressmen had to get over the same obstacle to effectiveness that troubled Lincoln and his executive counselors; that the Constitution, institutions, and laws punished retrospectively only. After Congress learned that constructive preventatives were wanted, it began to provide alternatives to futile but hazardous treason statutes and prosecutions, and fruitful but perilous martial-law impositions. The search led

---

quacy of the Constitution," *NE*, XXI (1862), 51–73; G. G. Van Deusen, "Some Aspects of Whig Thought and Theory in the Jackson Period," *AHR*, LXIII (1960), 305–22.

4. James G. Randall, *Constitutional Problems Under Lincoln* (rev. edn., Urbana, Ill., 1951), 77. On Congress generally, see Joseph Cooper, "The Importance of Congress," *RUS*, LIV (1968), 53–68; on Congress's self-consciousness in 1861 and after, see Albert Gallatin Riddle, *Recollections of War-Times: Reminiscences of Men and Events in Washington, 1861–1865* (New York, 1895), 111, 143; Michael Les Benedict, "The Right Way: Republicans, Congress, and Reconstruction" (Ph.D. diss., RU, 1970), *passim;* Herman Belz, *Reconstructing the Union: Theory and Policy During the Civil War* (Ithaca, N.Y., 1969), chs. 2, 4, 7–8; Phillip Paludan, "John Norton Pomeroy, State Rights Nationalist," *AJLH* (1968), 275–93.

Congress to explore middle regions of offenses and punishments between the unruffled civilian heights that Taney insisted were habitable even in wartime, and the murky martial depths that Union generals probed in the South as occupation commanders and in the North as executors of martial law. Many congressmen found Taney's topography too unrealistic to respect. But Lincoln's route proved to be too rugged and too uncertain for the nation to risk traveling frequently, without better guidelines than existed when the War began.

Soon after convening, the 37th Congress impeached the United States district judge for Tennessee, West H. Humphreys, for numerous offenses, including treason. Humphreys had favored secession and became a judge in the Confederacy's courts, dealing harshly with stubborn southern Unionists. In June 1862, when his trial came due in the Senate, he did not appear. After brief proceedings, the Senate found Humphreys guilty of all major charges. It ordered him removed from office and barred from future government employment. For the first time a federal judge stood impeached and convicted for treasonable activities. Now it was up to the federal courts to deal with Humphreys by means of a judicial trial for treason. But no trial ever occurred.[5]

The House later excluded Ohio's Representative Alexander Long as a result of disloyalty charges. Thereafter, Congress used exclusion rarely. But the latent power was there.

In 1863, Democrats angry with the Emancipation Proclamation toyed with a plan to seize control of the House by excluding Republican representatives. Their notion was to have the sympathetic Clerk of the House, Emerson Etheridge, leave key Republicans off his roll at the convening of the 38th Congress in December. Democrats would exploit the confusion and northern whitelash, reverse the administration's emancipation policy, and restore McClellan to top command and thence to the White House. Then the War could end on southern terms with respect to slavery. Lincoln sniffed out the plot, however, and let slip news of his knowledge. Fearful, the schemers gave up their project.[6]

---

5. John Oscar Tobler, "The Constitutional Controls of Congress over the Federal Judiciary" (Ph.D. diss., JHU, 1939), 128–9; CG, 37 Cong., 2 sess., 2277, 2942–53. Loyalty-oath requirements initiated since 1861 already barred Humphreys from holding a federal job.

6. According to House Speaker Schuyler Colfax, Lincoln warned him of the plot during the first days of December 1863. The President wrote, "The main thing, Colfax, is to make sure you have all our men there [in

It occurred to some congressmen that impeachment might be a better way than exclusion to get at colleagues who fit some definition of disloyalty. But here too roadblocks were in the way. A weighty tradition had it that the Constitution allowed impeachment only of civil officers, and that congressmen did not fit that category.[7] Instead of relying on any of these uncertain procedures, congressmen resorted to a mix of old and new devices to bear on alleged disloyalty among officials and legislators. It included investigatory committees and statutory loyalty-oath tests.

The Constitution required that all national and state officials take an oath to uphold it, but specified a text only for the President. The first Congress's first law (June 1, 1789) was an oath of office for lesser officials: "I . . . do solemnly swear . . . that I will support the Constitution of the United States."[8] Within a month after Sumter, without conference, every cabinet officer required subordinates to add some statement of intention to remain loyal to the Union. Then Congress assembled. The antidisloyalty concern produced, without debate, a loyalty-oath statute, reflecting the pervasive belief that secession had occurred because the nation lacked adequate links between government, citizens, and officials.[9] On August 8, 1861, Lincoln signed into law the

---

Congress]. Then if Mr. Etheridge undertakes revolutionary proceedings let him be carried out on a chip, and let our men organize the House. If the worst comes to the worst a file of 'Invalids' [convalescent combat veterans] may be held convenient to take care of him." Colfax to ? (probably John Hay), Dec. 8, 1863, Nicolay Papers, LC. See also C. Gibson to Missouri's Governor Gamble, Jan. 6, 1863, Gamble Coll., MoHS, on an earlier manifestation of similar concerns, and for background, Hans L. Trefousse, *The Radical Republicans: Lincoln's Vanguard for Racial Justice* (New York, 1969), 264; Belz, *Reconstructing the Union*, 151 n., 173–4 n.; and by the same author, "The Etheridge Conspiracy of 1863: A Projected Conservative Coup," *JSH*, XXXVI (1970), 549–67.

7. H. M. Hyman and M. Borden, "Two Generations of Bayards Debate the Question: Are Congressmen Civil Officers?" *Delaware History*, V (1953), 225–36. Despite this precedent, in 1864 Congress required its members to subscribe the same loyalty oath that in 1862 it had prescribed for civil officials; H. M. Hyman, *Era of the Oath: Northern Loyalty Tests During the Civil War and Reconstruction* (Philadelphia, 1954), ch. 3.

8. Note also that the Constitution forbade any "religious test" ever to be required as a prerequisite for public office. Art. VI; *SAL*, I, 23; H. M. Hyman, *To Try Men's Souls: Loyalty Tests in American History* (Berkeley and Los Angeles, 1959), chs. 1–5.

9. Charles Fenton Mercer, *An Exposition of the Weakness and Inefficiency of the Government of the United States* (London, 1863), 8, is only one of many arguments to this effect.

new oath for persons in any way connected with the central government. It pledged future loyalty to the United States plus renunciation of any contrary state resolution or statute. In addition to dismissal from public service, false subscriptions incurred such penalties for perjury as judicial processes might impose.

It is the essential quality of 1861 that this promise of future loyalty should have appeared to be revolutionary, and that its abjuration of contrary state statutes or resolutions seemed to bridge the federal system in manner to prevent future secessions. "Here, you will observe, is a most important and striking provision," enthused Peleg Sprague to a grand jury. "This [oath requirement] is a most explicit renunciation of the deadly heresy of a paramount state sovereignty."[10]

Whatever the 1861 formulation did to state sovereignty theories, apparently it accomplished almost nothing against disloyal practices. Despite subscriptions by officialdom and, subsequently, by contractors, passport applicants (passports were a Civil War innovation), steamboat pilots, and others who required favors or licenses from the government, the statute neither exposed traitors nor punished perjurers. Concern continued about disloyalty; a concern which certain congressional committees fostered and broadcast.

One result was that a tougher, "ironclad" test oath became law in July 1862. It required signers to swear to their past as well as future loyalty. The 1862 oath test applied to all federal (civil and military) officers and almost anyone else having business with national agencies. In occupied areas, southern white (Negroes needed to sign no Union loyalty oaths) had to swear to the oath (often amended unofficially to meet cases) as a preliminary to intercourse with occupation authorities. Since Union military government officials controlled travel and trade, mail, commodities priorities, turncoating for battle captives, office-holding and suffrage, militia membership, and the practice of licensed professions, the extension southward of the ironclad oath ran subscriptions into the millions.

Early in 1864, after hectic debate, congressmen imposed the ironclad-oath test on themselves. Still later, having already bound

---

10. Peleg Sprague, *What Is Treason? A Charge . . . to the Grand Jury* [*Mass.*] . . . *March, 1863* (Salem, April 1863), 7. SAL, XII, 326, has the August 1861 oath text. Discussion is in Hyman, *Era of the Oath,* ch. 1.

federal grand and petit jurors by oath requirement, the Congress required attorneys in the nation's courts to subscribe the ironclad-oath test as a condition of practice.

Several states, especially along the Unionist-slaveholding border, many counties, and an impressive number of municipalities also enacted "treason" statutes and loyalty-oath laws. Loyalty tests commonly faced state officials, voters, teachers, preachers, licensed tradesmen, and professionals.[11] Though grown extensive in a very short time, the congressional and state loyalty-oath laws failed to comfort patriots. A proposition was widespread that pro-Confederates in northern jurisdictions were numerous and unpunished. Perjuries were frequent. False swearers sometimes faced military trials. But to the indignation of Union soldiers and northern patriots, none of the many perjurers came to judgment before national civil courts, as the 1861 and 1862 oath laws specified.[12] Congress continued to search for ways to prevent and punish disloyalty.

Between 1861 and 1863, legislators successfully sidestepped the overprecise treason clauses of the Constitution and the too-rigorous death penalty specified in the 1790 treason statute. Congress substituted property confiscation statutes. These involved money fines, permanent loss of slaves and other personal property, and alienation of real-estate titles during but not beyond the lifetimes of proved offenders. In effect, confiscation laws, like loyalty-oath tests, were Congress's first efforts to reconstruct the rebel states' future electorates.

Confiscation was a familiar belligerent right under concepts of international wars, with domestic antecedents stretching back to the American Revolution. This comforting familiarity was not enough for the President and many congressmen, however. The application of confiscation to domestic rebels required creation in Congress of the same sort of duality that the Supreme Court resorted to in the Prize Cases. Congressmen were willing to see to rebels' deaths in combat as a matter of domestic, "municipal" law.

---

11. See Hyman, *Era of the Oath*, chs. 1–2; Edward D. Tittman, "The Exploitation of Treason," *NMHR*, IV (1929), 128–45; W. N. Trenerry, "The Minnesota Rebellion Act of 1862," *Minnesota History*, XXXV (1956), 1–10; H. H. Wubben, "The Maintenance of Internal Security in Iowa, 1861–1865," *CWH*, X (1964), 401–15. Note that for some states these were the first steps in the direction of regulating trades and professions.
12. H. M. Hyman, "Deceit in Dixie: Northern Reaction to Southerners' Evasions of Union Loyalty Tests," *CWH*, III (1957), 65–82.

But disloyalists' property, especially land titles, required greater delicacy. Therefore in the 1861 and 1862 Confiscation Acts they specified that penalties were to come into play only after federal courts brought in guilty verdicts in individual litigations. In short, Lincoln and the Republican majority in Congress did not tear themselves away from constitutional and criminal law guidelines long antedating the Civil War. So far as procedures to determine accused disloyalists' guilt were concerned, whatever the novelty of the subject matter, except temporarily in military occupation zones the Congress held antidisloyalty laws to unradical patterns centering on enforcements in and by national courts.[13]

On the surface, the President and Congress devised a neat partnership in which the national judiciary was to join as an essential element. Executive agencies, especially the Army, would deter disloyalty by martial-law applications in the North and in military-occupation areas of the South. At the same time, Congress's new antidisloyalty statutes would penalize persons immune from military jurisdiction. Resulting punishments of disloyalists after trials in federal courts would, it was hoped, dissuade other straddlers from falling the wrong way, without requiring creation of costly, distasteful coercive bureaucracies.

But in almost all respects the new statutes proved to be duds, reflecting the patchwork mixture of sovereign and belligerent powers in the laws, and the distaste almost everyone involved felt concerning enforcement. Known miscreants remained untouched by perjury, treason, or confiscation prosecutions.[14] Conflicting, half-comprehended imperatives tore at congressmen of both parties and at executive and judicial officers, and produced what appeared to be timid behavior with respect to enforcing the confiscation laws. Eager to punish rebels and suppress disloyalists, willing to expend treasure and, eventually, even to free slaves if necessary to kill the rebellion, congressmen and other officials simultaneously revered property, as states defined it. This intense,

13. Randall, *Constitutional Problems*, chs. 12–14; SAL, XII, 284, 317, 589, 696; U.S. v. Griener, 26 Fed. Cas. No. 15, 262 (1861), 36; U.S. v. Greathouse, *ibid.*, No. 15,254 (1863); J. Syrett, "The Confiscation Acts: Efforts at Reconstruction During the Civil War" (Ph.D. diss., UWis, 1971), *passim*.

14. Rev. W. S. Dutton, "Ought Treason Against the United States to Be Punished?" NE, XXIV (1865), 778; Edward McPherson, *The Political History of the United States of America During the Great Rebellion* (2nd edn., Washington, 1865), 387–8; David R. Wrone, "Abraham Lincoln's Idea of Property," *Science and Society*, XXXIII (1969), 54–70.

tenacious, compelling property-consciousness was magnified because of lawyers' rise to prominence in politics.[15]

Once enacted the confiscation laws received little enforcement. Partly this was due to the small number and overburdened work loads of government lawyers, who by terms of the statute would prosecute. More important, federal attorneys from Bates down never pushed confiscation prosecutions very hard because they distrusted proceedings (known as "in rem" actions) against property; Bates positively obstructed confiscation proceedings when he could. Further, during most of the War the great part of rebels' property was untouchable in portions of the South still unoccupied by Union troopers. And complications kept intruding. Property confiscations conflicted with presidential pardons and amnesty, with the uncertainty surrounding the legal nature of the War, with emancipation, and with the treason law still on the books. All of which justified Von Holst's verdict that these punitive laws, "brought to the surface by the civil war . . . [led] to a whirlpool of conflicting conclusions. . . . [D]octrines of constitutional law . . . were not clearly stated and sharply defined by reason of the civil war, but were rather obscured thereby."[16]

Why this confusion at a time when professionals in the law were heightening their influence on every level of government, and when the absence from Congress of the seceded southern delegations eased passage of deterrent and punitive statutes? Part of the reply is that the literature of law was silent, incomplete, or contradictory on many matters which the War dredged up. Further, the sense of urgency that hung over Washington pushed men into hasty decisions. Considering the novelty of many ques-

---

15. D. G. Morgan, *Congress and the Constitution: A Study of Responsibility* (Cambridge, Mass., 1966), 133; Mark DeWolfe Howe, *Justice Oliver Wendell Holmes: The Proving Years, 1870–1882* (Cambridge, Mass., 1963), 201 and ch. 8; Maxwell Bloomfield, "Law vs. Politics: the Self-Image of the American Bar (1830–1860)," *AJLH*, XII (1969), 306–23. Miss Patricia Allan, a doctoral student of Professor W. R. Brock, University of Glasgow, participated in my RU seminar, 1969–70. Her seminar papers, to be part of her Glasgow dissertation, shed new light on these complex questions.

16. Hermann Eduard Von Holst, *The Constitutional Law of the United States of America*, tr. Alfred Bishop Mason (Chicago, 1887), 156–7; Alfred H. Kelly and Winfred A. Harbison, *The American Constitution: Its Origins and Development* (3rd edn., New York, 1963), 412–16; Henry D. Shapiro, *Confiscation of Confederate Property in the North* (Ithaca, N.Y., 1962); Glenn M. Linden, "Congressmen, 'Radicalism,' and Economic Issues, 1861–1873" (Ph.D. diss., UWash, 1963), 216–22.

tions with which legislators dealt, and the increased volume and complexity of public business, no wonder slippage occurred.

Still further, the energetic new breed of congressmen who were busily and successfully reshaping Congress's committee structure in a manner to hold military leaders to obedience and to win from the President a full share in the nation's governance did not give a high priority to overseeing confiscation proceedings. They employed their suddenly freed legislative and investigatory facilities to deal with other War questions culminating in civilian controls over the military, internal security, emancipation, conscription, and Reconstruction. Congress attended also to long-delayed nonwar matters which the South's secession opened for solution, including judicial circuits, national court jurisdictions, tariff, banking, homestead, and revenue, along with entrepreneurial encouragements.

Another factor leading to ambiguities in confiscation law enforcement was that in 1861 a substantial number of congressmen were novices at legislative construction. Many Republicans who were elected with Lincoln in 1860 possessed neither parliamentary deftness nor expertness in Congress's internal machinery. Stated another way, party cohesion adequate to elect men *to* Congress did not simultaneously produce party leaders or party discipline *in* Congress. Time was needed for them to emerge. Meanwhile, imperfect statutes resulted.

The secession of the southern congressional delegations magnified these factors. Seceders included many of Congress's experienced parliamentarians and constitutionally minded men. Each of the twenty-two southern senators who went with their states had served in Congress more than ten years, fourteen had extensive legal training, six had been judges. The resulting upsets within Senate and House internal governments left leadership in the hands of few veterans, eventually enlarged the power of the Speaker in the House and the influence of party caucuses in the Senate, and decreased states' reins over their congressmen as well as legislators' competence in constitutional complexities.[17]

---

17. James A. Garfield, "A Century of Congress," *AM*, XL (1877), 60–2; Morgan, *Congress and the Constitution*, 133–4; David J. Rothman, *Politics and Power: The United States Senate, 1869–1901* (Cambridge, Mass., 1966), ch. 2; Richard Bolling, *Power in the House; a History of Leadership in the House of Representatives* (New York, 1968), 46, 48.

Struggling to cope with novel subjects like confiscation, martial law, and loyalty tests about which "experts" knew little, novice lawmakers had simultaneously to master lawmaking machinery which veterans found balky, and which had been in uncomfortable evolution long before the Lincoln Administration moved into the seats of power.

In Woodrow Wilson's estimation Congress's rise in importance after Sumter resulted from "an immensely increased efficiency at [internal] organization, and . . . the redoubled activity consequent upon the facility of action secured by such organization."[18] These improvements centered in the standing committee and caucus structures of both Houses and in the functions and power of the House Speaker.

Dramatic prewar contests of choice of a Speaker had reflected sectional tensions and tests of narrowly balanced party strength rather than arrangements for achieving comprehensive legislation. Speakers had exercised relatively little influence over legislative traffic; committee service lacked attractiveness except as a means to fulfill constituents' narrow desires; seniority bore little influence. Then secession provided Republicans with a clear majority in Congress. There was opportunity to achieve legislation of national purpose and impact, from war matters to banking, homestead, and tariff. Granting that partisan wants never ceased to be politicians' imperatives, national needs leaped to first priority. A member of the first wartime House, Albert Gallatin Riddle recalled that his colleagues of 1861 swiftly accustomed themselves to "great measures" in place of pettifogging factionalism, gained "confidence in themselves as legislators of the Great Republic," and proved themselves "equal to the extraordinary demands upon them." Of such men, George Julian recalled that they "were not the intellectual equals of the famous leaders who figured in the great crisis of 1850, but they were of a different and generally a better type. They were summoned to the public service to deal with tremendous problems, and [were] lifted up and ennobled by the great cause they were commissioned to serve." Admitting errors, Julian asserted nevertheless that by the decade's

---

18. Woodrow Wilson, *Congressional Government: A Study in American Politics* (15th edn., Boston, 1913), 47.

end the congressional work begun in 1861 had taken hold "on the very springs of our national life."[19]

When the 37th Congress assembled in July 1861, instead of the inconclusive ballots for a Speaker so common during preceding years, the new House selected Galusha Grow of Pennsylvania for the post on its first vote. Despite the bright auguries for effective party leadership and discipline within the Congress, Grow was not able to do more than keep pace with swift currents. He lent the Speakership to the committee and caucus operations which his party mates were conducting, especially with respect to committee chairmen and, because of his command of the Rules Committee, to agenda priorities. Defeated in the Democratic electoral resurgence of 1862, Grow turned over to Schuyler Colfax a Speakership filled with potentialities for channeling the power of the House, and Colfax and his successors made the Speakership the single most powerful congressional office.[20]

Even under Grow, however, more than ever before the Speaker became a controller of legislative traffic and a counterweight against centrifugal committee development. The committee evolution intertwined with the rise in the Speaker's powers so that after Sumter each nourished the other.[21]

Prewar congresses had worked primarily through floor debates. Behind scenes, Congress had operated by means of many single-purpose temporary "select" committees, relatively few standing committees, and resort to the Committee of the Whole. Congressmen served ordinarily on several short-lived select committees at one time. Long before Sumter a few semipermanent

19. George W. Julian, *Political Recollections, 1840–1872* (Chicago, 1884), 355; Riddle, *Recollections*, 69. And see as modern restatements, Neill MacNeill, *Forge of Democracy: The House of Representatives* (New York, 1963), 29; Bolling, *Power*, 29–50.
20. James T. Dubois and Gertrude S. Mathew, *Galusha A. Grow: Father of the Homestead Law* (Boston, 1917); M. P. Follett, *The Speaker of the House of Representatives* (London, 1909), 97; George B. Galloway, *History of the House of Representatives* (New York, 1961), 41–8.
21. Follett, *Speaker*, 241–2; Lauros G. McConachie, *Congressional Committees: A Study of the Origins and Development of Our National and Local Legislative Methods* (New York, 1898), 93–4, 108; Nelson W. Polsby, "The Institutionalization of the House of Representatives," APSR, LXII (1968), 144–68. Note how easily Edward McPherson became House Clerk after exposure of the "Etheridge conspiracy" resulted in dismissal of that conservative incumbent; Trefousse, *Radical Republicans*, 264. Note also that the 1864 revision of House rules gave the Speaker control over CG reporters, who thereafter were considered House officers rather than journalists. See FMSB218, Box 160, N. P. Banks PP, LC.

standing committees had taken form, reflecting especially the increasing size of the House and the complexities of public questions. Standing committees allowed the accumulation of expertness. Although by more recent gauges seniority was weak and unbinding, the growth of standing committees made them particular preserves of congressmen from safe districts. Chairmen of these relatively stable groups gained autonomy, patronage, and prestige. The Civil War encouraged the trend toward standing committees, diminished the resort to "select" committees, and emphasized the importance of seniority. Riddle recalled of the 1860's: "Everything now depends on the committees. If a man has no place on an important committee, he can secure no place on the floor [of the House], unless his constituency stand by him for a series of years, a thing which seldom occurs at the North. In the growth of the public business, there is a growing necessity to depend more and more upon the standing committees."[22]

Some prewar "joint" committees, with membership from both houses, had dealt primarily with routine or ceremonial tasks, and were almost always temporary. For example, conference committees were charged with reconciling the variant texts of a bill. After 1860 the increase in the number of inexpert legislators increased the need for harmonization. Beyond this factor, the Civil War magnified the importance of joint committees generally. Some became standing committees of particular value for investigating legislation and watchdogging executive operations. These joint standing committees allowed concentration of information, expertness, and talent and avoided duplication of effort or energy. Joint standing committees created after Sumter inquired into such basic matters as the conduct of the war, emancipation, the restoration of the seceded states, and southern outrages.

Today Senator Fulbright's judgment is accepted as a truism that Congress's investigating power, including punishment of re-

---

22. Riddle, *Recollections*, 222–3; and see Bolling, *Power*, 35; *Precedents of the House of Representatives of the United States*, comp. Asher C. Hinds (Washington, 1908), IV, 951. In mid-July 1861, the House authorized a select investigating committee to sit through a recess of Congress in order to inquire into Army contracts; *ibid.*, V, 111–112. Wilson, *Congressional Government*, 102, described America's government since the 1860's as "government by the chairmen of the standing committees of Congress." But see Von Holst, *Constitutional Law*, 191 n.; Emile Boutmy, *Studies in Constitutional Law, France, England, United States*, tr. E. M. Dicey (London, 1891), 78–81.

calcitrant witnesses by contempt proceedings, is "perhaps the most necessary of all the powers underlying the legislative function."[23] But in 1861 such processes were novel and imprecise. In the absence of reliable literature on the theme, Americans of the Civil War years knew vaguely that Parliament's committee investigations during the seventeenth century had provided the seed for American colonial practices; that with independence, states' legislatures assumed investigative powers including punishment for contempt; and that the Continental Congress, the Confederation Congress, and Congress under the 1787 Constitution also exercised these powers. Thereafter, despite Congress's occasional employments of investigative committees, little clarification occurred. Protections due to witnesses, including a right to refuse testimony for fear of self-incrimination, created a gray area. Another uncertain subject involved a committee's capacity to punish defiant witnesses for contempt beyond the time span of that particular Congress. Similarly, the limits of committees' jurisdiction over executive and judicial personnel were unclear, while the capacity of courts to review committees' decisions was an unasked question.

In 1857, Congress had provided some statutory underpinning for investigative functions. Contrary to British practice, a law of that year specified that a witness was punishable beyond the life of that legislature if he refused to appear, to respond, or to produce demanded papers.[24] With the 1857 law to inspire confidence, and with experience gained from its inquiry into the 1859 John Brown raid, Congress entered the Civil War armed with an augmented investigative weapon, without curbs on committeemen's conduct save those derived from political imperatives.[25]

Considering this boundlessness, and in light of the fact that procedural standards of the 1860's in civil courts were shockingly

---

23. William E. Fulbright, "Congressional Investigations: Significance for Legislative Process," *UChiLR*, XVIII (1951), 441; Alan Barth, *Government by Investigation* (New York, 1955), ch. 1; Ada C. McCown, *The Congressional Conference Committee* (New York, 1927), 12 and *passim*.

24. *SAL*, XI, 155; In re Chapman, 166 US, 661 (1891), sustained the statute. See Bernard Schwartz, *A Commentary on the Constitution of the United States* (New York and London, 1963), I, ch. 4, for a recent survey.

25. Kilbourn v. Thompson, 103 US, 168 (1881), which probably limited by exercise of judicial review the investigating function and contempt powers of Congress, lay two decades in the future. Of course, Barenblatt v. U.S., 360 US, 109 (1959), suggests that these problems are not yet solved. See Telford Taylor, *Grand Inquest: The Story of Congressional Investigations* (New York, 1955), 1–57.

low by modern standards, it is not remarkable that some investigating committeemen should have played the fool and ogre, or that the Republican majority in Congress should have exploited the rise in investigating committee significance. But despite the tenacious contrary tradition, the uplift in committee thrust and over-all congressional vigor did not result in abrasive contests between legislators, President, and jurists.

The first standing joint investigating committee in Congress's history was the Civil War's famous Joint Committee on the Conduct of the War. Always maintaining useful personal and political ties with leading committeemen, Lincoln let the Committee look where he preferred not to—into reverses at Ball's Bluff and both Bull Runs, the Fort Pillow massacre, tactics at Petersburg, McClellan's Peninsular strategy, and the Army's Negro-return policy.[26] Lincoln never shielded from Committee inquisitors generals who displayed the arrogance of the sword toward civilian superiors. Until 1863 the War Department lacked adequate internal machinery to perform such delicate tasks on its own. The political polarization of commanders such as McClellan meant that any disciplining by Lincoln had to seem partisan. Beyond lay the greater cost that the Army's officer corps would split into hostile factions if the Commander-in-Chief played open politics with chief commanders.

Accepting the critic's public role, Congress's committees, including the Joint Committee on the Conduct of the War, helped Lincoln to conduct the War far more than they hindered him. In the essential matter of civilian domination over the military, the Committee prevented contests between the Army's nominal civilian overlords and those in uniform. The result was that the President's overlordship never came up for grabs. And, finally, the Committee served as an essential bridge between Capitol Hill and White House, of a sort almost totally lacking before the War.[27]

In most congressmen's priorities, surveillance over public fiscal health and morality was second only to civilian domination

---

26. Hans L. Trefousse, "The Joint Committee on the Conduct of the War: A Reassessment," *CWH*, X (1964), 5–19; Benjamin P. Thomas and Harold M. Hyman, *Stanton: The Life and Times of Lincoln's Secretary of War* (New York, 1962), ch. 12.

27. "The complete concert of action now existing between the Congress and this [War] Department leaves no room to doubt that any legislation required to attain efficiently the desired purpose [of military victory] would be given." Stanton to Ethan Allen Hitchcock, March 11, 1862, owned by and used with permission of Mr. John S. Stark, Cincinnati.

of the military services. Primarily, this meant concern about contracts involving the armed forces. The 37th Congress and its successors made themselves "huge committee[s] of ways and means," reported Representative Riddle. Both the House Ways and Means and the Senate Appropriations Committees gained the right to report bills at any time, and by 1865, divided the money-raising and the money-allocating responsibilities into two committees each. These committees developed bookkeeping checks over the burgeoning executive departments, especially the Army, Navy, and Treasury, involving minute specifications of the ways Congress expected its appropriations to be spent, in place of lump-sum allocations common in prewar years.[28]

While standing committees scrutinized government agencies and budgets, special investigating committees looked hard at contractors who received the money. The 37th Congress's Committee on Contracts quietly unearthed frauds, indiscretions, and irregularities involved in equipping the Union's early forces; the Joint Committee on the Conduct of the War reinforced the contract-conscious colleagues as it probed the financial dealings of generals and contractors.[29]

These developing committee forms, functions, and powers won contemporary congressional, presidential, and public approval, and scholars of Congress's evolution echo the judgment.[30] Connected in effectiveness, House and Senate Republicans and their War Democratic coadjutors left antiwar Democrats in grumbling minority positions on committees. The wartime spur to committees thus helped to break the prewar deadlock of democracy on Capitol Hill.

Theoretically there were more pleasant and symmetrical ways to achieve this essential improvement than the unsystematic committee growth. But a century ago no one knew what they were. Indeed, throughout the War and Reconstruction, the appeal to perfection was irrelevant. Few Republican voices—certainly not Lincoln's—demanded it. In Congress as in the White House, the goals were adequacy, effectiveness, and promptness. Republican makeweights were less fearful of Lincoln's imposition of

---

28. Riddle, *Recollections*, 42; Joseph P. Harris, *Congressional Control of Administration* (Washington, 1964), 56–7.

29. Virgil C. Stroud, "Congressional Investigations of the Conduct of War" (Ph.D. diss., NYU, 1954), 138–51; House Report No. 2, 37 Cong., 2 sess., I.

30. McConachie, *Congressional Committees*, 242; see ns. 24, 25, *supra*.

martial law in the North or of military governments in the South than of his caution in suppressing disloyalty in both sections and in controlling the Union's generals.

In this context, Republican congressmen's often-professed concern over the rise in executive functions and powers was aimed less at the President's positive acts (although the rhetoric of the criticism made these the ostensible target) than at his apparent failures to act effectively and swiftly. By contrast, Democrats' diatribes against alleged excesses of congressional and executive power meant opposition to the exercise of all effective power.

Stated in Godkin's words, Congress was unawed by the "glamour thrown round the presidential office by the war." Let Democrats excoriate the President's internal-security policies as threats to liberty and state rights. The Republicans' job was different.[31] It was to spur the President to greater vigor, to continue through congressional investigations the monitor's function over the military, and to provide sharper antidisloyalty and Army-control weapons for President and Congress to use.

Adequate provision did occur. Achievement of workable ways proved to be possible because of the awareness of President and legislators concerning these wants and the responsiveness of Congress's invigorated internal machinery.[32] Proudly self-conscious of their worth—"If the rebellion should be crushed, Congress will have crushed it," said Fessenden—the lawmakers accepted themselves in the dual role of state's men and nation's representatives, with more attention going to the nation than ever before.[33] It was all quite different from, and better than, the numb weakness of the secession winter.

---

31. E. L. Godkin, in *The Nation* (April 5, 1866), 423–4.

32. Stroud, "Congressional Investigations," *passim;* McConachie, *Congressional Committees,* 38, 99, 174–5, 313, 318.

33. See Francis Fessenden, *Life and Public Services of William Pitt Fessenden* (Boston, 1907), I, 254; Galusha A. Grow letter, May 16, 1862, in New York *Tribune,* May 20, 1862; John Y. Simon, "Congress Under Lincoln, 1861–1863" (Ph.D. diss., HU, 1960), esp. ch. 11 and conclusion (used with permission). William Riker, "The Senate and American Federalism," *APSR,* XLIX (1955), 452–69, noted the development of a centralized federalism due to the increased prestige and power of senators. During the sixties earlier trends grew more definite of senators refusing to resign on instructions from states' legislators, rejecting states' instructions, and responding more to Senate than states' imperatives. Further, the practice grew of senators canvassing directly their states in search of votes, leading to lessened dependence upon local vote-getting machineries.

Chapter XII

Shaping the Topography of War

Until they learned better, the President and congressmen were inclined to let military stars govern the Union's armies. In 1861 generals complained that the Bull Run debacle resulted from lack of adequate discipline among the citizen-soldiers, and the indiscipline resulted because Washington civilians were diluting military law. Since appeals from courts-martial death sentences could by statute and tradition travel from regiments to the White House, the salutary effect of swift capital punishments following serious offenses was lost, according to uniformed commanders.

Still in their period of apprenticeship, Lincoln and War Secretary Simon Cameron lent support in Congress to legislation aimed at satisfying the generals. A law of December 24, 1861, gave division commanders final determination in appeals from death sentences imposed on soldiers by courts-martial.[1] Then Lincoln's understanding increased of the fact that, as he described it in mid-1862 to a French friend of the Union, "With us every soldier is a man of character and must be treated with more consideration than is customary in Europe."[2]

---

1. *SAL*, XII, 330.
2. Abraham Lincoln to Count Agénor-Étienne de Gasparin, Aug. 4, 1862, in *Collected Works of Abraham Lincoln*, ed. Roy P. Basler *et al.* (New Brunswick, N.J., 1953), V, 355; hereafter cited as Lincoln, *Works*.

In this context "more consideration" was a July 17, 1862 amendment to the 1861 statute. The amendment required the President to review every death sentence which courts-martial imposed on soldiers and each major prison term which military commissions set for civilian offenders against military-law or martial-law regulations.[3] In addition to Lincoln's and Congress's sensitivity to the civilian politics involved with the Union Army, the new legislation reflected also the wartime ingathering to Washington of accomplished lawyers. For the executive branch, especially the War Department, the effects were profound.

Cameron's successor as Secretary of War, Edwin M. Stanton, who took up the portfolio in February 1862, was central to this development. One of the nation's most effective trial and corporation lawyers, Stanton recruited some outstanding colleagues for the War Department.[4] With Congress's support in the form of Senate consent to appointments, House approval of appropriations, and joint accord in legislation, combined with Lincoln's encouragements, these lawyers devised administrative apparatuses and procedures more likely to achieve civilian control over generals and justice for soldiers and civilians than anything that existed before Sumter or until World War II.

The vexatious questions of appeals from courts-martial death sentences and military commission prison sentences illustrate the impact of these experts on Army institutions. In order not to alienate soldiers or their concerned families, the lawmen around Lincoln insisted that despite the Army's growth, appeals from military tribunals had to be in civilians' hands. This point of view received its most forceful expression from War Department Solicitor William Whiting. He worked out with congressmen the July 1862 law returning to the President final appeal determination.

Whiting was also trying to develop himself into one of the Department's several civilian monitors over the Army. He had two weapons. The more important was the swift accumulation of what he described as "military jurisprudence," which outstripped Army officers who were lawyers and befuddled those who were not. Second, Whiting was the Army's chief defense counsel. If officers were sued for alleged excesses over civilians, Whiting

---

3. *SAL,* XII, 598.
4. See comment in *ALRev,* XVI (1882), 236.

might choose not to defend them in civil courts unless they had co-operated with him in courts-martial and military-commission appeals.[5]

Stanton and Whiting were joined in the War Department's legal secretariat by patent attorney Peter Watson, former cabinet officer Joseph Holt, constitutional scholar Francis Lieber, and lawyers-become-generals Ethan Allen Hitchcock and Henry W. Halleck. From 1861–65, no university law faculty or private firm in the nation equaled this association of lawyers. Halleck and Hitchcock knew better than to shake too abruptly or roughly the regular soldier's ways or the War Department's bureaucratic habits, which alone made the volunteer masses an effective armed horde. Slow and cautious steps were all that was possible. But as emergencies arose, the necessity of action became manifest.[6]

In the spring of 1862 the conferees pressed upon friends on Capitol Hill the need to centralize and standardize practices of military justice in courts-martial and military commissions. The administrative instrument they elected to employ was a long-moribund Army office, the Judge Advocate General, which had never enjoyed much prestige among uniformed careerists. Its incumbent was unable to rise to the War's demands, and, further, was a McClellan supporter.

On July 17, 1862, as part of the statute which afforded the President appeal jurisdiction from courts-martial and military commissions, Congress established within the War Department a new Judge Advocate General and Holt accepted the post. Despite his martial title Holt remained a civilian, although in 1864 Congress gave him the rank of brigadier general. By terms of the 1862 statute, Holt enjoyed direct access to the President in order to lodge with Lincoln appeals from courts-martial and military commissions.

Holt's responsibility was to make military and martial law administration more uniform, humane, and effective, so that both military justice and martial efficiency might increase, and fast

---

5. William Whiting, *The War Powers of the President and the Legislative Powers of Congress, in Relation to Rebellion, Treason and Slavery* (2nd edn., Boston, 1862), ix; see too pertinent ms., "Proceedings of the War Board," Stanton Papers, LC.

6. B. P. Thomas and H. M. Hyman, *Stanton: The Life and Times of Lincoln's Secretary of War* (New York, 1962), 152–63, 368.

enough so that Union soldiers and their politically potent home-front connections should not create political crises. And last, Holt was to be one of several civilian sentries within the Army yet over it who President and Congress hoped would control the uniformed giant.

Holt won fair success. The Kentuckian had in his favor firm backing from Lincoln, Stanton, and Republican congressional makeweights, plus lengthy political experience and prestige from his career in Buchanan's lame-duck cabinet. After assembling a staff of subordinates into a Bureau of Military Justice in the War Department, and assigning judge-advocates to all field commands, Holt imposed a reporting procedure within the Army. Thereafter, transcripts of every court-martial and of military-commission proceedings involving civilians came to his desk. His peculiar access to the President increased possibilities for executive clemency in deserving cases.[7]

Army field commanders complained that Holt was too gullible and Lincoln too lenient; that bluecoats' discipline was deteriorating while disloyal civilians were growing arrogant. As a result of the sensitivity of Republican congressmen to the Army's wants a law received Lincoln's signature on March 3, 1863, that permitted corps commanders to be the final appeal level on death sentences imposed by courts-martial.[8] Perhaps Lincoln welcomed relief from the awful decisions involved in these appeals, and from the political pressures they generated. With information gained from Holt's reports, he could still interfere in exceptional instances and did so. By this time almost all field commanders had accepted essentially civilian limits on the military establishment. McClellan's brand of arrogance, a symptom of early days, was out. To be sure, among professional Army officers—and by 1864 West Pointers had most top commands—the habit of autonomy was difficult to alter for field commanders. What changed was the adequacy of military and martial law procedure, of the

---

7. William F. Fratcher, "History of the Judge Advocate General's Corps, United States Army," *Military Law Review*, IV (1959), 89–122; Ransom H. Gillette, *The Federal Government: Its Officers and Their Duties* (New York, 1871), 304–9; SAL, XII, 598, XIII, 144.

8. SAL, XII, 735. Ohio's Senator Wade wrote General Rosecrans, Feb. 9, 1863: "I believe [it is] just such a law as you desired should be passed. . . . I shall therefore advocate passage of such a law." Rosecrans Papers, UCLA. The statute applied also to military commission verdicts, but its stress was on courts-martial.

process due to soldiers or civilians numbering eventually into the millions, who became subject to soldiers. Civil War statutes improved these procedural standards. The civil lawyers in Congress, the War Department, and the White House became aware of evils in military law's ways and corrected them, and, uneasy over the limitlessness in military occupation commanders' powers, tried to confine them by such means as the bureaucratic reform in the JAG office.[9]

A second essential to raised procedural standards was the creation by the legalists in Washington of a standard, applicable literature on military law, intended to diminish sharply the erratic characteristic of earlier War months. Soon after he became Judge Advocate General, Holt commenced circularizing Army commands with "opinions" he and his staff rendered in the most significant courts-martial and military-commission appeals reaching Washington. By presidential orders, these opinions were assembled, printed, and circularized throughout the Army. They became the standards employed in thousands of courts-martial and military-commission proceedings. Holt's catechismal arrangement made military law manageable for mere company commanders.[10] In addition to his personal satisfaction in his achievement, Holt was pleased that on July 28, 1866, Congress made his rank and office permanent.[11]

Francis Lieber's contribution is more important. Early in the War he established close connections with the War Department and with prominent Republican congressmen, especially Sumner. At Stanton's and Halleck's requests, and with the cooperation of an Army board headed by Ethan Allen Hitchcock, Lieber worked to lessen the confusions Union field commanders felt about their powers as occupation officials in the South, especially concerning guerrillas in border areas. Two years after Sumter, Lieber presented to the Army his famous "Instructions for the Government of Armies of the United States in the Field."

---

9. Robert Brugger, "Military Law on Trial: The Impact of the Civil War on a Juridical Institution" (M.A. thesis, UMd, 1967), ch. 5, and *passim.* (Used with permission.)

10. Joseph Holt, *Digest of Opinions of the Judge Advocate General of the Army* (Washington, 1865), hereafter cited as Holt, *Digest.* Legal reaction is in *ALRev,* I (1867), 559; and see Brugger, "Military Law," 121–3.

11. *SAL,* XIV, 332. See Holmes's estimation, *ALRev,* I (1867), 559–60.

As General Orders 100, the War Department transmitted Lieber's "Instructions" to every Army command; Holt ordered all field legal officers and commanders to employ it.

Lieber's pioneering compilation provided Americans—and, later, Europeans—with history's most precise foundation on which to build military-occupation policies. Lieber cautioned commanders to honor humanitarian restraints as tactical situations allowed, to eschew "military oppression," and to defer to considerations of "justice, honor, and humanity, virtues adorning a soldier even more than other men, for the very reason that he possesses the power of his arms against the unarmed."[12]

Last of this trio of significant contributions to the literature on the military's place and power in America—a literature that would have lessened danger, acrimony, and heartbreak had it existed in 1861—was Whiting's *War Powers*. Like Holt's *Digest*, Whiting's "book" appeared piecemeal. Soon after Sumter, Whiting commenced pamphleteering in support of Lincoln's arbitrary arrests. At the request of "private friends" who probably included Lincoln and Sumner, Whiting turned to more systematic analyses of constitutional problems as they arose, including arbitrary arrests, confiscation, conscription, emancipation, and Reconstruction. When he became War Department Solicitor, Whiting was privy to facts so strikingly different from legal theories he had taught at Harvard Law School that he published his scattered writings as a book.

Whiting's *War Powers* was a manual for government lawyers, a store of arguments for the supply of Republican political campaigners, and a cornucopia of views about international and "municipal"—i.e., domestic—laws of war. Whiting was an ardent Republican and emancipationist. He built on Holt's and Lieber's work designed for the Army, but reached out to Republican-Union campaigners and citizens. Whiting intended his *War Powers* to

---

12. *OR*, ser. 3, III, 148; Frank Freidel, "General Orders 100 and Military Government," *MVHR*, XXXII (1946), 552–6; Charles E. Magoon, *The Law of Civil Government in Territory Subject to Military Occupation by the Military Forces of the United States* (Washington, 1902), 11–34; Brugger, "Military Law," 125. Note that General Orders 100 served American Army officers in the Philippines thirty-five years after Appomattox; see Root's testimony in House Report No. 596, 57 Cong., 1 sess. In 1865, Holt's guide advised the uniformed law officers of the Army that military occupation situations ran according to "the will of the general who commands the army." Holt, *Digest*, 75.

bridge the military and home front, to maintain soldiers in subjection to civilians, and to keep Republicans in charge of politics.

Unlike Sidney George Fisher, who also preached a doctrine of popular sovereignty as exhibited in elections, but who argued a need to alter existing ways, Whiting tied his constitutional theories to existing constitutional and political institutions, sanctifying what the President and Congress were and had been doing, including emancipation and confiscation. Fisher was a constitutional theoretician. Like Holt and Lieber, Whiting was a propagandist with portfolio whose product became policy.

Joel Parker, the Royall Professor of Law at Harvard, condemned *War Powers* as "a tissue of miserable sophistry, bad law, and if possible, worse logic."[13] But the Supreme Court's 1863 Prize Cases decision and 1864 Vallandigham verdict lent implicit support to Whiting's pragmatic stress. He appealed more than his critics because he stressed the law's capabilities rather than limits. "The Constitution, as interpreted by our lawyers, is as great a puzzle as the old problem of motion was to the Greek sophists," wrote the editor of the Boston *Commonwealth* in an appreciation of *War Powers;* "Mr. Whiting will leave with posterity the great credit of having discovered that *solvitur ambulando,* or 'Jump up and try' method, which is swiftly transforming the compromises of the Constitution into statutes of freedom."[14]

After publication of this literature and creation of Holt's new office, most Union Army officers chose to perform in a manner conformable to prescriptions set down by the executive aides. But not all did. Congress and President tried to understand what was still wanted in order the better to exert civilian control. One way was for Washington to regularize Army provost marshals' functions.

Traditionally, regular Army field unit commanders assigned officers temporarily as provost marshals to enforce discipline and to guard soldier-prisoners. After Sumter, in almost every field headquarters, provosts swiftly transcended simple military policemen's functions. In northern areas, provosts' liquor- and prostitu-

---

13. Whiting, *War Powers* (1862), prefaces and introductories, *passim,* esp. 11–13, 17–21, 27–32; Parker, *The War Powers of Congress, and of the President* (Cambridge, Mass., 1863), 59; and see John N. Pomeroy, "Recent Works on the United States Government," *Nation,* XIII (Oct. 12, 1871), 242.
14. Aug. 21, 1863 (with thanks to Herman Belz).

tion-control regulations (which often were results of civilian reformers' pressures) resulted in military-commission trials of civilian violators of camp regulations, and mixed the Army with civilian politics. Apprehensions of bounty-jumpers, deserters, and draft evaders brought provosts into accords with northern civilian police, resulting in arrests of civilians who assisted Army male-factors. Moving southward, provosts' duties included charge of refugee Negroes and captive Confederate soldiers, intelligence accumulation (runaway slaves and would-be turncoat rebels were rich sources of information), and counterespionage and anti-guerrilla operations. Some high-level provosts in Army of the Potomac headquarters commanded regiment-size military police units and employed undercover agents and *agents provocateurs* recruited from among Union soldiers, rebel turncoats, and private detectives in security work ranging from sabotage prevention to blockade enforcement.[15]

Busy field provosts also administered their unit commanders' camp regulations, division or corps commanders' military govern-ment orders, and Washington's directives on confiscation, con-scription, disfranchisement, emancipation, and Reconstruction (the last in accord with Lincoln's proclamation of December 8, 1863). In order to carry out these duties, provosts had to decide which white southerners should enjoy opportunity to swear loyalty to the Union or be a nonjuror; which, having sworn, could receive mail, buy or sell scarce commodities and at what prices, employ freed Negro labor at what wages and other conditions, receive travel passports, keep draft animals, practice licensed professions or trades including preaching, and vote and hold office in restored "loyal" local governments. Where appropriate, provosts assumed charge of municipal fire and police depart-ments and home-guard units. In areas where civilian judges abandoned local courts or Union provosts closed them, some commanders created provost courts.[16]

---

15. David Sparks, "General Patrick's Progress: Intelligence and Security in the Army of the Potomac," *CWH*, X (1964), 371–84; Edwin C. Fishel, "The Mythology of Civil War Intelligence," *ibid.*, 344–67.

16. Wilton P. Moore, "The Provost Marshal Goes to War," *CWH*, V (1959), 62–71; *Inside Lincoln's Army: The Diary of Marsena Rudolph Patrick, Provost Marshal General, Army of the Potomac*, ed. David Sparks (New York, 1964); and Harold M. Hyman, *To Try Men's Souls: Loyalty Tests in American History* (Berkeley, 1959), ch. 7, describe the evolution of the provost's stature after Sumter.

This unplanned augmentation of provosts' functions became rehearsals for reconstructions. In some field commands, provosts prescribed wages, hours, and housing conditions for freedmen. Where northern humanitarian-missionary organizations essayed to raise Negroes' literacy levels and technical skills, provosts protected buildings and participants—*if* local provosts and their commanding officers were sympathetic to the efforts.[17]

Reports flowing into Washington during 1861 and 1862 illuminated these developments in occupied southern areas. Halleck, Hitchcock, and other West Pointers in the top War Department echelons knew that the regular Army tradition, which Union Army officers imitated, was to assign lesser officers and convalescent, wounded, or superannuated veterans as provosts. They also became uneasy that field-command arrangements insulated provosts from their control. On every level from corps to company, provosts were subordinates of unit officers, not of the War Department and White House. Efforts by Holt to impose a measure of uniformity into the military justice picture by centralizing JAG administration suggest that Lincoln, Stanton, and heads of concerned congressional committees were aware of the need to cut directly from the Potomac to basic field levels. But surgery had to be very deft. Clumsy or importunate interference with field commanders' subordinates exposed the Lincoln Administration to charges of political interference. Battle results rated higher than occupation administration.

Unless generals openly defied presidential and congressional prerogatives, as Frémont and McClellan chose to do, Washington waved a small stick. In March 1863 Halleck advised General Rosecrans that "experience has proved that all matters of local police should be left to the civil authorities, and that Provost Marshals should be charged only with matters of military police and that their powers should be confined within narrow limits. This is necessary to avoid abuses of power."[18] Necessary perhaps; but not achievable, events indicated.

In April 1864 there was an exchange between General Sherman and Holt. Sherman was at Chattanooga, ready to begin

---

17. Willie Lee Rose, *Rehearsal for Reconstruction: The Port Royal Experiment* (Indianapolis, 1964), ch. 10; Frank L. Byrne, " 'A Terrible Machine': General Neal Dow's Military Government on the Gulf Coast," *CWH*, XII (1966), 5–22.

18. March 20, 1863, Stanton Papers, LC.

his risky thrust toward the Atlantic. Saboteurs harassed the expedition. Sherman's military commissions pronounced death sentences on captured guerrillas. Some of these transgressors claimed a right to appeal to the President. In a report to Holt, Sherman invoked Congress's 1863 statute which gave generals final review power:

> The question arises daily and I expect to execute a good many spies and guerrillas . . . without bothering the President. For many spies and villains escape us in the time consumed by trial, review and remission to Washington, and we all know that it is very hard for the President to hang spies even after conviction, when a troop of friends follow the sentence with earnest and ex parte appeals . . . Our . . . detachments have so little faith in the punishment of known desperadoes that a habit is growing of 'losing prisoners in a swamp,' the meaning of which you know. . . . [U]nless a legal [i.e., a swift] punishment can be devised you will soon be relieved of all such cases.[19]

When Sherman wrote this firm statement the Judge Advocate General's staff was active and Holt's opinions, Lieber's codifications, and Whiting's pamphlets were circulating. Lincoln's amnesty and Reconstruction proclamations were issued. Sherman, however, acted on the premise that his provosts were "his" to order and that civilian offenders, having "appealed to war . . . must abide its rules and laws."[20] So long as Sherman and other generals won battles, and accepted civilian direction in other basic policies such as emancipation, they received no complaint from War Department or White House.

By the close of 1862 the McClellan position dramatically lost backing in the Army, and conservative spokesmen employed increasingly an antimilitaristic idiom that they had muted while "Little Mac" was in the saddle. Fervent appeals issued from the antiwar Democracy to check the new uniformed nobility. Under Republican domination it was allegedly corrupting the northern

---

19. April 6, 1864, in *MH*, XIX (1914), 35.
20. *The Sherman Letters: Correspondence Between General and Senator Sherman from 1837 to 1891*, ed. Rachel Sherman Thorndike (New York, 1894), 230.

character already corroded by democracy's excesses; corruption the deeper because bluecoats, including black bluecoats, were ruling southern white civilians.[21]

Antimilitary yearnings of this sort won unsatisfying returns. Evidence was too obvious that the Union Army was composed not of dictatorship-bent militarists but of a fair cross section of American society with numberless connections to the home front. Even critics of northern democracy complimented the North's soldiers on their continuing commitment to democratic ways. Therefore it made sense for Republican leaders to reply to conservatives that the Union Army was sustaining the Constitution, not ruining it,[22] and therefore deserved trust as an occupation force as well as a combat force.

Once McClellan was gone from the Army, Lincoln accepted the thesis that military-occupation commanders enjoyed near-plenary power within their lines. The highest American courts affirmed this view.[23] But judges enjoyed the luxury of waiting for history to sort itself out. By contrast, Lincoln had to employ power, not precedents. With respect to the Civil War field commanders, Congress, courts, and President understood the wartime reality.

Lincoln came to the heart of the matter when a jurisdictional tangle between Army and Treasury Department field personnel snarled Union operations in occupied Florida. The President sent his private secretary John Hay to untie knots and soothe ruffled tempers. But Lincoln saw to it that Hay passed on to General Gillmore, the commander, this encouragement: "It is desirable for all to cooperate, but if irreconcilable differences of opinion shall arise [between military and civilian officials], you are master."[24]

What distinguished Lincoln's role in these matters was his

21. See Charles Astor Bristed, "The Probable Influence of the New Military Element on Our Social and National Character," *United States Service Magazine*, I (1864), 594–602; S. S. Cox, *The Nation's Hope in the Democracy—Historic Lessons for Civil War* (Washington, 1864), *passim.*
22. J. W. Edmonds, "What Shall Be the End?" *CM*, II (1862), 2; George Augustus Sala, *My Diary in America in the Midst of War* (London, 1865), I, 288–9.
23. Lincoln, *Works*, VI, 487–8; on courts, Scott v. Billgerry, 40 Miss., 119 (1866); Dow v. Johnson, 100 US, 158 (1866); U.S. v. Diekelman, 92 US, 520 (1875).
24. Jan. 13, 1864, J. G. Nicolay Papers, LC.

quiet insistence on mastering the uniformed "masters." To do so by direct confrontations of the Frémont or McClellan sort involved Republicans and War Democrats in fearful party strains and could make the Army a partisan cat's-paw. Instead Lincoln encouraged his White House coterie and congressional supporters to continue improvising appropriate administrative and institutional checkreins of the sort represented by the Judge Advocate General's office; and to increase the supply of procedural guides that Holt, Lieber and Whiting assembled for field officers to study and, it was hoped, to obey.

The process is illustrated in the "provost court" and "provisional court" developments. Union military commanders rarely closed local civil courts in occupied rebel regions, although martial-law proclamations suggested that all civil authorities should be replaced. Vacancies occurred more frequently on civil law benches when incumbents became refugees, than from policies of Union officers. Faced with the requirement to govern as well as to conquer, and under orders to govern within states' law codes and institutional frameworks as much as possible, Union generals resorted to provost courts to substitute for absent or unacceptable judges and justices of the peace, on the lowest civil judicial levels. By 1863 the Holt-Lieber-Whiting literature had filled in some hiatuses about occupation matters that had existed in 1861. Generals took comfort that this literature sanctioned the provost court expedient.[25]

By mid-1864 more than four thousand provost judges were holding courts in the occupied South. Employing for enforcement provost marshal detachments from local field or garrison commands—in some instances provost judges were simultaneously marshals—judges dealt in both civil and criminal law and accepted Negro complaints and testimony. Theoretically provost courts were not supposed to supplant courts-martial or military commissions or serve as civil courts of record. Some did, however, whether from judges' ambitions or ignorance is unclear. In any event, it appears obvious why provost judges should have been erratic. They were unconstrained by any uniform code (save as they employed the laws of the state where they held court), were

---

25. Jecker v. Montgomery, 13 Howard, 515 (1851); Leitsendorfer v. Webb, 20 Howard, 176 (1857); Mechanics and Traders Bank v. Union Bank, 22 Wallace, 276 (1874); Planter's Bank v. Union Bank, 16 *ibid.*, 483, and esp. 504.

uninformed by declaration of precise Reconstruction goals until the President's December 8, 1863, proclamation, and were never guided by Congress. Further, they were often tempted by opportunities for self-enrichment inherent in confiscation and trade-control proceedings, and were cursed by overfrequent transfers. At best provost judges were useful expedients. The worst is suggested by the judgment of War Department investigators who combed carefully through the provost court mélange in occupied Louisiana and concluded "that no military commander should be permitted to establish such courts."[26]

Lincoln and his coadjutors agreed. As Washington came to see matters, provost courts suffered from the same defects as the provost marshals. Both were insulated from central direction and instruction. In civil lawyers' estimations provost courts involved the further offense of placing laymen in positions where only persons trained in the mysterious science of the law should perform. Therefore, in Louisiana, the showcase state of developing executive Reconstruction policies, Lincoln proclaimed in October 1862 the establishment at New Orleans of a United States Provisional Court, directly under his authority. He named as judge Charles A. Peabody of New York. Although Peabody was a civilian, his court was as much a creation of the President's war powers as the armies that were penetrating the South. Salaries for Peabody and expenses of his court came from War Department funds. Lincoln was bent on a procedural, not a constitutional change—but sometimes the two were inseparable.

The fact that the Provisional Court novelty came into existence at all indicates that Lincoln was aware of the deficiencies of the ad hoc provost courts. The most impelling reason for establishing the Provisional Court was to set civilian judges, even of quasi-military character, over wholly martial provost judges. Louisiana's Provisional Court was to be a complete court of record, satisfying to civil lawyers at the White House, War Department, and Congress, and was to accept jurisdiction of matters that before the War were docketed in federal district and circuit courts and state and local tribunals. But most important, the Provisional Court innovation created an appeal level from decisions of the provost courts. Civil courts had no tradition of

---

26. Smith-Brady Commission ms. report, 125–7, RG 94, NA; Stanton to Grant, May 19, 1865, in Secretary of War Executive Letters, LXIX, 21, RG 107, NA; Holt, *Digest*, 386.

accepting appeals from military courts of any sort, and the contrary Milligan decision was still far in the future.[27]

Judge Peabody made no attempt to obfuscate the martial, executive, exceptional constitutional base of his court. In two cases before him in 1864 involving New Orleans civilians, one white and one Negro, on charges respectively of murder and arson, Peabody heard defense counsels' arguments that he had no jurisdiction and that Louisiana state law, forbidding Negro testimony, must govern. Further, the lawyers claimed that the Provisional Court was not legitimate, for Congress had not created it and no appeal to higher civil courts was possible from its decisions. Peabody admitted that in prewar years the national government "in the ordinary walks of life" did not touch one out of a hundred Americans. But civil war had vastly increased the work in which federal officials were engaged. The Union soldiers' occupation of Louisiana was analogous to that of any foreign army in enemy land. Bluecoats had brought into Louisianans' lives "the living federal power," including new courts. Thereupon Peabody declared guilty and sentenced both defendants.[28]

---

27. Elizabeth Joan Doyle, "New Orleans Courts under Military Occupation, 1861–1865," *Mid-America*, XLII (1960), 185–92; Lincoln, *Works*, V, 467–8, VIII, 400–5; Frank Moore, *Rebellion Record* (New York, 1869), X, 341–6; on July 28, 1866, Congress stipulated that the Provisional Court's records should be transferred to the U.S. District Court of Louisiana, by then restored; *SAL*, XVI, 344. Certain sufferers from the Provisional Court's decisions argued that the 1866 statute created the same appeal succession that a federal district court enjoyed. The result was the case of The Bark Grapeshot, 9 Wallace, 129 (1870), which sustained the Provisional Court's wartime decisions, and by implication, the legitimacy of the Provisional Court.

28. U.S. v. Louis; U.S. v. Reiter, in *ALReg*, XIII (1864–65), 534. Quotations are from Peabody, *United States Provisional Court for the State of Louisiana: Its Warrant and Jurisdiction* (New York, 1864), 25 (also in AHA, *AR* [1896]). Peabody relied heavily in this opinion on the findings of his court's prosecuting attorney, George D. Lamont. Lamont admitted that the Provisional Court was a war-born novelty in American jurisprudence made necessary when Union soldiers swept away all Louisiana courts. Of course "the authority of this court is derived from the military power alone," Lamont stated. No matter that it was a civil war that was raging and not one between nations. War was war. Its "accidents" formed history; "Its actual existence is a fact in our domestic history." Lamont, *Argument in the Cases of August Reiter . . . and Jean Louis . . . on the Jurisdiction of the [Provisional] Court, and the Principles of the Military Law* (New York, 1864), 6–7.

Subsequently, "regular" jurists agreed with arguments in favor of the President's authority to create the Provisional Court.[29] But Lincoln's first purpose was to create by appeal procedures a higher degree of civilian control over the Army's provost courts, and in this respect the Provisional Court was not successful. After its establishment neither the Provisional Court judges nor Washington managed to direct provost courts in Louisiana.[30] The Provisional Court was less useful in winning civilian mastery over generals than the JAG office, the Holt, Lieber, or Whiting compendia, or the congressional investigating committees. Its story reflects primarily sensitivity in Washington to the need for mastery.

Nevertheless, by the close of 1863 more precision and conformity existed within the Army with respect to civilian Washington's wishes than was conceivable during the first year after Sumter fell. During that first year Generals McClellan and McDowell assigned provost marshals to return runaway Negroes to masters, no matter how openly disloyal the latter might be; Frémont and Hunter armed southern Negroes; and Butler straddled. In 1863, Congress had added to the Articles of War a prohibition against any Army personnel enforcing the 1850 fugitive slave law, which as a national law had immediately wider if less dramatic application than Lincoln's edict on emancipation.[31] Antidisloyalty statutes and the Holt-Lieber-Whiting compendia offered Army and conscription officials improved procedural

---

29. Salmon P. Chase, Chief Justice of the United States, speaking in 1867 to members of the North Carolina bar, stressed that by conquering any portion of the rebel domain "[t]he national military authorities took the place of all ordinary civilian jurisdiction or controlled its exercise. All courts, whether state or national, were subordinated to military supremacy, and acted, when they acted at all, under such limitations and in such cases as the commanding general under the directions of the President, thought fit to prescribe. Their process might be disregarded and their judgments and decrees set aside by military orders. . . . The military tribunals, at that time, and under the existing circumstances, were competent to the exercise of all jurisdiction, criminal and civil, which belongs under ordinary circumstances to civil courts." In *Reports of Cases Decided by Chief Justice Chase in the Circuit Court of the United States for the Fourth Circuit, 1865–1869*, ed. Bradley T. Johnson (New York, 1876 [new edn., ed. Ferne B. Hyman and H. M. Hyman, New York, 1972]), 133. See too Chase's specific approval of the Louisiana Provisional Court, in The Bark Grapeshot, 9 Wallace, 129 (1870).

30. Smith-Brady, 125–7.

31. *SAL*, XII, 354; *OR*, ser. I, VIII, 522–3.

standards to employ in dealing with northern soldiers and southern whites and Negroes; Congress's committees and the Judge Advocate General's personnel allowed Washington's civilians to check with fair precision on performance.

This improved reporting and procedural system, combined with the new instructional media, suggest that President and Congress were successfully controlling the swollen military establishment. Other supports for this judgment emerge from a brief glance at the unique phenomenon of soldiers voting in state elections. Soldier-voting kept state legislators and congressmen keenly sensitive to intra-Army developments, for citizen-soldiers from each state could be counted on to express opinions by ballot on the adequacy of civilian monitorship. Conversely, generals had to keep weather eyes open for states' reactions to uniformed behavior. Congressmen—almost always states' men—were sure to look critically on generals' ways and means when they affected adversely the lawmakers' uniformed constituents.[32]

The 1787 Constitution (Article I, section 4; Article II, section 1) states that with respect to elections for congressmen "The times, places, and manner of holding elections . . . shall be prescribed in each State by the Legislature thereof"; with respect to presidential electors, "each state shall appoint [the proper numbers of electors] in such manner as the Legislature may direct," but Congress may determine the time for choosing them. Congress had left qualifications for voting such as age, residence, and property wholly up to each state and its subdivisions to define. Before the Civil War men physically absent from voting districts simply lost the right to vote. Early in the War, several states' legislatures decided that their soldiers in the field could vote by absentee ballots for congressional candidates and Presidential electors, though not for state or local officials. State constitutions and statutes required physical residence for enjoyment of the latter privilege.

In those states where local voting requirements for state officials were simply statutory, revisions looking toward absentee soldier balloting were relatively easy to arrange. But where residence was a factor of a state's constitution, changes were less quick. It took time before states' lawmakers realized the obstruc-

---

32. O.E.M., "Soldiers and Suffrage," *United States Service Magazine*, IV (1865), 542.

tions in the way of soldiers voting by absentee ballots for local candidates.

The general political pattern was that Republican-Union local and state party organizations supported soldier-voting; Democrats opposed it. These party positions were soundly based, for, uncoerced and independent, bluecoats generally sustained the Lincoln Administration and the Republican-Union party.

This striking freedom of choice reflected in part the scrutiny which states kept on their soldiers' voting ways. The closest student of soldier-voting (who in 1864 as a private in a Vermont regiment cast his vote for Lincoln) noted that in many states fear existed that Union soldiers would vote "as the colonel said." Therefore:

> . . . there were put into all the acts for soldiers' voting . . . very stringent provisions to secure the soldiers from undue influence by their officers. Many of the acts provided that the votes should be taken by commissioners appointed by the State; some provided that the votes should be announced when they were cast; and in various ways it was sought to prevent undue influence upon the soldiers in the casting of their votes in the field. . . . Elections in the field were subjected to no undue influence.[33]

In a few states, jurists pronounced against a specific statute allowing voting by soldiers in the field. But as a Pennsylvania judge noted, "While such men fight for the constitution, they do not expect judges to sap and mine it by judicial construction."[34]

Nor, concerning soldiers' voting, did "such men" allow Army provosts or other elements in the military discipline establishment who obstructed bluecoats' access to their states' polls to go unobserved by states' officials. The upshot was a continuing interaction of home front and military camp, an invigoration of

---

33. Josiah Henry Benton, *Voting in the Field: A Forgotten Chapter of the Civil War* (Boston, 1915), 320, and see chs. 1–3. Some Confederate states allowed absentee graybacks to vote. But because Confederate politics allowed no choices on basic issues, their arrangements are omitted; E. McKitrick, "Party Politics and the Union and Confederate War Efforts," in *The American Party Systems: Stages of Political Development,* ed. W. N. Chambers and W. D. Burnham (New York, 1967), 117–51.

34. Quoted in "[Advisory] Opinion of the Judges of the Supreme Court [of Vermont] on the Constitutionality of 'An Act Providing for Soldiers Voting,' " in 37 Veazey (Vermont), n.s. 2 (1864), 676.

states' dignities and self-consciousness despite the growth of national institutions and powers, and a wholly unanticipatable community of interest between the nation's civilian "rulers" of the armed forces, with the governors, lawmakers, and party leaders of almost all northern states. This community of interest between national and state political leaders reflected itself in Congress's statute of February 25, 1865, that Lincoln signed happily: "No military or naval officer . . . of the United States, shall order, bring, keep, or have under his authority or control, any troops or armed men where any general or special election is held in any State, unless it be necessary to repel the armed enemies of the United States, or to keep the peace at the polls."[35]

In later years Democrats argued that soldier-voting in states' elections and Congress's acquiescence in the presence of soldiers at polling places were a Republican conspiracy to undo democracy. But James Blaine's counterthrust is impressive, that had it existed, this alleged conspiracy would have mitigated against passage of such a statute.[36] Instead, the 1865 statute was a product of the civilian voice within the Army and the civilians' reins upon the Army, and both nourished the democratic process and the federal system. The President's and Congress's efforts involved very little bureaucratization or innovations such as civil-service isolation from politics. The War was becoming a revolution with respect to slave abolition and was achieving unprecedented organizational forms and mass in agricultural, production, and communications technologies, as well as in humanitarian, welfare, and charitable reform associations. But though public administrators increased greatly in number, and improved efficiency characterized the internal life styles of the Congress and White House establishments, the nation accommodated itself to the Civil War in ways basically familiar, including spoils appointments.[37]

These fundamentally unaltering characteristics along the

35. *RS*, 2002.
36. James Blaine, *Political Discussions, Legislative, Diplomatic, and Popular, 1856–1886* (Norwich, Conn., 1887), 246–59.
37. P. Van Riper, *History of the United States Civil Service* (New York, 1958), 553–4; and see Max Weber, *Essays in Sociology*, ed. and tr. H. H. Gerth (New York, 1946), 196–216; Allan Nevins, *The War for the Union: War Becomes Revolution, 1862–1863* (New York, 1960), chs. 9, 19–20; *ibid.*, *The Organized War, 1863–1864* (New York, 1971), chs. 4, 8, 12.

Potomac helped to shape configurations of military occupation-reconstruction policies which Lincoln's generals were working out in the shrinking Confederacy. Civilian Washington's traditionalism linked the civilian and military worlds, laws, politics, and spirit, and further tied the Civil War to Reconstruction.

Chapter XIII

Military Government and Conscription: Terrible Machines, Capital When Under Good Control

No one has bettered Halleck's description of Lincoln's military governors as "civico-military" officials.[1] Lincoln cared little about categorizing them precisely. He used them—or tried to—as he used the new Provisional Court judges and Holt's judge advocates: to counterweigh provost marshals, military commissions, and combat commanders. In short, military governors of rewon rebel states became investments in civilian direction of the War and shaping of the peace.

Initial inspiration for appointing military governors came from a general, Ambrose Burnside, who, very early in 1862, complained that occupation problems at New Bern, North Carolina, were inhibiting combat plans. He wanted Lincoln to "relieve . . . him from much that is tiring and harassing to him," Burnside's secretary noted.[2] Edward Stanly, Lincoln's first military governor, soon reached Burnside's "capital"; an indication of how

---

1. Henry W. Halleck to Francis Lieber, Apr. 18, 1865, Lieber Papers, HL.
2. Entry May 18, 1862, D. R. Larned ms. diary, LC, and see Edward Stanly to Stanton, Jan. 10, 1863, Stanton Papers, LC.

swiftly adaptation to the War's pressures was occurring and how sensitively Lincoln took advantage of the desire of most generals to slough off problems caused by the War's complexities. An energetic veteran of five terms as Whig congressman from North Carolina, leavened by a second career as a San Francisco lawyer, Stanly had offered his services to Lincoln as soon as Burnside's forces scratched out the coastal toe holds. They agreed that Stanly's most useful contribution would be to entice Carolinians back to national allegiance; to initiate a reconstruction, in short.

Lincoln's understanding of Stanly's purposes differed sharply from Burnside's; Stanly's was different from either. Stanly envisaged North Carolina as a state in being, wanting only elections of congressmen to resurrect its federal relationships. The United States Army in New Bern was a tool to stabilize, not unsettle, prewar state patterns in master-slave race relationships, as well as to reverse secession. He perceived no inconsistencies or contradictions in becoming governor of a "state" by a stroke of Lincoln's pen, and of the same time being for pay purposes a brigadier general of United States volunteers.

Once in New Bern, Stanly not only lifted obviously civil weights, as Burnside anticipated, but interfered in military matters as well. In addition to dealing with rationing, travel permits, and loyalty-oath subscriptions, Stanly regulated provost courts, provost marshals, home-guard and militia units, and Army-protected schools for Negroes (which he closed). Further, in August 1862, Stanly announced elections in the rewon enclave of North Carolina for all officials including congressmen.[3]

The civil-military, racial, and Reconstruction elements in Stanly's election call touched tender political and constitutional nerves. In September 1862, Lincoln issued his Emancipation Proclamation, by terms of which southern districts and populations returning to loyalty by January 1863 escaped penalties for rebellion, excepting emancipation. By late 1862 military governors were also on duty in occupied portions of Louisiana, Mississippi, Tennessee, and Arkansas. Lincoln encouraged them to follow Stanly's lead with respect to "state" elections and to have congressmen in Washington before the new year, thus entwining Reconstruction and emancipation, for, though it was not Lincoln's purpose, congressmen from "loyal" southern districts might help

3. Norman D. Brown, "A Union Election in Civil War North Carolina," *NCHR*, XLVIII (1966), 381–400.

to reverse emancipation by statute or, more agreeably, to preserve it.

Largely through careful examinations of Army and military governors' reports, Lincoln was coming early to an understanding of how to wage psychological warfare. From mid-1862 through December 1863, his successive proclamations on emancipation, amnesty, and Reconstruction were wagers that in areas where Union Army power was great, white southerners' self-interest in retaining white monopolies on voting and office-holding would outweigh affection for the Confederacy.[4] During 1862–63 the military governorships became rough laboratories for various patterns of state restoration. With respect to race, military governors chose cautious courses, and preferred lily-white suffrage standards likely to leave political power where it had always been. On the latter score, military governors employed loyalty tests that inquired only into subscribers' future intention, not past Unionism, thus leaving "galvanized" rebels undisfranchised. Such minima allowed quick action but not much change, in part because they left unaltered the host of state-defined civil (i.e., private) relationships. Stability in these relationships was dear to lawyers and familiar to laymen.

In reports to the White House, ideas of this standpat sort, stressing swiftness in rehabilitating southern whites, at first received sympathetic audition. Lincoln picked up from military governors ideas which they had evolved for a single area and, under the "war power" umbrella, developed a general if admittedly preliminary Reconstruction policy.

His proclamation of December 8, 1863, on amnesty, pardon, and Reconstruction allowed initiation under his military protection of secession-renouncing state constitutions and governments in the occupied South. When 10 per cent of the number of voters, as defined by states' laws, who had cast ballots in 1860 (whites only, of course) subscribed to a specified oath of future loyalty, a viable electorate formed unaltered except as to slavery from the presecession complexion. Oath-takers received the President's general amnesty. Persons excepted from amnesty by terms of his proclamation could seek his individual pardons.

---

4. Harold M. Hyman, "Civil War Turncoats: A Commentary on a Military View of Lincoln's War Prisoner Utilization Program," *MA*, XXII (1958), 134–8, suggests the success of these appeals among captured rebel soldiers.

State-making machinery compatible with the President's standards commenced quickly to move because the Army and the military governors sustained them with guns and funds.[5] But, even as these devices functioned, signs grew that the President was creating states about which significant northern opinion was uncertain or antagonistic.

Alternative modes of state restoration or alteration were operating at the same time as Lincoln's. In the unseceded but deeply divided border states processes were more ostensibly "civilian" than was true farther south where the presidential proclamation dominated, but in fact, along the border as in the deeper South, renascent political processes were dependent, for maintenance of order at least, on the Union Army.

Notwithstanding, Louisiana, Maryland, Missouri, and West Virginia diverged from the President's prescriptions. In those states districting received some democratization and loyalty tests were tougher than the one Lincoln had stipulated, for they required subscribers to attest to past Unionism. Augmenting opinion on the border was that the old racial-suffrage order should give way. Sometimes in advance of constituents' views on biracialism, sometimes responsively, significant elements of Lincoln's party rushed or drifted into opposition to the President's Reconstruction governments.

The upshot was that delegates elected from Lincoln's "restored" states, with few and inconclusive exceptions, did not gain seats in House or Senate. Further, in the midst of a most uncertain presidential election year (the world's first popular election to take place during a war), when stakes of balloting were as high as they have ever been, Republican leaders put forward an alternative, the Wade-Davis bill, to the President's Reconstruction policy.[6]

Thereafter to the eve of Appomattox, Lincoln experienced a swift escalation in his views on race and Reconstruction. His

---

5. Robert J. Futrell, "Federal Military Government in the South, 1861–1865," *MA*, XV (1951), 181–91; H. M. Hyman, *To Try Men's Souls: Loyalty Tests in American History* (Berkeley and Los Angeles, 1959), chs. 7–8.

6. On Wade-Davis bill, see below, ch. XVI; Herman Belz, *Reconstructing the Union: Theory and Practice During the Civil War* (Ithaca, N.Y., 1969), ch. 8. On border states see relevant essays in *Radicalism, Racism, and Party Realignment: The Border States During Reconstruction*, ed. R. O. Curry (Baltimore, 1969), *passim*.

ascent restored harmony within the Republican-Union party coalition in Congress, in its manifold states' echelons, and in its private benevolent, missionary, and patriotic associations. In early 1864, a flaccid, secret suggestion that token suffrage of Negro Union Army veterans was desirable in Louisiana was as far as the President dared or cared to go. But a year later Lincoln announced publicly that suffrage for literate blacks as well as for all black ex-bluecoats had become his firm, open policy for Louisiana, and that similar advance was in the cards for all the crumpled Confederate states. In brief, by Appomattox the War had moved the President and his party chieftains into racial attitudes radically different from what existed at Sumter. Possessed of a constitutional view unlikely to spur or constrain national action within the reconquered states save as northern politics supplied goads or reins, the Lincoln of April 1865 was as different from the man who in March 1861 had sworn to uphold the Constitution of the un-United States, as the reunited nation he intended to serve until March 1869.[7]

Back in early 1863, even emancipation was too much for Stanly and many northern whites. Stanly resigned from his hybrid position. Lincoln did not appoint a successor in North Carolina, although elsewhere military governors remained on their jobs. Stanly had been the pioneer. His tight-mindedness about race limited his usefulness. The contentions he entered with generals and with agents of northern Negrophile associations proved to be more trouble than his worth to the President. And yet, race aside, Stanly discerned clearly broad ways to reunion which his peers emulated in other states.[8]

Contentions were bound to spring up between military governors and Army area commanders. Lincoln wanted military governors to wrest as much power as possible from the Army brass, and simultaneously to keep Reconstruction an intrastate, not a national, political problem. In the latter purpose the military governors failed. The several state-level Reconstruction efforts forced themselves into national politics with resulting intra-Republican party hazards.

---

7. Cf. Ludwell Johnson, "Lincoln and Equal Rights: The Authenticity of the Wadsworth Letter," *JSH*, XXXII (1966), 83–7, and H. M. Hyman, "Lincoln and Equal Rights for Negroes: The Irrelevancy of the 'Wadsworth Letter,'" *CWH*, XII (1966), 258–66.

8. Brown, "Union Election," *passim;* and see Hyman, *To Try Men's Souls*, chs. 7–9.

The best contemporary summation of these matters is in advisory memoranda from General Halleck in Washington, to General Rosecrans, who was frequently at odds with military governor Andrew Johnson. Several lengthy instructions from Stanton to Johnson, specifying what the general controlled and what remained to the military governor, had failed to end the tangles. While Stanton worked on Johnson, Halleck tried to educate Rosecrans. After summarizing the contest between the Army commander and the military governor, Halleck reminded Rosecrans that both he and Johnson derived authority from Lincoln's war powers. Spelling out the functional arenas in which Johnson was supposed to work (and by implication, in which Rosecrans should not interfere), Halleck wrote:

> To mitigate as much as possible the evils resulting from a government [in Tennessee] purely military, and to restore to the loyal people and to those who are willing to return to their allegiance, the benefits of a civil government, the President directed Military Governor Johnson to restore the civil authorities, courts, and jurisdictions, so far as the circumstances . . . might render it practicable. This had been done, and . . . the military . . . will not interfere with the authority . . . of the loyal officers of the state government, except in case of urgent and pressing necessity.

Halleck understood that in the last analysis the general would define "urgent and pressing necessity." But in the Civil War's context "it is not always easy to accurately define the dividing lines between these . . . jurisdictions—the civil and the military," Halleck continued. Then, probably without believing the notion, Halleck asserted that granting good will, Rosecrans and Johnson could arrange an amicable distribution of functions.[9]

Unfortunately, more was necessary than co-operative spirit, although that vital element was always in short supply. Accumulated expertness and firm policy guidelines were wanted. Too

---

9. Halleck to Rosecrans, March 20, 1863; Stanton to Johnson, April 2, 1863, Stanton Papers, LC. Two years later, in the postassassination honeymoon that Johnson enjoyed, Halleck recalled incorrectly that he had always thought well of Johnson's wartime work as military governor. Halleck credited Johnson with "the good sense to always act right . . . to produce harmony in the clashing elements of the military and civil authorities in Tennessee." Halleck to Lieber, Apr. 18, 1865, Lieber Papers, HL.

frequently Lincoln had to cope with rasping substantive questions.

Stated another way, military governors of imperfect perception, such as Stanly and Andrew Johnson, found it compelling that the forms should prevail of civilian primacy. But this involved them in disputes over shadows. The substance of civilian domination was there because generals who subordinated themselves to direction from the White House and Congress came to the top; because Lincoln and congressional leaders employed constitutional and political pressures and evolved appropriate administrative machinery to keep high officers obedient; and because after McClellan no sharp divergences in aims existed between civilian and military leadership. Lincoln held only one civilian official, himself, superior to commanders of field forces. He understood intuitively the insight of twentieth-century scholar T. V. Smith, who during World War II was United States military governor in Sicily: "Military government is government nevertheless."[10]

But of course Smith had the advantage not only of his experience but also of his time. Complex military-occupation matters demand sophisticated preparation and quality personnel. By contrast, Lincoln's contemporaries brought to their unprecedented task the amateurish habits of the Jacksonian persuasion.[11] With all the talent the War attracted to the Potomac, Lincoln was never able to recruit military governors who were as able or inventive as combat commanders. The result was that the military-governor innovation, intended partially at least to keep Reconstruction out of politics and to centralize power in Washington in order to deny too much to occupation generals, diffused

---

10. T. V. Smith, "Government of Conquered and Dependent Areas," in *Civil-Military Relationships in American Life*, ed. Jerome Kerwin (Chicago, 1948), 91. Tragically, despite his own experience as a wartime military governor, Lincoln's successor in the Presidency disguised even from himself that the post-Appomattox crop of "provisional governors" he established in the South were also products of the President's war powers and were subject to military and political imperatives. See Salmon P. Chase to Johnson, May 17, 1865, in John Russell Young Papers, LC; James G. Randall, *Constitutional Problems Under Lincoln* (rev. edn., Urbana, 1951), ch. 10.

11. See the Sept. 1863 message to Banks in *Collected Works of Abraham Lincoln*, ed. Roy P. Basler *et al.* (New Brunswick, N.J., 1953), VI, 465–6.

power further. Throughout the North differences increased over occupation-reconstruction policy; a trend that continued after Appomattox.

One occupation commander, General Neal Dow, stated these ambiguities when late in 1862 he wrote that a military government was "a terrible machine, capital, like fire, when under good control . . . but awful as a conflagration when it escapes beyond the bounds of truth and right. . . . How few men there are really fit to be entrusted with such power."[12] As always, the problem was to find those who deserved trust, and then to give it.

No systematic study exists even today of the Civil War military governors. The known record suggests that wartime battles between generals and military governors required dangerous interventions by the President, cabinet heads, party leaders, and generals because the stakes of military occupations grew very large. Begun so adventitiously, military governments became cockpits for fighting basic constitutional, political, and racial battles. In brief, the military governments were not merely rehearsals for *a* reconstruction. They were variant forms which reconstructions could assume depending on decisions about race and suffrage that northern voters made or would make. Links between northern politics and military reconstruction tied together constitutional questions which the War allowed the Army to raise but not to answer.

Questions of this sort had to arise unless the conservative Democratic constitutional proposition received acceptance that once the Confederacy surrendered all was as it had been when it took to arms. But at Appomattox the southern states' relationships to the nation was still unclear; the position of southern Negroes remained undefined in their states' laws and the nation's Constitution. If the nation's wartime needs required emancipation, might not Reconstruction politics reverse emancipation? If not, where did Negroes land between slavery and equality in states' laws?

Civil War America trusted Lincoln's generals more than it

---

12. Quoted in Frank L. Byrne, " 'A Terrible Machine': General Neal Dow's Military Government on the Gulf Coast," *CWH*, XII (1966), 22. On quality, see Stanton's outburst to S. L. M. Barlow, quoted in Benjamin P. Thomas and Harold M. Hyman, *Stanton: The Life and Times of Lincoln's Secretary of War* (New York, 1962), 363.

trusted Lincoln's military governors (as after Appomattox it trusted General Grant more than Andrew Johnson's "provisional governors" or Johnson himself). Still, considering the total absence in 1860–61 anywhere in American national government of apparatuses relevant to the restoration of states, and the paralysis in 1861 throughout white America involving race relationships, the military-government innovations of the War worked better than appeared likely. At least they developed centers where defeatist southern whites could become "loyal" citizens and where southern Negroes could add muscle to the North's armies, together aiding substantially the surge of combat commands toward Appomattox. And, of course, that was the primary purpose of all efforts.

After several false starts, in March 1863 the United States government resorted reluctantly to conscription. The initial uncertainty reflected prewar national defense arrangements in the Constitution and statutes, which had created dual military apparatuses in the regular Army and the states' militias, paralleling the federal system. By the end of 1862 manpower needs became so pressing as to require alterations in habitual ways, extending even to race, America's most sensitive preoccupation. In January 1863, as part of the emancipation edict's provisions, Lincoln approved recruitment into the Union Army of Negroes—the South's Negroes primarily, for there were too few black northerners to count much in military terms. On March 3, 1863, Congress created a national conscription to run everywhere the flag flew and to draw in blacks as well as whites.

Beyond its primary function as a manpower supplier, the Civil War draft machinery, as modified in March 1863, became a major presidential checkrein over field generals, military-government commanders and home-front officers in charge of internal security, blockade maintenance, and war prisoners. This by-product of the North's rising need for men was issued because the Lincoln Administration had relied on volunteering for the regular Army and for the organized states' militia regiments, as specified in the Constitution and in statutes dating back to 1795. But the traditional mode was inadequate and troublesome.[13] A "militia

---

13. Lincoln's May 3, 1861 call for three-year volunteers was less firmly based on the Constitution's specifications, but Congress ratified his

draft" of July 17, 1862 had proved equally unsuccessful, and its
inadequacies derived from its reliance on state might and men.
Yet, when proposals for a national draft came forward, the President, the War Secretary, and Republican party leaders remained
states' men as long as possible.[14]

Close parallels exist between the movement toward a
national draft and the essentially local management of internal-
security operations. The Lincoln Administration persisted longer
than was desirable in efforts to achieve security and manpower
standards without disturbing overmuch customary national-state-
individual relationships or creating a coercive bureaucratic
apparatus.

The efforts failed. It was necessary to resort to alterations in
federal relationships and to wholly national administrative arrangements, as was evident on March 3, 1863, when Lincoln
signed the national conscription law. According to one judgment,
this law "must . . . be considered as the decisive step in the
elimination of state control over the militia as a check on the
general government's military power. This important result is as
directly traceable to the Civil War as the freeing of the slaves or
the adoption of the fourteenth amendment. Henceforth it was the
able-bodied male citizen's membership in the national forces, no
longer . . . the [states'] 'militia,' which carried with it the paramount obligation to military service."[15]

Evidence is scanty on how this "drastic act" (Randall's
phrase) assumed its final form in Congress. Probably the White
House–War Department coterie of lawyers-in-government and
field commanders available for consultation joined with congressmen as architects of the 1863 conscription bill. Certainly recollections were fresh that alternatives allowing local control over the

---

action; see Randall, *Constitutional Problems*, 244; John Quinn Imholte,
"The Legality of Civil War Recruiting: U.S. versus Gorman," *CWH*, IX
(1963), 422–9.

14. According to Randall the "militia-draft" law of July 17, 1862
"merely employed the [prewar] militia system, instead of creating a purely
national army; and, instead of providing a nationwide method of conscription, reliance was placed upon State laws which were to be supplemented by presidential regulations." Randall, *Constitutional Problems*,
245–6; and see Bernard Schwartz, *A Commentary on the Constitution of
the United States* (New York, 1963), II, 219; Fred A. Shannon, "State
Rights and the Union Army," *MVHR*, XII (1925), 65–6.

15. Howard White, *Executive Influence in Determining Military
Policy in the United States* (Urbana, Ill., 1925), 40.

draft and its internal-security concomitants were fatally defective.

In mid-February 1862 Secretary of War Stanton had taken over the jerry-built military-manpower and antidisloyalty contraptions, to try to dominate what Seward and Cameron had created but not controlled. The new Secretary established special commissions to check on civilian prisoners and required Army prison commanders to report regularly on their charges. Then, in midsummer, with the first wartime congressional and state elections coming on, and a draft imminent under the old, state-dominated system, Stanton created a corps of "special provost marshals" with the intention of centralizing draft enforcement, under nominal command of the prominent legalist Simeon Draper. Despite their War Department connection and martial title, as uncommissioned civilians Draper's men could not be disciplined from Washington. As if to point up the actual center of strength in the security apparatus, Lincoln's order of September 1862, suspending the habeas corpus writ privilege, contained authority to all United States marshals, and to "superintendents and chiefs of police, of any town, city, or district . . . to arrest and imprison any person or persons who may be engaged by any act of speech or writing in discouraging volunteer enlistments or in any way giving aid and comfort to the enemy, or in any disloyal practice against the United States."

The special provost-marshal experiment did not fail because it created local independence in antidisloyalty work; it failed because local independence already existed.[16] Draper never tried very hard to win obedience from the hodgepodge of local officials and volunteers he nominally controlled. Army officers involved in suppression of disloyalty scorned the hybrid upstart in the War Department. And vigilantes went their own bloody ways. Yet the 1862 Draper expedient faced the proper direction of seeking relatively centralized control and responsibility for conscription and internal security. Almost two years after Sumter, Congress finally linked these essential matters.

It created by statute (March 3, 1863) a totally military Provost Marshal General Bureau in the War Department and a field staff of Assistant Provost Marshals located in every congres-

---

16. *OR*, ser. II, vol. 2, 291–2, 333–5, ser. III, vol. II, 586–903. Gerald I. Jordan, "The Suspension of Habeas Corpus as a War-Time Political Control Technique" (Ph.D. diss., UCLA, 1941), 193–4.

sional district, including those redeemed by Union combat and occupation commands.[17] Massachusetts Senator Henry Wilson had rushed this bill through the upper house at the tag end of a fatiguing lame-duck session when senators' attention was sporadic and superficial.[18] A few days later it came up on the House floor, where looser parliamentary ways and the larger numbers of Representatives defied Republican leaders' efforts to push the bill through. With banking, conscription, and habeas-corpus legislation before them, House Democrats were alert and touchy. They charged that on behalf of blacks the Republicans were linking purse and sword against states and whites, and were making mockeries of state rights by giving ultimate powers to national Provost Marshals and military courts-martial. Overcoming opposition in the House, Republican floor managers won (149–115) passage of a bill differing slightly from the Senate's.

On February 28, the Senate took up the House draft, which somewhat limited martial authority over civilians. Administration leaders accepted the meager changes, and, by a 35–11 majority, the conscription bill passed the same day. On March 3, 1863, along with the banking and habeas corpus bills, the conscription measure received Lincoln's signature.[19]

The new Bureau's chief job was to make conscription national, acting directly on individuals rather than through states' militia echelons. One of the prickliest portions of the bill was the provision for Provost Marshals to apprehend soldiers and civilians for acts impeding or avoiding conscription and to punish them in military courts. Another was the designation of the new draft boards' decisions concerning exemption for physical disability as final, presumably without appeal to civil courts. Congress had

17. *SAL,* XII, 731–7; Donald G. Morgan, *Congress and the Constitution: A Study of Responsibility* (Cambridge, Mass., 1966), ch. 6. Note that I capitalize the Provost Marshals created under the 1863 law, to set them off from the field armies' military policemen and from Draper's 1862 corps.

18. Randall, *Constitutional Problems,* 247; *CG,* 37 Cong., 3 sess., 976–8; *Diary of Gideon Welles,* ed. John T. Morse (Boston, 1911), I, 397.

19. *CG,* 37 Cong., 3 sess., 1114–17, 1220–2, 1248–9, 1260–2, 1267–78, 1291–3; *SAL,* XII, 731. It is difficult to comprehend Randall's meaning in *Constitutional Problems,* 270, that the debates showed that "Congress gave particular attention to the matter of constitutionality." Indeed, an opposite judgment appears justifiable. But the heavy vote in both houses in favor of the law does bear out Randall's point that a consensus obtained in Congress that the law squared with the Constitution.

come to the brink of modern times by creating in the draft boards national administrative commissions.[20]

At Grant's suggestion Lincoln named Colonel James Barnett Fry Provost Marshal General. Fry's staff work with Buell had become an Army byword for excellence. In Washington, Fry became a member of the informed, informal circle close to Lincoln. Employing War Department contingent funds (Congress had provided no special budget for the new Bureau, a pattern subsequently to be repeated for freedmen's care), Fry set up a Washington staff within a month after the law's passage and organized an enrollment apparatus throughout the northern and border states and in the occupied portions of the southern states.[21] For the first time in America's history the nation made itself the base of military manpower.

This is not to suggest that the Provost Marshal Bureau ignored America's state-centered political realities. Congressmen, governors, and local political chieftains played patronage roles in appointing a Provost Marshal and his staff for each Congressional district, including for every enrollment subdistrict a civilian physician and a "commissioner," who with the Provost Marshal constituted the district's enrollment board. But once appointed, all these officials came under the district Provost's orders, and he was responsible only to the regional Assistant Provost Marshal General, who, in turn, served Fry. Washington had bypassed the field generals as well as the states.

Bypassing did not mean isolation from area commanders any more than from states. To be sure, district Provost Marshals employed special agents, private detectives, and spies in order to apprehend deserters and to ferret out obstructionists. But Provosts had also to call on field commanders if more force was wanted, or on states' home-guard units, although the commoner connection was with the national Army.

In most commands intimate links grew common between generals' provosts and Fry's Provosts. Both sought to punish and prevent "treasonable practices"; combat commanders were anxious to insure a smooth inflow of drafted men. Generals like

---

20. Jack Franklin Leach, *Conscription in the United States: Historical Background* (Rutland, Vt., 1952), 170–1. Federal judges enjoyed draft exemption but not state jurists; *CG*, 37 Cong., 3 sess., 978–9, 999. The exemption for the federal judges passed in the Senate by two votes.

21. See James Barnett Fry, *Military Miscellanies* (New York, 1889), *passim.*

Sherman, who had found military-occupation tasks distasteful, developed field-provost units only as traditional military police-men. Such generals let Fry's Provost Marshals, under orders from Washington, take on occupation duties which field provosts dealt with in neighboring commands.

All field commanders became accustomed to the Provost Marshals treading close on combat troopers' heels. Conscription apparatuses sprang up soon after military actions became mili-tary occupations and governments. Efficiently directed from Washington, the Provost Marshals corralled control of much of the internal-security work that had grown up irrationally since Sumter, largely because by mid-1863 disloyalty centered on oppo-sition to the draft and to emancipation, especially to the Negro recruitment feature of the latter.

Relatively centralized, the Provost Marshal General innova-tion was a bureaucratic conscription apparatus that, even in light of the 1863 draft law's commutation clauses, was the most decent the world had known. The decline of local influences meant less favoritism and influence-peddling. Greater efficiency and fairness meant more likelihood of apprehending actual spies and saboteurs without vigilantes' excesses. Fry's opinion that the 1863 draft law brought together the government and the people, and nurtured mutual confidence, was more than the apologia of an interested participant.[22]

No conscription arrangement could please everyone. The intrusion of uniformed Provost Marshals into northern localities with orders from Washington to take young men into the Army and to arrest civilians who interfered raised resentment. Severe inequities and endless bickerings persisted in matters of quotas, exemptions, and substitutes; the midsummer 1863 rioting testi-fied to deep resentments about the draft, especially its link to Negro elevation. But compared to what preceded it the 1863 draft law was efficient and equitable. In contrast especially to the 1862 "militia draft," with its local-level enforcement and chaotic inter-nal-security arrangements, the 1863 reform was a logical step by a nation looking to its people.

The conscription statute was no "master plan." But, obedient to its terms, Provost Marshal Bureau officers initiated more regu-lar reporting procedures concerning detained persons. The new

22. *OR*, ser. III, vol. 5, 601.

Provost Marshals were interested almost exclusively in disloyalty that might impede the draft. Many words and deeds that earlier would have brought about arrests went unpunished, an improvement aided by availability of Holt's, Lieber's, and Whiting's works and by Holt's Judge-Advocate and Bureau of Military Justice specialists. Harmless victims of the internal-security apparatus were able to gain hearings, and often release, more quickly than had been true earlier. Indeed, considering the nearly complete absence of national police institutions when the Civil War started, what grew up by mid-1863 was a creditable adaptation to what was possible, appropriate, and effective.[23] It is the measure of the vacuum in Washington in 1861 that greater liberty as well as security was obtained when national soldiers, not local officials, conducted security matters.[24]

Congress's power to conscript individuals into military service to serve in a war, whether or not the war is formally declared as the Constitution prescribes, immediately engaged the attention of antiwar leaders. New York's Democratic Governor Horatio Seymour was contemplating resorting to his state's courts for an injunction against the draft law's operation when the 1863 rioting weakened his resolution. But in Pennsylvania, a keystone state indeed, writs did issue from state judges directing national Provost Marshals to release state citizens from Army service and alleging that the 1863 draft law was unconstitutional. By Sep-

---

23. L. M. Haverstick, "The Conscription Act of March 3d," *CM*, V (1864), 110–15, discusses defects in the law as well as postwar aspirations. Scholarship has regrettably ignored the 1863 draft law. General data is in Joseph C. Duggan, *The Legislative and Statutory Development of the Federal Concept of Conscription for the Military Service* (Washington, 1946). Randall, *Constitutional Problems*, ch. 9, is essential.

24. By 1863 Lincoln and Stanton understood better than many states' governors, county sheriffs, and village constables that antidisloyalty work should be the nation's monopoly, though political weights were too heavy against achieving national hegemony. Their understanding is the more remarkable in light of the absence of historical confirmation now available, that localism in loyal-security matters leads to excess, cruelty, and partisanship. National controls made possible, not automatic, a better chance to watch the watchers. See *M&P*, VI, 104; Hyman, *To Try Men's Souls*, ch. 13; John D. Roche, *The Quest for the Dream: The Development of Civil Rights and Human Relations in Modern America* (New York, 1963), and Milton R. Konvitz, *Expanding Liberties: Freedom's Gains in Postwar America* (New York, 1966), *passim*.

tember 1863, Fry inquired of Stanton and Lincoln "whether the interference of the [Pennsylvania] State Courts with persons held in military custody [as draft evaders] shall be acquiesced in, or resisted by force." And, secretly, in anticipation that national troops would soon invade states' courts and that an appropriate case would come before him, Chief Justice Taney prepared an opinion without a case, declaring the draft law unconstitutional.[25]

Washington prepared for confrontations involving the national Army against federal and state courts, which could only benefit the Confederacy. Simultaneously, Lincoln and congressional leaders tried to work out better ways to sustain the nation without an "open rupture" (Whiting's phrase) with any judges. "The stern demands of military necessity were to be reconciled with the maintenance of [individuals'] civil liberties, and with the preservation of local self-government," the War Department Solicitor asserted.[26]

While efforts (discussed in the following chapter) proceeded in Congress to work out such a reconciliation, word came from Pennsylvania that they might be too late. Three drafted Pittsburghers sought preliminary injunctions in the state's courts against Congress's 1863 law, alleging that the Constitution did not provide for a direct connection between nation and individual when it came to raising armies, and that Congress had not declared war by the Constitution's prescriptions. In November 1863, a hasty assembling of the Pennsylvania Supreme Court resulted in a 3–2 verdict allowing the preliminary injunction. The majority's consensus was that Congress could raise a military force only through individual volunteering and "federalizing" states' militias. (Both had proved inadequate.) Further, the majority asserted inaccurately that Lincoln's September suspension of habeas corpus had closed national courts so that appeals such as this had to be heard in state courts.[27]

Within a month, a totally unfettered statewide election took

---

25. Fry, in Stanton to Lincoln, Sept. 13, 1865, Letterbook III, pt. 1, Stanton Papers, LC; Maj. Divens, Asst. PMG, Buffalo, N.Y., to Seymour, Aug. 6, 1863, Lincoln Papers, vol. 119, LC; Carl B. Swisher, *Roger B. Taney* (New York, 1935), 570–1. The Pennsylvania situation is in Kneedler v. Lane, 45 Pa., 238 (1863).

26. Whiting, *War Powers* (1871), 159.

27. Kneedler v. Lane, 45 Pa., 238 ff. (1863); J. L. Bernstein, "Conscription and the Constitution: The Amazing Case of *Kneedler v. Lane*," ABA *Journal*, LIII (1967), 708–12.

place in Pennsylvania. A prominent issue in the campaign was this litigation, since the "swing-man" on the state's Supreme Court retired and his elected successor must determine the matter when the permanence of the injunction came up for decision. Pennsylvanians chose a new judge whose public position was againt the recent majority. In December 1863, a motion before the Pennsylvania Supreme Court to dissolve the temporary injunction resulted in a reversal, with the effect of sustaining Congress's 1863 draft law. Ever since, national and state jurists have sustained Congress's plenary power to raise armies in ways the Congress deems appropriate.[28]

Lincoln and his coadjutors faced the Pennsylvania threat burdened with a concern that federalism and judicial review—two revered bases of American life worth the Civil War to preserve—might be destroying the Union. The remedy worked out in Washington was to build bridges between individuals and nation, and between states' and national courts. These new connectives were to make possible fairer hearings for the nation's wartime laws, including conscription, when they were attacked in states' courts, and improved protection for national officers, especially Fry's Provost Marshals, when they faced suits as a result of enforcing those laws. To their credit the Lincoln Republicans constructed an appropriate span in time for service; the Habeas Corpus Act of March 3, 1863 was the bridge, an essential element of which was the enlargement of national court jurisdiction.

---

28. *Ibid.*, and see John N. Pomeroy, *An Introduction to the Constitutional Law of the United States* (New York, 1868), 300–304; J. W. Delahant, "A Judicial Revisitation Finds *Kneedler v. Lane* not so 'Amazing,'" ABA *Journal*, LIII (1967), 1132–5, which contains a full case law survey. Note Ex parte Coupland, 26 Tex., 386, which sustained the Confederate draft law.

Chapter XIV

The Not-so-placid Concern
of Judicial Organization

Frankfurter's and Landis's judgment that "the Civil War put
out of men's minds such placid concerns as judicial organization" requires correction. Confiscation, emancipation, disloyalty, military governments, Reconstruction, and racial relationships, as well as a mix of nonmilitary matters, inspired wartime
Congresses to give nervous priority to judicial organization. During the Civil War Congress began a twelve-year-long systematic
augmentation in the jurisdiction and powers of the federal judiciary that, according to Frankfurter and Landis, "seems revolutionary."[1]

Yet, according to a tenacious contrary scholarly tradition,
Republicans of the Civil War and Reconstruction decades assaulted rather than enhanced the federal judiciary. At once after
Sumter, Republicans were supposed to have begun gerrymander-
ing judicial circuits, jockeying the numbers of justices on the
Supreme Court, and rigging federal-court jurisdictions in order to
prevent negative judgments about actions and laws that were
allegedly unsupportable. The presumed upshot was that, cowed
and puny, the Supreme Court slipped by unconstitutional laws

---

1. Felix Frankfurter and James M. Landis, *The Business of the
Supreme Court: A Study in the Federal Judicial System* (New York, 1928),
55, 65.

and administrative actions and the federal judiciary started to slide to its nadir.[2]

Since Dred Scott days and the Merryman misadventure, a resentful Republican backlash had developed in which reverence for constitutional forms appeared to crack. Even cautious, scholarly William Pitt Fessenden grumbled, "Were I in Lincoln's place a small scruple would not detain me from what was needful." One of Lincoln's cabinet included in a report to Congress the charge that "the judicial machinery seemed as if it had been designed not to sustain the Government, but to embarrass it."[3]

But such utterances should not be confused with party or popular determination to hamstring national courts or judges. Reverence for Constitution, courts, and law remained unimpaired; even Dred Scott and Merryman did not revive the old Jefferson-Jackson antipathy to judicial review. On December 3, 1861, when Lincoln addressed Congress, he did not attack the Court or Taney, although close subordinates felt free to do both. Instead he suggested that the time was ripe for a long-overdue reformation in the circuit organization of the federal judiciary to accommodate decades of commercial and territorial expansion. Further, Lincoln advocated that the appellate jurisdiction of the Supreme Court expand, not diminish, to include claims litigation.[4]

Historians have attended to subsequent resolutions of New Hampshire's Republican Senator John P. Hale, directing the Judiciary Committee to inquire into the "expediency and propriety of abolishing the present Supreme Court." But the chairman of that committee, Lyman Trumbull, buried Hale's resolution without difficulty. On the scale of political power real-

---

2. Stanley Kutler, *Judicial Power and Reconstruction Politics* (Chicago, 1968), 6. Kutler has argued ably that the tradition fails to fit post-Appomattox facts. I add that it fails also to match wartime realities. The most complete treatment is Ferne B. Hyman, "The 'Chase' Court and Reconstruction: An Historiographical Analysis" (M.A. thesis, Loyola University of Los Angeles, 1970).

3. Charles A. Jellison, *Fessenden of Maine: Civil War Senator* (Syracuse, 1962), 131–2; *M&P*, VI, 101–2.

4. *Collected Works of Abraham Lincoln*, ed. Roy P. Basler *et al.* (New Brunswick, N.J., 1963), hereafter cited as Lincoln, *Works*, V, 43; James G. Randall, *Constitutional Problems Under Lincoln* (rev. edn., Urbana, Ill., 1951), 9 n.; *CG*, 37 Cong., 2 sess., 26–8; David M. Silver, *Lincoln's Supreme Court* (Urbana, Ill., 1956), 43; Robert Trimble, *A Review of the American Struggle in Its Military and Political Aspects* (London, 1864), 24–5.

ities Hale hit zero.[5] Congress, obedient to Lincoln's request, in July 1862 apportioned more equitably judicial districts that since 1837 had been gerrymandered to favor the slaveholding states.[6] The 1862 circuit reform helped to preserve the dignity and usefulness of the federal judiciary, and the discussions reveal a commitment in Congress to the importance of those courts so strong that discerning and informed men fought hard in committees and on House or Senate floor to place their states in one circuit or another. Further, changes were imminent in the Supreme Court's roster due to death and retirement. Replacements were likely to come from the lower federal courts, and the location of an aspirant's circuit could determine his political eligibility.[7]

At the same time that congressmen reapportioned circuits, they discussed increasing the number of Supreme Court judges. Professor David Silver has suggested that "it was no coincidence" that the Prize Cases were before the Supreme Court when this discussion came on in Congress; implying that the numbers matter was a form of blackmail. But no evidence exists that one affected the other.[8] The Democratic opposition was calm about the numbers-alteration possibility, which would please mercantile communities across the nation. When, on March 3, 1863, Congress created in the far West a new Tenth Circuit and a tenth Supreme Court position to fill the place, legislators' agreements were far more general than contentions.[9]

Meanwhile, by statute of June 19, 1862, Congress began reversing the Dred Scott decision, fulfilling the Republicans' 1860 campaign plank.[10] As was true of the reapportionment of federal court circuits and numbers of jurists, the 1862 free-territories law evoked almost no antijudiciary rhetoric, a characteristic notable also in the extensive debates on antidisloyalty, conscription, and confiscation statutes. Indeed, the pattern emerges of constantly increasing dependence on and employment of the federal courts,

---

5. *CG*, 38 Cong., 1 sess., 753; Richard H. Sewell, *John P. Hale and the Politics of Abolition* (Cambridge, Mass., 1965), 195.

6. *SAL*, V, 176 (1837).

7. See debates in *CG*, 37 Cong., 2 sess., 124, 187–8, 288.

8. Silver, *Lincoln's Supreme Court*, 105; *SAL*, XII, 576.

9. Charles Warren, *The Supreme Court in United States History* (rev. edn., Boston, 1937), II, 378–81; *SAL*, XII, 794.

10. This June 1862 law (*SAL*, XII, 432) declared that territories were forever free from slavery.

for, as noted earlier, congressmen and President made them the primary enforcement apparatuses for these punitive statutes. During consideration of the 1861 confiscation act, the 1862 loyalty-oath bill, and the 1863 draft law, a "let-the-courts-do-it" attitude suffused Capitol Hill. As a result, dramatic constitutional discourses so long a feature of prewar House and Senate dwindled after Sumter.

The essential point is the White House–Capitol Hill consensus that the Civil War must restore the rule of law nationwide. Improved judicial organization and enlarged review responsibilities for national judges were means to that end. Lawmakers became confident that mistakes in drafting laws were forgivable because judges would repair errors. Leading lights in both parties, lacking leisure to mull over technicalities, were pleased to let the robed nobility make ultimate decisions about the distasteful public questions which the War forced politicians to raise. Far better for Congress to let judges bear ultimate responsibility.[11] By 1863 the Lincoln Administration felt confident that its improvements in and appointments to the federal circuit courts and Supreme Court lessened the Calhounite biases (as Republicans saw it) that in the Dred Scott and Merryman instances had marred the performance of the national judiciary.

Another factor impelling Republicans to resort to federal courts was that judicial enforcement was traditional and inexpensive. Never the spendthrifts of legend, Republicans were products of an anti-institutional age that abhorred coercive bureaucracies and were prisoners of Victorian fiscal imperatives. The unavoidable, enormous military expenditures distressed even pro-War congressmen, who were therefore the more eager to restrain secondary costs. As a result, enforcement of Congress's major punitive statutes fell to existing administrative personnel and to federal attorneys and judges. Legislators did not balance increased functions with proportionately enlarged budgets or staffs, however, even when, as in the case of enforcement of long-

---

11. Riddle, in *CG*, 37 Cong., 2 sess., 500 (Jan. 27, 1862); Donald G. Morgan, *Congress and the Constitution: A Study of Responsibility* (Cambridge, Mass., 1966), 127 and *passim;* Maxwell Bloomfield, "Law vs. Politics: The Self-Image of the American Bar," *AJLH*, XII (1968), 306–23, suggests the pervasive readiness among men of law for such roles. See too John Sherman's comment, Feb. 5, 1863, that courts would decide emancipation's legality and that few congressmen "will not submit with patience and respect to that decision." *CG*, 37 Cong., 3 sess., 735.

delinquent international-slave-trade prohibitions, American officers at last became energetic after Sumter.[12]

Consider in this connection the requirement that all federal civil and military officials subscribe loyalty oaths as a prerequisite to employment. As part of hiring procedures, departmental clerks filed signed oath forms along with letters of recommendation and patronage data, and that was all. A tiny number of persons incurred punishments by refusing to sign oaths or by altering phrases involving past aid to the Confederacy; a very small contingent faced accusations and, sometimes, proofs of perjured subscriptions. But all this occurred without creation of a separate loyalty-testing officialdom.

In apparent incongruity, lawmakers who believed fervently in the Constitution's adequacy to do anything the War required, at the same time professed, equally passionately and without hypocrisy, that these powers must be exercised without overtasking the government's fiscal structure. Loyalty and sound currency were inseparable moralities all during the War and Reconstruction years. Congressmen could rarely ignore the North's supposedly empty Treasury or the outflow of gold occasioned by War expenditures. To men of this mind, sovereignty could not result from an empty purse. They felt passionately that monetary imbalance would topple the nation as surely as a Confederate conquest of Washington or unquenched antidraft riots in New York City, and must incur moral costs too high even for salvation of the Constitution and the Union.

The result was that in War-centered matters, narrowly defined, Republicans drew from the Constitution sanctions for antidisloyalty, confiscation, conscription, emancipation, military-occupation, and Reconstruction policies. With respect to non-War matters, Congress approved also the innovations in bankruptcy proceedings, in tariffs, in banking and currency systems, in homestead provisions, and in subventions to states for higher education and to entrepreneurs for transcontinental communications. Congress resorted to national courts for enforcement of these innovations in the sense of individuals' litigations or punitive prosecutions, but it allowed no grand money outlays, large

---

12. Robert Marcus, "Wendell Phillips and American Institutions," *JAH*, LVI (1969), 41–58; George F. Hoar, *Autobiography of Seventy Years* (New York, 1903), I, 254–9; Warren S. Howard, *American Slavers and the Federal Law, 1837–1862* (Berkeley, 1963).

bureaucratic growths, or coercive, regulatory enforcement innovations. Lawmakers professed to believe that they had left basically unaltered the nation's relationships to state-chartered corporations and associations, and to individuals. As one scholar encapsulated the complex story: "governmental powers remained rudimentary while the economy proliferated."[13]

This continuing constraint is visible in the concern of the President and many congressmen, including "Radicals," that the confiscation laws not affect title to real property beyond the lifetime of offenders whose disloyalty had been proved in court. It is equally evident in the pressure for a national bankruptcy law enforceable through federal courts in restored rebel states; and in the 1862 law subsidizing through land donations primarily private construction of a transcontinental railroad. Professor Wallace D. Farnham has made clear how this last law's supporters insisted that the government "subsidize without governing, that it transfer the nation's resources . . . without ensuring justice and order."[14]

Still another impulsion toward Congress's resort to the national courts lay in a growing antipathy to state courts and judges. This estrangement derived from the secession and slaveownership supports developed in southern states' courts, and the fiscal and constitutional heresies flourishing in some northern and western states which those states' jurists did not condemn. It appeared distressingly clear that elected states' judges lacked will and ways to withstand popular pressures, however distasteful,

---

13. Bray Hammond, *Sovereignty and an Empty Purse: Banks and Politics in the Civil War* (Princeton, 1970), chs. 1–2; and see Paul B. Trescott, "Federal Government Receipts and Expenditures, 1861–1875," *JEH*, XXVI (1966), 206–22; Irwin Unger, *The Greenback Era: A Social and Political History of American Finance, 1865–1879* (Princeton, 1964). To be sure, military occupations and wartime Reconstruction efforts involved costs, bureaucracies, and functional pioneering. But essentially they were accommodated in and by private welfare associations and/or the Army's budgets, manpower resources, and primary purposes; Leonard P. Curry, *Blueprint for Modern America: Nonmilitary Legislation of the First Civil War Congress* (Nashville, 1968), chs. 4 and 6, on non-war data.

14. Farnham, " 'The Weakened Spring of Government': A Study in Nineteenth-Century American History," *AHR*, LXVIII (1963), 680; Henry D. Shapiro, *Confiscation of Confederate Property in the North* (Ithaca, N.Y., 1962), *passim*; Lincoln, *Works*, VII, 228–9, 292–5, wherein the President ordered a disloyal southern woman arrested, but the disposition of her confiscated house was to be left to the courts; Charles Warren, *Bankruptcy in United States History* (Cambridge, Mass., 1935), 97.

issued by conventions or legislatures. In northern cities local judges shared in the "money machines" of corrupt politics, allegedly corrupted Catholics, and disloyal antidraft rioters.[15]

Outstanding among northern cities in regard to fiscal immorality, according to shocked opinions of Lincoln's contemporaries, was Dubuque. Eager to attract railroads, Dubuque had exceeded statutory limits on its bonded indebtedness, then tried to evade payment, raising the specter of contract-clause unenforceability. Initially, Iowa judges held Dubuque to account. Then they bowed before angry popular reaction and sustained the city's evasion. Resorting to federal courts, bondholders were delighted in 1863 when, in Gelpcke v. Dubuque, the United States Supreme Court reversed the state jurists and issued national writs of mandamus requiring the Iowa counties involved to pay the debt. Whereupon Iowa judges enjoined county officers from obeying the national writs.[16]

Worried commentators saw analogies between Dubuque's fiscal recklessness, New York City's antidraft riots, and southern states' secessions. It startled concerned patriots to learn that the Supreme Court had to pioneer dangerously across the federal system in order to restrain Dubuque, as Lincoln had to venture in attempts to quell secession in the South and disaffection in the North. Expressing this uneasy surprise, Rhode Island Chief Justice Bradley admitted that "the action of our States [and cities through delegated states' police powers] has not yet passed into

---

15. John Alexander Jameson, *The Constitutional Convention: Its History, Powers, and Modes of Proceeding* (New York, 1867), iii; and see on Jameson's book, W. Barry, "American Political Science," *Old and New*, III (1871), 304; William M. Wiecek, "The Reconstruction of Federal Judicial Power, 1863–1875" (M.A. thesis, UWis, 1966), 18–19, on antipathy to state courts, and Wiecek's article of the same title, *AJLH*, XIII (1969), 333–59. Other data is in W. R. Blackard, "The Demoralization of the Legal Profession in Nineteenth Century America," *Tennessee Law Review*, X (1940), 315–16; C. K. Yearley, *The Money Machines: The Breakdown and Reform of Governmental and Party Finance in the North, 1860–1920* (Albany, 1971), intro., ch. 1.

16. A second resort by bondholders to the United States Supreme Court resulted (1867) in an extraordinarily stern statement directed to state judges, prohibiting further interference with national judicial writs, and, finally, Dubuque paid off. Gelpcke v. Dubuque, 1 Wall., 175 (1863); Von Hoffman v. Quincy, 4 Wall., 535 (1867). See Samuel Bowles, "The Relations of State and Municipal Governments, and the Reform of the Latter," *JSS*, IX (1877), 140–6; James B. Thayer, "The Case of *Gelpcke v. Dubuque*," *HLR*, IV (1891), 311–20.

written history." And it repelled thoughtful men that state and national judges responded to differing imperatives, that still another aspect of the federal system was imperfect. The proposition that the dual court systems were immune to polarizations affecting the political branches of national and state governments had retained currency. But the War was revealing that even the marvelous symmetry commonly attributed to courts and laws was illusory. If, to believers in a rule of law, secession was the extreme perversion of federalism, conflict between state and national courts was only a little less repellent and hazardous.[17]

To be sure, the 1863 Gelpcke v. Dubuque litigation was not the first national judicial consideration of cities' debt limits or of political democracy's "sacreligious hands grasp[ing] even at the ermine," in the words of E. W. Huffcut, a senator from Indiana in the 1890's. But implications in the Gelpcke case inspired the first sustained, sophisticated inquiries into America's urban-blind constitutionalism, in the same manner that the Merryman case illuminated lacunae and impelled Fisher, among others, to initiate appropriate research.

The first result of the Gelpcke lash was John Norton Pomeroy's 1864 volume, *An Introduction to Municipal Law.* A practicing New York City lawyer, Pomeroy was a fervid nationalist, Lincoln supporter, and preacher of the adequate Constitution theme. His *Municipal Law* was an adoration of the Union. But he refused to go along with those who were willing to abandon law in localities in order to save the nation. The War must restore respect in the North as well as the South for a rule of law, or the military effort was wasted. Indeed, abandonment of law on a false plea of necessity or in the face of popular demands must lead to defeat and anarchy.

Useful at once by those who were anxious to restrain popu-

---

17. Charles Bradley, *The Methods of Changing the Constitutions of the States, Especially That of Rhode Island* (Boston, 1885), unnumbered prefatory page; and see Senator Sherman's comment, Dec. 9, 1862, *CG,* 37 Cong., 3 sess., 26, 30–1; George Wharton Pepper, *The Border Land of Federal and State Decisions* (Philadelphia, 1889) *passim;* Joel P. Bishop, *Commentaries on the Criminal Law* (Boston, 1868), I, xv–xvi. Today few informed persons assume that identical interests move national and state courts; see comments by William Brennan, "Some Aspects of Federalism," *Proceeding, 16th Annual Meeting, Conference of Chief Justices* (Chicago, 1965), 57–60. For background see Mitchell Wendell, *Relations Between the Federal and State Courts* (New York, 1949).

lar excesses, especially in cities, Pomeroy's volume was superseded in 1867 by John F. Dillon's *Law of Municipal Corporations.* Probably the greater thrust of Dillon's technical compendium derived from his intimacy with the Iowa situation. He was a law professor in that state's university, former Iowa supreme court judge, and later, United States circuit court jurist. His *Municipal Corporations* was to be widely used by lawyers for fifty years. It is a powerful plea in favor of limiting what cities might do under delegated states' police powers and for state judges to resist political pressures.[18]

What emerges is the sense that within two years after Sumter, some men who supported the nation's martial effort to prevent the slaveowning states from evading national responsibilities through secessions were beginning also to conclude that a desirable "Reconstruction" required national limitations on all states' invasions of private rights. State invasions in the form of state-sanctioned secessions, chattel ownership of one human being by another, or cities' excessive employment of delegated state powers, as in the Gelpcke instance, were almost equally unpalatable.

Within two decades after Appomattox, the conviction that the states were limitable beyond confines set in 1787, and that the national courts were the best agency to hold them in, had become an "old legality." But in the early 1860's it was an exciting new legality, increasing cautiously in Congress. Legislators came to worry noticeably about what Yale president and law professor Theodore D. Woolsey described as "democratic abstractions." The result, Woolsey wrote, was a "more liberal construction of the general Constitution, so as to throw larger powers into the hands of Congress, and to look to the [national] Government for help in difficulty."[19]

---

18. On pre-Gelpcke precedents, see especially "Remarks on the Opinion of Chief Justice Black in the Case of Sharpless . . . vs. . . . Philadelphia," *ALReg,* II (1853), 2–20; Huffcut in AAPSS *Annals,* II (1892), 565; Pomeroy, *An Introduction to Municipal Law* (New York, 1864), esp. 402–3; Dillon, *The Law of Municipal Corporations* (2nd edn., New York, 1873), ix–xii; Phillip S. Paludan, "John Norton Pomeroy, State Rights Nationalist," *AJLH,* XII (1968), 277. C. Fairman, *Reconstruction and Reunion, 1864–88* (New York, 1971), 918–1116, offers rich details on Gelpcke.

19. David Brewer, *Protection to Private Property from Public Attack: An Address . . . Yale Law School, on June 23, 1891* (New Haven, 1891), 7, 10; Theodore D. Woolsey's unpaginated preface (Jan. 1874), to Francis Lieber's *Civil Liberty and Self Government* (3rd edn., Philadelphia, 1875),

The 1863 Iowa litigation, decided in the same court session as the Prize Cases, suggested that Congress could look to the nation's courts, especially the Supreme Court, to stand against local follies that states' judges sustained. As the United States Supreme Court's Reporter noted, in Gelpcke that bench had enforced "high moral duties . . . upon a whole community, [which was] seeking apparently to violate them."[20] Taney's failing health —he was probably absent during the Gelpcke hearing and decision—was an added element justifying cautious trust in the Supreme Court; the Merryman episode was unlikely to be repeated.

Administration leaders recalled vividly a potential crisis of August 1861. Men of a Minnesota regiment on duty near Washington petitioned the United States Supreme Court for a habeas corpus writ in the name of one of their number, on the ground that he was illegally in the service and that the President's call for three-year enlistments was unconstitutional because it increased the size of the Army without Congress's prior approval. Georgia-born Justice James Wayne received the petition and hurriedly notified Adjutant General Lorenzo Thomas. Conferences followed at the White House. The weight of a judgment by Wayne adverse to the government's right to enlist soldiers by means of presidential fiat added to the millstone of the recent Merryman opinion and Bull Run reverse, would have been very heavy. Taken together, the instances of the disloyal Maryland civilian and of the loyal Minnesota soldier could have cut out from under the nation its capacity to wage the Civil War.

Justice Wayne discharged the writ and the soldier-appellant went briefly to a military guardhouse. The War Department ordered that he not suffer a court-martial. A planned appeal from Wayne's action to the whole Supreme Court, in which the soldier was to have as counsel the redoubtable lawyer and conservative Democrat, Maryland Senator Reverdy Johnson, did not come off. Soon the soldier was back with his regiment and he and it served honorably throughout the remainder of the War.[21]

---

has the quoted phrase, and see also Woolsey's "Nature and Sphere of Police Power," *JSS*, II (1870), 97–114; Charles Warren, "Federal and State Court Interference," *HLR*, XLII (1930), 351–2; W. F. Swindler, *Court and Constitution in the Twentieth Century: The Old Legality, 1889–1932* (Indianapolis, 1969), ch. 1.

20. 1 Wall., xiv (1863).

21. John Quinn Imholte, "The Legality of Civil War Recruiting: U.S. Versus Gorman," *CWH*, IX (1963), 427–8 suggests, unverifiably, that

Wayne's happy stand did not at once dissipate the suspicion with which, in 1861 and 1862, White House and Capitol Hill viewed the Supreme Court. There the venerable Chief Justice hung on, anxious to swing with him enough of his robed brethren to make the Merryman doctrine constitutional law. Of necessity, the Lincoln Administration continued the internal-security and recruitment policies which Taney condemned and Wayne approved.

In order to thwart Taney, cabinet officers determined to avoid treason prosecutions as long as possible. By mid-1861 awareness had grown that it was a crime difficult to prove, that convictions would create martyrs, and that defeats for the government would make it ridiculous—so Attorney General Bates, whose reverence for legal procedures was well known, summarized the arguments. On another occasion Bates wrote that Clement L. Vallandigham's petition to United States courts for release from military arrest, was "only a peg on which to hang a denunciatory speech against the Administration and the War Office in particular." Stanton's assistant, Peter Watson, a gifted lawyer, was moved to warn the War Secretary and President that "This Department stands no chance in a game of shuttlecock with the lawyers before disloyal judges."[22]

But what made sense along the Potomac did not necessarily control officials elsewhere. For example Bates, lacking statutory authority over district attorneys—an 1861 statute allowed the Attorney General, who was not to become a Department head until 1870, only administrative superintendence over district attorneys and marshals—was incapable of substituting personal leadership and could not keep them at heel.[23] Army officers released Merryman and other offenders as part of the general

---

Wayne declared constitutional the August 6, 1861 statute. See also Silver, *Lincoln's Supreme Court*, 16–18; SAL, XII, 326 for the August 1861 statute.

22. Carl B. Swisher, *Roger B. Taney* (New York, 1935), 554–71; Marvin R. Cain, *Lincoln's Attorney General, Edward Bates of Missouri* (Columbia, Mo., 1965), 46; Edward Bates's summary in OR, II, vol. 5, 190–1; on Vallandigham, Bates to Stanton, Jan. 19, 1864, Stanton Papers, LC; Peter Watson to Holt, May 13, 1863, Holt Papers, LC; and see Seward to T. O. Howe, Aug. 15, 1864, copy in Stanton Papers, LC.

23. John P. Frank, "Edward Bates, Lincoln's Attorney General," *AJLH*, X (1966), 35; M. L. Hinsdale, *A History of the President's Cabinet* (Ann Arbor, Mich., 1911), 217.

prison-sweeping of early 1862, whereupon the hyperactive federal attorney in Baltimore had him and sixty others indicted for treason.

At first Taney welcomed the news of an opportunity to throttle again the runaway engine of national government. But, aging and ill, Taney drew back from having the treason cases go forward, even when his health temporarily improved. In the Chief Justice's view the Maryland atmosphere had become polluted. Harassed by arbitrary arrests and in many instances excluded from polls and jury duty by national and state loyalty tests, Maryland's antiwar Democracy was becoming unable to resist effectively even the thrust toward emancipation. Taney feared that such a population could not supply a jury willing to decide against the government in a treason case.[24]

These were the last opportunities Taney enjoyed to exploit a treason trial. But lesser litigations forecast the route he intended to travel if a treason trial allowed an opportunity to curb the government's excesses, as he saw them.

In the Merryman confrontation, Taney hit hard at the fact that the President rather than Congress had suspended the habeas corpus writ privilege. But by early 1863, Congress's approval for and incorporation of Lincoln's internal-security activities moved Taney to damn both Houses on Pennsylvania Avenue. Consider a relatively trivial case that came before him on circuit in mid-1863. Despite Congress's assignment of enforcement to national courts, under the 1862 statute, confiscation proceedings as punishment for evading the blockade which Lincoln had imposed by executive fiat involved aspects of War-altered life that Taney found most repellent. Worse, in the case at hand the evidence against the defendants had issued from secret agents of an Army provost marshal's staff who had bored into a smuggling ring. Functioning successfully as *agents provocateurs* and employing paid informers, the military spies exposed the outlaws.

Taney denounced the detectives' techniques rather than the culprits. In a display of astonishing illogic, considering Congress's statute and the evidence against the miscreants, Taney decided that their seized property was not subject to confiscation and that

---

24. Swisher, *Taney*, 557–9; Charles L. Wagandt, *The Mighty Revolution: Negro Emancipation in Maryland, 1862–1864* (Baltimore, 1964), *passim*.

the Army agents were personally responsible for damages and costs that the smugglers had suffered.[25]

The Chief Justice had a great antipathy also to Treasury bureaucrats who collected the taxes that sustained the War and who supervised commerce controls between northern areas and the occupied South. Congress had authorized the Secretary of the Treasury to license even intrastate trade south of Annapolis, Maryland, in order to choke off some of the goods that nurtured the Confederacy. A Marylander who lived south of Annapolis applied for a permit to ship home goods from Baltimore. Treasury agents refused permission. The owner then assumed the name of a man who possessed a coveted license and sent the goods off. Discovered and his property seized, the owner petitioned for redress in the United States District Court in Baltimore. After an unfavorable verdict, in mid-1863 he took an appeal to the circuit court where Taney sat.

Taney reversed the decision and ordered the disputed property returned to the petitioner. As the basis for this upset, Taney returned to a proposition he had advanced with respect to Merryman, that except in rarest emergencies the punishment of all crimes must be the result of trial proceedings, and that only a judge could define an emergency situation.

On this point almost all lawyers, including Lincoln, agreed with Taney that the loss of property title even by disloyal persons required utmost tenderness. But Taney went on to inquire first if the Treasury regulations properly carried out Congress's purposes, and then whether the interdiction of Marylanders' intrastate trading was within Congress's competency, war or no war. To both these larger questions he replied in the negative. The Treasury trade regulations exceeded and altered intentions of the congressmen, Taney declared. Treasury agents were transforming their administrative role into that of lawmakers, "changing the law . . . not according to the judgment and discretion of the legislature, but according to the discretion and judgment of the Secretary [of the Treasury]." Taney insisted that Congress, not the Treasury, must interpret Congress's will, and that he as judge would hold up matters until Congress did its job, despite its unconcern at the executive regulations.[26]

---

25. *Memoir of Roger Brooke Taney* (Baltimore, 1872), 436–43; Richmond, Va., *Record*, Sept. 3, 1863.

26. Phillip G. Auchampaugh, *Fundamental Principles of the Ward*

Having decided that the Treasury rules under review were excessive because they were administrative rulings, Taney moved on. Suppose that the unfortunate rules were products not of Treasury officers but of Congress itself? Taney stated that "they could not be sustained by a court of justice, whose duty it is to administer the law according to the Constitution of the United States." Trade totally within a state was not subject to congressional control. The existence of war did not modify the tight distinction between inter- and intrastate commerce that Taney discerned "so plainly set forth in the Constitution that it had never been supposed to be open to controversy or question"—a remarkable statement from the jurist whose reputation had grown during the preceding thirty years as a critic of looseness in the Constitution's distinctions between the two.

Taney hastened to add that he was not attempting to dictate to President or Congress how to wage war. But then he came to the conclusion that

> A civil war or any other war does not enlarge the powers of the Federal Government over the States beyond what the compact has given to it in time of war. A state of war does not annul the 10th article of the Amendments to the Constitution. . . . Nor does a civil war or any other war absolve the judicial department from the duty of maintaining with an even firm hand the rights and powers of the Federal Government, and of the States, and of the citizen, as they are written in the Constitution, which every judge is sworn to support. . . . [T]he regulations in question are illegal and void. . . . The seizure of the goods . . . because . . . [the appellant] refused to comply with them, cannot be sustained.[27]

These cases settled only the fates of the litigants. Although some of the fundamental questions which Taney wished to confront came to the whole Court, it slid by taproot issues, as in the momentous Prize Cases.[28] Taney went along with his Supreme

---

Case Upheld in a Forgotten Opinion of Chief Justice Taney in 1863 (Reno, Nev., 1945), 4, 5, 8, and *passim;* Swisher, *Taney,* 567–8.

27. Auchampaugh, *Fundamental Principles,* 5, 8.

28. Samuel Shapiro, *Richard Henry Dana, Jr., 1815–1882* (East Lansing, Mich., 1961), 119–20 and n.; S. Bernath, *Squall Across the Atlantic: America's Civil War Prize Cases and Diplomacy* (Berkeley, 1970).

Court colleagues in sustaining the legitimacy of the despised blockade, dissenting only on whether President or Congress should have invoked the blockade—for Taney an echo of his Merryman concern that Congress's primacy remain unimpaired. A bare minority of the jurists, including Taney, quibbled that offenses against the blockade could not have occurred until July 1861 when Congress affirmed presidential trade restrictions in force since the preceding April. John C. Hurd offered the neatest summary: When cards came down as in the Prize Cases, Taney "accepted the political situation without being able to change it."[29]

Relief at the decision in the Prize Cases was widespread in official Washington. Taney had failed to spark an open expression of the sort that he had pioneered in Merryman's case. Although some of his colleagues agreed privately with him, only public votes decided cases.[30]

By 1863 the federal courts had proved to be more co-operative, restrained, and respectful than the 1861 Merryman confrontation had suggested was possible; the two-score states' courts were the arenas in which War policies were receiving deadly flank attacks and in which states' judges were too permissive about intrastate excesses. Congressmen felt few restraints when criticizing decisions by federal judges. But many inhibitions came into play when obnoxious states' courts and judges were involved.

A century ago congressmen were states' men. Many were lawyers and veterans of practice in state courts. All were tied closely to their states' parties, treasuries, and voters. Sharp wrenches were required for these men to open avenues from state to national courts. Distaste at the immoral behavior of Iowa judges in the Gelpcke case helped to amass the energy. Outraged patriotism supplied the greater force when state judges issued writs against draft enforcement, blocked antidisloyalty arrests, and required the release of individuals from federal military service and/or custody.[31] Worst of all were states' jurists who

---

29. John C. Hurd, *The Theory of Our National Existence as Shown by the Action of the Government of the United States Since 1861* (Boston, 1881),263–4; Randall, *Constitutional Problems*, chs. 2–3; Prize Cases, 2 Black, 635 (1863).

30. John Catron to Taney, Feb. 26, 1863, in *LH*, I (1958), 52.

31. See as examples In re Kemp, and In re Griener, 16 Wis., 382, 447 (1863). Note that President and Congress carefully included state judges not national jurists, as draftable, and described which states' judges might

encouraged or connived with arrested persons to lodge damage suits or contempt proceedings in state courts against conscription and internal-security officers.

Naturally the written record in which men admit sordid purposes is sparse. But evidence infers that such motivation existed.

Former Iowa Chief Justice Charles Mason fretted over the internal-security policies which federal and state officials maintained in his state, ignoring evidence that these policies permitted Iowa to escape the turbulence so common in neighboring Kansas and Missouri. In Washington during 1861–62, Mason concluded that the strengths the Union exhibited were actually fatal weaknesses. Constitutional liberty was dead if a President could assemble an army by proclamation and if soldiers could arrest civilians. Lincoln's bypassing of Taney's Merrryman judgment, and Congress's 1862 legal-tender law, especially outraged Mason.

Despite Mason's conniving through his back-home connections, Iowa judges failed to exploit opportunities likely to embarrass the Lincoln Administration. But Mason never lost hope that the robed nobility of the states would save America from the nation.[32]

Philadelphia lawyer Charles Ingersoll was the type of litigant for whom Mason yearned. A devout Buchanan Democrat and a rigid nay-sayer about all questions then before the public, Ingersoll responded first to the Merryman confrontation by anti-administration pamphleteering, thereafter resorting to lawsuits in order to hamstring the national government. In his state's lower court Ingersoll secured a verdict against Congress's 1862 legal-tender law as destructive of a contractual stipulation requir-

---

be subject to penal clauses in the 1862 confiscation act; *M&P*, VI, 96, 98–9. See also John Phillip Reid, *Chief Justice: The Judicial World of Charles Doe* (Cambridge, Mass., 1957), 197–200; John McNulty, "Chief Justice Breese and the Illinois Supreme Court: A Study of Law and Politics in the Old West" (Ph.D. diss., HU, 1961 [used with permission]); Emma Lou Thornbrough, "Judge Perkins, the Indiana Supreme Court, and the Civil War," *IndMH*, LX (1964), 87–8.

32. Entry, Feb. 16, 1862, and see entries April 29, Aug. 8, Dec. 13, 1861; July 20, 1862, in *Life and Letters of Charles Mason, Chief Justice of Iowa, 1804–1882*, ed. Charles Mason Remey (Washington, 1939). See also W. I. Toussaint, "Charles Mason's Influence on Iowa Jurisprudence," *Annals of Iowa* (summer 1968), 372–87; H. H. Wubben, "The Maintenance of Internal Security in Iowa, 1861–1865," *CWH*, X (Dec. 1964), 401–15.

ing payment in specie. Ingersoll admitted to an intimate that he hoped the federal attorney would take an appeal to higher courts so that Ingersoll might win a general judgment of unconstitutionality against this statute. Indignant, Ingersoll's confidant protested that such a decision would leave the government powerless to continue fighting. "But we don't want the government to carry on this war," Ingersoll replied.[33]

Many Ingersolls were active; many Masons were waiting for appropriate suits to come up. Even a small number of lawsuits and verdicts announcing the unconstitutionality of congressional and presidential policies made continuing enforcement erratic, because judges' decisions in private litigation controlled public policy.

As had been the case since 1789, during the 1860's federal courts enjoyed only very rare "exclusive" jurisdiction, and "original" jurisdiction only in diversity litigation. These aside, almost all so-called "federal" questions *had* to begin in state courts, with only narrow appeal routes open to highest national tribunes. In short, prewar judicial arrangements made almost all national wartime policies subject to testing and thwarting in the court echelons of every state. It was a discouraging prospect.

Lawsuits lodged in states' courts against national military and civil security, conscription, and revenue officers accentuated the most worrisome aspect of these conditions. Plaintiffs were civilians arrested and imprisoned for some act or word equated with disloyalty, including blockade or trade-control violations. Released after a brief period after subscribing to an oath of future loyalty, several recent "political prisoners" initiated lawsuits against named national officers, claiming unlawful seizure, false arrest, kidnaping, assault and battery, or libel and slander. Other times, when despite writs from state judges to release individuals, national officers persisted in an arrest or imprisonment or retained alleged minors in the Army, state court con-

---

33. *A Philadelphia Perspective: The Diary of Sidney George Fisher, Covering the Years 1834–1871*, ed. Nicholas B. Wainwright (Philadelphia, 1967), 431; and see Roosevelt v. Meyer, 1 Wall., 512–17 (1863); I. F. Greenberg, "Charles Ingersoll: The Aristocrat as Copperhead," *PMHB*, XCIII (1969), 190–217; Ingersoll, *An Undelivered Speech on Executive Arrests* (Philadelphia, 1862). Note Lincoln's concern about emancipation and legal tender as the two targets of judicial attacks, in George S. Boutwell, *Reminiscences of Sixty Years in Public Affairs* (New York, 1902), II, 209.

tempt citations were issued against them. Noncomplying national officers faced prison and money fines in addition to penalties for assertedly violating private rights. Defendants included cabinet Secretaries Cameron, Seward, and Stanton, as well as Army lieutenants. Suits against the latter were especially shrewd hits. Few junior officers could shrug off threats of heavy fines, and none wished to suffer imprisonment. No statutes existed to require federal attorneys, themselves locally-oriented, to intercede on their behalf, and the nation's law officers were too few to do more than protect the highest-ranking officials. Other times, Bates recruited special counsel. But budgets were slim. In effect, national officers were naked in the interstices of federalism. Little wonder that some unknowable number of low- to mid-rank officers hesitated to perform duties because of threatened damage suits. State courts were dominated by what Whiting and others close to Lincoln believed were unfriendly judges, hostile litigants, and treasonable grand juries, especially in the border states and in occupied southern regions, and were simply not providing fair trials.[34]

Support for Whiting's analysis derives from the fact that almost no complainants completed suits. Cutting off the life of a suit in mid-passage served better to impede enforcement of a detested policy or to harass an obnoxious officer, since no risk existed of a verdict against the plaintiff. This is not to say that all plaintiffs aimed only to harass or that all Army officers were innocent of charged offenses. The point is that reasonable men in Washington and across the nation, employing the best available information, believed that many lawsuits were contrived for mean ends.[35]

Within the Army, the result of this belief was anger at the plaintiffs' abettors, the states' judges. It is impressive that prominent civilians, learned in the law, shared this anger; it is fortunate that they brought forth wholesome fruit from this seed of bitterness. But they waited what seems now to have been a dangerously long time, due to the tenacious state-centeredness that dominated legal professionals. Bates phrased the common

---

34. War Department, Policy Book, 26–7, 37–8, 48, RG 110, NA; Whiting's ms. opinion, July 14, 1863, Stanton Papers, LC.

35. See review by E. W. Huffcut of Samuel Miller's *Lectures on the Constitution* (1891), in AAPSS *Annals*, II (1892), 565; Ezra C. Seaman, *The American System of Government* (New York, 1870), vi–viii.

view that "someday" after the Confederacy capitulated, "a flood of [damage] actions" would commence. The fact that some suits began soon after Sumter caught almost everyone off balance and, combined with habeas corpus petitions, appeared to prove the obstructive purposes of the plaintiffs and petitioners.[36]

Francis Lieber illustrates the War's educative process on this score and the growth of ill-feeling between national and state courts. In prewar years Lieber had extolled existing forms of judicial review as "a very jewel of . . . liberty, one of the best fruits of our political civilization." But the leap of antiwar zealots to states' courts and their "unceasing harping upon constitutionality" at best became an "intolerable nuisance," he recalled later. At worst, and the worst was always close to the surface, it threatened disaster when in states' courts unsavory men tried to transform the nation's Constitution into "a boulder in the road," Lieber complained to Sumner.[37]

The result of such reactions was legislation, beginning with the March 3, 1863 habeas-corpus-indemnity-removal law, that in Frankfurter's and Landis's estimate made the Civil War and Reconstruction "a turning point in the history of the federal judiciary." Thereafter, between 1863 and 1875, successive Congresses wove the federal courts more intimately than ever before "into the history of the times."

Even today, when lawmen have scholarly resources available virtually undreamed of a century ago, the improved allocation of jurisdiction between national and state courts is an enormously difficult technical task and a tender political assignment. In the midst of the Civil War, the Lincoln Administration felt impelled to examine, for virtually the first time since 1789, basic nation–state court jurisdictional divisions. Lincoln's lawmakers achieved a remarkable improvement in the harmony and utility of federal courts.[38]

---

36. Stanton to Lincoln, Sept. 13, 1863, Letterbooks III, pt. I, Stanton Papers, LC; also Randall, *Constitutional Problems*, 186–9; Bates to Trumbull, Jan. 7, 1863, Attorney General's Letterbooks B and C, 310–11, RG 60, NA; "The Writ of Habeas Corpus and the Army," *Pittsburgh Legal Intelligencer* (Dec. 14, 1866), 396.

37. Francis Lieber, *Civil Liberty and Self-Government* (3rd rev. edn., Philadelphia, 1875), 164; to Andrew D. White, Feb. 24, 1867, and to Sumner, Nov. 25, 1865, Lieber Papers, HL; Paludan, "Pomeroy," 275–7.

38. Frankfurter and Landis, *Business of the Supreme Court*, 55; "Allocation of Jurisdiction Between Federal and State Courts," *Proceedings,*

Perhaps even these pressures could not have spurred Congress to action if implications in the new (1863) conscription bill had not become apparent before its passage. Many officials who would run the new draft knew that state court lawsuits and writs were impeding vigorous, uniform administration even of the arrangements obtaining in 1861 and 1862. When Congress created a wholly national drafting organization to replace the hodgepodge then on the books, the states' courts would throw up even higher road blocks against effective operation. In addition to conscription, during the 1862–63 winter increasing numbers of suits in states' courts questioned emancipation, Negro enlistment, and fiscal policies, as well as recruitment and internal security.[39]

If Lincoln, Whiting, and leading Republican-Union congressional leaders had been less tender about state rights, it is difficult to see how they could have avoided employing national troops against states' courts, which is what some thoughtful patriots and many critics of American life and institutions expected.[40] New York's Governor Horatio Seymour raised this specter explicitly with respect to the 1863 draft law. Seymour insisted publicly that the national government must carry on the Civil War without a national draft, that Provost Marshal General Fry halt draft operations until state and national courts decided whether or not Congress's 1863 draft law was legitimate, and that every drafted man have a way out of the national Army through state courts' habeas corpus writs. Should a New York court decide that the national law was excessive or that a New Yorker was unjustly in uniform, Seymour threatened to have the state's military force enforce the New York court order. A national conscription could not function under such conditions; indeed, continuation of the Union's search for survival was impossible if Seymour's prescription became accepted.[41]

15th Annual Meeting, Conference of Chief Justices (Chicago, 1963), 4–18; Wiecek, "Reconstruction of Federal Judicial Power," 18–19.

39. William Whiting, *War Powers Under the Constitution of the United States* (Boston, 1871), 159, and see 358–89 for a sample of Whiting's official opinions on these suits; see also War Department, Policy Book, 26–7, RG 110, NA.

40. See as example of expectation of clashes, John J. Freedman, *Is the Act Entitled 'An Act for Enrolling and Calling Out the National Forces, and for Other Purposes,' Passed March 3, 1863, Constitutional or Not?* (New York, 1863), 7.

41. William B. Hesseltine, *Lincoln and the War Governors* (New York, 1948), 301; Eugene C. Murdock, "Horatio Seymour and the 1863

Lincoln did not have to overawe antiwar governors or state judges. Congress provided an alternative to armed confrontations between nation and states on these intermixing matters, so that the federal system became less an unbridged every-government's-land in which odds were heavy against the nation's survival.

Draft," *CWH*, XI (1965), 117–41; Murdock, *Patriotism Limited, 1862–1865; The Civil War Draft and the Bounty System* (Kent, O., 1967), ch. 8 and *passim;* Benjamin P. Thomas and Harold M. Hyman, *Stanton: The Life and Times of Lincoln's Secretary of War* (New York, 1962), 283; Lincoln, *Works*, VI, 370; and see Randall, *Constitutional Problems*, 269–70, 274.

Chapter XV

The Habeas-corpus-indemnity-removal Law, March 3, 1863: To Wait the Verdicts of the Courts

O n March 3, 1863, a new law increased national court removal jurisdiction with respect to certain litigation then maturing in state courts, and federal courts' ministerial review power concerning some classes of civilian prisoners in military custody. Lincoln signed the landmark habeas-corpus-indemnity-removal statute the same day he subscribed the new national draft law. Instead of President or Congress employing what lawyer William Cocke called the "inevitable encroaching power of the sword" to protect national officers, including draft officials who were being sued in states' courts, they discerned the infinitely subtler rein of the national courts. The nation's judges, not its soldiers, would contest with states' judges; laws with laws; legal procedure with procedure. Passage of the habeas-corpus-indemnity-removal law argues that only two years after Sumter, the President and Congress discerned advantages and opportunities in the federal system along with frustrations and pitfalls; that even for Radical Republicans, victory required not only suppressing rebels and reuniting states, but also maintaining the national government's tripartite divisions and federalism's nation-state intricacies.[1]

---

1. William Archer Cocke, *A Treatise on the Common and Civil Law, as Embraced in the Jurisprudence of the United States* (New York, 1871),

This sensitivity is the more remarkable in that prewar jurisdictional allocations between national and state courts had been few, and largely state centered. In the early 1860's, the best information available was that the Constitution's stipulations and Congress's 1789 Judiciary Act had established very limited national court appellate jurisdiction, in instances of litigation deriving from treaties, congressional laws and admiralty or maritime matters, and especially from litigants' diverse state domiciles.[2] Though in 1789 Congress created lower federal courts, the lawmakers explicitly provided for concurrent state court jurisdiction of many subjects which the Constitution allowed to national tribunals, specified that state laws and rules of procedure govern in diversity litigation, and did not provide appeals from state supreme courts to the federal lower courts. If litigants' diverse state residences, or a "federal question" as specified under the Constitution's Article III, existed in a litigation under way in a state court, and the state court denied the national prerogative in question, the 1789 statute allowed (but did not require) the United States Supreme Court to take up the case.[3]

Long before the Civil War, national and state court concurrency created difficulties. New England state courts exhibited marked unwillingness to sustain Jeffersonian economic legislation culminating in the embargo; southern state courts ignored treaty provisions with Indian tribes and national laws affecting merchant sailors who were black; northern state tribunals shrugged off duties the fugitive slave law imposed.[4] In sum, the

---

xiii, 168; Stanley Kutler, *Judicial Power and Reconstruction Politics* (Chicago, 1968), 126.

2. Mitchell Wendell, *Relations Between the Federal and State Courts* (New York, 1949), 50–1; Bernard Schwartz, *A Commentary on the Constitution of the United States* (New York, 1963), I, 345–8; *SAL,* I, 73, sec. 12; John Norton Pomeroy, *Introduction to Constitutional Law* (New York, 1868), ch. 6.

3. Charles Warren, "New Light on the Federal Judiciary Act of 1789," *HLR,* XXXVII (1924), 49–53; Ray Forrester, "The Nature of a Federal Question," *TLR,* XVI (1942), 362–74; Joseph K. Angell, *A Treatise on the Limitations of Actions at Law and Suits in Equity and Admiralty; with an Appendix Containing the American and English Statutes of Limitations* (5th edn., Boston, 1869), 19.

4. C. Herman Pritchett, *The American Constitution* (New York, 1959), 128–9, 130; Prigg v. Pennsylvania, 16 Peters, 539 (1842), made nonconcurrency Supreme Court doctrine, at least for a while. In 1855, efforts failed in Congress to create a removal bill that would bypass northern state courts hostile to federal fugitive slave law enforcement: *CG,* 33

dual court system never became a system in any finished sense. Especially with respect to criminal law, state courts were by far the more important in the lives of the great majority of Americans. No writ, including habeas corpus, issuable by a national judge, could pry loose a state's prisoner except briefly to offer testimony in a federal court trial involving matters other than the prisoner's offense under his state's laws, which meant that most Americans in trouble had no place to go beyond a state's courts. "Here the state authorities have the jump on the national Constitution," Professor Amsterdam has concluded.[5]

Popular distrust of particular states in certain matters before 1860 had sometimes moved Congress to enlarge national court jurisdiction modestly. When New Englanders opposed to Jefferson's embargo and Madison's war initiated private lawsuits in state courts to inhibit federal customs collections and commerce regulations, Congress retaliated in an 1815 customs statute. It allowed federal-officer-defendants in state trials to shift suits to a national district court even if diversity of citizenship was not an element and regardless of amounts of money involved, and enjoined state judges to "proceed no further in the cause." Encouraged by Congress's support, Joseph Story and John Marshall employed Supreme Court opinions to plead for greater removal provisions from states' courts to national inferior courts and Supreme Court, and to encompass fully all federal questions even if state courts had come to final judgments. Indeed, in 1816 Story insisted that Congress had no option; it bore responsibility

---

Cong., 2 sess., App., 210 *ff.*, 26. See Osborn v. Bank of U.S., 9 Wheat., (1824); J. B. Heiskell, "Conflict Between Federal and State Decisions," *ALRev*, XVI (1882), 743–5.

5. Anthony G. Amsterdam, "Criminal Prosecutions Affecting Federally Guaranteed Civil Rights: Federal Removal and Habeas Corpus Jurisdiction to Abort State Court Trial," *UPLR* (1965), 801 and *passim.* Amsterdam's substantial essay provides the skeleton for the following treatment. Cohens v. Virginia, 6 Wheat., 264, asserted the U.S. Supreme Court's right to review convictions for state crimes when a federal question was involved. See also *Federalist Papers*, Nos. 80, 81; Ex parte Bollman, 8 US, 75 (1807); Ableman v. Booth, 21 Howard, 506 (1859); and the comment in Robb v. Connolly, 111 US 624, 637 (1883): "upon the State courts, equally with the courts of the Union, rests the obligation to guard, enforce, and protect every right granted or secured by the Constitution of the United States, and the laws made in pursuance therefore, whenever those rights are involved on any suit or proceeding before them." Note too that in the 1860's the national Bill of Rights was not allowed as a restraint on states: Barron v. Baltimore, 7 Peters, 243 (1833).

to provide the federal judiciary with this imperial jurisdictional highway.[6] But he was far too early. Only the Civil War and Reconstruction inspired Congress to begin provision, and the task was to take from 1863 to 1875 for systematic completion.

To return to the prewar chronology, in the 1833 antinullification Force Act Congress provided President Jackson with authority to employ the military power of the nation (including states' militias called into federal service), and allowed removal of customs suits from states' courts. To effect removal, a national revenue-officer-defendant in a state court, before trial commenced there, had to petition the United States circuit court for a habeas corpus (cum causa) writ. A writ could issue: "in all cases of a prisoner or prisoners, in jail [by states' authority], where he or they shall be committed or confined on, or by any authority or law, for any act done, or omitted to be done, in pursuance of a law of the United States, or any order, process, or decree, of any judge or court thereof."[7]

In 1842, as a result of the famous McLeod murder case, the need became evident for the nation to extricate from a state's prison aliens who claimed that their alleged offense against a state was legitimate under the law of nations. Then in 1855 proslavery senators tried to increase removals from northern state

---

6. *SAL*, III (1815), esp. sec. 8. Story in Martin v. Hunter's Lessee, 1 Wheat., 304 (1816); Story, *Commentaries on the Constitution of the United States* (2nd edn., Boston, 1851), II, 427; Marshall in Osborn v. Bank of U.S., 9 Wheat., 819 (1824). A succinct account is in William M. Wiecek, "The Reconstruction of Federal Judicial Power, 1863–1875," *AJLH*, XIII (1969), 333–59. Obviously variant pagination will indicate reference to Wiecek's far fuller M.A. thesis (UWis, 1966) of the same title. On specifics, Catherine M. Tarrant, "The Janus-faced 1863 Habeas Corpus Act" (SHA paper, 1971), a foretaste of her RU 1972 Ph.D. dissertation, "A Writ of Liberty or a Covenant with Hell?: Habeas Corpus in the War Congresses, 1861–1867," is essential, and I base substantial portions of this chapter on her work.

7. *SAL*, IV, 632–4. In Harris v. Dennie, 3 Peters 292 (1830), the U.S. Supreme Court rebuked states' officers including judges for impeding national officials from performing assigned duties. See also Warren, "Federal and State Court Interference," 345–50. Note that within a year South Carolina declared the 1833 law unconstitutional; State v. McReady, 2 Hill, 1 (1834), and that the precedent Corn Tassel execution and the case of Cherokee Nation v. Georgia, 5 Peters 1 (1831) would not have been embraced by the 1833 law, which dealt only with state interferences with federal revenue matters. Joseph C. Burke, "The Cherokee Causes: A Case Study in Law, Politics, and Morality," OAH paper, 1968 (copy used with permission), offers trenchant analysis.

courts of litigation involving federal fugitive slave commissioners. Antislave extensionists blocked the bill, condemning it as a centralizing enlargement of national court jurisdiction.[8]

These sporadic, sparse instances of attention to federal court jurisdiction questions and additions to the 1789 statute involved the removal remedy for only very limited classes of people and occasions. They did not alter federal-state court relationships very much, or greatly increase appeal roads from the latter to the former. Such alteration and augmentation had to wait till the Civil War's dangers and opportunities forced passage of the March 3, 1863 habeas-corpus-indemnity-removal law.

Unquestionably, as Professor Randall suggested, the congressmen who created this landmark statute were after immediate benefits rather than long-range improvements in federal-state relationships or the augmentation of national judicial power. He suggested also that Congress's purpose was totally to immunize national officers, who were being sued by private plaintiffs in state courts for such offenses as trespassing, illegal arrest, false imprisonment, and assault, from the consequences of their official actions. But War Department Solicitor William Whiting made it clear that Congress's first object was to indemnify and protect such officers, not to immunize them.[9] Congress's second "great object" was to legitimize and discipline the internal-security practices which the Lincoln Administration had developed since Sumter, that Taney had said only Congress could allow.

On the second point, Congress specified in the 1863 habeas corpus law that the President "is authorized" to suspend the writ privilege whenever during "the present rebellion" he judged that the public safety required the action. This phraseology left uncertain whether Congress was blanketing the arrest procedures which executive officers had been developing and following. What was not arguable was that Congress had acted; that is, not arguable unless courts declared unconstitutional this well-based section of the 1863 statute, an unlikely prospect.[10]

---

8. *SAL,* V, 539 (1842); Amsterdam, "Criminal Prosecutions," 808 and n.; Wiecek, "Reconstruction," 337 n., for other data.

9. Opinion, July 14, 1863, Stanton Papers, LC; James G. Randall, *Constitutional Problems Under Lincoln* (rev. edn., Urbana, Ill., 1951), 129–31, 214.

10. *SAL,* XII, 755, sec. 1. Almost at once after Appomattox, a Pennsylvania court declared this section of the 1863 law to have expired: Cozzens

Indemnification of national officers facing suits in state courts, Whiting's first "great object" of the statute, went back to Anglo-Saxon times. Civil War congressmen who were lawyers were able to resort almost without discussion to ancient principles of the common law for support. Officers who exploited their powers to profit or to oppress could not cloak themselves behind commissions or orders, and properly were subject to civil and/or criminal prosecutions, the tradition had it; officers who carried out lawful duties in a decent manner were entitled to government protection in the form of counsel and financial indemnity against consequences.[11]

This indemnity process was relatively simple in England, where Parliament's statutes ran through the land and subordinate courts did not deny the legitimacy of Parliament's legislation. But as with everything in America, federalism made it necessary for Congress to deal with two dozen states. Each contained independent courts, several of which were questioning the validity of national policies. Congress had to expand indemnity procedure to a judiciary act.

In this sense the March 1863 statute was an omnibus measure. But it was neither impetuous nor vindictive. Instead it possessed good political sense and constitutional insight. Justification for this description emerges from the context of the momentous legislative sessions in which the bill became law, and from the interwoven concerns and fears of its supporters.

Congressmen who created this law had been elected with Lincoln. Veterans of parliamentary battles since Sumter, these men were considering, simultaneously with the indemnity and habeas-corpus question, the conscription bill, with its Provost Marshal General centralizing feature. Republicans had to ponder the results of the fall 1862 state and congressional elections, involving strong Democratic upsurges, and the knowledge that on January 1, 1863, Lincoln's emancipation decree had become operative, initiating recruitment of Negroes into the Union's

---

v. Frink, reported in *ALReg*, n.s., IV (Sept. 1865), 700–702; and see Johnson v. Jones, 44 Ill., 142, reported in *ALRev*, II (1867), 184.

11. Randall, *Constitutional Problems*, 186–9; *SAL*, XII, secs. 4–7. Whiting held that under the 1863 law, the $100,000 which Congress appropriated to carry out its provisions was employable only for the hire of special counsel, not to pay damages if a federal (not state) court levied them against an officer found guilty as charged: Opinion, July 14, 1863, Stanton Papers, LC.

armies. Further, each state government that bluecoats—including blacks—were resurrecting southward was re-establishing civil courts, where except for secession and war matters, pre-Sumter state laws would resume sway.[12] Those laws, as well as those of certain unseceded loyal states, forbade arming Negroes and imposed capital punishments on violators. In short, by 1863 the Union Army's need for black manpower from the South was forcing the President and his executive subordinates to violate the laws of a dozen slaveholding states. National martial thrusts were shattering what Howe described as the profound "pre-War constitutional commitment to silence and [national] disability" about slavery. Lincoln's emancipation decision was a "resounding renunciation of the old neutrality" about federalism and political rights, which the nation had humbly observed.[13]

Emancipation and conscription were very likely to stall not only in resurrected state courts in the South but also in border and northern states. Provost Marshal administrators of the new national draft would enlist and arm blacks in defiance of several states' laws, and impeding litigation would follow. Always the Merryman specter refused to fade away. Similar attacks seemed likely on emancipation and conscription. Legitimacy was needed for existing security operations and for the more vigorous policies needed to sustain a national draft and Negro enlistments.

With respect to its second major purpose in enacting this law, Congress aspired to control as well as to legitimize security matters. Legislators involved in the habeas-corpus-indemnity-bill construction aimed at civilian domination over the ever-enlarging military hierarchy, especially the Provost Marshal General centralization they were considering simultaneously. In some measure, the lawyerlike penchant for procedural certainty and uniformity in government operations played a prominent part in shaping the March 1863 habeas corpus statute.[14]

---

12. Note that on December 8, 1863, Lincoln "suggested as not improper" the renascence of state courts and laws in each Reconstruction military government: *M&P*, VI, 214; and see Garrett Davis's statement of connection between these matters, *CG*, 37 Cong., 3 sess., 529–34.

13. Mark DeWolfe Howe, "Federalism and Civil Rights," *MHSP*, LXXVII (1965), 26. I advance Howe's argument from 1865–66 to 1862–63.

14. William Whiting, *War Powers Under the Constitution of the United States* (43rd edn., Boston and New York, 1871), 377: "It is obvious that there ought to be some way by which, in all cases, officers who have committed homicides, or other acts of violence, in the discharge of their

During the eighteen months separating the 37th Congress's July 1861 special session from the spring 1863 lame-duck days, legislators had worked over and over issues finally embraced in the momentous 1863 habeas corpus law. After so many repetitions, little debate was necessary when formal construction of a statute was under way. No Republican parliamentary coup was needed to jam the habeas-corpus-indemnity bill through the allegedly unsuspecting House and Senate.[15]

Republicans Thaddeus Stevens and Lyman Trumbull represented substantial sentiment on Capitol Hill when they demanded rigorous enforcement of executive antidisloyalty policies, along with greater regularization and civilian control of them and of the Army as a whole. The Republicans intended partially to rein in the uniformed giant by resort to the federal judiciary, which at the same time could protect soldiers against state court harassments.

Certain configurations of what became the March 1863 statute took form early. In December 1861, separate bills fell into House and Senate hoppers (none passed then) ordering dismissal of "political prisoners" except those indictable under existing federal criminal statutes, and approving past habeas corpus suspensions by the President as well as other suspensions to come.[16] Stevens introduced a bill on December 8, 1862, which peremptorily dismissed suits in states' courts when defendants were federal civil or military officers whose alleged offenses derived from presidential or congressional orders. His bill passed the House. But when it reached the Senate impenetrable obstacles to passage had risen, in the form of legislators' reverence for state prerogatives and procedures. The Stevens provision gave way to one by Trumbull for national officer-defendants to appeal for removal of their cases from state to federal courts.[17]

Senators of both parties objected to the novelty in Trum-

---

duties, should be protected under the law; and some procedures by which the same rules of law should be applied in all parts of the country. It would be discreditable to the administration of justice if the same act should be pronounced a crime in one State, and a justifiable act of duty in another. Hence there ought to be some mode of applying uniform rules of law, by one tribunal, to all like cases, wherever they arise."

15. Randall, *Constitutional Problems*, 190–1, typifies the position that a coup occurred.

16. *CG*, 37 Cong., 1 sess., 40; 2 sess., 91, 3106; 3 sess., 536.

17. *Ibid.*, 3 sess., 321.

bull's proposal that allowed national lower courts to take up from state courts certain civil and criminal cases and to consider them anew. Bayard of Delaware reminded his colleagues that the 1815 law, upon which Trumbull leaned for a precedent, "was confined to acknowledgedly constitutional powers of the [national] Government in relation to its custom-house . . . [and] its revenue affairs." But the 1863 proposal allowed removal in litigation about matters whose dubious constitutionality was a reason for state court litigation. Any defendant could claim that his acts for which he was on trial came under some wartime order and thereby prostrate the criminal jurisdiction of states' courts, Bayard warned.[18]

The Trumbull form passed the Senate. House variations required a conference committee. Agreement in the conference committee returned the bill to both houses. Passage, and Lincoln's subscription, occurred on March 3.[19]

The new law required the Secretaries of State and War to furnish lists of "political prisoners" within twenty days after incarceration occurred, to federal circuit and district judges (or their equivalent in territories and the District of Columbia). If the succeeding federal grand jury did not indict listed prisoners, the judge of that court was to discharge them on their subscribing an oath of loyalty, and, if the judge ordered it, a bond for good behavior. Further, Congress stipulated that "every officer" in charge of prisoners obey these judges' orders of discharge or suffer a five-hundred dollar fine and six months' imprisonment. If the Secretaries failed to supply the required lists within the twenty days, Congress specified a petitioning procedure to bring to a federal judge's attention the names of unreported prisoners, whereupon the preceding discharge arrangements were to be effective.[20]

Scholars have looked two ways at these provisions. Kelly and Harbison praise them guardedly for converting arbitrary practices into regular procedures and for regularizing arrests without unduly restricting executive procedures. But they remark also that the statute made little essential difference in the arbitrary arrests, because Stanton was laggard in supplying the lists and Holt interpreted narrowly the definition of political prisoner,

---

18. *Ibid.*, 538.
19. *Ibid.*, 1460, 1462.
20. *SAL*, XII, 755–6, secs. 2–3.

excluding from lists finally submitted the names of civilians under trial by military commissions.[21]

Stanton's orders to Holt called for assembling the lists within the twenty-day time limit. But in the spring of 1863 all energies were bent on mounting operations soon to climax at Gettysburg and Vicksburg. Ninety days after Lincoln signed the bill into law, Holt transmitted the laggard accounting of civilian prisoners.

Holt's narrow interpretation of political prisoners reflected professional agreement among the law-trained Washington executive leadership that civilian prisoners facing courts-martial and military commission trials for purely military offenses under the 57th Article of War, as much Congress's product as any statute, deserved no place on Holt's lists, for they were untriable by civil courts. Such criminals included proved bushwhackers, guerrillas, saboteurs, and spies, whom civil law could not touch by contemporary understandings soon substantiated in the 1864 Vallandigham case in the United States Supreme Court. If Holt's lists left unreported any prisoner who deserved a civil judge's attention, Congress's petition procedure was available.

More important is the fact that since February 1862 the War Department had anticipated Congress in examining prisoners and releasing those whose offenses were slight, by means of special investigating commissions composed usually of a senior Army officer and a prestigious civilian, almost always a lawyer. These commissions reviewed systematically charges against civilian prisoners and ordered their release when evidence was inadequate for civil or military prosecution.[22] In short, by the time Congress acted, executive personnel had done or were doing a

---

21. Alfred H. Kelly and Winfred A. Harbison, *The American Constitution: Its Origins and Development* (3rd edn., New York, 1963), 443; William B. Weeden, *War Government: Federal and State, in Massachusetts, New York, Pennsylvania, and Indiana, 1861–1865* (Boston and New York, 1906), 352–3.
22. *Sen. Exec. Doc.* 23, 38 Cong., 2 sess.; Benjamin P. Thomas and Harold M. Hyman, *Stanton: The Life and Times of Lincoln's Secretary of War* (New York, 1962), 157–8, 375–6. On the question of civil courts' jurisdiction over sentences of military commissions under the 57th Article of War see Ex parte Vallandigham, 1 Wall., 243 (1864); Ex parte Milligan, 4 Wall., 2 (1866), and Stanley I. Kutler, "Ex parte McCardle: Judicial Impotency? The Supreme Court and Reconstruction Reconsidered," *AHR*, LXXII (1967), 835–8 and *passim*.

fair share of the job Congress wished done, which is why the 1863 listing provisions made little difference.

In the sections of the 1863 law involving removal of suits from state to federal courts, Congress stipulated that an officer-defendant's orders to arrest persons and to search or seize property should be a defense. In short, Congress did not limit removal protection to acts done under any one statute. Instead Congress blanketed all official acts a national officer performed under orders. The sued officer could petition for removal of his case from the state court to the nearest federal circuit court and the state judge must accept the shift. In the federal court, "the cause shall proceed . . . in the same manner as if it had been brought in said court by original process, whatever may be the amount in dispute or the damages claimed, or whatever the citizenship of the parties, any former law to the contrary notwithstanding." If a state court had already rendered a verdict against the federal-officer-defendant, he might appeal to the national circuit court for a writ of error and have a new trial under the nation's judicial dispensation. Congress stipulated further that suits must begin against national officers within two years of the alleged false arrest and imprisonment.[23] The federal system now had a bridge, however narrow, for certain state defendants and even prisoners.

Randall and Swisher concluded that the 1863 law was hasty and extreme war legislation. But Alfred Conkling, a contemporary student of jurisdiction, described the 1863 law as "a studiously devised and carefully framed act" well constructed "to meet the exigencies of the rebellion then at its height."[24] Conkling's evaluation leads to an admonition by Justice Frankfurter: "Framers of judiciary acts are not required to be seers; and great judiciary acts, unlike great poems, are not written for all time. It is enough if the designers of new judicial machinery meet the chief needs of their generation."[25]

---

23. *SAL*, XII, 757–8, secs. 4–7; Wiecek, "Reconstruction," 338.

24. Randall, *Constitutional Problems*, 214; Carl B. Swisher, *Roger B. Taney* (New York, 1935), 443; Alfred Conkling, *A Treatise on the Organization, Jurisdiction, and Practice of the Courts of the United States in Suits at Law* (5th rev. edn., Albany, 1870), 80 n.

25. Felix Frankfurter and James M. Landis, *The Business of the Supreme Court: A Study in the Federal Judicial System* (New York, 1928), 107.

The March 1863 formulation fares well by Frankfurter's gauges as well as by contemporary measures. Its passage by united Republicans, many of whom were top-notch lawyers, suggests agreement on fundamentals. Alfred Conkling noted during the 1870's that Congress intended this statute "to evoke the dormant forces of the [national] Judiciary in aid of the Executive," and in his opinion the legislators aimed very accurately.[26] Whiting's informed judgment was that by 1863 the President, many congressmen, and most federal judges had learned a great deal about the "strange and alarming" ways of war, including the fact that relatively few states' judges were equally sensitive if only because of their unceasing involvements in local politics. Doctrines of the Constitution's adequacy, rare in 1861, and "confined to a few individuals, have now become so general among our most eminent [national] judges, lawyers, and legislators" as to warrant risking the habeas-corpus-indemnity law's removal innovations, Whiting happily recorded.

Whiting was correct. No more Taney-Lincoln confrontations occurred. The increased national court jurisdiction provided by Congress prevented constitutional crises. Ordinary court processes and familiar political procedures, including elections, avoided clashes between nation and state. The enlargement of national court jurisdiction was more than a duration-only step. It was the beginning of an end to some of federalism's twilight zones which had helped to bring on the Civil War.[27]

Probably Congress and the President would have trusted high national judges less if they had known what engaged Chief Justice Taney. Silently and gloomily observing affairs during 1861–63, Taney prepared opinions-without-cases declaring unconstitutional the nation's conscription, emancipation, and legal-tender policies.

---

26. Conkling, *Treatise*, unnumbered prefatory page; *CG*, 37 Cong., 3 sess., 554, 1479.

27. Whiting, *War Powers* (1871), 159–60; Roy Franklin Nichols, "Federalism versus Democracy: The Significance of the Civil War in the History of United States Federalism," in *Federalism as a Democratic Process: Essays by Roscoe Pound, Charles H. McIlwain, Roy F. Nichols* (New Brunswick, N.J., 1942), 75; Frankfurter and Landis, *Supreme Court*, 55; Wiecek, "Reconstruction," 358–9.

Professor Swisher concluded in 1935 that Taney was engaged in a sort of professional exercise. But it is equally reasonable to believe that Taney intended actually to employ these opinions when litigation came up along the widened jurisdictional roads the Lincoln Administration was providing. If this is the correct estimation, then by contriving the 1863 law the Republicans had delivered themselves, the Union, and Negro slaves into Taney's hands.[28]

Taney's general views were no secret. Any increase in national court jurisdiction to encompass war-centered litigation in state courts opened opportunities for Taney to speak officially against them. Probably many congressmen supported what became the 1863 habeas corpus law on the assumption that Taney had not much longer to live and would not benefit from the augmented jurisdiction.[29] Nevertheless, he had gone along in the Prize Cases and the Vallandigham petition. It may have been that congressmen and President decided that with all hazards balanced, even with Taney the United States courts were better arenas for protecting bedrock policies than the courts of most states.

A measure of the risk which, more or less unknowingly, Congress took in the 1863 habeas corpus statute is available from examination of the secret Taney opinions, especially the one on conscription. It reveals the existence of a paradox in his understanding of the Civil War. He believed privately that it was fundamentally and unpleasantly altering all relationships between nation, states, and individuals. However, his undelivered opinion on the 1863 conscription statute was a fully developed expression of the view that events since Sumter could alter nothing. In terms of the classic compact theory, Taney asserted that the functional orbit of the nation must never override those of the states. Going backward from his own strongly nationalist opinion in Ableman v. Booth (1958), Taney pointed to the Tenth and Eleventh Amendments "to show . . . that the states were

---

28. In 1966, Professor Swisher agreed orally that the alternative analysis is equally logical, of Taney preparing these opinions with intention actually to employ them at first opportunity, in contrast to his view of 1935 in Swisher, *Taney*, 571.

29. Lincoln agonized over the choice of Taney's successor because he was certain that emancipation, Reconstruction, and legal tender would face Supreme Court scrutiny; George S. Boutwell, *Reminiscences of Sixty Years in Public Affairs* (New York, 1902), II, 29.

still sovereignties in their character . . . [and] that the Federal government has no inherent, and original powers of sovereignty. It has only what the States delegated—and any exercise of sovereign power beyond these limits would be a usurpation of State Sovereignty—and consequently illegal." Any effort by the national government to coerce a seceded state back into the Union constituted treason against that state, he insisted.[30]

Americans owed basic allegiance not to the nation but to their respective states. The states had not delegated to Congress a power to enact any measure akin to the 1863 conscription law. This law illicitly merged into one national force the distinct military institutions that the Constitution authorized; the regular Army and the states' militias. The latter must never lose their discrete identities, even when temporarily in federal service. Congress could not at its whim amend and abrogate sections of the Constitution which referred to the states' militias.

To be sure, the Constitution (Article I, section 8) also stated without qualification that Congress might raise and support armed forces. But surely these sparse, general words did not obliterate all the specific clauses in the Constitution that undergirded the states' unalterable dominations of militia organizations.

It was the heart of Taney's judgment on the Civil War's impact on the Constitution that the arrangements of 1787 were exclusive and fixed. Under them the national government could do certain things and no others. War, rebellion, or insurrection did not open new arenas for the national government to enter, such as conscription did, acting directly on individuals. It "makes the Constitution of no higher authority than an act of Congress,— and every provision in it liable to be repealed and altered or disregarded whenever in the judgment of a majority of the Legislature

---

30. Quotations in Phillip G. Auchampaugh, "A Great Chief Justice on State and Federal Power: Being the Thoughts of Chief Justice Taney on the Federal Conscription Act," *Tyler's Quarterly Historical and Genealogical Magazine*, XVIII (1936), 77. Charles Grove Haines and Foster Sherwood, *The Role of the Supreme Court in American Government and Politics, 1835–1864* (Berkeley and Los Angeles, 1957), 488–95, review Taney's opinion and I follow closely their treatment and the Auchampaugh text, as well as the manuscript opinions in the Taney Papers, NYPL. An earlier version of the opinion on conscription is in the "oddments" folder, Taney Papers, LC, and was discovered by Michael Conron. See also Schwartz, *Commentary*, II, 219.

the public interest would be promoted by the exercise of the powers not conferred."[31]

Adequate only for a certain sort of war, the Constitution's specifications were unmodifiable as to the ways Congress might elect to wage such a war, Taney insisted. Champions of a looser construction, who argued that Congress could adopt measures unspecified in the Constitution, were establishing "a temporary or provisional government." To prevent such usurpation the national judiciary stood in the way. Judges "can never be called on to execute or enforce laws or recognize as justifiable assumptions of powers which the Constitution has not conferred," he concluded.[32]

Taney's undelivered opinion returned to themes that he had stressed in Merryman's case. In mid-1863, as in mid-1861, Taney was holding fast to pre-Sumter constitutional configurations. Yet everywhere contrasts with what had existed two years earlier were immense.

Merryman's petition came up a few weeks after the United States government had proved itself too weak to succor even the puny garrison of a single fort—in 1863, mass armies were maneuvering on fronts separated by a thousand miles. In 1861 abolitionists lacked real hope of achieving their aim—by 1863 partial abolition and Negro enlistments existed by virtue of an exercise of Commander-in-Chief powers which shaded all actions of Lincoln's White House predecessors back to Washington into insignificance, and which blazed a new trail into the civil liberties arena for Presidents to take. At half a dozen points around the shrinking Confederacy, military officers were establishing "loyal" local and state governments, convening state constitutional conventions, and enforcing disfranchising policies designed to exclude untrustworthy residents. Under the Army's protection, experiments were in process involving the employment of freed Negroes as tillers of abandoned agricultural properties. In cooperation with volunteer civilian groups, soldiers were seeing to it that some Negroes were gaining at least rudiments of common school educations. In a few racially unsegregated classrooms educators were pioneering new frontiers of pedagogy and curtailing racial prejudice, reformers hoped. Because so much of this

---

31. Auchampaugh, "A Great Chief Justice," 82.
32. *Ibid.*, 83.

was repugnant to him, by 1863 the Chief Justice became the more convinced that the 1861 war aim—reunion—was too dear to continue to strive for.

Randall concluded that Taney would not have carried his brethren if a high court test of the conscription law had taken place.[33] Nevertheless, considering the hazards involved in opening new roads into national courtrooms, the Lincoln Administration's insistence on employing legal processes in order to carry on the War and on living within the Constitution reflects compelling convictions. This insistence that the nation not enter into combats against any courts found expression by such conservative leaders in Congress as Trumbull, and by Bates in the Cabinet. Bates, lobbying for an indemnity bill, was determined to maintain both "the judicial peace of the country and . . . the reasonable safety of the [national] government." The "Radical" abolitionist spokesman Whiting wrote that "it was essential to preserve the power and dignity of the General Government unimpaired, and at the same time to avoid open rupture with the [states'] courts; hence it was desirable to meet and foil the secret enemies of their country by the use of [national] *judicial* weapons."[34]

The multiplication of such expressions is not difficult. Of confiscation law enforcement, in 1863 Bates reminded a federal attorney, "all . . . *must be done in or by the Courts;* and happily, with such proceedings you are familiar." Of emancipation, Lincoln's 1863 proclamation on Reconstruction raised the specter of reversibility, for the President specified that southern whites swear to abide by emancipation "so far as [it is] not repealed, modified, or held void by Congress or by decision of the Supreme Court." Of loyalty-test constitutionality, in 1867 another Attorney General cautioned a district attorney to "wait the verdicts of the courts."[35] Forty years later Supreme Court Justice John Marshall Harlan recalled Horace Binney's description of how the courts engaged the imaginations of war-weary men of

---

33. Randall, *Constitutional Problems,* 274. The World War I draft law received Supreme Court approval; Selective Draft Law Cases, 245 US, 366 (1918).

34. Edward Bates to Lyman Trumbull, Jan. 7, 1863, Attorney General's Letterbooks B and C, 311, RG 60, NA; Whiting, *War Powers* (1871), 159.

35. Bates to E. Delafield Smith, Jan. 10, 1863, Attorney General's Letterbooks B and C, RG 60, NA (italics are Bates's); Chief Clerk M. F. Pleasants for Attorney General Henry Stanbery, Feb. 26, 1867, Letterbook F, *ibid.;* and see Stanbery to A. H. Garland, Feb. 5, 1867, *ibid.;* M&P, VI, 219.

the sixties, who wanted the law and the courts to become "the great moral substitute for force in controversies between the people, the states, and the Union."[36]

This mood dominated congressmen as well as high executive officers. "I . . . thank God—the judgment of a court does still in the estimation of the public no less than in the estimation of the Law 'impart absolute verity,'" Wisconsin Senator T. O. Howe lectured Seward, after Seward, fearful of state judges' partisanship, suggested that guilty persons escape prosecutions.[37] Such evidence argues that a major impact of the Civil War and Reconstruction was augmentation, not diminution, of the national judiciary. It argues also that greater equality before law as a basic quality of the restored nation was tied to this effect.

In 1863 the idea of equality of each American before his state's law, and, if an alternative forum was necessary, before his nation's bar, where the relevant state laws might apply or, in certain circumstances, the nation's, as actuality rather than a phrase, was novel in American jurisprudence. Derived from prewar abolitionist theory, it found initial formal expression in Sumner's abortive 1863 proposal for a thirteenth amendment, in defense of which he argued that equality before law underlay the Declaration of Independence. Despite Sumner's defeat, his concept was attracting Lincoln and other Americans who pondered the Civil War's meaning. By 1863 the equality theme was so much part of Republican weaponry that the Senate spent half its time considering derivative implications and proposals, Senator Reverdy Johnson complainingly estimated.[38] In such contexts the March 8, 1863 habeas-corpus-indemnity law was very much part of a picture of reasoned congressional adaptation to the Civil War's impacts.

Events occurring soon after passage of this statute centering on the spectacular Vallandigham case suggest the general awareness among national jurists of Congress's unbellicose attitude

---

36. Quoted in *Dinner Given by the Bar of the Supreme Court of the United States to Mr. Justice John Marshall Harlan, December 9, 1902,* (New York, 1902), 26.

37. Aug. 22, 1864, Howe Papers, SHSW; Seward to T. O. Howe, Aug. 15, 1864, Stanton Papers, LC.

38. Sumner, *Works,* VIII, 81-2, IX, 380-93; Sumner, *Universal Emancipation Without Compensation* (Washington, 1864), 14-15; Reverdy Johnson in *CG,* 38 Cong., 1 sess., 1156, 2801-3.

toward them. Ohio's Clement Vallandigham had become a center of antiwar, right-wing Democratic party strength. He sharply criticized an order of the new Ohio Department military commander, Ambrose Burnside, who ordered his arrest. A military commission declared him guilty of expressing disloyal sentiments. Vallandigham's counsel refused to admit the Army court's jurisdiction over a civilian and sought a habeas corpus writ from the United States Circuit Court in Cincinnati, which refused to issue it.

Vallandigham's arrest was reported to executive and judicial officers in harmony with War Department's policies and the March 3, 1863 statute. When the Ohioan's lawyer sought a Supreme Court review of Vallandigham's case by means of a writ of certiorari, he learned that the Justices were unwilling to transcend the letter of what existing laws and precedents allowed; the Court denied itself jurisdiction in an appeal from a military commission trial. Lincoln ordered the nettlesome Ohioan released and banished into Confederate lines. When Vallandigham returned to the United States in the hope of again becoming a center of anti-Lincoln votes, the President saw to it that Union Army officers let him alone.

Ohio's Senator John Sherman noted that Vallandigham enjoyed not one but two opportunities to be heard before national civil courts. It was remarkable, the Senator continued, that a nation in the midst of a great war should concern itself at all with protective procedures for loyal citizens, much less openly disloyal ones. For himself, Sherman was proud of the Congress's priorities, which he believed represented popular will.[39] Certainly they represented at least a commitment to litigation as a substitute for force.

---

39. Randall, *Constitutional Problems*, 177–9, 186–99; Lorraine A. Williams, "Northern Intellectual Reaction to Military Rule During the Civil War," *The Historian*, XXVII (1965), 342–5; Sherman in *New York Times*, Aug. 2, 1863; Ex parte Vallandigham, 1 Wall., 243 (1863). See also Roger Bridges, "The Constitutional World of Senator John Sherman, 1861–1870" (Ph.D. diss., UI, 1970), 89–93; Frank L. Klement, *The Limits of Dissent: Clement L. Vallandigham & the Civil War* (Lexington, Ky., 1970), chs. 12–13.

Chapter XVI

Litigation:
The Great Moral Substitute
for Force

A year after Lincoln announced emancipation of slaves and the enlistment of Negroes into the Army (September 1862, January 1863), nine months after he signed into law the conscription, Provost Marshal General, and habeas-corpus-indemnity-removal bills (March 1863), he issued (December 8, 1863) a proclamation on amnesty, pardon, and Reconstruction. Thereafter, Reconstruction alternatives took form from the President's proposal, the "first in the field," Eben G. Scott noted.

Many congressmen had been and remained keenly sensitive to Reconstruction implications, especially with respect to race, if only because reconstructed southern states' courts touched race relationships as well as Congress's arrangements on courts' jurisdictions, among many other matters such as conscription and confiscation. Alfred Conkling hit the mark in his statement that, like the President's Reconstruction proclamation, Congress's 1863 removal law aimed "to readjust the shattered political fabric" once the War ended victoriously.[1]

---

1. Eben G. Scott, *Reconstruction During the Civil War in the United States of America* (Boston and New York, 1895), 275; Alfred Conkling, *A Treatise on the Organization, Jurisdiction, and Practice of the Courts of the United States* (Albany, 1870), unnumbered prefatory page.

In his December 8 proclamation Lincoln stipulated that disloyal persons wishing to "resume their allegiance to the United States and to reinaugurate loyal State governments" would receive his pardon, relieving them of the consequences of their guilt "except as to slaves." The only condition facing rank-and-file rebels was subscription of a specified oath of future loyalty containing also a promise to "abide by and faithfully support" all congressional confiscation laws and presidential emancipation edicts "so long and so far as not repealed, modified, or held void by Congress or by decision of the Supreme Court."

The same day, having already pleased militant Republicans by implying that national state-remaking initiative would fill rebel state vacuums,[2] Lincoln presented his "state of the Union" message to the newly assembled 38th Congress. Its members were the first legislators elected wholly on wartime issues. The results of the fall 1862 balloting encouraged antiwar, Negrophobe Democrats who had appealed to constituents as opponents to the Emancipation Proclamation. Many informed men feared that northern discouragement and racism were strong enough to make the President reverse course and withdraw the emancipation edict.[3] In order to thwart reversal, Francis Lieber's General Orders 100 (April 1863) contained injunctions derived from American, international, and natural laws against men once slaves being reduced again to bondage.[4] Lieber and like-thinking men were relieved and pleased that by the end of 1863, when he issued his Reconstruction proclamation, Lincoln had determined to hold as fast as he could against any rollback for emancipation. It had become a moral impossibility, Lincoln stated, a position agreeable to all Republicans.

This decision involved considerable political risk. The precarious Republican–War Democrat "Union" party coalition needed

---

2. *M&P*, VI, 213–14. That Lincoln's statement harmonized with the general constitutional views of Radical Republicans about southern state vacuums, however described, is noted in Herman Belz, *Reconstructing the Union: Theory and Practice During the Civil War* (Ithaca, N.Y., 1969), 170–1 and *passim*.

3. Forrest Wood, *Black Scare: The Racist Response to Emancipation and Reconstruction* (Berkeley, 1968), chs. 1 and 2; Benjamin R. Curtis, *Executive Power* (Boston, 1862), 16–19.

4. *OR*, ser. III, vol. 3, 153, secs. 42–3. Lieber referred to postliminy, a civil law doctrine by which a person is returned to a status which he held before unlawful deprivation occurred of that status.

little reason to break. Lincoln gambled that enough northerners, including Union soldiers, agreed with him that military victory for the Union was more likely with emancipation than without it. Lincoln still flirted with colonization chimeras. But they were losing out in favor of still-dim comprehension that finer alternatives existed, including biracial coexistence on terms other than master-slave. The question was, what terms?[5]

Lincoln's December message to Congress grappled forthrightly with the manifold opportunities and danger involved in emancipation and Reconstruction. He advised congressmen that events since January proved prophets of doom wrong about the consequences of arming Negroes. Black bluecoats had not indulged in excesses, as two centuries of white folklore insisted Negroes would if they had weapons. Therefore employment of Negro soldiers would continue. As Union armies advanced, slaves would become free men as firmly as executive power could make the transformation.

The President defended his linking of emancipation to Reconstruction in the proclamation issued that day. Turncoating southern whites must accept emancipation as well as reunion as preconditions to receiving his individual pardon or blanket amnesty. Only amnestied or pardoned people should participate in their states' Reconstruction efforts, Lincoln insisted.

In effect, Lincoln defined "loyalty" as willingness not only to live pacifically within the restored federal union but to do so with free blacks as co-residents, including those who were presently Union soldiers, the most obnoxious blacks by far, according to white conservatives' racial stereotypes. Lincoln had accepted the abolitionist constitutional base that federalism and slavery were inherently incompatible, Lieber's thesis that antislavery followed the flag, and Sumner's argument that national power was adequate not only to displace rebel state governments, constitutions, and personnel but also to reform them.

The destiny of all War policies and aims was up to soldiers more than to statesmen, Lincoln reminded the congressmen. If

5. Robert H. Zoellner, "Negro Colonization: The Climate of Opinion Surrounding Lincoln, 1860–1865," *Mid-America*, XLII (1960), 131–50; James M. McPherson, "Abolitionist and Negro Opposition to Colonization During the Civil War," *Phylon*, XXVI (1965), 391–9; William G. Cochrane, "Freedom Without Equality: A Study of Northern Opinion and the Negro Issue, 1861–1870" (Ph.D. diss., UMinn, 1957), chs. I–II.

the Confederacy survived the War, emancipation would be as dead as the Union. All meaningful accomplishments about emancipation and Reconstruction depended basically on "the war power [of the Constitution], . . . still our main reliance," Lincoln noted. He stressed his injunction in the Reconstruction proclamation addressed to southern whites to treat freedmen decently with respect to conditions of life, labor, and education in the new states, at the cost of the national military power again intruding.

Then the President referred again to the possibility of the "cruel and astounding breach of faith" involved in revoking emancipation—it weighed heavily in his thoughts. He would not willingly travel any road back to slavery, but he could not block Congress or courts. Congress need not admit delegates-elect from states rebuilt by his mode, and could contravene by legislation what he created by proclamation. Similarly, "supreme judicial decision" might affect or even reverse presidential commitments. Where the freedom road led no one knew precisely. But Lincoln promised that his administration would not reverse.[6]

Standpatters in matters of race and state rights criticized the December 1863 statements as centralizing, revolutionary, and tyrannical. The minuscule number of racial equalitarians in the North and abroad criticized them because they lacked provisions for intrastate political equality for freedmen. Worse, even though he would not support retrogression, the advances by Lincoln's blueprint were reversible in the frighteningly near future. The elections of 1864 could place in the White House a President of opposite mind about emancipation and enhance further the Democratic phalanx in Congress. Taney was dying. A replacement named by an antiwar President elected in 1864 might well swing the Supreme Court against emancipation. Meanwhile, southern states' courts being rebuilt by the Union Army (including Negro soldiers) were likely to declare the emancipation edict void. The President's Reconstruction policy assumed continuation of existing state law codes except for slaveholding, in order to encourage defection from the Confederacy and to stabilize property relationships, and because American lawyers knew no other kind of Union save one where each state's laws governed even national courts operating in that state, except as Congress specified exclusivity for a national statute. How, other than by frequent, unsettling, and expensive military interferences, could

---

6. *M&P*, VI, 189–91.

freedmen, even Union Army veterans, gain the minimally decent justice Lincoln had pleaded for, in state tribunals where blacks' testimony and jury service were excluded?

Undimmed by the War, the northern popular conviction was that all substantive questions would and should come up at polls and in courts.[7] "Popular" here means individuals and groups to whom the President and congressional leaders (especially those congressmen who were lawyers) were most sensitive—the Army, the legal profession, and the extensive northern membership of benevolent, charitable, humanitarian, missionary, patriotic, and sanitary organizations.[8] Temporarily at least, many of these northerners had come to distrust southern whites; a cynical attitude widespread in the Union Army and Union party. A successful Reconstruction must restore respect for all law from the Constitution down. Surely this was an absurd aspiration in light of notorious perjuries among oath-sworn southern whites who would staff state and local courts as judges and jurors. It required no savant to see that the nation's needs, the loyal states' rights, and the social strength deriving from the law's equitability were best served in the national courts. Therefore, untutored but perceptive contemporaries approved Congress's resort to the federal courts in the 1863 habeas corpus law and in precedent bankruptcy, confiscation, revenue, and loyalty-testing statutes.[9]

In March 1864, as election tensions grew larger, Maryland's Congressman Henry Winter Davis voiced this common cynicism

---

7. No evidence exists to affirm or deny that Lincoln knew of Taney's undelivered opinion declaring his Emancipation Proclamation unconstitutional. For other matters see Bingham's query, March 12, 1862, *CG*, 37 Cong., 2 sess., 1193, 1204–5; Philadelphia *Freedmen's Bulletin*, I (1865), 64; Frank L. Klement, "Midwestern Opposition to Lincoln's Emancipation Proclamation," *JNH*, XLIX (1964), 169–83; Mark L. Krug, "The Republican Party and the Emancipation Proclamation," *JNH*, XLVIII (1963), 98–114; William D. Mallam, "Lincoln and the Conservatives," *JSH*, XXVIII (1962), 31–45; Lorraine A. Williams, "Northern Intellectual Reaction to the Policy of Emancipation," *JNH*, XLVI (1961), 174–88.

8. *Speech of Major-General John A. Logan, on Return to Illinois After Capture of Vicksburg* (Cincinnati, 1863), 24–5, offers a perfect illustration.

9. *Ibid.*, and see Harold M. Hyman, "Deceit in Dixie: Northern Reaction to Southerners' Evasions of Union Loyalty Tests," *CWH*, III (1957), 65–82; Daniel Agnew, *Our National Constitution: Its Adaptation to a State of War or Insurrection* (Philadelphia, 1863), 29–30. Lincoln alluded to this distrust in December 1863; *M&P*, VI, 189–91.

about southerners' reliability on a larger stage. The Lincoln Reconstruction policy lacked adequate national civil guardianship over office-holding and voting in southern states, save that would-be balloters and officials must swear to abide by emancipation, and courts or a future President or Congress could stipulate against it, Davis told Representatives. If and when either occurred, loyalty-oath-takers were released from all obligations, for no man was bound by an illicit oath.

Further, Lincoln's way was too vague in its structure, too military in its instruments, and too inadequately democratic in its requirement that voter-participants number only 10 per cent of those within any state who voted in 1860. The result could be only paramilitary hybrids unknown to the 1787 Constitution, and overswollen executive authority destructive of all states' rights. Worse, the possibility existed that courts, including those of Lincoln's Reconstruction states, might declare the abolition proclamation invalid. Therefore it was "safer [for Congress] to make it [the proclamation] law." Let each Negro's fate "be determined by the writ of habeas corpus," i.e., by litigation in which the standing in courts and in the testimony of black Americans would be on the same level of quality as whites. Let Congress require that each restored state's constitution prohibit slavery. If necessary, "we will go to the people of the United States on that question," Davis concluded, with the fall elections and an emancipation amendment to the Constitution in mind.

Meanwhile, he wanted Congress to prevent future secessions and civil wars by safeguarding through national legislation freedmen's private rights, standing, and avenues of redress in states' courts built by the President's formula. Of course, permanent military governments southward could win the precious goal of permanent Union, Davis noted. But he so hated military domination over civilians that he criticized Lincoln for excess employments of soldiers in Reconstruction. Better to allow national civil courts to have the Reconstruction job. Let them protect the altered legal condition of the Negro by the pacific techniques of the law. Court's habeas corpus writs authorized by Congress, not the President's extraordinary, untrustworthy loyalty oaths, should provide that protection across the gaps in the federal system which emancipation had illuminated.[10]

---

10. March 22, 1864, in *CG*, 38 Cong., 1 sess., App., 82–5. See supporting statement of freshman Representative Ignatius Donnelly (Minn.), May

It is not easy to understand how the Davis position warrants description as "Radical" or why historians have accepted contemporary partisan Democratic accusations that it was so. It bypassed the favorite "Radical" assertion that southern states had reduced themselves to some kind of subordinate territorial condition. Davis was only suggesting that, with respect to emancipation and Reconstruction, Congress require that enforcement rest primarily in the hands of federal judges. By early 1864 this was a well-marked way, and became the basis of the Wade-Davis bill. Davis's gambit allowed Congress to leap over disruptive questions of the status of returning southern whites, blacks, and states; a large bonus for Republicans in an election year. Litigation also obviated a need for postvictory military occupations, an obnoxious as well as expensive recourse.

Among Republicans, the Davis propositions were less divisive than tradition suggests. By early 1864, President, general, and congressman believed that the nation served itself best by relying on national courts, as they shared belief that postwar America would retain familiar state lines and property conditions except for the southern Negro's elevation from slave.

To see to the permanence of this happy elevation, antislavery vanguardsmen pushed hard for an abolition amendment to the national Constitution. This amendment pressure increased greatly from the time (December 1863) when Lincoln warned his countrymen that a future President, Congress, or Supreme Court might rescind emancipation based only on his war powers proclamation.[11] During the spring weeks of 1864 representatives and senators introduced five abolition amendments. Senator Sumner's Select Senate Committee on Slavery and the Freedmen brought forward an amendment proposal which stipulated that all Americans enjoyed equality before law including that of their states. Acknowledging that the particular phrase was a stranger

---

2, 1864, *ibid.*, 2036–9; and the cogent analysis in Martin Ridge, *Ignatius Donnelly: The Portrait of a Politician* (Chicago, 1962), 79–80; Belz, *Reconstructing*, ch. 8.

11. Most members of the 38th Congress agreed with shrewd constitutionalist Reverdy Johnson that Lincoln's Emancipation Proclamation had force only in occupied areas; *CG*, 30 Cong., 1 sess., 1480, and see Kaufman v. Barb, 26 Arkansas, 24 (1870). Lincoln's December 1862 message to Congress had suggested gradual compensated emancipation culminating in 1900, plus federally subsidized colonization. But he did not push to pass these through Congress. *M&P*, VI, 139–41.

in American jurisprudence, Sumner, perhaps to exploit Lincoln's growing interest in the Declaration of Independence, asserted that it was implicit in the Declaration.

Congressmen preferred the familiar antislavery formula contained in the Northwest Ordinance, which the Senate's Judiciary Committee chairman, Lyman Trumbull of Illinois, resurrected for an abolition amendment. Democratic defenders of slavery as a state-defined private property, chiefly border states' men, resorted to the Fifth and Tenth Amendments—the Bill of Rights!—and insisted that abolition by a national constitutional amendment violated states' police powers over domestic concerns. The Senate passed Trumbull's amendment resolution handily and quickly (38–6, April 8, 1864). But Sumner had touched a sensitive northern nerve in his equality-before-state-law formulation.

In mid-June, 1864, when party platforms were building and presidential nominations under way, the Trumbull thirteenth-amendment proposal failed (95–65) to win the two-thirds vote needed to pass the House, and was tabled. In effect, the fall 1864 elections would decide for or against subsequent passage through Congress of an abolition amendment, and determine whether the Civil War was to be a revolution or not. If the amendment passed and the Union Army persisted to unconditional victory, the nation would be basically different from the society that in the first weeks of 1861 had come frighteningly close to adding to the Constitution a thirteenth amendment perpetually and unamendably protecting slavery in the states. If the abolition amendment failed—that is, if Lincoln and Republicans lost the 1864 election—then the War would mean only something less, perhaps even down to Dred Scott's shameful level.[12] In short, emancipation remained actually, not theoretically, revocable any time from December 1863, when Lincoln pointed to the possibility that Congress or courts could reverse his proclamation, to some unknowable time after the fall 1864 elections, unless he and Republicans won them. Among Republicans Lincoln's insight was

---

12. Howard Devon Hamilton, "The Legislative and Judicial History of the Thirteenth Amendment" (Ph.D. diss., UI, 1950), ch. I; Charles Sumner, *Complete Works* (Boston, 1900), VIII, 81–2; Gerald S. Henig, "Henry Winter Davis: A Biography" (Ph.D. diss., CUNY, 1971), 302–8; Willmoor Kendall and George W. Carey, *The Basic Symbols of the American Political Tradition* (Baton Rouge, 1971), 94 and *passim*.

widespread that emancipation and Reconstruction were tied together. Fear of retrogression about emancipation inspired support for the proposed constitutional amendment. It "would settle the whole question of reconstruction," argued one champion, Henry Everett Russell: "there could not then arise questions touching the validity of acts by which slaves are declared freemen. There would be nothing left to hang a doubt upon. . . . Freedom being thus made the law of the land, there would be no longer reason for differences . . . among conscientious and capable men, as to the proper mode of reinvesting the States usurped by the rebellion with their rightful powers as kindred republics of the nation."

Then Russell illustrated an impact of civil war. Potentials in the Constitution capable of transforming it from the covenant with hell, of prewar abolitionist imagery, to a charter of enlarged liberties had become visible. "In fine, the Constitution itself is all bristling with arguments for this [thirteenth] amendment," he wrote. He turned to the Fifth Amendment, long a mainstay for slavery extensions into national territories and for rigorous federal fugitive slave laws. Now the Fifth Amendment's due-process clause must become a positive bar against slavery's existence under states' laws, instead of a positive requirement that the national government sustain slavery in states and extend it into all federal territories. Once the proposed thirteenth amendment reinforced the Bill of Rights, the Fifth Amendment would have a "significance unknown before," the writer insisted. "Oh, how the rebellion has interpreted for us and commented upon the Constitution."[13]

---

13. Henry Everett Russell, "The Constitutional Amendment," *CM*, VI (1864), 323, 325. This awareness percolated high in Republican ranks. Lieber publicly touted the Amendment in similar terms: "We live in a time of necessary and searching reform. We cannot avoid its duty. Things have already changed. They must be readjusted. The harmony of the great polity has been rudely disturbed; it must be restored in some way. The Civil War, imperiling the existence of our country, has laid bare the roots of evil in our polity, and shown what some elementary errors must lead to when legitimately [i.e., logically] carried out. We have discovered that a part of our foundation has given way, and that repairs are needed. Let every one contribute his share to the reconstruction." See Francis Lieber, *A Letter to Hon. E. D. Morgan, . . . on the Amendment of the Constitution Abolishing Slavery* (New York, 1865), unnumbered prefatory page; and see John Sherman, *CG*, 37 Cong., 3 sess., 735, on commitment to judicial review of emancipation.

Lincoln's depiction, in his December 1863 Reconstruction proclamation, of the Supreme Court as a threat to emancipation, proved to be temporary. By mid-1864, with Taney's decline, Republicans were happy again with legal processes and in the belief that national courts were harbors, not hazards. If states' courts, judges, and juries were demeaning the rule of law, especially by allowing race to interrupt equality in procedures due (i.e., due process) to each resident of that state, ways out of states' courts were wanted; if states' lawmakers or constitutional conventioners exceeded bounds, checks more certain than decisions by transient majorities were in order. Interventions by national judges were the key.[14]

As stated by legal writer Edward F. Bullard, this proposition expressed itself in a conviction that equality of a state citizen before his state's law must exist across the nation, or intrastate uniformity—the essence of civil procedure in law—was impossible. Bullard noted that ever since 1789, in states where slavery existed the writ of habeas corpus did not exist for Negroes or for those few whites who ventured into courts to represent blacks. Congress must create a law "giving to every person the benefit of that writ, without regard to color." Then with habeas corpus nationalized, state reconstructions could proceed as Lincoln had spelled out, with greater safety than he had provided. If former masters refused to let black people go, Negroes would have a realistic recourse to national courts instead of the hopeless appeal to state judges and juries composed of owners' friends. Bypassing local courts where black men's testimony was inadmissible lifted the level of all Americans' rights.

Pressures deriving from these insights resulted (July 4, 1864) in a statute of Sumner's inspiration admitting Negroes' testimony in national courts. But until Congress provided a bridge from state to national courts for ordinary citizens (the 1863 habeas corpus act applied primarily to officials), no man would know confidently the status within states of three million black people. Bullard was optimistic that, once national habeas corpus writs were available to Negroes, the Supreme Court would no

---

14. John Norton Pomeroy, *An Introduction to Municipal Law* (New York, 2nd edn., 1883 [originally published 1864]), 402–3; Woodrow Wilson, *Congressional Government: A Study in American Politics* (Boston, 15th edn., 1903), 34; George F. Hoar, *Autobiography of Seventy Years* (New York, 1903), II, 255–7.

longer be "the fortress of slavery" but become instead "the bulwark of freedom."

The oppressed of Bullard's concern were not the Merrymans or Vallandighams or even the national officers who were facing damage suits in the states' courts. Indeed, odds are that even Negroes were not central in his priorities. He worried over the quality of equality of all Americans before state law. Historically, virtually independent states had diminished equality for many Americans, and were likely to continue the habit unless the nation interposed. Once Congress did its duty and enlarged bridges between states' and nation's courts, "the habeas corpus [writ], now sighed after by traitors, will then become to the oppressed the angel of deliverance," Bullard concluded.[15]

In sum, by 1864 courts' appellate jurisdictions had become a party matter tied to racial attitudes. Democrats wished generally to keep Negroes subject wholly to states' laws and courts. A few Republicans were pioneering a new frontier of nationally applied equality-before-law concepts, whose theoretical bases derived from Jacksonian abolitionism. States' habits of barring Negroes' testimony, limiting Negroes' rights to sue, and excluding Negroes from juries among many other demeaning disabilities, substantially prevented equality as a right, and diminished blacks' responsibilities as free men under law.

As anonymous Negro commentators of 1889 described this growth of justice and jurisprudence as a party divisor among Republicans, a "civil-rights man" had come into existence. Earlier, white men had not needed him and blacks had inadequate political support or muscle to create him. The War made him possible. But in 1864 civil-rights men were weak in numbers and impact even within the Republican party, where a Sumner often pleaded alone, or nearly so, for the rights of all Americans. Among Democrats, the civil-rights man was anathema. In the words of the Negro writers, "One party [Republican] for the time being, has placed him [the civil-rights man] in quarantine, in one or another of its [the nation's] judicial harbors. . . . The other [Democrat] has banished him into an infirmary called the State courts. There he will . . . die an unnatural death."

In 1864 the auguries favored hope about the alchemical

---

15. Edward F. Bullard, *The Nation's Trial: The [Emancipation] Proclamation: Dormant Powers of the Government: The Constitution a Charter of Freedom and Not "A Covenant with Hell"* (New York, 1863), 60–1.

possibilities of enlarged federal court jurisdiction; it was the right year for gambles.[16] Significant Republican sentiment existed in favor of bringing Negroes into the states' rules of government which held between white men. The only way to accomplish this swiftly was for Congress to recruit that ancient writ, habeas corpus, into freedom's service and, by adapting it belatedly to the federal system, make it actually a writ of liberty. Meanwhile the pressure would continue for an abolition amendment, which the habeas-corpus-appeal device would complement.

How large a jump such visions contained is evident by the fact that even the limited removal provisions of the March 1863 habeas corpus act met what Professor Randall described as the "intense opposition . . . on the part of state courts."[17] Kentucky's Supreme Court decided that Congress could neither expand nor contract national court removal jurisdiction, and therefore it would not obey the 1863 habeas corpus statute. Indiana's highest court stated that Congress had no constitutional right to regulate state courts' jurisdiction, and Hoosier judges would allow Congress no implied power in this arena.[18]

Some federal jurists were also anxious to hold jurisdiction where it had been before the War. About the time that the thirteenth-amendment proposal failed to pass the House, United States Circuit Judge Leavitt, in Ohio, heard a case involving Ohio land the Army had rented for pasturage. A horse thief, apprehended there and prosecuted in Leavitt's court, pleaded that his crime was against Ohio's laws, not Congress's. Leavitt agreed. Within a state, the 1787 Constitution allowed national jurisdiction only over places sold with consent of a state's legislature for erection of forts, arsenals, and similar purposes. A field temporarily leased for fattening cavalry mounts remained within a state's jurisdiction, Leavitt decided.[19]

---

16. [The Brotherhood of Liberty], *Justice and Jurisprudence: An Inquiry Concerning the Constitutional Limitations of the Thirteenth, Fourteenth, and Fifteenth Amendments* (Philadelphia, 1889), 111; David Donald, *Charles Sumner and the Rights of Man* (New York, 1970), 153–4; John Bascom, "The Three Amendments," AAPSS *Annals* (Jan.–June 1906), 597.

17. James G. Randall, "The Indemnity Act of 1863: A Study in the War-Time Immunity of Governmental Officers," *MichLR*, XX (1922), 596.

18. Short v. Wilson, 1 Bush. [Ky.] 350 (1866); Warren v. Paul, 22 Ind., 176 (1864).

19. U.S. v. Tierney, 28 Fed. Cas. No. 16517 (1864), 159–60.

Litigation: The Great Moral Substitute for Force

The Republican ideal had moved away from Leavitt's dualism. Taney's assertion in Ableman v. Booth of the primacy of national laws in contests with branches of states' governments was more attractive. The repellent fugitive slave statute that Taney had sustained in the Ableman litigation became in 1864 another casualty of the War. What remained was recollection of Taney's great enlargement of national courts' authority, and the reciprocal lessening of states' courts power to obstruct national policies. Quite logically, the Republican strategy of 1864 was to strengthen the Ableman mode by extending comprehensively the habeas corpus outreach of the national courts.[20] Therefore Republicans admired decisions in federal lower courts and in some state courts, between 1863 and 1865, which sustained the March 1863 habeas-corpus-removal law.[21]

So far as Republicans were concerned, the best sort of state judge was exemplified by Pennsylvania's Chief Justice George W. Woodward. Early in 1864, Woodward heard a case involving a state-chartered insurance company which had decided that policyholders in reconquered regions of the Confederacy had resumed legitimate status as citizens and were entitled to recover benefits. But would-be heirs in loyal states contested the decision. Woodward concluded that a private entrepreneurship could not establish the status of governments. Even states' courts must wait for instruction "which the political departments of the Federal Government [will] have adopted." Admittedly the men in Washington had not done a consistent or complete job of harmonizing their "various, discrepant, and sometimes inconsistent measures" on this score. But imprecision did not relieve from Congress the responsibility to set the Confederate states' status.[22]

The rebel states, once defeated, would contain greatly altered and expanded biracial citizenries resulting from the War.

---

20. Arthur Bestor, "The Two Habeas Corpus Acts of the Fifth of February, 1867, and Their Untoward Sequel, the McCardle Case" (OAH paper, 1966), 107; W. M. Wiecek, "The Reconstruction of Federal Judicial Power, 1863–1875," *AJLH*, XIII (1969), 342.

21. In re Fagan, 8 Fed. Cas. (1863), 947; In re Dunn, *ibid.*, 93; In re Dugan, 6 D.C., 131 (1865); In re Oliver, 17 Wis., 703 (1864).

22. Fifield v. Insurance Company of Pennsylvania, in *Pittsburgh Legal Journal*, XII (July 18, 1864), 17–19. But note that a year later Judge Thompson of the same court decided that the existence of rebellion was a fact to be determined judicially: Commonwealth v. Frink, in *ALReg*, XIII (1864–65), 700–2.

The specter of emancipation's revocability, the sluggish process of an emancipation amendment, the unsavory developments in Army-dominated Louisiana (the most fully developed of the presidentially rebuilt states), and the possibility of Democratic success in the fall 1864 elections explain why in mid-1864 Representative Henry Winter Davis and Senator Ben Wade sponsored their famous reconstruction bill.

As finally evolved, the so-called Wade-Davis bill modified the President's antecedent Reconstruction policy, but did not significantly alter it. Certainly, as Belz has shown, it was no radical attack on the President. It required subscription by a majority (not 10 per cent) of "white male citizens" in a rebel state to an oath to support the 1787 Constitution. Thereupon a "provisional governor" of the President's choice would invite the sworn majority to elect delegates to a state constitutional convention. Delegates to the convention must swear to the "ironclad test oath" of past loyalty which in July 1862 Congress had prescribed for federal military and civil officers.

Most important, the Wade-Davis bill tried to stabilize emancipation until wholly civil "republican" state governments rooted in the South, and to build in equality before law in the provisional state governments that would create the permanent forms. Each provisional governor was to see to it that "no [state] law or usage whereby any person was heretofore held in involuntary servitude shall be recognized or enforced by any court or officer in such State; and the laws for the trial and punishment of white persons shall extend to all [such] persons." Further, "all persons held to involuntary servitude or labor in the States aforesaid are hereby emancipated and discharged therefrom, and they and their posterity shall be forever free." Still further, the bill ordered that "if any persons or their posterity shall be restrained of liberty under pretense of any claim to such service or labor, the courts of the United States shall, on habeas corpus, discharge them." Wade and Davis also specified that offenders against this or other congressional antislave provisions "or any [emancipation] proclamation of the President," face on conviction a fifteen-hundred-dollar fine and prison for five to twenty years. Slaveowning was to be a new federal crime in the ex-rebel states; federal courts were to see to the equality before states' laws of all citizens; Reconstruction was to be a reform process leading to more democratic, republican state governments in the South. In essence, Wade and Davis had created a new judiciary act for Reconstruction so that at least in the ex-rebel states, emancipation and justice would proceed more surely, cheaply, and decently.[23]

A few Democratic congressmen made the habeas-corpus-removal provisions a special target. Illinois Democrat James Cameron Allen, a former state judge, condemned them as destructive of state rights and of "the civil liberty of our own race." But such demurrers were useless in the face of the Republican-Union coalition's conviction that Lincoln's plan was inadequate and insecure, that ratification for a constitutional amendment on emancipation was too far in the future, and that a congressional law of the Wade-Davis sort was wanted at once. It passed the Congress on July 2, 1864, the same day Lincoln signed into law Sumner's bill admitting Negroes' testimony in all national courts.[24]

Lincoln pocket-vetoed the Wade-Davis bill. He had no burning objections to it, but he hoped not to disturb the southern state governments building under his December 1863 plan. With the elections so close he wanted if possible to alienate neither northern racial conservatives nor progressives. Therefore Lincoln issued an explanatory proclamation for his decision to pocket-veto:

> . . . while I am (as I was in December last, when . . . I propounded a plan for restoration) unprepared by a formal approval of this bill to be inflexibly committed to any single plan of restoration, and while I am also unprepared to declare that the free State constitutions and governments already adopted and installed in Arkansas and Louisiana shall be set aside and held for naught . . . or to declare a constitutional competency in Congress to abolish slavery in States, but am at the same time sincerely hoping and expecting that a constitutional amendment abolishing slavery throughout the nation may be adopted,

---

23. Belz, *Reconstructing*, 233–43; M&P, VI, 222–6, secs. 10, 12, 13. Sumner proposed that the Emancipation Proclamation become a statute; Edward McPherson, *The Political History of the United States of America During the Great Rebellion* (2nd edn., Washington, 1865), 317, but this suggestion gained little support.

24. James C. Allen, in CG, 38 Cong., 1 sess., 1739; Donnelly, *ibid.*, 2038; Belz, *Reconstructing*, 236–9.

nevertheless I am fully satisfied with the system for restoration contained in the [Wade-Davis] bill as one very
proper plan for the loyal people of any State choosing to
adopt it.[25]

But the immediate effect of the veto was more important
than his reasons for vetoing. Angrily replying in their famous
"manifesto," Wade and Davis noted that Lincoln's explanatory
proclamation was a sport, "unknown to the . . . Constitution."
Notwithstanding the President's explanation, "the bill did not
therefore become a law; and it [the bill] is, therefore, nothing."
Arkansas and Louisiana were Lincoln's mere martial creations,
rotten boroughs overripe with patronage corruption, and Congress had properly prevented their chosen delegations from taking seats. The Wade-Davis manifesto demanded: "What the
[southern] State courts would say of the [President's emancipa-
tion] proclamation, who can doubt? . . . What the [United
States] Supreme Court would say, who can tell? When and how
is the question to get there? No habeas corpus lies for [a slave]
in a United States Court; and the President defeated . . . the
extension of that writ to his case."[26]

The results of the 1864 elections justified the assumptions of
Lincoln, Wade, Davis, and the substantial northern opinion they
and their party represented that politics, legislation, and litigation
remained the ways to win goals. The intraparty differences Republicans displayed so candidly until very near the balloting time
proved to be far less rending than those which had disrupted the
Democracy four years earlier. Republicans turned a common
front against the defeatist foe.[27]

One of the most remarkable but least remarked aspects of
the election was that it was held at all. A century ago as now,

---

25. *M&P*, VI, 222–3.
26. *American Annual Cyclopaedia and Register of Important Events
of the Year 1864* (New York, 1869), 307–10 n.; New York *Tribune*, Aug.
5, 1864.
27. *Collected Works of Abraham Lincoln*, ed. Roy P. Basler *et al.*
(New Brunswick, N.J., 1953), hereafter cited as Lincoln, *Works*, VIII,
100–1; *The Radical Republicans and Reconstruction, 1861–1870*, ed.
Harold M. Hyman (Indianapolis, 1966), lvii–lx, 153.

nations where elections occurred suspended them throughout emergencies, especially wars. As in 1860 and 1862, in 1864 the United States enjoyed constitutionally no alternative to holding elections. This mechanical rigidity was accounted by some determinedly insensitive observers to be another basic defect in American governmental arrangements. Such commentators held that after three years of bloody mass war, racial upsets, and financial outlays, it was absurd to allow by ballot the possibility of a Confederate victory which had thus far not been won on the battlefield.

Yet in 1864 constitutional habits remained firm. Almost no one took seriously suggestions for extraconstitutional devices to avoid contests. The election proceeded without violence, unfettered and uncorrupted by existing standards. Negroes voted in many states. Most marvelous, tens of thousands of Union soldiers voted by absentee ballots in their states' elections or were furloughed home in regimental masses in order to vote. They voted overwhelmingly for Republican-Union candidates, including Lincoln. In short, Union soldiers decided that the War should continue on the basis of the Republican platform, including permanent abolition of slavery and rejection of any contrived "armistice" with the Confederacy that might allow rebel governments to outlast hostilities. The civilian overlords of America's gigantic military institutions, a generation born during Napoleon I's career and come to maturity during the rise of Napoleon III, were so confident of their creation as to allow common soldiers a chance to vote out of office everyone from the Commander-in-Chief down. It was an unprecedented phenomenon.

An enduring impact of the War and a structuring of Reconstruction, the 1864 election confirmed Americans' presuppositions about postwar America. After victory, as during the War, the re-United States would retain their open characteristics. Decision-making (and, if desired, refusal to admit the need for decisions) about basic matters would continue to occur publicly in institutionalized elections and through party institutions. Taken together, the lessons of 1864 were that two-party politics arranged in states and localities were the proper ways to carry on peace because they were coping with the unimaginable weights of the Civil War. The election was a reaffirmation of national constitutional adequacy made possible by the efforts of the right states, the right causes, and the right candidates. Surely no future issue or occasion could be too fragile or dangerous to risk in ordinary politics. Walt Whitman offered this confident tribute to America's constitutional-political ways:

> What have we here if not, towering above all talk and argument, the . . . last-needed proof of democracy. . . . That our national democratic experiment, principle, and machinery could triumphantly sustain such a shock, and that the Constitution could weather it, like a ship in a storm, and come out of it as sound and whole as before, is by far the most signal proof yet of the stability of that experiment—Democracy—and of those principles and that Constitution.[28]

At the least the popular decision favoring Lincoln and the Union-Republican coalition was a setback for those who advocated abandoning the War and reversing emancipation. But the racist tide could return, and Lincoln exploited the election victory to press for passage and ratification of the abolition amendment, so that Reconstruction might not again escalate to crisis levels. "If [other] questions . . . remain, we would adjust them by the peaceful means of legislation, conference, courts, and votes," the President advised Congress a month after the 1864 balloting.[29]

Lincoln's confidence in these "peaceful means" rose further when Chief Justice Taney died, late in 1864, and the President replaced him with Salmon Portland Chase. Nevertheless, Lincoln continued to support the abolition amendment. He did not want emancipation to depend only on his war-powers edict of two years earlier.

Yet, as Wade and Davis had noted, his December 1863 Reconstruction proclamation enjoyed only this same martial support. Obviously Lincoln felt less urgent about the foundations of Reconstruction; indeed, as he had specified in his veto statement on the Wade-Davis bill, he hesitated to commit himself or the nation to any single Reconstruction course. Unlike emancipation,

---

28. *Walt Whitman's Civil War*, ed. Walter Lowenfels (New York, 1961), 285, 290; Harold M. Hyman, "The 1864 Election," in *History of American Presidential Elections*, ed. F. Israel and A. M. Schlesinger, Jr. (New York, 1971), II, 1155–7. On soldiers' voting and resulting litigation, see Josiah H. Benton, *Voting in the Field: A Forgotten Chapter of the Civil War* (Boston, 1915), *passim*.

29. *M&P*, VI, 254–5; and see Lincoln, *Works*, VII, 380–1, 499–502; VIII, 250, 386; see too *Works of William H. Seward*, ed. George H. Baker (New York, 1853–84), V, 493–4.

Reconstruction was plastic, especially concerning race relationships. Wade and other congressional party leaders closed ranks with the President.[30] Evidence was increasing that he was advancing to "Radical" heights.

On April 11, 1865, the President espoused publicly—not in timid secrecy as he had done a year earlier—that in any Reconstruction, Negroes as well as whites should receive public schooling, and that in Louisiana, at least "the very intelligent" Negroes and black veterans of the Union Army vote. "What has been said of Louisiana will apply generally to other [southern] States," the President continued. And he advised that the national authority should continue to play a part in reconstructing the South even after the surrender, now imminent, of all rebel forces.[31]

Opportunity to work out details stretched to March 1869. In early April 1865, President, Congress, and Supreme Court were staffed with men who agreed on essentials, including decent treatment for freedmen through access to schools, courts, and ballots. Four years before, the same President and some of the same congressmen had felt forced to agree to a proposed amendment perpetually sanctioning the institution of slavery where it then existed. Now an amendment abolishing slavery nationwide was on its way to passage and ratification. The President, Congress, and populace had abandoned at last compensated emancipation and colonization schemes to which they had clung so stubbornly. Lincoln's career and those of most of his party leaders in Congress offered no indication that they championed what was impossible to win through politics or that they risked venturing too far in advance of what public opinion allowed. Auguries for effective politics were fair indeed. Then, three days after Lincoln's speech on Reconstruction, Booth's bullet changed the odds.

---

30. Wade's remarks, Jan. 9, 1865, *CG*, 38 Cong., 2 sess., 165.

31. Lincoln, *Works*, VIII, 400–5; VII, 243. Variant views on the significance of this April 11, 1865, address are explored in an exchange I enjoyed with Professor Ludwell Johnson, in *JSH*, XXXII (1966), 83–7; *CWH*, XII (1966), 258–66; *ibid.*, XIII (1967), 66–73; *ibid.*, 282–3.

Chapter XVII

Reconstruction:
On *Every* Putrid Spot?

Lincoln's murder only briefly dimmed the optimistic mood that swept in with news of Appomattox. It derived in significant part from contrasts between the nation's futile flounderings during the 1860–61 secession winter and the smooth swiftness with which in 1865 the government coped with the assassination and Andrew Johnson's succession. No administrative crises, frantic punishments, or halts in wrap-up military operations occurred. Civilian control remained firm over the immense military establishment. The Union's armies gathered in Washington after Lee's surrender not to awe civilian overlords, but to celebrate with them in a grand review. Then bluecoats returned pacifically to the civilian society with which they had never cut connections. Demobilization, historically the moment of greatest risk involved in establishment of a military dictatorship, went off without hint of a coup. General Sherman's armistice with Confederate General Joseph Johnston was an unwarranted intervention into policy-making which Sherman's civilian and military superiors properly disavowed. But it was foolish, not sinister.

Victory initiated also the almost immediate disappearance of conscription, internal-security, and trade-control apparatuses so distasteful even to stanch patriots. Recollections of unfettered wartime elections, especially those of the preceding autumn, added to these evidences of federalism's durability and democ-

racy's vigor, impressed persons here and abroad who had anticipated their demise. The nation that was too puny in 1861 to
succor the garrison of a single fort by early 1865 had rolled back
the Confederacy's European-scale armies across a continent; the
society that in 1861 was willing to freeze southern states' slaves
in servitude as irrevocably as constitutional law allowed, in 1865
was considering and would ratify a new Thirteenth Amendment
to eliminate the cancer everywhere in the land.[1]

The exciting characteristics which the Thirteenth Amendment possessed to its admirers in 1865 are difficult to recapture
now. Republicans who wrote, spoke, and pleaded for passage
and ratification of the Amendment were a vanguard for racial
justice and a political majority concerned with the continuing
morality of political, social, and legal processes. To such men the
Amendment not only prevented slavery for blacks; it enriched
freedom for whites. By its ratification all Americans won release
from the uncertainties of slave-based national politics. Now the
search for success—a goal directed for many Americans as much
toward the acquisition of virtue as goods—would remain open.
Then, in states—which was the level of government that counted
in terms of effects on individuals' lives—the Jacksonian imperative, equality before law, would exist. The new Amendment
would end a class of unfair advantages and special privileges,
and decrease outrageous constraints or oppressive disadvantages.
In such improved intrastate environments unfettered individuals
could work out decent destinies, and the marketplace would
enforce itself as before. States would no longer impose on individuals the desperate disabilities that slavery represented; the
nation's Supreme Court and Congress would not again issue a
Dred Scott decision or a fugitive slave recapture statute.[2]

---

1. Raoull S. Narroll, "Lincoln and the Sherman Peace Fiasco—An-
other Fable," *JSH* (1954), 459–83; Benjamin P. Thomas and Harold M.
Hyman, *Stanton: Lincoln's Secretary of War* (New York, 1962), 423;
Carl J. Friedrich, *The Impact of American Constitutionalism Abroad*
(Boston, 1967), 5; Karl Marx and Friedrich Engels, *The Civil War in the
United States* (New York, 1961), 276; *The Radical Republicans and Recon-
struction, 1861–1870*, ed. H. M. Hyman (Indianapolis, 1966), liii–lxi;
Heard Round the World: The Impact of the Civil War Abroad, ed. H. M. Hy-
man (New York, 1968), 231–302. Eric Foner, *Free Soil, Free Labor, Free
Men: The Ideology of the Republican Party Before the Civil War* (New
York, 1970), *passim*.
2. Richard Weiss, *The American Myth of Success from Horatio
Alger to Norman Vincent Peale* (New York, 1969), ch. 1; Timothy L.

By these measures the primary immediate impact of the Civil War was to be the abandonment of secession as a state's right and of legal codes on slave property as states' wrongs. The Republicans of 1865 without hypocrisy employed constitutionally conservative configurations for the Thirteenth Amendment. Unlike the abortive unamendable 1861 Crittenden-style "compromise" amendment, its 1865 successor was open-ended. It allowed for whatever future alterations political democracy prescribed; it required no positive national actions, no innovative thrusts from Washington, and, presumably, no coercive, bureaucratic, enforcement apparatus supported by taxes. It "merely" prohibited one special category of state-defined private property and authorized Congress to enforce that prohibition. Responsive action was up to each state. If, as was expected, the recent Confederate states set their houses—legal codes concerning residents' rough equality in ordinary civil relationships—in order, the nation needed to take no further action. The enforcement clause was a trigger that a state might pull, but Congress hoped and expected that none would. In Pennsylvania Senator Edgar Cowan's words:

> The breaking of the bond by which the Negro slave was held by his master; that is all. It was not intended to overturn this Government and to revolutionize all the laws of the various States everywhere. It was intended, in other words, and a lawyer would have so construed it, to give to the Negro the privilege of the *habeas corpus;* that is, if anybody persisted in the face of the constitutional amendment in holding him as a slave, that he should have an appropriate remedy to be delivered.[3]

And so Appomattox said to most Americans that the need for further uncomfortable change was ended. The War had done an inestimable service by striking from legitimate constitutional-

---

Smith, *Revivalism and Social Reform in Mid-Century America* (New York, 1957), 236; James Willard Hurst, *The Legitimacy of the Business Corporation in the Law of the United States, 1780–1970* (Charlottesville, Va., 1970), *passim;* Hans Trefousse, *The Radical Republicans: Lincoln's Vanguard for Racial Justice* (New York, 1969), 298–300.

    3. CG, 39 Cong., 1 sess., 499 (Jan. 30, 1866), and see *ibid.*, 322, 476–80; cf. with Frederick Douglass, in *The Equality of All Men Before the Law Claimed and Defended in Speeches by Hon. William D. Kelley, Wendell Phillips, and Frederick Douglass* (Boston, 1865), 39. Note that the state initiative was a feature also of the Fourteenth and Fifteenth Amendments.

ism the very concept of confederacy, John Lothrop Motley noted to Lieber. But it diminished not at all Americans' addiction to constitutional bases for political positions and in 1865 the visitor William Dixon was struck by the way victorious northerners clung still to written law "as to a rock in the midst of a storm." By this measure at least, America after Appomattox was unchanged from the prewar scene. The 1787 Constitution was complete now that the Thirteenth Amendment was in train of ratification.

Looking wistfully back to 1865 from the centennial decade 1876, *The Nation's* editor E. L. Godkin recalled this golden promise. "When these things are taken into account . . . the Constitution may be fairly considered as having existed in . . . a provisional or experimental stage down to 1861." War had created a nation out of the uncertainties that had staggered into secession. Now the Thirteenth Amendment, whose substance was wildly improbable in 1861, had "cleared up matters which for seventy years had occupied, to the serious injury of great interests, a large proportion of the acutest minds of the country in fruitless logomachy." But the real amendment to the Constitution had occurred at Gettysburg and was reaffirmed at Appomattox, Godkin concluded. Lincoln's bluecoats killed off slave-property and state-sovereignty doctrines, and, so doing, finished the job left uncompleted by the too-timid framers of 1787. Total battlefield victory allowed Congress to take hold "resolutely of all the serious obscure or ambiguous passages in the instrument, and of all compromises which had proved difficult or impossible of execution, and eliminate . . . them."[4]

This sense of finality exhibited itself again and again in the months surrounding Appomattox. The Freedmen's Bureau, usually described as a spearhead of postwar Reconstruction begin-

---

4. John Lothrop Motley to Francis Lieber, June 12, 1866, LI 2912, Lieber Papers, HL; Anthony Trollope, *North America* (London, 1862) I, 367–8, and see his *The Present Condition of the Northern States of the American Union* [1862 or 1863], in *Anthony Trollope, Four Lectures*, ed. M. L. Parrish (London, 1938), 29–64; William H. Dixon, *New America* (London, 1867) II, 294–5; E. L. Godkin, "Some Things Overlooked at the Centennial," *Nation* (Sept. 2, 1887), 226. See also [J. C. Hurd] *The Centennial of a Revolution: An Address by a Revolutionist* (New York, 1888), *passim;* Jacobus ten Broek, *The Antislavery Origins of the Fourteenth Amendment* (Berkeley, 1951), 130 and *passim.*

nings, fits better into this context of wartime finality and imperatives, some of which carried over into peace.

Since mid-1862 increasingly incompatible elements in statutes and military orders concerning rebels' property, including slaves, cotton, tobacco, and land, had become apparent. Congressman Thomas Eliot advocated creation in the War Department of a new Bureau to take on temporarily the manifold weights involved. Democrats denounced the notion as socialistic, Fourieristic, Owenistic, and erotic. New York's Democratic congressman John W. Chanler, a Negrophobe, proposed seriously that since blacks were unimprovably inferior a permanent Bureau was wanted rather than a temporary one. Conversely, a thin racial-equalitarian chorus was raised in favor of government doing nothing at all for freedmen, on the basis that self-help plus minimum aid from private charities would immediately repair slavery's corrosions.

What emerged mixed military and civilian sectors with public and private resources. In the Freedmen's Bureau statute (March 8, 1865) Congress named the War Department as the new Bureau's home. It alone possessed personnel trained appropriately, out of occupation experience, for the uncertain tasks ahead. Army salaries were already funded, a fact which satisfied the sharp fiscal consciousness of many congressmen and allowed Congress without hypocrisy to create a Bureau virtually without a budget, and to stipulate that it end its existence one year after hostilities ended; coincidentally, this worked out to be almost precisely a calendar year after the bill became law.[5]

In many ways the Bureau's curious mixtures of men and measures represented precisely the spirit of sixty-five. It was to be a middleman between freedmen and white society's contending elements. The Bureau was to live off surplus Army funds and the cash, kind, and personnel which the volunteer educational, missionary, and relief societies provided. The Army's invaluable links with the volunteer associations with interest in the Negro's mind, body, and soul would result in the supply of the money, men, and materials to improve the first, protect the second, and save the third.

---

5. O. O. Howard in *Pennsylvania Freedmen's Bulletin* (Feb. 1865), 12, 39, 61; Chanler in *CG*, 39 Cong., 1 sess., 85 and see also *ibid.*, 38 Cong., 1 sess., 1156, 2801–3; William S. McFeely, *Yankee Stepfather: General O. O. Howard and the Freedmen* (New Haven, 1968), ch. 5, esp. 86.

Reconstruction: On Every *Putrid Spot?*

The Bureau was a novelty in American administrative history, markedly different from the muscleless Department of Agriculture or Bureau of Indian Affairs. The national government enjoyed a clear right to deal with Indians, but the only constitutional base for the Freedmen's Bureau was the war power. On the face of it, the Bureau could interfere with the Age of Lincoln's most sacred cows; state-defined private properties including land titles, labor and education codes, and race relationships. The paramilitary Bureau courts received limited concurrent and removal jurisdiction respecting states' judicial processes. Little wonder that during the first (and, presumably, last) year of operations in 1865, the Bureau was one reason some commentators confused this temporary construction with a permanent move toward centralization in federal-state relationships.

Centralization was never the Bureau's effect. Since Sumter, the Army's military government–Reconstruction enterprises had used rather than replaced most states' civil and criminal law codes and employed southern civil officials and institutions especially on local levels. Except for slaves, Army officers interfered very little with private properties, and Bureau personnel followed this practice. The Bureau rarely introduced national substitutes for local public or private orphan asylums, old age homes, and jails, although it experimented with schools. A Louisiana Bureau agent noted in a case concerning a Negro youth who had been assaulted that it was "the wish of the [national] Government and my instructions contained in [Bureau] Circular letter No. 24 . . . that these cases be decided by the state courts therefore I respectfully transfer this case to your [Louisiana state justice of the peace] jurisdiction." In the White House, in Army and Bureau headquarters, and in most Bureau field offices, the commitment against national monopoly in freedmen's affairs was tenacious, quiet, and consistent. By Appomattox, increasing numbers of Republicans in Congress and local party echelons, in the Army, and in the Freedmen's Bureau assumed that the nation's wartime goal—stability for the Union—required that each state's residents enjoy equally rights and responsibilities as defined by that state.

This widening assumption had it that all slave clauses in southern state and local laws were void. General A. H. Terry, commanding U.S. troops in Virginia, expressed it succinctly in June 1865: "People of color will henceforth enjoy the same personal liberty that other citizens and inhabitants [of Virginia] enjoy; they will be subject to the same restraints and to the same punishments, for crime, that are imposed on whites, and to no others." In Washington, reading Terry's policy statement, General O. O. Howard, newly assigned to head the Freedmen's Bureau, noted, "I like the letter and spirit of this Order, and wish it were universal." Within two years it would become "universal" on Capitol Hill, though temporarily.

The work of United States courts, returning to circuit operations in southern states during 1865, fed this augmenting assumption. Fears that the War had created whole categories of irresponsible persons, whether white debtors or black freedmen, diminished. These court decisions and opinions stressed continuities in private legal relationships including insurance policy coverages, indebtednesses, and estate conveyances within southern states. "The acts of all the officers, agents, and employees . . . of each one of the late Confederate States, would be recognized as valid by the Federal tribunals, provided those acts were not in aid of [secession, slavery, or] the war against the Federal Government," Chief Justice Chase's circuit reporter, Bradley T. Johnson, summarized these national court decisions.[6]

---

6. *Reports of Cases Decided by Chief Justice Chase in the Circuit Court of the United States for the Fourth Circuit, 1865 to 1869,* ed. Bradley T. Johnson (New York, 1876 [new edn., ed. Ferne B. Hyman and H. M. Hyman, New York, 1972]), iii–iv. The Terry Order #77, June 23, 1865, with Howard's comment, is owned by W. E. Layton, Wash., D.C., who graciously supplied a copy and permission to use it. Ten years after Appomattox, the U.S. Supreme Court created in Murdock v. Memphis, 87 US 590 (1875), a conformable "rule," by terms of which it would not review a state court judgment in a criminal case for which independent, adequate state grounds existed for conviction, even though a federal question was involved. This self-denying national court obeisance to state court autonomy has only recently been even partially undercut: see U.S. v. Shotwell Manufacturing Company, 355 US, 233 (1957), and Jackson v. Deno, 378 US, 368 (1964). On lawyers, see H. M. Hyman, "Law and the Impact of the War: A Review Essay," *CWH,* XIV (1968), 51–9; other data in *Radical Republicans and Reconstruction,* ed. Hyman, 188–99; J. Thomas May, "The Freedmen's Bureau at the Local Level: A Study of a Louisiana Agent," *Louisiana History,* IX (1968), 8–9; see Gen. H. G. Wright to Prov. Gov. A. H. Hamilton, Oct. 10, 1865, in C. W. Ramsdell, *Reconstruction in Texas* (New York, 1910), 79–80. The full text of the letter is in the Texas State Archives; RU doctoral student Jane Scarborough supplied its text; and see Howard Rabinowitz's unpublished "From Exclusion to Segregation: Southern Welfare and Correctional Policy, 1865–1890" (used with permission); McFeely, *Yankee Stepfather,* 73 and n., 153; Robert H. Bremner, "The Impact of the Civil War on Philanthropy and Social Welfare," *CWH,* XII (1966), 301–3.

Reconstruction: On Every Putrid Spot?

The Freedmen's Bureau meshed neatly with the state centeredness and the concerns about continuums that dominated Washington and the northern legal community, and with the emotional commitment northward favoring stability in the nation's errant southern states. Soon after Appomattox, civil government had resumed almost everywhere in the southern states. At President Johnson's orders, Army occupation commanders assigned private litigation, except when Negroes were involved unfairly to their detriment, to the renascent civil courts; Freedmen's Bureau agents co-operated with state or local authorities or officers of private philanthropic associations to arrange matters concerning freedmen.

This state-local focus on the part of Bureau agents fit precisely the popular "grasp of war" theory identified with federal attorney Richard A. Dana and accepted in the Supreme Court. Seemingly that theory had the nation's military supplanting all rebel, civilian, state and local governments. But as Dana and most contemporaries understood the "grasp of war" idea, coexistence was in order, not replacement.[7] To be sure, the President and Congress had stipulated that certain southerners were incapable of holding offices. Even such pronouncements allowed numerous amnesties and pardons for the offense of rebellion, however.

The upshot was that in 1865 it appeared reasonable and decent to conclude that almost nothing unfamiliar need be created in order to cope with the millions of suddenly freed Negroes. In Brock's apt phrase, "Imagination could hardly grasp that the difficulties of the Union preserved might be as formidable as those of the Union dissolved."

The nightmare question of what to do with emancipated blacks had for decades held even emancipationists back from pushing the reform. So acceptable were Freedmen's Bureau conglomerate arrangements, so strong was the antipathy against broad-gauged national concerns, so persistent was Jacksonian anti-institutionalism, that with few exceptions even the old antislavery vanguard shut up shop soon after Appomattox. Its brave veterans had won all they wanted; the excision of legal slavery from the American scene. The Army-centered wartime network

---

7. For Dana, see *Arguments and Addresses of Joseph H. Choate*, ed., F. C. Hicks (St. Paul, Minn., 1926), 57–8; C. F. Adams, *Richard Henry Dana: A Biography* (Boston, 1891), 330–1.

of private welfare associations, including the Sanitary and Christian Commissions, went out of existence almost as swiftly as the Union Army. In short, in April 1865 the American people had made a Niagara-leap by reversing secession and excising slavery. No commitment existed to continue revolutionary adventures, or to replace marketplace self-regulations by coercive bureaucratic novelties. Americans of the Appomattox year were buoyantly confident not only because the nation had defeated the rebels but also because that victory allowed the nation to return to prewar "symbolic" leadership in place of the wartime "instrumental" leadership, to use Talcott Parsons's index.[8]

As most Americans understood their Constitution, it had no commitments to Negroes as such. The Constitution's wartime performance justified popular optimism because with the War won, secession squelched, and slavery killed, the nation and the states—all states—would continue their workable involvements in the federal system. In fact, by reaffirming the permanent nature of the United States, the Civil War enhanced further the pre-eminence of the Union's states.

Little wonder that victory celebrations were spirited and prolonged.[9] An overwhelming sense emerges from innumerable editorials, speeches, and sermons that the Civil War had fundamentally improved America's constitutional and political ways. Americans accepted this view of enhanced strength so overwhelmingly that in 1865 and the decade following, few were interested in preparing systematic constitutional analyses about the locus of sovereignty or the theoretical lineaments of more desirable governmental arrangements, of the sort that had attracted much effort and thought in 1861–63. Those were years of weakness, frustration, and despair. But 1865?

To be sure, even in the victory year Orestes Brownson expressed doubts in his book on the tendencies and destiny of the American republic and Constitution, begun soon after the War

---

8. W. R. Brock, *The Evolution of American Democracy* (New York, 1970), 143. And see also Talcott Parsons, *The Social System* (Glencoe, Ill., 1951), 400–6; R. D. Marcus, "Wendell Phillips and American Institutions," *JAH*, XVI (1969), 41–58.

9. N. P. Banks, *An Address . . . at the Customhouse, New Orleans, on the Fourth of July, 1865* (n.p., n.d.), 15; on lack of commitment to Negroes, Carl B. Swisher, "Dred Scott One Hundred Years After," *JPoli*, XIX, (1957), 172; Bray Hammond, *Sovereignty and an Empty Purse: Banks and Politics in the Civil War* (Princeton, 1970), v.

started. But "looking back across the War-Gulf," the title of an 1870 article by Robert Dale Owen, became a litterateur's habit years after Appomattox, not in the year Lee gave up. The idea of Appomattox initiating what Arthur E. Sutherland called "uncomfortable change" would have fallen flat in 1865.[10]

Americans expected instead comfortable, smooth progress. Slavery and secession had made politics irrational and constitutionalism enfeebling. The death of both allowed confidence to exist again in the possibility of a science of politics and society and in the possession of a machineless rule of law, despite worry whether the freed Negro would be as dangerous to national and party unity after Appomattox as the slave had been before Sumter; whether Louisiana would play Kansas's disruptive pre-war role after hostilities. But these and other Reconstruction matters were not surprises as secession had been in 1861. By 1865 reconstructions had been under way for four years as bluecoats occupied increasing parcels of rebels' real estate. Full discussions had attended their evolutions. Arguments on the confiscation statutes, presidential and congressional policies on emancipation, amnesty, pardon, and state-rebuilding, elections, and the Thirteenth Amendment were broad educations. No literature was required in 1865, apparently, to clarify Reconstruction alternatives, as a necessary literature had come slowly, painfully, and fitfully into existence after 1861 to mark out wartime paths. By Appomattox, men were confident that the Constitution, which had reversed secession and undergirded the War, was adequate to restore states.

Once the initial shock passed of total military defeat, an augmenting white southern chorus, encouraged by President Johnson's policies and northern anti-Negroism, was heard. Its

---

10. Arthur E. Sutherland, *Apology for Uncomfortable Change, 1865–1965* (New York, 1965), 19; Howard M. Jones, *The Age of Energy: Varieties of American Experience, 1865–1915* (New York, 1971), ix; Robert Dale Owen, "Looking Back Across the War-Gulf," *Old and New,* I (1870), 579–89; on sovereignty, John C. Hurd, *The Theory of Our National Existence, as Shown by the Action of the Government of the United States Since 1861* (Boston, 1881), is dedicated to "the Sovereign: Whoever He, She, or They May Be." See also Herman Belz, "The Constitution in the Gilded Age: The Beginnings of Constitutional Realism in American Scholarship," *AJLH,* XIII (1969), 113–14; Orestes Brownson, *The American Republic, Its Constitution, Tendencies, and Destiny* (New York, 1865), and John F. Jameson, *A Treatise on Constitutional Conventions* (Chicago, 1867 [actually 1866]).

theme was a perversion of Lincoln's insistence since 1861 that secession was constitutionally inadmissible. Now southern whites said he had always been correct; secession had never occurred, and therefore the national government could not "reconstruct" any southern state. Instant Reconstruction followed the flag, the theme ran; state sovereignty secessionists now extolled exclusive national military power.

Shrewd southern lawyers added the engaging lure of restoring immediately long-suspended commercial links North and South. If civil governments did not exist in the rebel states could northern insurance companies demand premium payments suspended by the War? Were private debts and other contracts held between northern and southern residents voided by statutes of limitations or by the War, or were they still enforceable?[11]

In 1864 and early 1865, when Lincoln pressed Congress to admit Louisiana, Republican lawmakers fended off this unacceptable product of extraconstitutional military might, as Senator Sumner derided it, and avoided also the hazards of Democratic constitutionalism. Let Republicans not get "lost in a discussion, worthy only of schoolmen, on the metaphysical entity of a State," Sumner pleaded. The "great unquestionable fact" was that the War came because states said they had seceded. Congress, the instrument of popular will, alone possessed jurisdiction over the reconquered regions. It must determine whether would-be returnees had reformed their internal conditions enough to warrant the nation's confidence and comradeship.

In March 1865 Sumner's threat to filibuster against Louisiana's entrance passed the question on to the 39th Congress. But the larger issue, with its hangover Wade-Davis undercurrent concerning Negro remedies in restored states to which Lincoln alluded on April 11, left Republicans nervous. Party leaders feared the effects of growing factionalism in their ranks as the demises of slavery and secession realized major common goals of diverse supporters.

Hungrily anxious to recoup support lost because of identification with secession and disloyalty, in 1865 northern Democrats

---

11. E. Surrency, "The Legal Effects of the Civil War," *AJLH,* V (1961), 145–65; *Chase's Circuit Court Decisions,* ed. Bradley Johnson, iii–xvii. See also Peter Kolchin, "The Business Press and Reconstruction, 1865–1868," *JSH,* XXXIII (1967), 183–96; Allen G. Bogue, "Bloc and Party in the United States Senate, 1861–1863," *CWH,* XIII (1967), 211–41.

insisted that northern states keep all state rights undiminished, and northern blacks under control, by readmitting without delay the excluded southern delegates-elect. In the 38th Congress's last session (March 1865) and in the 39th Congress's initial meeting (December 1865), Republican congressmen frustrated this crass design. Thereafter, deeply resentful Democratic politicos insisted that a constitutional revolution had already occurred; a theme they hammered into history during ensuing years. Listing allegedly revolutionary changes between Sumter's depths and Reconstruction's heights, in 1867 Ohio congressman George H. Pendleton assembled this catalogue:

The old republic	*The new republic*
1. Equality of states.	1. Ten states blotted out . . .
2. The Federal government limited to national and internal affairs only.	2. The Federal government touches even private affairs . . .
3. Equal branches of the government.	3. Congress omnipotent . . .
4. Reverence for Constitutional rights.	4. Nonexistent; *viz.*, military arrests and suspension of the [habeas corpus] writ.
5. Delegated powers.	5. Federal government now has all.
6. The Constitution the fundamental law.	6. Now no Constitution at all.
7. Plain, simple, cheap government; army 15,000.	7. Huge debt and army of 100,000.
8. Freedom of thought.	8. None.
9. Freedom of reason.	9. None.
10. Internal peace.	10. None.
11. Freedom of debate in Congress.	11. Congress now ruled by a caucus.

Harvard's acidulous Joel Parker insisted in classroom and pamphlet that any post-emancipation "reconstruction" equaled revolution. Acknowledging that slavery had been the "root and cause of the rebellion," Parker argued that nevertheless the nation had no constitutional way to define the legal relationships it would establish with the recently rebellious states.

Relatively few northerners were immediately impressed by Pendleton's absurdities or Parker's abstractions. Instead, questions of the sort implicit in the Freedmen's Bureau received attention. These centered on what role the nation must play in Reconstruction, rather than whether the United States could participate at all. Thus the "adequacy" school of constitutional thought, developed after Sumter by Fisher and others, carried over after Appomattox.

But adequacy concepts did not define Republicans' Civil War and Reconstruction goals. Instead the doctrine insisted that the constitutional vehicle was competent to move where political direction stipulated. A few Republicans like Sumner had brooded over Reconstruction terms since 1861. By the end of the War Sumner had enveloped under a "state suicide" rubric notions such as the Constitution's requirement that Congress guarantee every state a republican form of government. Republican conservatives of Trumbull's stature found themselves agreeing from the strict letter of constitutional law, with positions Sumner derived from the Declaration of Independence and from judgments about racism's immorality.

Unlike secession, Reconstruction did not ruffle the northern business or legal community. Renascent state and national courts (including Freedmen's Bureau tribunals) in southern states were retying contractual knots and maintaining social control.[12] The

---

12. C. O. Lerche, "Congressional Interpretations of Guarantee of Republican Form of Government During Reconstruction," *JSH* (1949), 191–211. George H. Pendleton in William A. Russ, Jr., "Public Opinion on the Political Results of the Civil War," *Susquehanna University Studies* (1969), 178. On Sumner, *CG*, 38 Cong., 2 sess., 1103, 1109–10; D. Donald, *Charles Sumner and the Rights of Man* (New York, 1970), 197–208. Other data in Joel Parker, *Revolution and Reconstruction: Two Lectures . . . Law School of Harvard College, January, 1865, and January, 1866* (New York, 1866), 3–4 and *passim*, and see the derisive review in *ALRev*, IV (1969), 164–5. On transition of "adequacy" thought after Appomattox, see *A Philadelphia Perspective: The Diary of Sidney George Fisher Covering the Years 1834–1871*, ed. N. B. Wainwright (Philadelphia, 1967), hereafter cited as Fisher, *Diary*, 511, 526–7; William Whiting, *War Powers* (43rd edn., New York, 1871), 229–49; Emory Washburn, "Reconstruction. The Duty of the Profession to the Times," *MLRep* (July 1864), 477–84; W. M. Grosvenor, "The Law of Conquest the True Basis of Reconstruction," *NE*, XXIV (1865), 111–31; and most precise, John C. Hurd, "Theories of Reconstruction," *ALRev* I (1867), 237–64; W. H. Ahern, "The Cox Plan of Reconstruction: A Case Study in Ideology and Race Relations," *CWH*, XVI (1970), 293–308; George S. Boutwell, *Reminiscences of Sixty Years in Public Affairs* (New York, 1902 [1968 reprint]), II, 92–3.

upshot of these essentially comforting trends was that Recon-struction tensions, which according to McPherson, "occupied the mind of every politician and reformer in the winter of 1864–1865," diminished sweetly in the buoyant Appomattox season. The big national fights were won. Even northern Negroes were interested primarily in local developments in the District of Columbia and in northern states.

Concern among Negroes and Negrophiles centered in the workings-out of Congress's 1863 law requiring District street railways to exclude no passengers because of color, and on analogous questions in Cincinnati, New York, and Philadelphia. One black pamphleteer, explaining why Philadelphia Negroes insisted on equal treatment on intraurban street cars, admitted that the question must appear petty to whites after the grandeur of such War issues as union and emancipation. But he admon-ished readers to realize that equal access to public transportation affected Philadelphia blue-collared blacks every day. Beyond this, the pamphleteer argued that equal access to public conveyances "is immediately connected with the great policy of equality before the law, which is now offering itself to the national acceptance."[13]

Events underscored the prematurity of the word "accept-ance." As Professor Ahern has pointed out, equal rights for blacks required government intervention on several levels of the federal system; whites' rights were won by reducing governments to laissez-faire inaction, at least so far as popular understanding went. Bitter political fights broke out in northern communities concerning improvements in blacks' legal positions.

In California, Connecticut, Iowa, Illinois, Indiana, Mary-land, Massachusetts, Ohio, and Pennsylvania the exclusion or segregation of Negroes on public transportation, the admission of blacks' testimony in state and local courts, and the desirability of Negroes voting were heated issues. These contests made even stanch wartime Republican-Unionists recoil. "It seems our fate never to get rid of the Negro question," Sidney George Fisher

13. James M. McPherson, *The Struggle for Equality: Abolitionists and the Negro in the Civil War and Reconstruction* (Princeton, 1964), 308; Eric McKitrick, *Andrew Johnson and Reconstruction* (Chicago, 1960), 15–41; *The Right Way* (Sept. 30, 1865), 56; Elsie M. Lewis, "Political Mind of the Negro, 1865–1900," *JSH*, XXI (1955), 189–91; on District street cars, see *SAL*, XII, 805 (1863); Washington . . . Ry. v. Brown, 12 Wall., 445 (1873). The black pamphleteer's statement is in *Why Colored People in Philadelphia Are Excluded from the Street Cars* (Philadelphia, 1866), 5, and *passim.*

complained in mid-1865. "No sooner have we abolished slavery than a party, which seems [to] be growing in power, proposes Negro suffrage, so that the problem—What shall we do with the Negro?—seems as far from being settled as ever."[14]

Unlike these close-to-home problems, Reconstruction appeared to be in train of acceptable solution through undramatic means. Without litigation or crisis politics, in 1865 the United States Supreme Court "solved" the question whether West Virginia was a state. Meeting for the first session under the new Chief Justice Chase, the Court included West Virginia in its roster of states. This simple action ended a need for President or Congress directly to involve the nation in the passionate, disruptive politics of that border state.

Resolutions for the southern states of uncertain status were to be far less swift and simple. But no important element in any party or branch of government supported seriously a proposition that the War and Reconstruction could or should lead to a stateless nation or to a centralized one in which states played merely subordinate, administrative roles.

What worried careful observers so that Appomattox's bright promise was diffused was less a threat of a central leviathan than threatening tendencies in states North and South. Evils within any states corroded healthy states and undercut the nation, congressman Albert G. Riddle insisted in 1862, and his theme, tuned then against secession and slavery, endured past Appomattox.

The need to preserve the internal integrity of all the states justified Congress in holding off Lincoln's lily-white, bluecoat-built rotten borough, Louisiana, and, beginning in December 1865, Andrew Johnson's Army-nurtured southern state creations, Sumner insisted; it justified carrying on the "grasp of war" to total victory, Senator Sherman argued.

This compelling, disquieting, tenacious concern over intra-

14. W. H. Ahern, "Laissez-Faire versus Equal Rights: Liberal Republicans and the Negro" (Ph.D. diss., NU, 1968), ch. v; Fisher, *Diary*, 499; and see L. A. Dew, "The Racial Ideas of the Authors of the Fourteenth Amendment" (Ph.D. diss., LSU, 1960), ch. 8; G. G. Barrier, "The Negro Suffrage Issue in Iowa—1865–1868," *Annals of Iowa*, XXXIX (1968), 241–61; Leslie H. Fishel, Jr., "Wisconsin and Negro Suffrage," *Wisconsin Magazine of History*, XLVI (1963), 180–96; Elmer Gertz, "The Black Laws of Illinois," ISHS *Journal*, LVI (1863), 472; I. Dilliard, "Civil Liberties of Negroes in Illinois Since 1865," *ibid.*, 592–3.

state ways North and South illuminates certain obscure features of the Reconstruction. It suggests why within a year after Appomattox, many men of Trumbull's and Sherman's sorts concerned themselves, their constituents, their states, their party, and their nation in efforts to forbid racially defined inequities in southern states and, in some contexts, nationwide. Whatever scholarly disagreements remain, it appears clear that this consensus did not result from exploitative, "vindictive" schemes for the white South or "radical" equalitarian plans for the black. However tenacious, the "familiar history" no longer stands scrutiny, though offered in the United States Supreme Court in 1945, "that much of this [Reconstruction] legislation was born of that vengeful spirit which to no small degree envenomed the Reconstruction era."[15]

Recent scholarship is correcting the Supreme Court's misuse of history. The problem remains to explain why any further Reconstruction occurred at all after Appomattox; why 1865's happy spirit of finality should have altered so swiftly, and by early 1867 become a five-to-ten-year-long sectional verdict favoring further thrusts within states by national authorities.

In mid-1865, odds were heavy against further national efforts to improve the Negroes' intrastate status. This was, Fisher asserted, a matter *"incapable* of any solution that will satisfy both North & South." Even if "enlightened opinion" northward insisted

---

15. On West Virginia, see an undated, unidentified clip from the Cincinnati *Gazette,* Whitelaw Reid Papers, LC, vol. 219, which states: "Mr. Chase's first official act as Chief Justice was to hold a consultation with his Associate Justices about the call of States on the docket. The Clerk was arranging the list, and Mr. Chase directed him to insert West Virginia in its proper place. With the exception of Mr. Catron all the Justices were present, and all concurred in the action. One question, therefore, upon which Mr. Thad Stevens and others have been accustomed to hold high debate . . . without ever having been formally raised, may still be considered as henceforth practically *res adjudicata."* See also Richard O. Curry, "Crisis Politics in West Virginia, 1861–1870," in *Radicalism, Racism, and Party Realignment: The Border States During Reconstruction,* ed. R. O. Curry (Baltimore, 1969), 103–4 and *passim;* Albert G. Riddle in *CG,* 37 Cong., 2 sess., 500; John Sherman to W. T. Sherman, July 24, 1864, W. T. Sherman Papers, LC; and see Roger D. Bridges, "The Constitutional World of Senator John Sherman, 1861–1869" (Ph.D. diss., UI, 1970), chs. 4–6; Charles Sumner, *Complete Works* (Boston, 1900), VII, 493–546; Henry Winter Davis to ?, May 27, 1865, posthumously published in San Francisco *Free American,* April 17, 1866; Screws v. the United States, 325 US 91 @ 140 (1945), Justices Roberts, Frankfurter, and Jackson dissenting.

that southern states accept political equality for their black citizens, "how can the North enforce its views? Only by such an exertion of the power of the general government as would be inconsistent with its [i.e. the Constitution's] plan & theory. . . . I can see no way out of these difficulties consistent with the preservation of the Union & free government."

But by mid-1866 the reluctant Republican majority in Congress found in federalism and democracy ways to do the nation's new work. Sumner's secretary, Moorfield Storey, insisted in 1914: "The reconstruction policy [of Congress] was largely framed and was supported by the most conservative men in the Senate like Trumbull, Grimes, Sherman, and the group that voted against [conviction in] the impeachment [of Andrew Johnson]. . . . [T]he [reconstruction] policy was adopted in view of the exigencies of the time by the sober judgment of the men who were then in control of the Republican Party, and Thad Stevens was only one force."[16]

Storey's accurate recollection, offered precisely midway between Appomattox and the present, fell into the deep shadows cast by a half-century of contrary historiography. It condemned Reconstruction and the reconstructing Republicans in essentially economic-moralistic terms, as corrupt, exploitive conspirators who saddled North and South, whites and blacks, with unnecessary, improper, and unconstitutional weights.[17]

Constitutional specialists have already played a pioneer's role in initiating re-evaluations of Reconstruction's men and measures. Their reassessments agree that Reconstruction's configurations, like the War's, took shape from prewar understandings of the Constitution's nature, of federalism's ways, and of democracy's means.[18]

In constitutional terms the Republican centrists who became the architects of Reconstruction were constrained conformists. They were deeply committed to returning the nation and all states as quickly and thoroughly as possible to prewar arrange-

---

16. Fisher, *Diary*, 499; William B. Hixson, "Moorfield Storey and the Struggle for Equality," *JAH*, LIV (1968), 541.

17. Larry Kincaid, "Victims of Circumstance: An Interpretation of Changing Attitudes Toward Republican Policy Makers and Reconstruction," *JAH*, LVII (1970), 63; and see *Radical Republicans and Reconstruction*, ed. Hyman, xvii–lxviii.

18. Kincaid, "Victims of Circumstance," 61, n. 40.

ments, secession and slavery always excepted. Appomattox made the return possible; the Constitution made it mandatory. This retrospective view of the War's impact inextricably linked post-Appomattox to pre-Sumter America.[19]

This assumption of continuums jars with the hard-set scholars' habit of assuming that vast constitutional changes occurred, beginning in 1861 and especially after 1865. Of course enormous technological, economic, and social alterations did take place. But in constitutional terms the War and Reconstruction merged them so smoothly into familiar antecedent patterns as to make many men confuse the rapid pace and novel purposes of War and Reconstruction measures with substantive alterations. Certainly, confident statements of War-induced changes are suspect.[20] It appears that continuums dominated more than changes. The pacesetting members of the Age of Lincoln sought consciously and consistently to retain their Jacksonian past. Reconstruction politics were institutionalized disagreements whether retention allowed accommodation of new social needs which were weighty enough to count in politics. Republicans carried on from wartime the idea that government on some level of the federal system could cope with what was wanted. Whether coping should occur, how swiftly, and how generously supported, created party strains. Democrats clung to the negativistic conservative banner. They insisted that public responsibilities were limited and did not involve the central government in defining and enforcing the civil and political rights of states' citizens.[21]

All positions reflected the nation's and states' War-swollen strengths. Paradoxically, among Republicans at least, the restoration autumn's constitutional climate involved both pleasure in these strengths and fears concerning their applications.

Republicans who had fretted about Lincoln's wartime state restorations became all the more agitated by Johnson's repetitions after the shooting stopped. In the nine months after Appomattox President Johnson, continuing employment of the war powers,

---

19. Timothy Farrar, *Manual of the Constitution of the United States of America* (Boston, 1867), ix.

20. On Reconstruction theories, see Hurd, "Theories of Reconstruction," 237–64; Ahern, "The Cox Plan of Reconstruction," 239–308; Benedict, "The Right Way," chs. 8–11.

21. See *Radicalism, Racism, and Party Realignment*, ed. Curry, xiii–xiv; Russ, "Public Opinion," *loc. cit.*

though insisting by December 1865 that the war was ended in virtually all contexts, kept the Army building "provisional" civil governments in the southern states. Negro and white Unionist suffrage grew in none; equality-before-law assumptions were mocked in "black code" provisions; recent rebels returned to top elective and appointive offices. Emancipation made the three-fifths clause of the 1787 Constitution obsolete, increasing sub-stantially the lower-house representation in Congress of the re-cently rebel states. With astonishing rapidity white Democratic party echelons, with higher levels staffed largely by recent Con-federates holding the President's pardons, re-established them-selves in those states; Republican organizations struggled to root themselves among the thin ranks of white Unionists and appealed for suffrage to extend to blacks in order that the rebel hegemony be better balanced.

Obviously, President Johnson was injecting the national power deeply and profoundly within the southern states. His pro-fessions against such intrusions by any branch of the national government were to come later when Congress exercised powers parallel to his own. The fact that Johnson played his duplex game without calling Congress into special session profoundly rasped Republicans' state-centeredness, antimilitarism, and dedi-cation to legislative leadership. The gathering lawmakers of De-cember 1865 were happily rid of the prewar fixation on state sovereignty, but they abandoned none of their reverence for all states' rights. Further, their assumption was that Congress, not the President—not any President—embodied the nation's invigo-rated will on all matters includng the disposition of the defeated rebel states. Congress was "people-chosen," the poet Whittier wrote. Wisconsin's Senator Timothy Howe summed up the "brave old Curmudgeon" nature of the 39th Congress: "The whole will of God was not clearly revealed to it. But the one thing it was most tempted to do [abandon emancipation and national concern for freedmen and southern white Unionists], and not doing . . . awoke Hell's ugliest clamor, it refused to do with an obstinacy which history will look back upon and I hope will gratefully count for heroism."22 The 39th Congress's Republicans admitted few re-

22. John Greenleaf Whittier, "To the Thirty-ninth Congress," in *The Right Way* (Jan. 20, 1866); T. O. Howe to niece Grace, March 5, 1867, Howe Papers #140, SHSW; Edwin M. Stanton in Boutwell, *Reminiscences*, II, 93, approving Army salary payments for Lincoln's "Military Governors"

grets at the War's thrusts within states. At the same time, in 1865 almost all these men agreed implicitly that people within the defeated rebel states, under the nation's nominal overlordship ("the grasp of war"), should do their own decent reconstructing conformable to the Thirteenth Amendment. The evidence suggests that in 1865 Reconstruction was not a contest over national blueprints. Very few congressmen saw anything amiss with the constitutional world in which the rebel states were as unrestricted as ever, except for secession and slaveowning. Sutherland remarks on this point: "one constitutional fact concerning the United States [before the War through 1865] is difficult to keep in mind a century later—the absence of the Thirteenth, Fourteenth, and Fifteenth Amendments. Some of the then unhampered State powers are startling today."[23] Indeed they are.

It is the core of the Civil War's impact, constitutionally considered, that in early 1865 virtually unhampered state powers were considered fundamental for liberty, federalism, and democracy. Almost no one foresaw in politically practical terms need for amendments beyond the Thirteenth, much less for two more within five years which enjoined the nation to sustain individuals' political and civil rights. Victorious Americans understood their constitutional arrangements to be so strong, so vigorous, so worthwhile because they had sufficed to win the War, as to require no further alterations. And this consensus fed further the general optimism of the Appomattox year. No need, no right, no way existed for the nation to be involved in crises as it was forced to be in 1860–61.

In December 1865 congressmen enjoyed a luxury unimagin-

---

and for Johnson's "Provisional Governors" in southern states, recorded that "The payments were made from . . . army contingencies because the[ir] . . . duties were regarded of a temporary character ancillary to the withdrawal of the military force, and to take the place of the [national] armed forces in the respective states." The entire executive Reconstruction process was provisional, Stanton believed: "My opinion is, that the whole subject of reconstruction and the relation of the State to the Federal Government is subject to the controlling power of Congress; and while I believe that the President and his Cabinet were not violating any law, but were faithfully performing their duty in endeavoring to organize provisional governments in those States, I supposed then, and still suppose, that the final validity of such organizations would rest with the lawmaking power of the government."

23. Arthur Sutherland, *Constitutionalism in America* (New York, 1965), 384.

able in 1861, and barely credible in 1863, when, respectively, the 37th and 38th Congresses came together. Because Appomattox had occurred, time existed in which to search the past for patterns to keep without fear of shackling the present or hazarding the future. Rush in state restorations by the new President was out of order. Haste combined with commitment to rigid constitutional positions had led to Sumter's shame; the congressmen of 1865 had reached Appomattox.[24]

The President's haste jarred also with the "personality" of the 39th Congress. E. L. Godkin and observers-from-within George Julian and Ignatius Donnelly agreed that the 39th Congress boasted no stars of the Calhoun-Clay-Webster magnitude. Systematic constitutional theories as bases for comprehensive legislative schemes were unlikely to attract the plain, hardworking, business-minded congressmen of 1865. More lawyers than ever filled their ranks. Like farmer and merchant colleagues, the lawyer-legislators were intent on doing the nation's work and satisfying their constituents' demands. Almost all congressmen were awed by Senator Reverdy Johnson's unmatched erudition in constitutional law and Senator Sumner's undimmed passions for good causes and unequaled knowledge of classical history. But peers of lesser learning rarely hesitated to outvote them.[25]

Simultaneously, uncertainty existed about what the nation's work was. The 39th Congress "did not comprehend precisely what it ought to do," Senator Howe admitted.[26] If a congressional consensus existed it was to cope piecemeal with actual difficulties as they became clear; if a national consensus is describable it was to return to as much normality as possible.

Of course tensions were developing from differences concerning the locus of leadership between President and Congress in defining details (if the southern freedman's status as voter, juror, licensed professional or craftsman may be described as "details"). Defending executive initiative in reconstructing the southern states, Democrats revived Jacksonian views about sepa-

---

24. Bridges, "Sherman," 81, n. 34.
25. On lawyers' numbers and influence, see Morgan, *Congress and the Constitution*, ch. 6; on Godkin, see William Brock, *An American Crisis: Congress and Reconstruction, 1865–1867* (New York, 1963), 51; Julian, *Political Recollections*, 352–7; Ridge, *Donnelly*, 103.
26. Howe to Grace, March 5, 1867, Howe Papers #140, SHSW.

ration of powers by terms of which presidential actions properly within constitutional spheres were immune from curtailment by Congress or courts.[27]

But the doctrine of separation of powers was dear also to Republicans. Congress possessed from the Constitution clear power to decide delegates' qualifications immune from presidential or judicial processes. During the War, as noted earlier, Congress had improved its internal government, especially the committees' and the Speaker's operations. The wartime Congresses had less lost leadership than shared it with Lincoln. Even the President's gamesmanship and Taney's adventures in judicial imperialism never relegated Congress to second place to either, much less to both. Now both men were dead; their offices were in the hands of novices. Of the nation's three branches of government, only Congress represented democracy's mandate and enjoyed amassed expertness. Its Republicans insisted that it should also enjoy leadership and not be rushed.

By a parliamentary device centering in the House Speaker's office, in December 1865 the 39th Congress's Republicans omitted the southern states from the roll and assigned the Reconstruction question to a new joint committee. So doing, they averted a crisis that insistence on immediate full-scale debate about constitutional abstractions must have provoked. In the opinions of informed persons, such a debate would likely have returned Congress to the catatonia of 1860–61. Endless rhetoric issued thereafter concerning the status of the southern states. But like Lincoln in 1861, Congress in late 1865 seized the initiative from rigid Democrats. Henceforward the nation's ordinary business proceeded while Congress, without unseemly haste, pondered the realities of constitutional life in applicant states of the South. This would be the only opportunity Congress could have, foreseeably, to gauge intrastate performances. Once states re-entered, national "war powers" evaporated, the 1865 consensus ran.

But in 1865 as in 1861 "adequacy" constitutionalism allowed the nation to deal with its concerns from a position of strength only if Republicans retained political control in Congress. Lin-

---

27. Montgomery Blair, *Speech . . . on the Revolutionary Schemes of the Ultra Abolitionists and in Defence of the Policy of the President* (New York, 1863), 3–7, 19; Smith, *Blair Family,* II, 244–5.

coln's Louisiana and Johnson's baker's-dozen "restored" states could incur among Republicans the damages the Democrats suffered from Buchanan's Kansas. Defecting rightward, such Republicans as Trumbull could rend the Republicans as Stephen Douglas had cleft the Democrats.

President Johnson's strategy was to use national war powers and executive pardon power in ways Lincoln never dared employ during the War, to resurrect wholly white, overwhelmingly Democratic state governments and parties southward. Then the President shifted constitutional positions to state autonomy, denying that the nation had any rights to require decent standards in civil, political, and racial relationships. Aiming that way in 1865, Johnson, still head of the wartime Republican-Union party, was building a national coalition of conservative white state Democratic parties. He was trying to recruit into it conservative Republican congressmen of Trumbull's stature.[28]

As signs of the President's constitutional swerve increased, Republicans as well as Democrats responded to its inherent appeals for a rearward-looking generation. The constitutional history of the United States had long accepted as a concomitant of federalism that almost all public social responsibilities were burdens for states and localities to assume, not the nation. A heavy phalanx of Republican politicos including Sherman and Trumbull, and of Republican theoreticians such as John Norton Pomeroy and George Washington Paschal, were state-rights nationalists, suspicious of any new functional path the nation traveled. If in 1865 Republicans were convinced that the vigorous "adequacy" constitutional doctrine carried over from the War, it was true also that Republicans were unsure how, why, or when the nation should exert its energies.

In December 1865 news from the British West Indies of the "Eyre Rebellion" of freed blacks there gave temporary pause even

---

28. A useful survey of recent literature is in the footnoting to Kincaid, "Victims of Circumstance," esp. ns. 42, 43. Special attention is deserved to Eric L. McKitrick, *Andrew Johnson and Reconstruction* (Chicago, 1960); Brock, *An American Crisis*; LaWanda Cox and John H. Cox, *Politics, Principle, and Prejudice, 1865–1868* (Glencoe, Ill., 1963); and Trefousse, *The Radical Republicans*, all *passim*. See also Hugh McCulloch to George Harrington, June 11, 1866, Harrington Papers, HL.

to Negrophiles among Republicans. Further, with the wartime volunteers dispersed, the nation's administrative resources appeared to be wholly inadequate for any but familiar caretaker tasks such as tariff collections; a Freedmen's Bureau was needed to cope with a new charge. Were there to be many new national charges?

Back in 1862, Emerson pontificated that the War was illuminating "every putrid spot" in American life.[29] He was noting not only the timid tinkering then under way in Washington concerning slavery, but also the wide-ranging, eclectic, vigorous reformist surge under way since Sumter on all levels of government and in private associations. This improvement phenomenon had roots in Jackson's time. Its sudden upsurge in 1861 involved cities, counties, and states in unprecedented scales of commitment and wholly novel functional arenas.

These enlargements of governments' roles suggest again how constitutional federalism determined the structure, alternatives, and destinies of Reconstruction politics. Many "reconstructions" were going on simultaneously North and South, involving applications of government's powers, resources, and institutions on some level or on several levels of the federal system, for improvement purposes. Ignorance and confusion manifested themselves repeatedly concerning which level of government was appropriate to a concern—can a county contain cholera? Similarly, prejudice and imperception obscured which instrument of government, as well as what level, was wanted in particular instances. When education occurred on these points, a brief percolation from locality to state to nation, and use of expert staffs organized in permanent commissions, becomes visible among perceptive would-be improvers.

Succeeding chapters seek to underline the fact that "Reconstruction" of the southern states was an aspect of attempts to

---

29. *Journals of Ralph Waldo Emerson*, ed. E. W. Emerson and W. E. Forbes (Boston, 1913), IX, 462; Phillip Paludan, "John Nortom Pomeroy, State Rights Nationalist," *AJLH*, XII (1968), 275–93; on Paschal, Jane Scarborough, "George W. Paschal: Texas Unionist and Scalawag Jurisprudent" (Ph.D. diss., RU, 1972). See also "Lesson from Jamaica," *Pa. Freedmen's Bull.*, I (Dec. 5, 1865), 88–9; B. Semmel, *Jamaican Blood and Victorian Conscience: The Governor Eyre Controversy* (Boston, 1963), *passim.*

remedy within many states evils and distresses that the War had exposed to view—Emerson's "putrid spots." Further chapters will imply that for many reconstructors, a curious mixture (by modern standards) existed of attitudes and commitments. The constitutional tradition that states had plenary powers to do whatever was required for the maintenance of public health, safety, and morals jarred with antipathy toward coercion and with deepening awareness of democracy's propensity for foolishnesses. Distrust came to dominate; a search for stability resulted. A drift developed soon after Appomattox to favor restraining states and their multitudinous counties and cities.

These factors help to explain why Radical Reconstruction never came into existence even in southern states. Republican Radicalism became a nay-saying stance. Instead of a positive program, it responded negatively to others' initiatives—to the "black codes" created in President Johnson's state restorations, for example. Radical Republicans did not cease being Republicans. Needs for re-elections kept Radicals marching not too far in advance of party peers or constituents, for fear of tumbling out of office. And many Radicals were only relatively and intermittently in a Radical posture.

As noted earlier, no centralized leviathan developed in Washington to replace state-centered federalism; no huge national, coercive bureaucracy substituted for local decision-making. The over-all War and Reconstruction result was not, as frequently intimated, an absolute increase in positive national powers and functions, but as Carl Friedrich perceived, "a decrease in [state and] local autonomy."[30]

To substantiate this interpretation of Reconstruction as incorporating War-linked concerns about intrastate functional adventures North as well as South, long excursions are necessary. These excursions include inquiries into states' police-power theory and practices, especially urban applications of delegated states' powers and state-level regulatory and data-gathering commissions. Thereafter, reactions to the upsurge in states' and cities' activities receive attention, as well as the simultaneous (or, better, parallel) recourses to national powers when more local or regional efforts failed to cope. Then, Reconstruction's turn comes round again at last.

---

30. Friedrich, *American Constitutionalism Abroad,* 49; Benedict, "The Right Way," chs. 1–8.

Chapter XVIII

The Great
Transatlantic Workshop

I n 1861, with the nation's survival at stake, Lincoln groped
for nationalist adequacy doctrine. He acted for two years on
the assumption that it existed before comprehensive formulation
occurred; it was practice without much theory. By contrast, long
before Sumter, the states' adequacy to cope with almost any
public want was accepted in American constitutionalism. This
state-power notion had roots in colonial times and in the nineteenth century was developed further by Lemuel Shaw, John Bannister Gibson, and Isaac Redfield. Its essence was the constitutional rightness of state interventions to encourage, prevent, or
contain certain actions; to replace marketplace self-adjustments
with alternatives. The aim was to assure the public health, safety,
welfare, and morals.

Because it was ready-to-hand in 1865, state-power constitutionalism supplied part of Appomattox's happy optimism and
basic political framework. Democrats insisted that state or local
treatment of residents was wholly the concern of the state of
residence. Republicans agreed that the recent rebel states *could*
and *should* deal decently with returned white Unionists and black
inhabitants, but pointed out that they were not doing so.

After Appomattox as never before, efforts proliferated actually to apply state powers. Advocates of state-power applications resorted overwhelmingly to local, county, and state Republican organizations. Democrats were not merely still tarred by

disloyalty's associative guilt; they appeared to be stuck in constitutional inhibitions, and admitted proudly the comparative immobility of the party.

Delighted that Appomattox had destroyed secession and slavery, Republicans were pleased also that the Union victory allowed abandonment of grand concerns. For most people who retained social concerns at all, attention shifted from catastrophes (except for cholera) to crudities, from apocalypses to adversities, from nation to neighborhoods; each improver centered now on "his little home-republic," Moncure Conway noted. Like the Age of Jackson, the time of Johnson treasured eclecticism about public distresses and localism in dealing with them. In politically meaningful terms awareness persisted of certain "putrid spots" only. Thus, Brownson's 1865 comment that "there is no social grievance of magnitude enough to enlist any considerable number of people . . . in a [national] movement to redress it," reflects the existence of constitutional readiness to cope on local or state stages with problems of lesser magnitude.[1]

These characteristics were appropriate to federalism's numerous governmental levels below the nation and for the primitive condition of governments' bureaucratic and personnel resources. As had been true of all preceding reformers including abolitionists, post-Appomattox reform activists had to learn to travel through federalism's intricacies, how to find the proper government level in search of budget, personnel, and authority, and when successful in these delicate maneuvers, how to exercise power usefully. The War had not altered the problems federalism posed to persons and groups advocating changes. Instead the

---

1. William C. DeWitt, *Sundry Speeches and Writings: Driftwood from the Current of a Busy Life* (Brooklyn, 1881) I, 74–6; *The Works of Orestes A. Brownson*, ed. H. F. Brownson (reprint edn., New York, 1966), XVIII, 192; on state police power history, see Harry N. Scheiber, "The Road to *Munn:* Eminent Domain and the Concept of Public Purpose in the State Courts," *PAH*, V (1971), 329–33; Christopher G. Tiedman, *A Treatise on the Limitations of Police Power in the United States Considered from Both a Civil and Criminal Standpoint* (St. Louis, 1886), 2; Ernst Freund, *The Police Powers: Public Policy and Constitutional Rights* (Chicago, 1904), *passim;* S. I. Kutler, "John Bannister Gibson: Judicial Restraint and the 'Positive State,'" *JPL*, XIV (1965), 181–97; W. G. Hastings, "The Development of Law as Illustrated by the Decisions Relating to the Police Power of the State," *APSR*, XXXIX (1900), 364, 5; Leonard W. Levy, *The Law of the Commonwealth and Chief Justice Shaw; The Evolution of American Law, 1830–1860* (Cambridge, Mass., 1957), 119, 234–72; Moncure Conway, "Sursum Corda," *The Radical*, I (1866), 292–3.

War greatly improved techniques available to Lincoln's generation for obtaining through politics what its determined members
wanted.

Wartime service in the Army, the Sanitary and Christian
Commissions, the YMCA, the Loyal Leagues, and the Protestant
churches' home-front network taught ways to gain such new
goals as communicable-disease containment as well as to combat old sins like slavery or liquor. These lessons centered on
marrying the goals, managerial talents, and professional expertness of voluntarily associated improvers to government's
powers.[2] First, however, political weight was needed to force
government into partnership. What sort of partnership, on what
level of government, were questions that were to make more
constitutional history.

From Congress down to the most rural hamlet, nineteenth-
century officials lacked adequate enforcement powers, tax resources, career bureaucrats, professional staffs, and information
sources. Solons relied largely on special-interest, self-serving
lobbyists for data. Distinguishing them from other lobbyists, post-
Appomattox reformers wished to purify more than to profit.
Their common denominator was participation in large-scale wartime efforts. Sumter initiated their on-job training; Appomattox
dispersed nationwide these veterans of public administration,
social services, and practical politics. An impressive number
became apostles of new reforms. Their efforts to win narrow-
horizon improvements initiated heated tests of political power. As
always, political debaters sought constitutional guidelines.

The diffusion and quality of these debates forcibly struck the
English traveler Samuel Smith, who in prewar times had toured
the slave states and written an "inside USA" summation widely
read in Britain. Soon after Appomattox, he returned and roamed
almost every state west of the Mississippi. Deeply impressed,
Smith declared:

> There is no country at the present day where the student
> of political and social science can learn so many lessons
> as in the United States of America. He comes into contact

---

2. C. D. Cashdollar, "American Attitudes Toward Social Catastrophe"
(Ph.D. diss., UP, 1967); David Brion Davis, *Ante-Bellum Reform* (New
York, 1967), 1–10; Emory Washburn, "Reconstruction: The Duty of the
[Legal] Profession to the Times," *MLRep*, XXVI (1864), 477–84; J. W.
Hurst, *Law and Social Process in United States History* (Ann Arbor, Mich.,
1960), 234–53.

there with a busy ferment of ideas to which the old world is a stranger. He hears every possible theory of human rights propounded; he sees every intellectual and moral force in fullest activity; in short, he sees human society possessing all the advantages of civilization, but unfettered by its traditions, working out for itself anew the social and political problems which the old world has been solving with tardy progress these last three thousand years.[3]

Perhaps because Reconstruction concerns rarely troubled them, Appomattox's heady optimism suffused would-be appliers of state power. If horizons were relatively local, no insurmountable obstacles appeared to exist no matter how complex the problem. In this context, Charles Francis Adams, Jr., the patrician Massachusetts railroad reformer, recalled his conversation with an Illinois farmer who wished his state to impose maximum rail rates. Adams advised the "Granger" that before any state should act in this arena, years of careful empirical data accumulation and analysis were necessary, and that knotty economic, legal, and constitutional questions were involved. Unimpressed, the midwesterner replied: "Why I don't think I should have any trouble in drawing up an act in half an hour which would settle the whole thing."[4]

Adams's farmer offered this hearty tribute to his state's sufficiency to cope because, during the War, ordinary people had learned that applied government power worked. It made sense to carry past Appomattox an assumption that the causes and cures for other social ills were achievable. Thus the coexistence of the nation's victory and state power constitutionalism allowed faith among laymen and intellectuals in the imminence of a science of society. What Keller described properly as "a time of striking public vigor" was in the making not because the spring of government was weak but because it appeared strong, at least on state and local levels.

Undimmed by foreknowledge of the frustrations of Reconstruction or of the tarnish of the Gilded Age, such confidence

---

3. Samuel Smith, *Reflection Suggested by a Second Visit to the United States of America, Being a Paper Read Before the Liverpool Philomathic Society, March 13, 1867* (Liverpool, 1867), 5.

4. C. F. Adams, Jr., *Remarks . . . on a National Railroad Commission, Before the Merchants Association of Boston, February 25, 1882* (Boston, 1882), 4.

made Civil War and post-Appomattox America very different from the crisis-shadowed place of traditional estimations. For example, Union Army veteran Lester Ward, happy in his post-demobilization move to Washington from his rural Pennsylvania town and secure in his government clerkship, commenced on his own to study government's "politico-social functions." He noted the increasing confidence he and his peers felt in their ability to control and organize social environments through applied government's powers. Largely uninterested in Reconstruction, Ward was unimpressed by doctrines of constitutional restraints, unawed by technical experts, and unrepelled by bureaucratic institutions. Instead he wished to employ all as foils against spoils politicos and as sources of rational public policies. Within a remarkably short time after Appomattox Ward was ready to begin a full study, not of constitutional abstractions so popular among prewar theoreticians, but of America's evolving society. It became his masterpiece, *Dynamic Sociology.*

At least in the victorious section, men like Ward and the anonymous Illinois farmer believed that they were correcting the past and could control the present; that, applied through political action, new social sciences would purify all American institutions including government, prevent repetition of the Civil War's strains and sacrifices, and initiate the social stability for which many yearned. The status of the freed Negro and of the crumpled Confederate states were simply two more problems which reason would solve. Even race would find rational expression in the new statistical and anthropometrical data the War had allowed. Regenerations within the North's states would parallel reconstructions of the South's.

E. L. Godkin, editor of *The Nation*, a periodical established in the spring of 1865 which rapidly became the new intellectual reformers' chief mouthpiece, addressed the American Social Science Association on these matters. Like *The Nation*, the Association began in 1865.[5] The Association's major initiator and first

---

5. J. S. Haller, "Civil War Anthropometry: The Making of a Racial Ideology," *CWH*, XVI (1970), 309–24; E. L. Godkin, "Legislation and Social Science," *JSS*, II (1870), 126; John G. Sproat, *The Best Men: Liberal Reformers of the Gilded Age* (New York, 1968), chs. 1–2; Morton Keller, *The Art and Politics of Thomas Nast* (New York, 1968), ix. On Ward, see his "Politico-Social Functions," *Pennsylvania Monthly*, XII (1881), 321–36; *Lester Ward and the Welfare State*, ed. H. S. Commager (Indianapolis, 1967), xxvi–xxvii. Mr. Thomas Haskell, my Rice University colleague, is

secretary, Henry Villard, acknowledged that it could never have come into existence before the demise of slavery and secession made rationality possible in politics and progress inevitable in society.

Such organizations and publications, in the Boston *Commonwealth*'s phrase, were "mouthpieces for epicures." According to *The Round Table*'s analysis, they attracted "the best men" who believed that their cities, states, and nation were on the brink of a rebirth of reform, who were educated enough to understand relevant war-amassed statistical and other data, who were leisured enough to support political action, and who were public-spirited enough to feel an obligation to serve. Yet something more than scientism, noblesse oblige, or elitism moved reformers of the late sixties. Consciences stirred by the nation's peril and the slave's humanity proved sensitive also to cholera victims, exploited children, and abused animals. Many men were concerned also by the threats to familiar ways posed by what they saw as Catholic-corrupted urban politics, corrupting pornography, and corruptible Protestants; by private entrepreneurs' rapacity and public officers' venality, and by the sudden visibility allowed by urban environments to epidemic declines in public health.

During the War some of these concerns became for the first time acceptable topics for respectable folk to chew over. After the War, it was time to do something about them. Henry Bowditch noted happily, "A popular writer sits beside the 'Autocrat of the Breakfast Table' and discusses sewerage in the 'Atlantic Monthly' with infinite gusto, and apparently to the satisfaction of all readers of this popular monthly."[6]

This busy spirit encouraged associations to form whose purposes, however disparate, led commonly to efforts to employ local or state governments' powers and/or resources for reform purposes. The inchoate nature of state-power constitutionalism attracted mutually competitive interests to seek to apply it against each other for what sometimes were contradictory or incongruous goals; in Lemuel Shaw's words, "It is much easier to perceive and

---

completing his Stanford University dissertation on the American Social Science Association. I am grateful for his insights into and criticism of data in this chapter.

6. Henry I. Bowditch, *Public Hygiene in America: Being the Centennial Discourse Delivered Before the International Medical Congress . . .* (Boston, 1877), 42; *Commonwealth*, Jan. 9, 1869; *Round Table*, III (Oct. 21, 1965), 105; Henry Villard in *JSS*, II (1870), 210.

realize the existence of this [police] power, than to mark its boundaries and prescribe its limits of exercise."[7]

Plasticity in supposedly complete state-power constitutionalism failed to upset most people, any more than Reconstruction's augmenting tensions lessened the popular belief in the War-perfected national Constitution. Illogicalities of this sort troubled only legal logicians like Francis Lieber.[8] State-power activists simply acted upon the assumption that constitutionalism was on their side.

Appomattox inspired members of numerous professions to incorporate self-protective associations and to seek through them establishment through state authority of educational and other qualification requirements for future practitioners. New labor unions sought to have their communities set industrial safety standards. Farmers wished to pit state resources against galling industrial and communications enterprises, whose management resisted stoutly. Religious groups set out to hold lines against liquor, vice, and pornography by alliances with local and state governments.[9] There was a general consensus that activist politics nourished good causes; that associational efforts were the way to impact on politics and to remedy a public ill. Odds appeared to be that the loner was ineffective if not obsolete; the prewar failures of abolitionists were sharp lessons on this score.[10]

However heady the Appomattox do-anything optimism, no

---

7. Matthew T. Downey, "The Rebirth of Reform: A Study of Liberal Reform Movements, 1865–1872" (Ph.D. diss., PU, 1963), iv–vi, 2–22; T. D. Woolsey, "The New Era," *NE*, XXV (1866), 179–99; Lemuel Shaw in Commonwealth v. Alger, 7 Cushing (Mass.), 53 (1851).

8. Francis Lieber, *A Letter . . . on the Amendment,* unnumbered prefatory page and *passim;* Lieber, ms. "Lectures on the Constitution," ca. 1866, Lieber Papers, HL; *Round Table,* III (Jan. 20, 1866), 40; S. S. Nicholas, *Conservative Essays, Legal and Political* (Louisville, 1867), III, 60–1; E. L. Godkin, "Some Things Overlooked at the Centennial," *The Nation* (Sept. 2, 1887), 226; [J. C. Hurd] *The Centennial of a Revolution by A Revolutionist* (New York, 1888), *passim.*

9. Raymond H. Merritt, *Engineering in American Society, 1850–1875* (Lexington, Ky., 1970), *passim;* Burton J. Bledstein, "The Intellectual, the Professional, and the Problem of Democracy in America" (AHA paper, 1968); Maxwell Bloomfield, "Law vs. Politics: The Self-Image of the American Bar (1830–1860)," *AJLH,* XII (1968), 306–23.

10. George Martin, *Causes and Conflicts: The Centennial History of the Association of the Bar of the City of New York* (New York, 1970), ch. 1; NYBA *Journal,* I (1870), 17–29.

matter how giddy the constitutional tradition of considering the federal union as one "wherein broad powers were left to the states" (Swisher's phrase),[11] the fact remains that prewar practice differed sharply from the theory of plenary state-police powers. No matter how jurisprudents offered opposite depictions, during pre–Civil War decades almost all states had remained dedicated to do-little practices.

Exceptions existed. Asylum construction, water supply provision, common school support, levee maintenance, canal and railroad subventions, and slave controls were functions which some states and subdivisions performed with fair regularity and consistency. On this score, any activity at all by governments left traces in the form of budgets, ordinances, and statutes. Absence of traces is commoner; absence so general that the 1837 edition of Bouvier's *Law Dictionary* (reissued in 1867) did not even list police power. As Oscar and Mary Handlin noted of the prewar half-century, "Important spheres of social action were . . . left . . . to voluntary associations without the capacity for coercion."[12] Illustration of this pattern is available through examination of one question, public health, which stood high among concerns of many post-Appomattox improvers, as it had in prewar and War times.

During the late eighteenth and early nineteenth centuries, America's state and local governments had managed to avoid

---

11. Carl Brent Swisher, "Dred Scott One Hundred Years After," *JPoli*, XIX (1957), 172. As an inescapable characteristic of residual sovereignty, states had derivative responsibility to employ police powers to safeguard citizens' health, morals, safety, and welfare, according to legal theory, which held also that intrastate police power actions could never collide with the narrow band of national interstate functions. If, despite such planetary imagery, collisions occurred, judges could rule out of order irrational clashes in a manner reminiscent of papal bulls against comets. Thomas Cooley, *Constitutional Limitations Which Rest upon the Legislative Powers of the States of the American Union* (Boston, 1868), 574; Edward S. Corwin, "The Basic Doctrine of American Constitutional Law," *MichLR*, XII (1914), 247, 252–3.

12. Hastings, "The Development of Law," 359–78; David J. Rothman, *The Discovery of the Asylum: Order and Disorder in the New Republic* (Boston, 1971), *passim;* J. R. Spengler, "Laissez-Faire and Intervention: A Potential Source of Historical Error," *JPE*, LVII (1949), 440–1; Oscar and Mary Handlin, *The Dimensions of Liberty* (New York, 1966), 7; Andrew Shonfield, *Modern Capitalism: The Changing Balance of Public and Private Power* (London, 1965), 302–4 and ch. 13, *passim.*

taking on much if any of their supposedly basic police-power responsibility involving public health. Popular interest rose dramatically only when calamities impended in the form of epidemics. Otherwise, crusades about the disposal of human wastes, pollution in upstream waterways, or quarantining of diseased immigrants were not in order. Unlike slavery, these technical subjects were unfit for parlors, classrooms, chapels, or newspapers, and the involvement of many individuals and associations was necessary before politics could magnify the concerns of a few into a cause for many.[13]

That any attention at all went to public-health matters during pre–Civil War decades was due to a tiny number of leisured, science-minded, public-spirited persons in a few urban centers, who usually styled themselves "sanitarians." Self-appointed stewards of the general interest, sanitarians shared Benjamin Rush's vision of "the time when our courts of law shall punish cities and villages for permitting any of the sources of bilious and malignant fevers to exist within their jurisdiction[s]."[14]

It took the Civil War to make less easy the states' habit of ignoring the mass-health responsibility that constitutional law asserted was always theirs, and to involve the nation in public-health efforts. Before the War, advance from what the framers reached in 1787 and from the dual federalism of subsequent constitutionalism proved to be all but impossible. The Constitution did not assign to the new nation "general welfare" responsibilities that contemporary European governments accepted as concomitants of nationhood. Instead, a rough consensus obtained that the states would provide for their publics' well-being as each thought was necessary and proper, which proved to be not very much.[15]

---

13. Dorman B. Eaton, "Municipal Government," *JSS*, V (1873), 3–11; cf. Powell v. Pa., 127 US, 678 (1888); Holden v. Hardy, 169 US, 366 (1898); Leroy Parker and R. H. Worthington, *The Law of Public Health and Safety and the Powers and Duties of Boards of Health* (Albany, 1892), 1–2.

14. Benjamin Rush quoted in Bowditch, *Public Hygiene*, unnumbered prefatory page; David F. Hawke, *Benjamin Rush: Revolutionary Gadfly* (Indianapolis, 1971), chs. 17–19.

15. In this connection, Congress's quarantine policies want brief examination. A 1796 act, which Congress reaffirmed in essentials in 1799 and 1832, provided not national efforts but federal assistance to states' officers in enforcing whatever quarantine standards state legislators deemed

Political imperatives, racial and social attitudes, and medical scientific information mixed to form the noncommittal constitutional amalgam that emerged from Philadelphia, which generations of congressmen were content to keep. The political push derived from the need to obtain approval for the new government. Unless the 1787 formulation satisfied enough citizens that it was no threat to local orientation, then anti-Federalists must have their way. Without an epidemic on hand, the public-health theme did not inspire national functional adventuring.[16]

But contrary to expectations at Philadelphia, states failed to pick up the slack. On this score the Constitution's framers, who had assumed that federalism allowed alternatives to national action not available abroad, struck out.

In part, their naïveté reflected the prevailing scientific conviction that yellow fever and smallpox, the most feared epidemic diseases, were coming under control. Therefore, sporadic local action was adequate to check them. A constitutional-political proposition followed that anticontagion responsibility belonged to the locality where infection existed.[17] This view reinforced prevailing attitudes that epidemic illnesses afflicted persons and groups of innately depraved and vicious characteristics, or that divine caprice beyond man's capacities to block invited epidemics.

---

appropriate. Since states' quarantine policies, such as they were, occasionally involved impediments to foreign and interstate commerce and transit of persons and commodities, Congress's consistent permissiveness and sensitivity to state pride is the more impressive. *SAL*, I, 474 (1796); I, 619 (1799); IV, 577 (1832); and see XIV, 357 (1866).

16. John Roche, "The Founding Fathers: A Reform Caucus in Action," *APSR*, LV (1961), 799–816; Bowditch, *Public Hygiene*, 1, suggests the minor-key characteristic of public health matters at Philadelphia. Ratification achieved, then the Constitution's unambitious prophylactic stipulations proved no bar to nationally financed and executed public-health activities when they occurred far from the settled East, were on a small scale, and involved obviously national interests. No one objected in 1802 and later when Army doctors in then-western states and territories, vaccinated Indians who lived on or near military posts against smallpox. Such precautions about soldiers' health enjoyed patent validity under the Constitution's clause (Art. I, sec. 8) dealing with the armed services. In like manner the treaty clause (Art. VI, sec. 2) blanketed public-health service which United States officials provided subscribing Indian tribesmen early in the nineteenth century. Morris Kagan, "Federal Public Health: A Reflection of a Changing Constitution," *JHM*, XVI (1961), 270–1.

17. Howard D. Kramer, "Effect of the Civil War on the Public Health Movement," *MVHR*, XLVIII (1948), 462.

The upshot was a judgment that there was not much useful for even local authorities to do about epidemics, and that Congress had no role to play beyond enforcing state-set standards about immigrants or quarantines.[18]

These constrained attitudes toward man, God, and government were revealingly illuminated in 1793, when a savage yellow-fever epidemic struck Philadelphia and elsewhere. Many municipal and country officials joined the exodus to safer hinterlands, leaving in the city the poor, who by terms of elitist folklore suffered infection because of innate racial, religious, or character deficiencies.[19]

A few men high in social standing remained in the infested city. They formed volunteer committees to replace or supplement depleted ranks of local officialdom. When the disease ebbed, the adventitious committees went out of existence, and as before, no national, state, county, or city officers were responsible to prevent or to warn about future recurrences of disease.[20] Yet this was a time when altering urban concentrations and communications innovations insured that epidemics would spread in a worse manner. One scholar estimated recently that these alterations, contracting space and time, clearly "called for legislative remedies on the local, state, and finally on the national level."[21] However clear the call retrospectively, during the first half-century of the nation's history lawmakers managed not to hear it, as illustrated in the timid quarantines Congress established in 1796 and subsequently.[22]

---

18. John Duffy, *Epidemics in Colonial America* (Baton Rouge, 1953); Bowditch, *Public Hygiene*, 5.

19. Symbolically, in 1794 Congress joined in this abdication of responsibility by enacting a statute which authorized it to meet at places other than the designated capital when epidemics threatened. *SAL*, I, 353.

20. Without their respective states' authority to do so, Baltimore in 1793 and Philadelphia in 1794 organized municipal boards of health to try to cope with the yellow-fever peril; both of these faded out of existence after that epidemic passed. James A. Tobey, *Public Health Law* (3rd edn., New York, 1947), 11.

21. J. A. Carrigan, "The National Board of Health, 1879–1883: A Significant Failure" (SHA paper, 1964, used with permission).

22. The 1796 quarantine law began as a bill which specified that Congress must take positive steps in quarantining, notwithstanding states' actions. The proposition offered in support was that interstate obstructions to commerce would develop from any epidemics. But this assertive version died in committee, and the final form of the statute began the tradition

Greater national governmental vigor received only nominal encouragement. Addressing Congress in 1798, President John Adams noted that epidemics were occasions when "the national interests are deeply affected." But his recommendation was that Congress should establish "suitable regulations in aid of the health laws of the respective states."[23] The need for even this minimal energy appeared soon to lessen. In 1805, scientist-President Jefferson told Congress that as understanding increased about the disease, states "charged with the care of the public health, and Congress [charged] with . . . the [regulation of] general commerce, will become able to regulate with effect their respective functions in these departments." Nothing, however, needed to be done immediately, Jefferson advised the legislators.

Congress did nothing, and neither did states. If laggard lawmakers felt shame at inaction (no evidence suggests they did) the Supreme Court of the United States comforted the passive. In 1824, the Court imagined that health statutes under states' police powers were common, enforced, and vigorous.[24]

Then in 1832 a new disease, cholera, unknown in Europe until the close of the Napoleonic wars, spread westward from seaboard American cities along the turnpikes, canals, and rivers that were conveying the thrust of this buoyant society. Unlike yellow fever, cholera afflicted rich and poor, pious and profane, white and Negro, Protestant and Catholic. In the face of its horrifying incursions, restraints loosened for a little while.[25] In the year of the nullification crisis, frightened congressmen appropriated federal funds to subsidize states in their unsystematic quarantine regulations; the first direct national intervention, however directionless it seems today.[26] By the 1830's medical opinion was

of states excluding immigrants by whatever standards appeared appropriate, with Congress's blessing. See Kagan, "Federal Public Health," 264–5; Harry S. Mustard, *Government in Public Health* (New York, 1945), 49–57; *SAL*, I, 474.

23. *M&P*, I, 271, for Adams. A survey of Presidents' messages to Congress on the public-health theme is in James A. Tobey, *The National Government and Public Health* (Baltimore, 1926), ch. 3; *SAL*, I, 619 (Feb. 25, 1799).

24. Gibbons v. Ogden, 9 Wheaton 1, at 202; *M&P*, I, 383.

25. Kramer, "Effects," 449; Charles E. Rosenberg, *The Cholera Years, 1832, 1849, and 1866* (Chicago, 1962), 41–7; André Siegfried, *Routes of Contagion*, tr. Jean Henderson and Mercedes Charasó (New York, 1965), 35, 47, 51, 85.

26. *SAL*, IV, 577; Kagan, "Federal Public Health," 266.

that prevention could limit cholera, although even the finest physicians, the best-intentioned Ladies Bountiful, and the most pious private charities lacked resources to do the job. Since the unpalatable ingredients of the new anticholera pharmacopia included mass quarantines of afflicted persons, neighborhood-wide disinfectings, and burning of contaminated dwellings and other private property, government must step in. In sum, medical imperatives had moved close to constitutional theory about the plenitude of states' police powers.

The most dramatic illustration occurred in New York City. During the 1832 cholera epidemic, the City's Board of Health, a creation of state legislation, assumed temporarily "many of the functions of . . . twentieth century government—hospital and welfare services, slum clearance, and food and drug control," the closest student of the subject wrote recently. Deriving extraordinary authority from the Board, public and private agencies created temporary tenements, hospitals, and asylums for the stricken. At least in the nation's largest city, constituted authority provided a center from which medical "experts," leagued with government, improvised defenses against the killer. But similar provisions proved to be inappropriate for most other communities. Talent and inspiration were too rare; fiscal strains were, or appeared to be, too great for villages and smaller urban centers to bear. And constitutional-political restraints hemmed in even New York City about the limits of state and city action during crisis, although the constitutional literature continued to stress the plenary aspects of state action. The 1832 cholera epidemic struck very hard, but it changed little.[27]

Between 1832 and mid-century, many sanitarians decided that local efforts to limit cholera were useless, and began to favor establishment of statewide public-health boards. Public attention

---

27. Rosenberg, *Cholera Years,* 13–98; Bowditch, *Public Hygiene,* 2–4; John Duffy, *A History of Public Health in New York City, 1625–1866* (New York, 1968). Nevertheless, Jacksonian America exhibited more compassion for the disease's victims and for other unfortunates, such as tenement basement dwellers who came to light during the cholera epidemic, than had been the case forty years earlier when yellow fever had last hit. A fair chorus raised that man's inhumanity to man, not God's verdicts about individual men, had made the plague's unchecked spread possible; Robert H. Bremner, *From the Depths, The Discovery of Poverty in the United States* (New York, 1956), ch. 1; Benjamin H. Klebaner, "Poverty and Relief in American Thought," *Social Service Review,* XXXVIII (1964), 382–99.

moved away from their concern, however, often in the direction of the more engaging antislavery-extension cause. Sanitarians and antislave reformers—sometimes the same people—discovered the complexities, frustrations, and opportunities in the federal system; both sighed after advantages British improvers possessed in Parliament's single stage.

Although cholera reappeared in scattered localities every year from 1849 to 1854, and in 1853 New Orleans suffered a terrible yellow-fever attack, neither disease involved whole states or regions. Public indifference thwarted efforts at creating permanent statewide health boards or even temporary "sanitary surveys," such as the one which Lemuel Shattuck sought in Massachusetts. Meanwhile other natural disasters and economic dislocations provided ample opportunities for benevolent societies to alleviate localized distress. In public health, compared to other nations the United States practiced purest laissez-faire principles.[28] Yet the law continued preaching simultaneously reverence for state-defined private property and the total adequacy of state governments that, with notable functional exceptions, remained inadequate and inactive.

Still, medical advances were weakening folklore about contagion and constitutionalism.[29] But how fast? Would federalism continue to frustrate mass public-health efforts when greater opportunity—i.e., greater disaster—impended?

The greatest crisis in American history, the Civil War permitted unprecedented play for sanitarians, for it generalized among patriots the sanitarians' basic proposition that public power must protect public interests. Many prewar social critics, especially abolitionists, had been anti-institutional—and ineffectual. Sumter transformed admiration for defiant ones into respect for effective group involvement with government.[30]

---

28. Leonard Krieger, "The Idea of the Welfare State in Europe and the United States," *JHI*, XXIV (1963), 560; Bowditch, *Public Hygiene*, 30–2.

29. Rosenberg, *Cholera Years*, 172; Kramer, "Effects," 449–50; and see Susan W. Peabody, "Historical Study of Legislation Regarding Public Health in the States of New York and Massachusetts," *Journal of Infectious Diseases* (supp. No. 4: 1909), 1–158; Hastings, "Development," 411–38.

30. John L. Thomas, "Romantic Reform in America, 1815–1865," *American Quarterly*, XVII (1965), 656–81, esp. 680–81; Lorman Ratner, *Pre-Civil War Reform: The Variety of Principles* (New York, 1967); R. D. Marcus, "Wendell Phillips and American Institutions," *JAH*, LVI (1969), 41–58; *The Nation* (May 23, 1867), 405–6.

As with internal security, so with the Union soldier's health; prevention of evil by anticipatory action and improvement by coercion became the preferred way very soon after Sumter. Responding swiftly and appropriately to opportunities, abolitionists and sanitarians enlisted in their support much the same evangelical, patriotic, and soldiers' welfare organizations. Sanitarians were far readier than abolitionists to use government through organized pressures, however, because long before Sumter the sanitarians had accepted the need for efficiency, funds, and power.[31]

This did not mean that government, in the form of the Army's career medical staff, was eager to use the sanitarians. Indeed, the War's initial impact was to weaken sanitarians' causes and organizations. Many physicians, the sanitarians' bedrock strength, went into military service. Then, because the United States Army's medical personnel and procedures failed to cope with the health needs of the mass Union Army which Lincoln called into being, the sanitarians recouped rapidly. Descriptions became common—public-health crusaders spread them— about the physical hazards to which military life exposed citizen soldiers. Meanwhile, church leaders, especially of evangelical sects, who busied themselves with missionary and relief enterprises among soldiers, home-front dependents, and freedmen, stressed spiritual dangers represented by the bluecoats' fondness for liquor, pornography, prostitutes, and tobacco.

Ardent abolitionists, sophisticated sanitarians, and exhorting fundamentalists combined the evangelical, legalistic, and rational bases of prewar reformism, in concerns about soldiers' mortality and morality. Surgical techniques, waste disposal, and venereal diseases, hitherto unmentionable in parlor or pulpit, became acceptable subjects when contexts were barracks or battlefields. And public-health zealots found themselves leading the first large-scale involvements in American history of the national and state governments with public-health matters.[32] Almost without ques-

---

31. George M. Frederickson, *The Inner Civil War: Northern Intellectuals and the Crisis of the Union* (New York, 1965), ch. 7; James B. McPherson, *The Struggle for Equality: Abolitionists and the Negro in the Civil War and Reconstruction* (Princeton, 1964), 3–98.

32. See John Chapman, "Prostitution: Governmental Experiments in Controlling It," [London] *Westminster Review*, n.s. XXXVII (1870), 119–79; Bremner, "The Impact of the Civil War on Philanthropy and Social Welfare," *CWH*, XII (1966), 294; George W. Adams, *Doctors in Blue:*

tion or protest, overleaping localities was in order. No more than
was true of the Army's medical careerists could the few, feeble
local public-health apparatuses cope with wartime burdens. Prewar constitutional shibboleths about the nation's almost nonexis-
tent role in public-health concerns went into discard for the
duration. The Army's needs thrust the nation into activities which
constitutional and political habits reserved to the states, though
most states had rarely if ever seen fit to do much about their
allotted duties.

Product of the reformers' readiness and the public's ner-
vousness about bluecoats' well-being, the Sanitary Commission
and the morals-oriented Christian Commission forced the Army
to accept them as semiofficial auxiliaries. At the War Department, Commission leaders became health and morals sentries
over the citizen soldiers, and linked local committees, often associated with churches, to states' legislators and to congressmen.
The Commissions were curious mixes of private and public
sectors, of civil and military personnel, and of systematic reforms and eclectic improvisations. They slipped and stumbled.
But they worked. Led by Unitarian minister Henry Bellows,
physician Elisha Harris, and urban architect Frederick Law
Olmsted, the Sanitary Commission applied to the Union's amassing armies mass-health practices far more effective than those
employed in the Crimean and Franco-Austrian Wars.

The Sanitary Commission invested its major efforts to
achieve sound public-health practices in Army installations
located in the North.[33] But ironically, the most intensive and
successful application of the new mass medicine occurred not in
the loyal North but in the military occupation zones, where conquest by the Union Army and rigid blockades (i.e., quarantines)
by the Union Navy spectacularly improved public-health practices and standards.

New Orleans was the major disloyal area which gained
medically from defeat. Since the turn of the century, New

The Medical History of the Union Army in the Civil War (New York,
1961), chs. 1–2; Kramer, "Effects," 450.

33. William Q. Maxwell, Lincoln's Fifth Wheel: The Political History
of the United States Sanitary Commission (New York, 1956); Richard H.
Shryock, Medicine in America: Historical Essays (Baltimore, 1966), ch. 4;
Kramer, "Effects," 462. When the War's pace allowed the luxury, Commission officials imposed higher education and experience criteria for
Army doctors and nurses—a step in the direction of licensing qualifications
that became common after Appomattox.

Orleans had suffered annual yellow-fever epidemics, culminating in four awful attacks during the early 1850's. When Union forces neared the city in April 1862, diehard rebel residents prayed that "General Yellow Jack" would best the bluecoats, but new sanitary practices combined with Yankee good fortune frustrated such aspirations. The pre-occupation naval blockade was the best quarantine ever organized in the new world. After the city's capitulation, Union Army–Sanitary Commission policies improved health conditions for and among unrepentant residents.

Some streets, markets, and drains had never been cleaned. New Orleans now surrounded slaughterhouses once suburban in location, which continued to dump unused by-products into the water supply. Urban householders tossed human wastes into open sewers; horse manure and offal accreted so deeply on streets and markets that doors could not open.

"Beast" Butler's provost marshals set thousands of war prisoners and "contrabands" to cleaning up these manifold messes. The city's health board became a potent adjunct of the Union Army, with jurisdiction over every dweller and entrepreneur concerning sanitary practices. Maintained throughout the War, these policies lowered New Orleans's sickness rates to record low figures.[34]

Naturally such direct thrusts were not in the cards for northern areas, except those very close to military installations. The War had hardly begun when parents and patriots demanded that Army camps be free of liquor, prostitutes, and pornography, ancient ills linked to current disloyalty. In mid-1861, Lincoln's Postmaster General ordered "treasonable" and "incendiary" materials excluded from the mails. Subsequently, Christian and Sanitary Commission agents, postal officials, Treasury personnel, and certain Union generals such as O. O. Howard and Neal Dow cooperated in liquor prohibition and antipornography efforts within Army camps and commands, and YMCAs in Northern cities employed the patriotic argument to force officials to close centers of visible sin.[35]

Distant but connected problems arose out of the outbreak in

---

34. Kramer, "Effects," 462; J. A. Carrigan, "Yankee versus Yellow Jack in New Orleans, 1862–1866," *CWH*, IX (1963), 248–257.

35. Paul S. Boyer, *Purity in Print: The Vice-Society Movement and Book Censorship in America* (New York, 1968), 4–5; James C. Paul and Murry L. Schwartz, *Federal Censorship: Obscenity in the Mail* (Glencoe, Ill., 1961), 17, 251.

1861 of "Texas fever" among cattle and horses entering Kansas from farther southwest. Kansas's lawmakers excluded afflicted beasts from entry to the state and from transit through it. But Kansas lacked enforcement personnel and resources. Thieves and prorebel smugglers undid the prophylactic and patriotic purposes of the state statute until national officers intervened.

In late 1861 the Union Army began to enforce Kansas's law because the Confederacy received stolen stock, the Army's frontier garrisons had no surplus stores with which to replace stolen beasts, and Indian victims of rustlers were growing restless as tribal herds shrank. Four years later (February 28, 1865) Congress authorized what Union soldiers had been doing since 1861; made interstate cattle- and horse-theft a felony punishable by a ten-thousand-dollar fine and two years' imprisonment, and ordered Army personnel to co-operate with state officials in blocking transit of sick and stolen beasts. Kansas had enacted (February 11, 1865) a law of its own, punishing intrastate theft, to supplement the inadequate one of 1861. As long as this unusual pattern continued of national-state, civilian-military, soldier-veterinarian accord, sick and stolen animals (often the same cattle) moved less frequently toward eastern cooking pots and Confederate kitchens.[36]

Such wartime successes in applying socially scientific ideas, and the constitutional heritage of state-police-power adequacy, helped to create the optimistic mood of Appomattox. What was not apparent was that wartime public-health successes were recorded only when national officers spurred states', counties', and cities' officials to action. New Orleans suggested that the nation and the city were the stages on which reform-minded men should perform. But constitutional law restrained the nation and ignored the city in favor of the states. Could the law's illusions and traditions advance to meet postwar needs?

In 1865 the answer appeared to be a clear affirmative. "The conception of the uses and powers of government . . . [were] settled, and . . . strengthened by the civil war," concluded the closest student of the development of states' police powers.[37]

---

36. *SAL*, XIII, 441–2; Kansas, *General Laws, 1861*, 280; *ibid., 1865*, 159–60. William E. Unrau, "Joseph G. McCoy and Federal Regulation of the Cattle Trade," *Colorado Magazine*, XLIII (1966), 32–43. Professor Unrau provided other information for which I am grateful.

37. Hastings, "The Development of Law," 359.

Invigorated by what Allan Nevins has called "the organized war," states and their subdivisions, especially cities, began such a busy functional pattern after Appomattox that new presidents of the American Bar Association made it a duty to survey the annual accumulation of states' police-power innovations. British reformers found themselves taking lessons from their Yankee opposite numbers, a sharp reversal of the prewar habit. According to one admiring Englishman:

> The United States are generally the *vile corpus* out of which by dint of many an experiment, essay, and strange vagary, the good comes by which we tardily profit. The American loves to dabble in those subjects which are somewhat vaguely known as "Social Science," and we believe that in one State or another in the Union . . . education, crime, legal reforms, sanitary improvements, and so on, has been further sifted than it has at home. . . . A little more attention to Yankee notions would not be thrown away. . . . [T]he great transatlantic workshop possesses models in working order of all our projected reforms.

He noted that Americans were working so usefully on questions of interest in England that whenever a reform demand rose in Parliament, Members should "at once inquire diligently—'Have they tried it in America? How does it work?' "[38] How indeed, did it work?

---

38. "Americans and Their Prisons," *Law Magazine and Law Review* (London), XXV (1868), 57–8; ABA *Reports*, III (1880), 82–3; Allan Nevins, *The War for the Union: The Organized War, 1863–1864* (New York, 1971), chs. 7–8.

Chapter XIX

The New Era

The post-Appomattox reform pulse worked especially vigorously in northern cities. Mushrooming commercial and industrial centers along the northern Atlantic, Great Lakes, and major river shores attracted talented, vigorous veterans of the War's civil or military services and entrepreneurial management. These new urbanites rose swiftly to prominence in businesses, professions, and local politics; especially of Republican varieties. They rejected the individualistic, haphazard politics of their party's antislavery pioneers. Hustle, efficiency, organization, and success were their catchwords. "Push, labor, shove" were Cincinnati's ways, Rutherford Hayes wrote happily after he moved there; "these words are of great power in a city like this."

Urban amenities delighted the newcomers. They saw their augmenting communities as new frontiers blessed with entrepreneurial and cultural resources unknown on farms or in provincial towns. In 1865 they felt themselves to be on the brink of "a new era," wrote Yale law professor Theodore Woolsey. Boston public-health champion Samuel Eliot described this "age of great cities" as a profound social motion equal to emancipation or reunion.

Here was the rub. It was fine to enjoy interior toilets, piped water, illuminants, and fuels; fire, police, and sanitary services; and urban shops and markets. But sometimes the city's advantages became offensive to the senses, dangerous to health, and repugnant to war-heightened notions of pure public service. Rising property taxes and insurance rates during and after the

War inspired muckraking exposures of corruptions and inadequacies in police and sanitation departments, which too often were mere party patronage preserves. Breakdowns occurred or were imminent in "the money machines," those traditional arrangements by which state and local governments raised and spent revenues and which nourished political party apparatuses.

The initial response was confident recourse by associated urban improvers to successive levels of government, in efforts to apply their state's delegated police powers, the most powerful nonwar weapon American constitutionalism knew, to the permanent cure of city ills. The message of 1865's Independence Day was clear. Now that the nation was safe and the states restrained, the city's turn for salvation and civilizing was due.[1]

What resulted was a fertile reform surge that exhibited no interest in abstractions. Its spokesmen wanted to apply power, not to debate whether its sources were private or public, local or national. They were confident that old immoralities and new technologies would bow to old police-power constitutionalism and new politics. Associated expertness enlisted in the public service would triumph in peace as in war. The "dynasty of dirt and sovereignty of sots," in the vivid phrase of Reverend Samuel Osgood, must and would give way to the new leadership.[2]

In 1865 that would-be leadership entered politics in an

---

1. *Civilising America's Cities: A Selection of Frederick Law Olmsted's Writings on City Landscapes,* ed. B. S. Sutton (Boston, 1971); Ernest S. Griffith, *The Modern Development of City Government in the United Kingdom and the United States* (College Park, Md., reprint edn., 1969), I, 11–20, 58–65; II, 425–31, and *passim;* see also C. K. Yearley, *The Money Machines: The Breakdown and Reform of Governmental and Party Finance in the North, 1860–1920* (Albany, 1970), xi and *passim;* Theodore D. Woolsey, "The New Era," *NE,* XXV (1866), 179; Samuel Eliot, *Functions of a City, Oration, July 4, 1865* (Boston, 1865), 11, 30; William O. Winter, *The Urban Polity* (New York, 1969), ch. 4; Harriet Plunkett, *Women, Plumbers, and Doctors; or, Household Sanitation* (New York, 1885), *passim;* Howard D. Kramer, "Effect of the Civil War on the Public Health Movement," *MVHR,* XLVIII (1948), 462; *Diary and Letters of Rutherford B. Hayes,* ed. C. R. Williams (Columbus, O., 1922), 270–2; Morton and Laura White, *Intellectuals versus the City, from Thomas Jefferson to Frank Lloyd Wright* (Cambridge, Mass., 1962), chs. 3–7.

2. Samuel Osgood, *New York in the Nineteenth Century* (New York, 1866), 40–1; Frederick C. Jaher, "Boston Brahmins in the Age of Industrial Capitalism," in *Essays in Social Structure and Cultural Values,* ed. F. C. Jaher (New York, 1968); Robert H. Wiebe, *The Search for Order, 1877–1920* (New York, 1967), 5; A. Fein, *Frederick Law Olmsted and the American Environmental Tradition* (New York, 1972).

organized manner. The 1863 antidraft riots had convinced patriots that links existed between disloyalty, Catholicism, Democratic party membership, and immorality. Old sins involving vice, liquor, and tobacco appeared to be connected to disloyalty, venal politics, and class radicalism. Failures of wartime Army–Sanitary Commission–Christian Commission efforts wholly to eradicate any of these cancers had led to formation in 1864 of a Citizens Association in New York City. Its elitist membership, drawn from among architects, educators, engineers, entrepreneurs, feminists, lawyers, ministers, and physicians, exhibited proprietary interests about the city whose political control they were losing to bosses and rings. They hoped through application of social-science techniques and of delegated state police powers to raise the quality of government by cutting off spoils and by increasing their city's useful functions.

These were not anti-institutional agitators, or intellectuals versus the city. Members of the Citizens Association and like organizations elsewhere shared a belief expressed in an October 1865 Boston *Round Table* editorial that the time was at hand "to unite thinking men of various schools and political ideas in the thorough study of our country, and their tendencies for good and evil."[3]

Many Association members were fresh from Sanitary Commission triumphs against mass diseases and once-haughty uniformed medicos. Optimistically, they made the Association's first goal the rescue of New York City's public-health bureaucracy, such as it was, from the city's political masters. This rescue required resort to the state's capital. The state possessed the solid place in the nation-state-territorial constitutional structure which cities lacked; the states' delegated police powers had created the city and its administration, and were the obvious source of reform power to tap. And, like Lincoln's internal-security and military-occupation officials of 1861–63, urban improvers of 1865 had no relevant scholarly and legal literature. Ordinary legal practice, concepts, and categories equipped no lawyers to serve urban reform interests. As expressed by attorney Louis Janin, a profes-

---

3. *Round Table*, Oct. 21, 1865; *JSS*, I (1869), 210; Robert D. Marcus, "Wendell Phillips and American Institutions," *JAH*, LVI (1969), 50–8; Raymond H. Merritt, *Engineering in American Society, 1850–1875* (Lexington, Ky., 1969), ch. 7; F. Goodnow, *City Government in the United States* (New York, 1904), 57–66.

sional astigmatism existed so that "Lawyers in . . . commercial and industrial communities seldom find application for the principles of ethical and philosophical law which arise out of the relations of government, and their libraries are but scantily supplied with works on these . . . unpractical branches of the law."[4]

Lawyer Matthew G. Upton tried to analyze the reasons for the law's blankness concerning urban matters. It reflected the Constitution's attention only to nation, states, and territories. Even though nation-state relationships had been studied intensively, the Civil War had occurred. In terms of comprehensive treatises, city-state relationships were wholly unstudied; "no effort . . . was ever made to define the relations of the state governments to their counties and cities comprising the commonwealths."

Upton sketched in some of those relations. He judged that states had won overwhelmingly an unfair advantage over their cities when the colony-states became the vehicles of protest and revolution against Britain. Composed and ratified when cities were merely swollen market villages, the independent states' constitutions built in overrepresentation for rural counties. The subsequent growth of transportation-industrial cities and of polyglot urban populations exaggerated enormously the weight nonurban sections played in city affairs. History's verdict was clear, Upton judged: "With the experience of nearly one hundred years it can now be seen that it was a great mistake not to have made provision for sovereign cities as well as sovereign states." Instead, states in which great cities grew increasingly assumed direction of those cities' basic departments and tax resources.

To illustrate the decline in urban self-rule, Upton pointed to Baltimore's loss of police-department control to the Maryland legislature, occasioned by the wartime disloyalty of the city's policemen. Patriots had cheered this intrastate centralization, and equivalent post-Appomattox analogies in Tennessee, New York, and other states. But, in Upton's view, Baltimore's fate was another step toward "the absolute destruction of municipal liberty."

A great city was an unprecedented mass of desirable functions, Upton continued. These gone or decayed, the city must die.

---

4. Louis Janin to Francis Lieber, Jan. 16, 1871, Lieber Papers, HL.

Profiteering politicians wounded the functional heart of urban life by tying elections to irrelevant national and even international issues. When voting for a mayor or city councilmen, urban residents should not be deceived into casting ballots because a President or Congress achieved a treaty with England or a law on Reconstruction. Such deception occurred in election after election, however, the result being further increase in states' dominations over their cities. "The [states'] politicians have long since brought about, by the total suppression of local issues, that centralization and consolidation [in states' capitals] which all pretend to abhor and denounce [when state–nation relations were involved]," Upton insisted.

Constitutional change would occur when city residents realized that "the actual issues of [urban politics were] police, an economical administration of the local funds, sewage, [and] hygiene [which] are totally forgotten and ignored." Even if honest, lawmakers in distant state capitals were unequipped to deal intelligently with a city's complex self-sustaining functions. Upton deplored the fact that throughout American history, no organized political force had gained enough strength to lessen state interferences in the government of cities systematically. A politics of efficient home rule must reform municipalities.

Even as Upton wrote, lawyer-reformers like John F. Dillon were trying to remedy the almost total lack of accumulated knowledge about "municipal corporations."[5] Slow digging was necessary before the lineaments of urban law and history emerged. Meanwhile, more immediate-minded improvers labored in political arenas.

Dorman B. Eaton, a Vermonter born in 1823, a graduate of the University of Vermont and of Harvard Law School, was the leading urban-reform tactician. Soon after Appomattox Eaton explained to the American Social Science Association how weak

---

5. Matthew G. Upton, "The Railroad and Other Problems or A Review of the Changes in the American Government," ms., HL, undated. Internal evidence suggests 1876–77 as the year of completion, but Upton probably began its composition in 1864 or 1865. See also John F. Dillon, *The Law of Municipal Corporations* (2nd rev. edn., New York, 1873), ix–xii; R. S. Guernsey, "Municipal Law and Its Relations to the Constitution of Man," *Archives of Electrology and Neurology* (pam. reprint, Nov. 1874), *passim;* T. B. Alexander, "Political Reconstruction in Tennessee, 1865–1870," in *Radicalism, Racism, and Party Realignment*, ed. R. O. Curry (Baltimore, 1969), 55; D. Klebanow, "E. L. Godkin, the City, and Civic Responsibility," *NYHSQ*, LV (Jan. 1971), 52–75.

in constitutional and political terms a "great city" was, and how complex its steps toward improvement. The basic problem was that except as users of states' delegated police powers, cities had no secure place in American constitutional structure, political machinery, and historical tradition. "There are no materials for [urban] policy [in American history]," Eaton complained; "no subjects for a [city-based political] party, no great republican ideas, no part of our original constitutional theories, within the city jurisdiction."

Nation and states monopolized engaging functions; only sordid, dull tasks remained for city servants. Combined with the tight-mindedness and tight-fistedness at Albany, this characteristic attracted to city employment primarily corruptible placeholders whose true chiefs were party leaders.

Administrative, budgetary, and constitutional autonomy of city from state was in order, Eaton suggested. He noted how New York City reform advocates faced the recurring charge from standfast opponents that "change [in existing state-city relationships] would be anti-American and hostile to the spirit of our republican institutions, because our municipal methods are a part of our original political system which patriotism and consistency requires us to maintain." This patriotic argument was untrue to history, Eaton declared: "This country has never created a municipal system."[6]

Eaton believed that the time was ripe to improve one essential aspect of the City's life and law, even though systematic rationalization of city-state relationships was not in the cards. He thought that the public-health question would serve as a yardstick, and would be likelier to win passage at Albany because of the science connection. Soon after Lee surrendered, Eaton drafted a bill which his friends introduced into the legislative machinery at Albany, creating a New York City health board exempt from party and even judicial interferences. Eaton insisted that

> . . . a thoroughly organized and efficient [urban] Board of Health must have extraordinary powers, and must not be subordinated to any other branch of the civil service, not

---

6. Dorman B. Eaton, "Municipal Government," *JSS*, V (1873), 3–5, 11; and see Isaac N. Arnold, "Recollections of the Early Chicago and Illinois Bar," in Chicago Bar Association, *Lectures* (n.p., n.d. [ca. 1880]), 38–40.

even to the courts. What it declares to be a nuisance—dangerous to life and detrimental to health—no one should call into question. When it orders a nuisance to be abated within a given fixed time no mandamus should avail to stay its action or the enforcement of its decree. A Board of Health . . . should make its own laws, execute its own laws, and sit in judgment on its own acts. It must be an *imperium in imperio.*[7]

Eaton was not shooting wildly in proposing that his Health Board be exempt from judicial review. After all, the 1863 draft law forbade appeals from board decisions under certain circumstances. A sensitive opportunist, he estimated that his offhand reference to the "nuisance" accusation would intrigue lawyers among state legislators. In 1865, the nuisance concept in American jurisprudence after sporadic pre–Civil War employments in northeastern states had long been forgotten. Now it was beginning again to attract professional attention.

Earlier, Eaton had recruited Albany's aid in a brief successful campaign against the City's Tammany-tied volunteer fire companies. Unable to suppress them through recourse to municipal officials, Eaton and Citizens Association colleagues had amassed impressive data from insurance firms on the indirect costs of the inefficient volunteer companies. In February 1865, the state legislature passed a bill composed by Eaton creating for New York City the Metropolitan Fire Commission and a professional fire-fighting force. A happy alliance appeared to have been made between City reform interests and the state's rural lawmakers, who between them, by employing the commission device then growing in favor among lawyers and other professionals, could crush spoilsmen. Urban and rural Republicans, Protestants, and patriots had apparently worked out ways to combat New York City's Catholic, Democratic masses. Little wonder that Eaton risked his public health bill at Albany.

But although the City's financial community, the American Social Science Association, Henry Raymond's *New York Times,* Godkin's *Nation,* and State Senator Andrew D. White supported Eaton's bill, it stalled in committee rooms. Upstate legislators

---

7. Quoted in Stephen Smith *et al., Dorman B. Eaton* (n.p., n.d.), 16–17; and see Charles E. Rosenberg, *The Cholera Years—The United States in 1834, 1849, and 1866* (Chicago, 1962), 189; John Duffy, *A History of Public Health in New York City, 1625–1866* (New York, 1968).

were unwilling to pass it, ostensibly because of the exemption from judicial review.

The generalized reverence for the judiciary cannot be over-emphasized. Eaton and other Citizens Association members were not men to exclude great property matters from judicial review casually. Eaton-style improvers had cheered the 1863 Gelpcke v. Dubuque decision in which the United States Supreme Court held the Iowa city liable for bonded indebtedness it had incurred. A vigorous public-health board involved substantial outlays. Unlike the Iowa situation, the New York City problem was to make its state authorize, not limit, expenditures; to make New York City not mix the projected health board with other municipal agencies; to make state and municipal judges allow the board to perform professionally, not politically.[8] It appeared inconsistent for Eaton to cheer the Supreme Court's decision limiting an Iowa city that was behaving immorally in fiscal terms, and in 1865 to seek immunity from state judicial review for his city's proposed health board.

He and other reformer-patriots were intensely dissatisfied with New York judges who, little better able to withstand party demands than unrobed politicos, had impeded conscription and arbitrary arrests and were too sensitive to local political pressures. Since the Citizens Association wished to cut patronage tentacles by establishing a professional health service, it made sense to try to excise judges as well as other place-holders.

Once it was clear that Albany would not stand for his constitutional novelty, Eaton backtracked. Perhaps he had intended to from the first, merely using judicial-review exemption as a bargaining device; perhaps he supposed that whatever judges decided about other public questions, as educated men they bathed in the light that social science cast and would sustain rational

---

8. See Gerald W. McFarland, "Partisan of Progress: Dorman B. Eaton and the Genteel Reform Tradition," *JAH*, LIV (1968), 807–8; Emory Washburn, "Reconstruction: The Duty of the [Legal] Profession to the Times," *MLRep* (1864), 477–84; "The Judiciary," *ALReg*, n.s. VI (1867), 513–21; James Willard Hurst, *Law and the Conditions of Freedom in the Nineteenth-Century United States* (Madison, Wis., 1956), 9. On Gelpcke, see the Preface to 1 Wall., at xiv, Charles Fairman, *Reconstruction and Reunion, 1864–88* (New York, 1971), 918–1116, and Dillon, *Municipal Corporations*, ix–xii. On nuisance, I am indebted to RU doctoral student Edward Weisel, for directing me to Cooper v. Randall, 53 Ill., 24; 59 Ill., 317 (1869, 1871).

exercises of public powers even if the tradition of "privatism" diminished. In any event, Eaton accepted a substitute provision specifically allowing judicial interpretation to determine whether a given situation justified emergency Health Board rulings.[9]

Even this concession could not have squeezed Eaton's bill out of Albany if news had not arrived of the impending threat of cholera in New York City. In February 1866, this spur transformed the Citizens Association proposal into law. Its passage suggests that America had matured since the preceding cholera epidemic of 1832. At that time, it was nullification that inspired inquiries about appropriate roles of government; cholera was still primarily a moral problem. But in 1866 the disease fell at once into a category of public responsibility akin to secession or disloyalty.

An impressive advance in public-health legislation, the new state law replaced the unco-ordinated existing health agencies in New York City with a unified, nonpartisan, professional Metropolitan Board of Health. Employing delegated state powers, officers were to mix executive, legislative, and judicial functions; were to create, issue, and enforce rulings which were to have the force of law. Under circumstances of its determination, the Board could condemn property, issue summonses, fix penalties, compel testimony under oath, and require co-operation from city and county police, firemen, teachers, sanitation workers, and port personnel. Contrasted with its predecessors or with any similar institution in the nation, the 1866 New York City Board was immensely powerful even in "normal" times. During emergencies the Board's powers could become almost limitless. If the Board managed the trick, then, for the first time, peculiarly urban resources were massed to meet a dreadful challenge to a city. An apolitical administrative apparatus, enforcing with the weight of law the latest scientific techniques, would take the field.[10]

By May 1, Board inspectors, including police and physicians, sniffed out 7600 threatening situations. Alarmed property owners

---

9. Elisha Harris, "Health Laws and Their Administration," *JSS*, II (1870), 176; Smith, *Eaton*, 17; Rosenberg, *Cholera Years*, 175–87, esp. n. 31.

10. Rosenberg, *Cholera Years*, 193; Howard D. Kramer, "History of the Public Health Movement in the United States, 1850–1900" (Ph.D. diss., SUI, 1942), 84–8; Gert H. Brieger, "Sanitary Reform in New York City: Stephen Smith and the Passage of the Metropolitan Health Bill," *BHM*, XL (1966), 407–29.

hauled away accumulations of filth which had lain untouched for years. The Board readied quarantine facilities, mobile disinfecting squads, and reserves of medical and food supplies.[11]

Then the Board faced attack in the courts. Now legal counsel for his Health Board, Eaton had assumed that by the time damage suits came up the plague would have ended and the Board's policies would have prevailed even if, subsequently, judges ordered money damages to offended persons. Instead, individuals who feared establishment of quarantine centers near their property, and garbage-removal contractors whose City Hall patronage connections were upset by Board regulations obtained anticipatory injunctions from complaisant city and state judges, who ruled that the Board could punish only past offenses. Eaton appealed to the state's highest court. There, the Board's enemies added the charge that it was acting as an illicit inferior court which the legislature had no right to create. Further, the anti-Board brief claimed that the statute creating the Board was unconstitutional because the Board's orders deprived innocent persons of property without procedures due by terms of the state's constitution.

Not so, New York's highest court decided. To be sure, the maligned statute allowed impressive powers to the Board; however, its orders required householders to do only what precedent statutes or the common law always required. In any event, on matters of great public moment "all presumptions are and should be in favor of the board." If the state's legislators wished to bestow quasi-judicial responsibilities upon their novel municipal health creation, the state's judges could not say no.[12]

It appeared possible in 1866 that the New York idea of a city health board, armed with plenary delegated state-police power and sustained by courts, would sweep the nation. Such was "the very essence and meaning" of 1866, noted a Louisiana physician

---

11. Harris, "Health Laws," 176–84; M. L. Benedict, "Contagion and the Constitution: Quarantine Agitation from 1859 to 1866," *JHM*, XXV (1970), 177–93.
12. Coe v. Schulz, 47 Barbor, 64 (1866). But judges could say maybe. Another case involved a Health Board contract with a private firm, to clean out every "sink" and privy in the city. According to the jurists the inclusiveness was excessive; an order to clean only obnoxious waste-collectors would have been all right. Gregory vs. . . . New York, 40 NY (Hand), 273 @ 279 (1869); see also Schuster v. Metropolitan Board of Health (1867), *Century Edition, American Digest*, XXV, 1136.

who was distressed that wartime New Orleans health improvements had vanished once the Union Army left the city.

The New York City Health Board inspirational message traveled internationally. Dr. Samuel Abbot, the American delegate to a world conference held at Constantinople in 1866 to discuss cholera epidemiology, noted how the 1865–66 disease was the first epidemic in history to be "exactly traced." American physicians who believed in contagion theory and their lay allies of Eaton's caliber had been excited in 1865 by the idea of rational scientific bases for international quarantine cooperation and for intranational legislation of the New York Health Board's type.[13]

But no other state managed the New York trick of creating a professional municipal health board armed with coercive anticipatory powers. Even in New York State, the City's Health Board remained unique. With respect to other reform purposes, many improvers feared that such amassed powers might fall into the wrong hands. Instead, they were content to recruit volunteers and to arm them with quasi-public authority enforceable only through courts rather than through commissioned experts of the Health Board sort. After their brief, brave innovation with the Health Board, most New York reformers reconsidered whether the source of power was public or private, and, turning against "new era" expansions of home rule for New York or other cities, they committed themselves to the nongovernmental sector.

Wartime journalists had described vividly the fates of animals trapped in battles. Although in urban communities wholly private humane societies antedated the Civil War, during the War urban gentlefolk became aware for the first time of the conditions endured by beasts of burden employed in their cities, and animals on the way to and in slaughterhouses. Since the 1820's in England, Parliament had curtailed inhumane practices common during shipment of cattle to slaughterhouses, and in 1824

---

13. S. M. Bemiss, "Sanitary Legislation in New Orleans," *New Orleans Journal of Medicine*, XXIII (1870), 201–33, 230–1; Rosenberg, *Cholera Years*, 207–11; Susan Wade Peabody, "Historical Study of Legislation Regarding Public Health in the States of New York and Massachusetts," *Journal of Infectious Diseases*, supp. 4 (1909), 196; Dr. Samuel L. Abbot, *Report to the International Sanitary Conference . . . Relative to the Origin, Endemicity, Transmissability, and Propagation of Asiatic Cholera* (Boston, 1867), iii and *passim*.

created a Royal Society for the Prevention of Cruelty of Animals. An American, Henry Bergh, met RSPCA volunteers in London in 1864. Soon after reaching the United States, he learned of the horrors cattle suffered in transit from Chicago to New York City slaughterhouses, resulting in injuries and disease among the ill-fated animals, and adding to the consumer's perils because sick and hurt beasts entered retail channels.

In 1865, members of the New York Citizens Association and the American Geographical and Statistical Society, plus former governor John Hoffman, historian George Bancroft, financier John Jacob Astor, Union Army veteran John A. Dix, and prominent attorney James T. Brady, joined Bergh in lobbying at Albany for a statewide law prohibiting the worst features in cattle transit. On April 13, 1866, the legislature passed a law which required a ten-hour unconfined resting and feeding period during each twenty-eight hours cattle traveled in the state. The animals' owners were to supply food and water. If they failed to do so the common carrier was to provide the nourishment and bill the delinquent owner, who also faced court prosecutions and a hundred-dollar fine, with half going to informers and half to the state. Six days later the legislators incorporated the New York City SPCA, and made misdemeanors of a long list of actions deemed cruel to animals including malicious beating, tormenting, wounding, or neglecting of beasts. Owners or drivers of super-annuated, diseased, or crippled animals must no longer loose them to rot in city streets, as was common.[14]

But the legislators provided neither funds nor staff for enforcement. Unsalaried volunteers of the NYSPCA were to fill the gap in the manner of the Sanitary or Christian Commission and Freedmen's Bureau. Bergh took on the SPCA presidency, with Bancroft second in command and Elbridge Gerry as counsel. They publicized the fact that butchers plucked live fowl clean of feathers and plunged live pigs into boiling water in order to loosen bristles; they thundered against cruel drivers, overtasked beasts, and tormented fowl; and they exposed bloody contests popular in urban slum areas, involving roosters, dogs, or bulls. Venal policemen and politicos received Society attention where

---

14. *New York State Laws*, 89 sess., II, 1210, 1456–7; Sidney H. Coleman, *Humane Society Leaders in America* (Albany, 1924), 23–49; Raymond A. Mohl, "The Humane Society and Urban Reform in Early New York," NYHSQ, LIV (1970), 30–49.

gambling and bribery were involved. During the 1866 cholera crisis, Bergh joined Health Board sanitarians in attacking putrid "swill milk" with which butchers fattened swine. As a result of the first year of the Society's operations, Bergh and his agents took 119 alleged offenders to court and obtained 66 convictions.

On April 12, 1867, it became an offense in New York State to pit beasts or fowls against one another in gladiatorial combats; New York City initiated the licensing of work dogs and required that impounded animals have adequate food and water. NYSPCA agents received deputy sheriff authority to arrest violators, with fines going to the Society's treasury.[15]

Bergh's successes in politics were echoed by triumphs in appeal courts of the same sort Eaton enjoyed. Jurists dismissed allegations of unconstitutionality levied against the new state legislation, allowed the Society a quasi-public character, and favored Society rulings as being within the limits of delegated police power. Like the Health Board, the SPCA was an allowable interference by the state with private property rights, and properly prohibited intolerable customs. Several states emulated the inexpensive, voluntaristic SPCA way in their cities.[16]

Anticholera investigations into urban slums had exposed to Citizens Association members appalling living and working conditions endured by tenement children. Although some Association leaders still concluded that degradation resulted from the natural depravity of Irish and Negroes, the general response was disgust that no protection in law existed for youthful unfortunates, and that no requirement existed that they attend the public schools. Sectarian charitable agencies competed acrimoniously to gain leadership of the new wave of interest; the New York Children's Aid Society, primarily a genteel benevolent association organized in 1853 to board a few vagrant or delinquent children on west-

---

15. *New York State Laws*, 90 sess., I, 843–6. Medical-scientific institutions were exempt from the law; Frank M. White, "The Decline of Cruelty . . .," *Munsey's Magazine*, XLIV (1910), 32–7.

16. People v. Tindale, 10 *Abbott's Practice*, n.s., 374 (1868); Davis v. SPCA, 16 *ibid.*, 73 (1874). In 1868, Illinois, Maine, Massachusetts, and New Jersey listed cruelties thereafter punishable by law, prohibited adulteration of animals' fodder, and echoed the New York 28-hour transit limitation; Massachusetts General Court, *Acts and Resolves* (1869), 68, 165, 493, 642–4; *Public Laws of . . . Maine* (1869–1871), 56; *Statutes of Illinois* (1818–69), 18; *Acts of the 91st Legislature of . . . New Jersey*, 492. A survey of this legislation and derivative cases is in *Century Edition, American Digest* (1897), I, 479–90 and ff.

ern farms, won out. Soon after Appomattox the Society's leaders, several of whom served also in the Citizens Association and the SPCA, transformed themselves into effective lobbyists. They won passage in Albany of the state's first compulsory education law. Like the SPCA statute, it contained no enforcement provisions. Enforcement lagged until Gerry adapted his SPCA experience and, in the early 1870's, organized a Society Against Cruelty to Children, whose unsalaried field agents enjoyed quasi-police powers.[17]

In these ways concerns (though not organizations) merged in New York City and elsewhere of secular idealists, professional public-health sanitarians, opponents of cruelty to animals, and generalized enemies to political corruption. Except for the Health Board, they continued voluntaristic Jacksonian and Civil War practices. What was different about the post-Appomattox scene was the rapid percolation of political activity from city and county to state levels, and in some instances to the Congress. This swift rise through the federal system reflected primitive perception on the part of some reformers that, however approved in city and state courts, local action was ineffective in the face of certain evils.[18]

Such perception is illustrated in the antivice upsurge that gained impetus during and after the Civil War. Evangelical fundamentalists and urban sophisticates alike judged that sin in cities corrupted politics and was as worthy a foe as disease. Appalled by vice in the Union Army and inspired by antiprostitution steps being undertaken in England, Anthony Comstock, a devout young Congregationalist, dedicated himself to the creation of boards of moral health. In the late 1860's he perfected municipal and county antivice societies, which generated enough political pressure through YMCA-Protestant church connections to

---

17. Jeremy P. Felt, *Hostages of Fortune: Child Labor Reform in New York State* (Syracuse, 1965), 4–6; Nathan Huggins, *Protestants Against Poverty: Boston's Charities, 1870–1900* (New York, 1971); Morton Keller, *The Art and Politics of Thomas Nast* (New York, 1968), 8. See also B. Wishy, *The Child and the Republic* (Philadelphia, 1968), chs. 9–11; Robert S. Pickett, *House of Refuge: Origins of Juvenile Reform in New York State, 1815–1857* (Syracuse, 1969), *passim;* R. A. Mohl, "Humanitarianism in the Preindustrial City: The New York Society for the Prevention of Pauperism, 1817–1823," *JAH* (1970), 576–99.

18. Daniel J. Elazar, "Urban Problems and the Federal Government: A Historical Inquiry," *PSQ*, LXXII (1967), 505–6.

force from Albany in 1873 passage of a law creating a New York City Society for the Suppression of Vice, staffed with unsalaried volunteers. They censored public entertainments, prosecuted vendors of pornography and contraceptives, and kept liquor sources in check. But vice was unrestrained nearby. Comstock and his emulators became itinerant police power evangelists, with the result that antivice organizations spotted the map.[19]

During the 1860's and 1870's such concerns escalated from city-wide to state arenas. But it proved to be all but impossible for reform activists in other states and with different concerns to adapt the form (administrative commission) and substance (coercive powers) of New York City's Health Board.

In 1869 Massachusetts created the first state public-health board after sanitarians convinced Bay State lawmakers that New York City's experiences proved the need to lift public-health policies to the state level. Massachusetts's existing arrangements were defective because diseases knew no city, township, or county boundaries. Despite the belief that epidemics were urban phenomena, evidence from wartime and postwar experiences proved that rural regions held no immunity. Now Massachusetts must respond rationally to socially scientific data. Earlier state laws, such as an 1862 antimilk-adulteration statute, had been "dead letters," because "no central [i.e., statewide] authority [existed] specially charged with their enforcement," commented Henry Villard, secretary of the young American Social Science Association.[20]

Doubtless Massachusetts deserved congratulations for achieving the 1869 breakthrough, which according to Mrs. Harriet Plunkett, an alert onlooker, "in the abstract [was con-

---

19. Details in Paul S. Boyer, *Purity in Print: The Vice-Society Movement and Book Censorship in America* (New York, 1968), 4–5; Fitzhugh Ludlow, "The American Metropolis," *AM*, XV (1865), 85–6; Kramer, "Public Health Movement," 138–9; Coral F. Brooks, "The Early History of Anti-Contraceptive Laws in Massachusetts and Connecticut," *American Quarterly*, XVII (1965), 5; Mayer N. Zald, *Organizational Change—The Political Economy of the YMCA* (Chicago, 1970), *passim*; John Chapman, "Prostitution: Governmental Experiments in Controlling It," [London] *Westminster Review*, n. s. XXXVII (1870), 119–79; John Burnham, "The Social Evil Ordinance—A Social Experiment in Nineteenth Century St. Louis," MoHS *Bulletin*, XXVII (April 1971), 203–17.

20. Henry Villard in *JSS*, II (1970), 241–2.

sidered] . . . a great step forward by all classes of people intelligent enough to appreciate their scope." The Massachusetts state-level public-health innovation was abstract enough. For, as the Bay State's new health board advised physicians and every local official including clergymen and teachers who in any way touched on public health matters, the duties envisaged for the state board "are rather advisory than executive." With this understanding governing its activities, the Massachusetts board served merely as a low-budget data-gathering center. In 1869 the state's sanitarians had achieved only the sanitary survey which Lemuel Shattuck had proposed in 1849.[21]

Similarly, in 1865 Massachusetts labor union spokesmen obtained from the state's lawmakers a mandatory statistical survey of industrial conditions. Four years later, Massachusetts created a bureau of labor statistics to do this job annually and professionally; a dozen other states followed the Bay State's lead.[22]

This timid tinkering left workmen, organized or not, in much the same position before law which had obtained before Sumter. As individuals they had recourse to courtroom litigation against employers in whose service injuries allegedly resulted. But in most states antique law codes required victims of industrial accidents to prove not only that they were not at fault, but also that no "fellow servants" were culprits. Some states' jurists (Illinois Supreme Court Judge Sidney Breese was outstanding), sensitive to altering social contexts, were adapting the crabbed fellow-servant doctrine to contemporary industrial realities.[23]

---

21. Plunkett, *Women, Plumbers, and Doctors*, 238–9, for the quotation; *JSS*, II (1870), 242–4, has the circular.

22. New York *Commercial and Financial Chronicle*, III (Sept. 15, 1866), 325; Carroll Wright, *Industrial Evolution of the United States* (New York, 1897), chs. 27–9; James Leiby, *Carroll Wright and Labor Reform: the Origin of Labor Statistics* (Cambridge, Mass., 1960), chs. 3, 4; Irwin Yellowitz, *The Position of the Worker in American Society, 1865–1896* (New York, 1969), ch. 1; *Address of the Printer's Grant & Colfax Club of the District of Columbia* (Washington, 1868), 1–2; David Montgomery, *Beyond Equality: Labor and the Radical Republicans, 1862–1872* (New York, 1967), 161–77.

23. John McNulty, "Chief Justice Breese and the Illinois Supreme Court: A Study of Law and Politics in the Old West" (Ph.D. diss., HU, 1961), *passim* (used with permission); L. M. Friedman and J. Ladinsky, "Social Change and the Law of Industrial Accidents," *CLR*, LXVII (1967), 50–82.

But many workmen became impatient and bitter as Massachusetts and its emulators collected statistics that made clearer the nature of these realities. Worker-litigants still had to endure expensive, slow, and uncertain litigation before redress was possible.

Massachusetts's Board of Charities developed a similar pattern. In part inspired by admiration that S. G. Howe, the Board's chief architect, felt for the work of the Sanitary Commission, the Board's immediate political genesis was in a state legislative committee investigation into veterans' pension frauds. A chaotic mélange had grown up in welfare matters. Because official and private organizations and jurisdictions overlapped and competed for public and private funds, and for legal jurisdiction over paupers, criminals, orphans, idiots, insane persons, inebriates, the blind poor, and veterans, these dependent classes suffered; donors and taxpayers received poor returns. Obviously, Massachusetts wanted "some general control of this expenditure," recalled F. B. Sanborn, Secretary of the new Charities Board from 1863 until 1868 (when Edward L. Pierce, the Negrophile friend of Senator Sumner, replaced him). According to Sanborn, the 1863 law creating the Charities Board was primarily the result of this adventitious perception of existing budgetary irrationality: "an accidental growth rather than a piece of premeditated legislation." Established and staffed with volunteers plus a paid Secretary and General Agent who served as bookkeepers reporting to the governor, like the 1869 health and labor bureaus the 1863 Charities Board was actuarial, not supervisory.[24]

Actuarial accumulations were all that most Victorian improvers desired. When the inferior position in law of respectable women attracted the attention of feminists, women's property rights in divorces became a special worry. During the Civil War concern grew about unrespectable females who victimized Union soldiers and profited from rigged divorces. Exposures and subsequent surveys of divorce frauds involving soldiers revealed that only five states collected divorce data at all. Nothing, grumbled prestigious Yale law professor Woolsey, "hinders the progress of reform so much as the almost absolute darkness in which the number of divorces is involved through nearly the entire Union." Therefore, reformers aimed to create official compilers of "moral

---

24. F. B. Sanborn, "Supervision of Public Charities," *JSS*, I (1869), 73–4; and see Sanborn's *Public Charities of Massachusetts* (Boston, 1876); Villard, in *JSS*, II (1870), 236.

statistics," in Woolsey's phrase. A prewar example existed in Connecticut's 1859 statute that required the State Librarian to publish the state's annual divorce figures, and Vermont (1862), Ohio (1865), and Rhode Island (1869) emulated the Connecticut way. The cheap, simple pattern was that states' lawmakers assigned this added duty to some existing official.[25]

A similar characteristic marked new state commissions dealing with professional standards. They were staffed and supported financially by the beneficiaries of the new body's powers. The wartime behavior of some lawyers and pharmacists had outraged other physicians and attorneys as well as the public. Lawyers even invaded military prisons to scout for moneyed clients of Merryman's and Milligan's sort, preceding initiation of antigovernment suits.[26]

After Sumter distressing evidence accumulated from Army–Sanitary Commission sources that "numberless quacks and mountebanks" infested pharmacists' ranks, and that among nations the United States was the most "dangerously exposed [to] . . . criminal incompetency" and venality among pharmacists. Conditions worsened after Appomattox. Unscrupulous drug peddlers' garish advertisements enlivened periodicals and earned pharmacists the nickname "medicine men." To counter, an 1868 resolution by the new American Pharmaceutical Association held that "The pharmacist must be made responsible to the government and the law." The Association's leaders created standards of minimum education and practice that called for establishment of state boards composed of pharmacists to monitor fellow practitioners, especially in cities, by exercise of delegated states' police powers. The absence of salaried, commissioned enforcement personnel was made possible because policing was supplied by the societies' officers.[27]

Other professions and trades combined public licensing and private regulation. However varied the details, the recourse is

---

25. Theodore D. Woolsey, "The Moral Statistics of the United States," *JSS*, XIV (1881), 133; Nelson Manfred Blake, *The Road to Reno; a History of Divorce in the United States* (New York, 1962), 117–91, 560–2.

26. *OR*, ser. II, v. 2, p. 151; Washburn, "The Duty of the [Legal] Profession," 477–84; A. P. Blaustein, "New York Bar Associations Prior to 1870," *AJLH*, XII (1968), 50–7.

27. G. F. Markoe, "Legislation in Regard to Pharmacy," *JSS*, V (1873), 122–35. Note that rural drug-dispensers were usually exempted from a need to attain these minima; the pharmaceutical reforms were urban centered.

common to the states' police powers, the formation of professional self-regulation, and the linkage to raised standards being evolved in new professional schools. The Civil War encouraged professional leaders to lean on their states as the source of correction for intraprofessional evils and as the base from which to halt the status declines being suffered by members of that calling.

Most improvers were concerned only with *their* cities, professions, and improvements. Different distresses failed to rouse them. For example, the public-health zealots of the New York City Citizens Association and the newly organized medical associators in a dozen states ignored the spread of "phossy jaw" among workers in match factories. During the 1860's and seventies, several European nations regulated or prohibited altogether the use of phosphorous in match production. But this silent killer, about which medical diagnosis was uncertain, failed to interest physicians here.[28]

Except for New York City's Health Board, Illinois's Granger commission, and a very small number of full-time police and fire departments in large cities, reformers created no new public bureaucracies or tax weights. Public-health maintenance, prevention of cruelty to animals and children, diminution of quackery and shysterism in licensed professions, and vice suppression moved only partially and gingerly into the public sector. Donations, not taxes, provided budgets for the new improvement agencies; uncommissioned crusaders filled meager staffs and operated in what, retrospectively, appears to have been a fog of tight-pocketed, good-intentioned bumbling.

Floundering in city halls and state legislatures was bound to happen. Expertise did not exist in many matters that men wished government to enter for the first time during and soon after the Civil War. The result of the absence of managerial talent in good causes was a paradox. In some instances, educated champions of the new social sciences performed less effectively or no better than unlettered advocates of traditional moralities such as Comstock or the rustic midwestern Grangers, who evolved new tools for state government to use.

However limited this police-power pioneering appears today, in the 1860's it excited its champions. At least some continuing

---

28. States and Congress ignored the matter until after the century's turn. R. Alton Lee, "The Eradication of Phossy Jaw: A Unique Development of Federal Police Power," *Historian*, XXIX (1966), 1–2.

acknowledgment of public responsibility replaced casual charity. In this sense the rational idealists of the Citizens Association, the sentimentalists of the SPCA, and the moralists of the Society for the Suppression of Vice responded similarly to Civil War currents that swept "the best men" toward greater responsibilities for decent conditions than were perceived in 1860.

Defective in essential ways, incapable of surmounting its innate eclecticism and organizational fragmentation, this "fertility of reform"—Thelen's phrase—nevertheless performed essential services. Perhaps the greatest was that of enduring. The men and measures of Appomattox's reform thrust accumulated experts, techniques, and jurisprudence which more sophisticated improvers could exploit. Appomattox's reformers applied dominant concepts of commercial and constitutional law to humanitarian corporations, releasing their energy, in the Hurstian concept, as governments' analogous provisions for profit-making corporations nourished their growth.[29]

These services exhibit themselves better now than a century ago. The Appomattox reformers never managed to get at the roots of urban problems; they never even understood the need to do so. Some concluded that political democracy could play no useful role in the new great cities. By 1867 Charles Francis Adams, Jr. accepted Macaulay's dour predictions of the political upsurge of "dangerous classes." Adams noted unhappily that European urban masses were restrained by aristocratic traditions, ignorance of their own power, exclusion from the ballot, and, finally, force. But in America's swelling cities "these uncontrollable masses of humanity seem likely first, and that not remotely, to make their power felt." Four years later Washington Gladden continued the theme that "the war against bad government begins here in New York" in ways analogous to the war against immoral government in southern states that had been going on since 1861. Gladden admitted that state-sponsored reforms were rarely glamorous, and any success at all reflected great credit on those who aroused the public conscience.[30]

---

29. David P. Thelen, "Social Tensions and the Origins of Progressivism," *JAH*, LVI (1969), 335; Hurst, *Law and the Conditions of Freedom, passim.*

30. Charles Francis Adams, Jr., "The Railroad System," *NAR*, CIV (1867), 491–2; Washington Gladden in *The Independent*, XXIII (Aug. 31, 1871), 4; E. E. Lampard, "American Historians and the Study of Urbanization," *AHR*, LXVII (1961), 49–61.

In constitutional terms, the city-state reform activists of the 1860's and 1870's deserve praise. Many reformers had become aware of the excessively local horizons to which their interests bound them initially and, like Comstock, moved effectively to higher stages.

Chapter XX

Essay, Experiment, and Strange Vagary

A merica has passed out of the phase in which it was observed by De Tocqueville, and the same . . . administrative institutions . . . will fit her no longer," the English scholar Goldwin Smith noted approvingly after an 1865 visit to the re-United States.[1] But, as the preceding chapter indicates, the common functional denominator of the new "administrative institutions" was data-collection and reporting. Smith measured the motion of the new state and local agencies rather than their impact.

Very soon after Appomattox even velocity became worrisome. Improvers feared that, by pioneering new functional arenas for states and especially cities to enter, they had opened dangerous ways to persons and groups less responsible than themselves, who retained control of public policies through politics. Even while Appomattox's "new era" optimism prevailed, Theodore Woolsey warned that "disaffected people" might misdirect voters and create undesirable police power exercises. But in 1865 he was hopeful that his sort would lead to rational goals and that social science would replace irrational, corrupt politics.[2]

These attitudes are illustrated by the fact that, except for New York's Health Board and Illinois's Granger commission,

---

1. Goldwin Smith to C. E. Norton, Aug. 30, 1869, *MHSP*, XLIX (1915), 154.
2. Theodore Woolsey, "New Era," *NE*, XXV (1866), 198.

states' lawmakers denied coercive powers to any administrative apparatuses. By 1870, the year of the Fifteenth Amendment's ratification, erstwhile reformers like Woolsey labored to prevent additional alliances of state and local government with coercive bureaucratic arrangements. A basic position of the anticoercion phalanx was that such recourses were harshly novel; in pre–Civil War America, for example, states did not set rates for common carriers.

History had another tale to tell. Before Sumter, governments on all levels of the federal system had influenced economic change and entrepreneurial directions, and a few states had superintended state-chartered private transportation operations, even sometimes to setting rates. But by 1870 history's precedents meant less to Woolsey and like-thinking men than present perils. Woolsey's 1865 reservation about demagogic misdirections became outright fear. He and others became convinced that disaffected, evil, or merely foolish people were voting their states, counties, and cities into irrational, immoral, restrictive, and undesirable functional novelties. Therefore Woolsey swerved sharply away from his permissiveness. Sharing Thomas McIntyre Cooley's concept of the need for and pre-existence of constitutional restraints on states, in 1870 Woolsey insisted to social-science practitioners that states' police-power exercises must hold always within decent functional boundaries and allowable procedural limits.[3]

Another illustration of this reaction to the actuality, rather than the theory, of applied states' police powers in cities and other local government levels is available in Supreme Court Justice Field's changing views on the proper functional limits states should respect in the federal system. When Lincoln appointed him in 1863, Field was a constitutional latitudinarian with respect to states' functional innovations. Between 1865 and 1871, he reversed ground. Crude anti-Negroism in the South, analogous anti-Oriental state policies in western states, and mid-

---

3. Theodore Woolsey, "Nature and Sphere of Police Power," *JSS* (1870), 97–114; Thomas Cooley, *Constitutional Limitations Which Rest upon the Legislative Powers of the States of the American Union* (Boston, 1868). See also Harry N. Scheiber, *Ohio Canal Era: A Case Study of Government and the Economy, 1820–1861* (Athens, O., 1969), *passim;* Sidney Fine, *Laissez-Faire and the General Welfare State* (Ann Arbor, Mich., 1956), 128–9.

western Granger excesses combined in Field's thinking with the Paris Communards' attacks on all existing bases for law and order. Field commenced his historic reconsideration of American constitutionalism, of the judicial function, and of the Civil War's impact on the permissible ranges of state action.

Linking the Yale professor and the California jurist, publicist Samuel Bowles's attitudinal shifts from 1865 to 1877 deserve note. In the earlier year, traveling across the re-United States, Bowles had supported whatever functional innovations local self-determination estimated were necessary by reason of wartime population shifts or altered agricultural-industrial pursuits, and the like. Thereafter his views on local decision-making changed swiftly. During the decade after Appomattox, what Bowles believed to be extravagances grew so common in cities, counties, and towns as to make local governments synonymous with corruption. Some states, notably the wartime Copperhead center Illinois and the postwar Radical-dominated Missouri, allowed their major cities home rule, contrary to the general trend. There, cities granted bonuses to Civil War veterans and commissioned street railways; functions not authorized by parent states' charters or statutes. The resulting municipal and county debts fed spoilsmen and contributed to financial instability.

Urban extravagances received spotty checks, in New England especially, where several state judges denied the validity of cities' alleged inherent rights to make such commitments. But elsewhere a doctrine of virtual city autonomy received impressive jurisprudential support, as by Michigan's prestigious Chief Justice Cooley in the 1871 Hurlbut decision. Bowles became pessimistic about litigation as a rein on cities, and resorted in 1877 to this hyperbolic warning:

> The real imperialism of our government has come to be in the cities, on the one hand, and in the federation [i.e., the nation] on the other. Nearly every State has a city or cities more powerful than itself. The State continues to make the general laws, but has so far surrendered the execution of them to the municipality, that, instead of [the State] being a coherent whole, it is little more than the loose framework for hundreds of independent municipalities; each with a shade of difference . . . ; each maintaining distinct machinery for doing the same things; and each in a sort of rivalry or race with all its neighbors for outward renown or the local currents of popular favor.

Bowles yearned for regularity, "logic, simplicity . . . economy, and a safe balancing of the powers of the three organizations of our Government"; a yearning familiar since Jackson's time among lawyers and literati. In Bowles's pretty system a state's governor and lawmakers "would, indeed, be a perpetual Social Science Congress," doing what came scientifically rather than as result of political tugs, and allowing local governments to pursue only allotted goals while holding to tight debt limits.[4]

And so concerns merged over reform limits, urban and state runaway democracy, corrupt politics, and separation of powers; over the fact that as Andrew Shonfeld has noted, "state legislatures tended to regard the management of public enterprises as merely an extension of the conventional political process." Restraints on state interventions were necessary, Treasury Secretary McCulloch declared in 1865, because, with functions escalated, governments were "corrupting the public morals" in a way that threatened fiscal stability and all property. The upshot was an augmenting consensus favoring the establishment of limits on what local governments and the states could or should do.

Many blamed the Civil War for these excessive recourses by undesirable individuals and groups to governments. It had initiated a period of moral laxity strikingly different from the good old days before Sumter, when self-reliance allegedly ruled, when almost no one expected service from government, and when each locality was jealous even of "foreign" officials from county seats or state capitals.[5]

In the demonology of the "best people," the worst exploiters of states' powers were southern whites who after Lee surrendered denied freedmen equal rights and responsibilities under law, and

---

4. Howard Jay Graham, "Justice Field and the Fourteenth Amendment," in *Everyman's Constitution* (Madison, Wis., 1968), 110–51; Samuel Bowles, "The Relations of State and Municipal Governments, and the Reform of the Latter," *JSS*, IX (1877), 140, 145–6; Blake McKelvey, *The Urbanization of America, 1860–1915* (New Brunswick, N.J., 1963), 100; J. and M. Blawie, "Town vs. State: Interposition and Secession in New England," *JPL*, V (1956), 102–3.

5. Hugh McCulloch, *Our National and Financial Future: Address . . . October 11, 1865* (Fort Wayne, Ind., 1865), 14. See also Maxwell Bloomfield, "Law vs. Politics: The Self-Image of the American Bar (1830–1860)," *AJLH*, XII (1968), 306–23; editorial, New York *Commercial and Financial Chronicle*, March 23, 1867; Andrew Shonfeld, *Modern Capitalism: The Changing Balance of Public and Private Power* (London, 1965), 305–6.

creators of states' "stay" laws. According to *The Nation*, these debt-collection suspensions between 1865 and 1867 were immoral kin to the "general burnings of writs, summonses, and judgments" which were allegedly common among debtors in southern and midwestern states.[6]

Equally immorally, several southern states' legislatures were juggling statutes of limitations on private debts. Although in 1864 Congress suspended states' statutes of limitation during whatever time period judicial processes were unavailable because of war conditions, the argument was common that statutes of limitation wiped out prewar debts owed by citizens of ex-rebel states to presumably loyal residents elsewhere. Some northern life insurance companies, by virtue of their states' laws, escaped prewar obligations owed southerners. Eventually, litigation in federal courts established that states' statutes could not transform the Civil War into an opportunity to evade contractual obligations. Critics denounced these exploitations of states' political and legal processes, criticizing especially judges who cravenly sustained such evils.[7]

Even titles to land, inheritances, and estates, the most sacred Victorian properties, were unsettled by certain states during and after the Civil War. Trusteeships, fiduciaries, and inheritances were vacated or equivocal because of heirs' or trustees' wartime absences in armed forces, or because of states' laws forbidding their lodgment in "enemies" or "aliens." Slaveholders' wills and manumission arrangements were voided by the Emancipation Proclamation and the Thirteenth Amendment, requiring adjustments of decedents' bequests.

Legal life styles in some states, especially in the semifrontier southern and western regions, had always been chaotic, at least by eastern, allegedly higher, legal standards. Court reporting

---

6. *The Nation*, IV (May 2, 1867), 345. See also Joseph E. Brown, *Argument . . . Before the Supreme Court of Georgia . . . on the Constitutionality of the Stay Law* (n.p., 1866?), *passim*, esp. 5, 40; Paul W. Gates, *Agriculture and the Civil War* (New York, 1965), ch. 13.

7. *ALRev*, II (1867), 188; "Effects of the Rebellion on Southern Life Insurance Contracts," *ibid.*, XI (1877), 221–32; "The Effect of the War on Statutes of Limitations," *Albany Law Journal*, III (March 25, 1871), 224–5; *ibid.*, VII (March 3, 1873), 158–9; on the 1864 statute, *Stewart v. Kahn*, 11 Wall., 492 (1870); *White v. Hart*, 13 *ibid.*, 646 (1872). Erwin C. Surrency, "The Legal Effects of the Civil War," *AJLH*, V (1961), 145–65, surveys these and other associated matters.

everywhere was uneven, sporadic, and often inaccurate. As a result of War conditions even this low level lowered. "It was hard enough to keep the [state] court within bounds when . . . decisions were reported," grumbled George W. Paschal. "What shall we have when they are dependent upon memorys [sic] . . . Heaven knows."

Population movements of whites and Negroes and the abolition of Confederate currency and bonds further complicated the task of establishing the worth of many private estates. Informal wills by soldiers and sailors, though usually honored, resulted in litigation, delay, and inconsistency. The post-Appomattox growth of quasi-public welfare, reform, and uplift societies broadened concerns about donors' wills, tax applicabilities, and fiduciaries' responsibilities.[8]

These developments appeared to prove that communistic antiproperty heresies had replaced Calhounite slavery constitutionalism. If law could not hold back immoralities masquerading under states' power rubrics, what was safe?[9]

Such concerns troubled many men of law, property, and theology more than Reconstruction per se. The common pattern between 1865 and 1870 was the Woolsey-like turn against government involvement in strange enthusiasms, made by Orestes Brownson, Thomas McIntyre Cooley, Sidney George Fisher, Octavius Frothingham, William Gannett, Washington Gladden, E. L. Godkin, Samuel Gridley Howe, and James Russell Lowell, among many others. By the close of the seventies, Darwinian and Spencerian concepts laid a veneer of newer scientism over consciences. William Graham Sumner's estimate of the limits of responsibility which social classes owed to each other castigated the "complicated products of all the tinkering, meddling, and

---

8. See "Property Titles in the South as Affected by the Late War," *De Bow's Review*, II (1866), 123–32; "Effect of the Rebellion on Powers of Sale in Deeds of Trust," *CentLJ*, I (1874), 35; quotation is in Neill H. Alford, Jr., "The Influence of the American Civil War upon the Growth of the Law of Decedents' Estates and Trusts," *AJLH*, IV (1960), 307, and see *passim*; George W. Paschal to W. P. Ballinger, May 4, 1863, Ballinger Papers, TSA (with thanks to Jane Scarborough).

9. W. A. Maury, "The Late Civil War: Its Effects on Jurisdiction, and on Civil Remedies Generally," *ALReg*, n.s. XIV (1875), 129–51. Professor Audra L. Prewitt kindly allowed me to read her 1972 Webb Lecture, University of Texas at Arlington, not yet in print: "Bar vs. Bench: New Fears in an Old Relationship." I am grateful for her kindness.

blundering . . . social doctors in the past." In their spirited search for social ills, untutored improvers had abandoned social science. Instead, "these products of social quackery" created strains Nature never knew, Sumner concluded.

His wholehearted negativism is acknowledged as a hallmark of the Gilded Age and after. Sumner-like attitudes were voiced vigorously from 1865 on. Harvard's Joel Parker had set the theme in an 1867 lecture: "improvements are not to be looked for in those who make flaming speeches about the march of knowledge, and who decry the . . . fundamental laws of the States and of the nation." But they never succeeded in blanketing the busy rhythms of active governments in cities, counties, towns, or states, which explains the repetitive characteristic of complaints.[10] In 1880 the incumbent American Bar Association president still echoed McCulloch's and Woolsey's 1865–70 end-of-the-new-era complaints. "For almost every . . . grievance, public or private, lately come into notice, some supposed remedy may be found in the new volume of [every state's] statute law," the Association head complained. In this "vast amount of legislation" he noted "some that is useful and in harmony with the spirit of progress; some that is amusing, not to say, absurd; much that right minded people, and especially lawyers, must condemn; many curious and original statutes; some whose policy will give the political economist and the moralist food for discussion; and some whose constitutional validity will certainly be denied by the courts."[11]

---

10. J. S. Haller, "Civil War Anthropometry: The Making of a Racial Ideology," *CWH*, XVI (1970), 309–24; William G. Sumner, *What Social Classes Owe to Each Other* (New York, 1883), 12–24, 95–8, 116–20; Joel Parker, *The Three Powers of Government . . . Lectures Delivered in the Law School of Harvard College and in Dartmouth College, 1867–68, and '69* (New York, 1869), 12. See also John G. Sproat, *The Best Men: Liberal Reformers of the Gilded Age* (New York, 1968), ch. 1–2 and *passim*; Washington Gladden in *The Independent*, XXIII (Aug. 31, 1871), 4; Octavius Brooks Frothingham, *Recollections and Impressions, 1822–1890* (New York, 1891), 114, 115; William H. Pease, "William Channing Gannett, A Social Biography" (Ph.D. diss., UR, 1955), 89; [Lowell], "Education of the Freedmen," *NAR*, CI (1865), 549; Henry George, *Social Problems* (New York, 1904), ch. 17; Henry F. Brownson, *Orestes A. Brownson's Latter Life: From 1856 to 1876* (Detroit, 1900), III, 490–1; J. D. Y. Peel, *Herbert Spencer: the Evolution of a Sociologist* (London, 1971), 2.

11. ABA *Reports*, III (1880), 82; Bruce Curtis, "William Graham Sumner 'On the Concentration of Wealth,' " *JAH*, LV (1969), 828–32.

From such eclectic halfway houses, critics of Civil War and Reconstruction impacts initiated and supported virtuous state-power applications and encouraged socially scientific functional novelties. Traditional constitutional doctrines of almost limitless state powers to define residents' wants served admirably. At the same time, commentators stressed the existence of new constitutional restraints on states and subdivisions, derived from the War and Reconstruction, in instances of corrupted or irrational popular vagaries.

Ignoring contradictions inherent in this subjective approach to constitutionalism, critics condemned as distasteful and immoral, and therefore unconstitutional, southern states' black codes, midwestern states' railroad rate regulations, and juggling anywhere with cities' or states' contract obligations, fiscal stability, or property titles. Inadequate procedures (due process) or bureaucratic coercion without redress (a refinement of the procedure concern) were other favorite targets. Allegedly haphazard legislative draftsmanship, higher tax costs, and ideological radicalism on the parts of lawmakers or administrators also received criticism.

Approval issued from the same sources when government and law supported the release of entrepreneurial energy. For example, without coercive bureaucracies, southern states co-ordinated levee systems and recruited white immigrants; these were estimable efforts. Data-collection by Massachusetts's railroad and labor statistics commissions delighted respectables; applied-science goals in midwestern land-grant colleges impressed them.[12] In short, critics of Reconstruction–Gilded Age "excesses" were opposed less to all government institutions and intrusions than to those of coercive nature or those which exceeded some treasured private formulation of public good. The concern was less with states' theoretical rights to regulate private entrepreneurial activities than with the probabilities of private wrongs resulting from actual regulations. In 1888 Cooley, just become chairman of the brand-new Interstate Commerce Commission, commented privately that every government commission was "a

---

12. Bert James Lowenberg, "Efforts of the South to Encourage Immigration, 1865–1900," *SAQ*, XXIII (1934), 363–85; Lillian Pereyra, "James Lusk Alcorn and a Unified Levee System," *Journal of Mississippi History*, XXVII (1965), 18–41; C. Wilson, *Black Codes in the South* (UA, 1965); G. H. Miller, *Railroads and the Granger Laws* (Madison, Wis., 1971).

new temptation to trickery." Lieber heaped praise on local self-government as the base for republicanism, but he and men of like mind feared power anywhere in the federal system. Legal codes and governmental habits that defined and protected property and held law and government to tight procedural channels were their measures of the good.[13]

All of which is to say that changes occurring in economic, industrial, and communications matters, and in ways of life, work, and play, unsettled sensitive contemporaries. They reached out to block displeasing manifestations, to gain happier ones, or to regain the happiest conditions they remembered, the calm of Jackson's time.[14]

But popular pressures continued to produce novel public policies. Various responses to railroad collisions, derailments, locomotive explosions, and roadbed washouts further illustrate this pattern of concerned thrust and cautious response. During the Civil War rail companies co-operated effectively and profitably the better to serve the Union Army. When peace broke out, co-ordination ceased. Accidents occurred frequently, especially in jerry-built urban street railways and suburban links to trunk lines, and inspired in half a dozen states demands that public authority step in where state-chartered private enterprise failed to tread responsibly. "The protection of life is too important . . . to tolerate further neglect in this matter," wrote the editor of New York's *Commercial and Financial Chronicle* in December 1865. He noted Pennsylvania's 1865 law, and similar ones in New York, New Jersey, Massachusetts, and Ohio, subjecting railroad personnel who purchased defective materials or who allowed substandard workmanship on rails or roadbeds to civil and criminal prosecutions. What was wanted was for states to create corps of trained metallurgists and engineers to inspect rail lines, to order improvements, and to prevent tragedies rather than to punish authors of accidents. In short, this business spokesman championed creation of tax-supported bureaucracies of technical

---

13. Thomas Cooley to S. M. Collum, Aug. 25, 1888, Michigan Historical Collection (photostat); and see Richard O. Curry, "The Abolitionists and Reconstruction: A Critical Appraisal," *JSH*, XXXIV (1968), 527–45; Sproat, *The Best Men, passim;* Francis Lieber, *Civil Liberty and Self-Government* (3rd edn., New York, 1911), 321.

14. John Garraty, *The Transformation of American Society, 1870–1890* (New York, 1968), 1; John M. Blum, *The Promise of America: An Historical Inquiry* (Boston, 1965), 26–44.

experts whose preventive rulings should invoke the state's authority, in the manner of New York City's Health Board, then much in the air.[15]

The 1865 interest in prophylactic lawmaking resulted only in New York's 1866 requirement that passenger cars have steel bumpers. On their own, several rail companies hired more signalmen, improved roadbeds, and replaced shoddy rails. But some entrepreneurs refused to co-operate. Perhaps states must establish "some uniformity of precautionary provisions" by means of "a wisely framed statute applying to all roads [within each state]," the *Chronicle* writer mused in 1867.[16]

States' intrusions into transportation involving innocent third parties were one matter; quite another when workmen were concerned. States' laws depicted employees as willing, responsible participants in contractual relationships with employers, about which no public authority properly was concerned save to enforce "master-servant" contracts. For their part, fair numbers of industrial workers derived inspiration and reason from the Civil War experience to join new labor associations then forming.[17]

Labor's generally patriotic wartime stance, including support of local Republican-Union party echelons, paid initial dividends after Appomattox. Congress forbade peonage in national territories, Massachusetts passed an antichild-labor law, New York buried several antistrike bills, and a number of states enacted eight-hour workday provisions. But, lacking enforcement, these hard-won victories generally failed to improve conditions.

There were demands in the mid-sixties from isolated Pennsylvania factory towns and mining villages that state laws lessen work hazards. Pennsylvania's coal-mining industry proceeded totally unregulated with respect to mine safety, until in 1869 a disastrous explosion initiated the first state legislative investigation of any industry. It revealed that no public agency or authority was responsible for mine safety. Until the disaster, "very few

---

15. *Commercial and Financial Chronicle,* Dec. 30, 1865.

16. *Ibid.,* July 6, 1867; and see S. G. Fisher, "The National Highways," *The Nation,* I (Oct. 5, 1865), 424–5.

17. Herbert G. Gutman, "Protestantism and the American Labor Movement: The Christian Spirit in the Gilded Age," in *Explorations in the History of American Radicalism,* ed. Alfred F. Young (DeKalb, Ill., 1968), 139–41.

people in that State had ever thought [mine safety laws] to be necessary," noted mining engineer Ecklay B. Coxe in the *Journal of Social Science*. Legislators hastily passed the first state industrial-safety statute. Coxe derided it as "defective and incomplete." Safety inspectors were required to possess no specific technical knowledge, they were easy prey for bribery by mine operators, and their nominations through politicians assured partisan control over investigations.

Soon, Pennsylvania's labor spokesmen felt the more deceived. That state's lawmakers had earlier (1865) authorized banks, railroads, and mines to organize their own armed police forces. Commissioned by the governor but paid by the respective companies, these para-official police units became centers of antiunionism during the violence that racked the state during the 1870's.[18] The coexistence of the police and mine-safety statutes suggests how incongruous and contradictory applications of one state's new functional vigor became.

Although intellectuals including keen legal commentators condemned such irrationalities, the priority of evil they assigned to labor is clear. Brownson, Godkin, and Woolsey, among other commentators, wrote and spoke out against labor unionism, or, at best, saw no constitutionally respectable role for unions to play. Unions were criminal monopolies violating the laws of almost all states. Therefore, laws like Pennsylvania's mine-safety statute, passed in response to union demands, were tainted as well as useless.[19]

Analogous response occurred to spectacular "kerosene horrors." During the War and Reconstruction, petroleum distillates

18. On peonage, *SAL*, XIV, 546; L. E. Murphy, "Reconstruction in New Mexico," *NMHR*, XLIII (1968), 99–115; Ecklay B. Coxe, "Mining Legislation," *JSS*, IV (1871), 20; and see H. Bischoff, "The Reformers, the Workers, and the Growth of Positive Government: A History of the Labor Legislation Movement in New York State, 1865–1915" (Ph.D. diss., UC, 1964), ch. 1; Gerald D. Nash, "The Influence of Labor on State Policy, 1860–1920," *California Historical Society Quarterly*, XLII (1963), 242; Richard Bardolph, "Bases of Labor Grievances, 1860–1865" (M.A. thesis, UI, 1941), 25–8, 50–90; David Montgomery, *Beyond Equality: Labor and the Radical Republicans, 1862–1872* (New York, 1967), chs. 1–4; *It Can Be Done: The Autobiography of James H. Maurer* (New York, 1938), 150–5.

19. E. L. Godkin, "The Labor Crisis," *NAR*, CV (1867), 186–8; David Herreshoff, *American Disciples of Marx: From the Age of Jackson to the Progressive Era* (Detroit, 1967), 45–6; Harold Schwartz, *Samuel Gridley Howe, Social Reformer, 1801–1876* (Cambridge, Mass., 1956); J. V. Reese, "Intellectuals and Organized Labor, 1865–1915" (SHA paper, 1969).

became common lubricating, illuminating, and medical agents, but little popular understanding existed about the highly combustible substances. Only producers' and merchants' consciences and consumers' caution made possible relatively safe production, storage, transport, sale, and use of the new materials. Unfortunately, unscrupulous entrepreneurs adulterated kerosene with cheaper naphtha, with results that were frequently fatal.

Ohio was the center of production and of tragedies. Responding to exposures of links between adulterators and injuries, in 1867 Ohio's lawmakers created "inspectors of illuminating oils." They were to examine all kerosene sold in the state or in transit through it. But the inspectors possessed only the "power" to seek indictments in Ohio's courts against alleged offenders, not to issue anticipatory prohibitions. Neighboring states imposed no standards and interstate bootlegging of adulterated illuminants thrived.[20]

Without worrying about the inconsistencies involved, gentlemen who would not allow Ohio coercive powers effectively to safeguard citizens were outraged that individuals' selfishness resulted in distress to innocent persons. This reaction is visible also with respect to traveling salesman prohibitions of the 1860's.

By 1865 the new transportation and communications media expanded producers' markets and justified employment of peripatetic vendors. During the War some "drummers" violated Union Army trade regulations, a number were rebel spies, and others bootlegged liquor and pornography into communities where both were forbidden. Southern whites feared the spread of racial-equality literature as earlier they had worried over abolitionist tracts. Local merchants won town, county, and city rulings and one state law (Maryland) against "foreign" salesmen. Everywhere such laws and ordinances existed, police officials added to their duties the antidrummer responsibility; no new enforcement apparatuses grew up. In rare instances these regulations entered into litigation; enforcement was rarely sustained. But the regulation galled.[21]

Sporadically, Massachusetts regulated certain prewar railroad practices, after temporary investigating commissions in-

---

20. Harriet Plunkett, *Women, Plumbers, and Doctors; or, Household Sanitation* (New York, 1885), 65–7; License Tax Cases, 5 Wall., 462 (1867).

21. Ward v. Md., 12 Wall., 418 (1871); Stanley C. Hollander, "Nineteenth Century Anti-Drummer Legislation in the United States," *BHR*, XXXVIII (1964), 479–500.

quired into special situations and recommended improvements. In 1869, the same year Massachusetts moved on the charities and public-health fronts, rail accidents inspired legislators to create a permanent railroad commission. But though the statute allowed the commission "general supervision" of all railroads in the state, the only specified function was investigation of accidents. The commission field staff consisted of three inspectors; its proudest accomplishment was selection of a uniform bookkeeping system for railroads to follow. Publicity, persuasion, and actuarial precision were to achieve decent operating practices; coercive rate-setting and enforcement by a state agency was undesirable; anticipatory interferences were inadmissible; order and science were the only proper standards.[22] "Were there in this country a great many more public investigations into alleged railroad abuses, and not nearly so many repressive laws, the conditions of affairs would be greatly improved," Charles Francis Adams, Jr. stated in 1879. His disgust at railroad entrepreneurs' excesses was less than his gratitude for their wartime accomplishments and wealth-producing effects. Therefore the unscientific restraints on railroad operations of the sort Grangers devised in Illinois reduced the greater good.[23]

Regulatory intrusions by midwesterners into corporate operations galled, especially when patriots recalled that wartime Copperheadism in those states had threatened the Union's survival as much as antidraft riots in eastern cities. Offensiveness increased when judges in Illinois and neighboring states bowed to popular pressures and issued judgments in favor of coercive railroad rate regulations.

A permanent, statewide regulatory commission, armed with coercive powers including rate-setting, was the way an Illinois constitutional convention set out to tame railroad, warehousing, and milling corporations. Shrugging off railroad spokesman Orville Browning's suggestion that critics of rail rates use horses,

---

22. Edward Chase Kirkland, *Men, Cities, and Transportation: A Study in New England History, 1820–1900* (Cambridge, Mass., 1948), II, 380, and see 239, 250; Kirkland's *Industry Comes of Age: Business, Labor, and Public Policy, 1860–1897* (New York, 1961), 127; Leonard W. Levy, *The Law of the Commonwealth and Chief Justice Shaw: The Evolution of American Law, 1830–1860* (New York, 1957), 119–255.

23. "The Era of Change," in Charles F. Adams, Jr., and Henry Adams, *Chapters of Erie, and Other Essays* (Boston, 1871), 349–52; Edward Chase Kirkland, *Charles Francis Adams, Jr.: Patrician at Bay* (Cambridge, Mass., 1965), 56, has the quotation.

conventioners adopted ideas of Reuben Benjamin, a recent immigrant from the Harvard Law School, and of Illinois Chief Justice Sidney Breese, who were trying to apply in this semi-frontier state the concepts of public power adequacy Shaw had spelled out in Massachusetts. Assuming possession of unlimited powers, the convention created the Granger commission. Its pioneering contribution to the art of government lay in its perma-nence, professionalism, and statewide power to investigate, to command papers and persons, to set rates, and to punish vio-lators. Anticipatory, coercive police-power applications had risen since the New York City Health Board to the jurisdictional level of a state.

The Illinois approach soon inspired emulations in nearby states and led railroad corporations and states into litigation in state and federal courts.[24] But the distaste which eastern com-mentators of Adams's sort felt at the coercive expression of Illinois's police powers is clear: "In the West the fundamental idea behind every railroad act was force; the commission repre-sented the constable," Adams grumbled.[25]

The same men who extolled New York's Health Board as a socially scientific institution for coping with distress damned the Illinois Granger commission and its offshoots as a communistic attack on property. They were pleased when state courts sustained rulings of the New York Health Board. But they were not happy with Louisiana decisions upholding as a public-health measure the state legislature's slaughterhousing monopoly, or when Illinois courts affirmed commission-set railroad rates, diminished injured industrial workers' responsibilities under ancient fellow-servant and contributory-negligence common-law doctrines, and assessed damages on railroads for injuries claimants suffered in crossroad collisions. California court decisions sustaining legislation advo-cated by valley farmers that regulated hydraulic gold mining in overshadowing highlands, and Iowa court rulings that approved

---

24. Harry N. Scheiber, "The Road to *Munn:* Eminent Domain and the Concept of Public Purpose in the State Courts," *PAH,* V (1971), 329–402; Charles Fairman, "The So-Called Granger Cases, Lord Hale, and Justice Bradley," *StLR,* V (1953), 594–6. See also John McNulty, "Chief Justice Breese and the Illinois Supreme Court: A Study of Law and Politics in the Old West" (Ph.D. diss., HU, 1961).

25. Kirkland, *Industry Comes of Age,* 117, has quotation; and see Robert S. Hunt, *Law and Locomotives: The Impact of the Railroad on Wisconsin Law in the Nineteenth Century* (Madison, Wis., 1958).

bonded debt evasions by the city of Dubuque, were equally un-palatable evidences of the states' declining moral standards.[26]

Illinois's Granger commission and provisions for enlarged home rule for cities were doubly obnoxious because inspiration came from the holiest-of-holies in the Jacksonian pantheon, a state's constitutional convention. Missouri pulled analogous tricks. In 1864–65 the "show-me" state's Republican Unionists embedded a rigorous test oath in a new constitution. The dis-claimer required voters, office-holders, and applicants for partici-pation in state-licensed trades or professions to subscribe to its rigorous denial of past disloyalty. Missouri judges sustained the validity of the statute passed conformably to the constitution's charge, whereupon litigants appealed to the United States Supreme Court, which for the first time accepted jurisdiction in litigation that alleged the unconstitutionality of a clause in a state constitution. The Chief Justice confided to a friend, "No doubt the Missouri oath is detestable . . . I thought and still think it safer [for the United States Supreme Court] not to interfere with the right of the State to regulate her own internal concerns."

Chase's dualistic view illustrates how Appomattox's happy portents for a regeneration of society North and South through applications of states' powers deteriorated into a search for order so strong that by 1872 Charles Francis Adams, Jr., E. L. Godkin, Washington Gladden, Horace Greeley, Carl Schurz, and Lyman Trumbull agreed with southern standpatters in racial matters that government must cease further interventions. The miscalled Liberal Republican movement that year spoke essentially to the proposition that intrastate stability took precedence over progress.[27]

· · ·

---

26. W. G. Hastings, "The Development of Law as Illustrated by the Decisions Relating to the Police Power of the State," *APSR*, XXXIX (1900), ch. 7; Gelpcke v. Dubuque, 1 Wall., 175 (1863); Granger Cases, 94 US, 113; Slaughterhouse Cases, 16 Wall., 18 (1873); Robert L. Kelley, *Gold v. Grain: The Hydraulic Mining Controversy in California's Sacramento Valley: A Chapter in the Decline of Laissez-faire* (Glendale, Cal., 1959).

27. Cummings v. Missouri, 4 Wall., 277 (1867); Chase to A. Long, Feb. 10, 1870, Letterbook Ser. 4, vol. 118, 11, Chase Papers, LC; George S. Boutwell to Francis Lieber, July 14, 1867, Lieber Papers, LI 980, HL; Washington Gladden in *The Independent*, XXIII (Aug. 13, 1871), 4;

As noted earlier, one of the most disappointing obstacles in the way of restraining states' functional activists proved to be the unwillingness of most states' judges consistently to invalidate what lawmakers created. The idea of an upsurge in judicial review somewhere in the federal system soon after Appomattox attracted persons who looked suspiciously on the states' and cities' unprecedented activities, but state judges, immersed in politics, could not check democracy.

Before the Civil War attitudes on the desirability of judicial review had been fluid even in the legal profession. One of the brightest lights in the law had been Pennsylvania's Judge John Bannister Gibson, whose career was a long affirmation of the need for judicial restraint. The War raised popular as well as professional interest in the judicial-review function. Then came history's first specific assignment by a state of review responsibility to its judiciary; in 1861 and again late in 1865 Georgia constitutional conventioners stipulated that "Legislative acts in violation of the fundamental law are void; and the Judiciary shall so declare them."[28]

Unique as an explicit stipulation, Georgia's kudos to its judiciary outraged perceptive Republicans. The Georgia judicial review provision was indecent because it set no limit to the judiciary's powers. "This is nothing less than destroying the constitutional fabric that has been reared," Lieber complained.[29]

Robert H. Wiebe, *The Search for Order, 1877–1920* (New York, 1967), 4; W. Gillette, "Election of 1872," in *History of American Presidential Elections,* ed. A. M. Schlesinger, Jr., and F. Israel (New York, 1971), II, 1303–74. See also Burton J. Bledstein, "The Intellectual, the Professional, and the Problem of Democracy in America" (AHA paper, 1968) used with permission; Matthew T. Downey, "The Rebirth of Reform: A Study of Liberal Reform Movements, 1865–1872" (Ph.D. diss., PU, 1963), 1–7.

28. "I do not care very much whether my conclusions are adopted or rejected. But I do care very much, about what seems to me to be a great peril of our country, in the growing habit of considering and deciding questions of constitutional law, under the disturbing influence of partisan politics." Theophilus Parsons to Charles Sumner, Dec. 9, 1865, vol. 75 #90 Sumner Papers, Houghton Library, HU. See too "The Judiciary," *ALReg,* VI (1867), 513–21; Stanley I. Kutler, "John Bannister Gibson: Judicial Restraint and the 'Positive State,'" *JPL,* XIV (1965), 181–97; Ethel Kime Ware, *A Constitutional History of the State of Georgia* (New York, 1947), 123–32; cf. R. O. Curry, "Crisis Politics in West Virginia, 1861–1870," in *Radicalism, Racism, and Party Realignment,* ed. Curry (Baltimore, 1969), 94 and n.

29. "Supreme Court," ms. memorandum, LI 463, Lieber Papers, HL; Prewitt, "Bar vs. Bench," *loc. cit.*

As events worked out, Georgia's state judiciary chose to play the restrained Gibsonesque role. This judicial timidity deeply disappointed legal professionals, including Harvard's Emory Washburn, who had predicted that as soon as the Confederacy collapsed, acceleration in state judicial-review activity would be the legal profession's entering wedge leading to political leadership for all men of the law. Granting Washburn's ambitions, no wonder forceful state jurists attracted attention.

Soon after Appomattox Kansas Judge David Brewer decided litigation concerning the wartime Kansas-Army-Congress accord against transit of sick or stolen cattle. Cattle trader Joseph McCoy denounced the notion of contagion rising from bovine travel as medically unsound. Medical men were divided on this point and McCoy received support from prestigious physicians. Since Indian cattle were among the ill wave which national soldiers and Kansas veterinarians wished to subdue, McCoy was able to exploit the Army–Interior Department struggle for control of the red men.[30]

On July 25, 1865, two Kansas civilians who traded horses which might have been stolen from Indians, and which certainly suffered from Texas fever, reported in Leavenworth that soldiers had taken the animals from them. They petitioned Judge Brewer for a writ against the Army. The county sheriff served the writ on the commanding officer at Fort Leavenworth. Two weeks passed without result, whereupon Judge Brewer threatened to hold the commander in contempt. Four days later the general appeared before the state judge and asserted that the horses were Indians' property and therefore outside any state jurisdiction. Brewer rejected this contention and gave the officer twenty-four hours in which to obey the writ. The general called for reinforcements.[31] Major General John Pope, in charge of the Department of the Missouri, supported the contention of the Fort Leavenworth garrison commander that Brewer enjoyed no jurisdiction. Brewer reported to arguments well calculated to appeal to post-Appomat-

---

30. Emory Washburn, "Reconstruction: The Duty of the [Legal] Profession to the Times," *MLRep*, XXVI (1864), 477–84; William E. Unrau, "Joseph G. McCoy and Federal Regulation of the Cattle Trade," *Colorado Magazine*, XLIII (1966), 34; "American Judges," *Albany Law Journal*, I (1870), 219; and see Henry E. Fritz, *The Movement for Indian Assimilation, 1860–1890* (Philadelphia, 1963), chs. 1–3.
31. Leavenworth *Daily Times*, Aug. 11, 1865.

tox sentiments generally and to regional attitudes about Indians. In a public letter addressed to Pope, the judge charged that

> You assume that these ponies belonged once to certain Indian tribes, and therefore state courts have no jurisdiction. Now let me ask by what law a military commander is authorized to decide whether certain stock . . . ever belonged to the Indian tribes? If in fact, these ponies never belonged to the Indians . . . your whole argument falls to the ground. . . . If the military authorities have a right to go up and down the streets and decide to whom the several articles of property they see belong, we may as well dispose of civil courts altogether.

With respect to jurisdiction, Brewer insisted that concurrency existed so far as national and state civil tribunals were concerned. If Pope or other military officers rejected his writs, Brewer threatened to call on the Kansas militia to enforce them.[32]

The Kansas judge did not have to transform his threat into action. Opinion was spreading fast in the state and in Washington in favor of unregulated cattle trade. In this instance the public-health question was too low-keyed to dam that pressure; the Army and Indian involvements mitigated against effective political supports for restrictions. Pope simply ceased enforcing the disputed regulations. Then, in Congress, in July 1866, Iowa Senator James W. Grimes, a determined opponent to all national vigor, attached a rider to an Indian appropriation bill which opened the Indian livestock trade to any "moral and loyal" American citizen who could secure a permit from a federal district judge and post a bond.[33] The Kansas and congressional statutes and the Army health regulations concerning movement of infected animals went into discard.

Another pattern of state action resulted from the reappearances in 1867 and 1868 of the dreaded "Texas fever." It inspired concert among states. In June 1868, Illinois Governor Richard Oglesby broadcast a call for a convention to assemble in Springfield, composed of delegates of state and municipal health boards, sanitarians' and citizens' committees, and cattle dealers from affected states. Within a month, representatives from twelve

---

32. David Brewer to John Pope, Aug. 19, 1865, in *ibid.*, Aug. 20, 1865, and see Unrau, "McCoy," 37–8.
33. *CG*, 39 Cong., 1 sess., 1491, 3506–9.

"cattle" states were in Springfield along with delegates from two dozen private sanitarians' societies, including several from Canada. After sharing information, the conventioners prepared a uniform law which, it was hoped, each delegation's state or province would enact. Illinois, Indiana, Iowa, and Missouri passed statutes which prohibited the entry of "Texas or Cherokee cattle" during certain months when infestation was great. Individuals and transportation companies who defied the statutes were liable to prosecutions, fines, and/or jail sentences. In 1868–73, this time to the satisfaction of elitist improvers, states' courts and lower national courts sustained these laws.[34]

However disparate their goals and tastes, Anthony Comstock and Citizens Association members agreed implicitly about the need for governments to censor publications and entertainments, to discourage dissemination of contraception information, and to impose liquor prohibition. In short, they wished to enlarge official restraints on private actions that corrupted individuals, politics, and society. Gentlemen (including publishers) approved Comstock's achievement during the late sixties and early seventies, of laws in several cities and states against these evils, and applauded the states' jurists who sustained these police-power applications.[35]

But occasions to applaud appeared to be dangerously infrequent. Like legislatures, states' judiciaries were weak reeds for gentlemen to use as staffs. From 1865 to 1880, "the growing reluctance of the [state] courts to interfere with the [states'] legislative power" caused prewar "wholesome checks . . . to crumble away." Therefore the efforts "of wise men should not be directed toward enlarging the sphere of [states'] legislation. Surely it will not be judicious or safe, to turn the whole law of the land into [states'] statutes, and to subject it to the dangerous process of their biennial revision."[36]

The popular election of state judges made them too sub-

---

34. Henry I. Bowditch, *Public Hygiene in America: Being the Centennial Discourse Delivered Before the International Medical Congress* (Boston, 1877), 42–3, 155–9, 328–9; for the convention. Cases are Frye v. CB&Q RR Co., 73 Ill., 399 (1874); RR Co. v. Husen, 95 US, 465 (1877); Minn. v. Barber, 136 US, 313 (1890).

35. Coral F. Brooks, "The Early History of Anti-Contraceptive Laws in Massachusetts and Connecticut," *American Quarterly*, XVII (1965), 5; James C. Paul and Murray L. Schwartz, *Federal Censorship: Obscenity in the Mail* (Glencoe, Ill., 1961), 17–21, 251.

36. ABA *Reports*, III (1880), 82–3; and see *ibid.*, IV (1881), 172–3.

servient to the politicians, George Boutwell and Francis Lieber agreed in 1867. Less independent of "rings" than politicians, who in emergencies could appeal directly to the people, judges had to wait until litigation existed before speaking, and then had no audience save litigants. To win re-election judges felt impelled to sustain popular measures against which allegations of unconstitutionality had been lodged. But if the "reckless and scandalous [state] legislation by which we have been inundated" could not, because of judges' timidity, be dammed in states' courts, where lay safe havens?[37]

---

37. Boutwell to Lieber, July 14, 1867, Lieber Papers, LI 980, HL; and see Phillip Paludan, "John Norton Pomeroy, State Rights Nationalist," *AJLH*, XII (1968), 284; Henry Bellows, *Historical Sketch of the Union League Club* (New York, 1879), 79.

Chapter XXI

Search for an Old Order

Secession had set men to musing about the need to have the nation's and states' constitutions "thoroughly restudied," as Supreme Court Justice Wayne reminded Judge Advocate Holt, Professor Lieber, and Secretary of State Seward in 1864. Keenly aware that the War was accelerating precedent pressures for change and creating new ones, and that appropriate adaptation was wanted in America's governing institutions, in 1861 Seward had proposed an extraordinary national constitutional convention. In 1865 Lieber circulated knowledgeable coadjutors, especially lawyers, to learn their ideas on War-wrought shifts requiring accommodation through ordinary amendment and political machineries.

Differences between the 1861 and 1865 approaches reflect the altered climate of constitutional opinion, and the availability by the time Lee surrendered of constitutional glosses and compendia of the sort Lieber and Holt composed. The thin quantity and careless quality of replies to Lieber's questionnaires illustrate the indifference to abstract questions prevailing in the Appomattox spring and summer. This indifference is visible also in law-journal articles and editorials of 1865–66, which dealt almost exclusively with "bread-and-butter" matters.[1] When lawyers, the

---

1. On William Seward in 1861, see *Round Table*, III (Jan. 20, 1866), 40; *CG*, 36 Cong., 2 sess., 341–6. On the 1864 meeting and Wayne's phrase, Charles Sumner to Francis Lieber, Feb. 19, 1864, Lieber Papers, HL, which collection contains also Lieber's 1865 questionnaires. Other data

professional class that logically should have been keenly sensitive to Lieber's constitutional interests, ignored them, the compelling nature of events adequate to change indifference to intense awareness may be sensed.

The states' functional upsurges, appearing as a major source of dangerous new infections now that slavery and secession were excised from states' rights, proved to be adequate to force the change. This infection, commentators insisted, kept the entire polity unsettled, prevented the longed-for complete re-establish-ment of social order, and nurtured further disorder. A solution, slowly, unsystematically, and unevenly evolved and applied, was for the nation somehow to rein in states, as well as for the states to restrain themselves and their county and city divisions. Per-haps in this manner old constitutional doctrines of plenary police powers, since Appomattox applied for the first time in large volume, would not overfavor some individuals and groups and fetter others.

This solution remained pinned to the notion that postwar America remained the society of individuals that, at least theo-retically, it had been since the Revolution. Wartime Americans had excised even slaveownership, that ultimate privilege, from the states and the Union. Postwar Americans could do no less than to retain the spirit and practice of Jackson's and Lincoln's times.

This romantic historical revisionism prospered in the post-Appomattox intellectual climate; by 1870 Spencer's ideas domi-nated American colleges and universities. Among many others, Henry George gave them expression when he suggested that "It is not the business of government to make men virtuous or reli-gious, or to preserve fools from the consequences of their folly." He followed with an admonition that government's role was only to "secure liberty by protecting the equal rights of each from aggression on the part of others." Anything more threatened the liberty of all. Similarly, Octavius Frothingham insisted that the task of his generation was not "to remold the age," but to under-

---

in Lieber, *A Letter to Hon. E. D. Morgan, Senator of the United States, on the Amendment of the Constitution Abolishing Slavery, Resolutions, Passed by the New York Union League Club, Concerning Conditions of Peace with the Insurgents* (New York, 1865), 11–12 and *passim;* Harold M. Hyman, "Law and the Impact of the Civil War: A Review Essay," *CWH,* XIV (1968), 51–9; Henry Hitchcock, *American State Constitutions: A Study of Their Growth* (New York, 1887), 12–36.

stand it, "to penetrate its meaning" through the new social sciences, which

> . . . favor the largest play of the social forces—the most unrestricted intercourse, the most cordial concurrence among men, free competition, free trade, free government, free action of the people in their own affairs—the voluntary system. The community, it is felt, has a self-regulating power, which must not be obstructed by toll-gates, or diminished by friction, or fretted away by the impertinent interference of officials. Ports must be open, customhouses shut; overlegislation is the bane.

Theorists neither led nor fed practical efforts to dam the legislative flow, however. As Robert Jackson wrote of the Dubuque debt-evasion effort that in 1863 brought the Iowa city as defendant before the United States Supreme Court, "there is no evidence that philosophical considerations weighed heavily on the court. . . . The evidence is that practical considerations were controlling."[2]

In this spirit, without concert, during the later 1860's and the seventies men across the reunited nation searched for practical remedies for specific sources of constitutional infection. Unlike Sidney George Fisher and other commentators of the early sixties who commenced their constitutional analyses because of democracy's aimlessness and government's weakness, the new wave plunged into study and writing because of democracy's vigor and governments' thrusts. A consensus emerged remarkably swiftly from these unco-ordinated inquiries that all evils issued from two founts of villainy—extravagant doctrines of

---

2. J. D. Y. Peel, *Herbert Spencer: The Evolution of a Sociologist* (London, 1971), 2; Henry George, *Social Problems* (New York, 1904), 173; Octavius B. Frothingham, *The Religion of Humanity: An Essay* (3rd edn., New York, 1877), 9; and see R. H. Gabriel, "Constitutional Democracy: A 19th Century Faith," in *The Constitution Reconsidered*, ed. Conyers Read (New York, 1938), 254. James Willard Hurst, *Law and the Conditions of Freedom in the Nineteenth-Century United States* (Madison, Wis., 1956), 6, defined this "pervasive view" as the belief that "the legal order should mobilize the resources of the community to help shape an environment which gave men more liberty by increasing the practical range of choices open to them and minimizing the limiting force of circumstances." See also Robert H. Jackson, "The Rise and Fall of Swift v. Tyson," *ABA Journal*, XXIV (1938), 609–14; R. Berthoff, *An Unsettled People: Social Order and Disorder in American History* (New York, 1971), 296–8.

limitless popular voice expressed in states' constitutional conventions and legislatures, and the involvement of states' judges in popular elections.

This consensus is the more remarkable in that before 1865 very little relevant scholarship existed about states' constitutional institutions, while counties and cities were virtually ignored. Prewar giants among American legal commentators, including Kent, Marshall, and Story had concentrated so completely on national-state relationships that in 1865 intrastate configurations were opaque. In the 1860's when majorities in state constitutional conventions and legislatures claimed limitless powers as a factor of numbers, no effective denial to the claim was available from law and jurisprudence.[3]

Recent history served better. Southern states' constitutional conventions and legislatures had initiated secession and civil war. By threatening further secessions, conventions in Maryland, Indiana, and Missouri had strained further the Union's resources. Even West Virginia's Unionist countersecession from Virginia troubled patriots, for it implied that all legal relationships could alter when majorities chose. Though patriots applauded Missouri's Unionists who succeeded in keeping that state aligned with the North, they found Missouri's wartime constitutions which required test oaths from lawyers, teachers, and numerous other licensed tradesmen and professionals distasteful. Missouri's loyalty-oath tests appeared to attack vested property rights which state-licensed persons (including lawyers) should enjoy in the exercise of their skills.[4]

In this pantheon of mixed evils, Illinois's 1862 convention (and its successors at the decade's end) overshadowed all others. Allegedly dominated by Copperheads, its members claimed what

---

3. Charles S. Bradley (former Chief Justice of Rhode Island), *The Methods of Changing the Constitutions of the States, Especially That of Rhode Island* (Boston, 1885), unnumbered prefatory page; Philip L. Martin, "Convention Ratification of Federal Constitutional Amendments," *PSQ*, LXXXII (1967), 65–6; E. P. Oberholzer, "Law Making by Popular Vote; or, the American Referendum," AAPSS *Annals* (1891–92), 44–47.

4. Phillip Paludan, "John Norton Pomeroy, State Rights Nationalist," *AJLH*, XII (1869), 281–3. Note that in 1866, for the first time in its history, the U.S. Supreme Court accepted jurisdiction of a case involving a state constitutional provision, and declared unconstitutional the Missouri test oath for teachers, Cummings v. Mo., 4 Wall. (1867); see also S. P. Chase to A. Long, Feb. 10, 1870, Letterbook ser. 4, vol. 118, p. 11, Chase Papers, LC.

John A. Jameson, an outraged Chicago judge, described as "inherent powers amounting almost to absolute sovereignty." In 1865 Jameson resigned from the judgeship in order to combat by legal arguments, which he assumed were ready-to-hand, this downstate perversion of Jacksonian popular sovereignty doctrines and Copperhead echo of Calhounite heresies. But to Jameson's surprise and distress no useful counterweighing scholarship existed.

Jameson transformed himself into a legal historian. In 1867 he published a pioneering inquiry that stressed limitations on allegedly limitless constitutional conventions. History and law proved wrong those who attributed plenary powers to any branch of state government, including constitutional conventions, he asserted. Conventions were bound by their charges from legislatures. Legislatures were limited by the negatives of states' bills of rights and by explicit and implied restraints deriving from a state's membership in the American federal system; limitations which several states' new or revised constitutions made explicit by formal acceptances of national supremacy.

The demand for his technical, awkward volume pleased Jameson. Attorney General James Speed recommended it. "The great truth taught and proved in the book is that [states'] constitutional conventions are normal to our institutions," Speed wrote, "and that the powers of such conventions can be as well and accurately defined [i.e., restrained], as the powers of any department of any organized government—the book will be of great service."[5]

Also that year, Timothy Farrar published his *Manual of the Constitution.* As strongly nationalist as ever, in his *Manual* Farrar continued to decry state sovereignty, whether emanating from constitutional conventions, legislatures, or electorates; whether resulting in secession or coercive railroad commissions. Such

---

5. On John A. Jameson, see supra, ch. VII, ns. 52–4, and his *A Treatise on Constitutional Conventions: Their History, Powers, and Modes of Proceeding* (4th edn., Chicago, 1887), iii–iv, and *passim;* Henry Bellows, *Historical Sketch of the Union League Club* (New York, 1879), 79; Bradley, *Methods,* unnumbered prefatory page; Oberholzer, "Law Making," 44–5; Walter Farleigh Dodd, *The Revision and Amendment of State Constitutions* (Baltimore, 1910), ch. 3; James Speed to Lieber, March 3, 1867, LI 3218, Lieber Papers, HL; B. J. Brodhead, "Accepting the Verdict: National Supremacy as Expressed in State Constitutions, 1861–1912," *Nevada Historical Society Quarterly,* XIII (1970), ii, 3–16.

claims remained "false doctrine and antagonistic practice, leading, and terminating in, treason, rebellion, and [civil] war."[6]

Lieber joined the antistate-power crusade, revising his prewar *Civil Liberty* in a way that won a complimentary preface from Woolsey. Dangers from "democratic abstractions" were met by such studies, Woolsey wrote; they taught that "safe liberty" existed only within limited government: "one which is articulated, one which by institutions of local self-government educates the whole people and moderates the force of [states' political] administrations, one which sets up within certain well-defined limits against United States power, one which draws a broad line between the unorganized masses calling themselves the people formed into bodies 'joined together and compacted' by constitutions and institutions."[7]

Then the Thirteenth and Fourteenth Amendments to the nation's Constitution enlarged categories of behavior which states might not practice. In 1868, the same year the Fourteenth Amendment was ratified, Thomas McIntyre Cooley published his *Treatise on the Constitutional Limitations Which Rest Upon the Legislative Power of the States of the American Union.* In terms of circulation, employments in politicos' arguments, jurists' opinions, lawyers' briefs, and law students' curricula, Cooley's *Treatise* quickly became the single most significant antistate-police-power weapon, and it held that pre-eminence for decades.[8]

Born in 1824, Cooley left his upstate New York farming family as a youth and in the mid-forties was reading law in Michigan. He commenced private practice there just when the Mexican War's successes reopened the slavery extension question. Cooley moved early into Free Soil Republicanism and at the same time rose swiftly to prominence as a lawyer. By 1865 he had attained a professorship in the state university's law school and elevation to Michigan's supreme court. Unlike Jameson, who studied limitations on states' constitutional conventions—the bot-

---

6. Timothy Farrar, *Manual of the Constitution* (Boston, 1867), 515; Charles E. Larsen, "Nationalism and States' Rights in Commentaries on the Constitution After the Civil War, "*AJLH,* III (1959), 360–69.

7. Woolsey's preface to Francis Lieber, *Civil Liberty and Self-Government* (3rd rev. edn., Philadelphia, 1875), p. 10.

8. Alan Jones, "Cooley and the Michigan Supreme Court: 1865–1884," *AJLH,* X (1966), 120, and see 105; Alan Jones, "Thomas M. Cooley and 'Laissez-Faire Constitutionalism': A Reconsideration," *JAH,* LIII (1967), 759.

tom of the state-power pool, as it were—Cooley attended to limitations on states from the top down, deriving from general, historical, and institutional contexts within the federal Union.

As judge and jurisprudent Cooley exhibited deep intellectual commitments to Jeffersonian-Jacksonian libertarian values, mixed with admiration for Burkean conservativism. Cooley translated these mixed notions into concern for appropriate government forms and functions. He believed that government's primary and almost total role was to prevent individuals from injuring one another by advantages derived from unfair privileges. This essential aspect aside, governments existed in order to further independence among individuals who would advance the common good. The happy prewar republic remained his lodestar, especially after the Civil War cut slavery from allowable properties under states' laws. Thus for Cooley the Thirteenth Amendment was a wise and necessary restraint upon states, enhancing real liberty and order for individuals in all states. The Amendment denied states the privilege of exercising irrational, arbitrary, unacceptable power. It reined in the people's voices in former slaveowning states in favor of wider national majorities and improved standards of decency.

Cooley previewed these attitudes when he spoke at the University of Michigan's new law school in 1863. Along with many Republican lights of the law, by 1863 he was anxious to anchor emancipation as a statute, or even better as an amendment. The War had opened these options. An antislavery restraint on states was essential if the continuing coexistence of states and nation in useful symbiosis was to occur. Local self-government with resulting swift popular checks on visible arbitrary power could flourish only if nation-state harmony existed.[9] In short, Cooley's adoration of democracy looked to recapture "the old landmarks" of restrained democracy. Temporary excitements of the sort that swept the southern states in 1860–61 or that dominated Illinois and other Granger midwestern states during the period Cooley composed his *Treatise* required antidotes.

He hoped that the law would provide them. When transient popular demands produced excessive political sensitivity or deep-rooted popular needs faced frustrating political insensitivity, the

---

9. *Ibid.*; P. Paludan, "Law and the Failure of Reconstruction: The Case of Thomas Cooley," *JHI*, XXXIII (1972), 597–614.

legal profession must restore acceptable balances. Litigation and jurisprudence would allow change without new rents in society's fragile fabric. He told his 1863 audience that "The lawyer is and should be conservative. However radical the change he may desire to make the lessons of our judicial history admonish him that they can only be safely brought about in the slow processes of time."[10]

With this hymn to deliberate speed in states' policies informing his research and writing, it is little wonder that *Constitutional Limitations* became a basic guide for Republican lawmakers in Washington and many states' capitals, as well as for judges and lawyers in courtrooms nationwide. It analyzed and catalogued every restraint on states which the author could extract from American history, law, and logic. Cooley harmonized old values with the post-Appomattox scene. He admired the implicit limitations on prewar governments that derived from their relative torpidity; after Appomattox he championed explicit limitations because of states' activities.

Stands taken by the Fourteenth Amendment's framers and by writers such as Cooley have been construed as defenses only of property; a crusade to tie laissez-faire to the Constitution.[11] As was true of the framers of the Fourteenth Amendment, Cooley hoped to protect individuals' rights, including property rights, against unwise exercise of states' powers; to prevent excess accumulation or undesirable exercise of public power on any level of the federal system. To Cooley and most men of his generation, property was the base of all civil and political privileges. This base was less secure because of the War's impact. Their way was to preserve government's purity and neutrality by restraining its functional excesses when they intruded too far into vital private relationships.[12]

---

10. Quoted in Alan Jones, "Constitutional Conservatism of Thomas McIntyre Cooley" (Ph.D. diss., UMich, 1960), 117, and see 141, *passim* (used with permission).

11. Jones, "Cooley and the Michigan Supreme Court," 120; and see Jones, "Cooley and 'Laissez-Faire Constitutionalism,'" 759.

12. ABA *Reports*, III (1880), 82; Howard Jay Graham, "The 'Conspiracy Theory' of the Fourteenth Amendment," XLVII (1938), 371–403; see too W. G. Hastings, "The Development of Law as Illustrated by the Decisions Relating to the Police Power of the State," APS *Proceedings* XXXIX (1900), 360; Phillip S. Paludan, "Law and Equal Rights: The Civil War Encounter—A Study of Legal Minds in the Civil War Era" (Ph.D. diss., UI, 1968), chs. 5–6; Jameson, *Constitutional Conventions* (1887), iv;

Few scholarly efforts aimed at altering policies have enjoyed the swift returns of this post-Appomattox constitutional literature. Reaching to the prewar past for values, it was "a pledge to the future"; a bulwark against "restless and impetuous spirits" who no longer respected ancient virtues, wrote one reviewer.[13] In order to instill respect, men of conformable views, armed with Fisher's, Cooley's, or Jameson's volumes, became effective activists in elections, in states' legislatures, constitutional conventions, and courts, and in Congress and national courts. Over a long haul their talent, tenacity, and amassed expertness were likely to outweigh contrary voices.[14]

One major phase of this unconcerted but sustained effort was to add new restrictions on state, county, or city functions, on allowable debt limits, and on tax rates and bases to states' constitutions. Surveying these matters for New York's Bar Association in 1887, Henry Hitchcock reported huge increases since 1865 in the sizes and complexity of states' constitutions. Before the Civil War these were brief instruments, skeleton outlines which legislatures could fill up at will. Since Appomattox, states' constitutions had become lengthy. Their clauses filled with specifications and details jealously worked out, like huge acts of legislation. As many whole and partial changes in state constitutions occurred in the twenty years since Appomattox as in all the decades from 1790 to 1860.

Most important in Hitchcock's view were the "notable changes in state constitutions, consist[ing] . . . of . . . restrictions upon the [states'] law-making power, the frequency and extent of which have so greatly increased of late years."[15] These restrictions had grown so great since 1865 that Hitchcock could not enumerate them all. Instead he offered impressionistic comparisons between prewar and postwar ways in Missouri. That

---

Jacobus ten Broek, *Antislavery Origins of the Fourteenth Amendment* (Berkeley, 1951). See too Hitchcock, *American State Constitutions,* 59; Gelpcke v. Dubuque, 1 Wall., 175 (1863).

13. AAPSS *Annals,* II (1892), 565.

14. Arnold M. Paul, *Conservative Crisis and the Rule of Law: Attitudes of Bar and Bench, 1887–1895* (New York, 1969), chs. 1–3; Clyde Jacobs, *Law Writers and the Courts* (Berkeley, 1954); Hurst, *Law and the Conditions of Freedom,* 6, and *passim.*

15. Hitchcock, *American State Constitutions,* 12–14, 24, 34, and see 27 ff.; James Schouler, *Constitutional Studies State and Federal* (New York, 1897), 210.

state's 1820 constitution, amended in 1855, contained only three restrictions on the legislature; the 1875 constitution had fifty-six restrictive sections of which many were multibarreled. In Missouri as elsewhere, these restraints excluded from legislative purview special laws on designated subjects including incorporations and test-oath disfranchisements of ex-Confederates; besides general laws on many municipal matters, especially debt limits and tax rates. One compilation of 1880 counted sixty kinds of exclusionary stipulations in force in various states, though no single state constitution contained all of them. Several states included in constitutions or amendments "stringent provisions" about the manner in which certain classes of bills must be introduced, entitled, enacted, amended, or repealed. These classes included county or municipal debt limits, requirements for repayments before further public debts could be incurred, loans of state funds to private persons, and frequency or lengths of legislative sessions. So many states altered constitutions to change annual sessions to biennial that by 1886 "a large majority" operated on the two-year rhythm, Hitchcock reported.[16]

Restraints on cities in some states' postwar constitutions, as well as contradictory, simultaneous "home-rule" permissiveness in other states, are noteworthy. As with states' constitutions generally, the creation of a new urban-focused legal literature gave form and direction to city-centered changes. Once again outrage at what appeared to be popular excess and public immorality inspired creation of the literature.

John F. Dillon was the Iowa state supreme court judge and law school professor who, exacerbated by the city of Dubuque's avoidance of municipal debts incurred under terms of the state's delegated powers, amassed a pioneering compilation of urban law and commentaries. Dillon's influential book breathed this spirit from its preface: "it has, unfortunately, become quite too common with us to confer upon our [municipal] corporations extraordinary powers, such as the authority to aid in the construction of railways, or like undertakings, which are better left exclusively to private capital and enterprise, and to create, in

---

16. Hitchcock, *American State Constitutions*, 33–9; Rosalind L. Branning, *Pennsylvania Constitutional Development* (Pittsburgh, 1960), 32, 37 ff.; W. E. Parrish, "Reconstruction Politics in Missouri, 1865–1870," in *Radicalism, Racism, and Party Realignment*, ed. R. O. Curry (Baltimore, 1969), 36.

their [cities'] corporate capacity, indebtedness . . . which must be paid by taxation."

With Dillon's text as guide, state after state increased constitutional and derivative statutory clauses designed to limit cities' functions, debt ceilings, voting-residence details, and tax structures. Nationwide, states' law codes and constitutions contained few references to urban matters before 1860. In the postwar decades urban concerns absorbed large shares of attention, if not respect. This growing attention reflected also the continuing distrust of cities felt in the increasingly overrepresented rural sections. As with Eaton in New York, farm counties' representatives worked in implicit concert with sophisticates of Bowles's, Cooley's, Dillon's, Hitchcock's, and Jameson's predispositions, to fetter cities' ways.[17]

These alterations, by dramatically enlarging the length and complexity of states' constitutions and statutes, placed political premiums on legal training and parliamentary expertness in operating under the swollen versions. By 1889 even Cooley felt that the pendulum had swung too far in the direction of overspecification and length in states' constitutions, with, ironically, advantages going to parliamentary gamesmen and party chieftains.[18]

Historian James Schouler offered counterargument. If, like Massachusetts, a state chose to keep its constitution spare, leaving to legislatures the task of filling society's needs, "constant and prolonged annual [legislative] sessions" must ensue, with attendant extravagance, politicking, lobbying, special instead of general laws, and corruption. Although state constitutions must avoid too close specifications, they must not be so lax and thin as to allow excessive discretion to "transient representatives of the people."[19]

Johns Hopkins professor J. Franklin Jameson found "deplorable" the prolix postwar constitutions and the numerous amendments necessary to keep them decently current. Fundamental instruments requiring frequent tinkering exposed them-

---

17. John F. Dillon, *The Law of Municipal Corporations* (2nd edn., New York, 1873), x; R. W. Skinner, "Constitutional Limitations Relating to Cities and Their Affairs," AAPSS *Annals*, XXVII (1906), unnumbered oversize fold; Hitchcock, *American State Constitutions*, 34.

18. Jones, "Cooley and the Michigan Supreme Court," 121.

19. Schouler, *Constitutional Studies*, 210 n.

selves to the political evils that the creators of lengthy, complex constitutions had sought to bypass. Further, this frequent revamping of supposedly fundamental documents diminished popular respect for constitutions, law, and order.[20]

No matter how constitutional commentators differed about the changing configurations of post-Appomattox state constitutions, they were pleased that as result of these efforts several states acknowledged subordination to the national Union and strengthened their judges' review powers. In prewar years, as noted, a swing existed away from state judicial review of state laws and city ordinances. Beginning in the late sixties this drift reversed.[21]

Some state jurists also enjoyed decreased subordination to politics represented by their longer terms specified in new or revised constitutions. At the nation's beginnings no state elected jurists. In 1860 two-thirds specified the practice. Pressures built thereafter to lengthen judges' terms in office in states' constitutions, so to diminish the frequency of exposures to popular demands. Hitchcock reported happily that from 1870 through 1885, "no state which had not already adopted the elective system [for state judges] has adopted it."[22]

But in the 1860's this improved equilibrium was in the future. If distrust was justified about unwise voting masses and about states' jurists who failed to tie down police power thrusts, where might distrustful men go for redress? To other men an opposite question became dominant. If states failed to provide a desired benefit, or if state restraints tied down men who wanted

---

20. J. Franklin Jameson, *An Introduction to the Study of the Constitutional and Political History of the States* (Baltimore, 1886), 194–5; and see Francis N. Thorpe, "The Political Value of State Constitutional History," *Iowa Journal of History and Politics* (1903 [pam. reprint, n.p., n.d.]), 10–13.

21. Ethel K. Ware, *A Constitutional History of the State of Georgia* (New York, 1947), 123; Stanley I. Kutler, "John Bannister Gibson: Judicial Restraint and the 'Positive State,'" *JPL*, XIV (1965), 181–97; D. H. Chamberlain, "The State Judiciary: Its Place in the American Constitutional System," in *Constitutional History of the United States as seen in the Development of American Law* (New York, 1889), 255; Brodhead, "Accepting the Verdict," 3–16.

22. Hitchcock, *American State Constitutions*, 54; Jameson, *Constitutional Conventions* (1887), iv; Thomas M. Cooley, *Changes in the Balance of Governmental Power. An Address to the Law Students of Michigan University, March 20, 1878* (Ann Arbor, Mich., 1878), 20.

action, where were better alternatives? As never before, men asking one or the other question, or both, turned to the national government for replies and satisfactions.

The turn to Washington appeared to be so dramatically large, in the opinions of some contemporaries, as to raise up new specters. From the vantage point of the mid-seventies, Yale's Woolsey encapsulated his enlarged concerns:

> We are coming . . . to believe in a more liberal construction of the general Constitution, so as to throw larger powers into the hands of Congress, and to look to the [national] Government for help in difficulty; and at this very time when the newest and wisest reforms in state constitutions are restricting [states'] legislatures in the sphere of their functions. The tendency is plainly toward a more centralized government by a freer interpretation of the United States Constitution.[23]

Those sharing Woolsey's fears assembled without difficulty rosters of national government functions initiated or expanded since 1861. These appeared to prove that the Civil War created a massive centralization in Washington with consequent diminutions in that Victorian holy-of-holies, respect for law. Prestigious Republicans such as Senator Fessenden saw Appomattox as the signal to return to normality. In December 1865 he told his colleagues that during the War "it became necessary all around to do certain things for which no strict warrant will be found; contrary, at any rate, to previous experience." Nevertheless Fessenden had trusted Lincoln and other high officers and had "upheld many things then that perhaps I would not uphold now because they are not necessary." Now peace had broken out; the imperatives of a written Constitution required everyone to "come back [to it] as fast as possible."[24] After Appomattox this centralization charge received renewed employment by opponents to any Reconstruc-

---

23. Theodore Woolsey, in Lieber, *Civil Liberty* (3rd rev. edn., 1875), 10.

24. J. Sherman to W. T. Sherman, Jan. 2, 1863, W. T. Sherman Papers, LC; William Pitt Fessenden in *CG*, 39 Cong., 1 Sess., 27. Note, however, Fessenden's swift return within several weeks, to an "adequacy" position with respect to race and Reconstruction; *ibid.*, 365–7; see too Stephen Field, *Reminiscences of Early Days in California* (1893), 191.

tion at all, especially, as matters developed, to one by Congress. Out of the centralization assertion came the tenacious historical tradition that wily entrepreneurs and avaricious political opportunists cynically exploited naïve racial equalitarians, and, employing the nation's excessively swollen powers, transformed prewar state-centered federalism into an American leviathan.[25]

Such a centralization-listing divides itself naturally into two parts. The first centers on the extraordinary executive orders resulting in Army-centered wartime improvisations, some of which thereafter became statutory. These included manpower recruitment resulting in conscription; internal security including arbitrary arrests, loyalty-test requirements, and travel, trade, and communications restrictions in the North; and impositions in occupied rebel regions of military governments, including after March 1865 the brand-new Freedmen's Bureau. Emancipation itself requires a high place in this agenda, along with the uncertain and not-too-logical pattern of property confiscations and disfranchisements.

With exceptions involved primarily in emancipation, in certain small classes of confiscations, and in Kansas's cattle-trade controls, almost all this impressive roster ceased to operate in loyal states immediately after the War. Of course antiwar Democrats were vociferous antinational sentries. But northerners like John Sherman and Judge Brewer, who while the War lasted were willing to accept the nation's thrusts, assumed that all emergency restraints evaporated with Appomattox, and they did. Judges and congressmen did not have to force executive officers to close the draft and internal-security operations. The ease with which cattle trader McCoy broke Army-Kansas controls on bovine traffic suggests the thin anchors of wartime impositions. Only a rare exception like the Freedmen's Bureau linked the War to the post-Appomattox scene in institutional terms.[26]

The second part of the centralization-listing focused on evidences of increased national activity in non-War functional arenas ranging from homesteads to tariff (not all of which could

25. David Dudley Field, "Centralization in the Federal Government," *NAR*, CXXXII (1881), 407–26; Roy F. Nichols, *Blueprint for Leviathan: American Style* (New York, 1963), 275; Bernard Weisberger, "Dark and Bloody Ground of Reconstruction Historiography," *JSH*, XXV, (1957), 427–47.

26. See chs. XX, XVII, above.

be entirely disassociated from the War, of course). Wartime Congresses provided paper-money issues (1861), railroad-construction subsidies (1862–64), homestead and higher-education subventions (1862), a national banking and currency system and an income tax (1863), and encouragements for contract-labor immigration (1864). Congress also established the Department of Agriculture (1862), the Bureau of Printing and Engraving (1862), the National Academy of Science and the Comptroller of the Currency (both in 1863), and the Office of Immigration (1864).[27]

One way or another, these wartime innovations outlasted the War. Some, like the 1863 national banking act, received postwar strengthening in the form of the 1866 national tax on state-chartered banks' notes. Others, like the Geological Survey, continued links between government and science long antedating Sumter.[28] But centralization did not occur. Cautious, conservative, informed Treasury Secretary Hugh McCulloch's December 1865 statement to congressmen was a reasonable description of what actually obtained: "The [national] government, in the great contest which has been recently closed, has not sought to increase its own powers, nor to interfere with the rightful powers of the [loyal] States. . . . It has been the crowning glory of the Constitution that this great war has been waged and closed without the powers of the [national] government being enlarged or its relations to the [loyal] States being changed."[29]

McCulloch was correct. National wartime assistances to agriculture, commerce, industry, and science incurred very small expenditures and involved governmental facilities and techniques familiar from prewar times. Protectionist tariff rates (1861), postal handling of commercial merchandise (1861), free mail-carrier service in cities, postal savings and money orders, and railway mail distribution (1862–64) needed little for initiation but authorization. Very few of the new functions required new administrative bureaus, sharp personnel enlargements, or innovative enforcement techniques. With the exception of the tax

---

27. Leonard P. Curry, *Blueprint for Modern America: Nonmilitary Legislation of the First Civil War Congress* (Nashville, 1968), *passim*.

28. Veazie Bank v. Fenno, 8 Wall., 533 (1869); Thomas G. Manning, *Government in Science: The U.S. Geological Survey, 1867–1894* (Lexington, Ky., 1967).

29. Secretary of the Treasury, *Annual Report* (1865), 4, 5.

Congress imposed on state bank notes, these aids to entrepreneurship of the sixties and seventies lacked coercive, punitive, or enforcement arrangements even when regulatory stipulations existed. Congress subsidized but did not supervise. In constitutional terms, the impact of events since Sumter was to sound loudly the message that the national government could achieve goals, old or new, through essentially traditional ways and means.

Although centralization did not occur, a few champions of centralization were on the scene. Procentralization authors included, among many others, familiar constitutional commentators Sidney George Fisher and James Russell Lowell, who wondered if through centralization a return to prewar virtues was possible. This patrician procentralization theorizing flourished during the immediate post-Appomattox years only; 1868 ended their flirtation. By contrast, civil libertarians, some of whom were Negroes, continued in the years 1868–80 to argue that civil rights required a muscular national presence.[30]

The elitist procentralization literature raised the question whether states deserved life any longer. They were unsuitable and uncontrollable vehicles for peace or war, the assertion grew. Delinquencies by and in states, exposed by the War, made clear that the arrangements of 1787 were unsuitable for the 1860's. E. L. Godkin wrote in favor of the national government taking on all functions which "experience has shown to be necessary for the popular safety, comfort, and progress . . . if it cannot be or is not done by the individual States. . . ." He argued that the nation's expanded functional range, represented by the new Washington bureaus, should persist after victory. Staffed with men of talent and inventiveness, insulated from provincial greeds, national administrators would "therefore [be] more conservative,

---

30. Wallace D. Farnham, " 'The Weakened Spring of Government':
A Study in Nineteenth-Century American History," *AHR*, LXVIII (1963),
662–80; see Woodward, "Seeds of Failure in Radical Race Policy," in *New Frontiers of American Reconstruction*, ed. H. M. Hyman (Urbana, Ill., 1966), 146–7; Richard Hofstadter, "The Genteel Reformers," *Columbia University Forum*, V (1962), 2–4. On Negroes, see *Justice and Jurisprudence: An Inquiry Concerning the Constitutional Limitations of the Thirteenth, Fourteenth, and Fifteenth Amendments* (Philadelphia, 1889), *passim*; Philip S. Foner, *The Life and Writings of Frederick Douglass*, IV (New York, 1955), 171; W. H. Ahern, "Laissez-faire versus Equal Rights, Liberal Republicans and the Negro" (Ph.D. diss., NU, 1968), *passim*.

than any State legislature can be." Scandals, debt repudiations, and other local crudities would diminish, he concluded, most inaccurately.

Godkin was confident that the national Constitution and administration, so improved, were alert to "new wants and new dangers." He hoped that men of his own high purposes and values would exploit the nationalizing opportunity inherent in the dynamic conditions the Civil War created. Such men would guide the popular energies and amassed powers of the nation and states into safe channels.[31]

Fisher expressed a similar fear that local governments and states were too parochial in outlook and too simple in bureaucratic forms to cope with the "large interests" which the War had exposed to view; local independence had allowed the South to sweep into secession and was keeping northern cities restive. Excessive democracy in southern hamlets and northern cities endangered precious values transcending the maintenance of traditional federalism.[32]

Different in purposes from these patrician observers, racial equalitarians insisted that the War had nationalized citizenship, liberty, and suffrage. Such men saw centralization as a way not only to restore the Union but to proclaim and expand liberty nationwide in ways transcending the extermination of slavery. One argument had it that prewar reverence for states had meant that slavery was untouchable save through violence. To prevent future state-protected evils, the nation must supersede states in all substantive matters, especially elections. For the War's duration these efforts had shifted the balance of governmental and constitutional power to Washington. It must remain there; Appomattox must not call retreat, but advance. The nation must become "the custodian of freedom" even at the expense of northern states' rights; certainly at the expense of southern.[33]

But in 1865, as noted, the freed Negro's status in southern states' laws appeared to be in train of simple, total solution as the

---

31. E. L. Godkin, "The Constitution, and Its Defects," *NAR*, XCIX (1864), 136, 339–40, 145.
32. Sidney George Fisher, "Duties on Exports," *NAR*, CI (1865), 147–62.
33. L. H. Putnam, *The Review of the Revolutionary Elements of the Rebellion, and of the Aspect of Reconstruction* (Brooklyn, 1868), 12–13, and *passim*; see also *Justice and Jurisprudence, passim*.

Thirteenth Amendment hastened toward ratification. Beyond this, few people seemed to think the subject of setting precise limits for national coercive power and intrusive functions very urgent; no one was expanding them.[34]

Of course, individuals and groups were seeking aids from and association with the national government, and were trying to prevent competing groups and persons from winning related prizes. Politics remained the "convenient method," in Brooks Adams's disgusted estimation, by which men made their way "against a majority."[35]

Perhaps, as Adams insisted in his disillusioned retrospection, national politics were too open. But the translation of political influence into appropriate governmental-administrative arrangements beyond simple subvention of entrepreneurial adventures proved to be a difficult, ambiguous, constrained task even for the most adept lobbyist or skillful crusader. Men who during the sixties and seventies conquered Washington in the sense of winning passage of pet schemes learned that Congress would sometimes, though reluctantly and rarely, expand executive functions. Lawmakers and cabinet officers were as ignorant as everyone else about appropriate techniques for new tasks; in others, ignorance mixed with unyielding anticoercion or dual federalism scruples. Further, public administration, unlike the law, did not codify its wartime advances and so forgot them.

Without curricula in colleges or career commitments by place-holders, after Appomattox the government's work was done without distinction, dash, or grand design. Possessing no better information-retrieval arrangements or accumulated wisdom than opposite numbers in states, counties, or cities, the men who performed the nation's jobs simply did not know how to cope with new assignments Congress made or tried to make, especially involving War-altered communications and racial relationships.[36]

Shaky constitutional underpinnings further inhibited the

---

34. Larsen, "Nationalism and States' Rights," 361; Isaac Redfield, "Proper Limits Between State and National Legislation and Jurisdiction," *ALReg*, XV, n.s. VI (1867), 193–202; Hyman, "Law and the Impact of the Civil War," *loc. cit.*

35. Brooks Adams in *American Constitutional Law, Historical Essays,* ed. Leonard W. Levy (New York, 1966), 130.

36. V. P. DeSantis, "American Politics in the Gilded Age," *RP*, XXV (1963), 553; Lester Lindley, "The Constitution and Communications Technology, 1860–80" (Ph.D. diss., RU, 1970), *passim.*

nation's way into new functional ranges and kept the duration of the nation's stay uncertain. After Appomattox, states' men in Congress and courts were almost always ready to recall that national constitutionalism stressed restraints. When attempting to accommodate administration and law to intensely dynamic industrial, technological, and racial relationships, proponents of increased national duties had to work within a theoretically static federal system. Constitutional supports were available only from familiar clauses in the 1787 document on commerce, postal service, taxing, and war. Even so, champions of adapting such traditional rubrics to new purposes faced reluctance within both parties. Innovation was unlikely to flourish when the dominant mood was unwillingness to venture far from familiar functional arenas or administrative and budgetary modes.

In light of these constraints, it is less surprising that centralization never occurred than that the claim received serious acceptance that it had. To be sure, in 1865 Congress created the Freedmen's Bureau and in 1866 extended its life. The Bureau possessed certain coercive powers and was charged specifically to involve itself in intrastate property and legal relationships. But from its inception the Bureau was also limited in time and incurably addicted to supplementing rather than replacing states' officers and procedures, and performed only in the recently slave states. Contrast is in order here with characteristics of another national agency that Congress made permanent rather than temporary, and that operated nationally not regionally.

In 1862 Congress established the Department of Agriculture. Objections to its creation emerged primarily not from Democratic defenders of the Tenth Amendment, but from Republican congressmen who feared that the nation's fiscal morality was strained enough by direct War costs. "The present time, of all times in the world, is the last when we ought to enlarge the organization of the [national] government," Fessenden grumbled. The Senator need not have worried as much as he did. Congress's parsimonious budgets and the restrained notions of the Department's chieftains resulted in the dull spectacle of "a bureau gone to seed," in the opinion of an 1866 *Round Table* editorialist. Seed distribution as patronage good will, and data collection as a socially scientific aid to husbandmen, hardly measured up to the high aspirations of the farm organizations and their congressmen who established the Bureau. Where were the scientific experiments, the controlled breeding of cattle, and the innovative cultivation techniques which American agrarians expected from the new Department? Not visible, the writer concluded sadly.[37]

The inspiration for the Department's creation and the working pattern its officialdom chose to follow fit the predominant yearning for prewar ways. Bucolic virtues received the nation's seal of approval by the Department's establishment, almost precisely when agrarian pre-eminence in the nation's economy and politics was tipping into decline.

During the 1860's and seventies spokesmen in American life were unwilling to perceive, much less to admit, this shift. Even the decennial census minimized urban significance, as example. This compelling retention of familiar values received reaffirmation in the failures of other callings to win national bureau establishment. On this score, the trend nationward of highly self-conscious associations in certain professions and trades, including labor unions and teachers' associations, received great impetus during the Civil War. By 1864 William H. Sylvis's International Moulders' Union made it clear that, like farmers, wage workers understood the advantages of institutionalizing a department of labor as a friend in the national government. This tentative consideration of 1864 became overt and urgent as demobilization and cancellation of military contracts upset prosperous wartime ways. In August 1865, a convention of labor spokesmen at Louisville petitioned Congress to establish a department of labor, for these reasons:

> Every department of the Federal Government is now and has been officered by professional men, and manufacturers. They are or have been employers of labor or counselors of employers. Naturally their sympathies are not with labor. There should be at Washington a department of labor to be officered by men who are of and with labor, the duty of that department to be the guarding of labor interests in every way known or which hereafter may become known.

Twenty years passed before Congress responded. In 1884 it created a Labor Statistics office of the sort developed in Massa-

---

37. *CG*, 37 Cong., 2 sess., 2016 (May 8, 1862); Daniel Elazar's comment in *Economic Change in the Civil War Era; Proceedings*, ed. David T. Gilchrist and W. David Lewis (Greenville, Del., 1965), 94–108; Farnham, "Weakened Spring," *loc. cit.; Round Table* (March 24, 1866), 184–5.

chusetts, similar in limited vision and impact to the Department of Agriculture.[38]

Even tentative, restrained considerations by congressional Republicans of labor's request for a bureau made Democrats raise the centralization bogy. The Democrats' partisan advantage, deriving from cherished constitutionalism, played a significant role also when associated pedagogues linked the 1865 Freedmen's Bureau to their desires for a national bureau of education.

Professional educators had stanchly supported the Union Army's unexpected schoolteacher role for Negroes in and out of uniform. Self-conscious in their new profession, career educators perceived opportunities in the military occupation zones for patriotic service, pedagogical experiments, and religious-humanitarian contributions. From classroom teachers on up through school-system directors and educational association leaders, the proposition was accepted as proved that literacy and loyalty were linked, that secession had occurred because demagogues misled illiterate southern voters, that in northern states inadequately educated citizens were prey to Copperhead doctrines, corrupt "ring" politics, and antiproperty demagogues; and that the War and Reconstruction were opportunities for advances in education, especially if the nation would play an appropriate role.[39] One Army officer insisted to Senator Sumner that Congress must plant free schools in southern states and must keep them there permanently "so that they may be as flourishing and as useful as the common schools of the North."

Such visions penetrated even the elitist councils of New England's American Institute of Instruction. Its president in 1865, Birdseye G. Northrup, asserted that if a national bureau of education had existed in 1860, responsible for creating nation-

---

38. In Gustavus A. Weber, *Bureau of Labor Statistics, Its History, Activities, and Organization* (Bur. Labor Statistics Bull. No. 319: Washington, 1922); and see U.S. Dept. of Labor, *Activities of the Bureau of Labor Statistics in World War II* (Historical Reports of War Administration, No. 1, Washington, 1947), 1–2; K. P. Fox, "The Census Bureau and the Cities; National Development of Urban Government in the Industrial Age: 1870–1930" (Ph.D. diss., UP, 1972), Intro. and ch. 1; R. Wiebe, *The Search for Order, 1877–1920* (New York, 1967), *passim*, esp. chs. 1–5.

39. J. P. Wickersham, "Education as an Element in Reconstruction," NTA *Proceedings*, VII (1865), 548; Daniel Coit Gilman to Charles Eliot Norton, Nov. 2, 1867, in Hugh Hawkins, *Pioneer: A History of the Johns Hopkins University, 1874–1899* (Ithaca, N.Y., 1960), 18.

wide curricula for "all the people, South as well as North, black
and white," it would have frustrated secessionists. According to
the overoptimistic *American Education Monthly* in 1864, "Now
the question is, *how* the nation can interfere in behalf of this
great work. That it should interfere is unquestionable, since its
first duty is . . . self-preservation and self-elevation." Only a
national bureau of education sparked by a national university,
which among other duties would license all teachers, could transform or create southern states into patriotic centers and elevate
northern voters.[40] In short, a nationwide reformation through
national education was in the cards. Congressional support in the
1862 Morrill Act of states' agricultural and industrial collegiate
education, and in 1864 of the National Deaf Mute College in the
District of Columbia, suggested that visions of a national cultural
subvention might become reality; no one remarked how thinly
the Morrill Act committed nation *or* states to budgets or innovative policies.[41]

Opposition existed among educators to a national presence
in education. Some insisted that state and local governments
could realize all desirable social aims. Prospects of biracial education in southern states under national aegis troubled some pedagogues. Catholics feared intrusions into parochial education. And
private-school administrators such as Harvard's Charles W. Eliot
fought tax-subvented competition requested by Cornell's Andrew
D. White. Opponents to a national board of education and a
national university adopted conventional constitutional arguments centering on the traditional state monopoly in education.[42]

40. Capt. H. R. Klause to Sumner, Oct. 23, 1865, vol. 75, #7, Sumner
Papers, Houghton Library, HU; J. W. Blessingame, "The Union Army as an
Educational Institution for Negroes, 1862–1865," *Journal of Negro Educa-
tion,* XXVI (1965), 152–8; Hyman, *Radical Republicans,* 190 ff.; B. G.
Northrup, in American Institute of Instruction *Lectures,* XXVI (1866), 16;
Martin Ridge, *Ignatius Donnelly; the Portrait of a Politician* (Chicago,
1962), 100–1; *American Education Monthly,* I (May 1964), 148 (italics
original).

41. J. W. Bulkley, "Town, County and State Associations," NEA
Proceedings and Lectures, V (1864), 185–8; S. H. White, "A National
Bureau of Education," *ibid.,* IV (1863), 180–4; "Industrial Colleges,"
American Education Monthly, I (April 1864), 116–17; "National Deaf
Mute College," *The Republic,* III (1874), 173–6.

42. Albertine A. Abrams, "The Policy of the NEA Toward Federal
Aid to Education, 1857–1953" (Ph.D. diss., UMich, 1954), ch. 1; S. S.
Greene, "The Educational Duties of the Hour," NTA-NEA *Proceedings,*
VII (1865), 483; A. D. White, *Report of the Committee on Organization,*

In March 1867 Congress created a Bureau of Education in the Interior Department, with Henry Barnard as commissioner. Thereupon, as with the Department of Agriculture, Congress starved its infant for funds, personnel, and space, the next year drastically reducing the commissioner's salary and his staff, from three clerks to two. Barnard's Bureau amassed statistics and circulated reports. Funds dried up even for such modest work. Obviously the national presence in education hardly disturbed the familiar states' monopoly. Within ten years after Appomattox, even most Republicans were committed against national intrusions into states' educational policies; the Freedmen's Bureau education functions were finished.[43]

In part the opposition derived from efforts by a few Republican congressmen to tie racial desegregation in education to Reconstruction. Thwarted by colleagues' unwillingness to venture into such interracial frontiers even with respect to the Freedmen's Bureau's work in the conquered South, Negrophile congressmen attempted to bypass the mixed-school bogy. One way around it was the suggestion that national civil-rights legislation, enforceable in federal courts, embraced educational matters; another involved effort by "radical" state governments in the South to set up state school systems open to both races, under Congress's sponsorship. These attempts of a very few Civil War and Reconstruction Republicans to commit the nation to a permanent education role were to fail. Even John Sherman, who originally supported the nation's role in public education, became an opponent, primarily because he did not trust states, especially southern states, to disburse federal funds wisely or honestly.[44]

Yet the notion that the nation did have roles to play in the

Presented to the Trustees of the Cornell University (Albany, 1867), *passim;* White, "The Relations of the National and State Governments to Advanced Education," *Old and New*, X (1874), 475–95; T. O. Howe, "Some Remarks on the Report of President Eliot upon a National University," *The Republic*, II (1874), 28–37.

43. *JSS*, III (1871), 207; John Eaton, Jr., "The Relation of the National Government to Public Education," NTA *Journal & Proceedings*, X (1870), 118; McKee, *Conventions and Platforms*, 171, 188.

44. Alfred H. Kelly, "The Congressional Controversy over School Segregation, 1867–1875," *AHR*, LXIV (1959), 537–64; Louis R. Harlan, "Desegregation in New Orleans Public Schools During Reconstruction," *AHR*, LXVII (1962), 663–76; Sidney Andrews, "The School Men and their Bureau," *Old and New*, I (1870), 373–9. On Sherman, see George Frisbie Hoar, *Autobiography of Seventy Years* (New York, 1903), I, 255–7.

post-Appomattox scene, different from the wartime pattern, proved to be tenacious. Reviving sporadically, this idea mixed with the enduring one of keeping states and their subdivisions to respectable functional limitations, and became part of the post-Appomattox Reconstruction.

Chapter XXII

Designing Suits
for Poltergeists:
Some Non-Reconstruction
Adventures

E xcept for the Freedmen's Bureau, whose duration and jurisdictions were always limited, all other national functional
innovations begun during the War and Reconstruction lacked
coercive provisions. All, including the Bureau, suffered from
inadequate budgets and accepted constraints imposed by traditional constitutionalism.

A clear relationship existed between funds and futility. For
example, in 1862 Congress enacted antipolygamy statutes for the
territories. But Mormon leaders were unworried. Enforcement
consisted only of prosecutions in national courts. Similarly, in
1862 Congress emancipated slaves in the District of Columbia
and the territories. But white New Mexicans, many of whom held
Indians in slavelike peonage, ignored the law, one resident noting
that "It neither provided a penalty for its violations nor a remedy
for those desiring to secure its benefits."

The Thirteenth Amendment and the 1866 Civil Rights law
created to enforce it worked no better in New Mexico, Republican
congressmen learned. In Washington, lawmakers were uncertain
even about peonage's technical definition. Nevertheless they enacted a bill, which President Johnson signed on March 2, 1867,

abolishing it. The statute required New Mexican civil and military territorial officers to enforce the prohibition. Enforcement efforts were perfunctory and futile. Therefore Congress passed another act (July 27, 1868), which assigned the United States Army to end peonage in New Mexico. But, like the Army and the Freedmen's Bureau in the southern states, General Sherman's Army command in New Mexico employed rather than replaced local civil officers. He announced publicly that there would be no military "interference" in civil matters; which meant no enforcement of the law. Ignorance in Washington concerning western conditions, the inability even of open-minded territorial officials to know what Congress wished, and the blocks in the way of enforcement created by territorial personnel and by Sherman, led to the failure.[1]

Contrast these flounderings with the pattern created by persons outside the government who, experts in specialized fields, worked out ways to advance interests. Entrepreneurs squeezed out from Congress financial encouragements without concomitant supervision by the nation. Similarly, with Congress's cooperation, moralists linked private associations and purposes to the nation's powers.

In this connection, Anthony Comstock complained that the United States mails undercut local and state antiobscenity provisions he had inspired. Back in March 1865, Lincoln's Postmaster General had informed Congress of the impending demise of wartime antivice mail censorship which had existed since Sumter without statutory sanction. Consensus existed in Congress that so long as sealed mail remained unopened, antiobscenity statutory censorship was as acceptable as antidisloyalty executive orders. Almost without debate, Congress passed and Lincoln signed a statute providing for the exclusion from mails of "obscene" unsealed material, and for criminal prosecutions against senders. The temporary wartime concern to safeguard soldiers had become a general, presumably permanent, commitment to protect all citizens' morals.

---

1. Wallace D. Farnham, "The 'Weakened Spring of Government': A Study in Nineteenth-Century American History," *AHR,* LXVIII (1963), *passim;* R. D. Poll, "The Twin Relics: A Study of Mormon Polygamy and the Campaign by the . . . United States for Its Abolition" (M.A. essay, TCU, 1939), ch. 5; Lawrence B. Murphy, "Reconstruction in New Mexico," *NMHR,* XLIII (1968), 101 for the quotation, and *passim.*

The 1865 law barred only obscene words from mails. Comstock wished all sexually stimulating representations excluded, including contraceptive and undergarment advertisements. In 1873 Congress replaced the 1865 statute with a more inclusive one which incorporated Comstock's wider horizons, and included provision for customs officers to censor printed material coming in from abroad. But Congress provided no enlarged budget. Therefore Comstock got himself appointed as an unpaid volunteer "special agent" of the Post Office Department, and used the office primarily to correlate states' and localities' censorship rules.[2] Comstock bent the national government to his purposes by arrangements familiar to New York's SPCA and Congress's Freedmen's Bureau volunteers who staffed "official" agencies. Like states' legislatures, Congress hesitated to adventure when high costs and/or bureau growth were involved, even when, as in late 1865, a new cholera invasion appeared imminent.

Public health improvers were already alert; Dorman Eaton was storming Albany on behalf of the New York Health Board, and another sanitarian cadre was in Washington. Its spokesmen requested President Andrew Johnson to assign to New York City surplus Navy hulks and nationally owned islands in New York's harbor for use as quarantine centers. The President refused because Congress had not specifically approved such assistance, and the sanitarian delegation tried their lobbying skill in Congress. Three months slipped by fruitlessly.[3]

Science as well as constitutionalism caused the slow motion in Washington. The American Medical Association was sharply divided about contagion theory, and this division confused congressmen about appropriate national action in a technical, traditionally state-power arena. Senators who accepted contagion

---

2. Coral F. Brooks, "The Early History of Anti-Contraceptive Laws in Massachusetts and Connecticut," *American Quarterly,* XVII (1965), 5; *SAL,* XIII, 507 (1865); *CG,* 38 Cong., 2 sess., 660–2; C. P. Magrath, "The Obscenity Cases: The Grapes of Roth," *SCR* (1966), 7–77. Note that Congress's "breaking seals" repugnance did not extend to violators against federal revenue laws; J. W. Landynski, *Search and Seizure and the Supreme Court: A Study in Constitutional Interpretation* (Baltimore, 1966), ch. 2. In 1868 the Attorney General approved the wartime exclusions; James C. Paul and Murray L. Schwartz, *Federal Censorship: Obscenity in the Mail* (Glencoe, Ill., 1961), 17–21; 251; *Att. Gen. Ops.,* XII, 399.

3. *CG,* 39 Cong., 1 sess., 615, 1587; New York Assembly, *Annual Report of the Commission of Quarantine: Doc. No. 55* (1866), 4, 16–17, 24–5.

theory attempted to push positive, coercive national action, and constitutional objections mounted sharply.

Minnesota's Senator Alexander Ramsey, convinced that railroads, rivers, and lakes tied inland states to cholera-carrying commerce, introduced a bill so novel as to rank with Eaton's Albany proposal against judicial review. It would form the Secretaries of War, Navy, and Treasury into a permanent federal commission with powers to set rigid quarantines at ports of entry, to establish sanitary cordons in interior areas, and to employ the Army and Navy to enforce its decrees. The War Secretary would be in charge and could employ Civil War–like health techniques and coercive instruments, of sorts unknown until our own times.[4]

Ramsey's spectacular innovation entered a Senate atmosphere already hot from Reconstruction frictions; War Secretary Stanton had ordered a uniform quarantine for the southern states. Rhode Island Republican Senator Henry Anthony closely questioned a champion of Ramsey's bill, Zachariah Chandler, on how far the proposed quarantine commission could go in enforcing sanitary cordons. Chandler replied that "all the powers at their command may be used if necessary"; even martial law impositions were in order. To which Anthony sputtered, "I would rather have the cholera than such a proposition as this."[5]

Subsequent debate reflected the fact that the Senate was inexperienced at best in creating administrative commissions (especially one drawn from among cabinet officers) to operate on the borderlands of intrastate and interstate commerce; constitutional opposition to merging distinct departments into any sort of commission rose. Iowa's Grimes, a leader in the successful fight against continuing the congressional-Kansas accord about diseased cattle, and an opponent to all national-power enlargements, was unimpressed by medical conclusions in favor of national quarantines; "certain physicians in the city of New York" should not dictate to Congress that it must abandon all powers "into the hands of a commission and . . . confer . . . upon

---

4. AMA *Transactions*, XVII (1866), 34–6; Howard D. Kramer, "History of the Public Health Movement in the United States, 1850–1900" (Ph.D. diss., SUI, 1942), 157–9; M. L. Benedict, "Contagion and the Constitution: Quarantine Agitation from 1859 to 1866," *JHM*, XXV (1970), 182–3; 187.
5. *Ibid.*, 185, on Stanton; other data in *CG*, 39 Cong., 1 sess., 2445.

. . . [it] all control over the military . . . and over the treasury," he declared.[6]

Reconstruction partisans raised questions of national power
and intrastate limitations. Anticivil-rights Republican Ira Harris
of New York asked Sumner whether the Ramsey bill was undergirded constitutionally by that "elastic . . . provision which requires Congress to guaranty to every State a republican form of
government." Wisconsin's Timothy Howe stated incautiously that
the War had ended simpler times of constitutional limitations
and medical ignorance. Grimes hit back: "I trust the time is
gone . . . to legislate in the manner which this bill proposes.
During the . . . war we drew to ourselves here as the Federal
Government powers which had been considered doubtful by all
and denied by many . . . statesmen. . . . That time . . . has
ceased and ought to cease. Let us go back to the original conditions of things, and allow the States to take care of themselves.
. . . Yes, sir, take care of their own cholera. My state will take
care of its cholera."[7]

A variation on the antinational theme received expression by
conservative Republican John B. Henderson of Missouri. He
objected to the uniformity the bill would create, as making
impossible adequate sensitivity to local variations. Chandler suggested that the proposed commission would accommodate such
differences. Grimes chimed in. The proposed bill would create a
"vast machine"; a ballooned national bureaucracy to control
everything everywhere within the nation.[8]

Other critics raised the specter of a national law voiding all
states' laws on quarantine. Then pioneering states such as New
York must regress to levels of less enterprising sisters. This
argument introduced the question of whether congressional
quarantines were justifiable at all under the commerce power.
Yes, asserted Edmunds. Howe argued accurately that federal-
state concurrency had never actually worked; the sixty-year tradition of Congress leaving quarantine policy to states had been
unconstitutional, not the new proposal as charged.[9]

Sumner made an analogy between cholera and smugglers.

---

6. *Ibid.*, 2445–6 for J. Grimes; 2484–5 for Charles Sumner; and see
1542, 2121, 2548–9, and 2585.
7. *Ibid.*, 2446, 2521.
8. *Ibid.*, 2586.
9. *Ibid.*, 2584.

The latter, penetrating into states, faced pursuit by national revenue agents. Surely national health officers should enter states if cholera did. Could Sumner really mean that cholera was commerce, asked Maine's Lot Morrill? "I do, certainly," Sumner replied, which left him open for the scholarly counterthrusts of Reverdy Johnson.[10]

The champions of national quarantine resorted to the plea of necessity. "I do not think we shall injure the Constitution if we keep out the cholera," Chandler remarked. Sumner picked up the familiar wartime adequacy theme. In 1861, if Lincoln had folded his arms Buchanan-style in the face of rebels, no congressional debate about cholera or anything else would be under way in 1866. Must victors of the Civil War admit helplessness in the face of "a foreign enemy"? "I do not believe that this transcendant Republic is thus imbecile," Sumner insisted. The Constitution and the "nature of the case" allowed Congress "ample powers to meet the enemy."

The cholera invasion that year was less horrid than earlier visitations. The inventive Ramsey bill failed in the Senate, by two votes. The bill that passed, like prewar precedents, authorized Treasury officers temporarily to aid states' personnel in combating cholera. Treasury Secretary McCulloch circularized field agents with information on the new statute; nothing much else was done.[11]

Hopes rose among sanitarians during the 1866 cholera scare that Congress would at least create a permanent, apolitical board of health for the nation, staffed with physicians, and armed like New York City's with emergency coercive powers, including that of defining when emergency existed. The decline in the cholera threat submerged this aspiration along with the Ramsey bill. By the decade's end, even champions of anticontagion concert had lost the nationalizing surge. In 1874 the *Nation* cautioned that any systematic co-operation among national officials must not supersede states' officers, who "are so obviously the ones most directly charged [by the Constitution] with the protection of the public health that there can be little ground for anticipating the successful enforcement of any scheme of national quarantine." In 1878, Congress stipulated that physicians in the national

---

10. *Ibid.,* 2582.
11. *Ibid.,* 2549, 2586; SAL, XIV, 357 (1866); Boston *Daily Advertiser,* June 1, 1866, 1.

Marine Hospital Service, assigned to examining immigrants, must not conflict with any state or municipal sanitary or quarantine regulations.[12]

Pressure during the seventies from the American Medical Association and a new American Public Health Association, in favor of establishment of a national board of health, resulted in 1879 in creation of a board to gather data, doubtless a useful service in this increasingly complex arena. Each state remained its own conscience with respect to its citizens' well-being.[13]

Industrial disasters turned attention sporadically to the desirability of a national mining bureau. The states' ineffectiveness in policing the new extractive industries was clear to the rising generation of technically educated, socially conscious engineers. These men saw themselves as society's natural leaders. Professional executives and optimistic rationalists, engineers were impatient with political-constitutional constraints. In 1866 Congress created mining legislation, though not a bureau. The new mining law used no national officials in a supervisory, directing sense, and maintained the uncoercive, low-budget, state-oriented posture which was the common characteristic of national functional innovations of the Civil War and Reconstruction. It allowed states and even counties to define adequate standards with respect to mine safety, ventilation, and record-keeping.[14]

This was the way congressmen assumed the nation's mine-safety responsibilities should be institutionalized. Maine's Senator Eugene Hale spoke for a generation when he insisted that "the chief function of Congress was to provide for an honest, economical, wise . . . public expenditure, to keep in the old paths and to leave others alone." Especially averse to "legal restraint," disliking new doctrines and policies, Hale favored "government by good nature."

In short, when John Bach McMaster criticized "individuals,

---

12. *The Nation*, Sept. 24, 1874, p. 204; *SAL*, XX, 37 (1878), XX, 37 (1878); XXVII, 449 (1893).

13. Jo Ann Carrigan, "The National Board of Health: A Significant Failure" (SHA paper, 1964). H. D. Kramer, "Effect of the Civil War on the Public Health Movement," *MVHR*, XLVIII (1948), 462, mistakes establishment of the National Board of 1899 for initiation of a national policy.

14. Raymond H. Merritt, *Engineering in American Society, 1850–1875* (Lexington, Ky., 1969), chs. 3, 5; "Preamble and Resolutions . . . Submitted to the Miner's Convention . . . Sacramento, January 10, 1866," broadside, HL; *ANJ* (Nov. 11, 1871), 204.

societies, [and] sects" for resorting to Washington rather than to states' capitals as "the righter of wrongs, the corrector of abuses, the preserver of morals," he worried needlessly.[15] Almost without exception, the nation's bureaucratic growth kept to Senator Hale's unadventurous and uncoercive pattern.

The cry rose early and often that a proposed new bureau had more intra- than interstate work to do, and was therefore unconstitutional. A generation raised on Marshall, Story, Kent, and Taney clung firmly to the maxim that divisions between intrastate and interstate relationships were crystal clear. By contrast, John Roche's vivid suggestion is generally accepted today that the problem of finding the dividing line is "rather like designing a suit for a poltergeist."

Becoming aware of the difficulties, congressmen found high national judges eager to share the tailor's role.[16] Consider again in these manifold connections Ohio's War-born petroleum industry, the clear source of "kerosene horrors" because of naphtha adulteration. In 1866 Ohio congressman Robert Schenck was involved in political wars with oil processors. Schenck hit at foes and simultaneously tried to protect public interests.

The House of Representatives, considering reductions in wartime excise rates, proposed to drop naphtha from taxed commodities. This would make it cheaper and increase its use in kerosene mixtures, Schenck feared. After talks with public-health activists, Schenck proposed an amendment to the pending revenue bill, making naphtha adulteration of kerosene a misdemeanor punishable in United States courts. Without discussion about this novel police function and augmentation of national

---

15. On Eugene Hale, see George Frisbie Hoar, *Autobiography of Seventy Years* (New York, 1903), I, 257–8; other data in McMaster, *The Political Depravity of the Founding Fathers*, ed. L. Filler (New York, 1964), 220; Beulah Hershiser, "Influence of Nevada on the National Mining Legislation of 1866," Nevada Historical Society *3d Biennial Report* (1911–12), 1267; Joseph Ellison, *California and the Nation, 1850–1869: A Study of the Relations of a Frontier Community with the Federal Government* (Berkeley, 1927), 54–87. The creation of a national park in 1872 conforms to this pattern.

16. John Roche, "Entrepreneurial Liberty and the Commerce Power: Expansion, Contraction, and Casuistry in the Age of Enterprise," *UChiLR*, XXX (1963), 691; Donald G. Morgan, *Congress and the Constitution: A Study of Responsibility* (Cambridge, Mass., 1966).

court jurisdiction, Schenck's clause became part of the 1867 revenue act.[17]

A Detroit petroleum wholesaler was indicted for violating it. His lawyers admitted the adulteration. They argued that the national statute was unconstitutional because intrastate kerosene adulteration could not be a federal offense; Michigan had set standards for kerosene purity, albeit without enforcement. The federal circuit court found the Detroiter guilty. He appealed to the United States Supreme Court. There, early in 1870, Assistant U.S. Attorney General Walbridge A. Field noted that since the 1830's Congress had exercised police functions "over certain instruments of agencies of commerce, for the protection of life and property." Further, in the 1867 License Tax decision, the Supreme Court had allowed Congress an intrastate thrust when exercising its revenue powers.[18]

Field was in trouble and he knew it. For months after he assumed responsibility in the case Field was unable to locate a copy of the pertinent Michigan statute. When was that law enacted, he asked a Detroit friend rather desperately in December 1869, "and in what volume and on what page [of the state's statutes] can I find it?"

Field had to cope with the allegation of unconstitutionality of the national revenue statute. Punishment by Congress for employing naphtha as an adulterant inside Michigan could rise under the taxing power only if Congress employed revenue legislation for intrastate policing. Therefore, Field broadened his brief to include the commerce power. But he could not find in the *Congressional Globe* indication that the lawmakers considered the obnoxious commodity an article in commerce; in fact, the reverse was the case. Further, no agreement existed then among judges and lawyers that congressional debates should count at all when construing statutes.

Field resorted to weak surmises. Maybe Congress intended to protect interstate common carriers from risks attending transportation of inflammable naphtha-kerosene mixtures; perhaps

---

17. *CG*, 39 Cong., 2 sess., 1218, 1259–60, 1436; *SAL*, XIV, 484, sec. 29; Harriett Plunkett, *Women, Plumbers, and Doctors; or Household Sanitation* (New York, 1885), 57.

18. U.S. v. De Witt, 76 US, 9 Wall., 41 @ 43–5 (1870). Field cited *SAL*, V, 626 (1843); X, 61 (1852); XIII, 63 (1864); XIV, 228 (1866); License Tax Cases, 5 Wall., 462 (1867).

Congress wished to guard national tax officers who, in pursuit of dutiable commodities, must encounter the dangerous adulterated mixture unless Congress's prohibition remained judicially unwatered.[19]

Chief Justice Chase, replying for a unanimous Court, would not allow Congress to limit states' police powers by labeling its law a revenue measure. It did not, in fact, aid revenue collection. Precedents which Attorney Field cited of earlier, valid congressional limitations on transportation within states of federally taxed goods failed "at the essential point" of including untaxed kerosene under the revenue power. Instead the questioned regulatory clause was "too remote and too uncertain to warrant us in saying that the prohibition is an appropriate and plainly adapted means for carrying into execution the power of laying and collecting taxes." When in 1868 congressmen had let the Schenck clause stand, though they repealed all other wartime exercise on illuminating oils, the intrastate policing purpose was all that explained the retention, for no revenue was in sight from the naphtha hangover. For support, Chase referred briefly to past decisions by Marshall and Taney, which "so fully explained" federalism as to make it "unnecessary to enter again upon the discussion."[20]

The rhetoric of this decision depicted the Court protecting the continuing functional vitality of a state within the federal system. But after this decision Ohio officers responsible for enforcing that state's 1867 inspection law became lax. Subsequent Ohio legislatures repealed the statute and substituted one which allowed petroleum entrepreneurs to inspect their own product and to certify to its safe purity without enforcement of penalties for fraudulent branding. Soon other states (Michigan in 1871, for example) passed laws which rejected the inspection certificates on Ohio's kerosene as unworthy of any faith or credit.[21]

Similar patterns mark the percolation of the humane impulse from city and state levels to the national scene. By 1870 a dozen states had emulated New York in linking volunteer private humane associations to public law. That year, Republican Senator Charles Drake of Missouri successfully sponsored in

---

19. Field to A. B. Maynard, Dec. 20, 1869, Instruction Book A, RG 60, NA; U.S. v. De Witt, 76 US, 41 @ 42–3; "Congressional Debates: Can They Be Referred to in Construing Statutes?" *WLR*, IX (1881), 242–3.
20. U.S. v. De Witt, 76 US, 41 @ 45.
21. Plunkett, *Women, Plumbers, and Doctors,* 57, 65–7.

Congress a bill creating a District of Columbia SPCA. So encouraged, the next year the House Agriculture Committee presented a bill requiring rest, watering, and feeding of cattle every twenty-eight hours in transit. Enforcement was vested in United States courts.

"The most able legal gentlemen in the House" had agreed about the bill's constitutionality under the commerce clause. It was justified further as a precaution needed to protect urban consumers, requested by several states' health boards whose staffs were concerned about diseased beasts coming to eastern cities.

Unexpectedly, several Republicans and Democrats opposed the bill on the House floor as an unprecedented violation of states' police powers that could lead to total national regulation of prices charged for meat, of farmers' ways of work, and of all property relationships. The Civil War's pressures might have justified the Union Army in analogous interventions. Now no warrant existed. Nevertheless, the bill passed the House but hung over in the Senate for the next session.

During the interval, SPCA lobbyists from several states tried to convert congressmen to more latitudinarian constitutionalism. With the bill's reappearance, an amendment was proposed exempting from its coverage states where adequate humane laws existed, in the hope that other states would pass anticruelty laws in order to keep out the national presence. The Senate passed the bill. In opposition were Democratic conservatives Bayard, Blair, and Saulsbury, and sometimes-"Radical" Republicans Schurz and Trumbull, now swung to Liberal Republican antifunctional conservatism. The House concurred in Senate changes and on March 3, 1873, the bill became law. It remained the only national action on the subject until 1903, although its ineffectiveness was clear long before, explaining why no one felt impelled to test it in the courts.[22]

By contrast, plaintiffs against the midwestern states' anti-Texas-fever statutes (which were enforced) did support litigation up to the United States Supreme Court once the epidemic waned,

---

22. *CG*, 41 Cong., 2 sess., 3143; 3 sess., 432–3, 462–4, 555, 1768–9; 42 Cong., 2 sess., 4236–7; *SAL*, XVII, 585 (1873). On enforcement, see HR 105, pt. 2, 43 Cong., 2 sess. (1875); and U.S. Attorney General G. H. Williams to L. Prince, March 24, 1874, Letterbook K, RG 60, NA: "[T]he act itself is so loose and indefinite in its terms that considerable difficulty will attend any effort to obtain a conviction under it."

claiming that the state laws were not valid internal police exercises but excessive blocks to interstate commerce. In the late seventies, reversing a long catalogue of state and national judges who had upheld the maligned laws as public-health measures whose necessity legislatures, not courts, must discern, the Supreme Court struck down the states' statutes.[23]

The telegraph's uncertain relationships with the national government offers the best-documented example of the ambiguities and hazards of the War and Reconstruction decades. In 1861 state-chartered private telegraph companies were objects of suspicion as sources of espionage. On January 31, 1862, on request from the War Department, Congress authorized the President to take possession of railroad and telegraph lines when military necessity required the expedient.[24] With Appomattox, Congress's 1862 emergency statute and similar Confederate provisions became null. What remained were states' general or special incorporation laws. None contained enforcement provisions, even when rare regulatory specifications existed; none coped with telegraphy's peculiar technology that made it different from familiar communications media.

This difference centered on the fact that telegraphers must read a message in order to transmit and receive it; in short, had to do precisely what Congress forbade postal officials from doing with sealed mail. As prestigious legal writers noted in 1865, the prized notion of privacy in business correspondence was in danger. And lawyers worried how telegraph operators fit into accepted categories of agency and contract. Existing legal compendia were not helpful.[25]

---

23. See Frye v. C. B. & Q. RR Co., 73 Ill., 399 (1874); Surface v. H. & J. RR Co., 60 Mo., 452 (1875–6); RR Co. v. Husen, 95 US, 465 (1877); Minn. v. Barber, 136 US, 313 (1890); Henry I. Bowditch, *Public Hygiene in America: Being the Centennial Discourse Delivered Before the International Medical Congress* (Boston, 1877), 52–3, 155–9, 328–9.

24. *SAL*, XII, 334 (1862). Thomas Weber, *The Northern Railroads in the Civil War, 1861–1865* (New York, 1952), chs. 7, 9; J. Cutler Andrews, "The Southern Telegraph Company, 1861–1865: A Chapter in the History of Wartime Communication," *JSH*, XXX (1964), 319–44. Lester Lindley, "The Constitution Faces Technology: The Relationship of the National Government to the Telegraph, 1866–1884" (Ph.D. diss., RU, 1971).

25. T[homas] D. W[oolsey], "The Law of Telegraphs and Telegrams," *ALReg*, n.s. IV (1865), 211. On congressional laws punishing postal employees for diminishing the privacy of mail, see *RS*, secs. 3891, 3892.

A few members of the 39th Congress were mildly interested in emulating European and British ways, and creating a telegraph bureau in the nation's postal system. In December 1865, Missouri's Senator B. Gratz Brown introduced this suggestion, and it attracted support from reformers of Emerson's stamp. But most senators were interested in encouraging state-chartered private enterprise, not in regulating or replacing it. Brown's proposal gave way to one by Ohio's John Sherman, providing that existing and future telegraph companies be privileged to lay lines across public lands, over navigable streams, and along military and post roads. Further, telegraph companies could use natural building materials along railroads' rights of way, and pre-empt forty acres of public land for every fifteen miles of line strung. In return, the subscribing companies were to give transmission priorities to government messages at rates determined by the Postmaster General. Signed into law on July 24, 1866, Sherman's bill stipulated also that after five years (i.e., 1871) the nation might purchase the affiliated companies.[26]

The men who tied telegraphs to railroads' rights of way knew that existing constitutional law considered railroads to be public highways; some jurists were moving to a concept of railways as post roads as well. Both ways, national interest was implicit. Congressmen wished to keep at least a possibility of expressing public interest in a positive manner. But while lawmakers welcomed constitutional doctrines which afforded them extensive rights to regulate, they were in no mood to do so immediately. The 1866 law fits the common pattern of national aids to entrepreneurship without restraints or coercion, of supports without a bureaucratic watchdog. Regulations of telegraphy must come from the states which chartered the companies, the congressional consensus ran.[27]

---

26. Thomas M. Cooley, "Inviolability of Telegraphic Correspondence," *ALReg*, n.s. XVIII (1879), 66; *Journals of Ralph Waldo Emerson with Annotations*, ed. Edward Waldo Emerson and Waldo Emerson Forbes (Boston and New York, 1914), X, 119–20; John Sherman, *Recollections of Forty Years in the House, Senate, and Cabinet* (Chicago and New York, 1895), I, 293–4; David A. Wells, *The Relation of the Government to the Telegraph* (New York, 1873), 24; *SAL*, XIV, 221–2; *CG*, 37 Cong., 1 sess., 3480–90, 3744–7. F. S. Lyons, *Internationalism in Europe, 1815–1914* (Leyden, 1963), 38–42, suggests foreign analogies.

27. James F. Hudson, *The Railways and the Republic* (3rd edn., New York, 1889), 130–41; Pensacola Telegraph Company v. Western Union, 96 US 1 (1877), and see *RS*, sec. 3964 (1872); Robert Luther Thompson,

In states, antipathy to Western Union's continued consolidations is reflected in the 1870 proposal by Representative C. C. Washburne, chairman of a House select committee on the telegraph, to have the national government purchase all state-chartered private telegraph companies as provided in the 1866 law. Washburne specified that the Postmaster General would operate thereafter a nationalized, unified telegraph system as part of the postal service, British style, through a permanent Bureau of Postal Telegraphs in the Post Office Department.

An alternative proposal by Gardiner G. Hubbard of Massachusetts provided that Congress create and charter a quasi-private corporation, the Postal Telegraph Company, closer akin to historic "national" banks than to a wholly public bureau. The Company was to provide personnel and equipment; the government offered clerical services and maintenance for machines and men.

In 1871, though President Grant threw his weight in favor of Washburne's public-ownership bill, neither it nor the Hubbard bills passed.[28] Efforts against passage took the form of subsidized pamphlets critical of government ownership or regulation, including one by David A. Wells, former United States special revenue commissioner and New York State tax commissioner. Wells argued that a government telegraph bureau would destroy federalism and create instead an "imperial and centralized" government, increase greatly spoils corruption along with the number of federal employees, diminish the chances for reforming the civil service, lead to government ownership of railroads, express companies, and who knew what else? He noted that since the War, congressional committees were compelling witnesses to appear and give testimony. Did Americans wish to have telegrapher-witnesses disclose business and personal secrets of clients whenever politically inspired committeemen specified?

Wells raised the specific bogy that Congress's committees and federal judges' subpoenas were requiring telegraphers to disclose contents of all messages on file, although investigators

Wiring a Continent: The History of the Telegraph Industry in the United States, 1834–1866 (Princeton, 1947), 446.

28. Wells, *Relation*, 6–10; "Select Committee on Postal Telegraph," HR 114, 41 Cong., 2 sess., 158–60; *ibid.*, no. 115, 15–19; Grant in *M&P*, VII, 150; and see Western Union Telegraph Company, *The Proposed Union of the Telegraph and Postal Systems* (Cambridge, Mass., 1869), 23, and *passim*.

were searching only for one or a few. These general commands were searches and seizures forbidden by the Fourth Amendment. This argument would have been virtually meaningless before the Civil War, when the Fourth Amendment, like the rest of the Bill of Rights, was "a largely unexplored territory," in the opinion of the best student of the subject.[29] To understand the telegraph industry's success during the late 1860's and 1870's at fending off national regulation, a brief excursion is in order to the Fourth Amendment's pre–Civil War history.

When the Civil War began, except for the tiny class of importers for whom it was no protection, the Fourth Amendment was irrelevant for Americans. Early Congresses (1799) authorized revenue officers to procure summonses from justices of the peace and to arrest suspected importers of undutied goods. The judicially sustained practice grew that customs officers could seize such goods and all of a suspect's books and papers, and enter offices, warehouses, and homes on the premise that importers' records were created from dealings with the United States government and therefore were never private papers.

Revenue needs had inspired Civil War Treasury officials to lessen losses from customs evaders. At the same time, as in antidisloyalty arrests, congressmen improved procedural protections, and threw "around importers protection which they had never had under the [1799] law," one informed customs official noted.[30]

A March 3, 1863 revenue law escalated seizure from an administrative to a judicial process. Instead of a lowly justice of the peace, now a federal district judge had to be satisfied that frauds existed before a warrant allowed customs personnel to search suspected persons, vehicles, and offices or to seize goods, books, and papers. In mid-July 1866, Congress provided that district judges could initiate as well as authorize seizure proceedings. A law of March 2, 1867 allowed a share (moiety) of the proceeds of seizure to informers; another to officers making the seizure. Other provisions of the 1867 law restricted authority to seize books and records (as distinguished from persons or goods) to federal marshals, who, unlike customs agents, were court

---

29. Wells, *Relation*, 42, 49–50; Landynski, *Search and Seizure*, 49.
30. Testimony in "Moieties and Customs—Revenue Laws," House Misc. Doc. 264, 43 Cong., 1 sess., 7 (1874). See also Landynski, *Search and Seizure*, 49, esp. n. 3, for prewar cases. The 1799 statute is *SAL*, I, 678.

officers. Further, in the 1867 statute Congress specified that mere suspicion, as allowed in the 1863 act to justify seizure, gave way to precise information. Last, the 1867 law required federal district judges to set precise time limits for retaining seized books and papers in courts.[31]

Litigious importers stressed the new laws' inhibitions more than their protections. In an 1870 decision, federal circuit court judge Clifford sustained the 1867 revenue act against charges that the seizure of books, invoices, and letters rendered the entire law unconstitutional in light of the Fourth and Fifth Amendments. Clifford declared that the nation's power to raise revenue included a right to prevent evasions of customs duties. No one disputed the government's right to seize smuggled goods. Why object to seizures of records which proved the smuggling? And Clifford noted that the 1867 law established better procedural standards, for Congress had made the judiciary an essential part of the punitive mechanism.[32]

Importers continued to allege the unconstitutionality of the 1863–67 revenue laws under the Fourth and Fifth Amend-

---

31. *SAL*, XII, 737 (1863); *ibid.*, XIII, 441 (1865); *ibid.*, XIV, 187, 546 (1866–67); "Report from the Committee of Investigation and Retrenchment," Senate Report #227, pt. 1, 42 Cong., 2 sess., 502 (1871); testimony, House Misc. Doc. 264, 43 Cong., 1 sess., 7–8 (1874).

32. Stockwell v. U.S., Fed. Cas. No. 13,466 (1870), 116–26. An 1868 law required income-tax delinquents to bring records before a Treasury assessor in response to his summons. Failing in obedience, the offender faced an order from United States district court judges to bring in the withheld records for inspection. One district jurist, Erskine, decided that the Constitution's assignment to the nation of the right to tax was plenary. Since the 1868 law specified a judicial procedure, no Fourth Amendment excess was involved as the defendant had alleged. *SAL*, XIV, 101 (1868), as dealt with in In re Meador, 16 Fed. Cas., No. 9,375 (1869). A partial result of this increased consciousness of Fourth and Fifth Amendment questions is visible in a bill that became law in February 1868. It protected witnesses against prosecutions, and secured their estates against attachment. Probably the congressmen who passed this bill were interested primarily in evoking testimony of one particular witness by diminishing his fears of self-incrimination—were extending immunity in a specific situation. But, subsequently, antisearch and seizure champions claimed that this law's purpose and effect were to create protection against the revenue procedures rather than criminal prosecutions. *SAL*, XV, 37 (1868); *CG*, 40 Cong., 2 sess., 1334; "Evidence Before the Committee on Ways and Means Relative to Moieties and Customs-Revenue Laws," House Misc. Doc. 264, 43 Cong., 1 sess., 73 (1873–74). See also Cephas Brainerd, *The Customs Revenue Laws: Suggestions for Their Amendment, in Regard to the Seizure of Books* . . . (New York, 1872).

ments.[33] Then federal courts and congressional committeemen asserted, with respect to telegraphs, powers exceeding anything customs agents had dared. Congressmen investigating disputed presidential election returns in 1876 demanded from E. W. Barnes, Western Union manager in New Orleans, copies of politicos' telegrams. Barnes refused, insisting that he was an employee of his company and not subject to Congress's orders. The subpoena he received was defective in form and substance, he argued, for it required him to deliver copies not of specific messages pertaining to the election results but of all messages transmitted during the preceding year. An order so sweeping constituted a general search warrant. Continuing, Barnes stated that a Louisiana statute, requiring operators to keep secret telegraph messages entrusted to them, took precedence over Congress's demand for testimony. A House judiciary committee declared Barnes in contempt. He produced the disputed records and the incident passed over.[34]

Almost at the same time, the United States Supreme Court decided the "Pensacola" case. The Pensacola Telegraph Company had tried to enjoin construction of lines by Western Union in counties where the Florida firm enjoyed monopoly rights by terms of a state charter. For a majority of the Court, Chief Justice Waite held that a state could not grant an exclusive right even for intrastate telegraph operations. By its nature, telegraphy involved interstate commerce, wherein Congress's power was plenary even if Congress chose to exercise it only as in the uncoercive 1866 statute. Waite insisted that the commerce power kept pace automatically with technology. He noted that Congress had provided that all railroads were national post roads, that the 1866 statute authorized and encouraged telegraph companies to build lines along post roads, and that post roads existed wholly in states as

---

33. Sherburne Blake Eaton, *A Discussion of the Constitutionality of the Act of Congress of March 2, 1867, Authorizing the Seizure of Books and Papers* . . . (New York, 1874); Cephas Brainerd, *Remarks Made Before the Committee of Ways and Means in Advocacy of the Changes in the Customs-Revenue Laws Proposed by the Merchants of New York, Boston, Philadelphia, and Baltimore* (New York, 1874); *SAL*, XVIII, 186 (1874), presents text of a resulting statute, that did not satisfy either pamphleteer.

34. *CR*, 44 Cong., 2 sess., 452–5, 602–8, 678, 694; and see Thomas M. Cooley, "Inviolability of Telegrams," *loc. cit.*; Counselman v. Hitchcock, 142 US, 542 (1892).

well as in national territories or districts. Therefore Florida had exceeded its police powers and was interfering with interstate commerce by granting a monopoly of telegraph operations to the Pensacola firm.[35]

Then, in 1878, on request of a grand jury, the criminal court of St. Louis served a Western Union telegrapher with a subpoena duces tecum, a writ or process requiring a witness to appear with books and papers likely to clarify the matter in litigation, even if he is not a party to the action. The telegrapher appeared, but refused to bring the required copies or to allow court officers to search his office for them. A law of Missouri as well as Western Union's instructions held him to secrecy, he insisted. Thereupon the court held him in contempt, and his counsel appealed to the state supreme court.

There, the telegrapher's counsel argued that the Barnes and Pensacola precedents sustained the Missouri telegrapher. The Fourth Amendment to the 1787 Constitution and the identical 11th section in Missouri's bill of rights forbade the search and seizure which the lower court's subpoena constituted.

But the state court, in a 2–1 decision, sustained the lower court's right to subpoena the telegram copies. The majority opinion shrugged off the Fourth Amendment question, asserting that telegrams were not private papers held in one's home, examination of which might constrain the owner to be his own accuser and thus violate the Fifth Amendment as well as the Fourth. Instead, by reason of having been read to a telegrapher, the message became something other than sealed mail entrusted to a post office. Courts could not exclude themselves from access to technologically novel means of communication, else evildoers would resort only to such innovative avenues. Missouri's statute requiring secrecy of telegraphers improperly excluded operators' testimony to courts of justice, the decision had it.[36]

---

35. Pensacola Telegraph Company v. the Western Union Telegraph Company, 96 US 1 (1877); New York State Chamber of Commerce, Special Committee on Customs Revenue Reform, *Addresses, July 4, 1877 . . . Before the Commission Appointed to Investigate the New York Customs House* (New York, 1877), *passim.*

36. Ex parte Brown, in *CentLJ*, VIII (May 9, 1879), 378. St. Louis lawyer Henry Hitchcock obtained a copy of the telegrapher's brief, and this account is derived from the detailed statement in Henry Hitchcock's "The Inviolability of Telegrams," *SLR*, n.s. V (1879), 478–80. Hitchcock read this analysis to the ABA's annual meeting in August of that year.

All of this served to link issues and alternatives, touched on since 1865–66, about the desirable relationships of certain businesses, especially the telegraph, to national and states' governments, and the safe limits for governments' thrusts into private communications. Telegraphy brought the unfamiliar question of white men's need for the Bill of Rights into postwar prominence. It helped shape the federal judiciary into a monitor over state and national actions, and into a potential protection for all individuals' rights instead of for those only of Negroes or of private enterprise.

On this score, note Justice Field's enlarged restraint on government in an 1877 opinion in which he insisted that sealed letters and parcels, like telegrams, remained private communications though entrusted to a third party. Therefore, because of the Fourth Amendment, postal agents might not examine parcels or letters although Congress authorized examination.[37]

As a result of the Missouri telegrapher's case, Cooley asked the fundamental question: Could copies of telegrams in custody of telegraph companies be brought into courts by subpoena before a congressional committee, without consent either of sender or receiver, and be employed as evidence? The Fourth Amendment applied to telegraph messages and operators, and therefore limited Congress's subpoena powers, Cooley insisted, else the framers' antipathy to general writs of assistance did not span the century. Telegrams were as much private papers as any letter entrusted to the postal service. To be sure, Congress properly required postmen to open packages and to read unsealed letters to see if obscene material was being forwarded. But sealed letters? Or telegrams? Never!

Admitting that some miscreants might avoid exposure under his tight strictures on telegraphed evidence, Cooley insisted that this was better than allowing officials to pry into masses of messages in search of one bit of evidence of alleged misconduct. In any event, telegraphers were bound by states' laws requiring inviolability of telegrams; the Fourth Amendment restrained Congress.

But as Henry Hitchcock noted, in 1879 no national statute required inviolability. Of thirty-eight states, eighteen ignored the matter. The remaining twenty dealt with secrecy in such diverse ways as to make Cooley's confident position uncertain at best.

---

37. Ex parte Jackson, 96 US, 727 (1877), @ 733.

And who knew if the Fourth Amendment actually restrained Congress's investigating committees, executive officers enforcing Congress's laws, or court officers obeying judges' writs? Hitchcock pleaded with Congress and the Supreme Court to bring forth statutes and decisions that would make Cooley's illusions real.[38]

Congress maintained the existing unsatisfactory statutory relationships, but the Court interpreted with energy and effect. In the mid-1880's it took up Fourth and Fifth Amendment questions respecting both telegraphers and importers, with which some men had been concerned since the mid-sixties.

New York City importers George and Edward Boyd supplied glass for federal buildings. By agreement with the government, the Boyds were to import, duty-free, glass of equal quality to replenish their store. Revenue agents charged that the Boyds fraudulently imported superior glass, subject to confiscation under the 1874 statute. Federal circuit court judges required the Boyds to produce records of the questioned transaction. This was self-incrimination, the Boyds' lawyer protested. Overruled, he complied with the court's order. The invoices the Boyds supplied helped the jury to find them guilty, whereupon the Boyds alleged to the Supreme Court that the 1874 act was unconstitutional under the Fourth Amendment because the lower court's order for their papers constituted a search and seizure.

These were difficult positions to sustain. The Boyds' dwellings and offices had suffered no physical invasion. As the procedurally improved 1874 act required, obedient to a federal court's order the Boyds had brought in the wanted records. Further, the 1874 law provided for a civil trial of the sort the Boyds received, and precedent had it that the Fourth Amendment did not apply to civil trials.[39] Last, existing constitutional law accepted relevant evidence no matter how obtained. In short, the Boyds were seeking a liberalized interpretation of the Fourth Amendment, to be won only if federal judges transcended habitual review limits and traditional notions of constitutional law.

The Court was willing. In 1888, Justice Bradley decided for the majority that the 1874 act substantively involved the Boyds in a criminal proceeding, although technically it was a civil trial.

---

38. Cooley, "Inviolability," 67, 71, 78, for respective quotations, and *passim;* Hitchcock, "Inviolability," 496, 500, 517.

39. 116 US, 616 (1886); Landynski, *Search and Seizure,* 50–1, and ch. II, *passim;* Murray v. Hoboken Land Co., 18 Howard, 272 (1855).

The lower court's order for the Boyds to produce records was substantially the same as a physical entry into their premises; a figurative search, in Professor Landynski's apt phrase. Bradley stated that it was an unreasonable search as well. Only illicit goods were contraband and thus subject to seizure. The Boyds' records were untainted, and therefore protected. Nor should the Boyds suffer punishment specified in the 1874 law if they or others in like circumstances refused to obey the order to produce records. Obedience to such orders involved defendants in the awful choice of obeying and incriminating themselves, or disobeying and, as the 1874 law stipulated, by silence admitting guilt.

In this manner Justice Bradley linked the Fourth and Fifth Amendments. Unreasonable searches and seizures were condemned by the Fourth in order to halt self-incriminating testimony, forbidden by the Fifth, he asserted. Bradley expanded the meaning of self-incrimination to include testimony offered by defendants' seized papers, and planted the roots of the twentieth-century doctrine that evidence illicitly secured is inadmissible in national courts.[40]

The Boyd decision has enjoyed accumulating luster. Its employment by the Warren Court as a major lever with which to widen individuals' right to privacy against intrusions hearkens back to Cooley's warning of 1868: "it would generally be safe for the legislature to regard all those searches and seizures 'unreasonable' which have hitherto been unknown to the law, and on that account to refrain from authorizing them, leaving parties and the public to the accustomed remedies."

Yet, as contemporary critics noted, Bradley had to expand the Fourth Amendment's meaning to include not only physical searches but all procedures involving private papers and government, and to place the whole under judicial scrutiny; a great leap forward in judicial review. He insisted that the government only had a right to seize contraband, not records proving importation of contraband, which, Bradley stated, forced importers to testify substantively against themselves. Tying together the Fourth and

---

40. 116 US, 616, @ 640–1 has Waite's and Miller's trenchant dissents on the opinion, not decision. Which brings matters to the current issue of admissibility of evidence derived from such electronic novelties as wiretap apparatuses; see Landynski, *Search and Seizure*, chs. 3 ff., esp. pp. 57–61, ns. 34–7.

Fifth Amendments, Bradley made the test of unreasonableness in a seizure the fact whether what was seized became evidence adequate to prove smuggling.[41]

Little need existed for Bradley to link the two Amendments. Doing so, he assigned to courts peculiar watchdog functions in defense of certain civil liberties, precisely when it was removing from Negroes the sentinels which Congress had posted in the several civil-rights and enforcement acts. By exceeding earlier exercises of judicial review the Court reined in Congress from defining the proper limits on revenue seizures and the necessitous relationships of telegraphy to the government.

Mid-twentieth-century imperatives have ennobled his sometimes illogical opinion into a necessary and proper defense of a right of privacy not specified in the Fourth Amendment. But in 1904 the Court all but repudiated the Boyd "rule" against admitting illicitly acquired evidence; until our own time, the majestic references to the Boyd case as a cornerstone of liberty occurred in unavailing dissents.[42]

The curious thing is that the statute the Court condemned in the Boyd decision had raised procedural protections citizens enjoyed against federal agents higher than ever before; far higher than American citizens enjoyed against states' officials.[43] Boyd is like Milligan—a great case for the wrong reason; a civil libertarian hallmark, that, when the cases were decided, resulted in decreases in protection, not increases. The Boyd case and others

---

41. Cooley, *Constitutional Limitations* (1883), 372–3; William M. Beaney, "The Constitutional Right to Privacy in the Supreme Court," *SCR* (1962), 216–17.

42. Adams v. N.Y., 192 US, 585 (1904); Olmstead v. U.S., 277 US, 438 (1928); Abel v. U.S., 362 US, 217 (1960). Cf. J. A. Scott, "Justice Bradley's Evolving Concept of the Fourteenth Amendment from the Slaughterhouse Cases to the Civil Rights Cases" *RLR*, XXV (1971), 552–69.

43. Recently, warrantless administrative searches, as in public health investigations and searches incident to lawful arrests, have received approval by the highest states' and national courts, threatening to vitiate the vitality of the Boyd precedent. See Wayne R. LaFave, "Administrative Searches and the Fourth Amendment: The Camera and See Cases," *SCR* (1967), 4, 21; Edward L. Barret, Jr., "Personal Rights, Property Rights, and the Fourth Amendment," *SCR*, (1960), 50; John H. Mansfield, "The Albertson Case: Conflict Between the Privilege Against Self-Incrimination and the Government's Need for Information," *SCR* (1966), 127; Leonard W. Levy, *Origins of the Fifth Amendment: The Right Against Self-Incrimination* (New York, 1968).

suggest that within a decade after Appomattox, high-bench review was on the way to becoming the Constitution's tailor, selectively fettering, in garments as tight as the jurists felt impelled to create, disagreeable power exercises by cities, states, and nation; and approving more agreeable modes. This judicial augmentation was precisely what critics of America's directions desired.[44]

---

44. See John N. Pomeroy, *Introduction to the Constitutional Law of the United States* (New York, 1868), 504, 507; S. I. Kutler, *Judicial Power and Reconstruction Politics* (Chicago, 1968), 87–8.

Chapter XXIII

Reconstruction:
Its Hour Come Round
at Last

Preceding chapters have viewed post-Appomattox concerns rarely included in Civil War and Reconstruction analysis. But they deserve the attention. If from 1861 to 1865 intrastate matters seldom held center stage, after Appomattox they dominated horizons. States' efforts to license professionals, contain cholera, regulate railroad rates, suppress pornography, and control inflammable illuminants informed parallel national attempts, and set implicit—sometimes explicit—configurations for national Reconstruction as well. Responding to state policies about Negroes, congressmen used much the same symbols and instruments of government as for other admitted concerns. The result was that national Reconstruction evolved conformably to alternatives, dimensions, imperatives, and constraints present in seemingly disparate national enterprises.

Significant parallelism between postwar national and state efforts derived also from the common constitutional institutions, language, and spirit that inspired numerous improvement efforts. Since the federal system had worked well enough to survive the War, the assumption obtained that somewhere within its levels it could cope with any problem. But whether by state or nation, coping had to be done constitutionally. Constitutional permissiveness was never absolute. Federalism's survival required continued reverence for all states. Government retained social order in as high priority after Lee surrendered as during the War. Citizens Association sophisticates and rural Grangers aimed at improvements, not unsettlements. The generation accepted constitutional, budgetary, and philosphical constraints on activist government, and found not discomfort but pleasure and encouragement in their presence.

Scholars have emphasized that American central, state, and local governments failed to meet postwar responsibilities. The argument is that the War and Reconstruction were the roots of failure for reform efforts during 1865–76, and in turn, the latter were failures concerning politics and democracy and especially race. According to this view, most recently repeated by Professor Wiebe, Reconstruction deserved final abandonment in 1877 because since 1865 and even 1861, American constitutionalism and public administration frustrated great expectations. Wiebe concluded that by 1877 the faith of Americans in their governmental and constitutional systems had fallen unprecedentedly low.[1]

This conclusion is difficult to sustain in the face of contrary evidence implicit in the numerous efforts by states and localities to accommodate the sixties and seventies. Statutory and administrative postwar creations exhibited vigor, inventiveness, and durability, at least when measured by what obtained before the War and by contemporary horizons rather than by aspirations of future critics. The judgment that the War and Reconstruction doomed other goals wants reconciliation with the fact that the War inspired Americans to seek other goals and that non-Reconstruction imperatives shaped Reconstruction more—far more— than Reconstruction molded other matters.

Like states' efforts to suppress adulteration of kerosene or to contain cholera, reluctant essays on the part of Congress concerning the South's states and Negroes were shaped by felt limitations on the allowable functions of government, despite the existence of constitutional theories of near-limitlessness (police power for the states; grasp of war powers for the nation). Americans did not welcome actually doing what their constitutional law, political theory, and public commitments said they could and should do. Especially after 1870, changing views in the

---

1. Robert H. Wiebe, *The Search for Order, 1877–1920* (New York, 1967), 5; and see Phillip S. Paludan, "Law and the Failure of Reconstruction: The Case of Thomas Cooley," *JHI*, XXXIII (1972), 606–11.

biological and social sciences hardened hearts and minds further against Negro-centered national efforts within states, and, with respect to state activities, against coercive economic regulations.

Yet neither nation nor states ever abandoned the constitutional law or the sense of social responsibility implicit in policies and institutions created during the post-Appomattox Reconstruction decade. Even constrained constitutionalism allowed maintenance of the War's great advances, at least, and were to pass them on to later generations.[2] Interest persisted sporadically in the possibility of Negro participation in this release until, tragically and mistakenly, after 1870 the conclusion dominated that the black promise was not worth much sustained effort.

By Christmas 1865, developments primarily but not exclusively in ex-rebel states raised the almost wholly unexplored question of the nature of Americans' civil rights as against state actions, deriving from national citizenship. The initial focus was on white men as well as black. The accelerated tendency after Appomattox for states to license physicians, lawyers, and teachers, among other professionals, was a reflection of the social science upsurge. Several border states with ambitious Republican-Union party organizations required past disloyalty disclaimers for professional licenses, voting, and office-holding. Individuals refusing to swear were self-excluded from the civil right of practicing professions—if it was a civil right. For example, Missouri Republicans won control of the state's several constitutional conventions and legislatures held during and immediately after the War. To bar Confederate veterans and sympathizers from polls and power and to admit blacks, the dominant party mixed professional licensing and suffrage details with loyalty-oath tests.

On behalf of nonsigners alert lawyers argued first in state courts, and then on appeals in national tribunals, that the oath prerequisites substantively transformed the state license procedures into unconstitutional ex post facto and bill of attainder devices. Further, they insisted that these misusages invoked national limitations on Missouri deriving from their clients' national civil rights and liberties incidental to their status as free

2. L. L. and J. Bernard, *Origins of American Sociology: The Social Science Movement in the United States* (New York, 1965), 38–55; R. Berthoff, *An Unsettled People: Social Order and Disorder in American History* (New York, 1971), chs. 2, 3, and *passim;* J. S. Haller, Jr., "The Physician versus the Negro: Medical and Anthropological Concepts of Race in the Late Nineteenth Century," *BHM,* XLIV (1970), 154–67.

Americans (a striking, simultaneous parallel to Negrophiles' arguments against black codes' carryovers of slave incidents). The First and Fifth Amendments protected all citizens against such state encroachments; the President's amnesties or pardons relieved ex-rebels from the penalties of disloyalty which states could set. In essence these lawyers delineated a state-wrongs constitutionalism requiring national judicial intervention against states on behalf of certain (white) individuals' civil rights.[3]

Lawyers who in 1865–67 contrived these appeals mixed federalism and constitutionalism in novel ways. Mixtures often are unclear. These clouded further when the element entered of the freedman's condition in southern states, as structured in the black codes. Republicans asserted that these black codes proved that Negroes' and southern Unionists' civil rights and liberties could exist only if ex-Confederates' rights and liberties as state citizens were constrained by disfranchising loyalty tests.

Under President Johnson's orders to the Army, all-white electorates composed largely of amnestied or pardoned former Confederate supporters, almost all of whom became Democrats, resumed political domination of the southern states, and accommodated in black codes the freed Negro's altered status. After reading South Carolina's new black code in November 1865, Attorney General James Speed told Lieber that "it is the old slave code minus the slave owners' responsibilities—poor as they were. The President I was told was shocked at the thing." And Lieber warned Senator Sumner, "You will have plenty, plenty of work in Congress."[4]

There were contemporary claims that the black codes returned freedmen to slavery; recent judgments seem equally awry that the codes' labor portions reflected simple Negrophobia on the part of Freedmen's Bureau agents, who drew up some planter-freedmen labor contracts which southern whites incorporated into

---

3. Harold M. Hyman, *To Try Men's Souls: Loyalty Tests in American History* (Berkeley, 1959), chs. 6, 8; Alfred H. Kelly, "Comment on . . . Hyman's Paper," in *New Frontiers of the American Reconstruction,* ed. H. Hyman (Urbana, Ill., 1966), 54–5; William E. Parrish, "Reconstruction Politics in Missouri, 1865–1870," in *Radicalism, Racism, and Party Realignment: The Border States during Reconstruction,* ed. R. O. Curry (Baltimore, 1969), 14–17; Cummings v. Missouri, 4 Wall., 277 (1867).

4. Francis Lieber to Charles Sumner, Nov. 17, 1865, Box 50, LI-3842, Lieber Papers, HL; William S. McFeely, *Yankee Stepfather: General O. O. Howard and the Freedmen* (New Haven, 1968), 199.

black codes.[5] The labor contracts and code clauses did favor white employers. But in all states contemporary labor law favored employers under Dickensian "master-servant" categories.

If imbalanced, Freedmen's Bureau labor contracts tipped on customary legal, not racial, pivots. And with respect to the freedmen the Bureau's labor contracts advanced at least one great step—Bureau courts were open to Negroes. By contrast, almost all black codes denied Negroes basic remedies as litigants or witnesses in state and local civil courts when whites were involved. If, as W. W. Davis believed, the Bureau's labor provisions were not "personal Magna Chartas . . . for the liberated race" in the sense of being wholly fair to black workers, the black codes' thrusts were totally unfair. By existing legal (not to mention moral) standards, the codes kept blacks crippled in workaday legal relationships. Unjust to blacks, the codes, as Arieli noted, appeared dangerous also to white workers and insulting to the nation which the Union's military success had nourished; to that "integral American nationalism . . . crystallized around social and moral, rather than political, concepts."[6]

Impacting on this enhanced moral sensitivity, the black codes educated northern whites to facts long familiar to slaves, slaveowners, and abolitionists, teaching that slavery was never a simple relationship. Over two centuries, numerous incidental customary and statutory constraints and disabilities had borne down on the slave in order that the master's property rights and social control remain unimpaired. Such incidents as the exclusion of black testimony, persisting in the "reconstructed" states' black codes, maintained profound differences between freedmen and free men.

These incidents of slavery had grown up in law and custom because, in order for the master wholly to command his human property's labor and to buy, sell, lease, and bequeath his slave, the slave had to be stopped from contracting out his own services

---

5. McFeely, *Yankee Stepfather*, 148–52; and see Gen. H. G. Wright to Gov. A. J. Hamilton, Oct. 10, 1865, Hamilton Papers, TSA, cited in part in Charles W. Ramsdell, *Reconstruction in Texas* (New York, 1910), 79–80; but its significance is overlooked.

6. William W. Davis, *Civil War and Reconstruction in Florida* (New York, 1913), 394; Arieli, *Individualism and Nationalism in American Ideology* (Baltimore [Penguin edn.], 1966), 316. A contrasting view is in Charles Wilson, *Black Codes in the South* (University, Ala., 1965).

or hazarding them in marriage, debt accruals, or litigation.[7] But persons incapable of entering into contracts could not be held to contractual responsibilities; individuals barred from litigating or testifying were irresponsible so far as law was concerned. Freedom involved responsibility. The black codes denied the latter and so diminished the former. Slavery's hangover incidental liabilities in the black codes exempted from the law's sanctions five million people only recently released from their masters' social controls. Therefore to many white Americans who cared little about Negroes in moral terms, the codes were malignant perversions of states' powers that threatened the basic social fabric in the barely restored nation.

Some unknowable proportion of northern white distaste for the black codes was, ironically, an emotional response to generations of southern white folklore about black inferiority. Oversold on the myth of Negro defectiveness, many northern whites favored accommodating freedmen into the only condition their law knew, equality in rights *and* responsibilities, so that each American was simply equal to all fellow citizens of his state in the law's benefits and burdens. At the close of 1865 political equality—the ballot—for blacks was still a distant goal even among Republican Negrophiles. Civil rights was the politically acceptable, racially comfortable, constitutionally decent cause to champion. The black codes made it an urgent cause.

Andrew Johnson's disinclination to forbid retention of slavery's derivative incidents in the southern states' constitutions and laws[8] created support among Republicans for equality of

---

7. R. K. Kohl, "The Civil Rights Act of 1866, Its Hour Come Round at Last: Jones v . . . Mayer Co.," *VaLR*, LV (1969), 275–6; John C. Hurd, *The Law of Freedom and Bondage in the United States* (Boston, 1858), *passim;* Eugene D. Genovese, "Rebelliousness and Docility in the Negro Slave: A Critique of the Elkins Thesis," *CWH*, XIII (1967), 299–304 and *passim.*

8. Chief Justice Chase advised President Johnson after the jurist toured the recently rebel states to end those residual incidents; Chase to J. G. Bennett, Jr., May 22, 1868, concerning advice Chase gave Johnson in 1865, in Chase Papers, Letterbook, ser. 4, vol. 117, pt. 2, 393, LC. Republicans' community and diversity of views were illustrated when in January 1866 Congress turned to the question of Negro suffrage in the District of Columbia. No doubt at all existed of adequate national jurisdiction. But though the House passed (Jan. 18) a bill to strike the word "white" from District voting requirements, the Senate's Judiciary Committee immured the proposal. As matters worked out, this modest bill was to be the 39th

men before law "at least so far as civil rights are concerned, in the rebel States," Charles Sumner told fellow Senators in December 1865. "This is done simply to carry out and maintain the Proclamation of Emancipation." Short of this commitment, "Emancipation will be only half done. . . . Slavery must be abolished not in form only, but in substance."[9]

Insistence on substantive equality before state law rather than nominal abolition was to hold fairly firm for a decade after Appomattox. A man without civil rights had no capacity to redress wrongs, E. L. Godkin asserted in an 1866 *Nation* editorial; "wherein does he differ from a slave?" In 1870 constitutionalist Elisha Mulford retained the premise that "The absence of the rights of man is characteristic of his existence, insofar as the germ of the nation is undeveloped and its form undefined." And in 1875 Theophilus Parsons insisted in his study of American's national rights that "to every man, and to every man alike, it [the Constitution] is a supreme law."

Of course it is possible to dismiss such statements as theorists' musings or cynical camouflage. But evidence makes such assumptions increasingly difficult to credit. Viewed constitutionally, the linked black-code–national-civil-rights questions led from Appomattox to the Thirteenth Amendment to the Freedmen's Bureau and Civil Rights statutes to the Fourteenth and Fifteenth Amendments, with Congress's several Reconstruction laws and the impeachment fitting logically in their chronological places.

This interaction is summarized in Virginia legal expert John Randolph Tucker's end-of-century restatement. In 1865 the fact that even abolitionists demanded the Thirteenth Amendment proved the War powers alone incapable of ending slavery constitutionally. But the inability of freedmen to function within southern states' legal-judicial systems because of the black codes struck to the root of the Thirteenth Amendment. The black codes raised again the 1857 Dred Scott specter, that Negroes were noncitizens. Defined by the Constitution and by judiciary acts since 1789, access to national courts existed only to citizens of diverse states. Had the War and emancipation merely cut millions of blacks adrift from slave-status certainty in states' laws, however

---

Congress's most "radical" black-centered proposal. *CG*, 39 Cong., 1 sess., 310–11.

9. *CG*, 39 Cong., 1 sess., 91 (Dec. 20, 1865); and see David Donald, *Charles Sumner and the Rights of Man* (New York, 1970), ch. II.

dreadful, and left them without remedies in any jurisprudence? Even to southerner Tucker this was beyond credence.[10]

Carl Schurz, touring the defeated states late in 1865, noted that some southern whites, anxious to get rid of Freedmen's Bureau courts which allowed blacks' testimony in instances where the re-risen state courts did not, endeavored to open the state courts to Negroes. Schurz heard such strategists assuring whites unsympathetic to the change that little would alter so long as all-white judges and juries determined "in each case . . . whether the testimony of negro witnesses was worth anything or not." When Schurz objected that, loaded against blacks, state courts were most unlikely to punish a white abuser of a black employee for assault and battery, he was told: "You must make some allowance for the prejudices of our people."

Northward, residual incidents of slavery in the black codes were so hard to stomach that Republicans were able to restore effective party concert in the post-Appomattox Congress by the time it convened in early December 1865. The consequent stand-off of southern delegates opened alternatives to Radicals' demands that Congress set positive standards for political rights within states, in favor of constraining negatively states' diminutions of civil rights. Opinion grew that Wade and Davis's 1864 criticisms of executive military Reconstruction were valid for 1865 and 1866. This opinion fed partially off worries over a second civil war developing cut of Reconstruction's instabilities, but centered more on fears of class, race, and religious tensions growing from the inferior status in state law for Negroes. Expecting tranquility with Appomattox, that generation suffered again the compelling Victorian fear of upset and anarchy. The rewon southern states were endangering again not only the brittle Union of states but also the fragile veneer of social stability. As noted, the December 1865 bloody "Eyre Rebellion" in nearby Jamaica, occurring thirty years after emancipation there,

---

10. *The Nation* (April 5, 1866), 422; T. Parsons, *The Political, Personal, and Property Rights of a Citizen of the United States. How to Exercise and How to Preserve Them* (Chicago, 1875), I, 3; Elisha Mulford, *The Nation: The Foundation of Civil Order and Political Life in the United States* (New York, 1870), 106–7; and see C. E. Larsen, "Nationalism and States' Rights in Commentaries on the Constitution After the Civil War," *AJLH*, III (1959), 360–9; Donald, *Sumner & the Rights of Man, passim;* J. R. Tucker, *The Constitution of the United States,* ed. H. St. G. Tucker (Chicago, 1899), I, ch. 7, esp. 340–3.

heightened American fears of analogous distress if freedmen remained less than free men under law.

These post-Appomattox concerns, looking backward to pre-surrender conditions, linked the War to the Reconstruction. The Thirteenth Amendment lost character as a finality and sought still-unreached goals because of imperatives deriving from the American past. In essence, Republicans remained where they were in mid-1864, when Henry Everett Russell advocated passage of an abolition amendment "To supplement and complete the work of reconstruction . . . to make impossible the pretence of a [state] power anywhere in the . . . United States to hold a person in bondage." Defending the enforcement clause of the Thirteenth Amendment against charges that states diminished themselves as a consequence of their ratification, Seward reminded a critic that "The objection you mention . . . is regarded as querulous and unreasonable, because that clause is really restraining [states] in its effect, instead of enlarging the powers of Congress."[11]

For a long time scholars preferred to slight the Thirteenth Amendment, a seemingly obvious result of the War, and to concentrate on the Fourteenth and Fifteenth Amendments' apparently greater complexities, in effect severing the War from the Reconstruction. But recent interpretive trends have returned closer to contemporary understandings.[12] Along with excesses visible in all states, the southern states' hangover incidents from slavery exhibited themselves glaringly. This heightened awareness of defects in the restored Union underlay the Republican commitment to join conduct and constitutionalism, freedom and federalism the more closely; the better to harmonize what Professor Graham called "the American Creed, the American Conscience, and the American Constitution."[13] Perception spread of

11. Carl Schurz in *Sen. Exec. Doc.* 2, 39 Cong., 1 sess., 34–5 (Dec. 19, 1865); Henry E. Russell, "The Constitutional Amendment," *CM*, VI (1864), 324; Seward in Edward McPherson, *A Political Manual for 1866 and 1867* (Washington, 1867), 23. See also B. Semmel, *Jamaican Blood and Victorian Conscience: The Governor Eyre Controversy* (Boston, 1963); G. M. Frederickson, *The Inner Civil War: Northern Intellectuals and the Crisis of the Union* (New York, 1965), ch. 8 and *passim*; L. M. Kincaid, "Victims of Circumstance: An Interpretation of Changing Attitudes Toward Republican Policy Makers and Reconstruction," *JAH*, LVII (1970), 63.

12. W. Brock, *An American Crisis: Congress and Reconstruction, 1865–1867* (New York, 1963), 2; Kincaid, "Victims," 63–6.

13. Graham, *Everyman's Constitution: Historical Essays on the*

theretofore largely unperceived facts about civil rights. Before Sumter little accumulated wisdom existed on the civil-rights theme. "We were content to have a constitution applicable as law," Hurd noted, "without caring to acknowledge any actual person as having the will and power to maintain it."[14]

In substantial part because the black codes hit sensitive nerve ends throughout the North, the wartime consciousness of intrastate inequalities persisted after Appomattox. Brownson concluded in 1865 that "Government ceases [henceforth] to be a mere agency, which must obtain the assassin's consent before it can . . . hang him, and becomes authority, which is one and imperative." And Lieber gave up his quip that defining national civil rights was as irrelevant as newlyweds defining love.[15]

What in the 1787 Constitution and in the post-Appomattox administrative-bureaucratic arrangements were relevant to a national civil-rights role? Republicans faced the indisputable fact that the 1787 framers had accommodated in the federal system national functions unrelated to intrastate civil-rights practices. In situations where states restrained civil rights, the national Bill of Rights, a noble catalogue of wrongs the national government must not commit, offered no help. Therefore the Republicans' attention went to some of the Constitution's long-ignored clauses. The injunction that the nation guarantee each state a republican form of government was not immediately helpful. Suggestions issued, especially from lawyer-legislators, that the Constitution's "full faith and credit" clause deserved application. Perhaps the clause would make states obey other states rather than having the nation evoke obedience. But they learned quickly that the

---

Fourteenth Amendment, the 'Conspiracy Theory,' and American Constitutionalism (Madison, Wis., 1968), 3, and see 5, 8. See also *Journals of Ralph Waldo Emerson*, ed. E. W. Emerson and W. E. Forbes (Boston, 1914), IX, 461–5; J. M. McPherson, *The Struggle for Equality: Abolitionists and the Negro in the Civil War and Reconstruction* (Princeton, 1964), chs. 10, 14.

14. J. C. Hurd, "Theories of Reconstruction," *ALRev*, I (1867), 239. See review of his *Theory of Our National Existence*, in *ALRev*, XVI (1882), 389–93.

15. Francis Lieber, *Civil Liberty and Self-Government*, ed. T. D. Woolsey (3rd edn., Philadelphia, 1911), 35–6; Orestes Brownson, *The American Republic* (reprint edn., Louisville, 1969), 71–2.

"lawyer's clause" of the Constitution—Robert Jackson's phrase—was recruited in 1787 from international commercial practices wherein one nation agreed reciprocally to respect usages and papers. At best, as jurisprudence from 1839 suggested, it afforded remedies for a minuscule number of merchants; states' black codes diminished millions of Americans.[16]

A generation had learned since 1861 the lesson that prewar abolitionists apprehended, that the quality of an American's life under law was determined less by his nationality than by his locality. For example, in 1864 Maine allowed defendants in criminal trials to testify in their own defense, or, as was traditional, to keep silent and so avoid the possibility of self-incrimination. In sharp contrast, almost all the black codes forbade blacks from testifying at all in civil or criminal litigation concerning whites. Comity was an absurd concept as a rights protection when federalism allowed such disparities and when national remedies were irrelevant.

The significant fact of 1865 was that the absurdity was commonly apparent; constitutional complexities had become political commonplaces. Old political organizations, especially the Republican party, entrenched welfare-missionary spokesmen such as *The American Freedman,* and new patriotic watchdog societies such as the Union Leagues spread the word widely.[17] Laymen and lawmen looked to the new Thirteenth Amendment to restore rationality to the federal system. Republicans concluded that the Amendment provided authority for the nation—Congress specifically—to attend to last rites for slavery's hangover incidents, the black codes. And slavery's persisting incidents performed for Congress the service of requiring the obsequies to be initiated without the painful difficulty of defining positively

---

16. See McElmoyle v. Cohen, 13 Peters 311 @ 328 (1839); Robert H. Jackson, "Full Faith and Credit—the Lawyer's Clause of the Constitution," *CLR,* LXV (1945), 1–45; Shirley A. Bill, " 'Full Faith and Credit' and Early American Federalism," *Journal of World History,* XL (1969), 722–54; C. O. Lerche, Jr., "Congressional Interpretations of the Guarantee of Republican Form of Government During Reconstruction," *JSH,* XV (1949), 191–8.

17. "How Shall We Protect the Freedman?" *American Freedman,* II (July 1866), 50–1; J. McPherson, *Struggle for Equality,* chs. 13, 14; Frederickson, *Inner Civil War,* 8–10; Carl B. Swisher, "Dred Scott One Hundred Years After," *JPoli,* XIX (1957), 152; J. N. Pomeroy, *An Introduction to the Constitutional Law of the United States* (New York, 1866), I, 151–4; *Maine Acts and Resolves* (1864), ch. 280, pp. 214–15; Paludan, "Law and the Failure of Reconstruction," 610.

national civil rights. Instead the black codes allowed Congressional Republicans to protect Americans' national civil rights in negative terms of thwarting intrastate inequities. Diversities between states—the essence of federalism—could continue. But within states free Americans should stand equally mature before laws.

This was a great gift to Republicans; before 1865 almost no attention had gone to national civil rights. Since colonial times Americans had become the world's experts in political-rights applications—the vote. Armed with ballots, long before Sumter free Americans had cut anything like "white codes" out of their society. In harmony with federalism's state-centered arrangements, voting qualifications including residence, property, and the like were set by states and their subdivisions and, save for race as an aspect of national citizenship, the Civil War and Reconstruction never shook this structure.[18] Political rights were known concepts and familiar, simple intrastate practices.

All certitudes vanished with respect to workaday civil rights. They had no agreed definition, accepted contents, or understood divisions between civil rights one enjoyed as a citizen of the nation as distinguished from those enjoyed as consequence of state citizenship. Did Missourians' civil rights include a teacher's inter-

---

18. Little scholarly attention has centered on what in law constituted a free American. In 1969–70 Patricia Allan, a doctoral student of William Brock of the University of Glasgow, participated in my Rice University seminar. Her work, now maturing in a Glasgow dissertation, is the basis for this discussion. See also Theodore Sedgwick, *Statutory and Constitutional Law*, ed. J. N. Pomeroy (2nd edn., New York, 1874), 557–9 and n.; H. Phillips, *The Development of a Residential Qualification for Representatives in Colonial Legislatures* (Cincinnati, 1921); J. B. James, *The Framing of the Fourteenth Amendment* (Urbana, Ill., 1956); J. ten Broek, *The Antislavery Origins of the Fourteenth Amendment* (Berkeley, 1951); W. Gillette, *The Right to Vote: Politics and the Passage of the Fifteenth Amendment* (Baltimore, 1965), all *passim*. J. and L. Cox, *Politics, Principle, and Prejudice: Dilemma of Reconstruction America, 1865–1866* (Glencoe, Ill., 1963), chs. 1, 2, 10, and *passim*, and M. L. Benedict, "The Right Way: Congressional Republicans and Reconstruction, 1863–1869" (Ph.D. diss., RU, 1971), have detailed how President Johnson and conservatives of both parties tried to depict Republicans as advocates of political rights for Negroes in order to isolate Radical champions of this advance. The scheme failed, due to the clear recognition of the primacy of the civil-rights issue. Note that the Test Oath decisions did not deny a state the power to require a retrospective loyalty oath as a voting qualification, but only as professional minima, i.e., as property.

est in the practice of his profession for which he needed the state's license, it in turn requiring him to swear that he had never aided the Confederacy? Did a Negro have a civil right deriving from his freed condition to sue or to testify in his state's courts, though the state's laws and customs forbade him from doing either? Who decided, state or nation?

The prewar constitutional consensus was so heavily in favor of the states deciding that West Virginia jurist Henry Brannon was only mildly hyperbolic when he noted that until the Thirteenth Amendment only Magna Charta restrained states. National civil rights had blanketed primarily the tiny number of Americans with interstate and foreign interests. One reason the Reconstruction of the South loomed high to northerners was less that blacks were involved than that everyone understood the preeminence of states and subdivisions in affecting all their citizens' lives. If a state unjustly curtailed a citizen's myriad daily pursuits and privileges, which, collectively, were his civil rights, until 1865 the sole remedies open to him were those his state provided.[19]

Before the Civil War only abolitionists insisted that all Americans, white and Negro, possessed civil rights which took precedence over states' disabilities, especially slavery. These "national" rights derived from eighteenth-century natural rights, the Declaration of Independence, and the Constitution, especially the equal protection of the laws and comity clauses. Antislavery constitutionalists insisted also that the Constitution cloaked every American with privileges and responsibilities of dual citizenship. By such interpretation, the minuscule body of national civil rights, best catalogued in 1823 by United States Judge Bushrod Washington, but including as essential the right to sue and to testify in suits,[20] penetrated to every individual in every state.

Such analyses criticized the legitimacy of states' slave codes and of national supportive acts which denied bondsmen all ordinary civil rights. The War escalated civil rights from state to nation, abolitionists argued; national civil rights had become "fundamental and elementary" restraints on what states could do to individuals, Timothy Farrar insisted.

---

19. Brannon, *A Treatise on the Rights and Privileges Guaranteed by the 5th Amendment to the Constitution of the United States* (Cincinnati, 1901), 3; A. H. Kelly, "The Fourteenth Amendment Reconsidered: The Segregation Question," *MichLR*, LIV (1956), 1051–8. Note that by early 1866 Congress achieved definitions.

20. *Ibid.*; Kelly in Hyman, ed., *New Frontiers*, 52; Corfield v. Coryell, 6 Fed. Cas. No. 3230 (1823), 546 @ 551–2, for Justice Washington.

A century later, distinguished scholars and jurists inquiring into modern applications of the Fourteenth Amendment have argued convincingly its framers' purpose to reach the abolitionists' prewar visions.[21] But in 1865 the Fourteenth Amendment did not exist. Its creation waited until it became apparent from the behavior of southern states that the Thirteenth Amendment, though it ended states' rights in slaves, did not begin freedmen's civil rights. When this became clear, the Thirteenth Amendment became *a* constitutional impact of the Civil War, leading through the Civil Rights Act of 1866 and the Fourteenth Amendment to loftier levels of rights, rather than the sole result that its supporters thought it was.

Reconstruction's primary impact and configurations were defined by December 1865 in the congressional emphasis on equality within a state of civil-rights practices, not Congress's last-resort employment a year and a quarter later of military power to secure those rights. From December 1865 on, Congress tried to hold to statutory, nonmilitary recourses. By excluding southern delegates-elect, Congress stipulated that under the President's terms, the recently rebel states were not reconstructing themselves satisfactorily. The southern states' black codes, interacting with the Thirteenth Amendment, gave Congress a Reconstruction agenda different from the wartime rehearsals represented by Lincoln's 1863 policy statement and the 1864 Wade-Davis bill. The "new" Reconstruction would transcend reunion, now won. It required Congress, even over presidential and judicial opposition, to explore shores of decent intrastate practices rarely seen earlier save by abolitionist pioneers.[22]

Congress's improved joint committee arrangements resulted in a swift accumulation of dramatic, pertinent data. It underscored the distresses caused by intrastate inequities in civil-rights performances. The impact of this evidence was to make very dubious Democrats' reiterated claims that southern states' civil rights infringements were unsubstantial and not the nation's business.[23]

Utterly seriously, standpat constitutionalists transformed

---

21. Timothy Farrar, *Manual of the Constitution of the United States of America* (Boston, 1867), 59; Kelly, "Fourteenth Amendment Reconsidered," 1054.

22. Kohl, "Civil Rights Act," 275–9; Cox and Cox, *Politics*, ch. 10.

23. Mulford, *The Nation*, 120; and see *Report of the Joint Committee on Reconstruction* (Washington, 1866), *passim;* Bowlin v. Ky., 65 Ky. 5, (1867).

this posture into the Democratic party's basic position. Delaware's Senator Willard Saulsbury tried to stem the 39th Congress's drift toward interest in intrastate civil-rights practices by arguing that the Thirteenth Amendment abolished ownership in humans, "and that I think ought to be sufficient for the lovers of freedom in this country." A wider, more permissive application of the Amendment's enforcement section could "wipe the States of this Union from existence, and . . . vest in Congress the power to legislate for the States." George Ticknor Curtis typified a large stream of conservative constitutionalism in his argument that the Thirteenth Amendment diminished states' powers not one whit beyond abolition; that the Amendment's enforcement section must not inspire the nation to exploit "a mere pretext" of humanitarian or libertarian concern.[24]

Constitutionalism of this sort helps to explain the Democratic party's rise in northern and border states and rebirth in southern states within a year after Appomattox, developing effective capacity to impede and limit Republicans' policies. But if Democrats aspired to victory instead of survival, they had to alter the treasured dream of returning the nation to 1860 in constitutional terms.[25]

Unlike Republicans, who received heavy ammunition from nationalist constitutionalists, Democrats derived poor nourishment from contrary-minded scholars. Reverdy Johnson, the party's best politician-constitutionalist, though a power in the Senate, never systematized his thought, and was never really confident about Democrats' brittle constitutionalism. To be sure, Democratic audiences were already committed to retaining unaltered old racial and nation-state relationships save for emancipation. Republicans had to move constituents toward new, untrodden functional arenas involving definitions of and protections for national civil rights.

The Republican motion forced most Democrats, including prominent southerners such as J. D. B. DeBow, to abandon 1860

---

24. *CG*, 39 cong., 1 sess., 42 (Dec. 13, 1865); Curtis, *Constitutional History of the United States,* ed. J. C. Clayton (New York, 1896), II, 370; Tucker, *Constitution,* II, 340–1; Larsen, "Nationalism and State Rights," 360–9; P. S. Paludan, "Law and Equal Rights: The Civil War Encounter— a Study of Legal Minds in the Civil War Era" (Ph.D. diss., UI, 1968), *passim,* esp. ch. 5.

25. J. Silbey, "A Respectable Minority: The Democratic Party, 1860– 1868" (AHA paper, 1968, used with permission).

and to accept 1865; to hold up the Thirteenth Amendment as the War's final impact while arguing that its enforcement clause gave the nation no charge to interdict slavery's surviving incidents. Less mobile southern whites recoiled from the Amendment because of its enforcement provision—the power potentialities were clear. Mississippi refused to ratify the Thirteenth Amendment because of the enforcement clause; Louisiana Unionist Michael Hahn noted how in December 1865 pardoned ex-rebels supported the Amendment until they read that section. Then, "considerable murmuring is heard," and ratification was "quite slow, hesitating, and reluctant." Explicitly or implicitly, southern states' ratifications proceeded on the basis that Congress must not actually apply the second, enforcement section of the Amendment.[26]

Such resentful acquiescence in the Thirteenth Amendment reinforced many northerners in distrust of former Confederates. By the end of 1865, despite Ohio's racial conservatism, John Sherman's share in this sentiment inspired him to remind his colleagues that the Thirteenth Amendment's enforcement section sought not favoritism to blacks before any state's laws but equitable status for citizens in all states. No American could be free

> . . . without the right to sue and be sued, to plead and be impleaded, to acquire and hold property, and to testify in a court of justice. . . . Congress has the power, by the express terms of this amendment, to secure all these rights. To say that a man is a freeman and yet is not able to assert and maintain his right, in a court of justice, is a negation of terms. Therefore the power is expressly given to Congress [in the Thirteenth Amendment's second section] to secure all their rights of freedom by appropriate legislation.[27]

In some states and national districts, Republicans had practical recent experience defining civil rights and employing state and national government's powers for their protection. New

---

26. M. Hahn, *Manhood the Basis of Suffrage: Speech Before the National Equal Suffrage Association* (n.p., n.d.), 2–3; P. M. Gaston, *The New South Creed: A Study in Southern Mythmaking* (New York, 1970), chs. 1–2; Cox and Cox, *Politics*, 169–71.

27. *CG*, 39 Cong., 1 sess., 41 (Dec. 13, 1865), and see in *ibid.*, 39,322, supporting statements by H. Wilson and Trumbull; Kohl, "The Civil Rights Act of 1866," 275–6; Mark DeWolfe Howe, "Federalism and Civil Rights," *MHSP*, LXXVII (1965), 24.

York, Maine, and Massachusetts had experimented with positive civil-rights legislation and during the War Republicans had initiated analogous reforms within national jurisdictions. The April 16, 1862 law abolishing slavery in the District of Columbia required admission of testimony in litigations "without the exclusion of any witness on account of color." A July 12 addition to this statute extended color-blind testimony admission to "all judicial proceedings in the District." Four days later, however, in deference to traditional legal procedures, politics' state orientation, and that year's battlefield reverses, Congress stipulated that "the laws of the State in which . . . [national Circuit or District] court[s] shall be held shall be the rules of decision as to the competency of witnesses in the courts of the United States, in trials at common law, in equity, and admiralty." It took two more War years, emancipation, and the final reversal of the Confederate tide for Lincoln and Congress to bar race as a reason to exclude a witness's testimony in national courts, notwithstanding contrary "forum state" regulations.[28]

A congressional drift favoring the rights of freedmen to testify in their states' courts was visible almost a year earlier. Congressman Ashley's abortive 1863 Reconstruction proposal provided that United States District Courts in a militarily occupied state were to enjoy general jurisdiction concerning all criminal and civil litigation until Congress recognized a reconstructed state government. The national courts were to conduct their proceedings according to that state's laws in force on the date of secession, except "that all [of that state's] laws, judicial decisions, or usages . . . which recognize or sustain slavery, or which exclude the testimony of colored persons, or which deny them the right of trial by jury . . . or abridge the freedom of speech or of the press, shall be utterly void in the courts of the United States within said districts."[29]

---

28. *SAL*, XII, pt. 2, pp. 377, 539, 588–9; XIII, 362. Congress did not reach Maine's accomplishment on self-defensive testimony rights in national courts until 1878; *ibid.*, XX, 30–1. See n. 31, below, on state civil-rights advances.

29. Herman Belz, *Reconstructing the Union: Theory and Practice During the Civil War* (Ithaca, N.Y., 1969), 176–87; and see Ashley's request to Stanton for comment (Dec. 24, 1863), and bill's text in Sec. War., Letters Received, Irregular Series 1861–66, File #A.36 IB 1863, Registered and Irregular Book, V, RG 107, NA (with special thanks to Stephen Carson).

Ashley's bill did not pass. But, supremely insensitive to the currency of such ideas, the black codes' framers excluded Negro testimony, jury service, and access to common litigation remedies. Other enduring discriminations against freedmen became visible upon Congress's scratching even slightly beneath the southern states' surfaces. For example, widespread concert by former slaveowners against selling or leasing land to former bondsmen accentuated the blacks' economic helplessness; the black codes denied him litigation remedies against whites.[30]

Republicans' increasing irritation with Andrew Johnson derived substantially from the fact that he forced them to enter delicate intrastate arenas. Many congressmen had assumed that when they created the Freedmen's Bureau they had separated race from Reconstruction; by the end of 1865 the two were rejoined.

The President's vexatious compression of tender racial and political elements contrasted sharply to his austere attitude when they were present in northern states during 1865 and early 1866. For example, he did not aid Connecticut Republican efforts to win votes for blacks there. Many onlookers believed that success in those efforts might have defused the civil-rights issue in northern states, because, armed with political rights, blacks could protect themselves. With respect to "lesser" civil rights, Johnson did not help New York, Maine, or Massachusetts Republicans who in 1865 through 1867 enacted pioneering civil-rights laws in their states.[31]

To Republicans, the President was a nonco-operative third of the separated power structure; he was to become actively

---

30. When it came, congressional intercession took the form of national restraints on states' restrictive policies rather than use of rebel whites' confiscated lands, as Thaddeus Stevens and O. O. Howard advocated. Kohl, "Civil Rights Act of 1866," 272; McFeely, *Yankee Stepfather,* 98–105, 131–2; L. Cox, "Promise of Land for the Freedmen," *MVHR,* XLV (1958), 413–40.

31. Milton R. Konvitz [and Theodore Leskes], *A Century of Civil Rights [with a Study of State Law Against Discrimination]* (New York, 1961), 155–6, and 158 n. Perhaps the small number of states following Massachusetts's lead inspired rights-conscious Bay Staters such as Sumner to insist on a national law; Donald, *Sumner and the Rights of Man,* 226–42. See also J. C. Mohr, "New York State's Free School Law of 1867: A Chapter in the Reconstruction of the North," *NYHSQ,* LIII (1969), 230–49; Kohl, "Civil Rights Act of 1866," 272–300; New York *Independent,* Oct. 5, 1865, p. 4.

hostile to congressional Republicans' evolving concerns. Like the President, in 1866 and 1867 the Supreme Court, in novel judicial imperialism, protected whites' civil liberties against national and state limitations, while blacks' civil rights remained ignored.

Within a year after the 39th Congress convened in December 1865, Republicans were powerless to stop the President's southern policy through intraparty maneuvers. They could, and did, use congressional machinery defensively in the face of Johnson's increasing intransigence on Reconstruction matters. Defense was to require Republicans to shift effort and energy toward political rights for southern blacks so that freedmen might protect their own civil rights without continued need for national intervention. Impositions of national standards for ballot purity in southern states were to lead Republicans to try similar monitoring in northern cities.[32]

---

32. J. W. Burgess, *Reconstruction and the Constitution, 1866–1876* (New York, 1902), chs. 1–4, esp. 54–61; A. Burke, "Federal Regulation of Congressional Elections in Northern Cities, 1871–1894" (Ph.D. diss., UC, 1968), 9, and *passim,* on connections between urban voting reform northward and the southern states' restorations; see also J. and L. Cox, *Politics,* ch. 10.

Chapter XXIV

Republicans'
Reconstruction Dilemmas
and Solutions

The President's December 1865 State of the Union message measured the widening gap between White House and Capitol Hill. Johnson appealed to the southern states to afford the protections of state law equally to their freedmen. But he denied that the nation had any role to play in securing civil rights.

A few days earlier, on December 4, the President had ordered his North Carolina "Provisional Governor" and subordinates, as much creatures of national war powers as any of Lincoln's military governors, to transfer duties to the popularly selected, presidentially pardoned or amnestied state and local officials, including judges. Soon after similar orders were issued for Alabama, Georgia, and South Carolina.

Such policies raised immediate attendant questions concerning Negroes' status in the lily-white state court systems built by the President since Lee's surrender. His commands had reshaped the southern states' constitutions into antisecession and abolition postures. He had enfranchised electorates and authorized the reestablished officialdoms. His State of the Union disclaimers against further national intercessions in the southern states seemed to mean that only the President enjoyed a right so to function. Further, his speech implied that having conducted *a* Reconstruction because a war had existed and been won, only he

433

could end the process by deciding when peace broke out; that no *other* Reconstruction was permissible; that the Congress was to be a less-than-equal passive recipient of his report.

Congress's refusal to admit delegates-elect from his "reconstructed" states, and creation of the famous joint committee on their restoration with Senator Fessenden in the chair, were signals from Republican congressmen that if the President was willing to relinquish the nation's "grasp of war" over the ex-rebel states before Congress could even consider the complex implications of the move, the Congress was not. The consensus grew on Capitol Hill and across the nation that Reconstruction was not complete because a dozen state entities existed in southern states as a result of the President's postwar employments of the nation's armed forces. Further, the Congress—and, as events were to underscore, most northerners—remained committed to the notion that in Reconstruction as in all else, normal electoral procedures, statutes, and constitutional amendments were the ways to manage the country; that the President's military proclamations were the constitutionally and historically novel and unpalatable alternatives. Throughout, the Republicans' antiprivilege Jacksonianism and antislavery origins kept sensitivity to the freedmen's condition high.[1]

In immediate terms, Congress could do little if anything about Tammany Hall's mismanagements of New York City, Dubuque's debt evasions, or Illinois's constitutional convention claims to limitlessness and home-rule permissiveness concerning its cities. As a result of the War, however, for the first time in America's history the nation enjoyed dominion, however temporary, over states within the "grasp of war." Those states existed by reason of the nation's policy—or at least the policy of one branch of the nation. By terms of the Thirteenth Amendment the nation retained antislavery responsibilities, Republicans insisted.

---

1. L. Kincaid, "Victims of Circumstance: An Interpretation of Changing Attitudes Toward Republican Policy Makers and Reconstruction," *JAH*, LVII (1970), 48–66; *The Radical Republicans and Reconstruction, 1861–1870*, ed. H. M. Hyman (New York, 1967), lvii–lxviii; *Andrew Johnson: A Profile*, ed. E. L. McKitrick (New York, 1969), *passim*. Johnson's relevant message, orders, and policy lines are in *Sen. Exec. Doc.* 26, 39 Cong., 1 sess., 47; *New York Times*, Dec. 25, 1865, p. 4; *M&P*, VI, 353–71. Theorists' debates are in J. C. Hurd, "Theories of Reconstruction," *ALRev*, I (1867) 237–64; C. Warren, *History of the Harvard Law School* (New York, 1908 [1970 reprint]), II, 288–9.

National intercessions having become necessary within those states because of the malignant residues of slavery, Republicans felt a compelling need to accommodate them to the Constitution.

By prevailing understanding the Constitution's war powers and the Thirteenth Amendment operated now in combination. The combined effect, as John W. Burgess noted in 1902, was an injunction to the nation—Congress specifically by the Amendment's terms—to see to the unfinished wartime work of emancipation, defined as unfinished because of southern state policies. It was unnecessary for contemporaries to view Reconstruction as an extraconstitutional offside. Nevertheless, the contrary judgment persists. As David Donald expressed it in 1970, "every [Republican] theory of reconstruction required the twisting of the words in the Constitution to purposes never envisaged by the framers of that document."[2]

Hazards attend confident assertions about the framers' intentions and the torsions of another time. In the Republicans' constitutional world of 1866 extraconstitutional notions equivalent to Rousseau's mass-will revolutionary legitimacy had little or no appeal. Even arguments that the War had reverted the rebel states to territorial condition or suspended them did not easily attract support. Unwilling to walk radical constitutional routes, Republicans agreed that rear-marching was impossible. The nation's right existed under the war power–Thirteenth Amendment combination for Congress to look within the rebel states and to see to it that the Constitution, as amended, followed the flag.[3]

Federalism's vigor and the quality of northern states' internal life were affected adversely by substandard constitutional practices in the South—this was the lesson the War taught. Therefore, Republicans saw the task of 1866 in terms similar to those they asserted against the Dred Scott decision in 1857; to seek wholesome improvements in some constitutional relationships while holding hard to major constitutional arrangements. In this sense, Republicans did not argue that the Thirteenth Amendment transformed the Constitution into a blueprint for a

---

2. John W. Burgess, *Reconstruction and the Constitution, 1866–1876* (New York, 1902), 64; David Donald, *Sumner and the Rights of Man* (New York, 1970), 227.

3. See Charles Sumner to R. H. Dana, Feb. 8, 1866, Dana Papers, MHS; CG, 39 Cong., 1 sess., 74 (Dec. 18, 1865); Alfred Kelly in *New Frontiers of the American Reconstruction*, ed. H. M. Hyman (Urbana, Ill., 1966), 50–3.

unitary nation with special status for southern states or for Negroes. Republicans insisted that abolition created a larger national citizenry, whose disabilities under states' laws required national attention because the interests of all citizens and of the federal system of states were involved.

Realistic descriptions of actual southern conditions provided Republican congressmen with more than bloody-shirt polemics. Touring newsmen, Freedmen's Bureau personnel, and local Republican-Union leaders kept green the practical, precise questions centering on state-individual relationships. Answers to these questions could hardly be important if they took the form of abstract theorizing of the sort so beloved before Sumter. Stated another way, Republicans revered the Constitution but were impatient with scholastics' constitutionalism.[4]

Whether embraced in grasp-of-war, conquered-province, state-suicide, territorial, or instantaneous resurrection theories which John C. Hurd surveyed ably in 1866, Reconstruction was power, process, and performance. Hurd comprehended that sometime between Sumter and Appomattox, American governments, which had long possessed constitutional powers to do certain things, had begun doing them. Ten years after Appomattox, Hurd wrote that "Fact—basic political fact—of existing power and will to make law—was and is and always will be the thing wanted; and this fact is now, for us, in our day, revealed." Inhibiting theories "and every . . . fiction and fantasy shall be swept off to the limbo of busted superstitions."[5]

Acute in certain insights, Hurd slipped badly in concluding that as the bases for the federal system, the states were among the Civil War's "busted superstitions."[6] His slip was caused by his

---

4. J. C. Hurd, *The Theory of Our National Existence* (Boston, 1881), unnumbered dedication page; E. L. Godkin in *The Nation*, IX (March 28, 1867), 255.

5. J. C. Hurd, *The Centennial of a Revolution: An Address by a Revolutionist* (New York, 1888), 100, and *passim*. See also Hurd's "Theories of Reconstruction," *loc. cit.*, and H. Belz, "The Constitution in the Gilded Age: The Beginnings of Constitutional Realism in American Scholarship," *AJLH*, XIII (1969), 113.

6. Hurd later derided as "goody-goody talk" United States Supreme Court Justice Miller's Slaughterhouse Case opinion in 1873, that "under the pressure of all the excited feeling growing out of the war, our statesmen have still believed that the existence of the States were powers for domestic and local government . . . was essential for the workings of our complex form of government, though they [congressmen] have thought

lawyerlike habit of forcing Civil War and Reconstruction ambiguities into precise categories conformable to the courtroom's all-or-nothing adversary system. Hurd was so entranced by positive governmental thrusts engaging his attention that he ignored matters "solved" by national inaction.

One such nonsolution involved the telegraph's relationships to the nation, discussed earlier. The upshot of two decades of Congress's sporadic considerations of telegraph-government connections was that there were almost no connectives, and states continued as the primary governmental level involved with encouraging entrepreneurs to accept risks in the new communications technology, not with regulating it.[7] Another example more directly connected to the Reconstruction theme concerned the nation's use of states' militias. Interests involved in this question included the roles of Negro militia units in some states and the regular Army's War-enhanced prestige and influence. In 1867 Congress authorized the President to call to national duty either regulars or state militiamen when local police were unable to handle civil disturbances. That year, President Johnson mustered certain states' militias to repel Fenian invaders. Thereafter, until in 1957 Eisenhower federalized Arkansas guardsmen in order to open Little Rock schools to Negro children, Presidents chose to employ only regulars.[8]

Ignoring such nonemployments even of recognized powers, Reconstruction focused on the nation's relatively positive thrusts within the defeated states. But those thrusts conformed to federalism's pre-existing configurations. Reconstruction would reconstruct states no matter which national branch or branches called the shots. And the states' internal policies defined the limits of the nation's responsive politics and the depth and direction of the nation's intrastate interests.

After Appomattox, as before, constitutionalism and politics remained intertwined. The ongoing politicization of the Constitu-

---

proper to impose additional limitations upon the States." Hurd, *Centennial*, 156, contains the Miller statement and Hurd's view.

7. L. Lindley, "The Constitution Faces Technology: The Relationship of the National Government and the Telegraph, 1866–1884" (Ph.D. diss., RU, 1971).

8. R. W. Coakley, "Federal Use of Militia and the National Guard in Civil Disturbances: The Whiskey Rebellion to Little Rock," in *Bayonets in the Streets: The Use of Troops in Civil Disturbances,* ed. R. Higham (Lawrence, Kan., 1969), 25–6.

tion and the constitutionalization of politics, as in the Thirteenth Amendment–black code interactions, constrained the most Radical Republicans as well as the most reactionary Democrats. Thus, emancipation's reversal and a treason trial for Jefferson Davis proved to be equally impossible. When passions overcame political rationality in the White House and the impeachment resulted, it proceeded as the Constitution directed, and the failure to convict by only one Senate vote was honored by the Republican managers. In the midst of the impeachment political nominating conventions conducted their business in conformity with the Constitution's electoral calendar.

The impeachment resolved Reconstruction's primary constitutional uncertainty: Who should decide what conditions justified the nation's confidence in a state's stability, democracy, and decency? So perceived, the impeachment was never a constitutional dead-end.[9] But if the impeachment resolved for Republicans the urgent question of Reconstruction leadership, their obedience to the Constitution throughout the impeachment illustrates also one of several inescapable dilemmas the Constitution-worshiping Republicans faced, and from which they never tried to escape.

Professor Kelly lists as the first of the Republicans' self-imposed constitutional dilemmas the separation-of-powers structure in the national government. With respect to the President, the impeachment lessened the separation while preserving it; preservation was Congress's purpose and triumph. The Supreme Court and Congress were never basically at odds, and Reconstruction Congresses continued on a greatly augmented scale the pattern of wartime resorts to and invigoration of the national judiciary. Even when the Court contradicted the congressional Republicans, despite popular support they acquiesced grudgingly.[10]

Federalism was the second of the "constitutional barriers" which by Kelly's analysis the Republicans' constitutionalism accepted as a dilemma for themselves. Unlike a President, states could not be squelched by impeachment; unlike the Court, they

---

9. W. Brock, *The Evolution of American Democracy* (New York, 1971), 147; M. Benedict, "The Right Way: Congressional Republicans and Reconstruction, 1863–1869" (Ph.D. diss., RU, 1970), chs. 15–17.
10. Kelly, in Hyman, ed., *New Frontiers*, 53–4.

could not be softened by placatory partnership. Short of "a revolutionary destruction of the states and the substitution of a unitary constitutional system," no way existed for Radical Republicans to achieve social or total equality within the southern states for national citizens. What Republicans could do within the Constitution was to work through thin alternatives national institutions offered in the form of the national courts or the Freedmen's Bureau to shield individuals within states. This limitation derived from the Republicans' primary purpose in Reconstruction —to restore the seceded states as quickly as possible. Constitutionalism of such a compelling sort meant that "the radical Negro program could be only a very limited one," Kelly argued.[11]

The Republicans managed to limit what states could do *as states* about diminishing citizens' civil and, later, political rights because of race or former slavery. Almost no one anticipated, when formulating the Fourteenth Amendment in 1866 or when ratifying the Fifteenth in 1870, that the rights specified in both postwar amendments would be interpreted to affect only the public acts of the small number of state officials rather than private actions. By contrast, the Thirteenth Amendment's prohibition against a single form of state-defined property acted against all private and official contractual, statutory, and customary relationships. In short, Republicans concentrated on restoring states to harmony with the Constitution and reached out only rarely and incompletely to individuals. The Thirteenth Amendment represented the most radical root-and-branch Republican adventure in altering federalism's relationships.[12]

The third constitutional dilemma in Kelly's catalogue derived from Republicans' compelling devotion to traditional civil liberties. Almost always it received expression in terms of reluctance to enhance government power on any level of the federal system, especially the national. Therefore, the obvious necessity to employ national power, if southern Negroes' civil and political rights were to be effective, had to overcome Republicans' distaste with lessening whites' civil liberties by use of power. Republicans looked for ways to secure civil and political rights without diminishing civil liberties. They did not treat southern whites as

---

11. *Ibid.,* 55.
12. M. A. Howe, "Federalism and Civil Rights," *MHSP,* LXXVII (1965), 24–5; Phillip S. Paludan, "Law and the Failure of Reconstruction," *JHI,* XXXIII (1972), 611.

conquered enemies or shunt aside southern state or local governing institutions even when reluctantly enacted Reconstruction
statutes allowed elbowing.

Disfranchisements of southern whites under Congress's
"military reconstruction" law were few. In fact, Congress
amended that law several times in order to force more whites to
vote. From first to last in the Civil War and Reconstruction, from
Merryman to McCardle, whites who obstructed this relatively
light national martial rule, by judicial assumptions of jurisdiction
or by Congress's own stipulations, enjoyed appeals to the nation's
courts. The Supreme Court's rulings in favor of whites' civil
liberties, as in the Milligan petition, the Missouri test-oath case,
and the Yerger military commission verdict appeal, buttressed
certain Bill of Rights guarantees. But these rulings also increased
odds against effective realization of the Thirteenth–Fifteenth
Amendments' civil and political rights purposes for blacks.

Incurably bound to the Constitution, Republicans could not
be "vindictive" against southern whites or "radical" about American society. On this score, Lieber remarked the notable absence
of punitive purpose or content in the Reconstruction statutes and
constitutional amendments. They dealt with liberty's enhance-
ment and added nothing even to the Constitution's treason or
sedition clauses.[13]

Other constraints Republicans faced tied national Reconstruction still more firmly to states' rights. However variant in
contexts and purposes, Presidents and Congresses from 1861 on
agreed that the nation's Reconstruction role was to spell out
general guidelines. States' citizenries would volunteer appropriate
specific responses. This reliance on intrastate voluntarism was
the familiar constitutional-political way akin to the habit in economic matters of Congress encouraging entrepreneurs to risk
capital rather than having the nation run business enterprises.
But the habitual resort to voluntarism gave the advantage of first
motion or no motion to the intrastate citizenries in control of
affairs. Thus, the Thirteenth Amendment merely specified that
slave property could no longer exist under states' laws. Beyond
this, states wrote their own abolition tickets. They chose to write
them in the form of the obnoxious black codes, inspiring in turn

13. Kelly, in Hyman, ed., *New Frontiers*, 56–8; "Amendments to the
Constitution" folder, Lieber Papers, HL, #s LI 166, 168.

further national stipulations that were linked to the intrastate responses.[14]

The fifth of the Republicans' self-imposed constraints kept them tied to the familiar techniques, instruments, and rhythms of open politics and party priorities. As in 1862 and 1864, in 1866 and 1868 and after, unfettered elections determined policies. Commitments to popular decision-making created other ties between the War and Reconstruction. The 39th Congress, elected in 1864 on War issues, managed to win majority support in 1866 for altered though derivative policies centering on electoral standards and civil-rights practices in the recently rebel states. National politics concentrated on state-defined electorates, on state-echeloned political parties, and on state's restorations to national relationships.

The passions of the critical congressional and state elections of 1866 measured how greatly the nation, political democracy, the party systems, and the states had strengthened since 1860. State-centered federalism no longer required futility when bedrock issues were up for decision. Instead politics and constitutionalism managed a rough harmony.[15] This harmony, a fundamental impact of the Civil War, allowed Reconstruction America to escape the basic hazard secession had created of a collapse in the political processes which the Constitution required.

Despairing of majority political support, some dour Democrats tried after Appomattox to collapse politics through Buchanan-style constitutionalism. They resorted sporadically again to unamendable-amendment proposals similar to Toombs's and Crittenden's distasteful secession-winter packages. Far-right Democrats refused to recognize that the War had discredited the idea of reversing by such means popular decisions whenever a minority—themselves—found them unpalatable.

---

14. See J. Q. Adams, Jr., *Speech . . . to South Carolina State Executive Committee* (Boston, 1868), 9.

15. H. M. Hyman, "Election of 1864," and J. H. Franklin, "Election of 1868," in *History of American Presidential Elections*, ed. A. M. Schlesinger, Jr., and F. Israel (New York, 1971), II, 1155–299; L. G. Kincaid, "The Legislative Origins of the Military Reconstruction Act, 1865–1867" (Ph.D. diss., JHU, 1968), chs. 2, 3 and *passim*.

Never able to believe that Lincoln's mudsills could crush the South's slave-sustained elites, since 1861 Charles Mason had supported the notion of a national referendum or convention to end the War without victory, to reverse emancipation, and to nullify the results of the 1864 election. As Appomattox neared Mason confided to his diary that he was still afire with his "great project." He believed that the Constitution "has been overstrained and shattered by the rough service to which it has been subjected of late. We need a radical change to bring it back to what it ought to have been originally and to what it would have been but for the erroneous expositions that were given of it by those who had power of administering it."

In November 1866 Mason resorted again to his idea for a national constitutional convention, this time to block by the imposition of a fundamental condition the purposes of the proposed Fourteenth Amendment. Mason worked out a scheme to substitute another amendment: "that there shall be impartial suffrage in all the States, and when this is adopted . . . the [southern] States shall be restored to their position." The Iowan expected that such an amendment would be distasteful to North as well as South and be rejected. In the confusion attending congressional debate, northern Democrats and conservative Republicans would coalesce, overthrow Republican leadership, and "when this is done, we will call a convention to amend the Federal Constitution." With conservatives in control at the convention, Mason believed, neither Congress's nor his own proposed amendment, looking to improved suffrage, would be "calculated to be perpetuated in the new Constitution, but [instead] will be a means of preventing such a result."

Mason's secret strategy is the frankest expression on record of conservative design to exploit the national constitutional convention device—the basic *vox populi*—for undemocratic purposes; to pervert the processes and aspirations of democracy for retrograde goals. Apart from its frankness it is not unusual, however.[16]

In 1866 New York Democrats proposed that voters substitute for the pending Fourteenth Amendment an unamendable amendment by terms of which citizenship definitions would re-

---

16. Entries, May 24, 1863, July 2, 1865, Nov. 11, 1866, in *Life and Letters of Charles Mason, Chief Justice of Iowa, 1804–1882*, ed. Charles Mason Remey (Washington, 1939) [unpaginated]. See also S. S. Nicholas, *Conservative Essays, Legal and Political* (Louisville, 1867), III, 60–1.

main forever for states to set. One Republican pleaded: "Let us run no such hazard again, but engross so deeply on the foundations of the Republic the lessons of the war that bad men in the future can read and understand them."[17]

Reviewing this lesson of the War, in 1865 Republican journalists exhumed as an historical curiosity the fact that back in secession's darkest days, Seward had advocated the calling of a national constitutional convention. However, his suggestion had fundamentally different purposes and context from Mason's and those of other retrograde Democrats. The Seward bid issued when the nation's weaknesses failed even to cope with single-state secessions. Long before Appomattox, Seward and other Republicans had lost interest in such proposals because the nation's War-won strength allowed political choices binding on all states. Further, Seward's proposition was for an extraordinary convention to study weaknesses in the 1787 Constitution, not to exploit them. His 1866 decision to support Andrew Johnson was a response to Republicans' constitutional dilemmas different from that which most of Lincoln's party mates chose.[18] But Seward was never a Charles Mason.

Republicans' antipathies to national fundamental conditions did not extend to state constitutions. In 1868 Congress passed a law to readmit certain southern states under a condition precedent assertedly sanctioned by the Constitution's clause requiring Congress to guarantee each state a republican form of government (Article IV, section 4). This condition was that each state agree, under penalty of renewed exclusion from representation, never to amend those states' constitutions "as to deprive any citizen or class of citizen of the United States of the right to vote in said State, who are entitled to vote by the constitution thereof herein recognized, except as a punishment for such crimes as are now felonies at common law, whereof they shall have been duly convicted under laws equally applicable to all the inhabitants of said State."[19]

---

17. General Charles Henry Van Wyck, in *Proceedings of the Republican Union State Convention, Syracuse, Wednesday, Sept. 5, 1866* (n.p., n.d.), 3.

18. *The Round Table*, III (Jan. 20, 1866), 40; *CG*, 38 Cong., 1 sess., 341–6; G. G. Van Deusen, *William Henry Seward* (New York, 1967), ch. 30; J. and L. Cox, "Andrew Johnson and His Ghost Writers," *MVHR*, XLVIII (1961), 460–79.

19. *SAL*, XV, 73; *CG*, 40 Cong., 2 sess., 2659 (May 29, 1868); and see W. Gillette, *The Right to Vote: Politics and the Passage of the Fifteenth*

Substantive differences exist between a perpetual national amendment of the 1861 Crittenden sort, intended to insulate slavery from the touch of political democracy, or the 1866 Mason expedient, and a reversible congressional statute designed to see to it that more people vote in states and so better control their own destinies.

Having tried to untie one Reconstruction knot created by their own constitutionalism, Republicans found that they had to advance further into the political rights arena for Negroes. The Fifteenth Amendment was to be the result. Republicans exhibited again their adhesion to positions familiar since the Thirteenth Amendment's formulation. The Republican reconstructors were decreasing states' options in dealing with state and national citizens, were adding common civil and political rights minima to all states' law codes, without compelling the nation positively to intercede. Instead the states defined their own delinquencies and triggered their own punishments. That was the essence of Republican Reconstruction. Had it worked, the scheme would deserve description as ingenious, brave, and laudable.

Having discovered the right way to reconstruct the South and to stabilize the nation in limitations on states rather than in enhancements of national duties, major Republican spokesmen were amused if irritated at Democrats' misreadings of the times. In March 1867 Godkin noted to Democrats how their efforts to bypass election results were backfiring. He admitted that Reconstruction was already tiresome to many northerners, but there was greater impatience with Democrats' retrograde constitutionalism. This impatience had been growing "ever since . . . Breckinridge uttered his [1860–61] jeremiads over the violation of the Constitution, while himself preparing to destroy it." The majority of citizens had become too much disgusted with "the whole plea of [Reconstruction's] unconstitutionality to listen even to a refutation of it."[20]

The Democrats soon became more adept. In 1870 when the proposed Fifteenth Amendment was before the states for ratification, an anonymous Louisianan misrepresented it. "When this

---

Amendment (Baltimore, 1965), ch. 1; C. O. Lerche, Jr., "Congressional Interpretations of the Guarantee of Republican Form of Government During Reconstruction," JSH, XV (1949), 191–211.

20. The Nation, March 3, 1867, p. 254; cf. Burgess, Reconstruction, 64; Donald, Sumner and the Rights of Man, 227.

becomes part of the Constitution there can be no doubt but that the right [of Negroes] to hold office becomes complete. . . . These Reconstruction measures can be repealed by future Congresses, the infamous [state] constitutions which have been forced upon the people of the South, through fraud and corruption, may be amended; but let the [Fifteenth] Amendment become a part of the Constitution of the United States, and it is riveted upon us forever."[21]

Of course the Fifteenth Amendment was no more unamendable than any of its predecessors. Indeed, it fit so neatly into the pattern the Thirteenth Amendment began of imposition of highly specific restraints on states without augmentations of national powers or institutions, as to allow Democrats to take advantage of the predictable pattern through exploitation of the same open-ended, state-centered politics by which, according to the Republican synthesis, all ultimate decisions should be made.

Alluding in 1869 to this sense of the Constitution's continuing openness that Republican stubbornness had helped to retain through secession and the War and Reconstruction years, abolitionist Samuel J. May recalled that since 1860 he had studied the Constitution "with greater care and deeper interest than ever before. . . . It seemed to me that every article of the Constitution usually quoted as intended to favor the assumptions of slaveholders admitted of an opposite interpretation." But because the opposite was true also, May finally had to pin his abolitionist and reconstructing conclusions to his faith in political democracy: "It seemed to me that it [the Constitution] might be whichever the people pleased to make it."[22]

May's perceptive faith suggests the need now to judge what "the people pleased to make" of their Reconstruction constitutional opportunities.

---

21. Broadside, N. P. Banks Papers, Box 65, LC. Gillette, *The Right to Vote,* 92–165, details ratification complexities.

22. Samuel J. May, *Some Recollections of Our Antislavery Conflict* (Boston, 1869), 143–4.

Chapter XXV

The Right Way?

I f the politics and constitutionalism of Reconstruction allowed
only limited impacts to the Civil War, nevertheless the
Union's survival, democracy's reaffirmation, federalism's invigoration, and slavery's death remained fundamental effects. Because these wartime successes occurred, Reconstruction's limits
were tied inextricably to prewar constitutional configurations.[1]

Republican constitutionalism was the source of belief that
there were few policy alternatives to curb intrastate excesses.
Force was the simplest. But recourse to armed might was always
politically and morally unappealing. Republicans wanted the
southern states to restore themselves; wanted northern as well as
southern states to curb their residents' and officials' unjust behav-

---

1. Republicans, including Radicals, "devised a program which, in
spite of much shouting, actually protected and reinstituted the main
elements of both [federalism and the Bill of Rights], imposing only a
series of legal-constitutional guarantees for Negro political and legal rights
which would inevitably be left to southern federal courts to implement.
Constitutional conservatism of this kind doomed nominal objectives of the
radical program and the nominal professions of radical congressmen to
failure. They were, in short, not revolutionary radicals at all. Instead, they
were rather conservative constitutional legitimists, operating well within
the Hamiltonian-Marshall tradition." Alfred Kelly, in *New Frontiers of the
American Reconstruction,* ed. H. M. Hyman (Urbana, Ill., 1966), 57; and
see M. L. Benedict, "The Right Way: Congressional Republicans and Reconstruction, 1863–1869" (Ph.D. diss., RU, 1970), chs. 8–9 and *passim;*
Phillip Paludan, "Law and the Failure of Reconstruction: The Case of
Thomas Cooley," *JHI,* XXXIII (1972), 611–14.

ior. Pressure increased sporadically for the nation to correct distasteful intrastate ways. Yet the nation allowed itself only a circumscribed, intermittent, and partial enforcement role.[2]

Specific and implied constitutional limitations far outweighing those that limited wartime uses of national power held Republicans in. The Bill of Rights remained a rein on national power, not a goad to its employment. True, by the mid-1860's some Americans were accepting views of liberty derived from Adam Smith, Bentham, and Mill as something more than the absence of restraints on an individual's physical freedom. Republicans asserted that liberty also involved civil rights; i.e., the absence of inequitable governmental interferences with private pursuits. Republican congressional leaders worked out ways within the Constitution to combine civil liberty and civil rights. Opposition spokesmen rejected the combination and insisted that liberty remained solely the physical and legal freedom of persons, not their rights to function equally under law once free.

It is clear that both views, combined with the negative, state-oriented nature of prevailing constitutionalism, mitigated against systematic creation and maintenance of any grand governmental interventions. There had been the "organized War" phenomenon to which Allan Nevins attended so well; there would be no "organized Reconstruction." The humanistic concerns of some northern whites for blacks could not find effective institutional expression in this constitutional context. When fears of a black exodus northward did not materialize, when southern whites substituted relatively unobtrusive customary and statutory ways to cow their black cocitizens in place of overt violence, and when many northern spokesmen lost the improvement urge so prominent since 1861, Reconstruction would ebb into near-disappearance.

Negrophobia tended to hold even the sparse Reconstruction institutions that the nation created to low throttle, and played a part in Reconstruction's brevity and incompleteness. But Republican constitutional constraints were the more potent seeds of failure. Possessed of numerous purposes but few expedients,

---

2. L. and J. Cox, "Negro Suffrage and Republican Politics: The Problem of Motivation in Reconstruction Historiography," *JSH*, XXXIII (1967), 303–30; G. M. Linden, "A Note on Negro Suffrage and Republican Politics," *JSH*, XXXVI (1970), 411–20; G. Blackburn, "Radical Republican Motivation: A Case History," *JNH*, LIV (1969), 109–26.

Republicans were too bound by constitutional restraints on the nation to allow it to restrain states any more than was absolutely necessary for national survival and social stability.[3]

It is not surprising that Congress was greatly constrained about providing appropriate administrative machineries for newly acknowledged responsibilities, when the states' analogous performances are considered. Constitutional law sanctioned states' functional competencies. Soon after Appomattox permissive "public-interest" doctrines added further strength to prewar state power theories. But, as noted, state and local lawmakers remained almost totally unwilling to create or sustain enforcement institutions equivalent to the near-plenary constitutional powers the states possessed. Clearly, the high degree of acceptance for states' theoretical constitutional adequacy was no index to the effective application of those powers.

Equally clearly, the nation's novel Reconstruction commitments were less useful as an index. Even when applying such traditionally national powers as postal censorship or foreign commerce control, policy-makers stumbled. But when the nation entered arenas that history had left almost unexplored, such as national civil rights, its officials and policy-makers floundered as gracelessly as states' men were doing, if more spectacularly.[4]

The nation proved no more willing than the states to amass

---

3. Benedict, "The Right Way," chs. 8–11; C. Vann Woodward, "Seeds of Failure in Radical Race Policy," in Hyman, ed., *New Frontiers*, 132–5; Roy Franklin Nichols, in *Federalism as a Democratic Process, Essays by Roscoe Pound, Charles H. McIlwain, Roy Franklin Nichols* (New Brunswick, N.J., 1942), 86–7; George Julian, *Speeches on Political Questions* (New York, 1872), 154; P. Paludan, "John Norton Pomeroy, State Rights Nationalist," *AJLH*, XII (1968), 275–94; Paludan, "Law and the Failure of Reconstruction," *passim;* F. S. Philbrick, "Changing Conceptions of Property in Law," *UPLR*, LXXXVI (1938), 716–17.

4. In 1970, the sheer impact of the national government as employer, armed forces administrator, subsidizer, and education overseer shaped race relations policies in private associations, businesses, and lower levels of government; enforcement responsibilities and mechanisms in the national government dealing with civil rights required a 1,115-page-long description and analysis. See U.S. Commission on Civil Rights, *Federal Civil Rights Enforcement, Report,* 1970 (Washington, 1970), esp. 3, 23, and *passim.* Of course, no equivalents existed in 1866. On its subject, see H. N. Schieber, "The Road to *Munn*: Eminent Domain and the Concept of Public Purpose in the State Courts," *PAH*, V (1971), 329–404; A. N. Cheleden, "The Governmental Regulation of Business Through the Doctrine of Public Interest in American Constitutional Law" (Ph.D. diss., UCLA, 1947), ch. 1.

expertness or to employ coercive enforcement powers. Though noble and novel compared to the prewar void with respect to national responsibilities for Americans' civil liberties and rights, the nation's Reconstruction commitments, forms, duration, and intensity resemble its agricultural and entrepreneurial encouragements, banking and tariff regulations, revenue and import arrangements, telegraph and public-health responses, and provisions for humane treatment of livestock in interstate travel.

Congressmen could not transcend for Negroes what they allowed white farmers or physicians. In 1868 a House railroad committee reported that Congress had been inquiring for forty years into the proper relationships which that vital industry should have with the national government, but that no decision was yet possible "for want of the necessary information upon which to act." Taking up the matter of the telegraph's proper responsibilities to public wants in 1866, Congress managed to work out no effective policy until after the turn of the century. The tentative character of public-policy commitments in 1860–80 limited the nation's capacity to cope with responsibilities old and new.[5]

Reconstruction could not escape such history. Its novelty was not in techniques but in the admission of a national role in intrastate rights protections.

Early in 1866 there was evidence that the nation had a rights-protection role by reason of southern state, county, and municipal policies, and that national officers protecting freedmen wanted protection themselves. Congress's joint committee on states' restorations and the Senate's judiciary committee, the primary sources of Reconstruction statutes, were chaired by conservative Republicans who were strict constitutionalists, Fessenden of Maine and Trumbull of Illinois.[6] A former state supreme court

---

5. HR #57, 40 Cong., 2 sess., 7–8 (1868); M. Ostrogorski, *Democracy and the Organization of Political Parties* (New York, 1922), II, 550; L. Lindley, "The Constitution Faces Technology: The Relationship of the National Government and the Telegraph, 1866–1884" (Ph.D. diss., RU, 1971), 9–10, 26–9; Farnham, "Weakened Spring," *loc. cit.*
6. M. Krug, *Lyman Trumbull: Conservative Radical* (New York, 1965), ch. 12 and *passim*; C. A. Jellison, *Fessenden of Maine: Civil War Senator* (Syracuse, 1962); W. S. McFeely, *Yankee Stepfather: General O. O. Howard and the Freedmen* (New Haven, 1968), 200, 211; R. L. Kohl,

judge and an architect of the Thirteenth Amendment, Trumbull
wrestled control of a Freedmen's Bureau extension proposal from
Radical Henry Wilson's Military Affairs committee, and on January 5, 1866 introduced the Bureau measure. The bill aimed
temporarily to protect freedmen's civil rights until states denying
them abandoned the unhappy course and until the second bill
Trumbull reported out of committee that day, the Civil Rights
bill, could set more permanent bulwarks interdependent with
the Army–Freedmen's Bureau's presence in southern states.

Trumbull and most of his party mates supported the Bureau
bill (37–10 in the Senate; 136–33 in the House), after long and
careful debate in order, as Burgess noted, "to preserve and protect
the *freedom* of the newly enfranchised." Congressmen were more
worried about freedom than about the freedman. A majority of
the nation's lawmakers had reached a consensus that freedom
was a dynamic, not a static condition, and that it had advanced to
combine liberty and rights. Unlike Indians or Chinese immigrants, who rarely reached the conscience of the Congress, the
South's blacks, as free men, were at the eye of national concern
as a result of the southern states' rebellions.[7]

Trumbull's Bureau extension bill illustrates connections between constitutionalism and policy. Carrying over through the
Thirteenth Amendment, wartime "adequacy" and "grasp of war"
convictions, Republicans concluded that slavery's persisting incidents allowed the nation power to act in ex-rebel states. But only
limited paths and instruments of action were permissible. With
respect to the Bureau's extension, congressmen stipulated that
the national presence remain inert until, because of state and
local action, free men could not receive the level of justice called
for by a state's laws, constitution, and customs. This condition

---

"The Civil Rights Act of 1866: Its Hour Come Round at Last," *VaLR*, LV
(1969), 283–4; W. R. Brock, *An American Crisis: Congress and Reconstruction, 1865–1867* (New York, 1963), 104–5.

7. See Bowlin v. Commonwealth, 65 Ky., 5 (1867); Judge Emmons's
grand jury charge, 30 Fed. Cas. No. 18,260 (1875), 1005–7; U.S. v. Rhodes,
27 Fed. Cas. No. 16,151 (1866), 785; In re Turner, 24 Fed. Cas. No. 14,-
247 (1867), 337–40; J. W. Burgess, *Reconstruction and the Constitution,
1866–1876* (New York, 1902), 66 (italics added). On this score, H. E. Von
Holst's comment in *The Constitutional Law of the United States of America*, tr. A. B. Mason (Chicago, 1887), 47, "It was thus not a legal, but a
political question, how the so-called reconstruction was to be accomplished," assumes significant hues.

obtaining, the congressional response was to connect defective state forums to the nation's Army-Bureau tribunals and civil courts.

In short, as the 1958 *United States Code* annotator implied, the first postwar year resurrected the ghost of 1787—the inability of "foreign" Americans to receive equal protection of a state's law and procedures due to all free residents by terms of that state's own laws and of interstate comity.[8]

Trumbull's resort to the Army and Freedmen's Bureau allowed Congress the luxury of using budget, personnel, and institutional resources that he knew were available. As an economy measure, as more rational public administration, and as a way to improve the quality of southern state justice, Grant advocated a closer merger of the Army and the Freedmen's Bureau than obtained in the latter's initial construction.[9] The Army retained close holds on the North's affection and respect; prewar views of it as an irrelevance no longer obtained. Congress responded to bluecoats' wants as Grant expressed them.

In seeking closer connections between the Freedmen's Bureau, the Army, the state courts, and the national courts, Congress and Grant had differing though compatible purposes. Congress aimed to stabilize the conditions of freedom, racially defined, especially in the former rebel states. Grant's first priority was to continue and improve protection for uniformed Army and Bureau personnel from liabilities arising in harassing damage suits. Congress wanted a sword, Grant a shield.[10]

One large class of suits in northern state courts claimed

---

8. James Speed to W. P. Fessenden, April 7, 1866, Attorney General's Letterbook E, RG 60, NA; Letterpress Copies of Letters Sent, Freedmen's Bureau Commissioner's Office, Vol. II, #s 50, 212, 296, 301, RG 105, NA; *U.S. Code, Annotated* (1958), secs. 1441, 5035.

9. E. McPherson, *Political History of the United States of America During the Period of Reconstruction* (Washington, 1880), 68; K. E. St. Clair, "Military Justice in North Carolina, 1865: A Microcosm of Reconstruction," *CWH*, XI (1965), 341–50.

10. On Treasury concerns similar to Grant's, with hope that Treasury agents enjoy indemnity and removal provisions of the 1863 Habeas Corpus Act, McCulloch to Trumbull, July 9, 1866, Letterbook 9, set E, 70–1, RG 56, NA; W. S. Rankin to Gen. G. C. Smith, Jan. 18, 1866, HR 39A–F13.7, RG 233, NA; J. B. Fry to Stanton, Jan. 6, 1866, Records of the House Committee on the Judiciary, HR 39A–F13.7, RG 233, NA, reproduced with permission of the House Clerk, in *The Radical Republicans and Reconstruction, 1861–1870*, ed. H. M. Hyman (Indianapolis, 1966), 305–6.

damages from Army personnel, many of whom were now discharged, for enforcing wartime antidisloyalty and draft operations; War Secretary Stanton was the most prominent "military" defendant among many. With respect to post-Appomattox responsibilities, in southern state and municipal courts whites initiated numerous suits against Army and Freedmen's Bureau personnel and inspired arrests of soldiers by sheriffs and city police for alleged breaches of local and state ordinances against interracial schools.

Attorney General Bates had prophesied to Senator Trumbull in 1863 that "a flood of [damage] actions, for real or supposed wrongs" committed by Army personnel would commence "as soon as the war begins to subside." But apparently no one expected the post-Appomattox flood to rise as swiftly and as high as it did. Congressmen and Army officers were uncertain concerning the enthusiasm with which Johnson's administration would enforce the 1863 Habeas Corpus-Indemnity law. The upshot was that the presidentially "reconstructed" states inhibited their own acceptances in part because in their courts certain white defendants encountered harassments roughly equivalent to black-code diminutions facing almost every Negro.

These resurrected state and local courts existed by reason of the nation's power and clemency. Their judges and court officers, almost all ex-Confederate supporters, were in authority because presidential amnesties or pardons remitted exclusionary punishments for their past disloyalty. Some of these state judges, holding that they were competent to decide whether Congress could properly remove litigation involving national officer-defendants from state to national courts, pronounced the 1863 Habeas Corpus law unconstitutional. Others interpreted it rigidly, so that the burden of proof facing defendant officers to extenuate their alleged offenses by producing specific presidential orders became untenable. The initiative in litigations was enjoyed by plaintiffs, a majority of whom were ex-rebels and recent disloyalists.

Men like Horace Binney, who believed that in the 1863 Act Congress had bridged a dangerous interstice of the federal system, worried that such state court interferences reopened probabilities of new breakdowns.[11] It was outrageous that in their

---

11. Charles C. Binney, *The Life of Horace Binney* (Philadelphia, 1903), 389; Griffin v. Wilcox, 21 Ind., 370 (1863); Short v. Wilson, 1 Bush 663 (1866); and see Martin V. Snowden, 18 Grat. 100 (1868) and Hogue v.

courts the same states whose black-code inequities threatened the Union's precarious stability denied the nation a pacific way to bypass the threat.

President Johnson was also the Army's Commander-in-Chief. Appealed to by Grant and Stanton, Johnson failed to intercede in the states of his creation on behalf of the freedmen and soldiers for whom he bore responsibility. Turning to Congress, Grant illustrated the essential harmony that continued between it, the Freedmen's Bureau, and the Army, which shaped the 39th Congress's monumental achievements of the critical year 1866.

On January 12, 1866, the same day Trumbull's committee reported out the Bureau extension and Civil Rights bills, Grant issued General Order #3 to all Army and Freedmen's Bureau commands in the late rebel states. It required unit commanders to "protect" Army personnel and veterans and occupiers of abandoned or confiscated lands from liability imposed in suits in state and municipal courts for legitimate wartime or postwar acts. Moving into the civil-rights arena, Grant ordered soldiers to protect also "colored persons from prosecutions in any of said States charged with offenses for which white persons are not prosecuted or punished in the same manner or degree." In these contexts protection meant that the Army would not permit states' judges, county sheriffs, or city police to serve summonses or writs or to enforce judgments if racial discriminations existed. Where prejudiced inequities obtained, jurisdiction must shift from state courts (and subordinate echelons) to Freedmen's Bureau paramilitary courts or to federal civil courts. Negroes could testify there; judges, jurors, and lawyers were sworn by terms of Congress's "ironclad test oath" law (July 2, 1862) to their past as well as future loyalty, and certain state court impediments to national policies could be disregarded.

This instruction placed the Army in harmony with concepts championed by such leading civilian legalists as John Norton Pomeroy, who by 1866 was reconsidering the meaning of due process as "primarily and principally, that regular course of judicial proceeding to which our fathers were accustomed at the time the Constitution was framed." Since 1787 the white American had enjoyed civil rights because his access to courts protected

---

Penn, 3 Bush 663 (1868); Bates to Trumbull, Jan. 7, 1863, Att. Gen. Letterbooks B and C, 310–11, RG 60, NA.

him.[12] Grant's Order #3 reaffirmed whites' rights of access and insisted that blacks also enjoy the substance of equal procedures due to all free men.

A month after Grant's order, the Freedmen's Bureau bill, which preached the same sermon, went to the President for signature. It extended the Bureau's lifetime indefinitely (the assumption was that the tenure would be brief), regularized its finances, and enlarged nationwide its welfare-medical-educational work. Congress centered attention on provisions applying only to the ex-rebel states, where, whenever

> . . . in consequence of any State or local law, ordinance, police or other regulation, custom, or prejudice, any of the civil rights or immunities belonging to white persons, including the right to make or enforce contracts, to sue, be parties, and give evidence, to inherit, purchase, lease, sell, hold and convey real and personal property, and to have full and equal benefit of all laws and proceedings for the security of person and estate, including the constitutional right of bearing arms, are refused or denied to negroes, mulattoes, freedmen, refugees, or any other persons, on account of race, color, or any previous condition of slavery or involuntary servitude, or wherein they . . . are subjected to any other different punishment, pains, or penalties, for the commission of any act . . . than are prescribed for white persons committing like acts . . . it shall be the duty of the President of the United States, through the [Freedmen's Bureau] commissioner, to extend military protection and jurisdiction over all cases affecting such persons so discriminated against.[13]

Extending the Bureau in this manner, Congress intended to translate the Thirteenth Amendment into machinery responsive to what states were doing and conformable to the Republicans' constitutional views. Within only a few weeks of the 39th Congress's assembly, Trumbull and his party colleagues had catalogued practices which should be equal for all free men. The Bureau bill reflected also Republicans' assumptions about dual federalism in the laws and courts of states and nation, which sanc-

---

12. H. M. Hyman, "Johnson, Stanton, and Grant: A Reconsideration of the Army's Role in the Events Leading to the Impeachment," *AHR*, LXVI (1960), 388; McPherson, *Reconstruction*, 122; J. N. Pomeroy, *An Introduction to the Constitutional Law of the United States* (2nd edn., New York, 1870), 161–2.

13. McPherson, *Reconstruction*, 73–4.

tioned as much interstate diversity in laws and procedures as the states wished to create, subject only to the Constitution's sparse constraints on states' actions, including secession and slave ownership.

By 1866 it had become a northern constitutional consensus that however diverse states' laws were from each other, within a state uniformity of remedies must obtain, or rational conduct of individual and national life was impossible. Prudent, responsible free men had to be able to foretell procedures in legal relationships in order to function within ordered courses. The alternative was the sort of periodic social disorder Americans observed in Europe and Latin America, from which they believed themselves exempt despite the Civil War's contrary evidence. Therefore a state should not refuse reasonably equal remedies to all its citizens. If it did, the nation must supply alternatives, or free Americans possessed of national as well as state civil rights would be remedyless like slaves, an unthinkable condition. When a state's laws were as patently inequitable as the black codes, they fell outside the broad category of mere diversity. When prejudiced state judges failed to apply equitably their own state's standards of civil and criminal statutes, precedents, and customs to "strangers" in the state, especially freedmen and Bureau-Army personnel, the nation must open its courts the better to protect its citizens.

But in the national courts, including the Bureau's, the preponderance of statutes, rules of procedure and decision, and precedents employed would be the forum state's, not the nation's. To illustrate the compelling hold which state rules of pleading and procedures had on that generation, consider states' statutes of limitations enacted to exploit wartime interruptions in commercial and judicial processes. Often, "foreign" creditors were rendered helpless by these evasions. War Department Solicitor Whiting drafted a bill in 1864 to suspend all state statutes of limitation retroactively to the War's beginning, including those affecting criminal prosecutions. Congress would not take that step. Instead, it suspended only state limitation statutes where the War actually interrupted legal life, especially debt collections, and allowed creditors to appeal from state to national courts where local prejudice allegedly miscarried justice. With respect to rules of procedure, evidence, and pleading which federal courts had to follow in such appeals, congressmen knew that policy since 1789 was for a national court to observe ways obtaining in the state where it was located. Omitting contrary instructions from its 1864 statute on state statutes of limitation, by implication Congress let the tradition stand with respect to this bedrock commercial concern, so that in 1870 Theophilus Parsons remarked that "These statutes are [still] expressed very differently in different states."[14]

The theme asserted during arguments on the Civil Rights bill by Indiana congressman Kerr, that it conferred on national courts "the power of judicial legislation. . . . That is to say, the Federal courts may . . . make such rules and apply such law as they please, and call it [federal] common law," was untrue. No corpus of national "common law" was developing out of these War and Reconstruction enactments save as the new amendments and statutes forbade certain state practices as defined by the states' own constitutions, laws, and procedures.

This fact of federalism suggests that former Supreme Court Justice Benjamin Curtis's comprehension, offered in a eulogy to Taney, had sunk deep into the concepts of the generation: "Let it be remembered . . . that questions of jurisdiction were questions of power as between the United States and the several States."[15] Tentatively in the 1863 Habeas Corpus law, and by early 1866 with quickening pace, the message sounded that the nation required pacific recourses when national interests were attacked in states. Grant's order and Trumbull's bills were appropriate reactions to the black codes and to state courts' harassments of national officials, freedmen, and white Unionists.

---

14. Theophilus Parsons to C. W. Sponner, Feb. 7, 1870, SS195, HL; Joseph K. Angell, *A Treatise on the Limitations of Actions at Law and Suits in Equity and Admiralty* (Boston, 1869), 19; Stewart v. Kahn, 11 Wall., 493 (1870); ms. draft of Whiting's bill, War Department, Solicitor's Office, Record of Cases Decided, #414, Whiting Papers, TSA, with thanks to Miss C. Tarrant; R. S. Guernsey, "Law Reform: Pleadings in United States and Elsewhere," New York *Daily Register* (June 23, 1873 [pam. reprint: n.p., n.d.]).

15. M. C. Kerr in *CG*, 39 Cong., 1 sess., 1271 (March 8, 1866); Benjamin Curtis, *Notice of the Death of Chief Justice Taney: Proceedings in the Circuit Court of the United States for the First Circuit* (1864), 9; Charles Fairman, "Does the Fourteenth Amendment Incorporate the Bill of Rights? The Original Understanding," *StLR*, II (1949), 22; and see Fairman's "Supreme Court and the Constitutional Limitations on State Governmental Authority," *UChiLR*, XXI (1953), 40; W. W. Crosskey's rejoinder in *ibid.*, XXII (1954), 1; and Fairman's reply, *ibid.*, 144. I refer again to Murdock v. Memphis, 87 US 590 (1875), in which the Court stipulated that it would not review a state court criminal conviction if independent state grounds existed favoring it, even though a federal question was involved.

Trumbull and Grant had worked out ways for like-thinking Republicans to live happily with the 1787 Constitution. The Bureau bill harmonized with the 1822 opinion by Justice Bushrod Washington concerning the privileges and immunities required by the comity clause for each citizen; with Chief Justice Marshall's 1833 Barron v. Baltimore decision, wherein the Bill of Rights was held to restrain the nation, not the states; with Story's 1842 Swift v. Tyson judgment on national law supremacy over certain state commercial law precedents; and with general views on the Thirteenth Amendment's intrastate impact on slave property. Aspiring to enforce equality in state rights through national power, and to dignify further the dual citizenship every American bore, Trumbull constructed the Bureau bill in ways that were to be common to subsequent Reconstruction efforts. These included defining negatively national civil rights, denying certain inequities in state legal procedures based on race, and employing for enforcement the national courts (and the Army as a sort of magnified posse), whose removal roads from states' tribunals Congress expanded.

The Bureau bill also previewed forthcoming Reconstruction approaches. Its punitive clause stipulated that violators who caused inequitable applications of a state's laws, after prosecutions in national courts would incur penalties up to one year's imprisonment and/or a fine up to one thousand dollars. And last, Congress built in a state-triggered turnoff mechanism. Equal treatment of state citizens in a state's civil and criminal procedures cut off the national presence "whenever the discrimination on account of which it [the removal] is exercised ceases," and at once after the ex-rebel state became fully restored. This "is as far as the country will go at the present time, & the very thing it is asking for," Trumbull advised a confidant.[16]

Was more than this hidden among the purposes of the Republican framers of the Bureau extension bill? William McFeely believes that early in 1866 Congress was rehearsing for the

---

16. Trumbull to W. Jayne, Jan. 11, 1866, Jayne Papers, ISHS (with thanks to Miss C. Tarrant). Text of the bill is in McPherson, *Reconstruction*, 74; and see *CG*, 39 Cong., 1 sess., 209, 211–12, 588–9. The most useful analysis, on which the following treatment leans heavily, is M. Benedict, "The Right Way," 184–215. For Barron v. Baltimore, 7 Peters 243 (1833); Justice Washington in Corfield v. Coryell, 6 Fed. Cas. No. 3230 (1823); Swift v. Tyson, 16 Peters, 1 (1842).

Reconstruction bill that matured a year later, involving the use of military courts. But he erred by considering the Bureau extension proposal in relationship to the impenetrable future; by not evaluating it in the known context of the 1863 Habeas Corpus law, of Grant's General Order #3, of the Civil Rights bill, and of national policy requiring use of state statutory law and rules of decision in federal civil courts and in the Bureau's tribunals as well.

On this last point, Bureau policy was that when state courts performed defectively, appropriate criminal cases should go to Army commissions and civil litigation to Bureau courts. Army and Bureau leaders insisted also on swift return of all cases to state or national civil courts when conditions warranted. Further, with respect to legal life styles, except for black-code inequities Bureau courts employed the forms of pleading, rules of decision, and criteria for evidence, testimony, and standing of litigants prescribed by the state where the Bureau unit was located. Bureau courts used Army officers as judges only when local civil officials were unavailable or unwilling to serve; martial law did not replace civil laws of state or nation. Instead, in a dynamic combination of congressional requirements and Bureau policy, mixing was the ordinary way of Bureau court business. Bureau justice was more civilian than military, more state and local than national.[17]

There was no deliberate escalation by Republican policy-makers from the Thirteenth Amendment to the Civil Rights and Bureau extension bills to the Military Reconstruction laws. Escalation occurred. But as in the Bureau extension bill the development stressed civilian rather than military justice; required in Reconstruction courts traditional respect for such sacrosanct matters as state-defined property titles, statutes of limitation, inheritances, and master-servant relationships.

Looking backward, not forward, believing that each expedient finally would stabilize state-based federalism, Republican

---

17. William McFeely's review of S. I. Kutler, *Judicial Power and Reconstruction Politics* (Chicago, 1968), in *YLJ*, LXXV (1969), 1092–103, contains misapprehensions on Republicans' military commission intentions. See O. O. Howard to E. M. Stanton, Dec. 1, 1866, Letterpress Copies of Letters Sent, Bureau Commissioner's Office, Vol. II, #794,903, RG 105, NA, on law employed. Donald Nieman's research in my 1971–72 RU seminar is a base for this treatment.

congressmen had no need to be the martial-minded conspirators of McFeely's depiction. Certainly opponents to the Bureau extension bill smelled out no such subtle theme as he suggests. Once President Johnson decided to stand publicly against the bill by means of a veto, he would hardly have refrained from using damaging evidence of the Republicans' alleged purposes, if he had had it.

The mix of politics, principle, and prejudice in Johnson's veto include his denial of the nation's adequacy to play any part in intrastate relationships, and his insistence that Congress could only accede to what he had done in resurrecting a baker's-dozen states. Johnson's assertion that freed Americans could be free Americans when their states' laws denied them the minimal remedies and responsibilities freedom entailed was contradicted daily by testimony accumulating before Congress's committees.

Significantly, the veto inspired congressional Republicans to attempt overriding, another constitutional exercise rarely performed in American history. Only a single Senate vote prevented the gambit from being effective. Republicans in Congress turned with renewed determination to extending the Bureau's life and work (a slightly revamped extension bill passed over another veto in mid-July, 1866), to passing the Civil Rights statute, and to formulating a fourteenth constitutional amendment that would answer present objections and future needs.

The Republicans' irritation with the President derived from their conviction that in the Bureau bill they had discovered a formula to preserve state-based federalism, not destroy it, and had answered Johnson's appeal in his December message for decency toward freedmen sensitively. By basing the bill on the nation's war powers which, presumably, Congress shared with the executive, the congressmen avoided clashes over the status of the President's southern states in favor of stipulating how those states should reconstruct themselves enough to deserve Capitol Hill recognition. Johnson knew that Congress intended the Bureau bill only as an interim fill-in for the Civil Rights measure then under consideration; that the two were Siamese twins.[18]

---

18. Brock, *American Crisis*, 106; the veto is in *M&P*, VI, 398–405; see comments in *CG*, 39 Cong., 1 sess., 364–6, 523; for the July 1866 bill see *SAL*, XIV, 173; McFeely, *Yankee Stepfather*, 239–43, 267; L. and J. H. Cox, *Politics, Principle, and Prejudice, 1865–1866* (Glencoe, Ill., 1963), chs. 8–10.

Anticipating that the President would approve the Bureau bill, after prolonged and intense debate congressmen included Bureau personnel in the enforcement machinery of the still-unpassed Civil Rights bill. In one as in the other, what was to be enforced were national assurances against discriminatory intra-state disabilities through broadened appeal roads from state to national courts. Republican congressmen felt that they had successfully accommodated the War's constitutional impact.

Congressmen were convinced that the dangers of 1866, like those of 1861, emanated from the states. Flanks protected by the "old" Freedmen's Bureau and Grant's General Order #3, on March 13 Congress passed the first Civil Rights bill in the nation's history. Unlike the temporary "war powers" Bureau, the Civil Rights bill, based on the Thirteenth Amendment, was to be a permanent addition to federal-state relationships. Therefore the Republican drafters concentrated on restraining, as softly and invisibly as possible, state diminutions of specified civil rights basic to the practice of freedom. Senator Henry Wilson set the theme; the Thirteenth Amendment and the Civil Rights bill referred "to the rights which belong to men as citizens of the United States and none other."

This seemingly simple formula was to complicate constitutional law from the 1873 Slaughterhouse decision to the 1968 Jones case on to the present, and basically affect the history of race relations and the quality of democracy. Certainly, as Professor Kelly makes clear, in 1866 Congress was not embarked on diminishing traditional dual-citizenship characteristics of Americans' lives.[19] In part for this reason, the Republican drafters of the 1866 bill did not define national "civil rights and immunities." Opponents to the proposal rang the changes on the impossibility of doing so.[20]

Congressmen could not make precise what constitutional

---

19. Wilson in *CG*, 39 Cong., 1 sess., 1294; Kelly, "The Fourteenth Amendment Reconsidered: The Segregation Question," *MichLR*, LIV (1956), esp. 1061 and ns. 46–7. In Jones v. . . . Mayer Co., 392 409 @ 421 (1968) the Supreme Court, revitalizing the 1866 Act, determined that it was re-enacted in the 1870 Force Act and that, enduring as cited, was effective in 1968, minus the words "any law . . . notwithstanding." Kohl, "Civil Rights Act," 284, 300. For criticism of Kohl's argument and of the Court's opinion in the Jones case, see Benedict, "The Right Way," p. 683, n. 53.

20. See esp. Kerr in *CG*, 39 Cong., 1 sess., 1270–1 (March 8, 1866).

law and history had left vague; national prescriptions could not define the sum of intrastate practices, procedures, and remedies then almost wholly uncodified. Instead Republicans assumed that as a consequence of the War, intrastate equality of legal treatment should exist in their constitutionally governed federal system, as intrinsic parts of each state's constitution, laws, and customs. Writing to Lieber, Horace Binney stated the assumption best:

> The question remains, what are the privileges and immunities of free citizens—or [of] subjects without personal disability [such as conviction for crime]? I answer in the words of the Declaration of Independence—that among these endowments by the Creator are life, liberty, & the pursuit of happiness. In other words, to do what all who are under no disability can do—disability by nature, or disability imposed by law on all in the same condition of freedom—that is, by equal laws, in the general sense; for unequal laws in the special sense, are not law but usurpation upon law. . . . [C]itizens generally are in like circumstances unrestrained, so are citizens emancipated from slavery. The privileges and immunities in all free citizens by . . . [reason?] of the law, became inherent in . . . the emancipated slaves, & without further act of law, than the emancipation itself. To sue and be sued, make contracts—acquire property, give evidence, &c, &c.[21]

The pervasiveness of these assumptions are illustrated by what the Republican majority included in its Civil Rights bill, concerning which *The Nation* editorialized: "In the name of heaven and humanity, what *are* civil rights if those which . . . [Congress] have enumerated are not included under that term?" Congress defined citizenship in a manner to inter Taney's 1857 Dred Scott exclusion of blacks from that status. Except as punishment for crimes, the bill continued, "such citizens, of every race and color [excluding untaxed Indians], without regard to any previous condition of slavery or involuntary servitude, shall have the same right, in every state and Territory . . . to make and enforce contracts, to sue, be parties, and give evidence, to

---

21. Horace Binney to Francis Lieber, Apr. 11, 1866, Box 51, LI-917, Lieber Papers, HL; and see Walter Lippman, *The Method of Freedom* (New York, 1934), 100–2; Paludan, "Law and the Failure of Reconstruction," 610–14.

inherit, purchase, lease, sell, hold, and convey real and personal property, and to full and equal benefit to all laws and proceedings for the security of person and property, as is enjoyed by white citizens, and shall be subject to like punishment, pains, and penalties, and to none other, any law, statute, ordinance, regulation, or custom, to the contrary notwithstanding."

Subsequent sections provided for exclusive federal district court trials of violators and set punishments of up to a thousand dollars and/or one year in prison. National district and circuit courts were to have concurrent jurisdiction of criminal and civil litigations begun in states' courts "affecting persons who are denied or cannot enforce . . . any of the rights secured to them by the first section of this act." But since the federal statute books were thin on many categories of intrastate behavior, especially crimes, federal judges should employ relevant state statutes and state judge-made "common law" not repugnant to the bill's purposes or to national equivalents.

Congress stipulated that any suit begun in a state court against a person enforcing the Civil Rights act or the Freedmen's Bureau bill, or against a person refusing to enforce state law inconsistent with the Civil Rights bill, was removable on defendants' option to the appropriate national district or circuit court. Removal procedures were those specified for national officer-defendants in the March 3, 1863 Habeas Corpus law.

Delighted at the opportunity to employ for civil rights protection mechanisms similar to those stipulated in 1850 for fugitive slave renditions, congressmen provided in 1866 that national attorneys, commissioners, and marshals enforce the Civil Rights bill with assistance from Freedmen's Bureau personnel "and every other officer who may be specially empowered by the President," meaning, apparently, the Army obedient to Grant's General Order #3. Now the government could be the plaintiff; enforcement officials could institute court prosecutions against violators; poor freedmen and junior civil and military officers would not have to stand the costs of litigation. And the historic bill closed with this further augmentation of national court jurisdiction: "That upon all questions of law arising . . . under this act a final appeal may be taken to the Supreme Court of the United States."[22]

---

22. SAL, XIV, 27; The Nation (Apr. 5, 1866), 422–3; and see U.S. Code, Annotated (1964), sec. 1982.

Again President Johnson decided to veto. He depicted Congress as creating a corpus of positive national civil rights instead of the negatively defined intrastate uniformity that lawmakers were actually trying to insure. The President charged with some justice that the Civil Rights bill gave blacks more than whites, but he ignored the fact that states took more from blacks than whites. Concerning slavery's hangover incidents, the President pretended that in the ex-rebel states the freedman "has equal power in settling [with whites] the terms [of life and labor] and if left to the [natural] laws that regulate capital and labor it is confidently believed that they will satisfactorily work out the problem. This bill frustrates the adjustment." The bill demeaned states, lessened federalism's vitality, increased centralization, and weakened the tripartite separation of powers along the Potomac, Johnson continued. Then the President promised that though he must veto the bill at hand, he would "cheerfully cooperate with Congress" in any measure to strengthen civil rights of all Americans "by judicial process throughout the United States."[23]

On April 9, the Senate (33–15) and House (122–41) overrode the veto. The nation's first Civil Rights bill was law.[24] Retrospectively, it appears difficult to credit the President's inability to see what an obscure North Carolina editor perceived; that Congress intended the Civil Rights law to "take away that objectionable feature from the Freedmen's Bureau, the committing of judicial powers to comparatively inexperienced agents," and to speed "the full restoration of those [southern] States to their lost equality in the Union."[25] All that the law stipulated was that in each state, free Americans enjoy the same remedies as other residents with respect to that state's own procedures and laws; that intrastate freedom be the condition of law. Nevada's Senator William Stewart hit the nail precisely during the debates: "When I reflect how very easy it is for the States to avoid the operations of this bill, how very little they have to do to avoid the operations of this bill entirely, I think that it is robbed of its coercive features."[26]

---

23. *M&P*, VI, 412–13.

24. *CG*, 39 Cong., 1 sess., 1809, 1861.

25. Raleigh, N.C., *Progress*, undated, quoted in *The American Freedman*, II (June 1866) 47.

26. *CG*, 39 Cong., 1 sess., 1785 (Apr. 5, 1866). On "robbing" note U.S. v. Blyew and Kinnard, 13 Wall., 642 (1872). The Supreme Court decided that black would-be witnesses to a Kentucky murder involving

This "robbing" derived from the Republicans' persistence on the Reconstruction way found in the March 1863 Habeas Corpus Act and the 1864 Wade-Davis bill, leading from injustices to better justice. Few nations have transferred equally beneficent wartime lessons to postwar contexts. Having made the shift and viewing it in satisfied manner, Republicans estimated that the War's final carryovers were well on their way to solutions, although final internment for slavery's intrastate incidents was still necessary. The Republicans assumed that they had all that was wanted to complete obsequies for the hated institution. Celebrating the Civil Rights bill's enactment into law, Freedmen's Bureau Commissioner Howard believed that it "will enable us to regulate the judicial features of our work without difficulty."[27]

---

whites did not enjoy the Civil Rights law's removal protections because the Negroes were not primarily "affected" in their personal or property rights by the fact that Kentucky statutes forbade Negro testimony in state courts. See also R. A. Webb, "Benjamin H. Bristow: Civil Rights Champion, 1866–1872," *CWH*, XV (1969), 51.

27. O. O. Howard to Gen. A. Baird, April 9, 1866, Letterpress Copies of Letters Sent, Commissioner's Office, Vol. II, #301, RG 105, NA.

Chapter XXVI

Wise Restraints
to Make Men Free

Howard was oversanguine. But it is the essence of mid-1866 that so many other influential, informed Republicans also believed that an end to ideology had been won. The Freedmen's Bureau Act, the Civil Rights law, and the Habeas Corpus statute provided what appeared to be appropriately effective minimal mechanisms for protecting the nation's citizens and officials with respect to certain state relationships and policies. As a bonus, these laws would enforce the proposed Fourteenth Amendment as well as the still-new Thirteenth.

A conservative tradition flourished at once that the new statutes and Amendments were unconnected. Jeremiah Sullivan Black, Buchanan's former Attorney General, insisted to the United States Supreme Court that the Amendments were wholly self-executing and that enforcement, even of the sort the Bureau and Civil Rights laws provided, was neither required nor permitted.

The counterargument, offered by Thaddeus Stevens in Congress and United States Attorney Benjamin Bristow before the Supreme Court, was better. From what Bristow described as "the history of the time . . . [and] the objects to be accomplished" by the Reconstruction Amendments and statutes, the conclusion is justified that Congress created the statutes as machinery for the Amendments.[1]

---

1. See *CG*, 39 Cong., 1 sess., 2459, for Thaddeus Stevens; for Benjamin Bristow, E. A. Webb, "Benjamin H. Bristow: Civil Rights Champion,

Bristow's test and assumptions argue that whatever else the Fourteenth Amendment was supposed to accomplish—jurists and scholars still contest this matter bitterly—high among Republicans' priorities was the need to make certain impacts of the Civil War and Reconstruction more permanent. At the heart of the matter were state restorations and improved relationships between the nation, states, and citizens of the sort spelled out in the 1866 Civil Rights law. Congress also wanted limits on the white South's increased congressional strength created by abolition of the three-fifths clause. By failing to represent "the whole number of persons in each State," a state initiated its own punishment of decreased congressional representation, and simultaneously possessed the means to cut it off.[2]

1866–1872," *CWH*, XV (1969), 48; Jeremiah Sullivan Black, *Constitutionality of the Civil Rights Bill: Argument for the State of Kentucky, the United States v. Blyew et al., for Murder* (Washington, 1871), 5, 24. A fateful refinement accepted by the Supreme Court in the Slaughterhouse Cases, 16 Wall., 36 (1873), and in U.S. v. Cruikshank, 92, US, 542 (1876), was that enforcement of the Amendments, especially of the Fourteenth Amendment's prohibitions against state abridgments of national citizens' privileges and immunities, was primarily up to states. With respect to the Amendment's due process and equal protection clauses, Justice Bradley in the Cruickshank decision held that Congress could merely provide machinery for defeating prohibited state actions. See C. B. Swisher, "Dred Scott: One Hundred Years After," *JPoli*, XIX (1957), 173; P. Paludan, "Law and the Failure of Reconstruction: The Case of Thomas Cooley," *JHI*, XXXIII (1972), 611.

2. Of the enormous literature on the purposes of the Fourteenth Amendment's supporters see esp. C. Fairman, "Does the Fourteenth Amendment Incorporate the Bill of Rights? The Original Understanding," *StLR*, II (1949), 5; W. W. Van Alstyne, "The Fourteenth Amendment, the 'Right' to Vote, and the Understanding of the Thirty-Ninth Congress," *SCR* (1965), 33, esp. n. 11. A. H. Kelly, "Clio and the Court: An Illicit Love Affair," *ibid.*, 119 *ff.*, esp. 133–4, offers the most penetrating and useful analysis, and I rely heavily on its data and conclusions. Here is the Amendment's text:

SECTION 1. All persons born or naturalized in the United States, and subject to the jurisdiction thereof, are citizens of the United States and of the State wherein they reside. No State shall make or enforce any law which shall abridge the privileges or immunities of citizens of the United States; nor shall any State deprive any person of life, liberty, or property, without due process of law; nor deny to any person within its jurisdiction the equal protection of the laws.

SECTION 2. Representatives shall be apportioned among the several States according to their respective numbers, counting the whole number of persons in each State, excluding Indians not taxed. But when the right to vote at any election for the choice of electors for President and Vice-President of the

As it was, the constrained Republican consensus of 1866 involved profound alterations in nation-state relationships. In addition to the Civil Rights law's catalogue, the nation now forbade—or would forbid once ratification occurred—certain inequitable intrastate practices which the states defined themselves. By the Fourteenth Amendment's terms the legal processes (procedures) due equally as protection and remedy to each national citizen were the laws and procedures of a citizen's state. Instead of formulating positively national civil-rights minima, as some Republican Radicals preferred to do, the Amendment forbade unequal deprivations of the broad, uncodified, vague mass of civil-rights practices which a state professed to afford equally to the generality of its citizens. Thus the Amendment assumed the familiar negative cast of the 1787 Constitution's Bill of Rights without specifying bills of wrongs for every state. The states would do that job. At a given moment a state's laws, constitutions, procedures, and customs would be the catalogue of what a

---

United States, Representatives in Congress, the executive and judicial officers of a State, or the members of the legislature thereof, is denied to any of the male inhabitants of such State, being twenty-one years of age, and citizens of the United States, or in any way abridged, except for participation in rebellion, or other crime, the basis of representation therein shall be reduced in the proportion which the number of such male citizens shall bear to the whole number of male citizens twenty-one years of age in such State.

Section 3. No person shall be a Senator or Representative in Congress, or elector of President and Vice-President, or hold any office, civil or military, under the United States or under any State, who, having previously taken an oath as a member of Congress, or as an officer of the United States, or as a member of any State legislature, or as an executive or judicial officer of any State, to support the Constitution of the United States, shall have engaged in insurrection or rebellion against the same, or given aid or comfort to the enemies thereof. But Congress may, by a vote of two-thirds of each house, remove such disability.

Section 4. The validity of the public debt of the United States, authorized by law, including debts incurred for payment of pensions and bounties for services in suppressing insurrection or rebellion, shall not be questioned. But neither the United States nor any State shall assume or pay any debt or obligation incurred in aid of insurrection or rebellion against the United States, or any claim for the loss or emancipation of any slave; but all such debts, obligations, and claims shall be held illegal and void.

Section 5. The Congress shall have power to enforce, by appropriate legislation, the provisions of this article.

state must not deny selectively to its free Americans. As in the Civil Rights law, states could turn off a national presence by equalizing official intrastate life styles. In the absence of a national monitoring system over state behavior, much less over private acts of the sort forbidden, the Amendment relied on individuals to secure their rights through private case-by-case litigation, alleging each time state denial of a claimed federal right.[3]

In one sense this formlessness reflected political realism. Even if Congress never again entered the intrastate civil-rights arena—a consummation devoutly desired, however varied the reasons, in almost all sectors of Capitol Hill—the Fourteenth Amendment, the Civil Rights law, and attendant legislation including the Freedmen's Bureau and Habeas Corpus statutes, apparently provided acceptable, on-hand, unabrasive enforcers in the national courts. In remarkable unity of purpose, in sensitive reaction to history reaching back to abolitionists' prewar frustrations and aspirations, and in nervous concern over the unfathomable future, the framers of the Fourteenth Amendment had created a virtually machineless machine.[4]

But in another sense the Amendment's framers struck out. Hindsight suggests that the most correct Republicans of 1866 were the Radicals, who, though supporters of the Fourteenth Amendment in its final form, insisted that it was inadequate to the nation's needs and duties, and criticized the Amendment's tight ties to the Civil Rights law's case-by-case litigation commitment.

Early in the War Senator Henry Winter Davis had stressed the need for national habeas-corpus levers to pry prisoners and litigants who were unfairly treated out of states' courts and jails,

---

3. Paludan, "Law and the Failure of Reconstruction," 611–14. Another decade passed of white resistance to the laws before, in the 1875 Civil Rights law, Congress prohibited private discrimination based on race. In 1883 the Supreme Court declared this 1875 extension unconstitutional. In our time private as well as official discrimination invoke national limitations on states. Kelly, "Clio and the Court," 149; Kelly, "The Congressional Controversy over School Segregation, 1865–1875," *AHR*, LXVI (1959), 537 *ff.*; and see Kohl, "Civil Rights Act," 283–4; M. L. Benedict, "The Right Way, Congressional Republicans and Reconstruction, 1863–1869" (Ph.D. diss., RU, 1971), 692, n. 30-a; Evans v. Abney, 396 US, 435 (1970).
4. J. ten Broek, "Thirteenth Amendment . . . Consummation to Abolition and Key to Fourteenth Amendment," *CalifLR*, XXXIX (1951), 171; Bernard Schwartz, *Statutory History of the United States: Civil Rights* (New York, 1970) I, 293, and see 310.

and he had returned to this insight in the 1864 Wade-Davis bill. Following a parallel track, Senator Sumner tried to waken the Constitution's "sleeping giant," the stipulation (Article IV, section 4) that the nation guarantee each state a republican form of government. Acknowledging that the meaning of the guarantee clause was as obscure as the definition of civil rights, Sumner insisted to Lieber in 1865 that "The time has come to fix meaning to those words. My point is that liberty, equality before the law, and the consent of the governed are essential elements of a republican government." Contrasted with the relatively placid posture the nation assumed in the Civil Rights law–Fourteenth Amendment formulations in which states defined the conditions of liberty, Sumner wanted the nation to set positive standards. And he insisted that Congress, not the federal judiciary, was properly the court in the last resort to determine intrastate conditions.

In addition to such congressional champions, self-assertedly apolitical legal giants reached similar conclusions. Isaac N. Redfield, the former Vermont chief justice, was an early reinforcement to the guarantee-clause ranks. He favored positive national enforcement of the Constitution's guarantee-clause responsibility. The notion evoked a passionate counterblast from Joel Parker, who insisted that the War "has given no new meaning to the [guarantee] clause of the Constitution." Parker worried that if the nation attempted actively to enforce civil liberty, individuals' civil rights would be lost as the state's primacy in the federal system and the nation's separation of powers lessened.[5]

---

5. Charles Sumner to Francis Lieber (Oct. 12, Dec. 13, 1865), in E. L. Pierce, *Memoir and Letters of Charles Sumner* (Boston, 1877–93), IV, 258–9, 269; see also G. S. Henig, "Henry Winter Davis: A Biography" (Ph.D. diss., CUNY, 1971), 252; C. O. Lerche, Jr., "Congressional Interpretations of the Guarantee of a Republican Form of Government During Reconstruction," *JSH*, XV (1949), 192–7; W. M. Wiecek, "The Guarantee Clause of the United States Constitution: 'A Sleeping Giant'" (Ph.D. diss., UWis, 1968), 158–73, now a book of the same main title (Ithaca, 1972); David Donald, *Charles Sumner and the Rights of Man* (New York, 1970), 260. On Republican factions, see Benedict, "The Right Way," 274–7, and L. G. Kincaid, "The Legislative Origins of the Military Reconstruction Act, 1865–1867" (Ph.D. diss., JHU, 1968), chs. 1–4 *passim;* other data in Emory Washburn, "Reconstruction: The Duty of the [Legal] Profession to the Times," *MLRep,* XXVI (1864), 477–84; I. F. Redfield, *Letter to Senator Foot upon the Points Settled by the War* (New York, 1865), *passim;* Joel Parker, *Revolution and Reconstruction: Two Lectures . . . . Law*

During 1866 the congressional Republicans harmonized the divergent but never exclusive approaches represented by the civil-rights-state-determination-"restoration" majority and the guarantee-clause-national-stipulation-"Reconstruction" champions; the former was clearly ascendant. Perhaps satisfaction in the accomplishments of 1866 explains best the Republicans' corporate unwillingness to travel then any road more rugged than the Civil Rights–Freedmen's Bureau extension–Fourteenth Amendment route that left the states masters of their fates.

This contemporary judgment was neither hypocritical nor irrelevant. Republicans built better than many contemporaries believed was possible in a nation only eighty years old, about whose governance so much was unclear. The Republican congressmen reflected deep existing divisions concerning the nation's quality and direction. But their nationalistic theory and addiction to interconnecting amendments and statutes help a century later to provide better equality.[6]

However, in 1866 most Republicans believed that they had won what we still struggle to achieve. They boasted, to cite NYU Law School Dean John N. Pomeroy, of having more clearly defined "the true relations of the nation and the states." And they asserted confidently, as the Attorney General of the United States assured a questioner about the Civil Rights Act's constitutionality, that the nation's judges would settle the matter as all others; that securing blacks' civil rights against states' actions did not lessen the traditional civil liberties which whites enjoyed.[7]

Republicans derived added pride from their Reconstruction approach because, developing in response to harsh state policies and state court judgments, it retained the uncoercive characteristics contemporaries admired. In sum, the Republican commitment was to law's due processes, both to provide national citizens with equality in their states' legal protections, privileges, and immunities, and to insure national officials better protection

---

School of Harvard College, January, 1865, and January, 1866 (New York, 1866), 80, and passim; and also by Parker, The Three Powers of Government . . . Lectures . . . in the Law School of Harvard College and in Dartmouth College, 1867–68, and '69 (New York, 1869), 12–17 and passim.

6. Schwartz, Statutory History, I, 9, 182.

7. Pomeroy, An Introduction to the Constitutional Law of the United States (2nd edn., New York, 1870), 504; Chief Clerk M. F. Pleasants [for the Attorney General] to J. L. Williamson, June 2, 1866, Attorney General's Letterbook F, RG 60, NA.

against antagonisms of state police, judges, and juries. The basic Republican method was to build, enlarge, and improve jurisdictional-removal bridges from state to national courts. It was a commitment and method so compelling that every congressional statute enacted during Reconstruction that dealt with the enforcement of national laws or the securing of rights under the 1787 Constitution contained clauses appropriate to these ends.[8]

On May 11, 1866, in an amendment to the now-creaking 1863 Habeas Corpus law, Congress tried the better to shield Army and Bureau officers from state court harassments, to block state judges from impeding operations of the national courts and laws, and to decrease dependence of the nation's civilian branches on the Army. In relationship only to acts committed before passage of the May 1866 amendment, national officers no longer needed to prove possession of direct orders from the President as justification for the alleged assault, imprisonment, search, seizure, or trespass. Any superior officer's instructions were to be considered as delegated orders from the President. A defendant could remove his case to a United States circuit court at any point in a state trial, even after judgment was levied against him. If a state court insisted on proceeding with the litigation, Congress provided that "all such further proceedings shall be void . . . and all [state] parties, judges, officers, and other persons, thenceforth proceeding . . . shall be liable [doubly] in damages therefor to the party aggrieved." Damage actions could proceed either in that state's appeal court or in the United States circuit court for that state.[9]

Congress responded also to complaints by other executive branches than the Army about state courts' interferences. In order to protect defendant revenue officers or individuals holding property titles derived from revenue clauses of other laws, in 1866 Congress permitted pretrial removals from state to national

---

8. William Wiecek, "The Reconstruction of Federal Judicial Power, 1863–1875" (M.A. thesis, UWis, 1968), 18; Wiecek's article of the same title, *AJLH*, XIII (1969), 333–59.

9. *SAL*, XIV, 46; and see Mayor v. Cooper, 73 US, 247 (1868). On defects in the 1863 Habeas Corpus law, see J. B. Fry to E. M. Stanton, and to James Wilson, Jan. 6, 1866, in HR 39A–F13.7, RG 233, NA, used by courtesy of the Clerk, House of Representatives.

courts, as well as removal in suits already begun. If a state court refused to obey a federal habeas corpus writ or to transfer records, the plaintiff had to commence his suit anew in national courts or incur nonsuit judgment. And the plaintiff's questioning in a state court of the revenue statute's validity justified removal of the suit to federal court.[10]

The symbiotic relationships growing between Congress and the national courts, in which the latter served the nation as the primary executor of federal law, is illustrated again in the July 27, 1866 Separable Controversies Act. It concerned matters not necessarily involved in Reconstruction or race, but which reflected also state court animosity to national jurisdictions. In annoying number and frequency, southern state judges were lending themselves to a legal fiction of nondiversity or inadequate diversity which shrewd plaintiffs' lawyers were asserting in order to defeat defendants' removals to federal courts. Under diversity requirements of the 1789 judiciary act, as interpreted rigidly in Marshall's 1806 Strawbridge v. Curtiss decision, shared residence in a state by any two defendants in a litigation aborted removal. Therefore plaintiffs contrived to join a fictional defendant resident of the same state as the actual defendant, who often was a national officer.

To curtail this shystering, the Separable Controversies law provided that in litigation involving at least five hundred dollars, a defendant could remove that part of the suit to federal courts which except for the technical lack of diversity allowed federal court jurisdiction. Wholly state issues stayed below in state courts along with other defendants.[11]

---

10. H. McCulloch to Trumbull, July 9, 1866. Letterbook to . . . Members of Congress, IX, set E, pp. 70–1, RG 56, NA: *SAL*, XIV, 171; Wiecek, "Reconstruction," 20–1, esp. n. 38. By providing also Supreme Court review for United States Court of Claims appeals (earlier, review was an administrative function of the Treasury Secretary) and augmenting also the bankruptcy and admiralty jurisdictions of the national judiciary, in 1866 and 1867 Congress further tightened its ties with the courts. *Ibid.*, 119–95, esp. 138 *ff.*; C. A. Wright, *Handbook of the Law of Federal Courts* (2nd edn., St. Paul, Minn., 1970), 10.

11. *SAL*, XIV, 306; Wiecek, "Reconstruction," 23–5; Wright, *Federal Courts*, 136; Strawbridge v. Curtiss, 3 Cranch, 267 (1806). In 1875 (*SAL*, XVIII, 470), Congress provided that if separability existed, the entire suit was removable; an arrangement enduring until 1948 (Wright, *op. cit.*, 136 n.). See also 28 US Code, Annotated, sec. 1441-C; J. F. Dillon, *Removal of Causes from State Courts to Federal Courts* (St. Louis, 1889), 24–6; J.

The Civil Rights statute and, by implication, the Fourteenth Amendment cast aggrieved national citizens and responsible national officers as plaintiffs in state courts. Evidence accumulated swiftly through the last half of 1866 that "foreign" plaintiffs often enjoyed little chance of substantive justice in state proceedings. Therefore, on March 2, 1867, the same day the exasperated Congress resorted to "Military Reconstruction," it further altered traditional nation-state judicial relationships in favor of the former. A "local prejudice" law of that date allowed nonresident plaintiffs, as well as defendants in state court litigation involving issues of national rights, to remove to national courts. Before state court proceedings began, either litigant could file in an appropriate federal court an affidavit "stating that he has reason to, and does believe that from prejudice or local influence, he will not be able to obtain justice in such state court."[12]

Meanwhile, on February 5, 1867, President Johnson signed two habeas corpus bills which, vitally altering the nature of the writ, set the outer limits for the constitutional impacts of the Civil War and Reconstruction that centrist Republicans wished to allow. The first of the laws amended the 1866 and 1863 Habeas Corpus statutes. Congress designed it like its predecessors to cope with the temporary impediments which southern state judges were raising by detaining defendant Army and Bureau officers. The 1867 amendment provided that when a suit begun in a state court was removable by terms of the 1863 and/or 1866 statutes, and state authorities (judges primarily) refused to release defendants (usually Army or Freedmen's Bureau officials) from state custody, the defendant could seek a habeas corpus cum causa writ from a national circuit court.

This statute had larger implications. The 1866 Civil Rights law applied the removals procedures of the 1863 Habeas Corpus

---

Clifford, in Sewing Machine Companies Case, 18 Wall., 583. E. Weisel, RU doctoral student, aided research on this statute.

12. *SAL*, XIV, 558 (March 2, 1867). In form, this was an amendment to the July 27, 1866 law. J. Field in Gaines v. Fuentes, 92 US 10 (1875), at 19; Wiecek, "Reconstruction," 25–8. Here, Dillon wrote, was new ground in that it afforded a right to a plaintiff to leave the state forum he had chosen originally. With some justice, critics insisted that any losing plaintiff's lawyer would raise the cry of prejudice. Nevertheless the new law so satisfied Congressmen's primary purpose that efforts failed to repeal it and the Supreme Court sustained its constitutionality. Dillon, *Removal*, 27–31; Chicago & N. W. Ry. Co. v. Whitton's Admr., 13 Wall., 270 (1871).

Act and of subsequent amendments. Therefore in effect Congress attached the "first" of the February 1867 Habeas Corpus laws to the Civil Rights statute; a citizen as well as officials could employ the new removal procedure after he exhausted state alternatives and other removal channels and was still in state custody.

The "second" Habeas Corpus law of February 5, 1867 was even more important. It amended not Civil War statutes but the historic limitation on national judicial power in the 1789 Judiciary Act that "the writ of *habeas corpus* shall in no case extend to [state] prisoners in jail, unless they are in custody under or by color of the authority of the United States, or are committed to trial before some court of the same." The 1789 stipulation barred federal judges from questioning state judges concerning persons in custody by using habeas corpus as a writ of error; the second 1867 law allowed removals "where any person may be restricted of his or her liberty in violation of the constitution, or of any treaty or law of the United States." State court detention became an independent basis for a federal judge to order removal, regardless of the point reached in the state trial, even if a verdict was in, and disregarding whether the prisoner had sought removal by other legislative or judicial means. Thus Congress transformed the historic writ into a tool more appropriate to federalism. Using it a national judge could re-examine at least some federal questions involved in the facts that had resulted in conviction by state jurists and juries.[13]

Salmon P. Chase was to say mistakenly of this law that it was "of the most comprehensive character. It brings within the habeas corpus jurisdiction of every [federal] court and of every federal judge every possible case of deprivation of liberty contrary to the National Constitution, treaties or laws. It is impossible to widen this jurisdiction." In 1868, legal scholar Pomeroy pointed to the "perfect [nationalistic] theory" incorporated into

---

13. *SAL*, XVI, 385, 385–7, respectively. Note the Court's reluctance to employ the augmented appeal jurisdiction in instances when state criminal convictions rested on independent state grounds, even if a federal question was involved; Murdock v. Memphis, 87 US 590 (1875). Wiecek, "The Great Writ and Reconstruction: The Habeas Corpus Act of 1867," *JSH*, XXVI (1970), 530–48; A. Bestor, "The Two Habeas Corpus Acts of the Fifth of February, 1867, and their Untoward Sequel, the McCardle Case" (OAH paper, 1966); C. Tarrant, "A Writ of Liberty or a Covenant with Hell: Habeas Corpus in the War Congresses, 1861–1867" (Ph.D. diss., RU, 1972), have other data.

the second 1867 law, allowing retention of state-national court concurrency in many matters but also establishing clear national court primacy in the newly opened civil-rights arena. Anything less would "reject the very idea of one nationality," Pomeroy asserted. And within fifteen years, an American Bar Association president, unhappy with the enormous growth in national court business which the second 1867 law encouraged, complained:

> As construed by the Federal Judges [1867–83], this provision has wiped out as with a sponge the proviso of the act of 1789; has clothed the district and circuit judges of the United States with power to annul the criminal processes of the states, to reverse and set aside by *habeas corpus* the criminal judgments of the state courts, to pass finally and conclusively upon the validity of the criminal codes, the police regulations, and even the constitutions of the states.[14]

Some hyperbole attends these observations. Almost all workaday aspects of life remained factors of state laws, procedures, and remedies. Unless a litigant could prove that his national rights were involved in them, no removal route opened by reason of Civil War and Reconstruction laws. And where situations such as litigants' diversity of residence allowed federal court jurisdiction in matters otherwise wholly state issues, national judges had as always to employ state laws, rules of procedure and precedents. "Here is plainly a vast field open for injustice and oppression by individual states, which the nation has now no means of preventing," Pomeroy warned.

Professor Wiecek insisted recently that the purposes of the law's framers are "unusually murky, even for a piece of Reconstruction legislation."[15] Congress was imperfect as legislative draftsman, but as navigator it deserves admiration. It aimed the second 1867 Habeas Corpus law, and the numerous other Recon-

---

14. Chase in Ex parte McCardle, 73 US (6 Wall.) 318 at 325–6; Pomeroy, *Introduction*, 507; Seymour D. Thompson, "Abuses of the Writ of Habeas Corpus," ABA *Reports*, VI (1883), 260–3.

15. Pomeroy, *Introduction*, 149–50; Wiecek, "The Great Writ," 539. On the score of murkiness, note Justice Jackson's comment: "Just what our forefathers did envision, or would have envisoned had they foreseen modern condition, must be divined from materials almost as enigmatic as the dreams Joseph was called upon to interpret for Pharoah." Concurring in Youngstown Sheet & Tube Co. v. Sawyer, 343 US, 579 (1952), at 634.

struction statutes linked to it, directly toward shores illuminated by the War. In continuing if sporadic search of viable rules of law for the centrifugal federal system, Republican congressmen pinned their hopes on state procedural conformity and intrastate procedural equality to enhance nationalism while retaining near-autonomy for states.[16] Convinced still that law and litigation would secure these ends, the lawmakers and their coadjutors, though frustrated by the resistance and impediments that rose up, drew back from the prospect of a more direct permanent national presence in states. Reviewing this scene in 1869, Amos T. Akerman agreed with Sumner that the United States was

> . . . never as national in practice as in theory. The late [constitutional] amendments certainly make it more national in theory. But I discover at Washington, even among republicans, a hesitation to exercise the powers [provided by the new amendments and connected statutes] to redress wrongs in the states. This surprised me. For unless the people become used to the exercise of these powers now, while the national spirit is still warm with the glow of the late war, there will be an indisposition to exercise these rights, and the "state right" spirit may grow troublesome again.[17]

It did. As Akerman indicated, Republicans were shocked at the whites' tenacious opposition to and frustration of their soft Reconstruction thrust; opposition which, as Freedmen's Bureau Commissioner Howard complained to Stanton, rendered "[freedmen's] citizenship a mere abstraction recognized technically, but utterly inoperative to secure them the exercise of the cardinal right[s] of a freedman or citizen."[18]

But even the well-documented southern white contumacy of the late 1860's never forced abandonment of the Republican commitment to prior litigation concerning state denials of federal rights before national intercession occurred. Potentialities in the Fourteenth Amendment's first section for positive national guarantees of intrastate due process and equality in legal privileges,

---

16. Note the 1872 "conformity act," by terms of which Congress specifically limited federal court pleadings and procedures to those obtaining in forum states save as direct contradictions existed with national opposites: *SAL*, XVII, 197 (1872), and see Wright, *Federal Courts*, 256–7.

17. To Sumner, April 2, 1869, Vol. 94, #4, Sumner Papers, HU; and see Benedict, "The Right Way," chs. 10–11.

18. Howard to Stanton, Dec. 1, 1866, Letterpress Copies of Letters Sent, Commissioner's Office, vol. II, #794, RG 105, NA.

immunities, and protections remained dormant for longer than appears now to have been reasonable. In Chief Justice Warren's 1966 opinion, the result was that Congress left the "advantages of time and inertia . . . [with] the perpetrators of the evil . . . [rather than with] its victims."[19]

If individual congressmen gained financially and/or politically from Reconstruction's workings out, the party majority in Congress adhered to their Reconstruction creations because they knew no more acceptable alternative. Their ties to notions of the rule of law and of state-centered federalism were too tight to modify them seriously in favor of more coercive national thrusts. Most Republicans were unable rationally or consistently to credit the vigor, variety, and viciousness of southern efforts to thwart the new Amendments and statutes. Misconceiving seriously the adequacy of governmental machinery to enforce law, as distinguished from constitutional adequacy, Republicans anticipated incorrectly the readiness of high national judges to leap with legislators from concerns over traditional civil liberties to new civil rights.

Regional resistance ranged from pettifogging obstructionism to individual and mass violence and intimidation directed against blacks and their white champions. In many instances, southern Negro victims who resorted to local police and state law found further hazard. Other obstructionists eschewed violence, as in the plot worked out by Francis P. Blair, Jr. He wanted Missouri conservatives to win writs from federal judges under the Civil Rights law, ostensibly to enforce national revenue statutes. Blair intended to use the writs against Missouri Republicans who dominated federally taxed liquor manufacturing. He expected the distillers to defy the writs, the judges to call in the Army, and Grant, thus involved, to break from the congressional Republicans.[20]

---

19. Warren, C. J., in S.C. v. Katzenbach, 383 US, 301 (1966), at 328; A. H. Kelly, "The Fourteenth Amendment Reconsidered: The Segregation Question," *MichLR* (1956), 1071–2; and see H. J. Graham, *Everyman's Constitution*, intro. 3–21, and *passim*.

20. F. P. Blair, Jr., to M. Blair, Dec. 21, 1866, item #1, Box 26, Blair-Lee Papers, PU; R. O. Curry, "Reconstruction Politics in Missouri," in *Radicalism, Racism, and Party Realignment*, ed. R. O. Curry (Baltimore, (1969), 18–19; Paludan, "Law and the Failure of Reconstruction," esp. 610–14.

In apparent deference to the Civil Rights law, Maryland's legislature repealed its black codes. Then it proceeded to indemnify state officials for expenses incurred in opposing the Civil Rights law and limited the jurisdiction of a state judge who asserted the validity of Congress's creation.[21]

Delaware supplied another variant. A Negro, accused of a crime, assaulted the state prosecutor. Delaware's statutes admitted blacks' testimony only if no competent white witness was available. In this instance the state prosecutor was also the chief witness with respect to the assault; the defense objected to his testimony, citing the Civil Rights law. Delaware's chief justice felt impelled to rule directly on the conflict between his state's law and the new national statute. Congress's Civil Rights law was unconstitutional "insofar as it attempts to prescribe rules of procedure, pleading, and evidence for State courts."[22] Of course, the Civil Rights law prescribed no such rules save as Delaware's failed the test of equal protection.

The United States Attorney General's office was the most glaring example of congressional reliance on inadequate enforcement institutions. In April 1866 Attorney General James Speed complained that "The entire legal labor of this Office, which is growing to be immense . . . devolves upon two persons." In prewar years even this minuscule professional staff, plus a few clerks, had so adequately performed the nation's legal work that Attorneys General maintained extensive supplemental private practices. "But now that Federal legislation superinduced by the altered conditions and new relations of the nation has grown into such massive proportions," private work was out and Speed needed trained assistance. He asked Congress for one more "Law Clerk"![23]

Speed was not disingenuous in implying that single reinforcement would permit adequate administration of the complex new laws; yet, if ever statutes needed systematic attention by competent lawyers, the Republicans' Reconstruction battery fit that bill. In April 1866 Speed anticipated that the President

---

21. C. L. Wagandt, "Maryland in the Post–Civil War Years," in *Radicalism*, ed. Curry, 153–61; *Pennsylvania Freedmen's Bulletin and American Freedman* (May 1867), 216.

22. State v. Rash, reported in *ALRev*, II (Jan., 1868), 345. The Civil Rights law received similar condemnations in several states' courts.

23. James Speed to W. P. Fessenden, April 7, 1866, Letterbook E, RG 60, NA; M. Storey and E. W. Emerson, *Ebenezer Rockwood Hoar: A Memoir* (Boston, 1911), 168.

would abandon obstructionism. Then southern white intransigence, taking its cue from the White House, would fade. Speed enjoyed slightly more control than earlier Attorneys General possessed over the semiautonomous federal attorneys in every congressional district, many of whom also followed White House winds, and he could hire distinguished private lawyers for extraordinary government litigation.

Such springtime hopes withered in the light of presidential obduracy, whereupon the accumulated defects of the nation's chief legal office evidenced themselves. They ranged from the fact that it lacked almost all professional reference books (yet successive incumbents failed to spend book-purchase budgets), to the self-enriching, fee-splitting corruptibility of many district attorneys. Despite the 1861 increase of the Attorney General's nominal authority, district attorneys remained unruly, a result of the unfortunate Bates years. Some district attorneys did not know how to conduct the simplest courtroom proceeding. Faced with responsibility to plead a Civil Rights law action, such spoilsmen floundered foolishly.[24]

In November 1865 the Attorney General had loaned to Horace Greeley the only complete text of South Carolina's black code in possession of the government, and had to wait until the publisher printed it before again enjoying possession of the entire text. Two years after Michigan passed an anti-adulteration statute for illuminants, the text was unavailable in Washington, although derivative litigation involving national interests was well under way. And concerning Congress's anticruelty-to-animals statute of March 1873, the incumbent Attorney General, doubtful of the validity of the "loose and indefinite" law, refused even to ask railroad companies' permission to have federal officers travel on their coaches while inspecting cattle-car conditions.[25]

---

24. Respectively, these matters are in Speed to Fessenden, April 7, 1866, Letterbook E, RG 60, NA; J. H. Ashton to R. Murry, Oct. 11, 1865, *ibid.*; J. H. Williams to James Garfield, then chairman of the House Appropriations Committee, Jan. 11, 1872, Letterbook A (Exec. and Cong.), *ibid.*, E. R. Hoar to S. A. Strickland, Apr. 20, 1869, Instruction Book A, *ibid.* See also National Association of Attorneys General, *The Office of Attorney General* (n.p., 1971), 19; M. L. Hinsdale, *A History of the President's Cabinet* (Ann Arbor, Mich., 1911), 217.

25. J. H. Ashton to Greeley, Nov. 18, 1865, Letterbook E, RG 60, NA: W. A. Field to A. B. Maynard, Dec. 20, 1869, Instruction Book A, *ibid.*; G. H. Williams to Lucian Prince, March 24, 1874, Letterbook K, *ibid.*

Energetic, talented, and innovative federal attorneys such as Amos Akerman and Benjamin Bristow existed. But most of their colleagues displayed less creative characteristics. Since the federal district attorneys and their nominal Washington chieftain shaped the contours of government litigation, often deciding which cases should be aborted or continue to maturity, the effects of these men on the legal and constitutional life of the times can only be conjectured.[26]

In 1872 the Attorney General asserted that Alabama's anti-mixed-marriage law did not violate the Civil Rights Act because the state punished equally whites and blacks desiring interracial marriage. Georgia's chain-gang sentences did not violate the Thirteenth Amendment's bar against involuntary servitude, according to an 1866 instruction from the Attorney General. Yet, in 1866 as in 1875, Attorneys General refused modestly to comment on state racial discriminations, including that of Negroes being denied a right to testify in state courts, because, ostensibly, federal judges, not attorneys, decided such matters.[27]

By no means were all federal attorneys hypocrites or racists. A few understood the defects in Congress's civil-rights enforcement construction; realized that, as Grant's Attorney General Akerman noted, "the sufferers of the crimes punishable by these Acts [of Congress] are, for the most part, poor and ignorant men, who do not know how to put the law in motion, or who have some well-grounded apprehension of danger to themselves from the attempt to enforce it." But Akerman's tentative proposal that Congress create full-time civil-rights surveillance officers fell flat.[28]

---

26. Webb, "Bristow," *loc. cit.*; E. Swinney, "Enforcing the Fifteenth Amendment," *JSH*, XXVIII (1962), 202–18. As example, Congress's 1867 antipeonage statute received little attention until near the end of the century, judicial comment did not issue until 1901. During the intervening thirty-five years, in the West where it counted, enforcement was so sporadic and uncertain as to make the statute virtually a nullity. Clyatt v. U.S., 197 US 207 (1901); P. Daniel, "Up from Slavery and Down to Peonage: The Alonzo Bailey Case," *JAH*, LVII (1970), 655; L. R. Murphy, "Reconstruction in New Mexico," *NMHR*, XLIII (1968), 99–115.

27. G. H. Williams to G. D. Allen, Aug. 11, 1873, Instruction Book D, RG 60, NA; O. H. Browning to President Johnson, March 28, 1868, Letterbook G, *ibid.*, on Kentucky; G. H. Williams to J. P. Southworth, Instruction Book C, *ibid.*, on Alabama; H. Stanbery to A. H. Garland, Feb. 5, 1867, Letterbook F, *ibid.*; E. Pierrepoint to Miss J. Huston, Oct. 11, 1875, Letterbook L, *ibid.*

28. Amos Akerman to C. Cole, Jan. 23, 1871, Letterbook H, *ibid.*

Like most Republicans of the late sixties and early seventies, federal law officers were satisfied with the Reconstruction way their congressmen discerned. This satisfaction extended to the consistently augmented parts and powers Congress assigned to the federal courts in Reconstruction and other national matters, and the heightened roles and authorities those courts assumed on their own. Attorney General E. R. Hoar's 1869 comment, "We must now get along as well as we can with the judicial system of the United States as we find it," expressed pleasure, not disappointment.[29]

Recent scholarship has reversed the traditional notion that Congress harassed, threatened, and intimidated the national judiciary so thoroughly as to justify ex-President Buchanan's lament that Chief Justice Chase dragged "the judicial ermine through the dust to propitiate radicals." A truer picture has emerged of Congress's frequent and systematic recourses to the national courts and to the latter's own generous jurisdictional increases.[30] This impressive bootstrapping, reflecting the prevalence of far more amity than acrimony between the federal courts and Congress, proved to be the source for Congress's basic error.

It derived essentially from the Supreme Court's unanticipated defenses of traditional—white men's—civil liberties beginning in the historic 1866–67 term, the first full sessions headed by Chase, just when Congress created the new civil-rights battery. Reaching back to wartime military arrests of disloyal civilians, in the famous Milligan decision the Court offered a ringing defense of civil-law supremacy. Treading next on Congress's toes, the Court ignored separation-of-power traditions. In the Garland decision, the Court voided its own 1865 rule, made obedient to Congress's earlier statutory requirement that lawyers practicing in federal courts subscribe the "ironclad" oath of past loyalty. Last, the Court thrust deeply into hallowed arenas of states' self-choices in the Cummings decision when it struck down a Mis-

---

29. Hoar to W. M. Bateman, Dec. 15, 1869, Instruction Book A, *ibid.*; G. F. Hoar, *Autobiography of Seventy Years* (New York, 1903), I, 254.

30. *Works of James Buchanan*, ed. J. B. Moore (Philadelphia, 1910), XI, 446. Cf. *ALReg*, n.s. VI (1867), 513; S. Kutler, *Judicial Power and Reconstruction Politics* (Chicago, 1968), chs. 5, 8, 9; H. Hollingsworth, "The Confirmation of Judicial Review under Taney and Chase" (Ph.D. diss., UT, 1966).

souri past loyalty-oath requirement specified in the state's new constitution for teachers and many other licensed persons.

In these decisions the jurists dredged up ancient common-law prohibitions contained in the Constitution against bills of attainder and ex post facto laws. Under certain conditions, the high Court proscribed civilian amenability to military justice while civil courts operated. But despite judicial restraint rhetoric[31] the Court was involved in an imperial adventure, not a meek restatement. Looking behind the stated intentions of Congress and a state constitutional convention, to qualify attorneys in national courts and Missouri teachers respectively, and re-examining in another landmark decision the realities of Indiana's wartime internal-security situation, the high Court performed substantive fact-finder roles. So doing, it employed judicial review techniques that Marshall and Taney never attempted. Congress was seeking the substance of intrastate civil rights; the Court stressed civil liberties.

White Americans enjoyed civil liberties primarily as the result of local government inactivity. But in 1866 the constitutional election process gave support to the proposition that national activism favoring all Americans' civil rights was necessary and proper.[32] Thrusting itself into modern history with its vigorous defenses of ancient liberties, the Court issued final decisions to Congress[33] and states concerning the legitimacy of their entries into new functional arenas ranging from teacher licensing to antitraveling-salesmen ordinances[34] to required watering

---

31. "The judicial can not prescribe to the legislative department . . . limitations upon the exercise of its acknowledged power. . . . The responsibility of the legislature is not to the courts, but to the people by whom its members are elected," Chase intoned for the Court in 1869. Veazie Bank v. Fenno, 8 Wall., 533 at 543 (1869).

32. Cf. H. M. Hyman, "Reconstruction and Political-Constitutional Institutions," and A. H. Kelly, "Comments on . . . Hyman's Paper," in *New Frontiers of the American Reconstruction,* ed. Hyman (Urbana, Ill., 1966), 36–7, 53–5.

33. As noted earlier, in the late sixties and early seventies the Court inhibited Congress's efforts to contain under the interstate commerce clause hazardous aspects of the new production and communications technologies; License Tax Cases 5 Wall., 462 (1867).

34. Concerning states' efforts under police powers to limit "foreign" traveling salesmen by imposition of discouraging and discriminatory municipal, county, and state license fees, some local merchants wished out-of-state salesmen to remain available, and joined wholesalers and manu-

stops for cattle in interstate commerce. Jurists of the Chase and Waite years were little impressed by congressmen's and states' reservations concerning the desirability of this imperial review growth, or by anti-Court language. The Supreme Court received steady support and continuing jurisdictional increases from Capitol Hill. A let-the-courts-do-it attitude permeated Congress, Representative Casserly complained during passage of the anticruelty-to-animals bill which he opposed. Whenever the constitutional question was raised in debate, "it is to the courts that we leave all questions finally."[35]

As the pattern of removal legislation makes clear, leaving it to the courts was precisely Congress's intention. The federal judges accepted the congressional nourishment happily, if even more slowly than many legislators wished, and under certain circumstances what Congress did not provide the jurists asserted on their own behalf. The reciprocation that rooted firmly in 1866–77 between the nation's lawmakers and jurists became a dominant public policy configuration of the remainder of the century.[36]

---

facturers in antilicensing associations. These organizations decided to defend Elias Ward, a New Jersey harness salesman who violated Maryland's licensing statute and suffered a prescribed fine. William M. Evarts, recently United States Attorney General and President Johnson's counsel in the impeachment, pleaded Ward's case in the United States Supreme Court after Maryland's highest court sustained the statute as a valid expression of a state's rights to garner through license fees, taxes otherwise uncollectible from nonresidents. In 1871, the United States Supreme Court decided instead that a state could not discriminate substantively against foreign tradesmen through license taxation, which bound states' taxing and regulatory powers in such fetters as national judges wished to tie. Ward v. Maryland, 12 Wall., 418 (1871). In 1887, in Robbins v. . . . Shelby County, 120 US, 489, the Court held substantively discriminatory a Tennessee statute that applied to citizens and non-Tennesseeans alike, for it impeded interstate commerce despite the equality, Justice Bradley stated. See Hollander, "Nineteenth Century Anti-Drummer Legislation in the United States," *BHR*, XXXVIII (1964), 494–500.

35. *CR*, 42 Cong., 2 sess., 4228–30, 4231–5; Congress was less virginal about police functions than Casserly indicated. In 1863 Congress allowed a Virginia railroad entry to the District of Columbia only if it excluded no person because of color; *SAL*, XII, 805 (1863); sustained in Washington, Alexandria, and Georgetown RR Co. v. Catherine Brown, 17 Wall., 445 (1873).

36. Issuing in 1881 his revised treatise on removals John Dillon wrote: "When considering the disposition of the Federal courts to strongly assert their own jurisdiction, the very high character which the Federal judiciary has always sustained, the great variety of questions coming before

By and large, national judges consistently sustained one after another of Congress's augmentations of removal powers for the federal courts. In the Supreme Court, for example, an 1867 decision upheld Congress's right to determine the national judiciary's exclusive jurisdiction. The next year, the Court determined that a state could not defeat removal to a national court as provided for by Congress, by confiding litigation to an inferior state forum such as a probate or domestic relations court, from which national judges normally rejected appeals. And it decided also that a state could not by statute bar removals to national courts if Congress allowed them, even if the state required a "foreign" corporation to promise not to seek removal of litigation as a condition of doing business there.[37]

But the Court's enlarged removal jurisdiction never brought the whole Civil Rights law, the keystone of the new Amendments' enforcement arch, in for adjudication. Therefore inferior federal judges and other law officers felt unsure about the nation's new civil-rights function, translated into concerns about constitutionality and jurisdictional proprieties. This interaction is best illustrated in an 1866 description by General E. O. C. Ord concerning a federal jurist in Arkansas, where state court inequities to blacks were distressingly clear and present. Acknowledging plaintively that "there is no other competent court [in Arkansas] which will do freedmen justice," the judge had confessed himself "doubtful of the jurisdiction of his Court [under the Civil Rights law]."[38]

Perhaps, if the United States Supreme Court had examined the 1866 Act reasonably soon after its passage, it would have sustained the statute. But, ironically, the Court withheld itself from decisional opportunities, in part because most lower federal courts (including Supreme Court members on circuit) forthrightly supported its validity and thus closed off final review opportunities. On circuit in 1867, Chief Justice Chase heard the

---

these courts . . . and the enhanced importance they have acquired through Congressional legislation extending their jurisdiction, both original and appellate," the new edition was justified. Dillon, *Removals*, unpaginated prefactory note; Kutler, *Judicial Power*, ch. 8.

37. The Moses Taylor, 4 Wall. (1874). See also Wiecek, "Reconstruction," 119–95.

38. Ord to Sumner, Dec. 29, 1886, v. 154, #26, Sumner Papers, HU.

appeal of a Maryland freedwoman, Elizabeth Turner, whose erstwhile masters kept her in service under the state's black-code apprenticeship statute. Chase pronounced the Civil Rights law constitutional. Brushing aside the conflict with the state law's apprenticeship façade, he looked into the substance of Miss Turner's life and found that despite emancipation, she remained the "property and interest" of her employers, little changed from her slave situation.[39]

In Kentucky, a white robber of a Negro woman's home claimed in local courts that she could not testify against him because Kentucky's laws forbade black witnesses against whites. She obtained removal under the Civil Rights law to Justice Swayne's United States Circuit Court, where a jury brought in a guilty verdict against the robber. His lawyer moved for arrest of judgment notwithstanding the verdict, arguing in legally logical alternatives that the indictment was defective; that if the indictment was sound Congress lacked jurisdiction; and that the Civil Rights law could not create rights or remedies because it was unconstitutional.

Swayne denied these allegations. Congress had enacted the Civil Rights law precisely to aid such persons as the Kentucky robbery victim. Kentucky's insistence that only the state and the criminal were involved in a robbery prosecution left this victim without a substantive remedy unless the nation opened its forums.

Turning to the question of constitutionality, Swayne noted that the Thirteenth Amendment was the first to restrain state action. He insisted that the nation's vengeanceless moderation in enacting the Thirteenth Amendment, plus the debts due to the South's blacks, be kept in mind when construing the Amendment's derivative Civil Rights law. In a brilliant historical analysis, Swayne tied the citizenship that the Act conferred on blacks with the equality in privileges and immunities the Constitution stipulated for all free Americans. It was time for the contrary Dred Scott majority view to disappear; time to disconnect Ameri-

---

39. Ex parte Turner, in *Reports of Cases Decided by Chief Justice Chase in the Circuit Court of the United States for the Fourth Circuit, 1865–1869*, ed. Bradley T. Johnson (New York, 1876 [new edn., ed. Ferne B. Hyman and H. M. Hyman, New York, 1972]), 157–61; Horace White, *The Life of Lyman Trumbull* (Boston, 1913), 274–5.

can jurisprudence from slavery's incidents. Employing Marshall-Story logic, Swayne reminded the petitioner that since 1789 United States Justices had declared against only three national laws. The Civil Rights law would not meet that fate in his court; "we entertain no doubt of the constitutionality of the act in all its provisions."[40]

Freedmen's Bureau Commissioner Howard noted in January 1867 that national courts could not accept jurisdiction of a removal appeal unless the appellant could prove to the federal judge that state tribunals discriminated racially; i.e., that the state denied a right and remedy to a national citizen. Discrimination was not easy to prove. Litigation was slow, expensive, and unsure. Violence aside, even states that provided nominal equality retained prejudiced juries, prosecuting attorneys, and police officers; almost everywhere southward blacks suffered severer penalties than whites for the same statutory criminal offenses while "flagrant crimes against the persons and property of freedmen go unpunished."[41]

Meanwhile, in contrast to Swayne's lower national court position, several state judges declared against the Civil Rights law's validity. A scattering of prosecutions began against a few for excluding Negroes' testimony, but because it was sporadic and uneven, even this weak enforcement pulse increased uncertainty about the law and therefore about the effectiveness of the moderate Republicans' Reconstruction edifice, and final pronouncements from the United States Supreme Court never came.[42] As state and individual impediments to Congress's state restoration program increased, officers executing the nation's laws and individuals supposed to be benefiting from their impact needed badly to know if the President intended to enforce them. Never speaking precisely to this point, between April and August of 1866 President Johnson exhibited increasing opposition to continuation of national presence within states, even though in the Civil Rights, Freedmen's Bureau, and removal statutes, among others,

---

40. U.S. v. Rhodes, 16 Fed. Cas. No. 16,151 (1866), 785; *ALRev,* II (Jan. 1868), 345, 233–50.

41. Howard to Stanton, Jan. 12, 1867, Letters Sent, vol. III, #56, RG 105, NA.

42. See Stanbery to A. H. Garland, Feb. 5, 1867, Letterbook F, RG 60, NA. U.S. v. Harris, 106 US, 629 (1882), decided negatively on the 1875 enforcement statute.

Congress required continuation. The President seemed not only unsympathetic to legislation which supposed the southern states still to be under national authority; he also assumed a right to set aside responsibilities assigned to executive officers by Congress.

In an April 1866 proclamation made almost simultaneously with the Supreme Court's Milligan decision (the full opinion in that case was issued in January 1867 along with the Test Oath decisions), the President proclaimed peace restored everywhere in the South. Where civil courts functioned, he released almost all civilian prisoners of the Army and ordered military trials ended for them.

But the Freedmen's Bureau courts were based on Congress's independent statute. Responsible observers in the South responded with proofs that southern state and local civil courts provided only travesties of justice for soldiers, blacks, and white Unionists.[43] Congress's contrary injunctions concerning Freedmen's Bureau court continuations faced Army officers with the dilemma of obeying either the President or Congress. Convinced that Congress had as much right to require Army enforcement of Freedmen's Bureau paramilitary courts as the President had to forbid it, Grant interpreted the President's proclamations as leaving martial law unabrogated with respect to the nation's commitments which Congress had specified in statutes, and circularized subordinates to support Bureau courts. On July 6, 1866, Grant issued General Order #44. It authorized Army commanders in the South to arrest and hold for trial—for state civil or criminal trial—persons accused of state and/or local offenses against whom appropriate civil authorities failed to act.

Odds are that Grant issued this order in order to avoid having the Army continue a cat's-paw between President and Congress. Any action of this sort had to affect politics; General Order #44

---

43. Judge Advocate General J. Holt's summary report to Adjutant General's Office, Sept. 14, 1866, Attorney General's Records, Letters Received from War Dept., Box 7, RG 60, NA. See also W. Brock, *An American Crisis: Congress and Reconstruction, 1865–1867* (New York, 1963); L. and J. Cox, *Politics, Principle, and Prejudice, 1865–1866* (New York, 1963); E. McKitrick, *Andrew Johnson and Reconstruction* (Chicago, 1960); J. McPherson, *The Struggle for Equality: Abolitionists and the Negro in the Civil War and Reconstruction* (Princeton, 1964); H. Trefousse, *The Radical Republicans: Lincoln's Vanguard for Racial Justice* (New York, 1969); D. Donald, *The Politics of Reconstruction, 1863–1867* (Baton Rouge, 1968), esp. 53–82.

followed the state-centered Republican Reconstruction profile, favoring a more positive national stance only when states' laws and officials were unjustly torpid or partisanly active.[44] At the

---

44. *Radical Republicans and Reconstruction*, ed. Hyman, 343–4; cf. "Aristotle in Blue and Braid: General John M. Schofield's Essays on Reconstruction," ed. J. Sefton, *CWH*, XVII (1971), 45–7; Nelson A. Miles to Sumner, July 21, 1867, vol. 155, #2, Sumner Papers, HU. For typical Army reaction, see Gen. J. G. Foster's Order #28 (Florida), April 27, 1866 (owned by the author):

HEADQUARTERS, DEPARTMENT OF FLORIDA,
TALLAHASSEE, FLA., April 27, 1866.

GENERAL ORDERS,
No. 28.

His Excellency the President, in his proclamation of the second instant, having declared that the insurrection, which heretofore existed in the State of Florida, is at an end, and henceforth to be so regarded:

And the Honorable Secretary of War, having with the approval of the President, declared, in orders of the 9th instant, that although the "President's proclamation does not remove martial law,"—"it is not expedient, however, to resort to military tribunals in any case where justice can be attained through the medium of civil authority;"

And the Constitution of the State of Florida, having provided that all the inhabitants thereof "are free and shall enjoy the rights of person and property without distinction of color;"

And the Courts being now organised in said State, and the officers and people, in general, "well and loyally disposed," so that the Constitution "and the laws can be sustained and enforced therein by proper civil authority, State or Federal;"

And the bill entitled, "An Act to protect all persons in the United States in their civil rights, and to furnish means for their vindication," having become a law,—

It is therefore ordered as follows:

I. All persons in this Department, now under military arrest, shall be turned over to the civil authorities for trial, except soldiers and those subject to military law, and such other persons as shall be detained by Special Orders hereafter to be issued from these Headquarters.

II. In future, Commanders of Districts and Posts will, when requested, assist the ministerial officers of the civil authorities in making arrests; but will arrest no citizen on their own order, except in the absence of the proper civil authorities, or upon their neglect or refusal to perform their duties; and in all such cases, unless the circumstances provided for in Paragraph III exist, they will immediately turn over the persons arrested to the civil authorities.

III. Should any case or cases arise in which a citizen, agent of the Freedmen's Bureau, or a Commander of a District, or Post, shall deem that justice will not be done before a civil tribunal, they will, respectively, report such case or cases, together with affidavits showing the necessity for military inter-

488

same time, however, the President had managed to define the battle in his—or at least in the white South's—favor. He had "forced the public debate on to the question of the proper mode of *restoring* the rebel states, not governing them."[45]

For these interacting reasons Republican congressmen, after the mandate of the 1866 election, sought viable supplements to their Reconstruction approach. State defiance of national law and order drove reluctant Republicans toward political control of those states. Of the national institutions relevant to Reconstruction's dynamics, the federal courts, seemingly uncertain by reason of the Milligan and Test Oath decisions, and the Army remained almost alone. Perhaps their loneliness helps to explain why in 1867 Republicans supported black voting in states.

Seventy years ago, John W. Burgess judged that the Republicans "made . . . a mess of it in 1867." Instead of following several paths at once, Congress should have simply retained the South under "Territorial civil government" and overseen "the nationalization of civil liberty [i.e., civil rights] by placing it under the protection of the Constitution and the national Judiciary." Deciding instead on Negro suffrage and Military Reconstruction, congressional Republicans fell into fateful error.[46]

Burgess forced Reconstruction alternatives into unrealistically exclusive segments. Territorialization, the Radicals' pet for years, had no general support. The national Army and judiciary already had roles to play. If they were not always those Congress assigned, they spoke directly to Republicans' general social concerns. In this context the Gelpcke v. Dubuque and Missouri Test Oath decisions, resulting respectively in national judicial restraints on cities' fiscal immoralities and on states' licensing power misuses, meshed rather than clashed with Congress's Reconstruction imperatives. Milligan's case was less a contempo-

---

vention, to these Headquarters, for consideration and the necessary action.

By Command of MAJOR-GENERAL J. G. FOSTER:

CHAS. MUNDEE,

Brevet Brigadier General & A. A. G.

45. Benedict, "The Right Way," 277; and see Kincaid, "Legislative Origins," chs. 3, 4. Ellsworth Elliot, Jr., *Yale and the Civil War* (New Haven, 1913), 13, noted the popular view of the Army as a national police on duty to prevent intrastate anarchy.

46. John W. Burgess, *Reconstruction and the Constitution* (New York, 1902), vii–ix, 111.

rary criticism of and obstacle to Reconstruction policy than subsequent scholars asserted. Seeking order rather than consistency,
ineluctably restrained by constitutional scruples, Republicans
created self-contradicting Reconstruction policies.[47] But they
were under no obligation to history to be neat.

They continued to view Reconstruction as only one measure
of the direction and style of American life. Aiming to restrain
certain state actions, Republicans remained prisoners of respect
for law and for states. Thus, greatly expanding national courts'
jurisdictions, Republican congressmen and judges forbore from
altering the Seventh Amendment's prohibition against re-
examination of facts determined by a state jury, in cases appealed to federal courts, by any rules of pleading, procedure, or
evidence save the forum state's. As Pomeroy noted in 1868, the
fact that federal judges must defer to states' laws and apply them
"is plainly a vast field . . . for injustice and oppression by
individual states, which the nation has now no means of preventing. This is a result which is dismaying, and a remedy is needed."

Pomeroy found the wanted remedy in the proposed Fourteenth Amendment's first section which, he believed, would "give
the nation complete power to protect its citizens against local
injustice and oppression."[48] But as 1867 opened that Amendment was still pending. With Reconstruction through litigation
frustrated and spasmodic, Congress was forced to continue
searching for a more effective way.

---

47. A. H. Kelly in *New Frontiers of the American Reconstruction*,
ed. H. M. Hyman (Urbana, Ill., 1966), 54–5; Kutler, *Judicial Power*, chs.
5–6.

48. Pomeroy, *Introduction*, 150–1. Note that the greatly enlarged
federal court jurisdiction did not alter obedience to the Seventh Amendment's stipulation that "no fact tried by a jury shall be otherwise re-
examined in any court of the United States, than according to the rules
of the common [i.e., state] law." In effect, this required national judges
accepting removal jurisdiction of a state case involving jury trial, which
included all criminal prosecutions as well as very many civil litigations, to
accept facts as found in inferior courts, and to employ the relevant state's
rules of pleading, decision, and evidence. See E. R. Hoar to G. S. Hilliard,
March 21, 1870, Instruction Book A, RG 60, NA, re Justices v. Murray, 9
Wall., 274 (1870).

Chapter XXVII

How to Set the Law
in Motion

In March 1867 congressional Republicans felt impelled almost unanimously to supplement, not replace, 1866's litigation approach to construction with the Military bill, including Negro suffrage. Carl Schurz best describes their reasoning: "after a faithful and somewhat perplexed wrestle with the complicated problem of reconstruction, [congressmen] finally landed—or it might be said, were stranded—at the conclusion that, to enable the negro to protect his own rights as a free man by the exercise of the ballot was after all the simplest way out of the tangle."[1]

The Republican problem was to find this "simplest way" in light of opposition from the President and southern whites to the 1866 formula. Military government over the ex-rebel region would have been simple indeed, as would total abandonment of new national duties, the most retrograde Democrats' solution. But incapable of descending to the latter alternative, Republican congressmen temporized on the former. George Julian understood Congress's reason for keeping to a muddy middle: "nothing could stay the prevailing impatience of Congress for speedy legislation looking to the early return of the rebel districts to their places [as states] in the Union."[2]

This constitutional imperative and the moderating effect of

---

1. Carl Schurz, *Reminiscences* (New York, 1907–8), III, 246.
2. George Julian, *Political Recollections* (Chicago, 1884), 306–7.

intraparty tensions mitigated against long-term national functional commitments and led to the decision in the Military Reconstruction Act (March 2, 1867) for Negro suffrage as a condition precedent to state readmission.[3] The Capitol Hill hope was that by exercising ballots in new state elections initiated under national, paramilitary authority, blacks would protect themselves thereafter against local and state inequities, quickly relieving the nation of responsibility. Individuals failing to receive adequate remedies by voting had recourse to the national courts, which retained traditional housekeeping configurations yet possessed the augmented jurisdiction Congress had been supplying.

Unless Schurz's and Julian's insights into Republicans' pressing time sense are stressed, as well as the constitutionalism discussed in preceding chapters, the curious mix of martial and civilian features, of intrastate initiative and national imperatives, and of racial equalitarian and standpat aspects in the Military Reconstruction Act are almost inexplicable. The Act's recent analyst, L. G. Kincaid, wondered why "the most sensible, astute, and talented politicians in the nation . . . unanimously supported a policy so difficult to implement in the South and to defend in the North?" And yet Congress's pre-eminent constitutionalist, Senator Reverdy Johnson, joined Republicans to repass the bill over the President's veto.

The centrist Republicans who dominated the lawmaking process aimed at swift state restorations conducted by biracial majorities, minimum disfranchisements, and maximum stability in property and social relationships. Republicans remained fixed on equality-before-state-law goals, expanded in 1867 out of necessity to include equality in political as well as civil rights. Faced with an increasingly clear need to provide in the South what Godkin called either "a good [national] police or . . . the admission of the blacks to such a share in the management of state affairs that they can provide a police for themselves," Republicans in effect temporarily changed the "or" to "and." The former was essential if the latter was to be won.[4]

---

3. Abolitionists and Radicals criticized the fact that southern "states" under white control determined if and when the readmission–Negro suffrage combination should begin; J. M. McPherson, *The Struggle for Equality: Abolitionists and the Negro in the Civil War and Reconstruction* (Princeton, 1964), 376.

4. *The Nation* (Nov. 29, 1866), 430; David Donald, *The Politics of Reconstruction, 1863–1867* (Baton Rouge, 1965), 64–82; A. H. Kelly,

Of national government institutions, only the Army and the courts were relevant to Congress's purposes. Notwithstanding the Milligan and Test Oath decisions, by March 1867 Congress believed that it had already placed the federal courts into a posture appropriate for the Reconstruction task. The Military Reconstruction bill established parallel, not exclusive work for the Army to perform.

Excluding Tennessee, which had already ratified the Fourteenth Amendment, the Act declared for the other ex-rebel areas that no legal state governments existed, that inadequate protection for life and property obtained there, and that the nation must encourage republican state governments as the Constitution stipulated. Without requiring that existing presidential, state, county, and municipal governments disappear—they were to remain "provisional"—the law divided the rebel states into military districts subject to Army authority. Each general assigned to Reconstruction duty by the President was responsible

> . . . to protect all persons in their rights of person and property, to suppress insurrection, disorder and violence, and to punish, or cause to be punished, all disturbers of the public peace and criminals, and to this end he may allow local civil tribunals to take jurisdiction of and to try offenders; or when in his judgment it may be necessary for the trial of offenders, he shall have power to organize military commissions or tribunals for that purpose; and all interference under color of State authority with the exercise of military authority under this act shall be null and void.

Subsequent sections required that military-commission trials of civilians proceed without undue delay and that no excessive punishments issue, that district generals review all sentences involving losses of property and liberty, and that the President review death sentences. Moving next to the Act's goals, Congress stipulated that without racial tests state residents form a new

---

"Comment on H. M. Hyman's Paper," in *New Frontiers of the American Reconstruction,* ed. H. M. Hyman (Urbana, Ill., 1966), 54–5; M. L. Benedict, "The Right Way: Congressional Republicans and Reconstruction" (Ph.D. diss., RU, 1971), chs. 10–11; L. G. Kincaid, "Legislative Origins of the Military Reconstruction Act, 1863–1867" (Ph.D. diss., JHU, 1968), 38, and see 130–156. Note that in early 1867 Congress also required equal suffrage racially defined in the District of Columbia and for Colorado and Nebraska territories.

constitution conformable to the United States' "in all respects." Once a majority of qualified residents approved the Fourteenth Amendment and ratified the new state constitution, Congress would readmit the state and the Military Reconstruction Act would cease applying there.[5]

Dissatisfied with the Act's timidity, Sumner wished Congress to create the new states rather than to give southern whites the initiative to shape essential features concerning which Congress retained only a negative voice, which political change might mute. He wished also for Congress to commit the new state creations to color-blind universal education systems. And he wanted the Army to protect a long-term national reconstruction of attitudes, not to rush the restoration of state institutional forms. But his proposals, like those of Thomas D. Eliot or Thaddeus Stevens, involved commitments of sorts for which, as Julian indicated, the Republican party was too impatient. And so the Radicals went along with the centrist Republicans for the best that Congress was willing to provide: "Reconstruction without machinery or motive power," in Sumner's apt phrase.[6]

The President's veto message rang the changes on themes he had made familiar in his veto of the bill establishing black suffrage in the District of Columbia. Congress was upsetting property rights, law and order, and judicial remedies in placing the nation's political destiny into hands unready for the responsibility. The President's veto of the Military Reconstruction bill, like that on the same day of the Tenure of Civil Offices measure, added to the tradition that Congress was breaking down federalism, separation of powers, and checks-and-balances constitutionalism. Further, the President argued that military reconstruction was unconstitutional because it established "the absolute domination of military rulers" in the South, where allegedly, martial substitutes would replace all civil laws including those of the federal courts. As Timothy Farrar's 1867 constitutional anal-

---

5. *SAL*, XIV, 429–9. Three weeks later, March 23, Congress enacted a supplemental amendment permitting Army commanders to initiate the constitutional conventions because southern whites remained deliberately idle, frustrating the Act's purposes. *Ibid.*, XV, 2–5. See also Charles Fairman, *Reconstruction and Reunion, 1864–88* (New York, 1971), 334–43, 594–5.

6. David Donald, *Charles Sumner and the Rights of Man* (New York, 1970), 288, and see 285–9.

ysis and congressional Republicans' votes suggested, these were dubious assertions, full of "errors of reasoning," in Reverdy Johnson's phrase.[7]

The President's decision to veto instead of pocketing or even signing the bill "is simply inexplicable" in terms of political rationality, according to M. L. Benedict's careful inquiry. Benedict's analysis makes clear that Johnson's veto of the Military Reconstruction bill led to Republican harmony in creating the March 23 and July 19 supplements in which the Army, instead of Johnson state authorities, initiated the required state constitutional conventions.

With the passage of these bills over the President's vetoes Republican Reconstruction policy, in responsive evolution since the Wade-Davis proposals of 1864, was fixed. And as Radical critics predicted, this policy bore seeds of frustration. Congress's Reconstruction laws left too much unchanged in the South and in Washington where, as the Military Reconstruction law carefully stipulated, Commander-in-Chief Andrew Johnson must oversee what he insisted was unconstitutional.[8]

"Let us pause here," the President stated in his veto of the Military Reconstruction bill, "to consider, upon this question of constitutional law and the power of Congress, a recent decision of the Supreme Court of the United States in *ex parte* Milligan." According to the President and his contemporary supporters as well as to generations of commentators, the unanimous Milligan decision, issued at the turn of the year with the Test Oath decisions, bore out every presidential premise.[9] But as with Taney's 1861 Merryman opinion, the Chase Court's 1867 Milligan stand could prove much or little.

Republicans insisted that, in Milligan, the Court considered Lincoln's wartime policies behind battle lines, in Indiana. Only the gratuitous obiter dictum by Justice Davis, in which four

---

7. *M&P*, VI, 498–511, and 472–98 on other vetoes. See also S. S. Nicholas, *Conservative Essays, Legal and Political* (Louisville, 1867), IV, 19, 79; Kincaid, "Legislative Origins," 286, on Reverdy Johnson; Timothy Farrar, *Manual of the Constitution of the United States of America* (Boston, 1867), 442–5, and H. T. Blake's review in *NE*, xxvi (1867), 725–38.

8. Benedict, "The Right Way," 327–36; P. Paludan, "Law and the Failure of Reconstruction," *JHI*, XXXIII (1972), 597–614.

9. *M&P*, VI, 504; 4 Wall., 2 (1867).

colleagues joined, implied that post-Appomattox congressional Reconstruction policies fell under the same judicial disfavor as the unanimous negative vote on the wartime scene. Congress's statutes were sustained wholly by grasp of war constitutionalism; Congress's jurisdiction was proper over the South, a region lacking proper state institutions, Republicans argued. And Justice Davis, shocked by indignant congressional reaction to his misleading musings, acknowledged privately that there was "not a word said in the opinion about reconstruction, & the power is conceded in insurrectionary States."[10]

James Buchanan understood that the Milligan decision did not condemn the Military Reconstruction bill. He lambasted Chase, among other Justices, for not traveling the whole retrograde route toward conservative, rigid constitutionalism. But, commenting in 1868 on Milligan ambiguities, John Norton Pomeroy noted that in Britain as in America, widespread civil unrest during the 1860's required that "the legality of every military arrest, trial, and punishment must be determined upon its own circumstances, and not according to any general and inflexible rules."[11]

Wise counsel, rarely followed then or since. Republican congressmen leaned toward Pomeroy's test. They provided by augmented national court jurisdiction for at least as much flexibility in the conduct of military arrests during the Civil War and Reconstruction, plus numerous other subjects, as litigation afforded. The 1863 Habeas Corpus Act gave the Supreme Court jurisdiction of Milligan's case; the February 6, 1867 Habeas Corpus law, which Congress enacted after the Milligan decision, provided the Court with jurisdiction of Ex parte McCardle, involving allegations of the Military Reconstruction law's unconstitutionality.[12] This continuing evidence of Republican respect for courts and constitutionalism clarifies Reconstruction contours

---

10. Quoted in S. I. Kutler, *Judicial Power and Reconstruction Politics* (Chicago, 1969), 67.

11. Benedict, "The Right Way," ch. 11; *The Life of James Buchanan*, ed. G. T. Curtis (New York, 1883), II, 655; R. H. Dana to C. F. Adams, Jr., April 14, 1867, in Adams, *Richard Henry Dana* (Boston, 1891), 334–5; Pomeroy, *An Introduction to the Constitutional Law of the United States* (2nd edn., New York, 1870), 480, and see 478 and n.; P. Paludan, "John Norton Pomeroy, State Rights Nationalist," *AJLH*, XII (1968), 280–1.

12. Kutler, *Judicial Power*, 94; Ex parte McCardle, 6 Wall., 318; 7 Wall., 506 (1869).

deriving from federalism and separation of powers traditions. Clearer evidence should not force paradoxical elements in Reconstruction constitutionalism into neat paradigms, however.

The Military Reconstruction Act helps to prove how committed Republicans were to presidential participation in the conduct of newly admitted national responsibilities. But that Act involved also the Republican commitment to rebalance the national vessel, long overweighted on the executive side. Memories were sharp in 1867 of the two-year period from Sumter's surrender to passage of the March 1863 Habeas Corpus Act when, with respect to antidisloyalty arrests, Lincoln was almost independent of the Congress. Now, two years after Appomattox, during which time Johnson had employed national military power in the South as largely as he wished, Congress was determined to share in the exercise of that power.[13]

Further insight into a specific application of these assumptions derives from re-examination of Chase's concerns about riding his circuit. It embraced Virginia, where Jefferson Davis's treason prosecution hung in suspense, in part due to Chase's absence but also because the Attorney General distrusted his ability to form a Virginia jury capable of honest verdicts. Chase refrained primarily because he would not hazard indignity to his office. He had first to be convinced that the military's presence meant no interference with national civil court processes, and that he would not be dependent on the President's instruments.

But with respect to riding circuit, Chase had no objection to the Military Reconstruction law, including the military tribunals Congress authorized in the South. Chase's major point was that the United States Supreme Court should not re-create Taney's dangerous error and confront the President. Like Congress Chase worried about the decline in separation of powers as a result of Andrew Johnson's southern policy, not about the Army so long as it served duly prescribed civil authority.

Chase noted also that in April and August 1866 the President had proclaimed peace almost everywhere in the South. Further, in legislation of July 23, 1866, Congress relieved Supreme Court Justices from circuit-riding. But the same day it

---

13. See *The Nation* (Feb. 14, 1867), 130; M. H. Carpenter, *Arguments in the Supreme Court of the United States, March 3 and 4, 1868, in . . . ex parte McCardle* (Wash., 1868), 79; Benedict, "The Right Way," ch. 11.

overrode Johnson's veto of the Military Reconstruction bill, and more than two months after the Milligan decision, Congress reallotted circuits to the Supreme Court Judges. Despite the revival of military court activity soon to result in McCardle's case, Chase saw no reason now to refrain from his circuit assignment. He acknowledged that on the surface the Military Reconstruction Act employed the Army in ways similar to those the President had adopted. But now Congress was requiring the Army to create conditions beneficial to the life of the civil law; the Army was acting under color of law as the federal courts did.

In Military Reconstruction Congress was sharing with President and Court in the exercise of national power that looked to its own swift extirpation.[14] The ambiguous, contradictory, and unpalatable elements in civil-military coexistence would be brief. Further, Congress would insure that the Army sustained agreed civilian goals, not suppressed them. Soldiers would help to improve intrastate remedies against local and state inequities, through assuring citizens' access to ballots and protection in litigation. Then Reconstruction would end, the sooner the better.

Chase's acceptance of civil-military court coexistence reflected the pervasive Washington view of Military Reconstruction as a stopgap. Enjoying the greatly increased jurisdictions Congress had provided, the national courts would see to long-term Reconstruction responsibilities envisaged in the Civil Rights–Habeas Corpus statutes; Military Reconstruction would be a catalyst leading to a re-United States, a role which southern whites were preventing the Fourteenth Amendment from performing. Then the nation would abandon the unwanted Reconstruction duty save as courts remained open to litigation.

In all this Republicans remained aware that their rewon Union of states required restraints on states' excesses. For this reason congressional impulses to curb national courts, especially the Supreme Court, lessened quickly after the Milligan and Test

---

14. *Reports of Cases Decided by Chief Justice Chase in the Circuit Court of the United States for the Fourth Circuit, 1865–1869*, ed. Bradley T. Johnson (New York, 1876 [new edn., ed. Ferne B. Hyman and H. M. Hyman, New York, 1972]), 132–5; Chase in *Albany Law Journal*, II (Sept. 24, 1870), 233. See also R. Nichols, "United States vs. Jefferson Davis, 1865–1869," AHR, XXXI (1926), 266–7; Kutler, *Judicial Power*, ch. 4; David Hughes, "Salmon P. Chase: Chief Justice" (Ph.D. diss., PU, 1963), 108–10; H. Hollingsworth, "The Confirmation of Judicial Review Under Taney and Chase" (Ph.D. diss., UT, 1966), 134–41.

Oath decisions. Grant's confidant General John A. Rawlins insisted publicly that the Army could live within the Milligan context. Pomeroy preached to lay and professional audiences against Congress diminishing national court authority. That must result in increases in the power of unpredictable state courts and judges, Pomeroy warned: "The laws of the General Government must operate within the states, and the officers of the general government must act within the jurisdiction of state tribunals. Remove the supervisory functions of the national judiciary, and these laws will become the sport of local partisanship; upheld in one commonwealth, they will be overthrown in another and all compulsive character will be lost."[15]

It was easier for legal scholars and congressmen to insist that the Milligan decision applied only to wartime presidential policies than for Army officers to perform comfortably under Congress's Military Reconstruction law. Democrats and southern whites spread the story that the Milligan decision did apply to present Army personnel. The number of damage suits increased sharply against military officers, with Milligan initiating one. Happy to let the Military Reconstruction law go unenforced or to distort its purposes, some anti-Negro Army officers used the

---

15. J. N. Pomeroy, "The Use of the Supreme Court," *The Nation*, VI (1868), 146–7; Paludan, "Pomeroy," 284; Rawlins, *Speech: General Grant's Views in Harmony with Congress* (Washington, 1868), 14, and see 11–16. On the same busy March 2 when Congress enacted the Military Reconstruction law, it eliminated special taxes on all state court writs, judgments, and other paper required by revenue acts of 1861 and 1864. The taxes had irritated state judges in Indiana, Kentucky, Massachusetts, Michigan, and Wisconsin, who declared them in violation of reciprocally tax-immune state institutions; later, Texas judges noted that they would have reached the same decision had not Congress repealed the tax provisions. But Congress's decision to roll back these taxes reflects more the Republicans' compelling respect for states than fear of states' judges. This repeal statute of March 2, 1867 suggests again the timidity with which Congress accepted the Constitution's duty to guarantee each state a republican form of government. The Military Reconstruction law's "grasp of war" underpinning allowed Congress to try to fulfill the duty; the state court tax repeal suggests that March 2, 1867 was a point in the politics of Reconstruction when several interconnecting paths led toward that common goal. Cf. Benedict, "The Right Way," 332–6, 671; C. O. Lerche, "Congressional Interpretations of the Guarantee of a Republican Form of Government during Reconstruction," *JSH*, XV (1949), 192–211. State tax data in *SAL*, XIV, 475 (1867); Cavasos v. Gonzales, 33 Tex., 133 (1870); Jones v. Keep, in *ALReg*, n.s. V (1866), 161.

Milligan decision as an excuse. Army officers were unsettled further when the Secretary of War admitted to Congress that for these reasons the Milligan decision made it difficult for the Army to punish murderers of soldiers in the South where civil officials failed to prosecute the villains and conspired with them. Rumors were endemic that the President's reference to the Milligan decision in his veto of the Military Reconstruction bill previewed oncoming assaults from Court and White House on the Freedmen's Bureau, Civil Rights, and Habeas Corpus laws, and on the still-pending Fourteenth Amendment.

Congress provided some comforting stability when on March 2 it overrode the President's veto of the Civil Tenure bill. Passed in retaliation against the President's 1866 purges of officeholders looking toward creation of a new conservative coalition, it took on deeper meaning.

The Tenure law provided that persons appointed by the President and confirmed by the Senate should not be removed without Senate concurrence. The President could suspend an official if the Senate was not in session, but must report the suspension to the Senate on its reassembly and ask its consent. Republican congressmen differed on the question of whether the Tenure bill embraced Lincoln holdovers such as War Secretary Stanton in Johnson's cabinet. But enough sentiment obtained to lock Stanton in to comfort those in and out of the Army who feared the quality of a Johnson-appointed successor, a pleasure increased by provisions in the Army Appropriations Act requiring Congress's assent to transfer orders directed to the commanding general from the President.[16]

In unhappy chronological conjunction, ambitions and events transformed efforts during March 1867 at stability into nervous

---

16. H. H. Penniman to Sumner, Dec. [?], 1867, vol. 155, #49, Sumner Papers, HL, on Mississippi; JAG Joseph Holt to Sec. War, Nov. 30, 1870, Letters Received, Box 10, RG 60, NA, on Milligan. The general Army picture is in J. Sefton, *The United States Army and Reconstruction, 1865–1877* (Baton Rouge, 1967), chs. 6–7. On Army unsettlement and hesitation to use military courts after Milligan, see E. M. Stanton to the President, Feb. 15, 1867, Letters Received, RG 60, NA; H. S. Fitch to O. H. Browning, Feb. 6, 1867, Andrew Johnson Papers, vol. 109, LC; report on military commission trial of ex-CSA Provost Marshal Pickett, for hanging captured U.S. soldiers, Executive Letters, vol. 75, 81–2, RG 107, NA. See also B. P. Thomas and H. M. Hyman, *Stanton: The Life and Times of Lincoln's Secretary of War* (New York, 1962), 515, 517–29; Kutler, *Judicial Power,* 91–3.

near crisis. All through spring and summer, the President and Attorney General Henry Stanbery interpreted the Reconstruction statutes to hamstring commanding generals. A central issue was a general's authority to remove from office provisional state civil officials who failed to enforce state and local laws when blacks and Unionists were the victims of illegality and violence. In late April, Mississippi resorted to the Supreme Court for a permanent injunction directed against the President and the Army commander in that state, to forbid enforcement there of the allegedly unconstitutional Reconstruction statute. But even Johnson and his Attorney General acknowledged that Mississippi's request was unprecedented and outrageous; no court could enjoin a President. Congress had required the President to execute a law constitutionally enacted with respect to procedure, Stanbery told the court. The Mississippi petition, without legal or historical merit, received no support in the Court.

Almost simultaneously, Georgia sought injunctions against enforcement of the Reconstruction statute in the state, naming the Secretary of War and generals from Grant down. Georgia's counsel stressed Congress's alleged obliteration of the state. Responding for the defendants, Stanbery insisted that the Court's jurisdiction ended at political matters, and the Congress's decision concerning Georgia's status was political. Accepting Stanbery's argument on May 13, 1867, the Supreme Court dismissed both petitions.

By denying the Georgia and Mississippi petitions, the Court avoided for its own convenience direct confrontation with Congress concerning the Reconstruction law's constitutionality. The jurists' grounds were historical and jurisprudentially proper; plaintiffs' counsel had misfired.[17]

Congress's Reconstruction authorizations to the Army appeared to have passed all foreseeable constitutional and political obstacles that the provisional southern states and the President could raise and the Supreme Court would entertain. Despite partisan contrary assertion, no judicial decision yet issued questioned directly the Reconstruction law or the Army's derivative policies in the South. In substantial confidence and good humor, therefore, on July 19 Congress passed over Johnson's veto an-

---

17. Kutler, *Judicial Power*, 77, 96–9; Hughes, "Chase," 119; 4 Wall., 475 (1867); 6 Wall., 50 (1868).

other supplement to the Reconstruction law. Directly contradicting the Attorney General's hamstringing efforts, it authorized Army commanders to follow Grant's precedent instructions and to remove provisional state and local officials who failed equally to enforce their states' civil and criminal statutes.[18] Retrospectively, along with the McCardle case and the impeachment, this amendment forms the context in which Reconstruction's beginning ended and in which Reconstruction's end began.

Under Congress's authorization and Grant's orders most Reconstruction commanders became involved in numerous details of life and labor including criminal-law enforcement, professional licensing, municipal police, and debt collections, without which more decent political action, racially defined, was impossible, according to General Sickles in South Carolina. Sickles suspended execution of debt-collection judgments and debt-imprisonment sentences issuing from all courts, including national tribunals. He explained to Grant that under the 1789 Judiciary Act federal courts were required to employ the procedures of forum state courts. But it was precisely to reform state procedures that Congress had ordered the Army to Reconstruction duty. Therefore Sickles had suspended existing state laws and derivative judgments that in his view were unfair to citizens. But it was all fruitless if national courts, employing state procedures, substantively reinforced that state's unjust processes and results. Federal courts obeyed Congress's 1789 order to use state procedures. Should not national judges obey also Congress's 1867 laws that the southern states' constitutions, laws, and procedures become at least as decent as those of other states?[19]

Though Grant and Stanton sustained Sickles and other generals, it was clear that Reconstruction matters had gone awry. Even Chase felt that however worthy the goals, Congress had given the Army too much latitude and had upset both power separation and national-state relationships. Whether Chase objected more to Sickles's intrusions into state and local commercial tax, debt, labor, and criminal matters, or into inferior national court procedures, is not known. But he believed fervently in the

---

18. *SAL*, XV, 14–16.

19. Grant to Sickles, Aug. 24, 1867, Commanding General's Letterbook, Letters Sent, 1866–68, 296–7, RG 108, NA; Sickles to Grant, Aug. 26, 1867, #16705, Andrew Johnson Papers, LC; Sefton, *Army and Reconstruction,* ch. 7.

maintenance of state governments as the base of the federal union. Chase revered the national judiciary as the pacific links for Union, and he saw nothing amiss in the tradition that national judges use applicable state pleadings and procedures. The Army as servants for Congress and the national courts was one matter; the Army as master of federal court procedures was quite another.[20]

Conservatives sniffed the shifting wind and discerned opportunity in the Army's intrusion into property and judicial matters. Lawyers and southern politicos picked up the theme that Reconstruction laws were unconstitutional not only as infringements on civil liberties but also as deprivations of property rights. "The [South's] only gleam of hope for the Constitution then was in the Supreme Court," recalled Alabama's conservative constitutionalist, Hilary Herbert.

But appropriate litigation in the sense of dramatic, politically compelling qualities did not come up every day. A Louisiana suit remained obscure in state courts even though it challenged the Army's power to set aside interest payments on a municipality's debt and despite plaintiff's argument that the suspension deprived good-faith bondholders of property in a manner the national Supreme Court had declared unconstitutional in the Gelpcke v. Dubuque decision.[21]

Nationwide political attention turned instead to William McCardle's suit. He was a Vicksburg newspaper publisher whose editorials encouraged violent resistance to racial-equality provisions of the Reconstruction statutes. Arrested and awaiting a military commission trial, McCardle sought release by means of a habeas corpus writ from the United States Circuit Court. Its judge denied his petition and remanded him to Army jurisdiction.

Responding sensitively to growing civil-law concerns among lawyers, Jeremiah Black and David Dudley Field, McCardle's

---

20. Hollingsworth, "Confirmation," 141; Hughes, "Chase," 116–17; A. Russell, "Avoidable Causes of Delay and Uncertainty in Our Courts," ABA *Reports* (1891), 217; and see n. 15, above.

21. *ALRev*, IV (1869), 139 [concerning Louisiana v. Health]; and see A. H. Stephens, *Address Before the General Assembly of . . . Georgia, 22nd February 1866* (Milledgeville, 1866), 5, 9; H. A. Herbert, *The Supreme Court in Politics: Paper, Alabama State Bar Association, Aug. 3, 1883* (Montgomery, n.d.), 14; P. C. Friese, *The Unconstitutionality of Congressional Action: An Essay on the Paramount Unwritten Law* (Baltimore, 1867), 27, *passim*.

counsel, without abandoning the basic theme of the Reconstruction law's unconstitutionality, played down civil-military aspects. In order to get the case to the Supreme Court the appellants had to overcome the Vallandigham and Milligan precedents, which, taken together, suggested that no Supreme Court jurisdiction existed in appeals from military authority and that only wartime executive extensions of Army courts over civilians were unjustifiable. Instead McCardle's counsel seized on Congress's 1867 Habeas Corpus law and insisted that it gave adequate jurisdiction to the Supreme Court to protect McCardle.[22]

Many elements made McCardle's case dramatic. Although the Attorney General had appeared very recently on behalf of the government and its officers in the Georgia and Mississippi injunction litigation, he refused to appear against McCardle. Grant obtained for the Army the services of Senators Lyman Trumbull and Matthew Carpenter. Only a week after denying itself competency to issue Georgia the requested injunction against the Reconstruction law, the Supreme Court accepted jurisdiction of McCardle's appeal. A decision was possible adverse to the congressional statutes now being militarily enforced. Further, events determined that judgment in McCardle's case must issue in the superheated politics of the nation's first impeachment, which in its unique way was also testing issues implicit in McCardle's case.

In short, McCardle kept the Supreme Court in the most exposed salient of Reconstruction politics. As Henry Dutton noted, McCardle's case involved the fates of the South's states and Negroes, of the President of the United States, and of the Army. Unique among the world's courts, the United States Supreme Court was to determine national policy, the destiny of races, and the quality and direction of a great society.[23]

Aware of context and implications, the government's counsel chose to fight McCardle's appeal on his selected battlefield. Carpenter boasted confidently that in his brief he had "avoided all talk of the rights of conquest, a theme that is very unpalatable to that [Supreme] court . . . & placed [Congress's] right to pass the [Reconstruction] law upon entirely peace powers of the

---

22. 6 Wall., 318 (1868); Kutler, *Judicial Power*, 100–101.

23. Henry Dutton, "Impeachment and Military Government," *NE*, XXVII (1868), 360–9; Sen. Doolittle to Manton Marble, Jan. 2, 1868, Marble Papers, LC; Stanbery to Grant, Dec. 31, 1867, RP #670220, RG 94, NA.

[national] government. This foundation is as solid as a rock, & if that Court decides the case upon judicial, not political, points, we have a sure thing."[24]

Congress made a surer thing of it. Over somnambulistic Democratic resistance and a tepid presidential veto—the impeachment was under way, after all—on March 27 Congress repealed the provisions of the February 1867 law that provided it appellate jurisdiction in McCardle's case. In April the Court acquiesced and dropped consideration of McCardle's appeal.

But it dropped only that litigation. Accepting Congress's jurisdiction limitation, Chase stipulated carefully that "Counsel [for McCardle] seems to have supposed, if effect be given to the repealing act . . . that the whole appellate power of the court in cases in *habeas corpus* is denied. But this is an error." Instead McCardle meant only that quite constitutionally, Congress determined the Court's jurisdiction, which it elected now partially to excise.[25]

While McCardle's appeal made its way to Washington, the President asserted his alleged right to independent control over the Army, i.e., to issue orders contrary to Congress's Reconstruction purposes. In August 1867, complying with the Tenure law, he suspended Stanton and named Grant ad interim successor. The President relieved from command Sickles and other generals who had actively enforced Congress's Reconstruction statutes. Wearing two hats as commanding general and temporary War Secretary, Grant saw to it that the Army kept in motion Congress's basic Reconstruction directives involving redistricting, voter registration, and new state constitutional conventions. In December when Congress reassembled, as the Tenure law required, the President reported Stanton's suspension to the Senate. It refused approval. The President refused in turn to readmit Stanton to the Cabinet. Grant turned the War Office keys back to Stanton, who occupied the Secretaryship in defiance of the President.

---

24. Matthew Carpenter to Stanton, Feb. 10, 1868, #56770, Stanton Papers, LC.

25. Kutler, *Judicial Power*, 101–4 and chs. 5–6; 7 Wall., 506, 516 (1869). See also Carpenter, *Argument in . . . ex parte Wm. H. McCardle* (Washington, 1868), esp. 73–9; *Argument of Hon. Lyman Trumbull . . . ex parte McCardle* (Washington, 1868), *passim;* E. B. Thompson, *Matthew Hale Carpenter: Webster of the West* (Madison, Wis., 1954), 89–95; Fairman, *Reconstruction*, 598.

Unable to reverse Reconstruction through appeals to voters, to standpat and retrograde congressmen, or to courts, the President, defying a national law, reached out for control over one of Reconstruction's two essential instruments, the Army. Therefore, despite the clear political hazards and ambiguities involved in the unprecedented move, the Republican center decided for impeachment, a wholly constitutional procedure.[26]

Johnson's obstructive replacements of Reconstruction generals and rejection of Stanton were last straws calling impeachment into action. Preceding chapters have surveyed the President's course with respect to numerous policies Congress intended should shape the quality and direction of post-Appomattox life. Laws on confiscation, test oaths, Freedmen's Bureau courts, Civil Rights, and Military Reconstruction had suffered Johnson's nonenforcements, malforming interpretations, or outright obstructions. Yet his piecemeal impediments had kept impeachment only a minority dream. Fall elections in 1867 and a worrisome business recession had disposed many Republicans against further political unsettlements and made impeachment the more unlikely despite the President's now-open appointments of conservative generals to commands in the South. Nevertheless, in early 1868 Johnson managed to transform the Republicans' search for stability into an impeachment consensus.[27]

It was easier to decide on the need for the act than to know confidently how to proceed or to anticipate the consequences of success. Since 1789 impeachments had been whistled up sporadically for Presidents, but never came to action. A very small number of lesser official fry had been impeached.

The Republican decision to impeach Johnson was hardly an expression of partisan contempt for the Presidency, as distinguished from the incumbent. M. L. Benedict, author of the best inquiry into the subject, concludes that the impeachment grew from Republicans' incapacity to be legislative despots or to conceive of Military Reconstruction without the Army's Commander-

---

26. Dutton, "Impeachment and Military Government," 360. Cf. J. E. Sefton, "The Impeachment of Andrew Johnson: A Century of Writing," CWH, XIV (1968), 120–47; H. L. Trefousse, "The Acquittal of Andrew Johnson and the Decline of the Radicals," ibid., 148–61.

27. Benedict, "The Right Way," chs. 12–14, and see Johnson's December 1867 message to Congress, in M&P, VI, 558–81, on the President's view of Negroes' ineradicable inferiority and unsuitability for responsible citizenship, and his weighing of resistance to the Reconstruction laws.

in-Chief commanding. In Benedict's judgment, "Historians should view the . . . impeachment for what it was, . . . one of the great legal cases of history in which American politicians demonstrated the strength of the nation's . . . institutions by attempting to . . . give a political officer a full and fair trial in a time of political crisis."[28]

This moral victory would have been impossible had the Constitution's sparse impeachment clause failed to work. Impeachment became another instance in the Civil War and Reconstruction when politicians and legal scholars reviewed history in order for the first time actually to apply a dormant part of the Constitution.

Fortunately for congressmen a useful literature was available by early 1868 as a result of abortive efforts at impeachment in 1867. In this literature, attitudes about the law and politics of impeachment—and impeachment mixed characteristics of a trial at law and of a political contest—were sharply variant. A narrow view, insisted on throughout the trial by Democrats and conservative Republicans, was that English and American precedents applied which allowed impeachment of an official only if he had committed an indictable criminal act. The broad view, taken up by Republicans, insisted that English precedents were not wholly applicable. There the House of Lords could punish as well as try any offender, including officials. Here Congress could only remove officials. Therefore American precedents failed to sustain a need for indictable crime as a reason for removal.[29]

History leans strongly toward the broad Republican position. "That an impeached official can be tried in a criminal court after his trial on impeachment does not imply [that] only those who can be tried in a criminal court can be impeached," Benedict concluded. "It means, rather, that where an officer *is* impeached for an indictable offense, the impeachment does not preclude a later indictment." The Constitution's framers and ratifiers had themselves carefully sidestepped their own double-jeopardy, jury-

---

28. Benedict, "The Right Way," 498, and see ch. 12. The following treatment exploits heavily Benedict's work.

29. T. W. Dwight, "Trial by Impeachment," *ALReg*, XV (1867), 257–83; W. Lawrence, "Law of Impeachment," *ibid.*, 641–80; C. M. Ellis, "Causes for Which a President Can Be Impeached," *AM* (1867), XIX, 88–92; Dutton, "Impeachment," 361. Benedict, "The Right Way," 499–502, surveys trial use of these points.

trial, and pardon provisions when dealing with impeachments, envisaging instead a special political process set to lawlike procedures.[30]

Perhaps any strictly legalistic analyses would have amused the Constitution's creators. As John Norton Pomeroy noted just before the Johnson impeachment got under way, the men of 1787 aimed actually to check unpredictable future power abuses at the highest political level, where discretion had to exist, else free government could not live. Therefore the framers wrote into the Constitution a brooding impeachment threat rather than a precise weapon.[31]

Impeachment's adversary features gave the President's counsel ample scope to develop the narrow tradition that an indictable offense was necessary for conviction, that the Tenure law did not cover Stanton, that the President had equal right with Congress to determine if a law was unconstitutional, and that by violating the disputed law the President aimed at a court test.[32] These lawyerlike arguments-in-the-alternative well suited the substantively political yet procedurally legal contours of the impeachment proceeding. Concerning Stanton's amenability to the Tenure law, Benedict's careful analysis convinces that by the final vote on its passage congressmen had "concluded [that] the bill protected Stanton after all," and that Johnson's retention of Stanton in the Cabinet "was . . . a virtual reappointment" acquiring tenured status. On the matter of the President testing a law he thinks is unconstitutional by violating it, no evidence exists that Johnson actually tried for a court test. Benedict properly raises the derivative query, what if after violation a court or the Congress finds the law constitutional? As a defense, the President's argument raised endless abysses for the survival potential of American government.[33]

This evaluation of the President's scattergun points suggests a need to re-evaluate also the Republicans' omnibus accusations against him. They too were equivalents to a lawyer's arguments-

---

30. Benedict, "The Right Way," 348, and see his documentation in ch. 12, *passim.*

31. Pomeroy, *Introduction,* 440–5, 482–92.

32. D. M. DeWitt, *The Impeachment and Trial of Andrew Johnson, Seventeenth President of the United States: A History* (New York, 1903), 195–9; J. G. Blaine, *Twenty Years of Congress* (New York, 1903), II, 352–4.

33. Benedict, "The Right Way," 459–64; Pomeroy, *Introduction,* 444–5, 482–92; Thomas and Hyman, *Stanton,* 589–90.

in-the-alternative aimed to sweep as wide horizons as possible. In terms of Republican intraparty factionalism in the House the impeachment articles sought to accommodate conservative and centrist waverers whose goals were won with the President's mark-time response to impeachment, and who therefore felt little or no compulsion to proceed on the unmarked road to conviction.

Mixtures of politics and law featured also the Senate's maneuvers in committee and on the floor concerning rules of procedure for the impeachment trial. If the Senate proclaimed itself a court then the presiding officer stipulated in the Constitution, the Chief Justice of the United States, could "vote" as well as interpret points of evidence and law. But if the Senate retained its noncourt character, the Chief Justice could not claim a vote. Deciding that the Senate was not a court, senators determined also that they had the power to overturn Chase's rulings on disputed questions of law and evidence.

But senators' efforts not to be bound by Chase's unpredictable rulings on law collapsed in the trial's first days. As Chase administered oaths to senators to do impartial justice, Democrats insisted that Ben Wade should not sit, since he would succeed Johnson if the President were removed. Chase ruled that Wade should sit, since the Senate was a court and his status as president of the Senate was irrelevant. The Chief Justice implicitly resolved in his own favor the matter of his right to vote. It all meant that the trial would proceed far more slowly than Republicans wished. The conservatives won time for reaction to set in.[34]

In constitutional terms, Edward S. Corwin concluded, "the impeachers had the better of the argument for all but the most urgent situations."[35] And there was the heart of the matter. For conviction of Johnson involved the nation's most urgent situations, ranging from the unhappy prospects of Wade as President supporting agrarian monetary and tariff heresies, of continuing racial instability southward, of Negro suffrage issues in northern states, and of political corruption everywhere. Republican centrists impeached the President for refusing to execute their stat-

---

34. Benedict, "The Right Way," 468–87.

35. Edward S. Corwin, *The President—Office and Powers, 1787–1957: History and Analysis of Practice and Opinion* (4th rev. edn., New York, 1957), 79. See also W. A. Dunning, *Essays on the Civil War and Reconstruction* (New York, 1898), 253–303. Benedict, "The Right Way," 752–3, offers excellent bibliographical analysis.

utes. If the impeachment swerved his course, conviction became unnecessary.[36]

While the trial was on Johnson made clear his intention to name a moderate general to be Secretary of War; forwarded to the Senate the Reconstruction constitutions of Arkansas and South Carolina, created by terms of Congress's Reconstruction laws which he said were unconstitutional, including ratification of the detested Fourteenth Amendment and provisions for blacks' voting; and ceased obstructing the progress of congressional Reconstruction in other provisional states by devious interpretations of the laws or other overt means. Politically, the seven recusant Republican senators who voted not to convict Johnson merely affirmed impeachment's victory. Little wonder that contrary to tradition, they did not suffer disastrously at the hands of their constituents or party. Little wonder also that history is redressing opinion concerning the senators who voted finally and unavailingly to convict. They were, Benedict concludes, "motivated by the same desire for impartial justice [or lack of it] that historians and partisans ascribed only to the recusants."[37]

Between die-hard Democrats convinced of the need to acquit the President and Radical Republicans determined to convict him, senators in the center wrestled to come to decision on ambiguous technical points. Days, weeks, and months passed in complex skirmishes on the admissibility of evidence and on such technical legal points as estoppel and the President's independent power of removal. An over-all review sustains Benedict's judgment: "After the events leading to impeachment . . . it is difficult to understand how anyone could have accepted at face value the moderate and reasonable interpretation Johnson's lawyers put on his activities." But because evidential disproofs of the President's inner intentions were impossible to evoke, because Republican senators wished to retain existing constitutional configurations, and because all senators wished to prevent the "Mexicanization" of the Presidency, Johnson benefited. He received the one vote needed to secure nonconviction; in mid-May the impeachment ended.[38]

A kind of quiet returned to the Potomac. The President, smarting from his one-vote escape and his inability to win the

---

36. Benedict, "The Right Way," 491; Trefousse, "The Acquittal of Andrew Johnson and the Decline of the Radicals," 148–61.
37. Benedict, "The Right Way," 496.
38. *Ibid.*, 517–18, and see ch. 17, *passim.*

Democratic party's 1868 nomination for a whole term, contented himself with giving a "little lecture on constitutional law" to such captive visitors as youthful political reporter Henry Adams. But the scholarly pose failed to conceal the stubborn activist. Immediately after the Senate vote, Johnson considered sliding in the detested Seward as War Secretary, but, fortunately dissuaded, named conservative General John Schofield. The Senate consented "inasmuch as . . . Stanton has relinquished his place." Mutual ill-humor aside, the President's belated acquiescence in the impeachment's verdict indicated that at last he had learned the lesson which Republican congressmen had been trying for two years to teach him. Now Reconstruction would proceed as Congress had prescribed.

A profound psychological release, the impeachment was another of the proofs accumulating since early 1861 concerning the Constitution's tough workability. In terms of early 1868, it allowed a procedurally pacific institutional readjustment between the nation's governing branches, badly skewed in favor of the White House by reason of the War, another item in the South's debits. It was an article of Republican faith that Reconstruction of the South also involved improved equilibrium between the nation's branches, which helps to explain Congress's devotion to increasing the federal courts' jurisdictions and powers.[39]

Contemporaries saw impeachment's nonviolent course and constructive outcome as proof of Reconstruction's terminal phase. From 1866–68 Congress had embodied in legislation the War's "logical results," according to publicist Samuel Bowles. Insuring the protection of these results without the second civil war which reasonable men feared, the impeachment began a two-year-long wrapping-up of the War's residuals. By 1870 Ignatius Donnelly believed that "not a single issue of the many which

---

39. Quotations and supplemental data are, respectively, in Ernest Samuels, *The Young Henry Adams* (Cambridge, Mass., 1948), 172–3; Thomas and Hyman, *Stanton*, 611, and see also 106–13. Other data in Fairman, *Reconstruction and Reunion*, 594–5; McKitrick, *Johnson*, 506; Alfred Conkling, *The Powers of the Executive Department of the Government of the United States* (Albany, 1866), *passim;* "The Shifting of Power: Balances and Checks in Government," *AM*, XXVII (1871), 665–70; H. Davis, *American Constitutions: The Relations of the Three Departments as Adjusted by a Century* (Baltimore, 1885), *passim.* Note that Johnson did not veto the March 11, 1868, "fourth" Reconstruction Act (*SAL*, XV, 41), allowing it to become law by reason of the ten-days rule. It allowed a majority of the votes actually cast to be sufficient to place into force a new state constitution; a device to overcome white no-voting obstructionism.

agitated us in the past remains alive today—slavery—reconstruction—rebellion—impartial suffrage—have all perished." However coarse, his perception required a view of impeachment as a constitutional process accompanied by enormous political hazards that had rasped the nation's tight nerves. Pressures increased on politicians to close off Reconstruction. These pressures played essential roles in determining impeachment's hairbreadth outcome, the 1868 presidential elections, the Fourteenth and Fifteenth Amendments' ratifications and enforcements, and the nature of certain Supreme Court judgments.[40]

Elections in 1868 confirmed 1864's heartening message: the Constitution's rigid balloting timetable was not a built-in disaster. In Reconstruction as in the Civil War, Americans assumed that their choices of national, state, and local officeholders would solve problems ranging from Reconstruction's final manifestations to New York City's corrupt politics.

Meeting in Chicago in March, while the final impeachment tallies were coming in, the Republicans nominated Grant and assembled a platform which touched on the party's needs while reflecting its principles. It congratulated the party on Reconstruction's success as measured by new southern state constitutions "securing equal civil and political rights to all, and regard[ed] it as the duty of the [national] Government to sustain those constitutions, and to prevent the people of such states from being remitted to . . . anarchy or military rule." Other planks defended the requirement of black votes in southern states and weaseled on loyal state biracial balloting practices. Still others denounced the heresy of debt repudiation.

However, no plank condemned the impeachment recusants. The party avoided internecine vendettas and contained impeachment within constitutional processes. In this context Grant's "let us have peace" spoke to both party and public concerns.[41]

The Democrats' platform preamble depicted the Constitution "as the foundation and limitation of the powers of the

---

40. "Ignatius Donnelly, Diary," ed. T. Nydahl (Ph.D. diss., UMinn, 1941), I, 372–3; G. S. Merriam, *The Life and Times of Samuel Bowles* (New York, 1885) II, 42–4.

41. Benedict, "The Right Way," 542–5; J. H. Franklin, "Election of 1868," *History of American Presidential Elections,* ed. F. L. Israel and A. M. Schlesinger, Jr. (New York, 1971), II, 1247–53, 1270–1.

[national] government." Demands followed logically from this premise for immediate and unconditional state restorations, universal amnesty, state control of suffrage standards South as well as North in order to end "military despotism and negro supremacy," abolition of the Freedmen's Bureau, and repeal of the President's power to define when state militias should enter national armed service. Acknowledging that slavery and secession were obsolete, the platform asserted that no other impacts flowed from the Civil War and Reconstruction.

But on several constitutional and jurisprudential points the Democrats resorted to basic deceptions and misstatements. No Reconstruction legislation "abolished" habeas corpus; its encouragements have been detailed. Milligan and McCardle suggest how far from "secret star-chamber inquisitions" the Reconstruction military commission proceedings were. Referring to McCardle, the Democrats charged that Republicans "abolished the right of appeal, on important constitutional questions, to the Supreme Judicial tribunal and threaten[ed] to curtail, or destroy, its original jurisdiction, which is irrevocably vested by the Constitution." As Chief Justice Chase had noted in his McCardle opinion, and within a year was to affirm in Ex parte Yerger, habeas-corpus appeals to the Supreme Court from military-commission proceedings under Military Reconstruction were as available as the Justices wished. Congress's jurisdiction juggling never approximated the effects the Democrats asserted.[42]

At least one major candidate's statement on Reconstruction constitutionalism was more revealing—and threatening—than the formal party platform. Before the Democratic convention met, Missouri's powerful presidential aspirant and close advisor to Johnson, Francis Blair, illustrated prospects for discord in the notorious "Broadhead" letter. Blair noted that militarily reconstructed states were adding to the Republicans' Senate numbers

---

42. *Ibid.*, 1267–9; Kutler, *Judicial Power*, 104–7; 8 Wall., 85 (1869). A Mississippian, Yerger had killed an Army officer. A military commission was to try him when he appealed to a U.S. Circuit Court, charging the unlawfulness of the military trial and its supporting legislation. The Circuit judge declared him to be lawfully incarcerated. Taking their hint from Chase's McCardle dictum, Yerger's counsel argued that the Supreme Court enjoyed both certiorari and habeas-corpus jurisdiction because the 1868 repeal of the 1867 Habeas Corpus Act allegedly restored the 1789 Judiciary Act's jurisdictional grant. The Supreme Court unanimously sustained this duplex argument.

so that even a Democratic House majority in 1868 could not undo their Reconstruction legislation. Therefore Democrats should construct an alliance between the President and the House majority they hoped to elect, which would overthrow the Reconstruction Act. The new President must declare it void in Johnsonian manner. But unlike the impeached lame-duck incumbent, his imagined Democratic successor must refuse to enforce Reconstruction laws and "compel the army to undo its usurpations at the South, disperse the carpet bag State governments, allow the white people to reorganize their own [state] governments, and elect Senators and Representatives." This issue was "one which embraces everything else that is of value in its large and comprehense results."

Strong medicine. But the retrograde Democrats gave Blair only the vice-presidential nomination. His acceptance speech was a shade milder than his Broadhead letter, which Republicans exploited shrewdly and, not unreasonably, as associated with the upsurge in unpunished anti-Negro violence southward. It all helped Grant and his party.

The election results suggest that Blair was not shooting wildly in anticipating a stronger Democratic House. Even Georgia and Louisiana, already restored by the Military Reconstruction law including Negro suffrage, went for Horatio Seymour, the Democratic nominee. He narrowly lost Alabama and Arkansas. Mississippi, Texas, and Virginia votes were not counted; the states were still reconstructing themselves. Three unseceded former slaveholding states went Democratic and the party was strong in New England, the midwest, and California. Like the Constitution, the two-party system was still vigorous.[43]

The firm Democratic showing increased the influence of those Republicans who insisted that Reconstruction's terminal stages were imminent. By the time of Grant's election, six ex-Confederate states were represented again in Congress, having qualified by means of Military Reconstruction. Before admission, each state had busily altered its constitution, laws, and institutions, and ratified the Fourteenth Amendment which in mid-1868 was added to the Constitution. Doubtless by more recent standards of interracial decency and democratic practices these

---

43. Franklin, "Election of 1868," 1255, 1262, 1279–81; Union Republican Congressional Committee, *Treasonable Designs of the Democracy* (Washington, 1868), 4–5; J. H. Silbey, "A Respectable Minority: The Democratic Party, 1860–1868" (AHA paper, 1968).

efforts were incomplete and inadequate. But by mid-nineteenth-century gauges they were the most wide-ranging accommodations in the world's history to the fact that large numbers of whites and Negroes would live in physical propinquity on terms other than master-slave, in a federal system that was also a political democracy and an economic capitalism. In harmony with other states which were creating or revising constitutions in post-Appomattox years, the new southern state constitutions acknowledged the Union's perpetuity and its supremacy for appropriate purposes. Similarly the new southern state governments fleshed out their infant constitutions with innovations such as acknowledgments of public responsibility for asylums, schools, roads, and professional licensing. Army orders requiring biracial juries in local civil courts were incorporated into the new constitutions along with substantial revisions of antiquated civil and criminal law codes. Whereupon Army commanders declared national authority inoperative by terms of the Military Reconstruction law and turned over to the new civil courts all poll lists, voter registrations, and military-commission records. Generals released civilian offenders against Army regulations and transferred to the new state authorities civilian prisoners who had violated the statutes either of the Johnson "provisional" state or the successor reconstructed state. In an effort to avoid jurisdictional tugs from both national and state courts, Army orders required that habeas-corpus orders from United States courts enjoy prompt obedience but that habeas-corpus writs from state judges receive response only that national jurisdiction was exclusive.[44]

All very well, asserted one House Republican. But what assurance existed, he asked, "that if we admit the State of Alabama under these circumstances the next election will not find it in the hands of the rebel [i.e., Democratic] party?" The 1868 election returns hoisted danger signals that no existing assurance was reliable.[45] Trying to construct constitutional assurances, Republican congressmen accentuated what was to be a fundamental party split.

---

44. Pertinent documents in *The Radical Republicans and Reconstruction,* ed. Hyman, 409–46. See also J. B. Scroggs, "Carpetbagger Constitutional Reform in the South Atlantic States, 1867–1868," *JSH* XXVII (1961), 475–93; M. J. Brodhead, "Accepting the Verdict: National Supremacy as Expressed in State Constitutions, 1861–1912," *Nevada Historical Society Quarterly,* XIII (1970), 3–16.

45. Quoted in Benedict, "The Right Way," 551.

Chapter XXVIII

Untying
the Reconstruction Knot

Success widened Republican divisions. Johnson's postimpeach-
ment docility, Grant's election, the dramatic improvements
in and restorations of half-a-dozen southern states, the withering
away of the Army there, the spectacle of Negroes voting and
assuming high offices, and the ratifications of the Fourteenth and
Fifteenth Amendments led ever-increasing numbers of political
activists to drop involvements. Social-science, religious, and welfare auxiliaries shifted attention, energy, funds, and talent toward other, usually local horizons. "Constitutional jurisprudence"
was swiftly becoming attuned to immediate concerns, noted
Columbia's former president William Duer.[1] Reconstruction was
less and less immediate.

In 1868 an immediately significant new literature helped
further to justify the retreat from southern Reconstruction.
Treatises by Cooley, Dillon, and Jameson, sustaining Republican

---

1. William Duer, *A Course of Lectures on the Constitutional Juris-
prudence of the United States* (New York, 1868), 19–21; J. G. Sproat, *The
"Best Men": Liberal Republicans in the Gilded Age* (New York, 1968), 4–44;
Radical Republicans and Reconstruction, 1862–1870, ed. Harold M. Hyman
(Indianapolis, 1966), 461–3; M. Conway, "Sursum Corda," *Radical*, I
(April 1866), 291–4; G. W. Julian, *Political Recollections, 1840–1872* (Chi-
cago, 1884), 330–1; Herman Belz, "The Constitution in the Gilded Age:
The Beginnings of Constitutional Realism in American Scholarship," *AJLH*,
XIII (1969), 111–13.

constitutionalism, as noted earlier, aimed respectively to fetter constitutionally all states' excesses, to diminish cities' misusages of delegated state police and fiscal powers, and to deny certain state constitutional conventioners' claims to plenary authority. The combined effect was to lessen Republican political cohesiveness. Democrats exploited the generalized mood these writings helped to spread, that all government power was prone to excess, and that improvers had plenty of work to do in northern communities and states.[2]

The Supreme Court's implicit support for Congress's Reconstruction policies offered in the 1869 Texas bond case, issued the same day as the McCardle decision, accentuated the euphoric yet divisive sense of Reconstruction's completed character. The case arose because unrestored Texas wished to recover certain national bonds which the state had received before the War. Rebel Texas authorities sold the bonds. To allow United States Supreme Court jurisdiction of the postwar appeal for the bonds' return by the Texas provisional government, Texas's status as a state required clarification. The Court majority accepted the argument put forward by Texas's counsel, George Washington Paschal, a scalawag jurisprudent whose 1868 legal treatise was an important addition to nationalist constitutionalism. Paschal argued that states were indestructible components of this perpetual Union. But secession placed Texas outside a state's proper relationships to the Union. Obeying the Constitution's requirement that every state enjoy a republican form of government, Congress, not the Court or President, would determine the essentially political course which Texas must follow in order to win respectability. The Supreme Court bought Paschal's package.

Democrats had hoped for another Merryman-Milligan windfall from the Court. Instead the Texas bond decision accepted into constitutional law much Republican Reconstruction constitutionalism; Chase and his majority colleagues even employed

---

2. T. M. Cooley, *Constitutional Limitations Which Rest upon the Legislative Powers of the States of the American Union* (Boston, 1868); John F. Dillon, *The Law of Municipal Corporations* (New York, 1868); John A. Jameson, *The Constitutional Convention: Its History, Powers, and Modes of Proceeding* (New York, 1867); Henry Wilson, "New Departure of the Republican Party," AM, XXVII (1871), 104–20; Charles Fairman, *Reconstruction and Reunion, 1864–88* (New York, 1971), chs. 17–18; Loan Association v. Topeka, 20 Wall., 655 (1875).

the Military Reconstruction statute to sustain their position—and Congress's—on state perpetuity.[3]

Obviously, in the Texas bond opinion Chase did not proclaim that the Reconstruction legislation was valid; that was not up for decision. For equally obvious reasons, Republican laymen and lawmen inferred that the Court had upheld all they had done. And they were happy that the looming threat of Supreme Court interference, especially of a Court-President offensive against Congress, was ended. Thereby, less alertness was in order for Reconstruction. More attention was justified toward "new North" concerns such as corruption and wastefulness in state and local governments. Commingling with the social science upsurge, a "liberal" Republican drift grew greater in such Republican centers as New York's Citizens Association and Union League, and in Missouri where venal Republicans outraged B. Gratz Brown and Carl Schurz. Republicans had never casually initiated national interventions into states. Now the Texas case rhetoric of indestructible states made future interventions into restored states the more difficult to justify. The tough Republican commitment to state rights within the nation was accommodating itself to a parallel commitment to minimal national thrusts.[4]

As Republicans fell away or contested among themselves for new directions, Democrats enjoyed an increasing sense of unity. Although a far-right wing remained adamant on the unacceptability of any Civil War or Reconstruction impacts, a larger accommodationist voice, responsive to the victor's reverence for state-centered federalism and abhorrence for runaway democ-

---

3. Texas v. White, 7 Wall., 700–732 (1869); and see White v. Hart, 13 Wall., 646 (1875); S. I. Kutler, *Judicial Power and Reconstruction Politics* (Chicago, 1968), 108–10; E. L. McKitrick, *Andrew Johnson and Reconstruction* (Chicago, 1960), 115–17; J. C. Hurd, *The Theory of Our National Existence* (Boston, 1881), 8–18; J. W. Scarborough, "George W. Paschal: Scalawag Jurisprudent" (Ph.D. diss., RU, 1971), ch. 5; George W. Paschal, *The Constitution of the United States* (Washington, 1868), v–xvi; P. Paludan, "Law and the Failure of Reconstruction," *JHI*, XXXIII (1972), 597–614.

4. Gideon Welles, ms. "Government in the Civil War: A Discussion of the Effect of the Civil War on the Government of the United States" (ca. 1878), UC; J. R. Tucker, "The Relations of the United States to Each Other, as Modified by the War and the Constitutional Amendments" ([Paper, Soc. Sci. Assn., 1877] Albany, 1877), *passim;* W. D. Farnham, " 'The Weakened Spring of Government': A Study in Nineteenth-Century American History," *AHR*, LXVIII (1963), 662–80.

racy, became audible. In 1868 it enjoyed a counterpart to the Cooley-Dillon-Jameson treatises.

Less legalistic, Edward Pollard's *Lost Cause Regained* was a shrewd political evaluation based on constitutional assumptions. A southerner, Pollard spoke to concerns about democratic excesses—Congress, in Reconstruction's context—paralleling those which Dillon and his coadjutors expressed about state situations. America's distresses and tensions were products of inadequately limited government, Pollard concluded. He would secure liberty better throughout the land by accepting certain impacts of the War and Reconstruction, including 1866's Civil Rights law. In Pollard's reconstructed Union, states must afford Negroes civil but not political equality. Electing safe men to local, state, and national offices, lily-white electorates would keep the nation within proper constitutional limits. Since northern whites were not really enthusiasts for blacks voting, once it was clear that civil equality obtained in southern states Republicans would abandon the unnatural quest for nationally guaranteed political rights.

Pollard's formula helped Democrats adapt state-rights traditions without abandoning them. Criticisms of national wrongs in Reconstruction and animadversions against the quality of northern universal suffrage became hallmarks of "new South" politics and history. It advanced to 1866 since it could not halt at 1861. But voluntarily it would go no further.[5]

Pollard-style strategy inspired many duration-only Republicans to return to former Democratic allegiance. Exploiting northerners' nervous Negrophobia, reviving Democrats had defeated Negro suffrage proposals in several northern states, scored heavily in 1867's off-year contests, and run up danger signals for Republicans to ponder in 1868's presidential and state balloting.

These accelerating crosscurrents tended to divide congressional Republicans sharply. A primary divisor remained the

---

5. Edward Pollard, *The Lost Cause Regained* (New York, 1868), *passim;* P. M. Gaston, *The New South Creed: A Study in Southern Myth-making* (New York, 1970), ch. 1; J. P. Maddex, Jr., *The Virginia Conservatives, 1867–1879: A Study in Reconstruction Politics* (Chapel Hill, N.C., 1970), 51, 64, and chs. 1–5, *passim.* On the precise coincidence of Pollard's stress on 1866, and most Republicans' commitment against discriminatory state laws, see M. L. Benedict, "The Right Way: Congressional Republicans and Reconstruction, 1863–1869" (Ph.D. diss., RU, 1970), 692–4; Paludan, "Law and the Failure of Reconstruction," 610–14.

centrists' hurried state restoration pace, as contrasted to the Radical insistence on going slowly. Radicals never managed to gain support for a long-term regenerative Reconstruction or to hold off very long a state restoration once the party weight swung toward that step. Therefore, when circumstances warranted, Radicals averred that a restored state remained amenable to national authority if it failed to provide equal political and civil rights. When Georgia's conservative-dominated state legislature ousted elected black members, Radical Republican congressmen argued that such backsliding automatically reversed the state's restoration and invited in again the national presence. But centrist Republicans held that Reconstruction was not an ongoing process. They echoed the Supreme Court about indestructible states. The party majority insisted that the secession almost ten years earlier had justified national intercessions only to the point of state restoration.

Whereupon, as noted earlier, Radicals tried to tie fundamental conditions to a state's restoration during the brief time it remained in the nation's grasp. In early 1868 Thaddeus Stevens brought from the House Reconstruction Committee a proposal that Congress impose fundamental conditions on Alabama's readmission. Its new constitution must unamendably limit the state's power to restrict voting by citizens properly enfranchised, including blacks, or to widen the franchise with votes of persons presently disqualified by terms of the Fourteenth Amendment, meaning upper-level ex-Confederates. Further, Stevens wished Congress to retain a right to annul any subsequent state statute or proposed constitutional amendment that would result in those undesirable results. If Alabama failed to obey Congress's orders the state must revert to Reconstruction's constitutional limbo.

Stevens was trying essentially to supplement the indirect, case-by-case, state-to-national court litigation approach to Reconstruction which, Military Reconstruction aside, Congress had built up so painfully. Instead of an individual Negro, denied a vote, having as his only remedy a confrontation against a state in a lawsuit, Stevens proposed that the nation safeguard whole classes of citizens against adverse state policies. By his fundamental conditions, open congressional politics would be an alternative avenue to the mysterious science of the law.

Here was a new departure indeed. Republicans, ranging from Godkin to Ohio's Bingham, objected vigorously to this extraordinary deviation from the state-autonomy pattern the party had held to since its birth. A restored state was the equal of all others, Republican critics protested. Any lesser status meant that the federal Union was gone, that the War had failed in its primary restoration purpose, or that despotic centralization had occurred as Democrats charged.[6]

Republicans unworried by constitutional ambiguities objected on grounds of enforcement difficulties. Only the Army had proved relevant to achieving swift state alterations. It was time for the Army to withdraw from intrastate duties, not to anticipate eternal Reconstruction assignments. Low-contoured national courts were the only right way to sustain the nation's presence and laws, the argument ran.

Still, Stevens raised enough doubts concerning Alabama to delay its restoration temporarily. In May, he brought up the fundamental condition question again in a restoration bill for that state, and soon after in a measure embracing also Arkansas, the Carolinas, Louisiana, Florida, and Georgia. This time Stevens omitted the permanent disfranchising clause as defined in the Fourteenth Amendment and the reservation to Congress of authority to void obnoxious state laws or constitutional amendments. Enforcement remained moot.

In the Senate, centrist Republicans were torn between Stevens's sharp logic and their commitment to haste in restoring states. Johnson's impeachment was ending. If he was not convicted, unrestored states would remain under his control by reason of Congress's Military Reconstruction statute. Johnson might repeat his efforts to undo the Army's work that had brought on the impeachment crisis. At the least the President was likely to lock in those states' offices as many white conservatives as possible. Therefore the centrists approved restoration bills embracing fundamental conditions. But in both houses of Congress, enforcement considerations were inconclusive.

Late in June 1868, after presidential vetoes were overridden, the omnibus restoration bills became laws. Centrist and conservative congressional Republicans had accommodated the conditions precedent to existing Reconstruction lineaments by omitting enforcement apparatus beyond the courts, and by establishing its

---

6. *CG*, 40 Cong., 2 sess., 2214–16; R. C. Sterne, "Political, Social, and Literary Criticism in the New York Nation, 1865–1881: A Study in a Change of Mood" (Ph.D. diss., HU, 1957), 58–60; Benedict, "The Right Way," 552–61.

hurried cadence. There would be no long probation period, no national educational system, and no mass confiscations or disfranchisements. Reconstruction as regeneration must depend almost wholly on such self-enforcement as blacks' ballots and lawsuits provided.

In light of the absence of enforcement machinery from the 1868 statutes and their successors and of the conviction of many Republicans concerning the finality of a state's restoration, the notorious fundamental conditions proved to be pious preachments to good behavior. But they represented neither ignorance nor deviousness on the part of congressional Republicans.[7] Rather, along with other drives the 1868 statutes reflected constitutional imperatives with which Republicans lived and which played a primary role in shaping Reconstruction's final contours.

As Henry Adams noted, this context became the seedbed for the Fifteenth Amendment. Through positive impediments to blacks' voting and through inaction concerning white vigilantism, southern state and local authorities allowed anti-Negro violence to mar the 1868 elections. Suggestions sprouted in Congress for reversing the restorations of the worst offenders, Alabama, Georgia, and Florida. But this reopened party sores about nation-state relationships and the quality of political democracy. Except to "old" Radicals of Sumner's stature, who believed that without amendment the Constitution armed the nation adequately as a source of libertarian power that could penetrate every state, creation of a new amendment appeared to be the right way to carry on the spirit of the Thirteenth and Fourteenth Amendments without entering again into fundamental condition or Military Reconstruction questions.

A new amendment had to win ratification in black-weary northern states. Therefore centrist Republicans rejected proposals to forbid predictable state subterfuges such as literacy, property, or residence tests. The argument that state-supported common schools were essential to republican forms of government fell flat. As far as possible, Republicans wished to avoid congressional and state ratification debates concerning citizens' "rights." The party steered resolutely away from suggestions that all elections should come under national regulation. In short, the Republican

---

7. Cf. Benedict, "The Right Way," 552–61; James G. Randall and D. Donald, *The Civil War and Reconstruction* (Boston, 1961), 618–19; *SAL*, XV, 72–4.

majority refused further to alter state-based federalism. Instead it
held the War's impact to the acceptable limit of prohibiting a
particular class of state wrongs. Passed by Congress in mid-1869,
ratified March 30, 1870, the Fifteenth Amendment bypassed the
thorny enforcement question posed by the fundamental condition
statutes and returned to familiar negatives on states. The Fifteenth Amendment's sparse text—"Section 1. The right of citizens of the United States to vote shall not be denied or abridged
by the United States or by any State on account of race, color, or
previous condition of servitude. Section 2. The Congress shall
have power to enforce this article by appropriate legislation."—
responded precisely to Republican congressmen's mixed
concerns.

Of course the Fifteenth Amendment's primary function was
to maintain minimally decent levels of political democracy in the
face of southern states' positive discriminatory activity. But
mixed with the Amendment in rising priority of concern was the
lowering quality of northern urban politics as evidenced by New
York City election frauds in 1868. It was becoming a common
assertion that this decline was caused by the states' inadequate
monitoring activity. Therefore in 1870–71, when Congress saw to
enforcing the Fifteenth Amendment in southern states, it included in the "Force Act" provisions for the conduct of national
elections in northern cities, soon after adding separate laws on
the urban theme. These election laws were based not on the new
Fourteenth or Fifteenth Amendments but on the Constitution's
authorities, dormant since 1789, for Congress to prescribe naturalization procedures and to regulate national elections.[8] The
Amendment, enforcement, and city-elections statutes were innately connected aspects of a broadly defined Reconstruction.
Both were tied to hangover governmental apparatuses, party
institutions, and constitutional attitudes which, facing great
changes, knew few responses. Both parties wanted new identities
but did not know where to find them.[9] The Republicans had won

---

8. H. Adams, "The Session," *NAR*, XVIII (April, 1869), 610–40; Secs.
19–20, Enforcement Act 1870, *SAL*, XVI, 144–5; naturalization law July
14, 1870, *ibid.*, 154–6; elections law Feb. 28, 1871, *ibid.*, 433–40; 1872
amendment to sundry civil appropriations bill, on elections, *ibid.*, XVII,
348–9.

9. Two excellent recent scholarly inquiries increase greatly insight
into these subjects. But W. Gillette, *The Right to Vote: Politics and the
Passage of the Fifteenth Amendment* (Baltimore, 1965), 46 and *passim*,

the Union's salvation along with the abolition of slavery. As George Julian realized later, with few exceptions that generation agreed with Lincoln's "one war at a time" rhythm. By 1870 it wanted stability and peace, not innovation.[10]

The search for stability helped firmly to connect the Fifteenth Amendment and the urban voting laws. Similar visions of national direction and quality were involved; visions deriving from the constitutionalism which the War and Reconstruction nourished among Republicans. The party might not know where to go, but it understood where it had been. Wendell Phillips told Congress in 1869 that prewar abolitionists' cynicism about a Union buoyed up only by faith in "the harmonious cooperation of the States" had become a general Republican attitude. The derivative question of 1870 and later was not, as Gillette suggests, "whether state or nation should validate the voter." Instead it was how the nation limited, if lightly, how the states should do the work.[11]

Unquestionably this was a great distance. Taking long looks back to the shameful winter of 1860, the achievements were gratifying. To be sure, the Fifteenth Amendment's enforcement section seemed to some Republicans to go too far. But the spirit of the times was that the new Amendment's ratification fittingly rounded out the historic decade of antislavery agitation, which for so long had seemed doomed to failure. "The rebellion is crushed, the black man is free, and the 15th Amendment will secure everyone's civil [and political] rights," George Wilkes wrote Sumner. Reconstruction was hardly worth discussion on Capitol Hill, Henry Adams noted of Grant's first Congress.[12] In

---

argues that the Amendment aimed to enfranchise northern, not southern, states' Negroes; A. Burke, "Federal Regulation of Congressional Elections in Northern Cities, 1871–1894" (Ph.D. diss., UC, 1968), iii, asserts that "It is essential that advocacy of national action in a matter so basic [as national regulation of cities' balloting practices] be free of all association with southern reconstruction." Both err. See R. A. Horn, "National Control of Congressional Elections" (Ph.D. diss., PU, 1942), 140–1 and *passim*.

10. George Julian, "Is the Reformer Any Longer Needed?" *NAR*, CXXVII (1878), 247; A. V. House, "Republicans and Democrats Search for New Identities, 1870–1890," *RP*, XXI (1969), 466–70.

11. Wendell Phillips, "We Ask of Congress," Boston *Commonwealth* (Dec. 4, 1869); Gillette, *Right to Vote*, 46. But see p. 49 on Gillette's inadequately stressed awareness of the southern Negro as the focus of the 15th Amendment. Cf. Paludan, "Law and the Failure of Reconstruction," 611–14.

12. G. Wilkes to Sumner, May 8, 1969, and F. Gillette to same, March

the White House Grant nourished the sense of Reconstruction's completed character. When he took office in March 1869, Georgia, Mississippi, Virginia, and Texas were still unrepresented in Congress. A year later only Georgia remained outside and Congress, with Grant's support, seated its delegation in February 1871. In this swift restoration, frequently involving conservative white Democratic domination of local and state offices, Grant's influence was heavy. Thereafter he operated on the assumption that the nation's Reconstruction role was all but ended; that the reconstructed southern state governments would handle their internal affairs. The President's annual messages from 1871 to 1876 refer only infrequently to southern developments. National interventions in the South were inadequate, over-restrained, "vacillating and erratic," Professor Carpenter concluded in 1970.

Precisely a century earlier, Henry Adams and George W. Paschal perceived the constitutional context that hemmed in Grant and his Congresses. With respect to the South, Reconstruction had reached its legal limits, Adams noted, and now its meanings were spreading nationwide. Congressional Republicans blended with their southern-state concerns unhappy appreciation of "the rapid progress of corruption in . . . [northern] state legislatures . . . and the evident failure of . . . self-government in great municipalities."[13]

Reacting to disclosures of 1868 election frauds in northern cities, in 1870 Republicans began, as noted, to apply for the first time

---

8, 1870, Sumner Papers, HU; Donald, *Sumner and the Rights of Man*, 351–4; Adams, "The Session," 613. Gillette, *Right to Vote*, 72, 76, suggests that Adams missed the point because Congress intended no enforcement. But Gillette presents no convincing evidence. Instead I read Adams to mean only that he feared power in the wrong hands, in Reconstruction of states as in voting corruption in cities. See also Benedict, "The Right Way," ch. 19; R. D. Owen, "Looking Back Across the War-gulf," *Old and New*, I (1870), 579–89; *Life and Writings of Frederick Douglass*, ed. P. S. Foner (New York, 1965), IV, 45; *Radical Republicans and Reconstruction*, ed. H. M. Hyman, 461–502; J. McPherson, *The Struggle for Equality: Abolitionists and the Negro in the Civil War and Reconstruction* (Princeton, 1964), ch. 18, esp. 428–30.

13. H. Adams, "The Session, 1869–1870," *NAR*, CXI (1870), 29–62 @ 42–3; G. W. Paschal, *Lecture Presented to the American Union Academy of Literature, Science, and Art . . . March 7, 1870* (Washington, 1870), 25, 29; J. A. Carpenter, *Ulysses S. Grant* (New York, 1970), 84–6.

the Constitution's old nationalization and national-election supervision authorizations. The situations in northern cities and in
southern states presented Congress with markedly differing problems. Southern officials and vigilantes impeded black voters, and
through violence, intimidation, and fraud decreased the number
of balloters. In New York City and other urban centers, city and
state officers including judges fraudulently naturalized unqualified persons, thereby ballooning voters' ranks. The upshot was a
coinciding demand for election reform in northern cities and for
national action for the South, short of Military Reconstruction or
fundamental conditions.[14]

Beginning in early 1870, at great and increasing cost to
Republican party unity, Congress commenced to pass derivative
statutes. The first, signed May 30, 1870, aimed to enforce the
Fourteenth and Fifteenth Amendments and the Constitution's
long-moribund elections clause. Major portions of this "Enforcement Act" or "Force Act" prohibited state officers from manipulat-
ing local laws in elections embracing national officials in order to
discriminate against voters on the basis of race. The law forbade
use of fraud or violence to deceive or intimidate voters. And it
proscribed masked groups from riding public highways or interfering with citizens' political or civil liberties. In the Senate,
Sherman added sections to correct a "grievance which has become of greater magnitude even than the denial of the right to
vote to colored people; and that is, the open, glaring, admitted
frauds by wholesale in the great cities of this country." Taken
together, the complex, lengthy provisions of the Enforcement Act
added frauds and voter intimidation to the list of federal crimes,
and subjected national, state, and local officials who committed
or sanctioned violations to prosecutions in national courts, the
primary enforcement machinery. The Army was a backstop en-
forcer of court orders.[15]

Despite its brave clauses, the Enforcement Act was punitive
retrospectively and individually only. But the same imperatives
that brought it into being inspired Republican congressmen to

---

14. Burke, "Federal Regulation," ch. 2; Horn, "National Control,"
137–50; E. Swinney, "Enforcing the Fifteenth Amendment, 1870–1877,"
JSH, XXVIII (1962), 202.
15. *SAL*, XVI, 140–6 (1870); U.S. v. Reese, 91 US 214 (1876), invalidated the heart of the statute. See Burke, "Federal Regulation," 56–61,
for details; 56–7 for Sherman.

consider nationalizing the central naturalization process by which immigrants became voting citizens. In 1795 Congress had stipulated that any common-law court could nationalize, and except for the Alien Act interlude state and local judges had monopolized the function. But the Fourteenth and Fifteenth Amendments ended the custom that states determined national citizenship.

Under Union League inspiration, Congress considered ways to shift naturalization proceedings, so widely and vividly prostituted by state and local judges, to national courts. Noting that the 1795 Act allowed whites only to be naturalized, Sumner won inclusion of African descendants, skirting Orientals, about whom western Republicans were sensitive. Signed July 14, 1870, the Naturalization law provisions added to the list of national crimes a long catalogue of election frauds, assigned exclusive jurisdiction in derivative prosecutions to national courts, and required federal marshals, already part of the court structure, to preserve order at the polls in national elections. In cities of over twenty thousand in population (sixty-eight existed in northern states; only ten in southern), application by two citizens that frauds existed required federal judges to appoint supervisors of voter registration from both political parties.[16]

No permanent new national enforcement bureaucracy came into existence; national court officers did the work. Even these limited muscles flexed only when states failed adequately to enforce state standards of voting probity involving national elections.

Content with such constraints, Republican party leaders had discovered—or rediscovered—what they believed was the right way to restore states while reforming cities. Affection for this tentative stance evidenced itself again in the February 28, 1871 Elections law, commonly labeled as one of the Enforcement Acts. Its inspiration derived from the observably useful impact in the 1870 elections of the Naturalization and Force Acts of that year. In early January 1871 New York Republican John Churchill proposed his Elections bill as an amendment to the latter. In effect, Churchill expanded portions of the Naturalization law into an effective national elections monitorship. Passed quickly through both Houses by party votes and signed by President Grant on

---

16. *SAL*, XVI, 254–6 (1870); Burke, "Federal Regulation," 62–9; Horn, "National Controls," 154–5.

February 28, 1871, the Elections law mixed Reconstruction's means and ends instructively.[17]

The 1871 Elections law was more preventive than punitive. It aimed to curb national election perversions made possible by a state's lethargy by seeing to it that only qualified persons voted as nation and states prescribed. Repeating essentially the Naturalization statute's complaint procedures, the Elections law allowed national judges no discretion about receiving complaints, so that the federal courts took on a quasi-executive role basic in the political process.

In each federal circuit, the judge was to appoint from among his commissioners a permanent elections supervisor; again, no bureaucratic growth occurred. The supervisor appointed temporary assistants as needed to check the validity of registration lists and voting procedures. Courts' marshals and deputies could assemble posses to aid supervisors, apprehend violators, and keep peace at the polls.

Except as lack of enforcement of state election and voter registration laws resulted in temporary supersession by national standards, none of these provisions displaced state personnel or procedures. Once the particular election ended the national apparatus disappeared save for the single chief supervisor in each circuit, who was also a commissioner. With respect to supplementing, not superseding, state processes the 1871 Elections law made state officers subject to national criminal prosecutions for neglecting election duties imposed by state or national laws, and gave federal courts exclusive jurisdiction through expanded habeas corpus removals to hear suits against national election officials begun in state courts.[18]

By early 1871 there was overwhelming evidence that through positive impediments and deliberate inactivity, southern state and

---

17. *SAL*, XVI, 433–40 (1871). I follow here Burke, "Federal Regulation," 3–6 and ch. 5. Employed effectively many times, sustained by the Supreme Court (Ex parte Siebold, 100 US, 371 [1880]), and repealed in 1894, the Elections law has a sharply different history from that of the Enforcement Acts.

18. Burke, "Federal Regulation," 6, 96–106. An interesting comparison of the 1871 Elections statutes and the 1965 Voting Rights Act is in *ibid.*, 7–9; and in B. Schwartz, *Statutory History of the United States: Civil Rights* (New York, 1970), I, 548.

local officials were fostering vigilante terrorism against politically active blacks. Up to this point Congress had addressed itself almost exclusively to official state actions. Now spirited debates on Klan viciousness brought Republicans to a new frontier of federalism within the context of the Civil War and Reconstruction. This involved a view of lawbreaking that lessened individuals' constitutional rights, as implicit results of states' transgressions and/or slothfulness; a step many Republicans took reluctantly and from which they retreated very quickly.

The Ku Klux Klan bill provided that "any person" who "under color" of a state's or subdivision's laws or customs deprived another person of constitutional rights was liable to criminal penalties and/or damages after litigation in national courts. Their jurisdiction was enlarged to cover this wider canvas, with procedures for appeal set to the manner of the 1866 Civil Rights law "and the other remedial laws of the United States which are in their nature applicable in such cases." In the Klan bill's second section, the Republican majority admitted the validity of an old Radical argument, that punitive individual litigation was a too narrowly legalistic remedy. The Klan situation needed preventive lubricants for unimpeded mass political action, including pre-balloting electioneering, assemblies, and unfettered speeches and writing. Therefore, in complex provisions Congress armed the President with authority to suppress conspiracies that threatened to deprive persons of civil and political rights or to interfere with national and/or state officers' executions of rights legislation, if state officers refused or were unable to afford adequate protection. In a lengthy catalogue of state wrongs, situations now labeled national felonies, the President could suspend the habeas-corpus writ privilege for a limited time and employ federalized state militia and national armed forces to see to the equal protection of national and state laws including those on elections and jurors' qualifications. Procedures specified in the Habeas Corpus and Civil Rights laws were to govern offenders' arrests. Grant signed it into law on April 20, 1871.[19]

This remarkable statute encapsulated the Civil War and Reconstruction experience concerning national protections for

---

19. Schwartz, *Statutory History*, I, 591–2; *SAL*, XVII 13 (1871); 48 *USCode*, secs. 1983, 1985, are current revised portions of this Act, not invalidated in U.S. v. Harris, 106 US, 629 (1883); Benedict, "The Right Way," 693–5, n. 30-a.

individuals' civil and political rights. Congress thus moved tentatively into modern times.[20]

Contemporary criticism ranged from the nearly hysterical condemnations of the Force Acts by southern whites and Democratic party spokesmen to measured objections by such unimpeachable Republicans as Senator Trumbull and John Norton Pomeroy. Soon picked up by the United States Supreme Court, a standard justification for the new-era "Liberal" Republicans' retreat from Reconstruction, 1872–77, ran like this *Journal of Social Science* editorial:

> By transferring to the general government a responsibility not belonging to it, and making it answerable to acts of violence committed by individuals, the Act necessarily transfers to it a power not its own, but one inherent in the States, and wielded by them with far greater effectiveness than by the general government. . . . The Act provides . . . a system of centralization. . . . We hear of the blessings of centralization with the same emotions with which we used to hear of the blessings of slavery. . . . The act to enforce the [fourteenth] Amendment thus becomes an Act to prolong the divisions which the Amendment was intended to terminate.[21]

But then and since there were other voices and attention is deserved to their contrary message. Negroes insisted that justice was impossible for a racial minority if the old jurisprudence, where nation and states remained isolated, flourished again. Oliver Wendell Holmes replied to Pomeroy that he shared his doubts about section 2 of the law (so would the Supreme Court). But other sections (3 and 4, which the Court sustained, and upon which in 1956 President Eisenhower leaned for authority to send troops into Little Rock), in which Congress empowered the Presi-

---

20. In June 1872 Congress expanded the 1871 Elections law to cover Congressional rural as well as urban districts, thus underscoring explicitly the connections between the Force and Elections statutes. But the Elections law extension gave supervisors less authority, pay, and independence from political party control than was true of their urban counterparts. SAL XVII, 348–9; Burke, "Federal Regulations," 6.

21. JSS, IV (1871), 200–201; John N. Pomeroy in *The Nation*, XII (April 20, 1871), 269–70: Trumbull in CG, 42 Cong., 1 sess., 578–9; Ex parte Reese, 91 US, 214 (1876); U.S. v. Harris, 106 US, 629 (1883). For Cooley, see Paludan, "Law and the Failure of Reconstruction," 611–14.

dent to use military force and to suspend habeas corpus, appeared to Holmes to be legitimate if novel uses of traditional national authority. The statute did authorize the President to act when states did not punish or prevent crimes against individuals under state law. But Congress's authority became effective only when state inaction or obstructionism frustrated the national Constitution and laws, or allowed private actions to injure individuals' national rights. If this general authority did not exist, then the federal system was as constipated as in 1860–61. Like law, federalism required remedies for wrongs, Holmes wrote, and others such as Carl Schurz and Hermann Von Holst expressed themselves similarly.

It was the consensus of 1871 that a desirable, moderate revolution had taken place and was finished. The prewar republic of arbitrary states had become a federal republic in which equal citizens could determine their own fates through improved self-government of states and nation. Holmes and men of like mind admired these impacts of the Civil War and Reconstruction because they made possible regularity and predictability in governmental processes, replacing the vexatious inconsistencies of petty principalities common in prewar decades. It was a question of law, not partisan emotion, Holmes wrote, or should be, and he counseled fellow lawyers against making adverse judgments without close study of the Enforcement statutes and related legislation.[22]

Acknowledging the comprehensiveness of the Enforcement Acts, Swinney concluded that they "were essentially in accord with the democratic credo," were genuinely and desperately needed, and were workable when determinedly and devotedly administered. The habeas corpus suspension clause, the center of disagreement, was employed only once; other provisions of the

---

22. For Holmes, see *ALRev*, V (1871), 749–51; M. A. DeWolfe Howe, *Justice Oliver Wendell Holmes: The Proving Years, 1870–1882* (Cambridge, Mass., 1963), II, 35–9. Carl Schurz stated in Congress, "The revolution [of the War and Reconstruction] found the rights of the individual at the mercy of the States; it rescued them from their arbitrary discretion, and it placed them under the shield of the national protection" (*CG*, 41 Cong., 2 sess., 3607), and for Von Holst, see Howe, *Holmes*, II, 39. For Negroes, see [Brotherhood of Liberty], *Justice and Jurisprudence: An Inquiry Concerning the Constitutional Limitations of the Thirteenth, Fourteenth, and Fifteenth Amendments* (Philadelphia, 1889), *passim*, and Paschal, *Lecture*, 25–9.

1870–71 legislation "were consistent with traditional usage," Swinney judged.[23]

The Enforcement laws were hardly dry in the *Statutes at Large* when the Republicans' tentative and restrained commitment to administering them commenced to ebb. Newer crises, such as the Panic of 1873 and the ensuing depression, demanded attention. Other villains were replacing state injustices to citizens; public debt repudiationists, money inflationists, low-tariff advocates, champions of public regulation of railroads and other utilities, and spoils men of national, state, and local officialdom appeared to be the greater evils. Increasing numbers of stanch Republicans from Grant down believed Reconstruction to be complete. Georges Clemenceau noted how widespread the sentiment was that the "emancipation revolution is now ended." Happy that America's Civil War and Reconstruction exported liberty abroad as well as to the South, Republicans pointed to England's 1867 Reform Act as a derivative extension of suffrage and shuddered at the way France punished Paris Communards. "In America we do these things better," boasted the Republican party's official publication.[24]

Like Jamaica's 1865 Eyre Rebellion, the 1871 Paris Commune uprising and the 1873 Panic alienated recent Republican government adequacy proponents. Officials of New York City's Association for Improving the Condition of the Poor were repelled by unemployed workmen's demands for state-sponsored public works projects, and committed its men, money, and influence to combat the upsurging lower orders. On news of the Commune, as remarked earlier, Justice Stephen Field, a consistent, influential Republican constitutionalist, became almost totally antistatist, with profound effects on the constitutional evolution of the Fourteenth Amendment and on the history of America's races, sections, and institutions. The belief spread that dangers to society from civil wars and reconstructions were not worth the benefits.[25]

---

23. E. Swinney, "Enforcing the Fifteenth Amendment, 1870–1877," *JSH*, XXVIII (1962), 203–4, 218.

24. "The Slaveholder's War and the Paris Commune," *The Republic*, VI (1867), 126–7; H. C. Allen, "Civil War, Reconstruction, and Great Britain," in *Heard Round the World; The Impact Abroad of the Civil War*, ed. H. M. Hyman (New York, 1969), 3–96, esp. 77–96; Clemenceau, *American Reconstruction*, ed. F. Baldensperger (New York, 1928), 299–300; Carpenter, *Grant*, 89.

25. H. Gutman, "The Failure of the Movement by the Unemployed for

The developing sense of Reconstruction's essentially complete condition was expressed vividly by the Republican party's 1872 nominating conventioners. As expected, Grant was selected again, with the old abolitionist Henry Wilson as his running-mate. The party platform called for vigorous enforcement of the Fourteenth and Fifteenth Amendments, which "should be cordially sustained because they are right, not merely tolerated because they are law, and should be carried out by appropriate legislation." However, the party consensus was that Congress had already enacted the "appropriate legislations." For this reason, a companion plank calling for amnesty to almost all ex-Confederates still disfranchised appeared harmonious with the plank on enforcement of the Amendments. But their contradictory character is evident.

The amnesty provision reflected the misnamed "Liberal" Republican schism. Bolting the party which some of them had helped to found, mixing anti-Grantism with spreading laissez-faire Spencerian and Darwinian views, Liberals elevated to constitutional dogma the conviction that public sector action was by nature wasteful, corrupt, and dangerous. Democrats accepted the Liberal Republican nominees and platform, and were delighted by their recent opponents' growing conviction that Reconstruction was not only ended but dead-ended; that it had been a fool's errand.

From this conviction derived the Liberal Republicans' and Democrats' shared platform plank against "any reopening of the questions settled by the thirteenth, fourteenth, and fifteenth amendments of the Constitution."[26] It boiled down to a general sharing of views among Republican factions (by 1874, Democrats, as always grimly reactionary on Reconstruction, were out

---

Public Works in 1873," *PSQ*, LXXX (1965), 254; H. J. Graham, *Everyman's Constitution* (Madison, Wis., 1968), 117.

26. Of the Liberal Republican penmen, lawyers, and career politicos, the most recent student of the 1872 election concluded that "Their genteel posture of impossible hope and unnecessary fear caused reaction under the guise of reform." W. Gillette, "Election of 1872," in *History of American Presidential Elections*, II, 1305, 1331, 1333, 1336; and see *The Radical Republicans and Reconstruction*, ed., H. M. Hyman, xvii–xxx; O. Olsen, *Carpetbagger's Crusade: The Life of Albion Winegar Tourgée* (Baltimore, 1965), *passim*; W. B. Fowler, "A Carpetbagger's Conversion to White Supremacy," *North Carolina Historical Review*, XLXXX (1966), 286–304; J. Logsdon, "Horace White: Nineteenth Century Liberal" (Ph.D. diss., UWis, 1966), ch. 9.

of coalition with Liberal Republicans) concerning enforcement of Reconstruction statutes. As Professor Swinney has emphasized, an erratic, dwindling pulse dominated Enforcement Act administration. Although the Enforcement laws were "essentially sound," implementation was difficult and sporadic even when the party commitment was relatively strong in 1871–73. Thin money appropriations kept too small the numbers of enforcement personnel, ranging from troops to marshals, and Grant rarely worried Congress on this score. After 1874 these laws were "virtually dead letters," Swinney concluded, in part because southern whites were willing to take risks to defy them and northern society was no longer in a mood to hazard very much to enforce them.[27]

The world of law played an important part among the influences that diminished Republicans' appetites for Reconstruction and helped to set its unrhythmical, dwindling pulse. The 1869 Texas decision had stressed state indestructibility. In 1871, the Supreme Court re-emphasized that jurisprudential line while offering implicitly a kind of truce in the long competition between national and state judges.

The 1871 case concerned the applicability to state judges of the 1863 national income tax, the first in the nation's history. Congress had subjected to taxation the incomes of federal and state jurists among other officials. Following Taney's lead, many national judges simply refused to pay the tax, because the Constitution stipulated that their salaries should not be lowered. The Treasury and Attorney General's Departments let this matter lie. After Appomattox, a Massachusetts judge sued the national tax collector because, assertedly, reciprocal tax immunity existed between officials of state and nation. When the Income Tax case moved up to the Supreme Court, all but one of Justice Nelson's Court colleagues concurred in his opinion that the Bay State judge was correct; that in the federal Union states must be free to choose instrumentalities. The nation taxing state judges, or states taxing national jurists, might diminish independence of choice.

Nelson went a long way toward implying that judges could limit their respective legislatures' taxing outreach and mode; i.e., that high-bench law should contain majorities' decisions. He and his coadjutors on the Court moved judicial review another step

---

27. Swinney, "Enforcing the Fifteenth Amendment," 202–18.

ahead on the path Marshall, Taney, and Chase had taken; a route with which few Republicans of 1871 found reason to quarrel. And the Income Tax case added to the sense of achieved state stability and semiautonomy on internal matters.[28]

Much the same estimate fits 1873's Slaughterhouse case, the Supreme Court's first evaluation of the Fourteenth Amendment. Historians have long asserted that the Slaughterhouse decision did not involve national Reconstruction. It is true that the litigation arose out of a near-monopoly grant of the indicated business ostensibly in the interests of New Orleans's public health, by Louisiana's "carpetbag" legislature. But by the broader definition of Reconstruction embraced throughout the present inquiry, and expressed by Justice Bradley among the commentators, questions of state police power and state amenability to national judicial review were central in the litigation.

New Orleans butchers not favored by the state statute sued. Unsuccessful in lower courts, they secured Supreme Court jurisdiction with a plea that the Fourteenth Amendment guaranteed against unequal state action in broad categories of privileges and immunities including access to entrepreneurial opportunities. In its historic 5–4 decision the Court's majority rejected the argument. All the judges ignored congressional debates, that, arguably, assumed in the Amendment's first section national protection against state infringement of a very broad body of ordinary rights. Instead the Court majority declared that the new Amendments aimed exclusively at elevating the Negro's legal condition but not by expanding the nation's interests in all intrastate private rights even when they suffered by reason of official state action. Holding hard to this narrow view, Justice Miller distinguished sharply rights deriving from state and national citizenship, limiting the latter very tightly. "The effect of his interpretation was to devitalize the [privileges and immunities] clause as far as the giving of additional protection to individuals was concerned," Swinney concluded.

In the same vein, Miller construed narrowly the due-process and equal-protection clauses as restraints on state police power legislation of the sort under review. Contrary assertions of the

---

28. Collector [Buffington] v. Day, 11 Wall., 113 (1871). See also *The Nation* (June 29, 1971), 445–6; Dobbins v. Erie County, 16 Peters, 435 (1842).

Court minority offered by Field were that the Amendment and related legislation reflected Congress's intention to place a dynamic, broad body of common rights, including economic interests, under national judicial protection.[29]

A few years after the Slaughterhouse decision, the Supreme Court broadened substantially the doctrine of state self-definition of citizens' rights, privileges, and immunities within the new Amendment's context. Successive Court pronouncements denied the right claimed under the Fourteenth Amendment by a woman to practice law, or, in another instance, to vote, where the state in question franchised and licensed men only. The Court decided also that males denied a jury trial or state licenses to sell liquor were not deprived of rights flowing from national citizenship. And the 1877 "Granger" decision's encomium to state police power/public interest constitutional adequacy added heavily to the conviction that with few exceptions, which the national courts would later define in very broad terms, states and localities would set intrastate conditions of life and labor.[30]

Such decisions seriously undercut the already dwindling Republican commitment to broad national responsibility. According to the Supreme Court, the murder of Louisiana blacks attempting to vote did not involve official state remissness or national interests defined in the postwar Amendments. Those Amendments did not create new national criminal codes, the Court decided; only a state could punish murder. Therefore, in 1875, the Court allowed state-courts' criminal convictions to stand if it could discern wholly adequate evidential grounds as defined by that state, even if a federal question existed, and in 1876 the Court declared unconstitutional significant sections of the 1870 Enforcement Act and keyed the nation's responsibilities under the Fifteenth Amendment to positive state suffrage infringements

29. 16 Wall., 36 (1873); C. B. Swisher, *American Constitutional Development* (2nd edn., Boston, 1954), 336–40; H. J. Graham, "Justice Field and the Fourteenth Amendment," in *Everyman's Constitution*, 113; J. A. Scott, "Justice Bradley's Evolving Concept of the Fourteenth Amendment from the Slaughterhouse Cases to the Civil Rights Cases," *RLR*, XXV (1971), 552–69; Paludan, "Law and the Failure of Reconstruction," 611–12.

30. See, respectively, Bradwell v. Illinois, 16 Wall., 130 (1873); Bartemeyer v. Iowa, 18 Wall., 129 (1874); Minor v. Happersett, 21 Wall., 162 (1875); Walker v. Sauvinet, 92 US, 90 (1876); Munn v. Illinois, 94 US, 113 (1877) and *ibid.*, 155 ff.

based on race, rather than to a broad spectrum of discriminations, intimidations, and impediments.[31]

Of these decisions, Professor Schwartz, arguing that the Court's strict interpretations "all but nullified" the new Amendments, holds "a close reader" to the perception that "the high-bench doctrines articulated in the[se] cases . . . were anything but manufactured by the Justices out of the whole cloth. The theme of limited power conferred [upon Congress] by the relevant amendments . . . runs through all the debates . . . from the Enforcement Act of 1870 to the Civil Rights Act of 1875. If, in the congressional debates, that theme was stated principally by the Democratic legislators, it was soon taken up by a Supreme Court whose members had, with one exception, been appointed by Republican Presidents."[32]

Like the Court and almost the entire legal profession, American whites generally concurred implicitly or explicitly in the decline of Reconstruction as a public issue. A de-emphasis on Reconstruction permeated seemingly unrelated scenes. In 1873 Congress authorized the first codification revision of national statutes in American history. Reformers among lawyers had long been interested in codification. They had enjoyed some prewar successes, principally in New York, which had excited the American Bar. Then the Holt-Lieber-Whiting wartime compendia, the post-Appomattox Cooley-Dillon-Jameson treatises, and the growing bar association and law school movements continued the profession's heavy drift toward systematic codifications.

Never assembled or codified, the nation's statutes were an eighty-year accumulation in which, commonly, riders and amendments to statutes dealt with subjects irrelevant to the main title. Clauses in a statute contradicted or canceled others, yet the altered or superseded matter remained in the printed collections. Spoilsmen slipped easily through the law's interstices, for no

---

31. Murdock v. Memphis, 87 US, 590 (1875); U.S. v. Cruikshank, 92 US, 542 (1876); and see U.S. v. Reese, *ibid.*, 214. Ex parte Siebold, 100 US, 371 (1880), and Ex parte Yarbrough, 110 US, 651 (1884), in which the Court sustained Elections law and Enforcement Act provisions concerning national elections deriving from independent Constitutional authority. Combined with the 1883 Civil Rights Cases decision, 109 US, 3, these meant that Fieldian concerns were beginning to win out, and that national judicial controls, selectively applied on both state and national actions, guided policy.

32. Schwartz, *Statutory History*, I, 537.

adequate index existed. Intelligent jurisprudence was chancy and rational legislation impossible in such conditions.

In 1873, codifiers achieved the noncoercive, inexpensive, unbureaucratic kind of reform that had become dear to the hearts of reformers. A *Revised Statutes of the United States* replaced the haphazard *Statutes at Large.* For the first time in the nation's history its statutes were grouped reasonably by functional categories.

But this triumph of the rational law reformer further minimized Negro-centered Reconstruction. Describing this unanticipated relationship, Professor Schwartz noted that while the 1873 codification substantively altered none of the civil-rights-enforcement statutes, it rearranged and separated these laws under unrelated titles. In the process, he concludes, Reconstruction laws "lost their distinctive, unified character."[33]

The 1873 revision made law more than ever a mysterious science beyond the mastery of ordinary citizens, and accentuated the consistent swing to let courts and attorneys decide the contours of public laws and the intent of public lawmakers. Leading legal observers expressed increasing distrust with the majority's will as embodied in statutes.[34]

The 1874 congressional and state elections reflected and fed the generalized indifference to, approval of, or despairing acquiescence in this trend of events. In southern states physical and economic coercion of black and white Republicans had become systematic and successful. The Enforcement Acts remained all but unenforced. More than half the House Republicans were defeated in the 1874 balloting. Lame-duck Republican congressmen determined to support proposals for a new Civil Rights law which Sumner had sponsored for several years before his death in 1874. Republicans intended the Civil Rights law to be his memorial.

The Civil Rights law which Grant signed on March 1, 1875 avoided the pitfalls of military enforcement, fundamental condi-

---

33. *Ibid.,* 803. Perry Miller, *The Life of the Mind in America* (New York, 1965), 239–65, mistook the Civil War's impact as one that diminished the codification surge; cf. M. Bloomfield, "Law vs. Politics: The Self-Image of the American Bar (1830–1860)," *AJLH,* XII (1968), 306–23; and see *ALRev,* VI (1871), 211–16.

34. See Howe, *Holmes,* II, 52; re Legal Tender Cases, 12 Wall., 457 (1871).

tions, and revocable state restorations, and it shifted attention from state to private denials of voting or office-holding on grounds of race to mundane aspects of daily living. Relying wholly on litigation for enforcement, the 1875 law declared that equality of access to state- or national-licensed facilities such as transportation, public accommodations, and places of amusement must not be denied to any person in the United States because of race. After intense arguments, Congress omitted schools and cemeteries.

Persons violating access were subject in the law's first two sections to civil damage lawsuits (action of debt) initiated by the victim, and to criminal prosecutions by the appropriate public prosecutor. On the civil side, an aggrieved individual could opt for proceeding under his state's civil-rights statute if one existed; on the criminal, only the new national standard was to be employed. Guilty verdicts could result in plaintiffs receiving up to five hundred dollars in damages plus costs, and in defendants incurring additional fines payable to the appropriate jurisdiction of from five hundred to a thousand dollars, plus jail terms of from thirty days to one year.

Further sections afforded exclusive national District and Circuit Court jurisdiction for these proceedings without regard for diversity of citizenship. Congress "specifically authorized and required" federal attorneys, marshals, and commissioners to institute actions against offenders. Failures in diligence on the part of federal district attorneys made them liable to the victim, after independent actions of debt, for penalties of one to five thousand dollars. The statute provided also that in United States courts grand and petit jurors should not suffer disqualification on racial grounds. Officials so discriminating were subject to prosecution and heavy fines. And last, the Civil Rights law specified Supreme Court review of resulting litigation, without regard to minimum sums in contest.[35]

In some ways this was an exciting, adventurous statute. It tied individuals' discriminatory actions to state and national gov-

---

35. *SAL*, XVIII, 335 (1875). Secs. 1 and 2, described above, were declared unconstitutional in the Civil Rights Cases, 109 US, 3 (1883). A. H. Kelly, "The Congressional Controversy over School Segregation, 1867–1875," *AHR*, LXIV (1959), 537–63, and J. M. McPherson, "Abolitionists and the Civil Rights Act of 1875," *JAH*, VII (1965), 493–509, are essential. See also A. D. White, "The Relations of the National and State Governments to Advanced Education," *Old and New*, X (1874), 475–95.

ernmental power that had made the discriminations possible or
had left them unpunished. Further, the 1875 law provided criminal as well as civil penalties for violation; a tough stance that
even the 1964 Civil Rights Act, which allowed only injunctive
relief, could not manage.[36] But up until 1883, when the
Supreme Court declared its essential link between individual
actions as factors of state power unconstitutional, the 1875 law
was a weak reed. Indifference of whites combined with the financial inability of blacks to sue let Jim Crowism grow virtually
unimpeded, leading to a half-century deferment in civil and
political rights.[37]

The Civil Rights law's provisions enlarging national court
jurisdiction were unadventurous, although novel in tying together
individual discriminations with state policy. Since the 1863
Habeas Corpus law it had become a congressional habit to increase national courts' jurisdictions in order to enforce other
substantive policies, and the 1875 Civil Rights statute was another example of this trend.[38]

The spirit of seventy-five expressed itself also in another
law, the Jurisdiction and Removal Act. It received the cordial
support of those few remaining Republicans who still regarded
the Negro's situation as a priority, and of the enlarging number of
interest-group colleagues who worried about states' economic interventions. According to Professor Wiecek, the Jurisdiction and
Removal Act was "the culmination of nineteenth century removal
legislation, finally giving plenary removal jurisdiction to the
federal courts."[39] The Supreme Court's Sewing Machine Company decision of March 1874 inspired Congress to action. The
Court interpreted the 1866–67 Local Prejudice and Separable

36. M. B. Nimmer, "A Proposal for Judicial Validation of a Previously
Unconstitutional Law: The Civil Rights Act of 1875," CLR, LXV (1965),
1394–426.
37. McPherson, "Abolitionists and the Civil Rights Act of 1875,"
509–10; J. H. Franklin, "The Enforcement of the Civil Rights Act of 1875"
(AHA paper, 1964); V. Weaver, "The Failure of Civil Rights 1875–1883,
and Its Repercussions," JNH, V (1969), 368–82; D. Hoeveler, "Reconstruction and the Federal Courts: The Civil Rights Act of 1875," Historian, XXXI
(1969), 604–17; C. Vann Woodward, American Counterpoint: Slavery and
Racism in the North–South Dialogue (Boston, 1971), passim.
38. Exceptions were the 1866 Separable Controversies and the 1867
Local Prejudice laws, noted earlier.
39. W. Wiecek, "The Reconstruction of Federal Judicial Power,
1863–1875," AJLH, XIII (1969), 340; SAL, XVIII, 470 (1875).

Controversies Acts to mean that diversity of residence was still essential for removal of an entire suit, even if a litigant alleged that local prejudice prevented justice.[40] Congressmen discerned menace in this Court judgment. "Granger" style state legislation directed against out-of-state entrepreneurs was difficult enough to combat in federal courts, still traveling the Munn road. In the Munn decision, the Supreme Court approved state regulations of business activities affected with a public interest, as legislators defined it. But in state forums, where judges were popularly elected, the pull of neighborhood and the push of interest-group, marketplace politics placed the "foreigner's" rights in serious hazard.

And so, with little significant concern about blacks in southern states, the Jurisdiction and Removal Act was created to serve human and corporate citizens in all states; to aid in a "reconstruction" wherein restraints on certain state economic actions, already under way, could grow more swiftly in national forums. The law authorized removal of all federal question suits and of diversity situations, even though neither party resided in the forum state. The courts thus received original and removal jurisdiction as broad as the Constitution's subject matters, and the judges would define the extents of those subjects. In Wiecek's words, "At one stroke, Congress accomplished a greater expansion of both removal and original jurisdiction, without debate or difficulty, than it had in the previous 86 turbulent years."[41]

Examining the pattern of removals under the 1875 law and under relevant clauses in the 1867 Habeas Corpus Act, Wiecek has made clearer how in the decades from 1880 to 1910 the national courts transformed themselves into eclectic monitors over national and state legislatures and courts of the sort Justice Field favored in 1873. The 1875 Jurisdiction statute was "the very natural result" of the Civil War and Reconstruction, the *Central Law Journal* declared. Since 1863 Congresses and Presidents had enlarged national court jurisdiction, until now for the first time it encompassed all federal questions. Surely, the *Journal* continued, this systematic augmentation reflected the growing awareness that the nation's constitutional law processes were the best way to restrain states' common law and political ex-

---

40. 18 Wall., 553 (1874).
41. *SAL*, XVIII, 470 (1875); Wiecek, "The Reconstruction of Federal Judicial Power" (M.A. thesis, UWis, 1966), 38.

cesses. With respect to Reconstruction, instead of even symbolic military cadres in the South, national judges and courts would attend to the nation's business.[42]

By 1875, national protection of individuals'—especially black individuals'—civil and political rights against state wrongs was dropping on the nation's agenda. Judges did not create the descent, but with rare exceptions they accepted it. They pronounced eclectically against national or state policies they believed to be unwise. The law assumed a schizophrenic character as jurists enlarged national arenas which allegedly plenary state police powers might not enter, and other times discerned exclusive intrastate characteristics for entrepreneurial activities so that national policy could not apply. Lawyers "forum-shopped" on behalf of clients who could afford costs, until by the early 1890's American governments could be caught up uncertainly in a web of negations. Simultaneously, judges accepted into constitutional law pseudoscientific folklore about race inequalities and anti-socialist fears about working-class radicalism. Despite the flurry of Republican interest in a new Elections Bill in 1890, the party continued the retreat from Reconstruction so frequently adverted to in the 1876 centennial and symbolized in 1877's "compromise." A quarter century later, the Fourteenth and Fifteenth Amendments had become almost irrelevant for Negroes.[43]

They are no longer irrelevant. But as Frankfurter cautioned concerning the 1875 Jurisdiction Act, "That the wisdom of 1875 is the exact measure of wisdom for today is most unlikely."[44]

---

42. "Our Federal Judiciary," *CentLJ*, II (1875), 553.

43. J. Roche, "Equality in America: The Expansion of a Concept," *North Carolina Law Review*, XLIII (1965), 249–70; A. M. Paul, *Conservative Crisis and the Rule of Law: Attitudes of the Bar and Bench, 1887–1895* (Ithaca, N.Y., 1960), 1–38; W. F. Swindler, *Court and Constitution in the Twentieth Century: The Old Legality, 1889–1932* (Indianapolis, 1969), 3–133; R. E. Welch, Jr., "The Federal Elections Bill of 1890: Postscripts and Prelude," *JAH*, LII (1965), 511–26.

44. Felix Frankfurter, "Distribution of Judicial Power Between United States and State Courts," *Cornell Law Quarterly*, XIII (1928), 503.

Conclusion:
How Far Are We Bound
in Honor?

In 1871, a federal attorney prosecuting Ku Klux Klansmen in a South Carolina courtroom for violating Congress's civil and political rights statutes was struck suddenly by a contrast. "Gentlemen," he said to the judge and jury, "we have lived over a century in the last ten years."[1]

His sense of time compressed, of swift change, and of achievements, however imperfect and uncompleted, speaks to our concerns. A century has passed since the "First" Reconstruction "ended." We have participated in the "Second" Reconstruction that ennobled the 1950's and 1960's. Swift changes, frustrated but substantial progress, and time compression mark our years. A basic characteristic of both Reconstructions is the nation's commitment to sustain individual civil and political rights against official state obstructions and derivative private impediments.[2] In

---

1. D. T. Corbin, *Argument in the Trial of the KKK before the United States Circuit Court, November Term 1871, Columbia, South Carolina* (Washington, 1872), 4.
2. On the nation's unprecedented posture of caring, see Amos T. Akerman to Sumner, April 2, 1869, Sumner Papers, vol. 94, #4, HU; *New National Era* (June 13, 1872), in *The Life and Writings of Frederick Douglass*, ed. P. S. Foner (New York, 1950–55), IV, 296–7.

both Reconstructions the national courts supply the basic enforcement and monitoring systems. Adding further to the sense of familiarity across the century is the fact that constitutional amendments, laws, and enforcement techniques created between 1861 and 1875 serve today. "It is . . . impossible to account fully for such limited successes as the Second Reconstruction can claim without acknowledging its profound indebtedness to the First," Professor C. Vann Woodward has concluded.

Noting also the "ambiguous and partisan motives" of Republicans who drafted and enforced the Civil War and Reconstruction legislation, Woodward discerns there the "seeds of failure in American race policy."[3] But, after reviewing the constitutional impacts of the Civil War and Reconstruction on the Constitution and the reciprocal role the Constitution played in shaping the War and Reconstruction, "race policy" explains less and less satisfactorily what Republicans achieved and failed to achieve a century ago. Granted the existence of deep and abiding racism; the haste with which Republicans dodged the "southern question" as soon as possible (and far sooner than was decent); and the complex, subtle, and frequently distasteful comminglings of public needs, party purposes, and private gains—in the face of these enormous impediments, further complicated by the politics and constitutionalism of federalism, there was considerable advance.

This progress took the forms it did because Republicans (including Radicals) of the Age of Lincoln were incurably Constitution-bound as well as nervously Negrophobic. Kelly suggests:

> We can very well understand the radicals' constitutional conservatism and the dilemmas their own doctrines posed for them, for after a lapse of a hundred years we find ourselves attempting once more, very much in the spirit of 1865 and 1866, to implement a program which will guarantee Negro political and civil rights in the South without rupturing the basic framework of federal-state relations or the guarantees of the Bill of Rights. A reading of that interesting and tragic book, the *Report of the United States Commission on Civil Rights, 1963*, ought to impress upon us how difficult a task that is—if, indeed, it is not an impossible one within the time-framework that appears to be

3. C. Vann Woodward, "Seeds of Failure in Radical Race Policy," in *New Frontiers of the American Reconstruction,* ed. Harold M. Hyman (Urbana, Ill., 1966), 183.

available to our country in the present crisis in race relations. The radicals of a hundred years ago rejected without
serious debate the argument for revolutionary legitimacy
as a substitute for constitutional legitimacy.[4]

Confirmed by an impressive mix of sources, Kelly's insights
illuminate the Reconstruction's terrain. Northerners had come to
hate slavery as the cause of secession. They did not love Negroes
or feel special obligations to them, but they comprehended no
status in law halfway between slavery and freedom. All Americans should exercise their rights as desired, and bear responsibilities as required. Therefore the War and Reconstruction became
a sustained effort for the nation to equalize within each state that
state's own provisions for personal and property protections
which all residents should enjoy. Since slavery was a legal condition, only the law's obliteration was necessary to secure those
rights. By 1871 some Republicans—whatever their motives—
saw that private discriminations could exist in states only by
reason of state inaction or action. But the realization came too
late.[5]

The intense focus on the state citizen's legal—not racial—
condition as the gauge of the national society's health suddenly
ebbed. The question of 1865, asked by Army officer Manning
Force, on Reconstruction duty in Mississippi, was: "How far are
we bound in honor, to supervise the State laws on the subject of
freedmen [?]" Even so early the question had the confines of his
self-reply—"I should like to quit at the earliest moment."[6]

By 1883, when the Supreme Court emasculated the Civil

---

4. Alfred H. Kelly, "Comments on H. M. Hyman's Paper," in *New Frontiers*, 57–8; cf. James G. Randall and David Donald, *The Civil War and Reconstruction* (2nd edn., Boston, 1961), 633. See also J. S. Haller, Jr., "Civil War Anthropometry: The Making of an Ideology," *CWH*, XVI (1970), 309–24; J. S. Haller, Jr., "The Physician versus the Negro: Medical and Anthropological Concepts of Race in the Late Nineteenth Century," *BHM*, XLIV (1970), 154–67; P. Paludan, "Law and the Failure of Re-construction: The Case of Thomas Cooley," *JHI*, XXXIII (1972), 597–614.

5. M. L. Benedict, "The Right Way, Congressional Republicans and Reconstruction, 1863–1869" (Ph.D. diss., RU, 1971), 695 (n. 30-a), offers the best analysis and bibliographical survey. See also C. B. Swisher, "Dred Scott One Hundred Years After," *JPoli*, XIX (1957), 172; U. B. Phillips, "The Central Theme of Southern History," *AHR*, XXIV (1928), 31.

6. Manning Force to Peter Force, Dec. 3, 1865, Force Papers, UWash.

Rights law, a generation had registered its concurrence with that reply. Once the War and Reconstruction secured permanence for the Union, freedom for slaves, and nominal equality in state legal procedures for national citizens, the permissible role for national power ended.[7]

Historical scholarship's skeptical stance has discounted the deep, steady, consistent, contemporary expressions of admiration for and satisfaction in what Americans won in their Civil War and Reconstruction. Yet, here and abroad, careful critics accounted it a large victory that legal and civil equality was the nation's goal at all. As the English commentator J. W. Probyn noted in 1870, the War and Reconstruction legislation "very happily . . . unite[d] the control of [i.e. by] the Federal Government, with very large rights and powers given to each State." States' prewar autonomy diminished without European-style centralization. Federalism—that rarest form of durable government—continued to flourish here.[8]

Despite the persistent contrary tradition that a vast centralization resulted from the War and Reconstruction, it is difficult today to substantiate the thesis. Bray Hammond's insight that the decades of 1860 to 1880 "fixed no sharp line dividing [national from state] authority but had left a recondite, meandering watershed marked by ambiguities at every step" was far superior to the brittle ideological abstractions concerning state sovereignty that made prewar politics abrasive and wartime survival risky.[9] Even in economic realms centralization did not result from the Civil War and Reconstruction, except in bits and pieces that fail to fit

---

7. Cf. W. G. Cochrane, "Freedom Without Equality: A Study of Northern Opinion and the Negro Issue, 1861–1870" (Ph.D. diss., UMinn, 1957); L. A. Dew, "The Racial Ideas of the Authors of the Fourteenth Amendment" (Ph.D. diss., LSU, 1960); J. M. Harrison, *The Man Who Made Nasby, David Ross Locke* (Chapel Hill, N.C., 1969), 195–6; "Ignatius Donnelly Diary, 1859–1885," ed. T. Nydahl (Ph.D. diss., UMinn, 1941), II, 1035–6; Paludan, "Law and the Failure of Reconstruction," 611–14.

8. J. W. Probyn, *National Self-Government in Europe and America* (London, 1870), 171–2; and see C. J. Friedrich, *The Impact of American Constitutionalism Abroad* (Boston, 1967), 48–9; Daniel Elazar, "Civil War and the Preservation of American Federalism," *Publius*, I (1971); D. Elazar, *The American Partnership: Intergovernmental Co-operation in the Nineteenth-Century United States* (Chicago, 1962), 333 and *passim*.

9. Bray Hammond, *Sovereignty and an Empty Purse: Banks and Politics in the Civil War* (Princeton, 1970), 363; cf. R. F. Nichols, *Blueprints for Leviathan: American Style* (New York, 1963), *passim*.

mid-nineteenth-century definitions of the word, much less those of the mid-twentieth.[10]

In a candid moment, Wisconsin's ex-Senator Doolittle, one of the myth's major disseminators, admitted its untruth. Addressing law school graduates in 1879, Doolittle surveyed the manifold roles that state and local governments had come to play since Appomattox in individuals' lives. He estimated that as in prewar times, far more than 90 per cent of a citizen's connections with government were with states and their subdivisions. Only the minority who traveled abroad, held national offices, or paid federal income taxes were touched by Washington. Now that Reconstruction was completed, "the republic [was] restored to its normal condition, [and] the burdens of the federal government . . . will once more . . . rest as lightly upon our people, . . . as they were before that terrible convulsion."[11]

Ironically, until recently scholars attended least to the branch of the national government that received the largest degree of monitorship over states out of the War and Reconstruction—the courts. The scholarly tradition lingered overlong that the national courts suffered severely in a losing contest with Republican Presidents and Congresses. Now it is clearer that Congress fought no wars with the national courts, especially the Supreme Court. As with the states, the nation worked out new patterns of partnership with the courts.[12]

---

10. *The Economic Impact of the American Civil War*, ed. R. Andreano (Cambridge, Mass., 1962), vii–xi and *passim; Economic Change in the Civil War Era: Proceedings of a Conference on American Economic Institutional Change, 1850–1873, and the Impact of the Civil War . . .*, ed. D. T. Gilchrist and W. D. Lewis (Greenville, Del., 1965), *passim.*

11. "Law Address of Ex-Senator James R. Doolittle, Delivered Before the Union College of Law at Chicago, June 6, 1879," ed. D. Mowry, ISHS *Journal*, XIX (1926), 77–93. James Bryce, *The American Commonwealth* (New York, 1959), I, 102.

12. So systematically did Congress nourish the Court's outreach, that in 1889, when Brazilian Emperor Don Pedro II was instructing his Minister to the United States, he ordered him to "Study with special care the organization of the Supreme Court of Justice at Washington. When you return we must have a conference on the subject. . . . [I]f we could create here a tribunal of the type of the Supreme Court . . . things would be better. Give every attention to this point." In P. A. Martin, "Causes of the Collapse of the Brazilian Empire," *Hispanic American Historical Review*, IV (1921), 23. See also Horace Helbronner, *Le Pouvoir judiciaire aux Etats-Unis: Son organisation et ses attributions* (Paris, 1872), 32–3 and *passim;* W. M. Wiecek, "The Reconstruction of Federal Judicial Power,

However useful Democrats found the centralization charge
—along with others alleging the deaths of checks-and-balances
and two-party politics—it should not have impressed scholars.
The War and Reconstruction allowed spectacular entrepreneurial
enrichment, in part because in many functional arenas the government remained rudimentary as a result of the Constitution's
tight hold on the dominant Republicans. Nevertheless a curiously
duplex vision afflicted the generation. Clearest comparative evidence proved that nothing like European-style centralization was
occurring, but prevailing rhetoric assumed that it was. By a
decade after Appomattox, just when the nation was abandoning
even sporadic enforcement of civil and political rights legislation,
the centralization myth was firmly established.

For example, a foreign diplomat made a wartime prediction
to Sumner that "from this time, your government and ours are
the same" because of the Civil War's huge public debt and supposed coercive bureaucratic growth. "These official establishments will govern your country, as such establishments govern
our countries," the foreigner predicted. Was he correct, Sumner
asked Edward Everett Hale?

Hale replied that such fears were excessive. Americans
forbade their nation a mass peacetime army and limited the new
bureaucracy safely as to duration, powers, and budget. "We can
make new [administrative] machinery when we want to," Hale
wrote, in accurate encapsulation of what occurred after Appomattox concerning freedmen's labor and education, mine safety,
railroad subvention, and cholera containment.

> Given two courses of national conduct the nation must al-
> ways select that which will employ the fewest people, that
> which will have least distinct corporate organization, and
> that which will finish its business the sooner. It was a pity,
> perhaps, to abolish the Freedmen's Bureau at the moment
> we did it; but the principle which abolished it was the true
> one; and the moment was only a question of weeks or
> months. To work by special [i.e., temporary] machinery
> . . . even if then the machinery be given away . . . this
> is the true policy of the Republic.[13]

1863–1875" (M.A. thesis, UWis, 1966), ch. 1. William E. Nelson, "State
Appeals to Federal Courts in the Early Republic" (OAH paper, 1972), used
with permission.

13. Edward Everett Hale in *Old and New*, XI (1875), 1–2, 4, 6, 20;
see also D. D. Field, "Centralization," *NAR*, CCXIV (1881), 407–26; T. M.

Conclusion: How Far Are We Bound in Honor?

An apposite example of this curious duality of vision concerning centralization is illustrated by events of the centennial year 1876. At the party convention, a few Republicans sought a platform plank approving creation of a national "bureau of industry," an idea with which the party conventions had flirted since 1864. The proposed bureau would set minimum wage and safety standards for workers in interstate commerce, and regulate returns for investors and fares for travelers and freight. Although in 1876 the proposal died, Democrats inveighed again, as they had since 1861, against Republicans' "corrupt centralism."

Even such eclectic pronational government activists as sanitarian Henry Bowditch accepted the anticentralization credo concerning Reconstruction's basics. President Hayes "will relieve the South of Federal bayonets," Bowditch wrote early in 1877. "The negroes will have their rights before the law, but will now have to defend themselves."[14]

Neither Hayes's installation as President (which after the disputed election's tensions delighted men whose memories of the secession winter's discouragement were sharp), nor Congress's repeal in 1894 of much of the remaining voting rights legislation, ended Reconstruction.[15] It ended when perceptions of new wrongs replaced those that had moved men of the War and Reconstruction to achieve what they did. Reviewing in 1889 "The Constitutional Results of the War of the Rebellion," the mulatto combat veteran George W. Williams catalogued his concerns: "The vexatious and dangerous problem of socialism; unrestricted immigration; private trusts; [and] the saloon question" headed his list. Then he reminded his audience: "We should not forget that the predominant spirit of our times is materialism, and the

---

Cooley, *Changes in the Balance of Government Power, an Address to the Law Students of Michigan University, March 20, 1878* (Ann Arbor, Mich., 1878), 3–25, esp. 21; W. Farnham, "The Weakened Spring of Government, A Study in Nineteenth-Century American History," *AHR*, LXVIII (1963), 662–80.

14. *Life and Correspondence of Henry Ingersoll Bowditch*, ed. V. Y. Bowditch (Boston, 1902), II, 56; Thomas Hudson McKee, *The National Conventions and Platforms of All Political Parties, 1789 to 1905* (6th edn., Baltimore, 1906), 164; Elizabeth Probasco Ward, *Life, Speeches, and Orations of Durbin Ward of Ohio* (Columbus, 1888), 434.

15. See Bernard Schwartz, *Statutory History of the United States: Civil Rights* (New York, 1970), I, 803–34, re Act, Feb 8, 1894, *SAL*, XXVIII, 36.

science of history shows that this is the critically dangerous moment in the life of a Nation."[16]

The "science of history" which Williams called up so familiarly was then initiating a significant, critically realistic re-evaluation of the Constitution's meanings to the latter decades of the century. Pioneers of this movement, including the first Ph.D.s to assess the War and Reconstruction, assumed that no one had preceded them in awareness of the Constitution's defects. For example, in Woodrow Wilson's 1885 analysis, he understood that the Civil War and Reconstruction had been "a rude shock." But he misjudged the nature, timing, and quality of responses.

> We of the present generation are in the first season of free outspoken, unrestrained constitutional criticism. We are the first Americans to hear our countrymen ask whether the Constitution is still adapted to serve the purposes for which it was intended; the first to entertain any serious doubts about the superiority of our own institutions as compared with the systems of Europe; the first to think of remodeling the administrative machinery of the federal government, and of forcing new forms of responsibility upon Congress.[17]

Hardly. Since the secession winter conformable criticism of constitutional arrangements had been part of America's life style. From secessionists upward, would-be pallbearers for the Constitution had declared its obsolescence and death. "The lamentations on that subject have never been silent," noted William Graham Sumner in a centennial review of American politics.[18]

Ironically, one of the most persistent dirges mourned the

---

16. George W. Williams, *The Constitutional Results of the War of the Rebellion: An Oration, Memorial Day . . . 1889* (Worcester, Mass., 1889), 19.

17. Woodrow Wilson, *Congressional Government: A Study in American Politics* (Boston, 1885), 5–6, 332. See also Herman Belz, "The Constitution in the Gilded Age: The Beginnings of Constitutional Realism in American Scholarship," *AJLH*, XIII (1969), 112–14.

18. William Graham Sumner, "Politics in America, 1776–1876," *NAR*, CXXII (1876), 86–7. Note that Sumner never subscribed to the view of democracy's degeneracy or of federalism's failure. "It is well, perhaps, to receive with caution this verdict of [i.e., by] dandyism; for of all adepts in impertinence the most accomplished are the nominal professors of politeness," wrote one shrewd observer. He concluded that the elitist critics of the Constitution who were so shocked at the new millionaires and the old politicos had forgotten that "We all came from the woods." E. P. Whipple, "Shoddy," *AM*, XXVII (1871), 343.

Conclusion: How Far Are We Bound in Honor?

Constitution's death or corruption as proved by the fact that it worked so vigorously during the Civil War and Reconstruction. In Harvard Law School lectures between 1867 and 1869, Joel Parker, exhibiting the same malaise that Taney expressed since Merryman's appeal failed to stop a war, asserted that along with state-centered federalism the national government's check-and-balance, separation-of-powers traditions were casualties of that War.

Reviewing Parker's jeremiad, Oliver Wendell Holmes wondered at its pessimistic flavor. Parker, Holmes said, "is like a voice from a past generation, though he does not, like many old men, moan over the good old time he is too filled with the evil of the present days to think of the evil of the past."[19]

Holmes had hit the essential point. By contrast with prewar constitutional conditions the impacts of the Civil War and Reconstruction had been to improve the Constitution; to make a more perfect—never a perfect—Union. Acknowledging failures, the War and Reconstruction's achievements deserved the critically approving evaluations which, in the decades from 1880 to 1910, issued from George Merriam, Moorfield Storey, and George Frisbie Hoar, among participants, and historians John Burgess, W. E. B. DuBois, and W. A. Dunning.[20]

In January 1865, when Union forces appeared to be on the edge of victory, Frederick Douglass told Boston abolitionists what Negroes wanted out of the War and Reconstruction. Irreversible emancipation, of course; thereafter, sharing by blacks of the legal conditions of freedom:

> What I ask for the negro is not benevolence, not pity, not sympathy, but simply *justice*. The American people have always been anxious to know what they shall do with

---

19. *ALRev*, IV (1869), 164–5, reviewing Parker's *The Three Powers of Government; the Origin of the United States and the Status of the Southern States, on the Suppression of the Rebellion; the Three Dangers of the Republic—Lectures Delivered in the Law School of Harvard College and in Dartmouth College, 1867–68, and '69* (New York, 1869).

20. George Merriam, *The Life and Times of Samuel Bowles* (New York, 1885), II, 424; W. B. Hixson, Jr., "Moorfield Storey and the Struggle for Equality," *JAH*, IV (1968), 539–41; George Frisbie Hoar, *Autobiography of Seventy Years* (New York, 1903), I, 254–9; John Burgess, *Reconstruction and the Constitution, 1866–1876* (New York, 1902), II, 245–6, and chs. 11–12, *passim*; W. E. B. DuBois, "Reconstruction and Its Benefits," *AHR*, XV (1910), 781–99; W. A. Dunning, *Constitution of the United States in Civil War and Reconstruction, 1860–1867* (New York, 1885), chs. 7, 10.

us. . . . I have had but one answer from the beginning.
Do nothing with us! . . . All I ask is, give him [the Negro]
a chance to stand on his own legs! Let him alone! If you see
him on his way to school, let him alone,—don't disturb
him! If you see him going to the dinner-table at a hotel, let
him go! If you see him going to the ballot box, let him
alone—don't disturb him! If you see him going into a work-
shop, just let him alone—your interference is doing him a
positive injury.[21]

Efforts to create the policy Douglass sketched in 1865 fell
somewhere between John Stuart Mill's determined laissez-faire
liberalism and Sir James Fitzjames Stephen's discovery of coercion as the bedrock tool of a modern nation. What emerged was a
sporadic national commitment to decent standards for citizens'
civil and political rights practices in their states; a reluctant
resort to certain limited coercive modes and institutions in attempts to have black Americans live uncoerced. It would have
been simpler for the nation to do nothing. Suggestions to this
effect spot the period.[22] But, happily, that generation chose the
tougher middle road and held to it, however reluctantly, unevenly, and briefly.

Even these constrained commitments to undeferred equality
were supposed to have corroded the Constitution. Reflecting in
1868 on the commonplace assertion that efforts growing out of
the War and Reconstruction were the sources of the Constitution's ills and of the corruption of politics, Loren Blodgett, a
Philadelphia lawyer, entered a Union League prize-essay contest.
The theme required him to analyze what was wrong with constitutional-political institutions, and to suggest remedies in light of
actual—not theoretical—institutional, legal, and monetary alternatives. Though he won the prize, Blodgett admitted finally that
despite his assiduous research and careful thinking on the subject, he was unable to suggest "a complete and adequate measure
of reform in the practical working of the existing forms of

---

21. Frederick Douglass, in *The Equality of All Men Before the Law
Claimed and Defended; in Speeches by Hon. William D. Kelley, Wendell
Phillips, and Frederick Douglass* (Boston, 1865), 39.
22. Cf. Rev. O. B. Frothingham, *The Let-alone Policy: A Sermon
. . . June 9, 1861* (New York, 1861); Stephens, *Liberty, Equality,
Fraternity* (New York, 1873), *passim*; G. W. Paschal, *Lecture Delivered to
the American Union Academy of Literature, Science, and Art . . . March
7, 1870* (Washington, 1870), 25–9.

political action. Many years of close observation have shown the defects of these forms in a strong light, but have indicated no other or better reliance than on the elevation and advancement of the people as a whole."[23]

There are worse judgments to make on the impact of the Civil War and Reconstruction, and of the Constitution on them. On the one hand, the "existing forms of political action" failed to translate into reality the substance of the Republicans' vision of equality for Americans before states' laws as a characteristic of national citizenship, and that vision dimmed. But on the other hand, it never disappeared. And its revitalization in our time suggests the correctness of Professor Bertram Wyatt-Brown's judgment:

> The Civil War was indeed a tragic, moral failure in many respects . . . but beyond that it was the only way for blacks to make that enormous leap from slavery to a kind of free peasantry, meager though that step toward restricted liberty appears in retrospect. In all of human history there has never been a painless avenue for any subject class or race to travel toward equality with former masters. In this grim context, the Union dead did not die in vain, though they left the larger task of racial democracy to future, thankfully less harried generations.[24]

---

23. Loren Blodgett, "Practical Defects of the Existing Forms of Political Action," in *Essays on Political Organization Selected from Among Those Submitted in Competition for the Prize Offered by the Union League of Philadelphia* (Philadelphia, 1868), 106. See too in the same publication, Charles Goepp, "Legal Organization of the People to Select Candidates for Office."

24. Book review in *NYHSQ*, LV (1971), 89.

BIBLIOGRAPHY, ACKNOWLEDGMENTS, AND RELATED MATTERS

A Note on Bibliography, Acknowledgments, and Related Matters

Reflecting this book's wide-ranging, eclectic research characteristic, the footnotes will, I trust, serve readers usefully as source references. Supplemental bibliographic guides to constitutional and legal history generally, and to Civil War and Reconstruction constitutionalism specifically, are in H. H. Bellot, "The Literature of the Last Half-Century on the Constitutional History of the United States," Royal Historical Society *Transactions*, 5th series, VII (1957), 159–82; James G. Randall and David Donald, *The Civil War and Reconstruction* (2nd edn., Boston, 1961), 703–88; Donald, *The Nation in Crisis, 1861–1877* (New York, [Goldentree Bibliographies in American History], 1969), entire; Charles Fairman, *Reconstruction and Reunion, 1864–88* ([VI, I, *The Oliver Wendell Holmes Devise History of the Supreme Court of the United States*] New York, 1971), footnotes *passim;* and *Perspectives in American History,* V (1971), *passim,* which was devoted entirely to essays on law in American history.

Despite the guidance these compilations and analyses offered, it was never easy during the creation of this volume to overcome research and bibliographical difficulties in the way of recapturing the letter and spirit of constitutional and legal history a century ago; never possible to shape a comfortably confident reply to Francis N. Thorpe's 1902 question, "What Is a Constitutional History of the United States?"[1]

Admitting this sobering yet exciting imprecision and inclusiveness about a specialization's boundaries, the bibliographical guides noted above, including this volume's footnote suggestions, serve to direct attention away from the history-for-use stress which for too long has dominated research and writing. During the past half-century, lawyers and social scientists have been the primary judges of constitutional and legal histories' means and ends. However admirable their achievements, these colleagues assumed that Clio's natural, necessary, and proper role was subordination to what Howard J. Graham described as "law office history." They saw history as a "blinding light" shining upon constitutional decision-making, and they approached historical research and analysis in a posture similar to that of the adversary's stance in litigation. Not surprisingly, in such hands constitutional history developed case-centered, partisan configurations. John Reid set the theme: "Since history is the lock and key of constitutional law, the determinants of constitutional history have usually been more judicial than historical."[2]

Case-centered sources for constitutional history shaped its literature, and litigation-focused research tools defined the sources. Research directions often are factors of library finding aids, and historians who labor primarily in law libraries in order to recapture legal and constitutional history have been and are prisoners of research tools and library arrangements created and maintained for lawyers. Few "old" books are catalogued at all in most law libraries. Ephemeral pamphlets, drafts of briefs, and prominent individuals' manuscripts, autobiographies, or diaries are rarely collected or retained. In short, law-library finding aids are categorized to aid lawyers in search of a manipulatable present, not to assist historians in re-creating a reasonably accurate past. This is not to complain of extra work involved for nonlawyers in law-library research; rather it is to state a his-

---

1. F. N. Thorpe in AAPSS *Annals*, XIX (1902), 259–65; and see E. R. James, "Some Difficulties in the Way of a History of American Law," *Illinois Law Review*, XXIII (1929), 683 ff.

2. John Reid, "Legal History," *Annual Survey of American Law* (1962), 750. See also J. R. Wiggins, "Lawyers as Judges of History," MHS *Proceedings* (1962), 85–104; J. G. Wofford, "The Blinding Light: The Uses of History in Constitutional Interpretation," *UChiLR*, XXXI (1964), 502–33.

torian's persisting problem, and to mourn that improvement seems distant.[3]

Law-office history was vigorous enough to overbear historians and engaging enough to seduce jurists into illicit affairs with the past. Little wonder that the offspring, in the form of historians' judgments about constitutionalism and jurisprudents' conclusions about history, were distorted.[4]

During the past decade, significant rehabilitation efforts concerning Civil War and Reconstruction scholarship and the constitutional history of that watershed period, have matured. It is evident that this newer wave, which buoys up my present effort, exploits law libraries as only one source of the past. Arthur Bestor's valid stress on "The American Civil War as a Constitutional Crisis," *AHR*, LXIX (Jan. 1964), 327–52, sheds a gentle, usefully balanced illumination on the mid-nineteenth century's dim and gory terrain. The ongoing reclamation of constitutional and legal history by historians, employing standards more in keeping with the discipline's methods and constraints than the lawyer's or jurisprudent's imperatives, suggests that rich research fruits remain to be plucked.[5]

Happily, accounts increase in number and quality of the Buchanan-Lincoln-Andrew Johnson presidencies, of major legislators and political leaders, and of the Taney-Chase-Waite chief justiceships. Recent scholarship scrutinizes the 37th–44th Congresses better than any earlier work, because it closely examines committee structures, styles, and procedures as well as floor speeches. But historians continue to shy off from attempting a full history of Congress, or even of particular congresses, and

---

3. William F. Fratcher, "The Decline of the Index to Legal Periodicals," *Journal of Legal Education*, XVIII (1966), 297–303; E. H. Pollack, *Fundamentals of Legal Research* (3rd edn., Brooklyn, 1967), esp. chs. 1–10 and *passim*.

4. A. H. Kelly, "Clio and the Court: An Illicit Love Affair," *SCR* (1965), 119–58; H. M. Hyman, "Law and the Impact of the Civil War: A Review Essay," *CWH*, XIV (March 1968), 51–9.

5. On these matters, see Paul L. Murphy, "Time to Reclaim: The Current Challenge of American Constitutional History," *AHR*, LXIX (Oct. 1963), 64–79; B. A. Weisberger, "The Dark and Bloody Ground of Reconstruction Historiography," *JSH*, XXV (Nov. 1957), 427–47; L. Kincaid, "Victims of Circumstance: An Interpretation of Changing Attitudes Toward Republican Policy Makers and Reconstruction," *JAH*, LVII (June 1970), 48–66; *The Radical Republicans and Reconstruction, 1861–1870*, ed. H. M. Hyman (New York, 1967), xvii–lxviii.

559

leave parallel state and local decision-making institutions woefully uninvestigated. Therefore, the inner life of the legislative process in Lincoln's Washington, in state capitols, in county seats, and in city halls remains unsatisfyingly two-dimensional. The Andrew Johnson impeachment has long suffered from the same flatness, but work on its history and law promises to remedy this defect.[6] A gratifying upsurge of interest in mid-nineteenth-century jurisprudence and constitutional thought is evident and, I hope, will continue.[7]

Unfortunately, equivalent progress does not appear likely in other, equally significant research arenas. Promising preliminary work on the functional limits which Americans a century ago allowed their national government appears to have halted.[8] Neither historians nor lawyers have dug deeply into contract, property, tort, and nuisance relationships on the civil side of the law, or into criminal law history as affected by the War and Reconstruction.[9] The great interest in southern state–United States relationships during the Civil War and Reconstruction decades has too long obscured the need for work on northern states, and within states, on city-county-state interactions. Similarly, the stress on highest-court decision has left questions that badly want answers concerning lower national and state courts and their incumbents largely unasked. Professor S. A. Bill has noted that these avenues and others deserve exploration because each generation, in its own ways, but with unseverable continuums to the past, tests again the Constitution's capacity to cope.[10]

---

6. M. L. Benedict, "The Law of Impeachment: An Historian's Estimate," and R. Berger's "The Law of Impeachment: A Lawyer's View," plus H. Trefousse's comments on both SHA (1972) Papers, are essential. Each is preparing a book on the Johnson impeachment. Irving Brant, *Impeachment: Trial and Errors* (New York, 1972), ch. VII, does not satisfy.

7. Herman Belz, "The Constitution in the Gilded Age: The Beginnings of Constitutional Realism in American Scholarship," *AJLH*, XIII (April 1969), 110–25; Belz, "The Realist Critique of Constitutionalism in the Age of Reform," *AJLH*, XV (Oct. 1971), 288–306.

8. W. D. Farnham, " 'The Weakened Spring of Government': A Study in Nineteenth-Century American History," *AHR*, LXVIII (April 1963), 662–80.

9. E. C. Surrency, "The Legal Effects of the Civil War," *AJLH*, V (April 1961), 145–65.

10. S. Bill, "The Really Crucial Matter: Proper Constitutional History," *Mid-America*, XLVIII (April 1966), 134.

The best moment to begin writing a book is when one has "finished" it. Then, if ever, accumulated insights are the most penetrating and expanded horizons the more inclusive.

Life does not allow this luxury. Instead, of necessity, at a certain point, one halts his effort of historical re-creation. I do so now in the uneasy awareness that I have made a beginning, not an ending, and that I know many more questions than answers.

During the past decade this was "the book" in my life and I will miss it. Everything I did professionally and much of my personal life as well, I fear, was affected by it. Members of my family and friends, including colleagues and students, suffered with me through its many phases of development. I thank them now for their patience and for what individuals among them taught me.

A succession of past and present graduate research assistants and seminar members, notably Patricia Allan, Michael Les Benedict, Roger Bridges, Barry Hoffman, Lester Lindley, Phillip S. Paludan, and Edward Weisel, served me diligently; Catherine Tarrant was an especially useful and tough aide and critic. I am grateful to them and to the institutions (University of Illinois, Rice University), which supplied stipends for the research assistants, and which nourished appropriate seminar environments. In a special class of research assistance, Mr. J. F. DePorry, formerly of the Library of Congress Manuscripts Division, came out of retirement to plow with me through mountains of National Archives records. His help was extraordinarily valuable.

Colleagues and administrators of the University of California, Los Angeles, the University of Illinois (especially of its Center for Advanced Studies where in 1965–66 I had the honor to be a Fellow, with simultaneous association with The Johns Hopkins University's Center for Research in American History), and Rice University co-operated generously to provide favorable conditions for learning and thinking. Summer grants from the Center for the Study of the History of Liberty in America, Harvard University, the Newberry Library, and the American Bar Foundation permitted me to exploit archives here and abroad. The National Endowment for the Humanities honored me with a Senior Fellowship, 1970–71, which allowed me to begin acquaintance with several branches of technical law at the Bates College of Law, University of Houston.

The opportunities and encouragements could have meant

little if archivists and librarians in the dozens of institutions indicated had not helped. I note my deep debt to all these guardians of the past, with special citation of Helen Welch Tuttle, formerly Head of Acquisitions, University of Illinois Library; Martha Orr Friedman, History Librarian, University of Illinois Library; Ferne B. Hyman, Social Science and Humanities Reference Librarian, Rice University Library; Carolyn E. Jakeman, Keeper of Printed Books, Houghton Library, Harvard University; and Mary I. Fry, Reader Services, Henry E. Huntington Library, San Marino, California. By no means least, I thank Sylvia Ross, whose secretarial skills, durability, and good humor relieved even frustrating working days.

The late Allan Nevins, who conceived this series, was always ready with encouragement and advice. Alfred Knopf and the editor for this volume, Ashbel Green, were patient, forgiving, and usefully demanding, and I am much in their debt.

Professor Alfred H. Kelly, Wayne State University, and Professor Stanley I. Kutler, University of Wisconsin, read the manuscript and offered tough criticism and encouragement. Without their responses, the useful qualities of what I have done would be less and the defects more numerous. Naturally, I am wholly responsible for the latter.

September 1972   Harold M. Hyman
                                                      Houston, Texas

INDEX

Index

iii

Index

Arkansas, 208, 278, 484, 510, 514, 521

armistice, 279

Army: civilian control of, 144–215 *passim*, 251, 266; and courts, 189–90, 219–21, 233, 238–41, 502–3; and civilian–military relationships, 65–86 *passim*, 141–71 *passim*, 194–5, 380, 392; and Congress, 144–5; courts-martial and military commission jurisdiction over civilians and soldiers, 85–6, 151–2 and *n*., 188–202, 217, 219, 254–5, 285–9, 294, 451–89 *passim*, 492–4; and Freedmen's Bureau, 285–9, 294, 385–93, 417–18, 450–64, 477, 486–9 *passim*; governance, including BMJ, IGO, and PMG, 141–70, 151–3, 191–202 *passim*, 250, 254; and internal security, 61–2, 65–98 *passim*, 147–8, 197–200, 219–20, 282–3; and Lincoln, 211–12; and Negroes, 27, 159, 164–7, 185, 194–203, 283; and peonage, 356, 391–2, 480 *n*.; and politics, 164–7, 194–203; and public health, 321–4, 380; and Reconstruction, 157–70, 198–215, 251, 278–82, 300, 417, 446–64, 471, 481–527 *passim*; and soldier voting, 203–5, 279; *see also* arbitrary arrests; civil liberties and civil rights; conscription; courts; emancipation; Force Acts; Freedmen's Bureau; habeas-corpus writs; Holt, J.; impeachment; internal security; Johnson, A.; Lieber, F.; Lincoln; loyalty-oath tests; martial law; military law; military occupations; Whiting, W.

Articles of Confederation, the, 129

Ashley, James, 430

Association for Improving the Condition of the Poor (New York City), 532

associations, 286, 289–90, 308–9, 313, 326–46 *passim*, 386, 516, 532; *see also* bureaucratization; censorship; cities; coercion; commerce power; federalism; functions; licensing; professional associations and licensing; states,

police powers; reform and reformers; social sciences; voluntarism; *and various societies*

Astor, John L., 337

Attorney General, U.S., 138 and *n*.; *see also* Bates, E.; Browning, O. H.; Hoar, E. R.; Speed, J.; Stanbery, H.; Williams, George H.; Cabinet, the

Bacon, Francis, 111

Bagehot, Walter, 106–10, 115, 125

Baltimore, 61, 81–2, 95

Bancroft, George, 32, 168, 337

Bank, U.S., 8

banking and currency, 381; *see also* fiscal stability concerns

Bankruptcy Act, 228–9

Barlow, S. L. M., 165, 166

Barnard, Henry, 389

Barnes, E. W., 407, 408

Barron v. Baltimore, 457

Bates, Edward, 74, 92–3, 103, 142–3, 179–80, 234, 241–2, 261, 452, 479

Bayard, James, 253, 401

Beecher, Henry W., 134–5

Bell, John, 32

Bellot, H. H., 554

Bellows, Henry W., 38, 322

Belmont, August, 119–21

Belz, Herman, 276 and *n*.

Benedict, M. L., 495, 506–8, 510

Benjamin, Reuben, 360

Bentham, Jeremy, 447

Benton, Josiah H., 204 and *n*.

bequests, decedents, 351

Bergh, Henry, 336–9

Bestor, Arthur, 8, 23, 87, 556

Bill, Shirley A., 557

bill of attainder, 482

Bill of Rights, in U.S. Constitution, 11–15, 19, 30–1, 36, 59, 66–80, 86, 119, 257–8, 270–1, 409, 423, 440, 447, 457; *see also* civil liberties and civil rights; coercion; Constitution, U.S.; functions

Bingham, John, 520–1

Binney, Horace, 102–3, 129, 260–1, 452, 461

Bishop, Joel P., 97–8, 159

Black, Jeremiah S., 465, 503–4

Index

A NOTE ABOUT THE AUTHOR

HAROLD M. HYMAN was born in New York City in 1924. After taking his A.B. degree at the University of California at Los Angeles, he did graduate work at Columbia University, and his doctoral dissertation, *Era of the Oath: Northern Loyalty Tests During the Civil War and Reconstruction,* won the American Historical Association's Albert J. Beveridge Award in 1952. He has taught at Earlham College in Indiana, at Arizona State University, at UCLA, at the University of Illinois, and is now William Hobby Professor of American History at Rice University in Texas. In 1959 he received the Sidney Hillman Award for his *To Try Men's Souls: Loyalty Tests in American History.* In 1962 he published a biography of Edwin McMasters Stanton, Lincoln's Secretary of War, begun by Benjamin P. Thomas before his death. In 1969 he was the editor of *Heard Round the World: The Impact of the Civil War Abroad.* Mr. Hyman is married, and is the father of two daughters and a son.

A NOTE ON THE TYPE

The text of this book was set on the Linotype in a new face called PRIMER, designed by Rudolph Ruzicka, earlier responsible for the design of Fairfield and Fairfield Medium, Linotype faces whose virtues have for some time now been accorded wide recognition.

The complete range of sizes of Primer was first made available in 1954, although the pilot size of 12 point was ready as early as 1951. The design of the face makes general reference to Linotype Century (long a serviceable type, totally lacking in manner or frills of any kind) but brilliantly corrects the characterless quality of that face.

Composed, printed, and bound by
American Book–Stratford Press, Inc.

Typography and binding based on designs by

WARREN CHAPPELL

Date Due

JK231   Hyman
.H9

A more perfect Union

Due Date	1st Ren.	2nd Ren.